Travelers'
"COMMENTS"

"Thanks for helping make our holiday extra special." ﾞ   ﾞuse)

Keｒ   Idaho

"Best we've ever stayed in — after 3 ﾝ   ﾝf the family."*
(ABC Reservation Service)

bￜ   ﾝￜns, Champaign, Illinois

"Very enjoyable stay! Nice innkeepers." (The Old Appleford Inn)

Elizabeth Wallraff, Minneapolis, Minnesota

"Thank you for being such good hosts. We enjoyed your home, the company and the great breakfasts." (Mr. & Mrs. Ron and Sandy Johnson, Bernaby, British Columbia)

Natash & Peter Fish, Vancouver, British Columbia

"We are veteran users of B&Bs. We were on our way to the beautiful Grand Canyon and called to get reservations. We received a warm welcome; enjoyed the guests; the hosts and hostess were delightful and they prepared a scrumptious breakfast . . . ; the accommodations were excellent . . ." (Touch of Sedona)

Dr. & Mrs. Frank Allen, Wolfeboro, New York

"Marlene and I wanted you both to know that you make us feel very welcome and at home at your place. You have a very special way of communicating with people and are very attentive to their needs . . . We urge you to keep on sharing your warmth and hospitality with your visiting guests . . ." (Mr. & Mrs. Ron and Sandy Johnson, Bernaby, British Columbia)

Marlene & Frank O'Donnell, Williamsville, New York

Travelers'
"COMMENTS"

"On our trip East, we stayed in many B&Bs — this was the most comfortable, enjoyable place we stayed — a reasonable price too! The hosts were charming." **(Riverview B&B)**

Elizabeth Wallraff, Minneapolis, Minnesota

"Excellent food, convenient kitchen facilities, very comfortable rooms, the "trashy novel' bookcase came in handy, enjoyed talking with the hosts and hostess." **(Brannon-Bunker Inn)**

E.E. Somerville, Massachusetts

"Just wanted to let you know we stayed in Quebec at an inn listed in your book. It was very clean, delicious food and Mrs. Riddell went out of her way to make us feel welcome. Great." **(Chateau Beauvallen at Mt. Tremblant)**

Roy Grosskopf, St. Petersburg, Florida

"Charlie and Hilda made us feel so welcome, like we were friends and not just guests. I'm looking forward to visiting them again in the future." **(Grandma's House)**

James & Betty Day, Martinez, Georgia

"Located close to the commons. Beautiful renovations done to bring to 1820 style with all the conveniences of home. Kay and Mike were helpful and friendly. Would definitely return." **(Hannah Davis House)**

C. Evans, Delray, Florida

"Great food — wonderful accommodations. Very gracious hosts. We're veteran B&B users — this was certainly one of the best." **(Cedaryn B&B, Redwood, Washington)**

Marilyn Hogan, Revton, Washington

Bed & Breakfast Hosts'
"COMMENTS"

"You're doing great work; keep it up."

Mr. E.J. Marsmann, Princely B&B,
Alexandria, Virginia

"Thanks so much. I enjoyed and learned from your book and I look forward to being listed in the guide."

Susan Risse, Blue Goose Bed & Breakfast,
Fairbanks, Alaska

"We look forward to another two seasons of lovely people who find us and return to us through your excellent guide."

Katherine Van Gelder, Harbor Breeze,
Harwichport, Massachusetts

"Your guide has been instrumental in bringing visitors to our area from other parts of the country. I recommend it to all my guests and local folks looking for B&B accommodations in other states, etc. Thanks for a job well done."

Vera Good, Rte. 1,
Blacksbury, Virginia

Thank you for the opportunity of being in your bed and breakfast guide. It has been very good for us in the past and we look forward to your new edition."

Fay & Donald Bain, Ashley Manor,
Barnstable, Massachusetts

"Sami Sunchild and all of the staff at the Red Victorian Bed & Breakfast Inn really appreciate being in your excellent book, The Bed & Breakfast Guide. People from across the globe have found their 'home in San Francisco' here and a large part of the credit goes to the exposure you gave us in your book."

Jeffrey Hirsch & Sami Sunchild, Red Victorian Bed & Breakfast Inn,
San Francisco, California

" . . . We look forward to sharing it (The Official B&B Guide) with guests, using it ourselves on the all too infrequent occasions we get away, and best of all welcoming guests who've found the Goose & Turrets through its pages. As a former editor and longtime publications person, I commend you on the balance you've achieved between economy, readability, attractiveness and ease of use. It's an eminently portable compendium that tells all one has a reasonable need to know."

Emily Hoche-Mong, The Goose and Turrets Bed and Breakfast,
Montara, California

Bed & Breakfast Hosts' "COMMENTS"

" . . *our business became more successful than we could have imagined in such a short period of time. This rapid success was due in part to our listing in your book, and we thank you for including us.*"

Pat Tichenor, Oak Spring Farm & Vineyard
Raphine, Virginia

"*Your Guide is one of the best on the market - I know - we use it frequently!*"

Patricia York, Saint Charles House
St. Charles, Missouri

"*Your book has been a valuable source of information for us. The French and Spanish explanations, have been greatly appreciated by our foreign guests.*"

Marjorie Bettenhausen, Seal Beach Inn
Seal Beach, California

"*We've been listed in several guide books, but have gotten the best response from your book. You've been a big help to us in getting established. Keep up the good work!*"

Rebecca Richardson, Richardson House
Jamesport, Missouri

"*Thank you for the opportunity to once again be a part of the National Bed & Breakfast Association. Best wishes for your continued success.*"

Joanne Hardy, Hill Farm Inn,
Arlington, Virginia

"*We were very pleased with the response from our listing in your guidebook and want to be sure that our membership is up to date so that we will be included in the new issue. Thanks so much.*"

David & Kay Merrell, The Summer House,
Sandwich, Massachusetts

"*Thank you for printing such an excellent guidebook. I know that I have had many guests from it and hope to be entering it again soon.*"

Sherry Cash, Westbourne Windansea B&B,
La Jolla, California

Bed & Breakfast Hosts'
"COMMENTS"

"We appreciate the opportunity to be in your book."

John & Dice Starets, Noble House,
Bridgton, ME

"We appreciate being included in your NBBA guidebook this past year. We'd like to extend our gratitude for the thorough research and high quality standards of your guide. We ask all our guests where they heard about us and a substantial number of our people had used your guide. Your guide is a considerable benefit to the traveler and subsequently to us. Thanks for a job well done."

Priscille & Richard Burdsall,
Baldwin Hill Farm, Gt. Barrington, Massachusetts

"Just a note to let you know that I appreciate the effort you put into your book. It is becoming a good vehicle for the somewhat more adventurous traveler."

Inge Ranzoine, Wellington B&B,
Victoria, British Columbia

"We have been very pleased with the number of referrals we have received from your guide and look forward to being a member for many years to come. Thank you for such a wonderful job . . ."

Margaret Ray, The Oaks B&B,
Christiansburg, Virginia

"We enjoy all the nice people who come to our bed & breakfast. All rooms are filled all summer and quite a lot in the off season."

Marion Rohrer, Maple Inn Guest House,
Paradise, Pennsylvania

"We wish you much success and are appreciative of all the support you give to the bed and breakfast inns."

Carol Johnson, Interlaken,
Lake Placid, New York

"You have a very excellent book and we are proud to be included in it."

Helen Sawyer, Bay View B&B,
New Carlisle West, Quebec, Canada

Newspaper & Magazine
"COMMENTS"

"The Bed & Breakfast Guide for the U.S., Canada, Bermuda, Puerto Rico and U.S.V.I. is easy to grasp, with big headings and a key to the code on amenities is on the bottom of each page. The book contains specifics for each place and a brief note written by the proprietor. The prices are specific down to pennies."

Betsy Wade, New York Times

"Tucked into the glove compartment of any family car . . . this (The Bed & Breakfast Guide for the U.S. and Canada) is a guarantee against not being without accommodations or putting in at a fleabag in desperation."

Boston Herald

"With the publication of The Official Bed & Breakfast Guide it's easier to locate lodgings that meet high critical standards. If you are looking for comfortable accommodations for your next vacation, it's time to pick up a copy of The Official Bed & Breakfast Guide."

Mature Outlook Magazine (Sears & Roebuck)

"The Official Bed & Breakfast Guide should prove an invaluable guide for active duty personnel as well as retirees and their families in planning an inexpensive, but comfortable vacation."

U.S. Navy News

"On the road, The Official Bed & Breakfast Guide might be just the book to help you find a bed for the night. Designed for French and Spanish speaking people too, the guide is easy to read in a hurry."

Country Living Magazine

"Vital for free-wheeling travelers to the U.S. and Canada is the National Bed & Breakfast Guide."

Finance Week, South Africa

The Official Bed & Breakfast Guide is Waldenbook stores third best selling travel guide according to U.S. News & World Report, June 1992.

THE OFFICIAL BED & BREAKFAST GUIDE

FOR THE
UNITED STATES, CANADA
& THE CARIBBEAN

Listings With Descriptions

Of more than
1,600 Bed & Breakfast Homes & Inns

Plus
Reservation Services With
An additional
7,000 plus Bed & Breakfast
Accommodations

Also Including
The Host Recommended
Restaurant Guide Section

By
Phyllis Featherston
& Barbara Ostler

THE NATIONAL BED & BREAKFAST ASSOCIATION, INC.
P.O. BOX 332, NORWALK, CONNECTICUT 06852

Copyright 1993 by Phyllis Featherston and Barbara F. Ostler

Library of Congress Cataloging in Publication Data

ISBN #09611298-5-9

Cover and Book Design: Christine Rooney

Typography and Graphics: R.I.S. Publishing, Westport, CT

Printed in the United States
Published by the National Bed & Breakfast Association
P.O. Box 332, Norwalk, Connecticut 06852

Distributed by The Talman Co., N.Y., N.Y.

DEDICATED TO CHARLES FEATHERSTON

FOUNDER OF

THE NATIONAL BED &
BREAKFAST ASSOCIATION.

PREFACE

The National Bed & Breakfast Association's sixth publication of *The Official Bed & Breakfast Guide for the United States, Canada and the Caribbean,* celebrates 12 years of bed and breakfast service to the traveler. We at the National Bed & Breakfast Association have often been mentioned as a solid resource for bed and breakfast information. Twelve years in the business and one of the oldest publishers of a bed and breakfast guide is perhaps the reason.

Over the years, we have remained true to our philosophy of what a true bed and breakfast is. Breakfast is always included in the price of a room and the B&Bs listed in our guide fall under two categories: a small, private home with less than 10 guest rooms or an inn, family-owned and/or operated, with less than 30 guest rooms. We do not list hotels, motels or hostels, even though today due to the increased numbers of bed and breakfasts in the competitive accommodations industry, many hotels and motels are now offering a complimentary continental breakfast for their guests. It is the individual and personal touch, and atmosphere that we feel gives the bed and breakfasts their uniqueness. The Associated Press, in an article about bed and breakfasts said, "bed and breakfast is the fastest growing segment of the hospitality industry which hastens to credit host and guest." This is the very heart of the business. When a host goes out of his way to make his guest feel welcome he makes the difference.

Over the past 12 years, we have seen the expansion of bed and breakfasts in both numbers as well as direction. They are no longer just for the adult couple as overnight guests. Today, the world of bed and breakfasts includes the business traveler, families, single people, wedding parties, reunions, visiting relatives, day and weekend seminars and functions. Travel agents have added bed and breakfasts to their list of accommodations for their clients. It is an industry full of potential. In a world where people are working harder and have less free time, when they do have time to relax and get away they want service and comfort and something different—the bed and breakfast is there for them.

We hope that you enjoy using this guide and find this sixth edition of *The Official Bed and Breakfast Guide* a valuable resource, referring to it for your personal, family or business travel use.

Sincerely,

Phyllis Featherston & Barbara Ostler

CONTENTS

CONTENTS *(continued)*

INTRODUCTION

<u>The Bed and Breakfast Guide of the United States and Canada</u> is the first guide to compile and list ONLY those privately-owned homes and small inns which provide a night's lodging and include in their rates a full or continental breakfast.

Traveling in a more formal way, using motels or hotels, etc., is expensive and often uneventful and dull. Your personal contacts most often are with a desk clerk or an elevator operator — in most cases, not very memorable and hardly to be compared with spending an evening with a Kansas farm family or in a fisherman's ocean-front home in Nova Scotia. Having used the B and B method of travel here and abroad, we speak from personal experience. We now count many of the B and B proprietors as friends, whom we would always be glad to revisit and whose warm hospitality we will always cherish.

Not all Bed and Breakfast homes and inns area the same. Some are big, some small; some are owned and operated by an experienced innkeeper, some by an energetic housewife whose family has grown and whose home has space now that it never had in the past. If your are looking for uniformity of accommodation, you will not find it here . . . but, this is the beauty of our Association! Bed and Breakfast homes and inns conform in certain important respects. They must be clean, provide either a full or continental breakfast, must adhere to the listed rates in the Guide — these rates will include all taxes and surcharges.

We want you to enjoy staying at B and B's as much as we do. We do not want you, our guests, to be disappointed in any way; therefore, we suggest to you the following:

1. Call or write to confirm that a room will be available.
2. Inspect the room before you take it. The proprietor will be agreeable.
3. Verify the room rate and the provision of breakfast.
4. If children are part of the group, verify their accommodations.

WE WISH YOU HAPPY TRAVELING WHILE STAYING AT THE BED AND BREAKFAST HOMES AND INNS IN THE UNITED STATES AND CANADA!!

Sincerely,

Phyllis Featherston & Barbara Ostler

INTRODUCTION

Le Guide des Pensions des États Unis et du Canada est le premier guide qui compile et enregistre seulement les maisons et les petites auberges qui fournissent le logement pour la nuit et qui comprennent dans leurs ratifs un petit déjeuner complet ou léger.

Le voyage cérémonieux, avec les motels et les hôtels, etc., coûte cher et c'est souvent monotone et enneuyeux. Vos rapports personnels sont le plus souvent avec un concierge ou un opérateur d'ascenseur - d'habitude pas trés mémorable et on ne peut pas comparer ces expériences à une nuit avec une famille à une ferme dans le Kansas ou la maison d'un pêrcheur au bord de la mer en Nouvelle Écosse. Nous sommes restés à ces pensions ici et à l'étranger, et nous parlons de nos expériences personnelles. Maintenant beaucoup de propriétaires de pensions sont nos amis à qui nous voulons refaire des visites et nous chérirons toujours leur hospitalité.

Toutes les pensions et les auberges ne sont pas les mêmes. Quelquesunes sont grandes, les autres sont petites; quelquefois il y a un hôtelier, parfois il y a une ménagére dont les enfants sont parties et les chambres sont libres. Si vous cherchez l'uniformité de logement, vous ne la trouverez pas ici . . . mais voilà la beauté de notre association! Les pensions et les auberges respectent certains réglements. Il faut être propre: fournir un petit déjeuner complet ou léger; rester fidéle aux tarifs du Guide — taxes et service compris.

Nous voulons que vous aimiez le séjour en pension autant que nous: Nous ne voulons pas que vous, nos invités, soyez déçus: alors nous vous recommandons le suivant:

1. Téléphoner ou écrire pour confirmer qu'une chambre vous attend.
2. Examiner la chambre avant de la prendre; le propriétaire le veut bien.
3. Vérifier le tarif et le petit déjeuner.
4. S'il y a des enfants dans le groupe, vérifier leurs chambres.

NOUS VOUS SOUHAITONS UN BON VOYAGE PENDANT VOTRE SÉJOUR DANS LES PENSIONS ET LES AUBERGES AUX ÉTATS-UNIS ET AU CANADA!!

À beintôt,

Phyllis Featherston & Barbara Ostler

INTRODUCTION

 <u>La Guía de Pensiones de los Estados Unidos y de Canadá</u> es la primera guía que compila y cataloga solamente las casas particulares y las posadas pequeñas que proveen alojamiento e incluyen en sus precios un desayuno completo o continental.

El viajar de un modo más formal, usando moteles o hoteles, etcétera, es caro y muchas veces, exento de acontecimientos notables, y aburrido. Sus contactos personales muchas veces son con un dependiente del escritorio del hotel o con un operador del ascensor — en la mayoría de los casos, no muy memorables y casi no pueden ser comparados con pasando una noche con na familia de una finca en Kansas o en una casa de un pescador frente al océano en Nova Scotia. Como hemos usado peniones cuando viajando aquí y en el extranjero, hablamos de una experiencia personal. Ahora contamos a muchos de los propietarios de las pensiones como amigos, a quienes siempre estarémos alegres de visitar otra vez, y cuya hospitalidad ardiente siempre la apreciamos.

No todas las pensiones son iguales. Unas son grandes, otras pequeñas; unas son propiedad de y manejados por un posadero experto, otras por una ama de casa enérgica cuya familia ha crecida y cuya casa ahora tiene el espacio que nunca lo tenía en el pasado. Si Uds.., buscan la uniformidad de acomodaciones, no la encontráran aquí...pero, iesta es la belleza de nuestra asociación! Las pensiones conforman en ciertos, respectos importantes. Deben estar limpias, proveer o un desayuno completo o un desayuno continental, deben adherirse a los precias que están en la Guía — estos precios encluirán todos los impuestas y sobrecargas.

Queremos que Uds. gozan se estancia en las pensiones tanto como nostotros. No queremos que Uds., nuestros huespedes, sean desilusionados de ninguna manera; por eso, les sugerimos lo siguiente:

1. Llamar o escribir para confirmar que habrá una habitación.
2. Inspeccionar la habitación antes de tomarla. El propietario asentirá.
3. Verificar el precio de la habitación la provisión de desayuno.
4. Si niños son parte del grupo, verificar sus acomodaciones.

 ¡Les deseamos un buen viaje mienetras que se queden en las pensiones de los Estados Unidos y dé Canadá!

Adiós,

Phyllis Featherston & Barbara Ostler

How To Start a B&B

In response to the many inquiries we have received regarding how to acquire and start a Bed and Breakfast home or inn, we have asked Mr. David Caples, an expert in the field of lodging and the Bed and Breakfast industry, for his input. In the following pages, Mr. Caples will give you some idea of the more important aspects of the business that you as a prospective innkeeper, should be aware of before starting out on your own.

We are sure you will find what Mr. Caples has to say interesting and informative.

How to acquire and start up a Bed and Breakfast.

When Bob (the innkeeper) Newhart awoke in the last episode of his famous TV show he found the Stratford Inn, its funky staff and curious guests to be nothing but a dream! Lucky for him as it turned out . . . and maybe a caution to other would be innkeepers.

Innkeeping is small B&Bs and country inns has reshaped itself significantly over the last thirty years of growth in the United States. Guests who in the early days accepted the idiosyncrasies of small inns as an adventure, now expect more gracious or upscale accommodations and value for the dollar. To meet these demands, innkeepers have had to sharpen their management, leadership and marketing tools.

Augmenting the above, the B&B industry has blossomed and is having an interesting tail wagging affect on the lodging marketplace. Early innkeeper pioneers of the 60-70's had a wide open field with plenty of demand and little supply. In 1980 it is estimated that there were five- to six-thousand inns domestically. The US Travel Date Center, in a study published in 1991, projects that the industry has grown geometrically to over 20,000 properties. Within its own ranks the choices of guests are so varied that the start-up and operation of an inn can not be taken lightly.

The quiet pressure from the rest of the lodging industry also is interesting. Industry giants such as Marriot (Courtyard) are visibly downsizing the number of rooms at their properties, suite ("inn") style facilities have swept the industry with success, chain operations now regularly offer a complimentary breakfast and resorts

by: David Caples

now have a 'Bed and Breakfast' package in their marketing arsenal. This is no longer a hobby or second investment opportunity . . . this is a hard ball entrepreneurial business.

The new innkeeper in the business is going to require an "unfair advantage" to compete successfully. A career change to Innkeeping carries a double indemnity in that it not only involves a change, but also demands a sizeable investment of personal savings. To gain this advantage there are several steps that prospective innkeepers can take.

1. *Ask yourself why?*

Do you want to escape the corporate hassle, stress and pressure of deadlines? Be the boss and let someone else do the hands on? Improve your financial condition? Create an opportunity for you and your spouse to work together?

Well, innkeeping may not be the panacea. The personal commitment is beyond what most individuals expect. Its a hands on, roll up your sleeves, physically demanding job that often doesn't provide minimum wage for the owner in profits. And there's stress in them 'thar cute little inns' that will put a marriage or a professional deal maker's psyche to the test. Remember, there's no Personnel Dept., no Marketing Dept., Purchasing Agent or bookkeeper except you!

What to do: Visit and stay in inns. Talk to innkeepers. See if you can arrange a short apprenticeship to see what its like. Ask other couples who work together for advice about how to divide job responsibilities.

2. *Why would anyone want to stay with me?*

The inn of our dreams (and Bob Newhart's too!) is often perfect in our mind. But putting it on paper and eventually opening the door can be a different animal altogether. What you like . . . and what may keep a guest interested for more than one evening can be very distant relatives.

The success of the product you create will be 70 percent you and your staff and 30 percent facility. That's what the big guys are starting to learn.

What to do: Try to answer the question. If you feel like your stretching the answer, start over again. Review competitive properties in B&B guides, Sunday travel section ads and your own travel experiences. How do your ideas stack up?

Continued . . .

3. Will this endeavor meet my financial goals?

Behind many a small inns success story is a second income stream (Don't quit your day job!). Many existing inns were purchased for prices above their ability to service the debt. Some start ups (especially when renovations are required) drain the new innkeepers resources to the point that there is no operating funds to market the inn once it is open.

What to do: Initiate considerable research on the geographical area, your site and the building for your potential inn. This, along with a competitive review, supply and demand analysis and pro-forma projections are basic steps in creating a Business Plan for your investment.

Members of SCORE (retired executives working with the SBA), industry consultants or a recognized B&B seminar can assist with the preparation of the plan.

To support a couple a minimum size inn is 10 rooms. Plan on having equity resources of 25 percent of the project cost and operating capital to cover negative cash flow that may exist during start up.

If you are purchasing an existing (operating) inn due diligence should be exercised to confirm revenue, expense and occupancy data provided by the seller. Assistance should be secured to properly evaluate the inn based upon the income it generates. The asking price for some inns the author has reviewed has no justification. They wait hoping you will be the next future innkeeper to buy with his heart instead of his calculator.

About the author:

*D*avid Caples is an innkeeper, lodging industry consultant, real estate broker and creator of the seminar and apprentice program "How to acquire and start up a Bed and Breakfast". A graduate of the masters program at Cornell Hotel School, Mr. Caples has managed a Sheraton Inn and Conference Center, a five room B&B, created a resort management company and currently operates the 20 room Elizabeth Pointe Lodge on Amelia Island, Florida. He can be reached at (904) 277-4851 for additional information.

BED AND BREAKFAST

HOMES AND INNS

IN THE UNITED STATES

ALABAMA

The Heart of Dixie

Capitol: Montgomery
Statehood: December 14, 1819; the 22nd state
State Motto: We Dare Defend Our Rights
State Song: "Alabama"
State Bird: Yellowhammer
State Flower: Camellia
State Tree: Southern Pine

At one time everything in this state relied upon King Cotton; however, with the coming of the destructive Boll Weevil in the early 1900's, the Alabama farmer had to turn to planting other crops, including the peanut, to survive. As a result, the peanut crop was so successful it revived the economy and today Alabama is often referred to as "The Peanut Capitol of the World."

Along Alabama's southern shores can be found beautiful beaches and resorts. Its chief seaport, Mobile, on the Gulf of Mexico, is an exciting and bustling seaport. Its harbor is filled with ships from all over the world. The lovely old homes there reflect the style and grace of the early Spanish and French settlers.

The largest and perhaps the wealthiest city in Alabama is Birmingham, often called The Pittsburgh of the South because of its great steel mills and heavy industry. This city, however, is also known for its pioneering work in health and medical research in open heart surgery.

Among some of the most famous citizens that came from Alabama are Helen Keller, George Carver, Hugo Black and Booker T. Washington. The first White House of the Confederacy was located in Montgomery.

ALABAMA

Ashville *

Sparks, Shirley   **Amenities:** 1,9,10,11,16,17   **Dbl. Oc.:** $58.85 - $80.25
P.O. Box 852   **Breakfast:** F.   **Sgl. Oc.:** $48.85 - $70.25
Hwy. 231 So. @ 9th, 35953   **Third Person:** $10.00
(205) 594-4366   **Child:** Under 12 yrs. - $5.00

Roses And Lace Country Inn—Built in 1890, this three-story B&B is in the National Historic Register. The house is filled with Victorian flare! Wrap-around porches, stained-glass windows, hand-carved mantels and traditional furniture make it an excellent example of southern craftsmanship.

Forest Home *

Inge, George   **Amenities:** 1,6,10,11,16,17   **Dbl. Oc.:** $60.00 - $75.00
P.O. Box 33, Hwy. 10 W., 36030 **Breakfast:** F.   **Sgl. Oc.:** $55.00 - $70.00
(205) 471-8024   **Third Person:** $15.00
   Child: Under 1 yr. - no charge

Pine Flat Plantation Bed And Breakfast—The present owner is a descendent of the original owner. All interior woodwork is hand-hewn heart pine. Fish ponds, trails and hunting on 900 acres. The house is furnished comfortably but elegantly with many antiques. Plantation home built in 1825.

Mentone

Kirk, Amelia   **Amenities:** 1,2,4,6,7,10,11,   **Dbl. Oc.:** $60.50
Hwy. 117, Box 284, 35984   16   **Sgl. Oc.:** $49.50
(205) 634-4836   **Breakfast:** F.   **Third Person:** $5.50
   Child: Under 5 yrs. - no charge

Mentone Inn—A historic mountain retreat on Lookout Mountain. A wrap-around porch on which to sit and watch the world go by. Natural wood in all 12 rooms. All have own baths. A quiet place to relax. Near Fort Payne and Desoto State Park.

N.E. Arab *

Allen, Billy J.   **Amenities:** 2,5,6,7,9,10,11,12,   **Dbl. Oc.:** $45.00
102 1st Ave., 35016   16   **Sgl. Oc.:** $40.00
(205) 586-7038   **Breakfast:** F.

Stamps Inn Bed And Breakfast—Located atop Brindlee Mtn. in beautiful Mountain Lakes region. This 1936 inn, renovated in 1988, has antique furnishings, colonial colors and wallcoverings throughout. Convenient to natural recreational areas, high-tech space- related areas & a nationally ranked shopping outlet center.

---

1. No Smoking	5. Tennis Available	9. Credit Cards Accepted	13. Lunch Available	17. Shared Baths
2. No Pets	6. Golf Available	10. Personal Check Accepted	14. Conference Rooms Avail.	18. Afternoon Tea
3 Off Season Rates	7. Swimmming Avail.	11. Reservations Necessary	15. Group Seminars Avail.	* Commisions given
4. Senior Citizen Rates	8. Skiing Available	12. Dinner Available	16. Private Baths	to Travel Agents

Orange Beach *

Gilbreath, Jerry M.   **Amenities:** 1,2,3,6,7,9,10,16   **Dbl. Oc.:** $100.00
Bozeman, Mrs. Jackie   **Breakfast:** F.   **Sgl. Oc.:** $100.00
23500 Perdido Beach Blvd., 36561   **Third Person:** $15.00
(205) 981-6156, (800) 48-ROMAR   **Child:** No children under 12 yrs.

The Original Romar House Bed And Breakfast Inn—An historic 1920s seaside inn with six private art-deco-appointed rooms, purple-parrot bar, bicycles, cypress swings and hot-tub spa. Full southern breakfast on ocean-view deck. Close to fine restaurants and shops. Relax in a charming atmosphere on the sea.

1. No Smoking	5. Tennis Available	9. Credit Cards Accepted	13. Lunch Available	17. Shared Baths
2. No Pets	6. Golf Available	10. Personal Check Accepted	14. Conference Rooms Avail.	18. Afternoon Tea
3 Off Season Rates	7. Swimmming Avail.	11. Reservations Necessary	15. Group Seminars Avail.	* Commisions given
4. Senior Citizen Rates	8. Skiing Available	12. Dinner Available	16. Private Baths	to Travel Agents

ALASKA

The Last Frontier

Capitol: Juneau
Statehood: January 3, 1959: the 49th state
State Motto: North to the Future
State Song: "Alaska's Flag"
State Bird: Willow Ptarmigan
State Flower: Forget-Me-Not
State Tree: Sitka Spruce

Alaska, the largest state in the United States, is a fast growing and bustling state. Purchased from Russia in 1867 by Secretary William Seward for $7,200,000, it was at the time thought to be a foolish act and was called Seward's Folly. Today, it has vast fishing and lumber industries and her new and huge pipeline brings her latest natural resource, oil, to her sister states in the Union.

Tourists find their way to Alaska by means of plane or automobile across the Alaskan Highway, or by ferryboat up from the southwest coast of Washington and Canada.

Alaska has thousands of wild and untamed wilderness acres. Fisherman and hunters hunt the salmon, tuna, brown bear and caribous. The highest mountain peaks of North America are in this state and are a constant challenge to mountain climbers.

In the remote regions of the Bering Sea coast you will find cities like Nome, once a gold rush camp housing thousands during the 19th century. Here you will also fine the famous Iditarod Trail which marks the end of the famous 1,000 mile Dog Sled Race which starts from Anchorage on the first Saturday in March.

Anchorage *

Dunlap, Betty	**Amenities:** 1,2,4,6,8,10,11,16,	**Dbl. Oc.:** $85.00
10661 Elies Dr., 99516-1136	17	**Sgl. Oc.:** $60.00
(907) 346-1957	**Breakfast:** C. & F.	**Third Person:** $25.00
		Child: Under 12 yrs. - $15.00

Alaska Cozy Comfort's B&B—A warm and cozy home located near golf course, walking trails, skiing, zoo. Minutes to shopping and dining facilities. Enjoy the city lights or view Mt. McKinley while enjoying a full meal. Check-in 5 p.m. to 10 p.m. Transportation available.

Anchorage

Kerr, Cathy	**Amenities:** 1,2,3,9,10,11,16,	**Dbl. Oc.:** $40.00 - $85.00
950 P. St., 99501	17	**Sgl. Oc.:** $40.00 - $85.00
(907) 272-3553	**Breakfast:** C.(winter), F.(summer)	**Third Person:** $15.00
		Child: Under 18 yrs. - $15.00

The Lilac House—An exceptional bed and breakfast, paying careful attention to details to make your stay memorable. Nearby restaurants, shops, museums and Coastal Trail. Beautiful furnishings, soothing atmosphere and quiet neighborhood. Great place to relax and unwind from your Alaskan travels.

Anchorage *

LaFever, Mary & Dick	**Amenities:** 1,2,3,9,10,17	**Dbl. Oc.:** $80.00
1406 W. 13th Ave., 99501	**Breakfast:** C. Plus	**Sgl. Oc.:** $60.00
(907) 258-7378		**Third Person:** $15.00
		Child: Under 14 yrs. - $10.00

Crossroads Inn B&B—Close to coastal trail and downtown. Cable TV, open year- round, office machines available for business travelers. Homey atmosphere, fireplace, quiet neighborhood, nearby restaurants. Hosts are long-time Alaskans, dedicated to your comfort.

Anchorage *

Stimson, Sandra J.	**Amenities:** 1,2,3,4,5,6,7,8,	**Dbl. Oc.:** $80.00
1610 "E." St., 99501	17	**Sgl. Oc.:** $65.00
(907) 279-7808	**Breakfast:** F.	**Third Person:** $15.00

Walkabout Town B&B—Our B&B is close to downtown and also near the spectacular coastal trail. Near all Anchorage tourist attractions. Easy access to Alaska's many fishing, boating, camping and hiking opportunities. Call to let us know when you've arrived and we will assist you.

---

1. No Smoking	5. Tennis Available	9. Credit Cards Accepted	13. Lunch Available	17. Shared Baths
2. No Pets	6. Golf Available	10. Personal Check Accepted	14. Conference Rooms Avail.	18. Afternoon Tea
3 Off Season Rates	7. Swimmming Avail.	11. Reservations Necessary	15. Group Seminars Avail.	* Commisions given
4. Senior Citizen Rates	8. Skiing Available	12. Dinner Available	16. Private Baths	to Travel Agents

ALASKA

Anchorage *

Truesdell, Linda & Daniel
4814 Malibu Rd., 99517
(907) 243-8818, 244-7233

Amenities: 1,2,3,8,9,10,11,16, 17,18
Breakfast: F. & C.

Dbl. Oc.: $85.00
Sgl. Oc.: $75.00
Third Person: $10.00
Child: $10.00

Glacier Bear Bed And Breakfast—One mile from the airport. Walking distance to fine dining, bike and hiking trails, public transportation and the world's largest seaplane base. All this makes your Alaskan experience truly enjoyable. Please visit us and enjoy our great land.....Alaska.

Fairbanks *

Risse, Susan & Ken
4466 Dartmouth, 99709
(907) 479-6973, (800) 478-6973

Amenities: 1,2,9,10,16,17
Breakfast: F.

Dbl. Oc.: $50.00 - $70.00
Sgl. Oc.: $50.00 - $70.00
Third Person: $10.00
Child: Under 16 yrs. - no charge

The Blue Goose Bed And Breakfast—Clean, comfortable rooms with antiques, quilts and old treasures. Convenient location near the University and the airport. On city busline. Full breakfast with Blue-ribbon Alaskan rhubarb pie baked each morning. We love Alaska and we love visitors.

Fairbanks *

Welton, Leicha & Paul
4312 Birch Lane, 99708
(907) 479-0751

Amenities: 1,3,8,9,10,11,14,16,17
Breakfast: F.
Dbl. Oc.: $48.00 - $85.00
Sgl Oc.: $40.00 - $75.00
Third Person: $10.00

Alaska's 7 Gables Bed And Breakfast—Centrally located on 1-1/2 acres in a spacious Tudor home with a floral solarium, garden, waterfall, cathedral ceilings and antique stained glass. Featuring gourmet food, jacuzzis, laundry, phones, cable TV, bicycles, skis and canoes. Rooms or apartments with new beds.

Gustavus *

Burd, Sandy
Box 37, 99826
(907) 697-2241

Amenities: 2,10,17
Breakfast: C. Plus

Dbl. Oc.: $50.00 - $70.00
Sgl. Oc.: $50.00
Third Person: $25.00

Good River Bed And Breakfast—Come explore Glacier Bay using my large log house as home base. Comfy beds, delicious breakfst of home-baked breads. Wild berry jams prepared fresh on the premises using local ingredients. Upbay tours arranged - also whale watching, kayaking and fishing. Free bikes.

1. No Smoking	5. Tennis Available	9. Credit Cards Accepted	13. Lunch Available	17. Shared Baths
2. No Pets	6. Golf Available	10. Personal Check Accepted	14. Conference Rooms Avail.	18. Afternoon Tea
3 Off Season Rates	7. Swimmming Avail.	11. Reservations Necessary	15. Group Seminars Avail.	* Commisions given
4. Senior Citizen Rates	8. Skiing Available	12. Dinner Available	16. Private Baths	to Travel Agents

ALASKA

Gustavus *

Unrein, Annie & Al
Tong Rd., Box 5, Gustavus (summer) 99826
Box 2557, St. George, UT (winter), 84771
(907) 697-2288, Fax: (907) 697-2289
(801) 673-8480, Fax:673-8481 (summer)

Amenities: 1,2,10,11,12,13,16, 17,18
Breakfast: F.

Dbl. Oc.: $144.00
Sgl. Oc.: $102.00
Third Person: $47.00
Child: No charge - $32.00

Glacier Bay Country Inn—A photographer's paradise, profesional's retreat and fisherman's dream. Peaceful storybook setting away from the crowds. Fresh seafood, garden produce, homemade breads and desserts. Boat tours, bikes, fishing, kayaking, whale watching and hiking.

Homer *

Seekins, Gert & Floyd
Box 1264, 99603
(907) 235-8996

Amenities: 1,2,3,7,8,9,10,11, 16,17
Breakfast: F.

Dbl. Oc.: $65.00 - $80.00
Sgl. Oc.: $45.00 - $70.00
Third Person: $10.00
Child: Under 12 yrs. - no charge

Homer Bed And Breakfast—Fantastic view: mountains, glaciers and beautiful Kachemak Bay. Modern cabin guest houses with complete kitchen facilities. TV and outdoor wood sauna. Birds, moose and wildflowers. Salmon and halibut charters. Referral agency for other B&B activities in the area.

Juneau *

Carroll, Charlotte
P.O. Box 20537, 99802
(907) 586-6378

Amenities: 1,2,8,9,11,16,17
Breakfast: C. Plus

Dbl. Oc.: $83.25
Sgl. Oc.: $72.15

Eagle's Nest Bed And Breakfast—It's your own two bedroom A-frame nestled in among the evergreens with your hostess right next door. Provided: BBQ, woodstove, TV, VCR, phone, washer/dryer and full outdoor hot tub. All uniquely Alaskan! Great fishing in the summer and skiing in the winter.

Juneau *

Urquhart, Judy
9436 N. Douglas Hwy., 99801
(907) 463-5886

Amenities: 1,2,3,6,7,8,10,12,14,15,17
Breakfast: F.
Dbl. Oc.: $75.00
Sgl Oc.: $70.00
Third Person: $10.00
Child: Under 5 yrs. - no charge

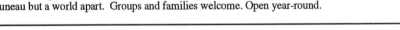

Blueberry Lodge B&B—Relax in a spacious hand-crafted log lodge overlooking an ocean waterway, wildlife refuge and an eagle nest. Library and three story living room. Located minutes from downtown Juneau but a world apart. Groups and families welcome. Open year-round.

1. No Smoking	5. Tennis Available	9. Credit Cards Accepted	13. Lunch Available	17. Shared Baths
2. No Pets	6. Golf Available	10. Personal Check Accepted	14. Conference Rooms Avail.	18. Afternoon Tea
3 Off Season Rates	7. Swimmming Avail.	11. Reservations Necessary	15. Group Seminars Avail.	* Commisions given
4. Senior Citizen Rates	8. Skiing Available	12. Dinner Available	16. Private Baths	to Travel Agents

ALASKA

Seward *

Freeman, Charlotte L.
Eagle Lane
P.O. Box 1734, 99664-1734
(907) 224-3939

Amenities: 1,2,10,16,17
Breakfast: F.

Dbl. Oc.: $55.00 - $75.00
Sgl. Oc.: $46.00 - $65.00
Third Person: 10.00

Swiss Chalet Bed And Breakfast—An old-time Alaskan offers gracious hospitality and comfortable, smoke-free atmosphere. Located one block off Seward Highway by the road to Exit Glacier. A five-minute walk to Le Barn Appetit Restaurant. Seasonal service May through September.

Seward *

Reese, Annette & Frances
Box 1157
Mile 1.7 Nash Rd., 99664
(907) 224-3614

Amenities: 1,2,3,4,8,9,10,11, 16,17
Breakfast: C.

Dbl. Oc.: $61.20 - $76.50
Sgl. Oc.: $51.00 - $66.30
Third Person: $10.20
Child: $10.20

The White House Bed And Breakfast—A country home with five large guest rooms surrounded by forests and majestic mountains. Four miles to Seward Boat Harbor and 10 miles to Glacier exit. Cross-country skiing in winter. Guest rooms, TV room and fully equipped kitchen on second level.

Tok *

Morgan, Lois
647 W. 1st St.
Box 527, 99780
(907) 883-5647

Amenities: 17
Breakfast: C.

Dbl. Oc.: $35.00
Sgl. Oc.: $30.00
Child: Under 10 yrs. - $5.00

Lois' Bed And Breakfast—Queen-size bed with Sealy mattress. Convenient location but away from center of town. Originally an Alaskan homestead.

Wasilla *

Carswell, Louise & Ross
2651 E. Palmer Wasilla Hwy., 99654
(907) 376-5868

Amenities: 1,8,9,10,11,16
Breakfast: F.
Dbl. Oc.: $68.25
Sgl Oc.: $52.50

Country Lakes Bed And Breakfast—Handy, yet scenic and peaceful. Guest rooms and back-yard deck overlooks a quiet waterway leading to nearby Lake Wasilla. Hosts are longtime Alaskans. We do spectacular seaplane, glacier and wildlife tours. Remote cabin stays also available.

1. No Smoking	5. Tennis Available	9. Credit Cards Accepted	13. Lunch Available	17. Shared Baths
2. No Pets	6. Golf Available	10. Personal Check Accepted	14. Conference Rooms Avail.	18. Afternoon Tea
3 Off Season Rates	7. Swimmming Avail.	11. Reservations Necessary	15. Group Seminars Avail.	* Commisions given
4. Senior Citizen Rates	8. Skiing Available	12. Dinner Available	16. Private Baths	to Travel Agents

ARIZONA

The Grand Canyon State

Capitol: Phoenix
Statehood: February 14, 1921; the 48th state
State Motto: God Enriches
State Song: "Arizona"
State Bird: Cactus Wren
State Flower: Saguaro
State Tree: Palverde

Arizona is a vacation land of wonder and beauty. It has one of the oldest communities in the country, going back to the 1100's. Inhabited then by the Hopi Indians, it still is a home for many American Indians today.

No other state has as many national monuments as this state. It not only boasts of the Grand Canyon, one of the natural wonders of the world, but also giant dams such as Coolidge, Glen Canyon, Hoover, Parker and Roosevelt.

Hundreds of visitors and vacationers come here every year. Many remain and make it their second home. Its warm and easy climate make it a haven for senior citizens.

London bridge was brought brick by brick from England and reassembled in the popular resort area of Lake Havasu.

Bisbee *

Waid, Gail
61 Main
P.O. Box 825, 85603
(602) 432-5900, (800) 421-1909

Amenities: 1,2,5,6,9,10,14,15,16,17
Breakfast: F.
Dbl. Oc.: $55.28 - $105.02
Sgl Oc.: $55.28 - $105.82
Third Person: $15.00

Bisbee Grand Hotel- A Bed And Breakfast Inn—A step back in time. Family heirlooms and antiques. Romantic, Victorian decor. Homelike atmosphere with inn privacy. Quiet old Western saloon downstairs. Located downtown, a town time forgot, in Mule Mountain of historic south Arizona. Walk everywhere. Enjoy a slower pace.

Flagstaff

Dierker, Dorothea
423 W. Cherry, 86001
(602) 774-3249

Amenities: 1,2,5,8,10,17
Breakfast: C.
(F. after 8:00 a.m.)

Dbl. Oc.: $43.50
Sgl. Oc.: $35.00
Third Person: $11.00

Dierker House—A charming home in old historic Flagstaff. Second-floor guest area with private entrance, sitting room and small kitchen. Excellent breakfast in downstairs dining room. Antiques, king beds and good lamps. Quiet area. Convenient for walking.

Flagstaff

Wanek, Ray
685 Lake Mary Rd., 86001
(602) 774-8959

Amenities: 1,2,8,9,10,16,17
Breakfast: C.
Dbl. Oc.: $64.80 - $100.00
Sgl Oc.: $54.00

Arizona Mountain Inn—Our old English inn is nestled in the pines three miles south of Flagstaff. Antiques, crystal and lace decorate each room and suite. A delicious continental breakfast is served in our lovely dining room. Relax in the quiet forest atmosphere.

---

1. No Smoking	5. Tennis Available	9. Credit Cards Accepted	13. Lunch Available	17. Shared Baths
2. No Pets	6. Golf Available	10. Personal Check Accepted	14. Conference Rooms Avail.	18. Afternoon Tea
3 Off Season Rates	7. Swimmming Avail.	11. Reservations Necessary	15.Group Seminars Avail.	* Commisions given
4. Senior Citizen Rates	8. Skiing Available	12. Dinner Available	16. Private Baths	to Travel Agents

ARIZONA

Lakeside *

Bartram, Petie
Rte. 1, Box 1014, 85929
(602) 367-1408

Amenities: 1,4,8,11,16
Breakfast: F.

Dbl. Oc.: $73.85 - $116.05
Sgl. Oc.: $63.30
Third Person: $21.10
Child: Under 12 yrs. - $10.55

Bartram's White Mountain Bed And Breakfast—Unique accommodations at affordable prices. year-round lodgings. Includes a seven-course country breakfast served in elegant style in a quiet, country setting. Each room specially decorated for comfort and appeal. A variety of house pets.

Phoenix *

Kelley, Mary Ellen & Paul
15 W. Pasadena Ave., 85013
(602) 274-6302

Amenities: 2,3,10,11,16
Breakfast: C. Plus

Dbl. Oc.: $98.00
Sgl. Oc.: $98.00
Third Person: $15.00
Child: $10.00

Maricopa Manor—Old-world charm in an elegant urban setting. Five luxury suites. Close to shops, restaurants and only 15 minutes from the airport. Art, antiques and spacious grounds. Gazebo, spa and patio amid palm and citrus trees.

Phoenix *

Trapp, Darrell
P.O. Box 41624, 85080
(602) 582-3868

Amenities: 1,2,3,4,5,6,7,9
10,11,12,13,14,
15,16,18
Breakfast: F. (winter)
C. Plus (summer)

Dbl. Oc.: $49.00 - $122.00
Sgl. Oc.: $49.00 - $99.00
Third Person: $12.00
Child: $12.00

Westways "Private" Resort-Inn—Convenient to I-17. Executive estate area. Contemporary Spanish design on designer-landscaped grounds. Deluxe queen-bedded rooms. Resplendently simple elegance. Guests rate us five stars. Casual Western comfort with class. "Where guests preserve their privacy."

Pinetop/Lakeside *

Horn, Margaret & Robert
453 N. Woodland Rd., 85929
(602) 367-8200

Amenities: 2,3,6,8,9,11,12,13,14,15,16,18
Breakfast: F.
Dbl. Oc.: $100.00 - $250.00
Sgl Oc.: $100.00 - $250.00

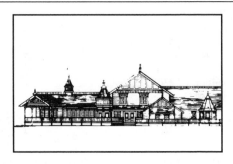

The Meadows Inn—"Celebrate the seasons" in the White Mountains. Classic elegance at this "world-class" Victorian country inn. Gourmet food, fine wines, romantic, private gardens and greenhouse, antiques, original art and verandas. "A magical place where peace of mind is normal."

1. No Smoking	5. Tennis Available	9. Credit Cards Accepted	13. Lunch Available	17. Shared Baths
2. No Pets	6. Golf Available	10. Personal Check Accepted	14. Conference Rooms Avail.	18. Afternoon Tea
3 Off Season Rates	7. Swimmming Avail.	11. Reservations Necessary	15. Group Seminars Avail.	* Commisions given
4. Senior Citizen Rates	8. Skiing Available	12. Dinner Available	16. Private Baths	to Travel Agents

ARIZONA

Prescott *

Faulkner, Morris
503 So. Montezuma
(U.S. Hwy. 89), 86303
602) 445-7991

Amenities: 1,2,4,5,6,7,9,10, 11,14,16
Breakfast: C. Plus

Dbl. Oc.: $54.00 - $125.00
Sgl. Oc.: $54.00 - $125.00
Third Person: $10.00
Child: Under 12 yrs. - $5.00

The Cottages At...Prescott Country Inn—Breakfast in your two- ,three- or four- bedroom cottage suite. Twelve charmingly decorated country cottages 3 blocks from center of town. Three fireplaces. BBQs. Queen and king beds. Free access to separate health club, pool, spa and tennis. World-class restaurants & theatre.

Scottsdale *

Curtis, Kathleen
P.O. Box 2214, 85252
(602) 941-1281

Amenities: 2,4,5,6,7,16,17, 18
Breakfast: C., F.,or C. Plus

Dbl. Oc.: $35.00
Sgl. Oc.: $25.00

Valley O'The Sun Bed And Breakfast—Established in 1983. Arizona's only Irish bed and breakfast. Ideally located in the college area of Tempe, yet close enough to Scottsdale to enjoy the glamour of its shops, restaurants and theatres. All guests enjoy glorious views and a hearty Arizona breakfast.

Sedona

Bruno, Fran & Dan
255 Rock Ridge Dr., 86336
(602) 282-7640

Amenities: 1,2,3,5,6,7,10,11, 14,15,16,18
Breakfast: F.

Dbl. Oc.: $95.00 - $125.00
Sgl. Oc.: $90.00 - $120.00
Child: $15.00

Bed And Breakfast At Saddle Rock Ranch—HISTORY * ROMANCE * ANTIQUES * ELEGANCE * Centrally located Old West movie estate. Magnificent views. Romantic rooms feature fieldstone fireplaces, canopied beds and antiques. Scrumptious breakfast and afternoon snacks. Warm and friendly hosts. Flower gardens, pool and spa.

Sedona *

Gillman, Lynn & Bob
80 Canyon Circle Dr., 86336-8673
(602) 284-0082

Amenities: 1,2,5,6,8,9,10,11, 16
Breakfast: F.

Dbl. Oc.: $94.95
Sgl. Oc.: $89.68
Third Person: $10.55
Child: $5.55

Cozy Cactus—Towering formations of red rock dominate the character of Sedona,known worldwide as an arts colony, an ideal retreat and a premier resort. Furnished with heirlooms and theatrical memorabilia; shared sitting rooms with fireplaces. Direct access to hiking area.

Sedona *

Pace, Lea
65 Piki Dr.
P.O. Box 552, 86336
(602) 282-2833

Amenities: 1,2,3,4,5,6,10,11, 14,15,16,17,18
Breakfast: F.

Dbl. Oc.: $75.14 - $108.29
Sgl. Oc.: $68.00 - $98.00
Third Person: $7.74
Child: $7.74

Sipapu Lodge—Experience Old West hospitality at its best! Sipapu Lodge is a ranch-style house featuring Anasazi Indian culture mixed with southwest memorabilia. Unique recipes are Lea's breakfast specialty. Vince is a massage technician and potter.

---

1. No Smoking	5. Tennis Available	9. Credit Cards Accepted	13. Lunch Available	17. Shared Baths
2. No Pets	6. Golf Available	10. Personal Check Accepted	14. Conference Rooms Avail.	18. Afternoon Tea
3 Off Season Rates	7. Swimmming Avail.	11. Reservations Necessary	15. Group Seminars Avail.	* Commisions given
4. Senior Citizen Rates	8. Skiing Available	12. Dinner Available	16. Private Baths	to Travel Agents

13

Sedona

Redenbaugh, Carol & Roger
150 Canyon Circle Dr., 86336
(602) 284-1425

Amenities: 1,2,5,6,7,9,10,15,16,18
Breakfast: F.
Dbl. Oc.: $100.23 - $200.45
Sgl Oc.: $79.13 - $179.35
Third Person: $21.10
Child: Under 3 yrs. - no charge

The Graham Bed And Breakfast Inn—The inn was built as a Southwest-style bed and breakfast inn with six unique guest rooms, some with fireplaces and Jacuzzis, all with private balconies and baths. Beautifully landscaped pool and spa area; local artist pieces; spectacular red rock views. Mobil - ****
award.

Sedona *

Stevenson, Doris & Dick   **Amenities:** 1,2,9,15,16   **Dbl. Oc.:** $85.00 - $95.00
595 Jordan Rd., 86336   **Breakfast:** F.   **Third Person:** $10.00
(602) 282-6462

"A Touch Of Sedona" — **Bed And Breakfast**—Eclectic elegance. Furnished with stained-glass lamps and antiques with a mix of contemporary. Old-fashioned breakfast with home-baked breads. Within walking distance of uptown.

Tucson *

Bryant, Deborah   **Amenities:** 1,2,3,4,5,7,9,10,   **Dbl. Oc.:** $95.00 - $125.00
1640 N. Campbell Ave., 85719   11,16,18   **Sgl. Oc.:** $95.00 - $125.00
(602) 795-3840   **Breakfast:** C. Plus (weekdays)   **Child:** Under 12 yrs. - no charge
          F. (weekends)

La Posada Del Valle—An elegant 1920s inn located in the heart of Tucson. Lush gardens and mature orange trees perfume the air. Patios for sunning. Five richly appointed guest rooms. Gourmet breakfast and afternoon tea. Within walking distance of the University of Arizona and University Hospital.

Tucson *

Florek, Phyllis   **Amenities:** 1,2,3,4,7,8,9,10,   **Dbl. Oc.:** $78.00 - $83.00
316 E. Speedway, 85705   11,14,15,16,18   **Sgl. Oc.:** $72.00 - $83.00
(602) 628-1800   **Breakfast:** F.   **Third Person:** $10.00

Casa Alegre Bed And Breakfast Inn—Distinguished 1915 home located between the University of Arizona and downtown Tucson. Scrumptious breakfast served in the formal dining room or poolside on the serene patio. Near historic, cultural and recreational activities. Fantastic birding and hiking.

1. No Smoking	5. Tennis Available	9. Credit Cards Accepted	13. Lunch Available	17. Shared Baths
2. No Pets	6. Golf Available	10. Personal Check Accepted	14. Conference Rooms Avail.	18. Afternoon Tea
3 Off Season Rates	7. Swimmming Avail.	11. Reservations Necessary	15. Group Seminars Avail.	* Commisions given
4. Senior Citizen Rates	8. Skiing Available	12. Dinner Available	16. Private Baths	to Travel Agents

ARIZONA

Tucson *

Fredona, Phyllis	**Amenities:** 1,2,4,5,6,7,8,10,	**Dbl. Oc.:** $50.00 - $70.00
Cummings, Albert	11,16,17	**Sgl. Oc.:** $50.00 - $70.00
2324 No. Madelyn Cir., 85712-2621	**Breakfast:** C. Plus	$5.00 extra for 1 night stay
(602) 326-4846		

The Gable House—Centrally located on an acre lot in a guiet residential neighborhood, this picturesque Santa Fe-style home with Mexican influence was home to actor Clark Gable in the early 1940s. Restaurants, shops, bus within easy walking distance. Experience Southwest charm.

Tucson *

Haberman, Larry	**Amenities:** 1,2,10,11,13,15,16,	**Dbl. Oc.:** $45.00
3150 E. Presidio Rd., 85716	17,18	**Sgl. Oc.:** $35.00
(602) 881-4582	**Breakfast:** F.	**Third Person:** $15.00
		Child: Under 12 yrs. - $10.00

Natural Bed And Breakfast—Attention is put on natural, non-toxic, non-allergenic environment. Only natural foods served. A private patio and professional massage are available. I offer a large living room with a fireplace inwhich to relax and recuperate. In the beautiful Southwest desert.

Tucson

Hymer-Thompson, Karen	**Amenities:** 1,2,16	**Dbl. Oc.:** $65.00 - $75.00
11155 W. Calle Pima, 85743	**Breakfast:** F.	**Sgl. Oc.:** $65.00 - $75.00
(602) 578-3058		**Third Person:** $10.00
		Child: $10.00

Casa Tierra Bed And Breakfast Inn—Rustic Mexican-style adobe home. Arched courtyard, colorful tiles, vaulted brick and viga ceilings. Quiet, secluded desert area 30 minutes west of Tucson. Near Desert Museum, Old Tucson and Saguaro National Monument. Hiking, mountain views, sunsets, birding and hot tub.

Tucson *

Mayer, Wanda & Kenneth	**Amenities:** 1,2,11,16	**Dbl. Oc.:** $47.00
7002 E. Redbud Rd., 85715	**Breakfast:** F.	**Sgl. Oc.:** $37.00
(602) 721-0218		

Redbud House Bed And Breakfast—Cozy retreat with view. Near restaurants and attractions. Living room for guests; king or twin bedroom; books, TV, newspaper and BBQ. Off-street parking. Short walk to large recreation center with Olympic-size pool and exercise facility that is open to the public for small fee.

Tucson *

Toci, Patti	**Amenities:** 1,2,3,4,10,11,14,	**Dbl. Oc.:** $94.08 - $115.98
297 N. Main Ave., 85701	15,16,18	**Sgl. Oc.:** $77.65 - $99.55
(602) 623-6151	**Breakfast:** F.	**Third Person:** $20.00
		Child: Under 12 yrs. - $15.00

El Presidio Bed And Brekfast Inn—Luxury inn in award-winning Victorian adobe mansion. Southwestern charm abounds in lush garden courtyards surrounding richly appointed guest house and suites. Near downtown in quaint historic district. Restaurants, shopping, museums nearby. Mobil 3-star rated 1992.

1. No Smoking	5. Tennis Available	9. Credit Cards Accepted	13. Lunch Available	17. Shared Baths
2. No Pets	6. Golf Available	10. Personal Check Accepted	14. Conference Rooms Avail.	18. Afternoon Tea
3 Off Season Rates	7. Swimming Avail.	11. Reservations Necessary	15. Group Seminars Avail.	* Commisions given
4. Senior Citizen Rates	8. Skiing Available	12. Dinner Available	16. Private Baths	to Travel Agents

ARKANSAS

Land of Opportunity

Capitol: Little Rock
Statehood: January 15, 1836: the 25th state
State Motto: The People Rule
State Song: "Arkansas"
State Bird: Mockingbird
State Flower: Apple Blossom
State Tree: Pine

Arkansas is a southern state with comfortable weather, warm enough to make the visitor feel unhurried and relaxed. There are beautiful rugged mountains and the Ozark Valley, where hot and cold springs invite tourists to come and soothe their aches and pains. The Buffalo National River flows across the norther boundary of Arkansas and through the Ozark Plateau. Here one can swim, canoe, fish and shot the rapids. Here, too, the Ozark Folk Center at Mountain View has preserved the ingenuity of the country people of this state ad their mountain music, crafts and folklore. Twenty-five million tourists each year come here to see and enjoy this center.

There are two large cities in Arkansas, Little Rock and Fort Smith. Perhaps one of the most unique towns in all of the U.S. is Texarkana, built just across from the state of Texas, yet on the border of both states. One half of the town is in Texas and the other in Arkansas.

Arkansas is the home of our 42nd president, William Jefferson Blythe Clinton, who was born here on August 19, 1946. Arkansas' national hero is Gen. Douglas MacArthur. He was born in Little Rock in 1880.

ARKANSAS

Eureka Springs *

Becker, Dr. Ralph	**Amenities:** 1,2,3,7,9,10,16	**Dbl. Oc.:** $79.55 - $112.70
211 Spring St., 72632	**Breakfast:** F.	**Sgl. Oc.:** $79.55 - $112.70
(501) 253-6022		

Crescent Cottage Inn—Famous 1881 Victorian. One of the few designated as a significant structure. Home of the first Governor of Arkansas. Superb mountain views, breakfasts. Antiques. On historic loop, a few minutes walk to town along Spring & Maple tree-lined streets. Private Jacuzzis. Queen beds.

Eureka Springs *

Dragonwagon, Crescent	**Amenities:** 1,2,9,10,11,12,	**Dbl. Oc.:** $125.00 - $175.00
Shank, Ned	14,16	**Sgl. Oc.:** $120.00 - $170.00
515 Spring St., 72632	**Breakfast:** F.	**Third Person:** $10.00
(501) 253-7444, (800) 562-8650		**Child:** Under 5 yrs. - no charge

Dairy Hollow House—A warm and indulgent country inn/restaurant. Fireplaces, flowers, hot tub and heavenly breakfast delivered daily to your door in a basket. Fresh seasonal, regional cuisine featured in our flower-filled restaurant. Lodging in our 1880s farmhouse or spacious main house.

Eureka Springs *

Gavron, Barbara
11 Singleton, 72632
(501) 253-9111

Amenities: 1,2,9,10,11,16,17
Breakfast: F.
Dbl. Oc.: $71.83 - $104.98
Sgl Oc.: $66.30
Third Person: $20.00
Child: Under 12 yrs. - $10.00

Singleton House—An old-fashioned inn with a touch of magic. Whimsically decorated with an eclectic collection of treasures and antiques. Breakfast served on the balcony overlooking the fantasy garden and fish pond. Historic district. Walk to shops. Separate romantic cottage with jacuzzi.

Eureka Springs

McDonald, Denise & Michael	**Amenities:** 1,2,3,5,6,7,9,10,	**Dbl. Oc.:** $77.00 - $99.00
263 Spring St., 72632	16	**Sgl. Oc.:** $77.00 - $99.00
(501) 253-7853	**Breakfast:** F.	**Third Person:** $20.00
		Child: Under 5 yrs. - $10.00

Bridgeford House B&B—Nestled in the heart of the historic district lies this delightful 1884 Victorian house. Each private room or suite has a private entrance, private bath, antiques, color TV and fresh coffee or tea. Gourmet breakfast served daily. Open all year.

1. No Smoking	5. Tennis Available	9. Credit Cards Accepted	13. Lunch Available	17. Shared Baths
2. No Pets	6. Golf Available	10. Personal Check Accepted	14. Conference Rooms Avail.	18. Afternoon Tea
3 Off Season Rates	7. Swimmming Avail.	11. Reservations Necessary	15. Group Seminars Avail.	* Commisions given
4. Senior Citizen Rates	8. Skiing Available	12. Dinner Available	16. Private Baths	to Travel Agents

ARKANSAS

Eureka Springs *

Simantel, Iris & William	**Amenities:** 1,2,6,7,9,10,11,14,	**Dbl. Oc.:** $58.00 - $105.00
35 Kings Hwy., 72632	15,16	**Sgl. Oc.:** $58.00 - $105.00
(501) 253-8916	**Breakfast:** F.	**Third Person:** $15.00

Heartstone Inn B&B And Cottages—An award-winning, turn-of-the-century Victorian inn in the historic district. Nine guest rooms with antique furnishings, private baths and entrances. Cable TV. King, queen and double beds. Two charming cottages next to the inn. Located on trolley route.

Fordyce

Phillips, James	**Amenities:** 1,2,5,7,9,10,11,	**Dbl. Oc.:** $60.00
412 W. 4th St., 71742	16	**Sgl. Oc.:** $55.00
(501) 352-7202	**Breakfast:** F.	**Third Person:** $10.00
		Child: Under 10 yrs. - $5.00

Wynne Phillips House—A gracious colonial revival mansion listed in the National Register of Historic Places. Furnished with antiques, Oriental rugs and family heirlooms. Enjoy rocking on the porch, a stroll beneath the arbors, or a dip in the lap pool.

Hardy *

Johnson, Peggy	**Amenities:** 1,2,5,6,7,9,10,16	**Dbl. Oc.:** $60.00
511 Main St., 72542	**Breakfast:** F.	**Sgl. Oc.:** $55.00
(501) 856-2983		

Olde Stonehouse Bed And Breakfast Inn—Native stone historic home with spacious porches for relaxing. One block to river. Old railroad town with quaint shops. Period antiques. Queen beds. Dinner and country music theatres, canoeing, golf, tennis, horseback riding, Mammoth Spring and Grand Gulf Street Park nearby.

Hot Springs *

Bartlett, Helen	**Amenities:** 1,2,4,9,10,16	**Dbl. Oc.:** $66.30 - $82.88
303 Quapaw, 71901	**Breakfast:** F.	**Sgl. Oc.:** $55.25 - $71.83
(501) 623-3258		**Third Person:** $15.00
		Child: Under 12 yrs. - $5.00

Vintage Comfort Bed And Breakfast Inn—A 1907 Queen Anne home where guests are pampered with Southern hospitality. Ideal for weddings and honeymoons. Hot Springs National Park, hiking trails and famed bath- house row. Oaklawn Horse Race Track.

---

1. No Smoking	5. Tennis Available	9. Credit Cards Accepted	13. Lunch Available	17. Shared Baths
2. No Pets	6. Golf Available	10. Personal Check Accepted	14. Conference Rooms Avail.	18. Afternoon Tea
3 Off Season Rates	7. Swimmming Avail.	11. Reservations Necessary	15. Group Seminars Avail.	* Commisions given
4. Senior Citizen Rates	8. Skiing Available	12. Dinner Available	16. Private Baths	to Travel Agents

ARKANSAS

Hot Springs *

Wilson, Lady Janie
906 Malvern Hwy., 71901
(501) 624-0896

Amenities: 3,4,10,11,16
Breakfast: C.
Dbl. Oc.: $50.00
Sgl Oc.: $45.00
Third Person: $5.00

Dogwood Manor—A 105- year- old Victorian in the National Registry Showplace of Architecture & Design. Custom draped, furniture of that era. Five lovely bedrooms, seven baths. Experience the luxury of yesteryear. Centrally located to bath house, row house, races, three lakes and hiking.

Kingston

Sullivan, MaryJo
HCR 30, Box 198, 72742
(501) 665-2986

Amenities: 1,4,9,10,11,12,17
Breakfast: F.

Dbl. Oc.: $55.00
Sgl. Oc.: $30.00
Third Person: $15.00

Fools Cove Ranch—A rustic setting high in the Ozarks. Fine accommodations and great food. Family farm with beautiful views and natural trails. A short drive to Buffalo River, Eureka Springs area and Branson, Missouri, or just rest and relax in comfort under large oaks. Corrals available.

---

1. No Smoking
2. No Pets
3 Off Season Rates
4. Senior Citizen Rates

5. Tennis Available
6. Golf Available
7. Swimmming Avail.
8. Skiing Available

9. Credit Cards Accepted
10. Personal Check Accepted
11. Reservations Necessary
12. Dinner Available

13. Lunch Available
14. Conference Rooms Avail.
15. Group Seminars Avail.
16. Private Baths

17. Shared Baths
18. Afternoon Tea
* Commisions given
to Travel Agents

19

CALIFORNIA

The Golden State

Capitol: Sacramento
Statehood: September 9, 1850: the 31st state
State Motto: Eureka (I have Found It)
State Song: "I love You, California"
State Bird: California Valley Quail
State Flower: Golden Poppy
State Tree: California Redwood

The gold rush of 1848 started millions of people moving to California. Today more people live in the state than any other state in the union.

Farmers here have created some of the largest and most productive farms in all of our country. Their fruits, vegetables and nuts are shipped all over the U.S. California has the distinction of having the highest farm income in the nation.

Visitors visit California by the thousands every year. The wonderful climate and diversified beauty of this state, from the majestic redwood forest to the north and the giant sequoias of the Sierra Nevadas to the beautiful beaches and deserts in the south, make it a favorite vacation land.

The movie industry, located around Los Angeles, has brought excitement and glamour here as well as entertainment for the entire country since the early 1900's.

One of the most famous events of the year is perhaps the Tournament of Roses Parade in Pasadena on New Year's Day.

Our 37th president, Richard Nixon, is a native Californian, born in Yorbe Linda.

CALIFORNIA

Alameda *

McCormick, Susan & Andrew
1238 Versailles Ave., 94501
(510) 523-9697

Amenities: 1,2,5,6,7,10,11,12, 13,14,15,16,17,18
Breakfast: F.

Dbl. Oc.: $82.50 - $137.50
Sgl. Oc.: $82.50 - $137.50
Child: Under 1 yr. - no charge

Webster House Bed And Breakfast Inn—Step back in time. Lovingly restored 1854 Gothic revival cottage. The oldest house on the island. Afternoon tea at 4 p.m., evening snack by the fireside. Breakfast served on the sun porch or on the deck by the waterfall. Bus or ferry to San Francisco every 30 minutes.

Anaheim *

Pischel, Anna Marie & Steve
856 So. Walnut St., 92802
(714) 778-0105

Amenities: 1,2,3,4,9,10,14,16, 18
Breakfast: F.

Dbl. Oc.: $65.00 - $90.00
Sgl. Oc.: $37.00 - $80.00
Third Person: $10.00
Child: Under 10 yrs. - $5.00

Anaheim Country Inn—A large and beautiful Princess Anne farmhouse built in 1910 on an acre of lawn and gardens. One mile from Disneyland. Graced by beveled lead-glass windows and charming turn-of-the-century furnishings. Hot tub and laundry room available.

Angwin *

Lambeth, Corlene & Harold
415 Cold Springs Rd., 94508
(707) 965-3538

Amenities: 1,2,3,5,7,9,10,11, 15,16
Breakfast: C.

Dbl. Oc.: $99.00 - $195.00
Sgl. Oc.: $99.00 - $195.00

Forest Manor Bed And Breakfast—A majestic English Tudor on 20 secluded acres above Napa Valley. Massive hand-carved beams, vaulted ceilings, fireplaces, decks and large pool/spa. Described as "one of the most romantic country inns, a peaceful wooded sanctuary and a small, exclusive resort."

Aptos *

Groom, Diana
6265 Soquel Dr., 95003
(408) 475-6868

Amenities: 1,2,3,5,6,7,9,10, 14,15,16,17,18
Breakfast: F.

Dbl. Oc.: $95.00 - $145.00
Sgl. Oc.: $85.00 - $135.00
Third Person: $15.00
Child: $15.00

Apple Lane Inn—A 1876 Victorian farmhouse on three acres. Antiques. Walk to beach, shopping and world-class restaurants. Full, elegant breakfast includes home-grown fruits and eggs. The best of the country and the coast, yesterday and today. Every visit an experience to remember.

Auburn *

Lynieks, Jean
164 Cleveland Ave., 95603
(916) 885-1166

Amenities: 1,6,8,9,10,14,15, 16
Breakfast: F.

Dbl. Oc.: $75.00 - $165.00
Third Person: $10.00
Child: Under 3 yrs. - no charge

Power's Mansion Inn—Our beautiful Victorian home offers you the hospitality of that era. Each room is furnished with period pieces and modern conveniences with the comfort of our guests our top priority. Come, let us pamper you!

---

1. No Smoking
2. No Pets
3 Off Season Rates
4. Senior Citizen Rates

5. Tennis Available
6. Golf Available
7. Swimmming Avail.
8. Skiing Available

9. Credit Cards Accepted
10. Personal Check Accepted
11. Reservations Necessary
12. Dinner Available

13. Lunch Available
14. Conference Rooms Avail.
15. Group Seminars Avail.
16. Private Baths

17. Shared Baths
18. Afternoon Tea
* Commisions given
to Travel Agents

CALIFORNIA

Avalon *
(Santa Catalina Island)
Michalis, Hattie & Robert
344 Whittley Ave.
P.O. Box 1381, 90704
(310) 510-2547

Amenities: 1,2,3,4,5,6,7,10,11,16,17
Breakfast: C. Plus
Dbl. Oc.: $110.00 - $150.00
Sgl Oc.: $90.00 - $135.00
Child: Under 14 yrs. - $10.00

Gull House Bed And Breakfast Home—Discover the romance of the island. You will return often. Uphill 1/4 mile from all harbor activities. Newly built "touch-of-class" contemporary suites and guest rooms. Breakfast at leisure on patio by the pool or under a large umbrella. Spa heated in season only. Great place.

Avalon *
(Santa Catalina Island)
Olsen, Jon
125 Clarissa Ave., 90704
(310) 510-0356

Amenities: 1,2,3,4,5,6,7,9,10,11,14,15,16,18
Breakfast: C. Plus buffet
Dbl. Oc.: $96.65 - $267.50
Sgl Oc.: $96.65 - $267.50

Garden House Inn—An elegant 1923 historic home. Steps to beach. Ocean-view terraces. Large garden patio for buffet breakfast. Wine and appetizers. Romantic and relaxed. Antiques. Mid-week discounts. AAA-approved. Cable TV, VCR and film library. Avalon Bay and Catalina Island are lovely.

Big Sur *
Bussinger, Robert
Hwy. 1, 93920
(408) 667-2331

Amenities: 1,2,7,9,10,11,12, 13,14,16,18
Breakfast: C. Extended

Dbl. Oc.: $180.00 - $850.00
Sgl. Oc.: $180.00 - $850.00
Third Person: $50.00
Child: $50.00

The Ventana Inn—Mobil four-star. Romantic. On 240 acres above the Pacific. Decorator-designed guest rooms with king or queen beds, terraces, A/C, phones, TV and VCR. Most with fireplace, some with hot tubs. Afternoon wine and cheese. Fireside lounge, Four-star restaurant, sauna and massage.

---

1. No Smoking	5. Tennis Available	9. Credit Cards Accepted	13. Lunch Available	17. Shared Baths
2. No Pets	6. Golf Available	10. Personal Check Accepted	14. Conference Rooms Avail.	18. Afternoon Tea
3 Off Season Rates	7. Swimmming Avail.	11. Reservations Necessary	15. Group Seminars Avail.	* Commisions given
4. Senior Citizen Rates	8. Skiing Available	12. Dinner Available	16. Private Baths	to Travel Agents

CALIFORNIA

Burlingame

Fernandez, Elnora & Joe
1021 Balboa Ave., 94010
(415) 344-5815

Amenities: 5,6,7,10,11,16
Breakfast: C.

Dbl. Oc.: $50.00
Sgl. Oc.: $40.00
Third Person: $10.00
Child: Under 6 yrs. - no charge

Burlingame Bed And Breakfast—We are three miles south of the San Francisco Airport. Restaurants, shops and buses are a block away. The train is six blocks away. Private upstairs quarters. King-size bed. Separate eating area. View of creek. Native flora and fauna. Italian, Spanish and French spoken.

Calistoga *

Beckert, Doris & Gus
3037 Foothill Blvd., 94515
(800) 942-6933

Amenities: 1,2,5,6,7,9,10,11, 16
Breakfast: F.

Dbl. Oc.: $122.45 - $177.70
Third Person: $39.57

Foothill House Bed And Breakfast—A country setting 1-1/2 miles north of Calistoga. Three cozy yet spacious suites. All rooms have private baths and entrances, fireplaces, queen beds and air-conditioning. Some Jacuzzi tubs. Complimentary wine and appetizer. Close to wineries, ballooning, spas and restaurants.

Calistoga

Dywer, Scarlett
3918 Silverado Trail, 94515
(707) 942-6669

Amenities: 2,5,6,7,10,16,18
Breakfast: C. Plus
Dbl. Oc.: $105.33 - $166.11
Sgl Oc.: $88.76 - $138.27
Third Person: $20.00
Child: Under 15 yrs. - no charge

Scarlett's Country Inn—A secluded farmhouse set in a quiet setting of green lawns and tall pines overlooking the vineyards. Three exquisitely appointed suites, one with fireplace and wet bar. Breakfast in room or by woodland swimming pool. Close to wineries and spas. Children welcome. Air conditioning.

Calistoga *

Layton, Christopher
1010 Foothill Blvd., 94515
(707) 942-5755

Amenities: 1,2,5,6,9,11,14,15, 16
Breakfast: C. Plus

Dbl. Oc.: $112.00 - $184.80
Sgl. Oc.: $112.00 - $184.80

Christopher's Inn—A most elegant inn with English country architecture. Ten rooms with Laura Ashley interiors. Fresh flowers adorn select antiques. Breakfast brought to your room. Fireplaces, patio gardens and croquet add special touches. Walk to spas and restaurants.

---

1. No Smoking	5. Tennis Available	9. Credit Cards Accepted	13. Lunch Available	17. Shared Baths
2. No Pets	6. Golf Available	10. Personal Check Accepted	14. Conference Rooms Avail.	18. Afternoon Tea
3 Off Season Rates	7. Swimmming Avail.	11. Reservations Necessary	15. Group Seminars Avail.	* Commisions given
4. Senior Citizen Rates	8. Skiing Available	12. Dinner Available	16. Private Baths	to Travel Agents

CALIFORNIA

Calistoga *

Mills, Earle
109 Wapoo Ave., 94515
(707) 942-4200

Amenities: 1,3,9,10,11,12,16
Breakfast: F.

Dbl. Oc.: $125.00 - $150.00
Third Person: $20.00

Brannan Cottage Inn—This romantic 1860 award-winning inn is mentioned in a book by Robert Lewis Stevenson. Just a short walk to the quaint main street of shops, spas and restaurants. Heavenly down comforters. Private entrances, rooms opening off of lovely gardens and candlelight dinners.

Calistoga *

O'Gorman, Debbie
3225 Lake Co. Hwy., 94515
(707) 942-6334

Amenities: 5,6,7,10,14,15,16,
17
Breakfast: C.

Dbl. Oc.: $77.98 - $100.08
Sgl. Oc.: $77.98 - $100.08

Hillcrest B&B—Breathtaking views. Hiking, swimming and wildlife. Forty acres. Family owned since 1860. Hilltop modern home decorated with heirlooms from family mansion. Rooms have balconies, fireplaces and rare artwork. Grand piano, silver, crystal and china. Family albums circa 1870.

Calistoga *

Swiers, Alma & Don
4455 N. Saint Helena Hwy., 94515
(707) 942-0316

Amenities: 1,2,5,6,7,9,10,11,
16
Breakfast: F.

Dbl. Oc.: $100.00 - $125.00
Sgl. Oc.: $90.00 - $115.00
Third Person: $20.00

Quail Mountain Bed And Breakfast—A romantic, secluded, luxury retreat located on 26 heavily forested acres 300 feet above the Napa Valley, with a vineyard on the property. Guest rooms have king beds and private baths and decks. Pool, spa, complimentary wine and a full, lovely breakfast with champagne.

Calistoga *

Wheatley, Meg & Tony
1805 Foothill Blvd., 94515
(707) 942-4535

Amenities: 1,2,3,10,11,15,17
Breakfast: F.

Dbl. Oc.: $104.50 - $115.50
Sgl. Oc.: $104.50 - $115.50

"Culvers," A Country Inn—A beautifully restored 1875 Victorian home. All rooms have an aura of days gone by. Furnished with antiques throughout. We offer a full country breakfast, afternoon sherry, pool, spa and sauna. Close to wineries and mud baths. Many good restaurants are close by.

Cambria *

Hitch, Penny
6360 Moonstone Beach Dr., 93428
(805) 927-3136

Amenities: 1,2,9,11,16,
18
Breakfast: F.

Dbl. Oc.: $115.00 - $153.00
Sgl. Oc.: $115.00 - $153.00

The Beach House—Located six miles south of Hearst Castle in the artistic village of Cambria. On the ocean. Private baths, some fireplaces and TV. Mountain bikes available. Enjoy beautiful sunsets while relaxing with other guests during the wine and cheese hour. Peaceful!

1. No Smoking	5. Tennis Available	9. Credit Cards Accepted	13. Lunch Available	17. Shared Baths
2. No Pets	6. Golf Available	10. Personal Check Accepted	14. Conference Rooms Avail.	18. Afternoon Tea
3 Off Season Rates	7. Swimmming Avail.	11. Reservations Necessary	15. Group Seminars Avail.	* Commisions given
4. Senior Citizen Rates	8. Skiing Available	12. Dinner Available	16. Private Baths	to Travel Agents

Cambria

Larsen, Anna
2555 MacLeod Way, 93428
(805) 927-8619

Amenities: 2,4,7,9,10,15,16
Breakfast: F.

Dbl. Oc.: $92.65 - $130.80
Sgl. Oc.: $92.65 - $130.80
Third Person: $21.80
Child: $21.00

Pickford House Bed And Breakfast—Eight rooms, some with fireplaces. King or queen beds. TVs. All rooms with antiques. Beach, shops and restaurants. Wine and cake at 5 p.m. in our 1860 bar. Well behaved children welcome. Hearst Castle — seven miles north.

*Capitola-by-the-Sea**

Lankes, Suzie
250 Monterey Ave., 95010
(408) 462-DEPO, FAX: (408) 458-0989

Amenities: 1,2,9,10,15,16,18
Breakfast: F.
Dbl. Oc.: $167.40 - $270.00
Sgl Oc.: $167.40 - $270.00
Third Person: $20.00

The Inn At Depot Hill—Stately 1901 railway station in quaint coastal resort. First place interior design award for the eight lavishly decorated rooms: Portofino, Paris, Delft, Cote d'Azur, etc. Fireplaces, TV/VCRs, stereos, phones, private patios and hot tubs. 1-1/2 blocks from Monterey Bay.

*Carlsbad**

Hale Celeste
320 Walnut Ave., 92008
(619) 434-5995

Amenities: 4,5,6,7,9,10,11, 14,15,16
Breakfast: C.

Dbl. Oc.: $93.00 - $165.00
Sgl. Oc.: $82.00 - $154.00
Child: Over 12 yrs. - no charge

Pelican Cove Inn — Feather beds optional. Fireplaces. Private baths and entries. Jacuzzi tubs. 200 yards from beach. Beach chairs and towels. Picnic baskets available. Amtrak and Palomar Airport courtesy pickup. Gift certificates. Sun deck, veranda and gazebo. Exquisite!

Carmel

Stewart, Dick
Monte Verde (between 5th & 6th)
P.O. Box 2619, 93921
(408) 624-7917

Amenities: 1,2,6,9,10,11,16,18
Breakfast: C.
Dbl. Oc.: $99.00 - $159.50
Sgl Oc.: $99.00 - $159.50
Third Person: $16.50

Happy Landing Inn — True Carmel charm with Hansel and Gretel architecture, antiques, fresh flowers and breakfast served to your room. Private and quiet yet near beach and town. A true taste of old Carmel.

---

1. No Smoking	5. Tennis Available	9. Credit Cards Accepted	13. Lunch Available	17. Shared Baths
2. No Pets	6. Golf Available	10. Personal Check Accepted	14. Conference Rooms Avail.	18. Afternoon Tea
3 Off Season Rates	7. Swimmming Avail.	11. Reservations Necessary	15. Group Seminars Avail.	* Commisions given
4. Senior Citizen Rates	8. Skiing Available	12. Dinner Available	16. Private Baths	to Travel Agents

Coloma *

Ehrgott, Cindi & Alan
345 High St.
Box 502, 95613
(916) 622-6919

Amenities: 1,2,10,15,16,17,18
Breakfast: C. Plus
Dbl. Oc.: $89.00 - $120.00
Sgl Oc.: $89.00 - $120.00
Third Person: $15.00
Child: $15.00

The Coloma Country Inn—Located in historic gold rush town - charming 1852 farmhouse on five acres surrounded by state park. Guest rooms offer queen or double beds, antiques, private baths and quilts. Afternoon tea in rose garden. Canoe on pond. White-water raft or hot-air balloon with your host.

Coronado *

Bogh, Elizabeth A.
1017 Park Pl., 92118
(619) 435-9318

Amenities: 2,3,9,10,16
Breakfast: C.
Dbl. Oc.: $85.60
Sgl Oc.: $64.20
Third Person: $10.00

Coronado Village Inn—One block from beach, town, restaurants and shops. Ten minutes to San Diego attractions. European in style. Decorated with antiques. Some canopy beds. Jacuzzis. New baths. The romance of yesterday mingled with today's comforts.

Coronado *

Kinosian, Bonni Marie
1000 Eighth St., 92118
(619) 435-2200

Amenities: 1,2,5,6,7,9,10,11, 12,13,14,15,16,17
Breakfast: F.

Dbl. Oc.: $175.00 - $350.00
Sgl. Oc.: $175.00 - $350.00
Third Person: $50.00
Child: Under 12 yrs. - no charge

Coronado Victorian House Bed And Breakfast Inn—Historic landmark in beautiful Coronado. Five minutes to San Diego, eight minutes to zoo, wonderful beach and shopping. Stained-glass doors, windows, claw-foot and Jacuzzi tubs. Delicious health and ethnic food. Visited by *People Magazine*. Beach walks, bikes and dance instructions.

---

1. No Smoking	5. Tennis Available	9. Credit Cards Accepted	13. Lunch Available	17. Shared Baths
2. No Pets	6. Golf Available	10. Personal Check Accepted	14. Conference Rooms Avail.	18. Afternoon Tea
3 Off Season Rates	7. Swimming Avail.	11. Reservations Necessary	15. Group Seminars Avail.	* Commisions given
4. Senior Citizen Rates	8. Skiing Available	12. Dinner Available	16. Private Baths	to Travel Agents

CALIFORNIA

Davenport

McDougal, Marcia
31 Davenport Ave., 95017
(408) 425-1818

Amenities: 1,2,3,9,10,12,13, 16
Breakfast: F.

Dbl. Oc.: $60.00 - $105.00
Sgl. Oc.: $60.00 - $105.00
Third Person: $10.00
Child: Under 10 yrs. - no charge

New Davenport Bed And Breakfast—Nine miles north of Santa, halfway between Monterey and San Francisco. Twelve ocean-view rooms. Ocean access. Whale watching January to May. Nearby state elephant-seal tours, beaches, hiking and favorite coastal restaurant.

Del Mar *

Holmes, Doris
410 15th St., 92014
(619) 481-3764

Amenities: 1,2,3,9,11,15,16, 17,18
Breakfast: C.

Dbl. Oc.: $75.00 - $150.00
Sgl. Oc.: $75.00 - $150.00

Rock Haus Inn—A romantic getaway to a quaint seaside village. Ten rooms, four with private baths and one with fireplace. Most have ocean view and down comforters. Stroll to beach, restaurants and Amtrak.

Elk

Triebess, Hildrun-Uta
6300 S. Hwy. 1, P.O. Box 367, 95432
(707) 877-3321

Amenities: 1,2,3,10,11,15,16
Breakfast: F.

Dbl. Oc.: $108.00 - $138.00

Elk Cove Inn—An 1883 Victorian with spectacular ocean views from cabins and main house. Fireplaces. Full gourmet breakfast. Ready access to expansive driftwood-strewn beach. Relaxed, romantic atmosphere in a rural village. Near Mendocino and Anderson Valley wineries. Nearby hiking and biking.

Eureka *

Benson, Diane & Leigh
1521 Third St., 95501
(707) 445-3951, (800) 331-5098

Amenities: 1,2,3,6,9,10,16,17, 18
Breakfast: F.

Dbl. Oc.: $81.40 - $141.35
Sgl. Oc.: $70.68 - $130.63
Third Person: $21.63

Old Town Bed And Breakfast Inn—An 1871 Victorian. Plush period decor with whimsy. Seven rooms, one with woodstove; five with private baths. Outdoor hot tub. Wine and chocolate. Cat in residence. Heart of the redwood empire and northern California coast. Historic Old Town district. ABBA inspected and approved.

Eureka *

Vieyra, Liliane & Douglas
1406 'C' St. (at 14th), 95501
(707) 444-3144, 442-5594

Amenities: 1,2,3,4,5,6,9,10, 11,12,13,14,15,16, 17,18
Breakfast: F.

Dbl. Oc.: $85.00 - $135.00
Sgl. Oc.: $85.00 - $105.00
Third Person: $30.00

"An Elegant Victorian Mansion"—Eureka's most prestigious and luxurious accommodations. Let spirited and eclectic innkeepers help you enjoy an acclaimed gourmet breakfast in the opulent splendor of a NATIONAL HISTORIC LANDMARK. Bicycles, croquet, ice cream sodas, sauna, classic movies and old cars.

---

1. No Smoking	5. Tennis Available	9. Credit Cards Accepted	13. Lunch Available	17. Shared Baths
2. No Pets	6. Golf Available	10. Personal Check Accepted	14. Conference Rooms Avail.	18. Afternoon Tea
3 Off Season Rates	7. Swimmming Avail.	11. Reservations Necessary	15. Group Seminars Avail.	* Commisions given
4. Senior Citizen Rates	8. Skiing Available	12. Dinner Available	16. Private Baths	to Travel Agents

Ferndale *

Torbert, Ken W.
400 Berding, 95536
(707) 786-4000

Amenities: 1,2,3,9,10,16,18
Breakfast: C. Plus
Dbl. Oc.: $90.00 - $200.00
Sgl Oc.: $75.00 - $185.00
Third Person: $20.00

The Gingerbread Mansion Bed And Breakfast—Victorian elegance abounds in this turn-of-the-century inn that offers nine large, romantic guest rooms completely decorated in antiques. The inn also offers four parlors, afternoon tea, bicycles, bedside chocolates and a formal English garden.

Fort Bragg

Bailey, Colette & John
615 N. Main, 95437
(707) 964-0640, (800) 382-7244

Amenities: 1,2,3,5,6,7,9,10,14,15,16,18
Breakfast: F.
Dbl. Oc.: $82.50 - $165.00
Sgl Oc.: $66.00 - $145.00
Third Person: $25.00
Child: $25.00

The Grey Whale Inn—Mendocino coast landmark since 1915. Fourteen spacious rooms. Each room has a special amenity: ocean, garden or hill views, fireplace, deck, patio, wheelchair access or whirlpool tub. Some have TV, refrigerator or in-room phones. Walk to beach and Skunk Train and dining.

Fort Bragg *

Sorrells, Anne   **Amenities:** 1,2,3,9,10,11,16   **Dbl. Oc.:** $77.00 - $137.50
561 Stewart St., 95437 **Breakfast:** F.   **Third Person:** $10.00
(707) 964-5555   **Child:** Under 7 yrs. - no charge

Avalon House—A 1905 Craftsman house. Quiet neighborhood. Three blocks from ocean and two blocks from Skunk Train. Six rooms with private baths, some with fireplaces, spas and ocean views. The Mendocino coast is famous for its scenic beauty and unspoiled environment; 150 miles north of San Francisco.

Freestone

Hoffman, Rosemary & Rogers **Amenities:** 1,9,10,15,16   **Dbl. Oc.:** $85.00 - $92.00
520 Bohemian Hwy., 95472   **Breakfast:** F.   **Sgl. Oc.:** $85.00 - $92.00
(707) 874-2526   **Third Person:** $15.00

Green Apple Inn—An 1860s farmhouse set in a meadow backed by redwoods. Located on five acres in the historic district of Freestone, between Bodega Bay and the Russian River. Nearby are excellent restaurants and small family wineries.

1. No Smoking	5. Tennis Available	9. Credit Cards Accepted	13. Lunch Available	17. Shared Baths
2. No Pets	6. Golf Available	10. Personal Check Accepted	14. Conference Rooms Avail.	18. Afternoon Tea
3 Off Season Rates	7. Swimmming Avail.	11. Reservations Necessary	15. Group Seminars Avail.	* Commisions given
4. Senior Citizen Rates	8. Skiing Available	12. Dinner Available	16. Private Baths	to Travel Agents

CALIFORNIA

Fremont *

Medeiros, Anne & Keith
43344 Mission Blvd., 94539
(510) 490-0520

Amenities: 1,2,9,10,11,16
Breakfast: C.

Dbl. Oc.: $69.55 - $80.25
Sgl. Oc.: $69.55 - $80.25
Third Person: $15.00

Lord Bradley's Inn—A Victorian nestled below Mission Peak, adjacent to Mission San Jose. Historic areas. Hikers' and kite fliers' paradise. Victorian decorated. Common room. Garden patio. Parking. Easy access to San Francisco by Bay Area Rapid Transit. Great for small weddings or retirement parties.

Geyserville

Campbell, Mary Jane & Jerry
1475 Canyon Rd., 95441
(707) 857-3476

Amenities: 1,2,5,7,9,10,11,16
Breakfast: F.

Dbl. Oc.: $100.00 - $145.00
Sgl. Oc.: $90.00 - $135.00
Third Person/Child: $25.00

Campbell Ranch Inn—Located in the heart of the Sonoma County wine country on a 35-acre hilltop. Spectacular views, beautiful gardens, tennis court, pool, spa and bikes. Large rooms, king beds and balconies. Full-menu breakfast and homemade dessert in the evening.

Georgetown *

Collin, Maria & Will
P.O. Box 43, 95634
(916) 333-4499

Amenities: 2,5,6,7,8,9,10,11,
12,14,15,16,17
Breakfast: F.

Dbl. Oc.: $85.00 - $115.00
Sgl. Oc.: $85.00 - $115.00
Third Person: $15.00
Child: Under 3 yrs. - $15.00

American River Inn—This jewel of the mother lode restored 1853 miners' hotel decorated with Victorian antiques. Gorgeous gardens, mountain stream. Jacuzzi, aviary bikes, croquet, golf, horseshoes, Ping-Pong, hammocks. Wine and cheese at 6 p.m. Georgetown is a Sierra foothills village.

Gualala *

Flanagan, Nancy & Loren
34591 So. Hwy. 1, 95445
(707) 884-4537

Amenities: 1,2,3,4,5,6,7,9,10,16
Breakfast: F.
Dbl. Oc.: $126.50
Sgl Oc.: $126.50

North Coast Country Inn—Rustic Rrdwood buildings on a forested hillside overlooking the ocean. Four large guest rooms, each with fireplace, antiques, private bathroom, deck, hot tub and view.

1. No Smoking	5. Tennis Available	9. Credit Cards Accepted	13. Lunch Available	17. Shared Baths
2. No Pets	6. Golf Available	10. Personal Check Accepted	14. Conference Rooms Avail.	18. Afternoon Tea
3 Off Season Rates	7. Swimmming Avail.	11. Reservations Necessary	15. Group Seminars Avail.	* Commisions given
4. Senior Citizen Rates	8. Skiing Available	12. Dinner Available	16. Private Baths	to Travel Agents

Guerneville *

Rechberger, Diane
12850 River Rd., 95446
(707) 887-1033

Amenities: 1,2,9,10,12,15,16
Breakfast: F.

Dbl. Oc.: $102.60 - $140.40
Sgl. Oc.: $102.60 - $140.40
Third Person: $15.00

Ridenhour Ranch House Inn—Near Korbel Winery. A 1906 farmhouse on 2-1/4 acres. American and English decor throughout. A hearty breakfast of homemade goodies. 1-1/4 hours from San Francisco, in the Russian River resort area. Children 10 years and over welcome. Two-night minimum on weekends.

Half Moon Bay *

Granados, Cindy
407 Mirada Rd., 94019
(415) 726-6002

Amenities: 1,2,5,6,9,10,13,16, 18
Breakfast: F.

Dbl. Oc.: $148.50 - $275.00

Cypress Inn On Miramar Beach—Located on a five-mile stretch of sandy beach. Every room has a private deck, fireplace, private bath and great ocean views. Just 1/2 hour from San Francisco. Gourmet breakfasts, afternoon tea and snacks. In-house massage therapist available.

Half Moon Bay *

Lowings, Anne
779 Main St., 94019
(415) 726-1616

Amenities: 1,5,6,9,10,16,18
Breakfast: F.

Dbl. Oc.: $71.50 - $148.50
Sgl. Oc.: $66.00 - $110.00
Third Person: $10.00
Child: Over 6 yrs. - $10.00

Old Thyme Inn—An 1890s Victorian on historic main street. Walk to shops, fine restaurants and beach. Inn has herbal theme, herb garden and guests are invited to take cuttings. Rooms decorated with antiques, prints and wallpaper. Fireplaces, double whirlpool tubs and great breakfasts.

Half Moon Bay *

Lowings, Simon
324 Main St., 94019
(415) 726-9123

Amenities: 1,5,6,7,9,10,14,16, 18
Breakfast: F.

Dbl. Oc.: $71.50 - $143.00
Sgl. Oc.: $66.00 - $132.00
Third Person: $10.00
Child: Over 6 yrs. - $10.00

Zaballa House—Oldest house in Half Moon Bay. Built by Estanislao Zabella, first city planner. Located in a garden setting, all rooms have garden views; some rooms have fireplaces and Jacuzzi tubs. If you like old oil paintings, grandfather clocks and flowers, stay here. Ask about the ghost.

Healdsburg

Jenkins, Genny
110 Matheson, 95448
(707) 433-6991

Amenities: 1,2,3,9,10,11,16, 18
Breakfast: F.

Dbl. Oc.: $85.00 - $155.00
Sgl. Oc.: $75.00 - $155.00
Third Person: $35.00
Child: $35.00

Healdsburg Inn On The Plaza—A 1900 brick Victorian, formerly a Wells Fargo stagecoach express station. Nine rooms with private bathrooms and queen-size beds. Fireplaces, solarium, afternoon refreshments. Convenient to shops, wineries and restaurants. Bicycling. Phones and TV available.

1. No Smoking	5. Tennis Available	9. Credit Cards Accepted	13. Lunch Available	17. Shared Baths
2. No Pets	6. Golf Available	10. Personal Check Accepted	14. Conference Rooms Avail.	18. Afternoon Tea
3 Off Season Rates	7. Swimmming Avail.	11. Reservations Necessary	15. Group Seminars Avail.	* Commisions given
4. Senior Citizen Rates	8. Skiing Available	12. Dinner Available	16. Private Baths	to Travel Agents

CALIFORNIA

Healdsburg *

Woodburn, Keill
321 Haydon St., 95448
(707) 433-5228

Amenities: 1,2,3,5,6,7,9,10, 16,17
Breakfast: F.

Dbl. Oc.: $80.90 - $162.00
Sgl. Oc.: $75.90 - $157.00
Third Person: $20.00
Child: $20.00

Haydon House Bed And Breakfast Inn—A beautifully furnished Queen Anne Victorian. Comfortable rooms, lavish breakfast and warm hospitality in a quiet and relaxing atmosphere within minutes of many award-winning wineries. Located in the heart of the Sonoma wine country. Within walking distance of historic plaza.

Idyllwild *

Jones, Barbara
26770 Hwy. 243
P.O. Box 1115, 92549
(909) 659-4087

Amenities: 1,2,7,10,11,16,17
Breakfast: C. Plus

Dbl. Oc.: $71.50 - $104.50
Sgl. Oc.: $60.50 - $77.00

Wilkum Inn Bed And Breakfast—Warm hospitality and personal comfort combine with an ambience of yesteryear, enhanced by handmade quilts, antiques and collectibles. In a pine-forested mountain village with unique shops, excellent restaurants, fine and performing arts. Hike or just relax.

Inverness *

Storch, Suzanne
75 Balboa Ave.
P.O. Box 619, 94937
(415) 663-9338

Amenities: 5,6,7,10,11,16
Breakfast: F.

Dbl. Oc.: $137.50
Sgl. Oc.: $132.00
Third Person: $15.00
Child: Under 1 yr. - no charge

Rosemary Cottage—Romantic seclusion in a French country cottage. Large deck overlooks view and garden. Spacious main room with view furnished with antiques. Wood-stove fireplace. Fully equipped kitchen. Bedroom has queen bed and private bath. Families welcome.

Ione *

Hubbs, Melisande
Cross, Patricia
214 Shakeley Lane, 95640
(209) 274-4468

Amenities: 1,2,6,10,11,15,16, 17,18
Breakfast: F.

Dbl. Oc.: $60.00 - $95.00
Sgl. Oc.: $55.00 - $90.00
Third Person: $15.00
Child: $15.00

The Heirloom—Down a country lane to a petite colonial mansion, circa 1863. Spacious private garden, century-old trees, heirloom antiques, enhanced by love of the arts, fireplaces, balconies, breakfast with French flair and gracious hospitality.

Jackson *

Beltz, Jeannine & Vic
11941 Narcissus Rd., 95642
(800) 933-4393, (209) 296-4300

Amenities: 1,2,9,10,11,16,18
Breakfast: F.

Dbl. Oc.: $90.23 - $128.70
Sgl. Oc.: $84.93 - $116.73

The Wedgewood Inn—A replica Victorian tucked away on wooded acreage. Six lavishly furnished guest rooms. Wood-burning stoves, antiques, balcony, terraced English gardens, spectacular gazebo and sparkling fountains. Secluded, yet central to all tourist areas and dining. Mobile rated - three stars.

1. No Smoking	5. Tennis Available	9. Credit Cards Accepted	13. Lunch Available	17. Shared Baths
2. No Pets	6. Golf Available	10. Personal Check Accepted	14. Conference Rooms Avail.	18. Afternoon Tea
3 Off Season Rates	7. Swimmming Avail.	11. Reservations Necessary	15. Group Seminars Avail.	* Commisions given
4. Senior Citizen Rates	8. Skiing Available	12. Dinner Available	16. Private Baths	to Travel Agents

CALIFORNIA

Jamestown *

Willey, Stephen
77 Main St.
P.O. Box 502, 95327
(209) 984-3446

Amenities: 3,6,8,9,11,12,13, 14,15,16,17
Breakfast: C. Plus

Dbl. Oc.: $86.40
Sgl. Oc.: $86.40
Third Person: $10.80

Historic National Hotel, B&B — One of the ten oldest and continuously operated hotels in California. Award winning restoration with 19th century gold rush atmosphere but 20th century comfort. Outstanding on premises restaurant, courtyard dining and, of course, the original saloon.

Kernville *

Andrews, Marti & Mike
119 Kern Dr.
P.O. Box 1725, 93238
(619) 376-6750

Amenities: 1,2,3,4,5,6,7,8,9,11,15,16,18
Breakfast: C. Plus
Dbl. Oc.: $85.00 - $95.00
Sgl Oc.: $75.00 - $85.00
Third Person: $16.00

Kern River Inn Bed And Breakfast—A warm, charming six-room country inn on the wild and scenic Kern River in Sequoia National Forest. Giant cinnamon rolls, fireplaces, whirlpool tubs and river views. Walk to restaurants, shops and parks. All-year fishing, white-water rafting or relaxing. Gift certificates.

Klamath

Hamby, Paul
451 Requa Rd., 95548
(707) 482-8205

Amenities: 1,2,9,11,12,16
Breakfast: F.

Dbl. Oc.: $60.00
Sgl. Oc.: $60.00
Third Person: $15.00

Requa Inn—A historic inn overlooking the Klamath River. Located in the heart of the Redwood National Park, one mile from the ocean. Near beaches and redwood trails. Open March to October. Full dinner menu — steaks and seafood.

Laguna Beach *

Taylor, Dee
1322 Catalina St., 92651
(714) 494-8945

Amenities: 2,3,10,11,16
Breakfast: C. Plus

Dbl. Oc.: $95.00 - $150.00
Sgl. Oc.: $95.00 - $150.00
Third Person: $20.00
Child: Under 10 yrs. - $10.00

The Carriage House—New Orleans-style inn two blocks from the Pacific Ocean. All are suites with private living room, bedroom and bath. Courtyard with flowers, fountain and birds. Parking. Breakfast served in the dining room or on patio. Wine, fruit and goodies. Quiet walk to restaurants and shops.

1. No Smoking	5. Tennis Available	9. Credit Cards Accepted	13. Lunch Available	17. Shared Baths
2. No Pets	6. Golf Available	10. Personal Check Accepted	14. Conference Rooms Avail.	18. Afternoon Tea
3 Off Season Rates	7. Swimmming Avail.	11. Reservations Necessary	15. Group Seminars Avail.	* Commisions given
4. Senior Citizen Rates	8. Skiing Available	12. Dinner Available	16. Private Baths	to Travel Agents

CALIFORNIA

Laguna Beach *

Wietz, Annette & Henk
741 So. Coast Hwy., 92651
(714) 494-3004

Amenities: 2,3,5,6,7,9,10,11,
14,15,16,18
Breakfast: C. Plus

Dbl. Oc.: $100.00 - $175.00
Sgl. Oc.: $95.00 - $170.00
Third Person: $20.00
Child: Under 10 yrs. - $10.00

Eiler's Inn—Experience European hospitality. Warm, yet elegant, rooms. Downtown location. Walk to restaurants and art galleries. Wine served in a beautiful courtyard with fountain. Exceptional breakfast. Living room with fireplace. Library with color TV. Great to relax and get away.

La Jolla *

Timmerman, Pierrette
7753 Draper, 92037
(619) 456-2066

Amenities: 4,5,6,9,10,11,16,
17
Breakfast: C.

Dbl. Oc.: $85.00 - $225.00
Third Person: $25.00

The Bed And Breakfast Inn At La Jolla—Deluxe accommodations are offered in this "Cubist"-style historic 1913 inn. Home of the John Philip Sousa family for seven years. Fresh fruit and flowers, sherry and terry robes await you in each guest room. Located near the cultural center and Museum of Contemporary Art.

Long Beach *

Brasser, Laura & Reuben
435 Cedar Ave., 90802
(310) 436-0324

Amenities: 1,2,9,10,11,16
Breakfast: F.

Dbl. Oc.: $95.00 - $104.00
Sgl. Oc.: $66.00
Third Person: $20.00

Lord Mayor's Inn—Elegant, award-winning, restored 1904 Edwardian home of Long Beach's first mayor. Spacious rooms with antiques, gardens, library, porches and off-street parking. Near the Queen Mary and World Trade Center. Enjoy ambience of years gone by with 10-foot ceilings.

Los Angeles

Moultout, Suzanne
449 No. Detroit St., 90036
(213) 938-4794

Amenities: 1,2,10,11,17
Breakfast: C.

Dbl. Oc.: $60.00
Sgl. Oc.: $50.00
Third Person: $25.00

Paris Cottage—A Spanish-style house located on a quiet street. Close to West Hollywood, downtown (Amtrak), Beverly Hills and beaches. Your hostess offers an attractive guest room and a shady yard with fruit trees. Hollywood Hills, CBS Studios, restaurants, theatres and museums are close by.

Lucerne *

Myers, Mervin
715 Pearl Ct., 95458
(707) 274-8009

Amenities: 1,2,3,4,5,6,7,9,10,
16,18
Breakfast: C. Plus

Dbl. Oc.: $60.00 - $164.00
Sgl. Oc.: $50.00 - $140.00
Third Person: $15.00
Child: Under 12 yrs. - $10.00

Kristalberg B&B—Majestic lake view, European/Victorian ambience; luxurious comfort; congenial, tri-lingual hosts; gourmet breakfast; fishing, boating, hiking, biking. Country tranquility.

---

1. No Smoking	5. Tennis Available	9. Credit Cards Accepted	13. Lunch Available	17. Shared Baths
2. No Pets	6. Golf Available	10. Personal Check Accepted	14. Conference Rooms Avail.	18. Afternoon Tea
3 Off Season Rates	7. Swimmming Avail.	11. Reservations Necessary	15. Group Seminars Avail.	* Commisions given
4. Senior Citizen Rates	8. Skiing Available	12. Dinner Available	16. Private Baths	to Travel Agents

CALIFORNIA

Mariposa

Fincham, Carol & Bruce
4605 Triangle Rd., 95338
(209) 966-4738

Amenities: 1,2,10,16
Breakfast: C. Plus

Dbl. Oc.: $70.85
Sgl. Oc.: $70.85
Third Person: $10.90
Child: Under 12 yrs. - $5.45

Finch Haven Bed And Breakfast—Quiet country home on nine acres with panoramic mountain views. Abundant wildlife! Private deck and bath. In the heart of gold rush country near historic attractions. Convenient access to spectacular Yosemite Valley and Yosemite National Park.

Mariposa

Foster, Gwen & Dick
3871 Hwy. 49 So., 95338
(209) 966-2832

Amenities: 1,7,10,11,17
Breakfast: F.

Dbl. Oc.: $45.00
Sgl. Oc.: $35.00
Third Person: $10.00
Child: Under 10 yrs. - $7.00

The Pelennor Bed And Breakfast At Bootjack—Created for the traveler seeking economical lodging. An hour to Yosemite National Park. Bagpipes and Scottish lore. Hot tub, lap pool and sauna. Four rooms. Honeymoon suite in the works. Jogging/walking path on 15 acres with pond.

Mariposa

Haag, Janice & Donald
5636 Whitlock Rd., 95338
(209) 966-5592

Amenities: 1,2,10,15,17
Breakfast: C. Plus

Dbl. Oc.: $50.00
Sgl. Oc.: $40.00
Third Person: $10.00

Winsor Farms Bed And Breakfast—A peaceful hilltop retreat. This one-story country home is seven miles from Mariposa, three miles off Highway 140 and 45 minutes to Yosemite National Park. You can also explore the gold rush history unique to this area.

Mariposa *

Renna, Susan
4990 8th St.
Box 1888 (mail), 95338
(209) 966-2439

Amenities: 1,2,6,7,9,10,11,12,
16,17
Breakfast: F.

Dbl. Oc.: $67.00 - $83.00
Sgl. Oc.: $67.00 - $83.00
Third Person: $17.00
Child: Under 5 yrs. - no charge

Villa Mont: Bed And Breakfast—A 1920s Spanish-style, in-town location. Guest rooms and one suite have queen-size and double-size beds, every room with TV. Wheelchair accessibility. Baths: one private, two guest rooms share one bath. Pool, patio, hot tub. Museums, shops and restaurants within walking distance.

Mariposa *

Starchman, Francie
5263 Hwy. 140, 95338
(209) 742-6161

Amenities: 1,2,8,9,10,11,16
Breakfast: C. Plus

Dbl. Oc.: $75.11 - $85.95
Sgl. Oc.: $64.21
Third Person: $10.90

Oak Meadows, Too Bed And Breakfast—Contemporary New England-style cottage with stone fireplace in guest parlor, original art, brass beds and quilts. Near Yosemite National Park. Close to restaurants and California State Mining and Mineral Museum. Central heat and air.

1. No Smoking	5. Tennis Available	9. Credit Cards Accepted	13. Lunch Available	17. Shared Baths
2. No Pets	6. Golf Available	10. Personal Check Accepted	14. Conference Rooms Avail.	18. Afternoon Tea
3 Off Season Rates	7. Swimmming Avail.	11. Reservations Necessary	15. Group Seminars Avail.	* Commissions given
4. Senior Citizen Rates	8. Skiing Available	12. Dinner Available	16. Private Baths	to Travel Agents

Mendocino

Ciancutti, Arthur	**Amenities:** 1,2,3,9,10,11	**Dbl. Oc.:** $93.50 - $143.00
9350 Coast Hwy. One, 95460	**Breakfast:** F.	**Sgl. Oc.:** $93.50 - $143.00
(707) 937-4752		**Third Person:** $15.00

Brewery Gulch Inn—Secluded 1860s farmhouse on 12 acres accented by delightful gardens. Five charming, antique-filled rooms. Hearty breakfast. "...serene and unhurried - a mythical sleepy hollow by the sea. Breathtaking." - *San Francisco Examine*r. One mile from village.

Mendocino

Erwin, Kathleen & Bill	**Amenities:** 1,2,5,6,9,10,11,14,	**Dbl. Oc.:** $65.00 - $145.00
44860 Main St.	15,16,18	**Sgl. Oc.:** $65.00 - $145.00
P.O. Box 626, 95460	**Breakfast:** F.	**Third Person:** $15.00
(707) 937-0246		**Child:** No charge for babe-in-arm

Mendocino Village Inn—An 1882 Queen Anne Victorian promising merriment and quiet repose. Good company, hearty breakfasts, fireplaces, ocean views; Headlands State Park and beach trails. Your home on the North Coast.

Mendocino

McConnell, Sallie & Jake	**Amenities:** 1,2,3,9,10,11,16	**Dbl. Oc.:** $80.00 - $190.00
11201 Lansing St., 95460	**Breakfast:** F.	**Third Person:** $25.00
(707) 937-0551		

Agate Cove Inn—Situated on a bluff above the Pacific Ocean with a breathtaking view. Cozy and romantic cottages with fireplaces, ocean views and private baths. Full country breakfast is served in this 1860s farmhouse with beautifully landscaped gardens.

Mendocino *

Reding, Joe	**Amenities:** 2,5,6,7,9,10,11,12,	**Dbl. Oc.:** $75.00 - $165.00
45020 Albion St., 95460	15,16,17	**Sgl. Oc.:** $75.00 - $165.00
(707) 937-0289	**Breakfast:** C.	**Third Person:** $15.00
		Child: Under 8 yrs. - $7.00

MacCallum House Inn—Located in the center of the village of Mendocino. Besides the main house, there are unique cottages on the grounds. There is an award-winning restaurant and bar on the premises.

Montara

Bechtell, Peggy & Bill	**Amenities:** 1,2,9,10,11,16	**Dbl. Oc.:** $80.00
1125 Tamarind St., 94037	**Breakfast:** F.	**Sgl. Oc.:** $70.00
(415) 728-3946		**Third Person:** $15.00

Montara B&B—Just 20 miles south of San Francisco on the scenic California coast! Semi-rural area with nearby hiking, beaches and horseback riding. Private entrance, private bath, fireplace, ocean view, phone and TV. Full breakfast served in a solarium overlooking the garden.

1. No Smoking	5. Tennis Available	9. Credit Cards Accepted	13. Lunch Available	17. Shared Baths
2. No Pets	6. Golf Available	10. Personal Check Accepted	14. Conference Rooms Avail.	18. Afternoon Tea
3 Off Season Rates	7. Swimmming Avail.	11. Reservations Necessary	15. Group Seminars Avail.	* Commisions given
4. Senior Citizen Rates	8. Skiing Available	12. Dinner Available	16. Private Baths	to Travel Agents

Montara *

Hoche-Mong, Emily & Raymond
835 George St., 94037-0937
(415) 728-5451

Amenities: 1,2,4,9,10,16,18
Breakfast: F.
Dbl. Oc.: $87.65 - $120.65
Sgl Oc: $87.65 - $120.65
Child: Under 12 yrs. - $10.00

Goose And Turrets Bed And Breakfast—One-half mile from beaches, 20 minutes from San Francisco Airport, 25 miles south of San Francisco. A historic home in a quiet garden. Fireplaces, down comforters, four-course breakfasts, bocce ball court and hammock. Near tidepools, golf, galleries and restaurants. French spoken.

Napa *

Delay, Lauriann
Weinstein, Andrea
1727 Main St., 94559
(707) 226-3774

Amenities: 1,2,3,4,5,6,9,10,11,15,16
Breakfast: F.
Dbl. Oc.: $109.00 - $163.00
Third Person: $20.00

Hennessey House Bed And Breakfast Inn—Charming Queen Anne Victorian on Main Street in downtown Napa in the heart of the Wine Country. This 10-room inn offers antique furnishings and private baths. Some rooms feature fireplaces and whirlpools, others have canopy or feather beds.

Napa *

Guidotte, Joanna
485 Brown St., 94559
(707) 253-7733

Amenities: 1,2,9,10,11,14,15, 16,18
Breakfast: F.
Dbl. Oc.: $82.88 - $160.23
Sgl. Oc.: $82.88 - $160.23
Third Person: $16.58

Churchill Manor—An 1889 three-story mansion surrounded by an extensive covered veranda with large, white columns. Carved-wood ceiling moldings, Corinthian columns, fireplaces and a mosaic marble-floored sunroom. Nine lovely guest rooms. Fine European antiques, Oriental rugs and chandeliers.

1. No Smoking	5. Tennis Available	9. Credit Cards Accepted	13. Lunch Available	17. Shared Baths
2. No Pets	6. Golf Available	10. Personal Check Accepted	14. Conference Rooms Avail.	18. Afternoon Tea
3 Off Season Rates	7. Swimmming Avail.	11. Reservations Necessary	15. Group Seminars Avail.	* Commisions given
4. Senior Citizen Rates	8. Skiing Available	12. Dinner Available	16. Private Baths	to Travel Agents

Napa *

Maddox, Sybil & Cheryl
7400 St. Helen Hwy., 94558
(707) 946-2785

Amenities: 1,2,5,6,9,10,11,16
Breakfast: C.
Dbl. Oc.: $110.00 - $150.00
Sgl Oc.: $110.00 - $150.00
Third Person: $25.00

Sybron House—Hilltop Victorian inn commanding spectacular view of entire valley. Antiques fireplaces, robes. Balconies, gardens, private tennis court (pro available). Near wineries, restaurants and shops. 4 rooms with private baths. Expanded continental breakfast and refreshments.

Napa *

Morales, Carol & Doug
1137 Warren St., 94559
(707) 257-1444

Amenities: 1,2,6,9,10,11,16, 18
Breakfast: F.

Dbl. Oc.: $121.55 - $176.80
Sgl. Oc.: $121.55 - $176.80
Third Person: $27.63
Child: Over 15 yrs. - $27.63

The Napa Inn—Queen Anne Victorian built in 1899. Quiet, historic neighborhood. The inn has four spacious guest rooms and two large suites with fireplaces. The parlor, dining room and six guest rooms are furnished in antiques. For hospitality and gracious surroundings, visit Napa Inn.

Napa *

Passino, Barbara
2200 E. Oak Knoll Ave., 94558
(707) 255-2200

Amenities: 1,2,7,9,10,11,16, 18
Breakfast: F.

Dbl. Oc.: $170.00 - $250.00
Sgl. Oc.: $170.00 - $250.00
Third Person: $25.00

Oak Knoll Inn—A beautifully built stone inn considered by many as the most luxurious and romantic in Napa. Suites have a king- sized bed, fireplace, bath and privacy. A Jacuzzi is available and wine. Wine-and-cheese hour provided.

Nevada City

Boko, Geri & Doug
449 Broad St., 95959
(916) 265-4660

Amenities: 1,2,5,6,7,9,10,15, 16
Breakfast: F.

Dbl. Oc.: $100.00 - $150.00
Sgl. Oc.: $100.00 - $150.00
Third Person: $20.00
Child: $20.00

Gramdmere's Inn—A warm French country atmosphere on beautiful grounds. Listed in the National Register of Historic Places. Located right above downtown Nevada City. Offers homemade gourmet breakfasts in a relaxed decor. Central air-conditioning.

1. No Smoking	5. Tennis Available	9. Credit Cards Accepted	13. Lunch Available	17. Shared Baths
2. No Pets	6. Golf Available	10. Personal Check Accepted	14. Conference Rooms Avail.	18. Afternoon Tea
3 Off Season Rates	7. Swimmming Avail.	11. Reservations Necessary	15. Group Seminars Avail.	* Commisions given
4. Senior Citizen Rates	8. Skiing Available	12. Dinner Available	16. Private Baths	to Travel Agents

CALIFORNIA

Nevada City *

Weaver, Mary Louise & Conley
109 Prospect St., 95959
(916) 265-5135

Amenities: 1,5,6,7,8,9,10,16,18
Breakfast: F.
Dbl. Oc.: $76.60 - $118.80
Sgl Oc.: $70.20 - $113.80
Third Person: $20.00

The Red Castle Inn—Since 1963, this four-story 1857 landmark inn has welcomed guests to the pleasure of its company. "Tops my list of places to stay" — *Gourmet Magazine.* Overlooks the queen city of the gold country. Terraced gardens. Sweeping verandas. Bountiful buffet. Seven guest rooms and suites.

Nevada City *

Wright, Mrs. Miriam
517 W. Broad St., 95959
(916) 265-2815, (800) 258-2815

Amenities: 1,2,5,6,7,8,9,10, 16,18
Breakfast: F.

Dbl. Oc.: $75.00 - $95.00
Sgl. Oc.: $75.00 - $95.00

Downey House B&B—Circa 1869. Light and comfortable soundproofed rooms with down comforters and full private baths. Lush garden with waterfall. Sunroom, veranda and parlor. Generous full breakfast. Walk to fine shops, restaurants, galleries, museums and theatre.

Newport Beach *

Palitz, Michael
2102 W. Ocean Front, 92663
(714) 675-7300

Amenities: 5,6,7,8,9,10,11,12, 13,14,15,16,18
Breakfast: C. Plus

Dbl. Oc.: $135.00 - $275.00
Third Person: $25.00

Doryman's Ocean Front Inn—Romance, luxury and resounding elegance await you at this exquisits Victorian ocean-front B&B. All rooms feature Italian marble sunken tubs, fireplaces and spectacular views of the beautiful Pacific Ocean. Enjoy breakfast in bed and a complimentary bottle of wine or champagne.

Nipton *

Freeman, Gerald
HC1, Box 357, 92364 (mail)
(619) 856-2335

Amenities: 2,9,13
Breakfast: C.

Dbl. Oc.: $48.15
Sgl. Oc.: $48.15
Third Person: $12.84
Child: Under 6 yrs. - no charge

Hotel Nipton—Located in the east Mojave national scenic area, 65 miles south of Las Vegas. Built in 1904, restored in 1986. Decorated with old photos depicting the history of the area. Beautiful views from front porch. Outdoor Jacuzzi for star gazing. The stars touch the horizon.

1. No Smoking	5. Tennis Available	9. Credit Cards Accepted	13. Lunch Available	17. Shared Baths
2. No Pets	6. Golf Available	10. Personal Check Accepted	14. Conference Rooms Avail.	18. Afternoon Tea
3 Off Season Rates	7. Swimmming Avail.	11. Reservations Necessary	15. Group Seminars Avail.	* Commisions given
4. Senior Citizen Rates	8. Skiing Available	12. Dinner Available	16. Private Baths	to Travel Agents

Ojai *

Nelson, Mary
210 E. Matilija, 93023
(805) 646-0961

Amenities: 1,3,5,6,7,9, **Dbl. Oc.:** $90.00
10 **Sgl. Oc.:** $80.00
Breakfast: C.

Ojai Manor Hotel—Originally a little brick schoolhouse and now Ojai's oldest building. The hotel is centrally located in lovely park-like surroundings. Six guest rooms share three baths.

Orland *

Glaeseman, Mary & Kurt
Rte. 3, Box 3176, 95963
(916) 865-4093

Amenities: 1,2,9,10, **Dbl. Oc.:** $58.75 - $78.75
11,16,17 **Sgl. Oc.:** $58.75 - $78.75
Breakfast: C. Plus **Third Person:** $15.75

The Inn At Shallow Creek Farm—The inn is a gracious farmhouse offering spacious rooms furnished with carefully chosen antiques, creating a blend of nostalgia and comfortable country living. Breakfasts feature old-fashioned baked goods and an assortment of local fresh fruits and juices.

Oroville *

Pratt, Jean
45 Cabana Dr.
P.O. Box 2334, 95965
(919) 533-1413

Amenities: 1,2,5,6,7,9,10,14,15,16,18
Breakfast: F.
Dbl. Oc.: $57.00 - $102.00
Sgl Oc.: $52.00 - $97.00

Jean's Riverside Bed And Breakfast—Romantic waterfront hideaway. Swimming, gold-panning and bird watching. Croquet on premises. Some private Jacuzzis and woodburning stoves. Goldminers' sourdough breakfast. Historical sites, shopping and restaurants minutes away. One hour north of Sacramento airport.

Pacific Grove *

Browncroft, Dawn Yvette
557 Ocean View Blvd., 93950
(408) 373-7673

Amenities: 1,2,6,7,10,14,15,16,17
Breakfast: F.
Dbl. Oc.: $137.50 - $225.50
Sgl Oc.: $115.50

Roserox Country Inn By-The-Sea—An intimate, historic Victorian set on the shores of the Pacific Ocean. All rooms have breathtaking ocean views. Wine/cheese by the fireplace in the parlor. Snuggle under down comforters and let the ocean lull you to sleep. Walk to aquarium and Cannery Row.

---

1. No Smoking	5. Tennis Available	9. Credit Cards Accepted	13. Lunch Available	17. Shared Baths
2. No Pets	6. Golf Available	10. Personal Check Accepted	14. Conference Rooms Avail.	18. Afternoon Tea
3 Off Season Rates	7. Swimmming Avail.	11. Reservations Necessary	15. Group Seminars Avail.	* Commisions given
4. Senior Citizen Rates	8. Skiing Available	12. Dinner Available	16. Private Baths	to Travel Agents

Pacific Grove *

Cherry, Joyce & Kent
225 Central Ave., 93950
(800) 753-1881

Amenities: 1,2,9,10,16,18
Breakfast: F.

Dbl. Oc.: $104.50 - $187.00
Sgl. Oc.: $104.50 - $187.00
Third Person: $22.00
Child: Under 6 yrs. - $49.50

Gatehouse Inn Bed And Breakfast—Historic 1884 seaside Victorian home, distinctive rooms, stunning views, private baths, fireplaces, delicious breakfasts, afternoon wine and cheese. Centrally located. Walk to Cannery Row and Monterey Bay Aquarium. Ten minutes to Carmel and world-famous golfing.

Pacific Grove *

Flatley, Susan
555 Ocean View Blvd., 93950
(408) 372-4341

Amenities: 1,2,9,10,11,16,18
Breakfast: F.
Dbl. Oc.: $104.50 - $203.50
Sgl Oc.: $104.50 - $203.50

Seven Gables Inn—Victorian mansion overlooking the Pacific Ocean. Furnished throughout with fine European and American antiques. All ocean-view rooms with private baths. Generous full breakfast and four o'clock tea served in an elegant parlor. Smoking in garden only.

Pacific Grove *

Purcell, Marjorie
321 Central Ave., 93950
(408) 372-3246

Amenities: 1,2,3,6,9,10,11,16, 17
Breakfast: F.

Dbl. Oc.: $99.00 - $165.00
Third Person: $20.00

The Old St. Angela Inn—This unique Cape Cod home, set among many Victorians, exudes warmth and charm. Within this historic home are rooms of distinctive individuality to provide you with comfort and serenity. Breakfast at the inn is truly a delight. Walk just 100 yards to the bay.

Palo Alto *

Hall, Susan & Maxwell
555 Lytton Ave., 94301
(415) 322-8555

Amenities: 1,2,9,10,11,16
Breakfast: C.

Dbl. Oc.: $107.80 - $192.50
Sgl. Oc.: $107.80 - $192.50

The Victorian On Lytton—This B&B offers a combination of forgotten elegance with a touch of European grace. All 10 rooms have sitting parlors and private baths. Fine restaurants and shops are one block away.

1. No Smoking	5. Tennis Available	9. Credit Cards Accepted	13. Lunch Available	17. Shared Baths
2. No Pets	6. Golf Available	10. Personal Check Accepted	14. Conference Rooms Avail.	18. Afternoon Tea
3 Off Season Rates	7. Swimmming Avail.	11. Reservations Necessary	15. Group Seminars Avail.	* Commisions given
4. Senior Citizen Rates	8. Skiing Available	12. Dinner Available	16. Private Baths	to Travel Agents

Palo Alto *

Young, Tricia & Scott
P.O. Box 4528, 94309
(415) 321-5195, Fax: (415) 325-5121

Amenities: 1,2,5,6,7,9,10,16, 18
Breakfast: F.

Dbl. Oc.: $99.00
Sgl. Oc.: $99.00
Third Person: $20.00

Adella Villa—Exclusive, secluded, one-acre 1920s estate. Pool, gardens, bicycles and barbecue. Piano in music foyer. 4,000-square-foot residence with all amenities. Antiques. Quiet atmosphere. Two bedrooms. Whirlpool tub. Close to Silicon Valley, San Francisco and Stanford University.

Placerville *

Thornhill, Doreen & Bill
800 Spring St., 95667
(916) 626-1882, (800) 831-4008

Amenities: 1,2,9,10,11,14,16, 17
Breakfast: F.

Dbl. Oc.: $81.00 & $86.40
Sgl. Oc.: $75.60 & $81.00
Third Person: $16.20
Child: $16.20

The Chichester House Bed And Breakfast Inn—Elegant 1892 Victorian built by lumber baron, D.W. Chichester. Enjoy fireplaces, fretwork, stained glass, antiques and relaxing hospitality. Three air-conditioned rooms with private toilet facilities and robes. Downtown Placerville. Near Bear Apple Hill and gold discovery site.

Pt. Reyes Station *

Bartlett, Julia
39 Cypress, Box 176, 94956
(415) 663-1709

Amenities: 1,2,3,10,16
Breakfast: F.

Dbl. Oc.: $95.00 - $120.00
Third Person: $20.00
Child: $20.00

Thirty-Nine Cypress—"Spectacular views of the Pt. Reyes Peninsula," *NY Times.* All redwood, Oriental rugs, library, original art and country gardens. Each room opens onto a private patio. Hot tub. Close to beaches and 140 miles of trails in Pt. Reyes National Seashore.

Point Reyes Station *

Gray, Karen
11561 Coast Rte. #1, 94956
(415) 663-1166

Amenities: 1,4,6,10,11,16
Breakfast: F.
Dbl. Oc.: $115.00
Sgl Oc.: $115.00
Third Person: $15.00
Child: $15.00

JASMINE COTTAGE

Jasmine Cottage—Tucked in a quiet country garden; lovely view and romantic seclusion; charming interior with full kitchen; garden room; library; wood stove; ideal for families; sleeps four plus crib.

1. No Smoking	5. Tennis Available	9. Credit Cards Accepted	13. Lunch Available	17. Shared Baths
2. No Pets	6. Golf Available	10. Personal Check Accepted	14. Conference Rooms Avail.	18. Afternoon Tea
3 Off Season Rates	7. Swimmming Avail.	11. Reservations Necessary	15. Group Seminars Avail.	* Commissions given
4. Senior Citizen Rates	8. Skiing Available	12. Dinner Available	16. Private Baths	to Travel Agents

CALIFORNIA

Porterville

Gifford, Rosemary
384 N. Hockett St., 93257
(209) 782-5580

Amenities: 2,9,11,16
Breakfast: C. Plus

Dbl. Oc.: $74.52 - $85.32
Sgl. Oc.: $74.52 - $85.32
Third Person: $16.20

Rosebed Inn And Gallery—Elegant private suites in restored Victorian home with amenities comparable to most five star hotels. Two rooms handicapped accessible. Designated smoking areas. Steps away from historic sites and city center. Porterville is a quaint rural community with friendly people.

Portola

Haman, Lynne & Jon
256 Commercial St., 96122
(916) 832-0107

Amenities: 1,5,6,7,8,10,17
Breakfast: F.

Dbl. Oc.: $43.42 - $65.13
Sgl. Oc.: $43.42
Third Person: $5.45
Child: No charge - $5.45

Upper Feather Bed And Breakfast—Small-town comfort and hospitality in casual country style. No TV or radio, but we have board games, puzzles and popcorn for relaxing. Walk to railroad museum, restaurants, wild and scenic river and national forest lands. Only one hour from Reno entertainment.

Pt. Reyes Station *

Bartlett, Julia
39 Cypress, Box 176, 94956
(415) 663-1709

Amenities: 1,2,3,10,16
Breakfast: F.

Dbl. Oc.: $95.00 - $120.00
Third Person: $20.00
Child: $20.00

Thirty-Nine Cypress—"Spectacular views of the Pt. Reyes Peninsula," *NY Times*. All redwood, Oriental rugs, library, original art and country gardens. Each room opens onto a private patio. Hot tub. Close to beaches and 140 miles of trails in Pt. Reyes National Seashore.

Rancho Palos Verdes

Exley, Ruth & Earl
4273 Palos Verdes Dr. So., 90274
(213) 377-2113

Amenities: 4,6,7,10,11,12,13, 16,17,18
Breakfast: F.

Dbl. Oc.: $75.00
Sgl. Oc.: $50.00
Third Person: $12.50
Child: Under 10 yrs.- no charge

The Exley House By The Sea—A cozy home in suburban Los Angeles. Friendly atmosphere; ocean front; private beach; many tourist attractions; restaurants; beautiful views; quiet.

Redding *

Goetz, Gail
1200 Palisades Ave., 96003
(916) 223-5305

Amenities: 2,3,4,9,10,11,17
Breakfast: C. Plus, F.(weekends)

Dbl. Oc.: $66.00 - $88.00
Sgl. Oc.: $61.00
Third Person: $10.00

Palisades Paradise B&B—A breathtaking view of the Sacramento River, city and surrounding mountain from this beautiful, contemporary home with garden spa, fireplace, TV/VCR and homelike atmosphere. Serene setting for a quiet hideaway, yet convenient to shopping, I-5, hiking and water sports.

---

1. No Smoking	5. Tennis Available	9. Credit Cards Accepted	13. Lunch Available	17. Shared Baths
2. No Pets	6. Golf Available	10. Personal Check Accepted	14. Conference Rooms Avail.	18. Afternoon Tea
3 Off Season Rates	7. Swimmming Avail.	11. Reservations Necessary	15. Group Seminars Avail.	* Commisions given
4. Senior Citizen Rates	8. Skiing Available	12. Dinner Available	16. Private Baths	to Travel Agents

CALIFORNIA

San Diego

Brown, Ann & John **Amenities:** 1,2,3,9,10,11,12, **Dbl. Oc.:** $150.00
1220 Rosecrans St., #199, 92106 13,16 **Sgl. Oc.:** $150.00
(619) 298-5432 **Breakfast:** C.

The Castaway Guest Yachts—Centrally located on Shelter Island in beautiful San Diego Bay. Each private yacht is equipped with a double bed, down comforter and private bathroom. Each yacht contains a fully equipped galley for cooking.

San Diego *

Helsper, Nancy & Charles **Amenities:** 1,2,3,4,5,6,7,9,10, **Dbl. Oc.:** $87.00 - $131.00
2470 Heritage Park Row, 92110 11,12,14,15,16,17 **Sgl. Oc.:** $82.00 - $125.00
(619) 299-6832 **Breakfast:** F. **Third Person:** $22.00

Heritage Park Bed And Breakfast Inn—Situated on a seven-acre park in the heart of Old Town. Eight antique-filled guest rooms. Evening refreshments. Nightly vintage films. Queen Anne Victorian mansion. Breakfast on the veranda. Walk to museums, shops and restaurants. Near ocean, Sea World and zoo.

San Diego *

Milbourne, Dorothy A. **Amenities:** 2,9,10,11,15,16 **Dbl. Oc.:** $65.00 - $85.00
2330 Albatross St., 92101 **Breakfast:** C. **Sgl. Oc.:** $65.00 - $85.00
(619) 233-0638 **Third Person:** $10.00
  Child: Under 12 yrs. - no charge

Harbor Hill Guest House—Enjoy a fantastic view of San Diego at this 1920s B&B inn. Ideal location for business, vacations, weekend getaways, honeymoons or family reunions. Main house can accommodate 16 adults, carriage house - a separate hideaway for two. Each level has a private entrance with kitchen.

San Diego

Seitz, Michael **Amenities:** 1,5,6,7,10,11,16, **Dbl. Oc.:** $45.00
25536 Pappas Rd., 92065 17 **Sgl. Oc.:** $39.00
(619) 788-9232 **Breakfast:** C. **Third Person:** $4.00
  Child: $5.00

Splendid Serenity—Located in the historic oaks of the Cuyamaca National Forest. Enjoy quiet relaxation after tourist attractions in the city. Guests may choose to use the services of the nearby golf, equestrian, tennis and swimming clubs or to visit the wild animal park.

San Francisco

Baires, Emma **Amenities:** 1,2,5,6,7,10,14,15, **Dbl. Oc.:** $55.50 - $83.25
McKenzie, Marina 16,17 **Sgl. Oc.:** $55.50 - $83.25
225 Arguello Blvd., 94118 **Breakfast:** C. **Third Person:** $15.00
(415) 752-9482 **Child:** $12.00

Casa Arguello—Comfortable rooms in cheerful, elegant flat. Fifteen minutes from center of town, near Golden Gate Park. Restaurants and shops are within walking distance. Public transportation.

---

1. No Smoking	5. Tennis Available	9. Credit Cards Accepted	13. Lunch Available	17. Shared Baths
2. No Pets	6. Golf Available	10. Personal Check Accepted	14. Conference Rooms Avail.	18. Afternoon Tea
3 Off Season Rates	7. Swimming Avail.	11. Reservations Necessary	15. Group Seminars Avail.	* Commisions given
4. Senior Citizen Rates	8. Skiing Available	12. Dinner Available	16. Private Baths	to Travel Agents

CALIFORNIA

San Francisco *

Bouagou, Aziz
135 Gough St., 94102
(415) 621-0896

Amenities: 2,3,9,10,11,14,16, 17,18
Breakfast: F.

Dbl. Oc.: $75.00 - $160.00
Sgl. Oc.: $75.00 - $125.00
Third Person: $25.00

Albion House Inn—The inn is in proximity to The Performing Arts Complex, Civic center. Minutes away from downtown, Fishermans Wharf, Chinatown, Mascone Center. Antique furnishings. Spacious living room with marble fireplace, grand piano, 15- foot beamed ceiling. A fabulous place to unwind in.

San Francisco *

Brennan, Pamela
525 Ashbury St., 94117
(415) 553-8542

Amenities: 1,2,11,17,18
Breakfast: F.

Dbl. Oc.: $58.00
Sgl. Oc.: $55.00
Third Person: $15.00
Child: Under 3 yrs. - $5.00

The Herb'N Inn—Spacious Victorian located right in the heart of Haight- Ashbury where everlasting 60s culture still lends character. Two blocks from GG Park and bus to downtown. A quiet garden off the large country kitchen, comfortable elegance and seasoned host await your visit. Restaurants.

San Francisco

Britt, N. A.
117 Park Pl., Richmond (mail), 94801
(510) 233-2385

Amenities: 1,2,10,11,12,13,14,15,16,17
Breakfast: F.
Dbl. Oc.: $295.00
Sgl Oc.: $235.00
Third Person: $100.00

East Brother Light Station—On an island in San Francisco Bay. A working lighthouse and historic landmark built in 1873. Four rooms. Dinner, breakfast and boat transportation included. Foghorns, views of San Francisco and Mt. Tam, fireplace, history tours, seabirds, seals. Unique.

San Francisco *

Karr, Rodney
1057 Steiner St., 94115
(800) 228-1647, (415) 776-5462,
FAX:(415) 776-0505

Amenities: 1,2,5,6,7,9,10,14,15,16,17,18
Breakfast: C.
Dbl. Oc.: $80.00 - $200.00
Sgl Oc.: $80.00 - $200.00

The Chateau Tivoli—A landmark mansion that was the residence of the owners of San Francisco's world-famous Tivoli Opera. Guests experience a time-travel journey back to San Francisco's golden age of opulence with the 1890s furnishings from the Vanderbilts, Gettys, etc.

---

1. No Smoking	5. Tennis Available	9. Credit Cards Accepted	13. Lunch Available	17. Shared Baths
2. No Pets	6. Golf Available	10. Personal Check Accepted	14. Conference Rooms Avail.	18. Afternoon Tea
3 Off Season Rates	7. Swimming Avail.	11. Reservations Necessary	15. Group Seminars Avail.	* Commisions given
4. Senior Citizen Rates	8. Skiing Available	12. Dinner Available	16. Private Baths	to Travel Agents

CALIFORNIA

San Francisco *

Kavanaugh, Robert
4 Charlton Ct., 94123
(415) 921-9784

Amenities: 2,10,14,15,16,17
Breakfast: C.
Dbl. Oc.: $127.50

The Bed And Breakfast Inn—A 10-room, intimate and luxurious inn located on a mews street in a trendy shopping area. Warm, helpful staff and lovely furnishings. This is the original B&B inn in San Francisco.

San Francisco *

Kreibich, Susan
5 Dolores Terrace, 94110
(415) 479-1913

Amenities: 1,5,9,10,11,16,17, 18
Breakfast: F.

Dbl. Oc.: $65.00
Sgl. Oc.: $55.00
Third Person: $10.00
Child: $10.00

Country Cottage Bed And Breakfast—A cozy country-style B&B in the heart of San Francisco. The four guest rooms are comfortably furnished in antiques and brass beds. It is located at the end of a quiet street away from the city noise. There is a small patio with trees and birds. Breakfast served in sunny kitchen.

San Francisco *

Kreibich, Susan
847 Fillmore St., 94117
(415) 479-1913

Amenities: 1,5,9,10,11,16,17, 18
Breakfast: F.

Dbl. Oc.: $75.00 - $125.00
Sgl. Oc.: $65.00 - $125.00
Third Person: $10.00
Child: $10.00

No Name Victorian B&B—Located within close proximity of all the famous San Francisco sights. Three of the five guest rooms offer private baths and fireplaces. A big breakfast is served. There is a hot tub for your enjoyment and complimentary wine is always available. Family apartment available.

San Francisco *

Moffatt, Ruth
431 Hugo St., 94122
(415) 661-6210, Fax: (415) 564-2480

Amenities: 5,6,7,9,10,11,17
Breakfast: C. Plus
Dbl. Oc.: Up to $62.00
Sgl Oc.: Up to $55.00
Third Person: $7.00
Child: $7.00

Moffatt House—Catch a view of fog-veiled Mt. Sutro from our simple 1903 Edwardian home, located just one block from the major attractions in Golden Gate Park. Enjoy complete shopping and excellent public transit to downtown and ocean beach. Safe area. Exercise club discount.

---

1. No Smoking	5. Tennis Available	9. Credit Cards Accepted	13. Lunch Available	17. Shared Baths
2. No Pets	6. Golf Available	10. Personal Check Accepted	14. Conference Rooms Avail.	18. Afternoon Tea
3 Off Season Rates	7. Swimmming Avail.	11. Reservations Necessary	15.Group Seminars Avail.	* Commisions given
4. Senior Citizen Rates	8. Skiing Available	12. Dinner Available	16. Private Baths	to Travel Agents

San Francisco *

Pritikin, Robert
2220 Sacramento St., 94115
(415) 929-9444

Amenities: 5,9,10,11,12,13,14,15,16,18
Breakfast: F.
Dbl. Oc.: $102.12 - $300.00
Sgl Oc.: $82.14 - $280.02
Third Person: $18.00

The Mansions Hotel—Rates include sumptuous breakfast, flowers in rooms, billiard/game room, superb dining, sculpture gardens and so much more. Celebrated guests include Barbra Streisand, Andre Sakhrov and Robin Williams. This small family-owned inn is indeed a magic palace.

San Francisco

Widburg, Monica & Ed   **Amenities:** 1,2,5,6,7,10,11,   **Dbl. Oc.:** $65.00
2007 15th Ave., 94116   16   **Sgl. Oc.:** $60.00
(415) 564-1751   **Breakfast:** F.

Located in a quiet, residential area with lovely ocean view, this charming home offers one room for B&B. Nearby ample parking and public transportation. Twenty minutes from airport.

San Francisco *

Yuan, George   **Amenities:** 1,2,9,11,16,17,18   **Dbl. Oc.:** $69.93 - $119.88
600 Presidio Ave., 94115   **Breakfast:** C. Plus
(415) 931-1875

The Monte Cristo—Part of San Francisco since 1875. Located two blocks from the elegantly restored Victorian shops, restaurants and antique stores on Sacramento Street. Each room is elegantly furnished with authentic period pieces. Convenient transportation.

San Gregorio *

Raynor, Lorraine   **Amenities:** 1,2,6,7,9,10,14,15,   **Dbl. Oc.:** $65.00
Rte. #1, Box 54, 94074   16   **Third Person:** $15.00
Hwy. 84 off Hwy 1, 94074   **Breakfast:** F.   **Child:** Under 12 yrs - $5 - $10
(415) 747-0810, Fax: (415) 747-0184

Rancho San Gregorio—Warm hospitality and home-grown products featured in our breakfast feast make this coastal country retreat a traveler's respite. Fifteen creekside acres, apple orchards, gazebo, gardens, patios and decks; 45 miles south of San Francisco; 45 miles north of Santa Cruz.

---

1. No Smoking	5. Tennis Available	9. Credit Cards Accepted	13. Lunch Available	17. Shared Baths
2. No Pets	6. Golf Available	10. Personal Check Accepted	14. Conference Rooms Avail.	18. Afternoon Tea
3 Off Season Rates	7. Swimmming Avail.	11. Reservations Necessary	15. Group Seminars Avail.	* Commisions given
4. Senior Citizen Rates	8. Skiing Available	12. Dinner Available	16. Private Baths	to Travel Agents

CALIFORNIA

San Jose *

Layne, Sharon
456 N. 3rd. St., 95112
(408) 298-3537,
FAX: (408) 298-4676

Amenities: 1,2,3,4,5,6,7,9,10,11, 12,13,14,15,16,18
Breakfast: F.

Dbl. Oc.: $82.50 - $137.50
Sgl. Oc.: $82.50 - $137.50
Third Person: $20.00
Child: $20.00

The Hensley House—Located in the historic district downtown. Restaurants, theatres, museums within walking distance. Historic Queen Anne high ceilings, antiques, hand-painted walls, two rooms have whirlpools, all have TVs and VCRs. Full gourmet breakfast. Fireplace, crystal chandelier and feather beds.

San Luis Obispo *

Dinshaw, Ann & Michael
1473 Monterey St., 93401
(805) 549-0321

Amenities: 1,2,3,9,14,16,18
Breakfast: F.

Dbl. Oc.: $53.41 - $92.65
Sgl. Oc.: $49.05
Third Person: $10.00
Child: Under 5 yrs. - $5.00

Adobe Inn—Southwestern decor with European atttitude and warm hospitality. Bountiful breakfast, patio garden, cozy, comfortable rooms. Near Hearst Castle, vineyards and beachs. Stroll to historic town, cafes, shops and theaters. Farmer's market every Thursday night all year.

San Rafael *

Soldavini, Linda Cassidy
531 'C' St., 94901
(415) 454-3140

Amenities: 1,4,5,10,11,16,17, 18
Breakfast: C. Plus

Dbl. Oc.: $65.00 - $85.00
Sgl. Oc.: $60.00 - $65.00
Third Person: $25.00
Child: Under 10 yrs. - $10.00

Casa Soldavini—A 1930s winemaker's home located in historic Mission San Rafael. Many activities close by. Family antiques, three private guest rooms, sitting room, VCR and TV. Large patio, BBQ, fruit and vegetable gardens. A hearty breakfast and snacks all day. Come stay with us soon.

Santa Barbara

Canfield, Carolyn
P.O. Box 20065, 93102
(805) 966-6659

Amenities: 1,5,6,7,10,11,16
Breakfast: C. Plus

Dbl. Oc.: $60.00
Sgl. Oc.: $45.00
Third Person: $10.00

Ocean View House—A private home within walking distance of the ocean. Two rooms decorated in antique charm; one with a queen bed and a den with a queen-size divan. Two TVs and an interesting collection. Breakfast on the patio while viewing the Channell Islands. Two-day minimum. A wonderful location.

1. No Smoking	5. Tennis Available	9. Credit Cards Accepted	13. Lunch Available	17. Shared Baths
2. No Pets	6. Golf Available	10. Personal Check Accepted	14. Conference Rooms Avail.	18. Afternoon Tea
3 Off Season Rates	7. Swimmming Avail.	11. Reservations Necessary	15. Group Seminars Avail.	* Commisions given
4. Senior Citizen Rates	8. Skiing Available	12. Dinner Available	16. Private Baths	to Travel Agents

CALIFORNIA

Santa Barbara *

Donaldson, Nancy	**Amenities:** 1,2,3,4,9,10,11,12,	**Dbl. Oc.:** $88.00 - $154.00
431 Corona Del Mar Dr., 93103	13,14,15,16	**Sgl. Oc.:** $82.00 - $110.00
(805) 962-1277	**Breakfast:** F.	**Third Person:** $33.00
		Child: $33.00

The Old Yacht Club Inn—The inn at the beach - Santa Barbara's first. Known for hospitality and fine food. Moderate rates include full breakfast, evening wine, bikes, beach chairs and towels. Reduced mid-week rates off-season. Two-night stay required if Saturday night included. Dinner available on Saturdays.

Santa Barbara *

Dunstan, Christine
36 W. Valerio St., 93101
(805) 569-1610

Amenities: 1,2,5,6,7,9,10,11,14,16
Breakfast: F.
Dbl. Oc.: $97.90 - $273.90
Sgl Oc.: $82.50 - $214.50
Third Person: $25.00
Child: $25.00

The Cheshire Cat Inn—Two elegant Victorian homes in the heart of Santa Barbara. Laura Ashley decor. English antiques throughout. Some rooms with Jacuzzi, fireplace or kitchenette. Bikes, outdoor spa, chocolates/liqueurs and full breakfast to all guests. Phones in room. Beautiful garden.

Santa Barbara *

Eaton, Jenise	**Amenities:** 1,2,3,4,5,6,7,9,10,	**Dbl. Oc.:** $90.20 - $181.50
1908 Bath St., 93101	13,14,16,17,18	**Sgl. Oc.:** $72.16 - $145.20
(805) 687-2300,	**Breakfast:** F.	**Third Person:** $20.00
USA (800)676-1622, CA (800) 549-1622		**Child:** $20.00

Blue Quail Inn And Cottages—Cottages and suites in a delightfully relaxing country setting. Close to town and beaches. Delectable full breakfast, afternoon wine and hors d'oeuvres, evening sweets and hot spiced apple cider. Bicycles, picnic lunches and gift certificates available.

Santa Barbara *

Harmon, Holli	**Amenities:** 1,2,3,4,9,10,11,14,	**Dbl. Oc.:** $93.50 - $181.50
1600 Olive St., 93101	15,16	**Sgl. Oc.:** $88.50 - $176.50
(805) 962-9336	**Breakfast:** F.	

The Parsonage—Charming 1892 Victorian, furnished beautifully with antiques and Oriental rugs. Romantic homeymoon suite with city and ocean views. Enjoy breakfast on the spacious sundeck. Centrally located within walking distance of the Mission, shops and restaurants.

1. No Smoking	5. Tennis Available	9. Credit Cards Accepted	13. Lunch Available	17. Shared Baths
2. No Pets	6. Golf Available	10. Personal Check Accepted	14. Conference Rooms Avail.	18. Afternoon Tea
3 Off Season Rates	7. Swimmming Avail.	11. Reservations Necessary	15. Group Seminars Avail.	* Commisions given
4. Senior Citizen Rates	8. Skiing Available	12. Dinner Available	16. Private Baths	to Travel Agents

CALIFORNIA

Santa Barbara

Miller, Marie
435 E. Pedregosa, 93103
(805) 569-1914

Amenities: 1,2,10,11,16,17
Breakfast: C.

Dbl. Oc.: $45.00
Sgl. Oc.: $45.00
Third Person: $10.00

Old Mission Inn—This is a Craftsman house built in 1895 with fireplaces in all the rooms. We are within walking distance of the Mission, museum, downtown Santa Barbara and many parks; in addition, we are 10 minutes from the beach by car.

Santa Barbara *

Montgomery, Michael
18 Bath St., 93101
(805) 963-4418, CA (800) 433-3097
FAX:(805) 966-4240

Amenities: 3,4,9,10,14,16,18
Breakfast: C. Plus

Dbl. Oc.: $65.00 - $115.00
Sgl. Oc.: $65.00 - $115.00
Third Person: $10.00
Child: Under 12 yrs. - no charge

Casa Del Mar—A Mediterranean-style inn at the beach. Located just 1/2 block from the beach near Stearns Wharf and the harbor. Intimate spa in hidden garden courtyard. Bungalow-style rooms of various types - queens, kings and suites. Many with kitchens and fireplaces.

Santa Barbara *

Pomeroy, Keith
111 W. Valerio St., 93101
(805) 682-3199

Amenities: 1,3,5,6,7,9,10,11,
14,16,18
Breakfast: F.

Dbl. Oc.: $93.50 - $148.50

The Bayberry Inn B&B—Enjoy a stroll on the spacious grounds; play croquet or badminton; retreat from the world in the beautifully appointed in-town inn. Experience the comfort and splendor of another era. Gourmet breakfast. Many guest rooms have fireplaces. Free bicycles to explore our lovely city.

Santa Barbara *

Slade, Mark
1136 De La Vina, 93101
(805) 965-6532

Amenities: 1,3,4,9,14,15,16
Breakfast: F.

Dbl. Oc.: $95.00
Sgl. Oc.: $85.00
Third Person: $10.00
Child: Under 12 yrs. - no charge

Arlington Inn—Just two blocks from the heart of town. Individually decorated rooms, antiques and charming old-fashioned decor. Guests enjoy a wonderful home-cooked breakfast. All rooms have a kitchen, walk-in closets and TV. Free local phone calls. Suites also available.

1. No Smoking	5. Tennis Available	9. Credit Cards Accepted	13. Lunch Available	17. Shared Baths
2. No Pets	6. Golf Available	10. Personal Check Accepted	14. Conference Rooms Avail.	18. Afternoon Tea
3 Off Season Rates	7. Swimmming Avail.	11. Reservations Necessary	15. Group Seminars Avail.	* Commisions given
4. Senior Citizen Rates	8. Skiing Available	12. Dinner Available	16. Private Baths	to Travel Agents

CALIFORNIA

Santa Barbara *

Stevens, Valli & Larry
340 N. Sierra Vista Rd. 93108
(805) 969-1272

Amenities: 1,4,5,6,7,10,11, 16
Breakfast: F.

Dbl. Oc.: $65.00
Sgl. Oc.: $65.00
Third Person: $30.00
Child: Under 18 yrs. - $20.00

Bed & Breakfast At Valli's View—This beautiful home in the Santa Barbara foothills has spectacular mountain views, sunny patio, porch swings, shady deck, fern gardens in a peaceful tranquil setting. Guestroom has mountain view, color TV and private bath. Fresh fruit and vegetables from garden when in season.

Santa Barbara *

Wilson, Gillean
121 E. Arrellaga, 93101
(805) 963-7067, (800) 676-1280

Amenities: 1,2,3,5,6,7,9,10, 15,16,18
Breakfast: F.

Dbl. Oc.: $110.00 - $220.00
Sgl. Oc.: $110.00 - $220.00
Third Person: $25.00

Simpson House Inn—Beautifully restored 1874 Victorian secluded on one acre of English gardens, yet a five-minute walk to downtown. Elegantly decorated with antiques, Oriental rugs and original art. Rooms with private decks and fireplaces. Bicycles, croquet and beach chairs.

Santa Cruz *

King, Helen
1025 Laurel St., 95060
(408) 427-2437, (800) 866-1131

Amenities: 1,2,5,6,7,9,10,11,14,15,16,18
Breakfast: F.
Dbl. Oc.: $93.50 - $148.50
Sgl Oc.: $93.50 - $148.50
Third Person: $16.50
Child: $16.50

The Babbling Brook Inn—Cascading waterfalls, meandering brook and romantic garden with gazebo grace an acre of pines, Rrdwoods and flowers. Site of 1796 mill and Indian village. Near beaches, historic boardwalk, redwood forest, narrow gauge steam train, wineries, golf and tennis. AAA - three diamonds.

Santa Cruz/Soquel *

O'Brien, Pat & Tom
2815 Main St., 95073
(408) 464-1137

Amenities: 1,2,3,4,5,6,7,9,10, 11,13,14,15,16,18
Breakfast: F.

Dbl. Oc.: $93.50 - $132.00
Sgl. Oc.: $86.50 - $127.00
Third Person: $20.00

Blue Spruce Inn—Our 1873 farmhouse, located on Monterey Bay, blends the flavor of yesterday with the luxury of today. Guests can walk to fine dining, unique shops and local wineries. Amish quilts and original local art make each room a place of quiet respite. Come visit soon!

---

1. No Smoking	5. Tennis Available	9. Credit Cards Accepted	13. Lunch Available	17. Shared Baths
2. No Pets	6. Golf Available	10. Personal Check Accepted	14. Conference Rooms Avail.	18. Afternoon Tea
3 Off Season Rates	7. Swimmming Avail.	11. Reservations Necessary	15. Group Seminars Avail.	* Commisions given
4. Senior Citizen Rates	8. Skiing Available	12. Dinner Available	16. Private Baths	to Travel Agents

CALIFORNIA

Santa Cruz *

Young, Tricia & Scott
P.O. Box 66593, 95067
(415) 321-5195, Fax: (415) 325-5121

Amenities: 1,2,6,7,9,10,11,15, 16
Breakfast: F.

Dbl. Oc.: $110.00
Sgl. Oc.: $110.00
Third Person: $20.00

Valley View—Secluded "unhosted" mountain retreat. Walls of glass overlook thousands of redwoods in forest. Hot spa on private deck. Cable TV, stereo, piano, fireplace and full kitchen. Includes breakfast. Two-night minimum. Ten minutes to Santa Cruz; 20 minutes to Silicon Valley.

Seal Beach *

Bettenhausen, Marjorie
212 Fifth St., 90740
(310) 493-2416

Amenities: 1,2,4,5,7,9,12,14, 15,16
Breakfast: F.

Dbl. Oc.: $158.05
Sgl. Oc.: $106.82
Third Person: $10.90
Child: Under 5 yrs. - $5.45

The Seal Beach Inn And Gardens—A historic French Mediterranean-style bed and breakfast country inn located in the quaint seaside village of Seal Beach. Ideally located between Orange and Los Angeles counties. A lavish gourmet breakfast is served.

Solvang *

Remak, Robert
1564 Copenhagen Dr., 93463
(805) 688-0559

Amenities: 1,2,3,4,5,6,7,9,10, 11,12,13,14,15,16
Breakfast: C.

Dbl. Oc.: $85.00 - $195.00
Sgl. Oc.: $85.00 - $195.00
Third Person: $12.00 (rollaway)

Tivoli Inn—Twenty-nine individually decorated and designed wood-burning fireplace suites. Complimentary basket of fruit and chilled bottle of local wine on your night of arrival. Complimentary continental breakfast served to your room every morning of your stay.

Sonoma *

Leese, Joe
18935 Fifth St. W., 95476
(707) 938-3129

Amenities: 1,2,3,9,10,11,16, 17
Breakfast: C. Plus

Dbl. Oc.: $81.00 - $135.00
Sgl. Oc.: $81.00 - $135.00
Child: Under 10 yrs. - $25.00

Sonoma Chalet Bed And Breakfast—Swiss-style chalet and country cottages located in the beautiful Sonoma Valley wine country. Romantic antique- filled rooms. Wonderful country farm setting near historic plaza and wineries. "Fairytale" honeymoon cottage available.

Sonoma *

Lewis, Donna
316 E. Napa St., 95476
(707) 996-5339, (800) 543-5339

Amenities: 2,5,6,7,9,10,11,14, 15,16,17
Breakfast: C. Plus

Dbl. Oc.: $86.90 - $152.90
Sgl. Oc.: $86.90 - $152.90
Third Person: $22.00

Victorian Garden Inn—Nestled beside a creek on an acre of gardens, paths and patios, this lovely, historic farmhouse and watertower is 1-1/2 blocks from Sonoma's Plaza and world-class wineries. Breakfast is served in your room, by the pool, or in the dining room as requested. Romance, privacy and comfort.

1. No Smoking	5. Tennis Available	9. Credit Cards Accepted	13. Lunch Available	17. Shared Baths
2. No Pets	6. Golf Available	10. Personal Check Accepted	14. Conference Rooms Avail.	18. Afternoon Tea
3 Off Season Rates	7. Swimmming Avail.	11. Reservations Necessary	15. Group Seminars Avail.	* Commisions given
4. Senior Citizen Rates	8. Skiing Available	12. Dinner Available	16. Private Baths	to Travel Agents

CALIFORNIA

Sonoma *

Musilli, Dorene
110 W. Spain St., 95476
(707) 996-2996

Amenities: 2,3,5,6,9,10,11,12, 13,15,16,17,18
Breakfast: C.

Dbl. Oc.: $77.00 - $126.50

Sonoma Hotel—To spend an evening here is to step back into a romantic period of history. Each antique-furnished room evokes a distinct feeling of early California while the emphasis on comfort is decidedly European. Short walks to wineries, historic landmarks and art galleries.

Sonora *

Miller, Janet
85 Gold St., 95370
(209) 533-3455, (800) 538-3455

Amenities: 1,2,3,4,5,6,7,8,9, 10,14,16,18
Breakfast: F.

Dbl. Oc.: $80.00 - $100.00
Sgl. Oc.: $65.00
Third Person: $15.00
Child: Under 5 Yr.s - $5.00

Lulu Belle's Bed And Breakfast—Charming 1886 Victorian with relaxing gardens and porch swing. Each of the five individually decorated guest rooms have private baths, entrances and air-conditioning. Enjoy delicious full breakfasts and hosts who enjoy making your visit special.

Springville *

Bozanich, Ann
33024 Globe Dr., 93265
(209) 539-3827

Amenities: 1,2,5,6,7,8,9,10, 11,12, 13,14,15,16, 18
Breakfast: F.
Dbl. Oc.: $85.00 - $95.00
Sgl Oc.: $75.00 - $85.00
Third Person: $25.00

Annie's Bed And Breakfast—Situated on five acres in the quiet beautiful Sierra Foothills. Beautifully furnished with antique furniture, feather beds and homemade quilts. Full country breakfast prepared on an antique wood cookstove. Close to golf, tennis, river, lakes, mountains, fishing and redwoods.

St. Helena *

Bartels, Jami
1200 Conn. Valley Rd., 94574
(707) 963-4001

Amenities: 2,4,5,6,7,8,9,10, 11,14,15,16,18
Breakfast: C.

Dbl. Oc.: $105.00 - $265.00
Sgl. Oc.: $105.00 - $265.00
Third Person: $25.00
Child: $25.00

Bartels Ranch And Country Inn—Internationally acclaimed 60-acre estate setting in world-famous wine country. Romantic and secluded; 10,000- acre view. Game room, library, bicycles and vineyard view. Three miles from St. Helena. Private and peaceful. Smoking limited. Children accepted by special arrangement.

1. No Smoking	5. Tennis Available	9. Credit Cards Accepted	13. Lunch Available	17. Shared Baths
2. No Pets	6. Golf Available	10. Personal Check Accepted	14. Conference Rooms Avail.	18. Afternoon Tea
3 Off Season Rates	7. Swimming Avail.	11. Reservations Necessary	15. Group Seminars Avail.	* Commisions given
4. Senior Citizen Rates	8. Skiing Available	12. Dinner Available	16. Private Baths	to Travel Agents

St. Helena *

Cunningham, Erika
285 Fawn Park, 94574
(707) 963-2887

Amenities: 1,2,3,5,6,7,9,10, 11,16
Breakfast: C.

Dbl. Oc.: $65.00 - $165.00
Third Person: $10.00

Erika's Hillside—Enjoy a peaceful and romantic retreat. Nestled on a quiet hillside overlooking the vineyards in the heart of the Napa Valley wine country. Hot tub, fireplace, private entrance, and private bath. European hospitality.

St. Helena *

Gevarter, Annette
9550 St. Helena Rd., P.O. Box 726, 94574
707) 944-0880

Amenities: 1,2,3,9,10,11,16
Breakfast: F.

Dbl. Oc.: $113.40 - $178.20
Third Person: $15.00
Child: $15.00

Hilltop House Bed And Breakfast—Located on 135 acres providing a unique mountain-top experience with a hang glider's view of the Mayacamas Mountains. Hot tub under the stars. Afternoon refreshments. Hiking trails. Beautifully furnished. We enjoy pampering our guests.

St. Helena

Jenkins, Genny
1407 Kearney St., 94574
(707) 963-4653

Amenities: 1,2,3,9,10,11,16, 18
Breakfast: F.

Dbl. Oc.: $85.00 - $150.00
Sgl. Oc.: $75.00 - $150.00
Third Person: $35.00
Child: $35.00

Cinnamon Bear Bed And Breakfast—Classic arts and crafts house, built in 1910 and furnished in that style with lots of bears. Comfortable parlor with fireplace, TV and VCR. Convenient to wineries, restaurants and shopping. Four rooms, queen- size beds and private bathrooms.

St. Helena *

Wild-Runnells, Lisa & John
399 Zinfandel Lane, 94574
(707) 963-1190

Amenities: 1,2,3,5,6,7,10,16, 18
Breakfast: F.

Dbl. Oc.: $128.00 - $161.00
Sgl. Oc.: $128.00 - $161.00
Third Person: $25.00
Child: $25.00

Shady Oaks Country Inn—Secluded and romantic among the finest wineries in the valley. Experience country tranquility and warm hospitality. Full gourmet champagne breakfasts; wine and cheese; private baths; immaculate; luxury linens; antiques. We assist with restaurant, tours and spas, etc.

Summerland *

Farned, James
2161 Ortega Hill Rd., 93067
(805) 969-5225

Amenities: 1,2,3,4,9,10,16
Breakfast: C. Plus

Dbl. Oc.: $60.00 - $130.00
Sgl. Oc.: $55.00 - $110.00
Third Person: $15.00

Summerland Inn—Five miles south of Santa Barbara in the picturesque town of Summerland. Stroll through antique stores, elegant shops and take a relaxing walk on the beach. All rooms have private baths, TVs and phones. Some have fireplaces.

1. No Smoking	5. Tennis Available	9. Credit Cards Accepted	13. Lunch Available	17. Shared Baths
2. No Pets	6. Golf Available	10. Personal Check Accepted	14. Conference Rooms Avail.	18. Afternoon Tea
3 Off Season Rates	7. Swimmming Avail.	11. Reservations Necessary	15. Group Seminars Avail.	* Commisions given
4. Senior Citizen Rates	8. Skiing Available	12. Dinner Available	16. Private Baths	to Travel Agents

CALIFORNIA

Tahoe City *

Knauss, Cynthia & Bruce
236 Grove St., 96145
(916) 583-1001

Amenities: 1,2,5,6,7,8,9,10, 11,17
Breakfast: F.

Dbl. Oc.: $75.60 - $113.40
Sgl. Oc.: $75.60 - $113.40
Third Person: $15.00
Child: $15.00

The Mayfield House—Built in 1932, the Mayfield House is one of the finest examples of old Tahoe architecture. The inn has five bedrooms, each with down comforters and pillows, lots of books to enjoy and fresh flowers. A full breakfast can be enjoyed in the breakfast nook or your room.

Tahoma *

Butler, Phyllis & Joel
6941 W. Lake Blvd.
P.O. Box 262, 96142
(916) 525-5000

Amenities 1,3,4,5,6,7,8,9,10, 11,12,13,16,17
Breakfast: F.
Dbl. Oc.: $81.00
Sgl. Oc.: $50.00
Third Person: $12.00
Child: Under 2 yrs. - $15.00

The Captain's Alpenhaus—A European-style country inn and gourmet restaurant with an Alpine bar and stone fireplace. Guest rooms and cottages with fireplaces nestled in pine woods. A cozy and quaint resort on Lake Tahoe's unspoiled west shore, five minutes from Emerald Bay, a scenic wonder.

Ukiah *

Ashoff, Marjorie & Gilbert
2605 Vichy Springs Rd., 95482
(707) 462-9515

Amenities: 1,2,5,6,7,9,10,11, 14,15,16
Breakfast: C. Plus

Dbl. Oc.: $105.00 - $150.00
Sgl. Oc.: $80.00 - $130.00
Third Person: $25.00
Child: $25.00

Vichy Springs Resort And Inn—A two-hour drive north of San Francisco. Quiet setting featuring wonderful cottages and rooms. Naturally sparkling mineral baths, hot pool, Olympic pool, 700 acres, trails for hiking, picnicking, bicycling, massage, herbal facials and landscaped grounds.

---

1. No Smoking	5. Tennis Available	9. Credit Cards Accepted	13. Lunch Available	17. Shared Baths
2. No Pets	6. Golf Available	10. Personal Check Accepted	14. Conference Rooms Avail.	18. Afternoon Tea
3 Off Season Rates	7. Swimming Avail.	11. Reservations Necessary	15. Group Seminars Avail.	* Commisions given
4. Senior Citizen Rates	8. Skiing Available	12. Dinner Available	16. Private Baths	to Travel Agents

CALIFORNIA

Ventura *
Gisela, Flender Baida,
411 Poli St., 93001
(805) 643-3600

Amenities: 1,2,3,5,6,7,9,10,11,16,18
Breakfast: F.
Dbl. Oc.: $120.00 - $170.00
Sgl Oc.: $110.00 - $160.00
Third Person: $25.00

"La Mer"—A most romantic European getaway in historic landmark overlooking spectacular coastline. Bedrooms have private baths and entrances and are furnished with European antiques to capture a specific country. Full Bavarian buffet-style breakfast. Mid-week packages available. AAA.

Westport
Grigg, Sally & Charles
40501 N. Hwy. One
P.O. Box 121, 95488
(707) 964-6725

Amenities: 1,3,9,10,11,16,17
Breakfast: F.

Dbl. Oc.: $55.00 - $120.00
Third Person: $10.00

Howard Creek Ranch—An 1867 rural, ocean-front ranch on 20 acres; magnificent views; beach; mountains; creeks; sauna; pool; hot tub; fireplace; antiques; flower garden; cabins; parlor with piano; near redwoods.

Whittier *
Davis, Coleen
P.O. Box 9302, 90608
(310) 699-8427

Amenities: 1,2,5,6,7,10,11,12, 13,14,15,16,18
Breakfast: F.

Dbl. Oc.: $60.00
Sgl. Oc.: $50.00
Third Person: $15.00
Child: Under 3 yrs. - $10.00

Coleen's CA Casa—Private entrances and baths; two suites with three bedrooms and private entrances. Microwave, refrigerator, off-street parking and complimentary beverages. Near the Queen Mary, Disneyland, Universal Studios, Knott's Berry Farm and the beach. Patio. Lunch. Dinner. Gourmet picnic baskets.

Yountville *
Packard, Louis & John
7433 St. Helena Hwy., 94599
(707) 944-8315

Amenities: 1,2,5,6,7,9,10,11, 16
Breakfast: F.

Dbl. Oc.: $127.10 - $160.25

Oleander House—Country French two-story home combining old-world design with modern amenities. Located in the heart of Napa Valley, guests enjoy spacious, high-ceiling rooms with private baths, balcony, fireplace, antiques, Laura Ashley wallcoverings and full gourmet breakfast. Outside spa.

1. No Smoking	5. Tennis Available	9. Credit Cards Accepted	13. Lunch Available	17. Shared Baths
2. No Pets	6. Golf Available	10. Personal Check Accepted	14. Conference Rooms Avail.	18. Afternoon Tea
3 Off Season Rates	7. Swimmming Avail.	11. Reservations Necessary	15. Group Seminars Avail.	* Commisions given
4. Senior Citizen Rates	8. Skiing Available	12. Dinner Available	16. Private Baths	to Travel Agents

COLORADO

The Centennial State

Capitol: Denver
Statehood: August 1, 1876; the 38th state
State Motto: Nothing Without Providence
State Song: "Where the Columbines Grow"
State Bird: Lark Bunting
State Flower: Rocky Mountain Columbine
State Tree: Blue Spruce

Colorado, with its majestic rocky mountains and its cool refreshing climate, is a state tourists love to visit. It has unusual natural beauty, historic mining towns and old Indian cliff dwellings. It also is the home for the U.S. Air Force Academy.

The capitol of the state is Denver known as the "Mile High City." It is a cosmopolitan city with a cultural and commercial center.

The Shrine of the Sun dedicated to the memory of Will Rogers is located high on the slopes of Cheyenne Mountain. Buffalo Bill's grave lies atop Lookout Mountain near Denver.

Fascinating cliff dwellings can be seen in the Mesa Verde, one of the nations major archeological preserves.

Skiing is the big winter attraction. At Vale, Aspen and other well known areas, millions of dollars a year are spent on this sport by vacationers.

Tourists can still ride the old-time locomotive between Durango and Silverton, and the Cliff Palaces of the Indians such as Mesa Verde are a constant source of pleasure for those who enjoy Indian history.

Arvada *

Thomas, Sue
6600 Simms (mail), 80004
(303) 431-6352

Amenities: 1,2,9,10,15,16
Breakfast: F.

Dbl. Oc.: $51.21 - $82.56
Sgl. Oc.: $51.21 - $82.56
Third Person: $51.21 - $82.56
Child: $51.21 - $82.56

The Tree House—A peaceful, romantic hideaway nestled in a 10- acre forest with wildflowers and animals. Twenty minutes from downtown Denver. Rooms have private baths, brass beds, handmade quilts, antiquing and four rooms have wood-burning fireplaces.

Aspen *

Dolle, Norma
124 E. Cooper St., 81611
(303) 925-8455,
(303) 925-6971

Amenities: 2,3,5,6,7,8,9,10, 11,16,17
Breakfast: C. Plus

Dbl. Oc.: $58.26 - $134.87
Sgl. Oc.: $48.26 - $124.87
Third Person: $16.85
Child: Under 14 yrs. - $10.79

Snow Queen Victorian Bed And Breakfast Lodge—A quaint family-run lodge built in the 1880s. It has a variety of rooms, most with private baths plus two kitchen units. Reasonably priced. In-town location within walking distance o fshops, restaurants and ski lift. Hot tub, fireplace, TV and phones.

Aspen *

Percival, Anthony
520 W. Main, 81611
(303) 925-7696

Amenities: 1,2,3,7,8,9,10,11, 16,18
Breakfast: C.(summer), F.(winter)

Dbl. Oc.: $60.00 - $102.00
Sgl. Oc.: $54.00 - $102.00
Third Person: $10.00

ULLR Lodge—Family owned and operated. Located in the residential west end. Walk to music tent and Aspen Institute. Ten-minute walk to town on free ski bus route. Emphasis on personal service and very clean rooms and apartments. We encourage quiet after 10 p.m.

Basalt *

Waterman, Martha D.
23484 Hwy. 82
P.O. Box 815, 81621
(303) 927-3309

Amenities: 1,2,4,6,7,8,10,11, 17
Breakfast: F.

Dbl. Oc.: $60.00
Sgl. Oc.: $45.00

Altamira Ranch Bed And Breakfast—The remodeled 1906 farmhouse is a charming contemporary home. The ranch borders the roaring Fork River and with a private pond provides great fishing. Guests appreciate our location minutes from Glenwood Springs and Aspen's year-round resort.

1. No Smoking	5. Tennis Available	9. Credit Cards Accepted	13. Lunch Available	17. Shared Baths
2. No Pets	6. Golf Available	10. Personal Check Accepted	14. Conference Rooms Avail.	18. Afternoon Tea
3 Off Season Rates	7. Swimmming Avail.	11. Reservations Necessary	15. Group Seminars Avail.	* Commisions given
4. Senior Citizen Rates	8. Skiing Available	12. Dinner Available	16. Private Baths	to Travel Agents

Breckenridge

Contos, Georgette & Peter
102 So. French St., 80424
(303) 453-5509

Amenities: 1,2,3,5,6,7,8,10, 16,17,18
Breakfast: F.

Dbl. Oc.: $77.00 - $99.00
Sgl. Oc.: $77.00 - $99.00
Third Person: $20.00
Child: Under 12 yrs. - $10.00

Cotten House—An 1886 Victorian home in National Historic District. Free bus to ski slopes. Nightlife, restaurants and shopping two blocks away. Cozy atmosphere with period furnishings. Comfortable TV room with beautiful view. Delicious full breakfasts. Home away from home.

Colorado Springs *

Clark, Sallie & Welling
1102 W. Pikes Peak Ave., 80904
(719) 471-3980

Amenities: 1,2,5,6,7,9,10,11,16,18
Breakfast: F.
Dbl. Oc.: $65.00 - $90.00
Sgl Oc.: $65.00 - $90.00

Holden House — 1902 Bed And Breakfast—Romantic storybook Victorian with antiques, views, fireplaces, tubs for two and more! Honeymoon suites. Centrally located to all the Pikes Peak Region, near historic district in residential area. Helpful hosts. Friendly resident cat, "Mingtoy." A relaxing retreat.

Denver *

Hillestad, Ann & Chuck
2147 Tremont Pl., 80205
(303) 296-6666

Amenities: 1,2,3,9,10,14,16,18
Breakfast: C.
Dbl. Oc.: $82.00 - $168.00
Sgl Oc.: $71.00 - $157.00
Third Person: $11.00

Queen Anne Inn—Colorado's MOST award-winning inn with numerous national "Best Of" honors such as *Country Inns* magazine. Luxurious, elegant, romantic and historic. Quiet downtown location. All private baths, phones, air-conditioning, music, art, heirlooms, flowers and views.

1. No Smoking	5. Tennis Available	9. Credit Cards Accepted	13. Lunch Available	17. Shared Baths
2. No Pets	6. Golf Available	10. Personal Check Accepted	14. Conference Rooms Avail.	18. Afternoon Tea
3 Off Season Rates	7. Swimming Avail.	11. Reservations Necessary	15. Group Seminars Avail.	* Commisions given
4. Senior Citizen Rates	8. Skiing Available	12. Dinner Available	16. Private Baths	to Travel Agents

COLORADO

Denver *

Peiker, Diane
1572 Race St., 80206
(303) 331-0621

Amenities: 1,2,3,4,9,10,12,13,14,15,16,18
Breakfast: F.
Dbl. Oc.: $89.00 - $174.00
Sgl Oc.: $78.00 - $174.00
Third Person: $20.00

Castle Marne - A Luxury Urban Inn—Minutes from the airport, convention center, business district, hospitals, shopping and fine dining. Each room in this Victorian mansion is a unique experience in pampered luxury. A local and national historic structure. Dinner and lunch available with 48-hour notice.

Durango *

Alford, David
16919 Hwy. 140, Hesperus, 81326
(303) 385-4537

Amenities: 1,2,7,10,11,14,16, 18
Breakfast: F.

Dbl. Oc.: $85.00 - $225.00
Sgl. Oc.: $60.00 - $195.00
Third Person: $25.00
Child: Under 2 yrs. - no charge

Blue Lake Ranch—This has evolved from a simple homestead to a luxurious country estate. Overlooking gardens, Blue Lake and the mountains. The ranch is a full retreat, 15 minutes from Durango. A magical experience in a magnificent private setting in all four seasons.

Durango *

Carroll, Crystal
495 Animas View Dr., 81301
(303) 247-4775

Amenities: 1,2,3,4,9,10,11,15, 16
Breakfast: F.

Dbl. Oc.: $55.00 - $75.00
Sgl. Oc.: $50.00 - $65.00
Third Person: $15.00

River House—Offers comfort in one of Durango's largest and finest homes. Enjoy vacation living at its best on the river with a view of the Animas Valley. Each room has a private bath. Begin your day with breakfsat in a huge atrium with a waterfall. Massage available.

Durango *

Verheyden, Debby & Greg
35060 U.S. Hwy. 550, 81301
(303) 259-4396, (800) 369-4082

Amenities: 1,2,6,7,8,9,10,11, 15,16,18
Breakfast: F.

Dbl. Oc.: $85.68
Sgl. Oc.: $74.97
Third Person: $16.07
Child: Under 7 yrs.- no charge

Logwood - The Verheyden Inn—"Come home to Logwood" with hosts Debby and Greg Verheyden. An appealing, rough-hewn retreat with a wrap-around porch. Logwood is constructed of red cedar logs. Five guest rooms complete with home-stitched country quilts. Full breakfasts are served for your enjoyment.

1. No Smoking	5. Tennis Available	9. Credit Cards Accepted	13. Lunch Available	17. Shared Baths
2. No Pets	6. Golf Available	10. Personal Check Accepted	14. Conference Rooms Avail.	18. Afternoon Tea
3 Off Season Rates	7. Swimmming Avail.	11. Reservations Necessary	15. Group Seminars Avail.	* Commisions given
4. Senior Citizen Rates	8. Skiing Available	12. Dinner Available	16. Private Baths	to Travel Agents

Estes Park *

Mansfield, Sue & Gary
P.O. Box 1910, 80517
(303) 586-4666

Amenities: 1,2,5,6,7,8,9,10,12,16
Breakfast: F.
Dbl. Oc.: $85.00 - $160.00
Sgl Oc.: $75.00 - $150.00
Third Person: $25.00

RiverSong—A romantic eight-room country inn, at the end of a winding country lane on 30 wooded acres. Breathtaking views of snow-capped peaks of the Rocky Mountain National Park. Most rooms have fireplaces and spacious soaking tubs for two. Hiking trails. A peaceful getaway!

Georgetown *

Schmidt, Sarah
605 Brownell
P.O. Box 0156, 80444
(303) 569-3388

Amenities: 1,2,3,8,10,16
Breakfast: F.

Dbl. Oc.: $62.19 - $78.55
Sgl. Oc.: $51.28 - $77.64
Third Person: $10.00

The Hardy House Bed And Breakfast Inn—Only one of over 200 Victorian homes in this historic mountain town. Enjoy hiking, biking and fishing anytime. Skiing in winter. Georgetown is only 45 minutes from seven major ski areas. Fine dining, great shops and museums all within walking distance.

Green Mountain Falls

Grant, Debra
10755 Ute Pass Ave., 80819
(719) 684-9063

Amenities: 1,2,3,5,7,9,12,13, 16
Breakfast: C.

Dbl. Oc.: $50.00 - $65.00

Columbine Inn—Perfect mountain getaway 15 minutes from Colorado Springs and all major sightseeing attractions. Built in 1908, the inn crosses comfort and casual elegance. Restaurant and outdoor dining deck open to the public.

Idaho Springs *

Jacquin, Steve
336 Crest Dr., 80452
(303) 567-4084

Amenities: 1,2,8,9,10,15,16, 18
Breakfast: F.

Dbl. Oc.: $85.00 - $125.00

St. Mary's Glacier Bed And Breakfast—From the deck of this hand-hewn mountain log retreat enjoy majestic views of the Continental Divide, a waterfall and lake. In the evening return to one of five romantic suites or enjoy the fireplace, hot tub or library. Just 45 minutes west of Denver off I-70. Reopening 6-1-93.

1. No Smoking	5. Tennis Available	9. Credit Cards Accepted	13. Lunch Available	17. Shared Baths
2. No Pets	6. Golf Available	10. Personal Check Accepted	14. Conference Rooms Avail.	18. Afternoon Tea
3 Off Season Rates	7. Swimmming Avail.	11. Reservations Necessary	15. Group Seminars Avail.	* Commisions given
4. Senior Citizen Rates	8. Skiing Available	12. Dinner Available	16. Private Baths	to Travel Agents

COLORADO

Loveland *

Wiltgen, Marilyn L.
217 W. 4th St., 80537
(303) 669-0798

Amenities: 1,2,4,5,6,7,9,10,
14,15,16,18
Breakfast: F.

Dbl. Oc.: $84.00 - $111.00
Sgl. Oc.: $52.00 - $101.00

The Lovelander Bed And Breakfast Inn—A beautifully restored Victorian. Enjoy a leisurely breakfast on the veranda. Or rise early for a hike or drive in Rocky Mountain National Park with a picnic basket packed just for you. Welcome to the sweetheart city, community of the arts!

Manitou Springs *

Podell, Shirley & Mel
336 El Paso Blvd., 80829
(719) 685-4265,
(800) 530-8253

Amenities: 1,2,4,5,6,7,9,10,16,18
Breakfast: F.
Dbl. Oc.: $82.28 - $131.64
Sgl Oc.: $71.31 - $120.67
Child: Over 10 yrs. - $15.00

Onaledge Bed And Breakfast—Selected one of the "Top 50 Inns in the USA" by *Inn Times*. Historic 1912 Onaledge speaks of romance. Honeymoon suites, private baths, private hot tub, suites, terraces, full gourmet breakfast. Near attractions and historic Cripple Creek gambling casinos. Scenic mountain views.

Manitou Springs *

Sharon & Wendy
Ten Otoe Pl., 80829
(719) 685-9684

Amenities: 1,2,9,10,11,16,17
Breakfast: F.
Dbl. Oc.: $66.00 - $110.00
Sgl Oc.: $66.00 - $110.00

Two Sisters Inn - A Bed And Breakfast—A gracious 1919 Victorian bungalow at the base of Pikes Peak. Lovingly restored with four bedrooms and a honeymoon cottage. Family collectibles, antiques and fresh flowers fill the sunny rooms. Gourmet breakfast. Walk to art galleries and mineral springs in historic district.

---

1. No Smoking	5. Tennis Available	9. Credit Cards Accepted	13. Lunch Available	17. Shared Baths
2. No Pets	6. Golf Available	10. Personal Check Accepted	14. Conference Rooms Avail.	18. Afternoon Tea
3 Off Season Rates	7. Swimmming Avail.	11. Reservations Necessary	15. Group Seminars Avail.	* Commisions given
4. Senior Citizen Rates	8. Skiing Available	12. Dinner Available	16. Private Baths	to Travel Agents

COLORADO

Minturn *

Leavitt, Jane
P.O. Box 100, 145 Main St., 81645
(800) 344-1750

Amenities: 1,2,3,4,5,6,7,8,9, 10,11,12,13,14,16
Breakfast: F.

Dbl. Oc.: $96.30 - $183.94
Sgl. Oc.: $96.30 - $183.94
Third Person: $20.00
Child: $20.00

The Eagle River Inn—Located in the heart of Vail Valley. One of Colorado's top-10 bed and breakfasts. Southwestern charm and hospitality. Homemade breakfast and wine and cheese buffet included.

Poncho Springs

Conrad, Judy & Russell
P.O. Box 457, 81242-0457
(719) 539-4861

Amenities: 1,2,9,17
Breakfast: C.

Dbl. Oc.: $37.00
Sgl. Oc.: $30.00
Third Person: $5.00
Child: Under 5 yrs. - no charge

Jackson Hotel Bed And Breakfast Inn—Come stay in a piece of Colorado history. An old stagecoach stop hotel built in 1878. Located in the upper Arkansas Valley where excellent white-water rafting is found in summer or skiing in winter.

Pueblo *

Trent, Kerrelyn
300 W. Abriendo Ave., 81004
(719) 544-2703

Amenities: 1,2,9,10,16
Breakfast: F.

Dbl. Oc.: $53.38 - $94.52
Sgl. Oc.: $47.82 - $88.96
Third Person: $11.12

Abriendo Inn—Outstanding estate home in a park-like setting. Enchanting atmosphere that you want to experience. All the comforts of today. Restaurants, antiques, galleries within walking distance. Mountains, fishing, rafting, golf and many attractions are minutes away.

Red Cliff *

Wasmer, Molly
101 Eagle St., 81649
(303) 827-5333

Amenities: 1,2,6,8,9,10,11,16, 17,18
Breakfast: F.

Dbl. Oc.: $85.00
Sgl. Oc.: $70.00
Third Person: $15.00
Child: Under 10 yrs. - no charge

The Pilgrim's Inn—A charming Victorian home located 15 miles from Vail. A place to meet and plan excursions, paint, write or meditate. Escape the city and relax on a sunny deck or in a hot tub. Mountain biking, skiing, camping or hiking in the National Forest that surrounds the inn. Massage available.

---

1. No Smoking	5. Tennis Available	9. Credit Cards Accepted	13. Lunch Available	17. Shared Baths
2. No Pets	6. Golf Available	10. Personal Check Accepted	14. Conference Rooms Avail.	18. Afternoon Tea
3 Off Season Rates	7. Swimming Avail.	11. Reservations Necessary	15. Group Seminars Avail.	* Commisions given
4. Senior Citizen Rates	8. Skiing Available	12. Dinner Available	16. Private Baths	to Travel Agents

COLORADO

Redstone *

Johnson, Rose Marie & Ken
0058 Redstone Blvd., 81623
(303) 963-3463, (800) 643-4837

Amenities: 1,3,5,6,7,8,9,10,11,12,14,15,16,17
Breakfast: C.
Dbl. Oc.: $82.84 - $177.35
Sgl Oc.: $82.84
Third Person: $20.00
Child: Under 12 yrs. - $5.00

CLEVEHOLM MANOR

Cleveholm Manor ("The Historic Redstone Castle")—Nestled high in the Colorado Rockies, you can relive the elegance, grace and history of the Manor House at Redstone with an enchanting overnight stay. One mile from town, where restaurants and shops are available.

Steamboat Springs *

Callsen, Kitty
46915 R.C.R. 129, 80487
(303) 879-5767,
Fax: (303) 879-8132

Amenities: 1,2,3,5,6,7,8,9,10, 11,12,13,15,16
Breakfast: C. Plus
Dbl. Oc.: $109.41
Sgl. Oc.: $109.41

The Country Inn At Steamboat Llama Ranch—We invite you to spend your vacation at our 85-acre llama ranch in the Rockies. The country inn is 20 minutes from the Steamboat ski area. Shuttle is available. Enjoy fishing, hiking, biking and cross-coutry skiing or just resting at our Western-style inn.

Telluride *

Maclean, Judy & Michael
100 Pennington Ct., 81435
(800) 543-1437, (303) 728-5337
Amenities: 1,2,3,4,5,6,7,8,9, 10,11,14,16,18
Breakfast: F.
Dbl. Oc.: $155.00 - $300.00
Sgl. Oc.: $155.00 - $300.00
Third Person: $16.23
Child: Under 12 yrs. - no charge

Pennington's Mountain Village Inn—A luxury B&B inn located on the 12th fairway of the Telluride golf course. Large rooms and suites enjoy spectacular views, private baths and decks. Amenities include spa, steamrooms, guest lockers, fireplace, lounge and happy hour with spirits and hors d'oeuvres.

1. No Smoking	5. Tennis Available	9. Credit Cards Accepted	13. Lunch Available	17. Shared Baths
2. No Pets	6. Golf Available	10. Personal Check Accepted	14. Conference Rooms Avail.	18. Afternoon Tea
3 Off Season Rates	7. Swimmming Avail.	11. Reservations Necessary	15. Group Seminars Avail.	* Commisions given
4. Senior Citizen Rates	8. Skiing Available	12. Dinner Available	16. Private Baths	to Travel Agents

Telluride *

Weaver, Denise & John
440 W. Colorado Ave., 81435
(303) 728-6282

Amenities: 1,2,3,6,8,9,10,11,16,17
Breakfast: F.
Dbl. Oc.: $65.00 -$180.00
Sgl Oc.: $65.00 -$180.00
Third Person: $15.00

Alpine Inn Bed And Breakfast—Victorian inn built in 1907, located in historic district. The inn has nine rooms decorated with antiques and homemade quilts. Within walking distance of ski slope and hiking trails. Breakfast served in the sunroom with spectacular views. Hot tub also available.

Winter Park *

Engel, Margaret
1035 Cranmer Ave.
P.O. Box 1305, 80482
(303) 726-4632

Amenities: 1,2,3,6,8,9,10,11, 16,17
Breakfast: F.

Dbl. Oc.: $75.00 - $95.00
Sgl. Oc.: $65.00 - $85.00
Third Person: $10.00

Englemann Pines—A contemporary mountain home furnished with antiques, down comforters and handmade quilts. We are near Winter Park ski resort, Pole Creek Golf Course and Rocky Mountain National Park.

1. No Smoking	5. Tennis Available	9. Credit Cards Accepted	13. Lunch Available	17. Shared Baths
2. No Pets	6. Golf Available	10. Personal Check Accepted	14. Conference Rooms Avail.	18. Afternoon Tea
3 Off Season Rates	7. Swimmming Avail.	11. Reservations Necessary	15. Group Seminars Avail.	* Commisions given
4. Senior Citizen Rates	8. Skiing Available	12. Dinner Available	16. Private Baths	to Travel Agents

CONNECTICUT

The Constitution State

Capitol: Hartford
Statehood: January 9, 1788; the 5th state
State Motto: He Who Transplanted Still Sustains
State Song: "Yankee Doodle"
State Bird: Robin
State Flower: Mountain Laurel
State Tree: White Oak

It was the early Indians that named this state after the long tidal river of Connecticut that flowed through the state into Long Island Sound.

This New England state is proud of its history and goes back to 1639 when as a colony it adopted The Fundamental Orders of Connecticut.

Yale University is the 3rd oldest institution for higher learning and was established in New Haven in 1701. In 1748, the first American Law School was established in Litchfield, Connecticut.

Connecticut is known as the gadget state and its Yankee Peddlers traveled all over selling the craftsmanship of its citizens in clocks, brasswear, button, firearms, pins and combs.

Today, visitors can stroll the cobbled streets of the restored Mystic Seaport and visit the old stores, sea captains' homes and museums. The whaling ships, The Joseph Conrad and the Charles Morgan are a visitor's delight. In Groton, Connecticut, the submarine capitol of today's naval world, the first nuclear submarine, the Nautilus, was built.

CONNECTICUT

Bolton

Smith, Cinde & Jeff
25 Hebron Rd., 06043
(203) 643-8538

Amenities: 1,2,5,6,7,8,10,15, 16,17
Breakfast: F.

Dbl. Oc.: $60.00 - $70.00
Sgl. Oc.: $45.00 - $55.00
Third Person: $10.00

Jared Cone House—Located in the center of Bolton. Queen-size beds. Scenic views. Bicycles and canoes available. Nearby antiques and berry farms. Full breakfast featuring our own maple syrup. Children welcome. No smoking in guest rooms.

Bristol *

Cimadamore, Cynthia
5 Founders Dr., 06010
(203) 582-4219

Amenities: 1,2,4,8,9,11,15, 16
Breakfast: F.

Dbl. Oc.: $100.00 - $144.00
Sgl. Oc.: $89.00 - $130.00
Third Person: $17.00
Child: Under 12 yrs. - $11.20

Chimney Crest Manor—A registered historic English Tudor mansion featuring five suites with A/C, color cablevision, queen beds, fireplace or kitchens. Mobil rated - three stars. Lodging near Litchfield Hills and Hartford. Romantic getaway packages or hot air balloon packages available.

Chester

Quoos-Momparler,
    Thayer & Michael
123 Main St., 06412
(203) 526-9770

Amenities: 1,2,5,6,7,8,9, 10,11,15,16,17
Breakfast: F.

Dbl. Oc.: $55.00 - $85.00 + tax
Sgl. Oc.: $45.00 - $65.00 &+tax
Third Person: $10.00 plus tax
Child: 5 & under - no charge

Chester Village Bed And Breakfast—Located in a friendly New England town with a storybook village setting, Chester Village B&B was originally a two-room Victorian schoolhouse built in the 1860s at the turn of the century. Two floors and a large veranda were added, establishing it as a hotel and bar.

Clinton *

Adams, Helen
21 Commerce St., 06413
(203) 669-1646

Amenities: 1,2,3,9,10,16
Breakfast: F.
Dbl. Oc.: $95.00
Sgl Oc.: $84.00

Captain Dibbell House—Our 1866 Victorian features a spacious parlor with fireplace, bedrooms furnished with antiques, heirlooms and auction finds, fresh flowers, fruit baskets, home-baked savories for breakfast and snacks. There is a gazebo overlooking the gardens and wisteria-covered footbridge.

1. No Smoking	5. Tennis Available	9. Credit Cards Accepted	13. Lunch Available	17. Shared Baths
2. No Pets	6. Golf Available	10. Personal Check Accepted	14. Conference Rooms Avail.	18. Afternoon Tea
3 Off Season Rates	7. Swimmming Avail.	11. Reservations Necessary	15. Group Seminars Avail.	* Commisions given
4. Senior Citizen Rates	8. Skiing Available	12. Dinner Available	16. Private Baths	to Travel Agents

CONNECTICUT

Cornwall Bridge *

Zandy, Lois
Rte. 7, 06754
(203) 672-6884, (800) 786-6884

Amenities: 1,3,4,7,8,9,10,11,
12,13,16,17
Breakfast: F.

Dbl. Oc.: $110.00
Sgl. Oc.: $99.00
Third Person: $10.00
Child: Under 5 yrs. - no charge

Cornwall Inn—A charming country inn dating back to 1810. Rooms at the inn are decorated with antiques and have private baths with either king or queen beds. Relax by the fireplace or on the terrace overlooking the pool. The inn is located along the Housatonic River.

Coventry *

Kelleher, Joy & Bill
41 North River Rd., 06238
(203) 742-6359

Amenities: 1,2,4,5,6,7,9,10,
11,16,18
Breakfast: F.

Dbl. Oc.: $65.00
Sgl. Oc.: $56.00
Third Person: $10.00
Child: Under 6 yrs. - $5.00

Special Joys—Featuring romantic Victorian or cozy colonial rooms. Caprilands Herb Farm, antique shops and University of Connecticut nearby. Antique dolls, toys, Steiff shop/museum on premises. Fine arts available; 35 minutes to Sturbridge Village. A real treat!

Middlebury *

Cebelenski, Susan
96 Tucker Hill Rd., 06762
(203) 758-8334

Amenities: 1,2,6,7,8,9,10,16,
17
Breakfast: F.

Dbl. Oc.: $61.60 - $100.80
Sgl. Oc.: $61.60 - $72.80
Third Person: $10.00

Tucker Hill Inn—Charming New England colonial. Large, spacious rooms are decorated for the period. Guests have described our breakfast as "The best breakfast in Connecticut." Antiquing nearby.

Mystic

Adams, Maureen
382 Cow Hill Rd., 06355
(203) 572-9551

Amenities: 1,2,7,9,10,11,16
Breakfast: C.

Dbl. Oc.: $65.00 & up
Sgl. Oc.: $65.00 & up

"The Adams House"—A quaint country setting, just 1-1/2 miles from downtown Mystic. This 1790 home has three fireplaces. Lush greenery on one acre. Fully air-conditioned. Antiques and period decor.

Mystic

Comolli, Dorothy M.
36 Bruggeman Pl., 06355
(203) 536-8723

Amenities: 3,10,11,16
Breakfast: C.

Dbl. Oc.: $75.00 & up
Sgl. Oc.: $75.00 & up
Third Person: $25.00 & up

Comolli's Guest House—Ideal for vacationers or business person who desires a homey respite while traveling. Immaculate home on quiet hill overlooking the Mystic Seaport complex. Convenient to Olde Mystic Village, the Aquarium, sightseeing, shops, restaurants and sporting activities. Cozy. Color TV

1. No Smoking	5. Tennis Available	9. Credit Cards Accepted	13. Lunch Available	17. Shared Baths
2. No Pets	6. Golf Available	10. Personal Check Accepted	14. Conference Rooms Avail.	18. Afternoon Tea
3 Off Season Rates	7. Swimmming Avail.	11. Reservations Necessary	15. Group Seminars Avail.	* Commisions given
4. Senior Citizen Rates	8. Skiing Available	12. Dinner Available	16. Private Baths	to Travel Agents

CONNECTICUT

Mystic

Keyes, Ruth
P.O. Box 237, 06372
(203) 572-0349

Amenities: 1,2,3,5,6,7,9,11, 16,18
Breakfast: F.

Dbl. Oc.: $95.00 - $169.00
Sgl. Oc.: $75.00 - $149.00 + tax
Third Person: $25.00 + tax
Child: Under 12 yrs. - no charge

Red Brook Inn—Enjoy colonial hospitality in a real country inn. We are located on 7-1/2 acres of wooded hillside providing seclusion and serenity. Early American antiques, fireplaces and down comforters are a few of the many amenities offered. Come join us soon.

Mystic *

Lucas, Kay & Ted
180 Cow Hill Rd., 06355
(203) 536-3033,
Fax: (203) 536-1326

Amenities: 1,2,9,10,11,14,15, 16,17,18
Breakfast: F.

Dbl. Oc.: $85.00 - $110.00
Sgl. Oc.: $80.00 - $105.00
Third Person: $15.00
Child: 5 - 10 yrs. - $10.00

"Brigadoon"—A traditional Scottish B&B in historic Mystic. Restored Victorian farmhouse, 1-1/4 miles from downtown Mystic. Relaxed, friendly atmosphere. Afternoon tea. Baileys or brandy in the evening. Delicious country breakfasts. Great for Victorian teas, showers and birthday parties.

Mystic

Mitchell, Nancy
711 Cow Hill Rd., 06355
(203) 572-0390

Amenities: 1,2,3,6,7,14,15, 16
Breakfast: F.

Dbl. Oc.: $95.00 - $125.00
Third Person: $20.00

Pequot Hotel Bed And Breakfast—Historic 1840 stagecoach stop on 23 wooded acres, 2-/2 miles to Mystic Seaport and Aquarium, 10 miles to Foxwoods Gambling Casino. Privacy with personalized service. Full country breakfast. Fireplaced bedrooms and parlor. Large screened porch.

Mystic

White, Patricia
25 Church St., Noank, 06340
(203) 572-9000

Amenities: 1,2,5,6,7,9,10,11,14,15,16,18
Breakfast: C. Plus
Dbl. Oc.: $117.60 - $195.00
Sgl Oc.: $117.60 - $168.00

The Palmer Inn—Two miles to Mystic. Historic turn-of-the-century mansion. An inn of gracious elegance and quiet charm by the sea. Children must be old enough to have their own room. Open all year. Gift certificates available.

1. No Smoking	5. Tennis Available	9. Credit Cards Accepted	13. Lunch Available	17. Shared Baths
2. No Pets	6. Golf Available	10. Personal Check Accepted	14. Conference Rooms Avail.	18. Afternoon Tea
3 Off Season Rates	7. Swimmming Avail.	11. Reservations Necessary	15. Group Seminars Avail.	* Commisions given
4. Senior Citizen Rates	8. Skiing Available	12. Dinner Available	16. Private Baths	to Travel Agents

CONNECTICUT

New London *

Rutledge, Julie & Ray
265 Williams St., 06320
(800) 347-8818, (203) 447-2600

Amenities: 1,2,3,9,10,11,15, 16,18
Breakfast: F.

Dbl. Oc.: $87.00 - $175.00
Sgl. Oc.: $82.00 - $170.60
Third Person: $16.80

Queen Anne Inn—Capture the essence of the historic Mystic-New London shoreline area in soothing Victorian elegance. Enjoy the ultimate in intimacy, romance and comfort. A memorable breakfast and afternoon tea await you. A/C, fireplaces, wrap-around porches and Jacuzzi. Call about activities.

New Milford *

Sproviero, Loli
Deana Berry
34 Bridge St., 06776
(203) 354-8883

Amenities: 4,9,11,16
Breakfast: F.

Dbl. Oc.: $77.28 - $105.28
Sgl. Oc.: $66.08 - $88.48
Third Person: $16.80
Child: Under 6 yrs. - no charge

The Heritage Inn Of Litchfield County—Renovated 1800s tobacco warehouse. Listed with the National Historic Register. Located in the downtown village of New Milford. We are within walking distance of shops, restaurants, movies and the historic town green. Enjoy a hot, hearty breakfast in our cozy atmosphere.

Norfolk

Zuckerman, Kim
Rte. 44, 06058
(203) 542-5100

Amenities: 2,3,4,5,6,7,8,9,10, 12,13,14,15,16,17
Breakfast: C.

Dbl. Oc.: $60.00 - $150.00
Sgl. Oc.: $50.00 - $120.00
Third Person: $20.00

Blackberry River Inn—A 225-year-old colonial inn located in northwestern Connecticut in the foothills of the Berkshires. Nineteen rooms, some with fireplaces. Serves fine continental country cuisine. Enjoy our relaxed, rural setting.

North Stonington *

Gray, Ann & Tom
32 Main St., 06359
(203) 535-1736

Amenities: 1,2,4,5,6,7,9,10,11,15,16,18
Breakfast: F.
Dbl. Oc.: $95.20 - $185.00
Sgl Oc.: $89.60

Antiques And Accommodations—A restored Victorian situated in a charming village 2-1/2 miles off I-95. Minutes from Mystic Seaport and Watch Hill beaches. Rooms furnished with antiques and canopy beds. Elegant four-course candlelight breakfast. Extensive gardens.

1. No Smoking	5. Tennis Available	9. Credit Cards Accepted	13. Lunch Available	17. Shared Baths
2. No Pets	6. Golf Available	10. Personal Check Accepted	14. Conference Rooms Avail.	18. Afternoon Tea
3 Off Season Rates	7. Swimming Avail.	11. Reservations Necessary	15. Group Seminars Avail.	* Commisions given
4. Senior Citizen Rates	8. Skiing Available	12. Dinner Available	16. Private Baths	to Travel Agents

CONNECTICUT

Old Lyme

Janse, Donald
11 Flat Rock Hill Rd., 06371
(203) 434-7269

Amenities: 2,5,6,7,9,10,11, 16
Breakfast: F.

Dbl. Oc.: $75.00
Sgl. Oc.: $65.00
Third Person: $12.00
Child: $12.00

Janse, Helen And Donald Bed And Breakfast—A large room with sitting area, antiques, air-conditioning and private bath. Custom saltbox. Park-like yard. Three miles from I-95. Quiet road. Vintage stone walls. Century-old maples. Near fine dining, shops, theatre and recreational sites. In-room bouquets and snacks. Special!

Plantsville *

Potter, Mary & David
184 Marion Ave., 06479
(203) 276-0227

Amenities: 1,7,10,11,16,17, 18
Breakfast: F.

Dbl. Oc.: $55.00 - $65.00
Sgl. Oc.: $55.00 - $65.00
Third Person: $20.00
Child: Under 10 yrs. - no charge

Captain Josiah Cowles Place—An 18th -century colonial with lovely gardens and grounds in friendly New England town just 30 minutes from Hartford and New Haven. Choose queen- size bed with working fireplace and private detached bath or king- size waterbed with private bath. Golf, skiing, tennis and hiking nearby.

Portland *

Hinze, Elaine
7 Penny Corner Rd., 06480
(203) 342-1856

Amenities: 1,2,4,6,8,10,16
Breakfast: F.

Dbl. Oc.: $55.00 - $75.00
Sgl. Oc.: $45.00 - $60.00
Third Person: $15.00
(rollaway/trundle)

The Croft—An 1822 Colonial situated on four picturesque acres. Barns, herb garden and picnic grove. One and two-bedroom suites with private entrances, baths, telephones, TV and refrigerator (one has a complete kitchen). Convenient to Wesleyan University. Every detail considered.

Ridgefield *

Mayer, M. M.
22 West Lane, 06877
(203) 438-7323

Amenities: 2,3,9,13,14,16
Breakfast: C. Plus

Dbl. Oc.: $128.80
Sgl. Oc.: $112.00
Third Person: $11.20

West Lane Inn—Surrounded by majestic trees and beautiful gardens. The entry to a charming and elegant inn. Some rooms with a fireplace, all rooms with private bath, color TV and telephone. Fine dining, antiques and boutiques within walking distance.

Sherman *

Johnson, Sallee
29 Rte. 37 E., 06784
(203) 354-4404

Amenities: 1,2,5,6,7,8,9,10, 16,18
Breakfast: F.

Dbl. Oc.: $64.80 - $91.80
Sgl. Oc.: $64.80 - $91.80
Third Person: $15.00

Barnes Hill Farm B&B—Circa 1835. Furnished with antiques. Situated on acres of fields and woods. Outside Jacuzzi. Open all year. Cross- country skiing on property. Candlewood Lake one mile away for boating and ice fishing.

1. No Smoking	5. Tennis Available	9. Credit Cards Accepted	13. Lunch Available	17. Shared Baths
2. No Pets	6. Golf Available	10. Personal Check Accepted	14. Conference Rooms Avail.	18. Afternoon Tea
3 Off Season Rates	7. Swimmming Avail.	11. Reservations Necessary	15. Group Seminars Avail.	* Commisions given
4. Senior Citizen Rates	8. Skiing Available	12. Dinner Available	16. Private Baths	to Travel Agents

CONNECTICUT

Simsbury *

Hohengarten, Kelly
731 Hopmeadow St., 06070
(800) TRY-1820

Amenities: 3,9,10,11,12,13,14, 15,16
Breakfast: C.

Dbl. Oc.: $110.00 - $150.00
Sgl. Oc.: $90.00 - $150.00
Third Person: $15.00
Child: Under 5 yrs. - no charge

Simsbury 1820 House Country Inn And Restaurant—Beautifully restored 19th-century country manor in the heart of scenic Farmington River Valley. Period antiques in guest rooms and in restaurant. Country weddings and custom business meetings our specialties. Antiquing, hiking and cycling close by. A romantic getaway.

Somersville *

Lumb, Ralph
63 Maple St., 06072
(203) 763-1473

Amenities: 1,2,6,10,11,14,16,17
Breakfast: C. Plus
Dbl. Oc.: $54.00 - $60.00
Sgl Oc.: $54.00 - $60.00
Third Person: $15.00
Child: Over 3 yrs. - $15.00

The Old Mill Inn—Gracious old New England home with cable TV, refrigerator, phone, stereo, fireplace and books. Beautiful muraled dining room overlooking the lawn and its surrounding gardens, flowering trees and shrubs. Convenient to shopping, restaurants, airport and many other attractions.

Storrs

Kollet, Elaine
418 Gurleyville Rd., 06268
(203) 429-1400

Amenities: 2,4,7,8,10,15,16
Breakfast: F.

Dbl. Oc.: $60.00
Sgl. Oc.: $40.00
Child: Under 5 yrs. - $5.00

Farmhouse On The Hill Above Gurleyville—An elegant Cape Cod house. Air-conditioned bedrooms. Within walking distance of University of Connecticut campus. We offer all activities at the university plus our sheep farm, fishing, bikes and exercise equipment. Nearby sports program or musicals available.

Thompson

Corttis, Ginny & Herb
235 Corttis Rd., 06255
(203) 935-5652

Amenities: 1,2,4,8,10,14,16, 17
Breakfast: F.

Dbl. Oc.: $75.00
Sgl. Oc.: $55.00
Third Person: $15.00
Child: $15.00

Corttis Inn B&B—A restored 1758 colonial located on 900 private acres. On-site cross-country skiing, hiking and nature trails. Period furnishings. Near Pomfret Prep School, old Sturbridge Village and Brimfield flea market. Four bedrooms and three baths.

---

1. No Smoking	5. Tennis Available	9. Credit Cards Accepted	13. Lunch Available	17. Shared Baths
2. No Pets	6. Golf Available	10. Personal Check Accepted	14. Conference Rooms Avail.	18. Afternoon Tea
3 Off Season Rates	7. Swimming Avail.	11. Reservations Necessary	15. Group Seminars Avail.	* Commisions given
4. Senior Citizen Rates	8. Skiing Available	12. Dinner Available	16. Private Baths	to Travel Agents

CONNECTICUT

Thompson *

Olson, Birdie & Ken
1084 Quaddick Town Farm Rd.,
06277
(203) 928-9530

Amenities: 1,3,4,7,10,11,17
Breakfast: F.

Dbl. Oc.: $67.20
Sgl. Oc.: $56.00
Third Person: $22.40
Child: Under 4 yrs. - no charge

Hickory Ridge—Spacious post-and-beam home situated in a rural setting of 3 wooded acres. Lake activities - 300 feet of lake frontage. Hiking on an additional 17 private acres. A nearby 1814 inn offers delightful cuisine. Children and pets welcome. Senior citizen and long-term discounts.

Tolland,

Beeching, Stephen
63 Tolland Green, 06084-0717
(203) 872-0800

Amenities: 1,2,5,6,9,10,11,14,
15,16,17,18
Breakfast: C. Plus

Dbl. Oc.: $56.00 - $100.90
Sgl. Oc.: $44.80 - $56.00

The Tolland Inn—An 1800 colonial on historic Village Green. Seven guest rooms and kitchen suite. Three common rooms and fireplaces. Antiques and handmade furniture. Convenient to Old Sturbridge, Hartford, UConn, Caprilands Farm and I-84. Wonderful home-baked breakfasts and p.m. tea by the fire.

Uncasville *

Samolis, Sandra
1851 Rte. 32, 06382
(203) 848-3649

Amenities: 3,5,6,7,9,10,
16,18
Breakfast: C.

Dbl. Oc.: $78.40 - $123.20
Sgl. Oc.: $78.40 - $123.20
Third Person: $11.20
Child: Under 1 1/2 yrs. - free

1851 Guest House—A four-room luxury B&B located 20 minutes from Mystic and 10 minutes from the Indian casino. In summer, breakfast is elegantly served in our Victorian gazebo surrounded by perennials and herbal gardens.

Westport

Scarella, Robin & Joe
18 Moss Ledge Rd., 06880
(203) 454-2933

Amenities: 1,2,4,5,6,7,8,10,
11,16
Breakfast: C. Plus

Dbl. Oc.: $85.00
Sgl. Oc.: $75.00
Child: Under 12 yrs. - $10.00

Top Of The Ledge—Gracious Georgian colonial. Spacious room with twin- or king-size bed, cable TV and private bath. Outdoor pool and exercise equipment available. Large living room for reading or sitting by the fireplace with evening refreshments.

Wethersfield *

Bottaro, Sophie & Frank
184 Main St., 06109
(203) 563-4236

Amenities: 1,2,5,6,9,10,11,14,
15,16,17
Breakfast: F.

Dbl. Oc.: $65.00 - $75.00
Sgl. Oc.: $65.00 - $75.00
Third Person: $10.00
Child: Under 2 yrs. - no charge

Chester Bulkley House Bed And Breakfast—Nestled in the historic village of Old Wethersfield, this classic Greek Revival brick house has been lovingly restored by the innkeepers to provide a warm and gracious New England welcome to the vacationer, traveler or businessperson.

1. No Smoking	5. Tennis Available	9. Credit Cards Accepted	13. Lunch Available	17. Shared Baths
2. No Pets	6. Golf Available	10. Personal Check Accepted	14. Conference Rooms Avail.	18. Afternoon Tea
3 Off Season Rates	7. Swimmming Avail.	11. Reservations Necessary	15. Group Seminars Avail.	* Commisions given
4. Senior Citizen Rates	8. Skiing Available	12. Dinner Available	16. Private Baths	to Travel Agents

*Woodstock , South**

Naumann, Richard
Becks, Sheila
94 Plaine Hill Rd., 06267
(203) 928-0528

Amenities: 3,5,6,9,10,11,12,13,14,15,16
Breakfast: C. Plus
Dbl. Oc.: $84.00 and up
Sgl Oc.: $61.60 and up
Third Person: $13.44
Child: Under 5 yrs. - no charge

The Inn At Woodstock Hill—Romance in the country. Restored country estate on 14 acres. Rolling farmland; 19 guest rooms with TV, phone and air-conditioning. Wood-burning fireplaces throughout. Decorated in Waverly chintz. Four-star restaurant. Outdoor dining, cozy bar. Come and make memories. Quiet getaway.

1. No Smoking	5. Tennis Available	9. Credit Cards Accepted	13. Lunch Available	17. Shared Baths
2. No Pets	6. Golf Available	10. Personal Check Accepted	14. Conference Rooms Avail.	18. Afternoon Tea
3 Off Season Rates	7. Swimmming Avail.	11. Reservations Necessary	15. Group Seminars Avail.	* Commisions given
4. Senior Citizen Rates	8. Skiing Available	12. Dinner Available	16. Private Baths	to Travel Agents

73

DELAWARE

The First State

Capitol: Dover
Statehood: December 7, 1787; the 1st state
State Motto: Liberty and Independence
State Song: "Our Delaware"
State Bird: Blue Hen Chicken
State Flower: Peach Blossom
State Tree: American Holly

Delaware is called the first state because it was the first to ratify the Constitution of the United States. It is the second smallest state; however, it has so much diversification in industry and economy that it is thought of as a big state. Factories boom in the north and beautiful farmlands grace the southern part of Delaware. Rivers, bays and oceans are all part of this state. If a pollster wants to get a reading on anything, he usually comes here first. In this state there is a cross section of Americans and American industry.

DuPont, the largest chemical company in the world, has its headquarters here and its research division.

Delaware also has its pleasure side too. The beaches along the Atlantic coast around Rehoboth and Bethany are great favorites with the tourists.

Bridgeville *

Straughen, Susan
303 Market St., 19933
(302) 337-3134

Amenities: 1,3,7,9,10,12,13,
15,17,18
Breakfast: F.

Dbl. Oc.: $50.00 - $75.00
Third Person: No charge
Child: No charge

Teddy Bear B&B—On US 404, 40 minutes from Chesapeake Bay and the Atlantic Coast. Resort area. Four square, 1920 home with three guest rooms sharing one bath. Gourmet cooks. Great hospitality and a down-home relaxed atmosphere.

Dover *

DeZwarte, Sherry & Carolyn
305 So. Governors Ave., 19901
(302) 678-1242

Amenities: 2,9,10,16
Breakfast: F.

Dbl. Oc.: $42.00 - $58.00
Sgl. Oc.: $35.00 - $50.00
Third Person: $10.00

The Inn At Meeting House Square—Located in Dover's historic district, this 1849 inn offers old-style hospitality, along with distinctive and quality accommodations. Four rooms, each with TV, phone and air-conditioning. Walk to historic sites, restaurants, business and government districts. AAA approved.

Lewes

Stafursky, Susan & Dick
330 Savannah Rd., 19958
(302) 645-5592

Amenities: 1,2,3,5,7,10,17
Breakfast: C. (Vegetarian)

Dbl. Oc.: $35.00 - $65.00
Sgl. Oc.: $35.00 - $48.00
Third Person: $8.00
Child: $8.00

Savannah Inn—Offers comfortable, casual accommodations in historic Lewes. Ocean, bay beaches and major resorts nearby. Vegetarian breakfast features homemade breads and fresh fruit. Rooms available year-round, but breakfast served only during summer. Fans in rooms.

New Castle

Burwell, Irma & Richard
206 Delaware St., 19720
(302) 328-7736

Amenities: 1,2,5,10,14,17
Breakfast: C.

Dbl. Oc.: $45.00
Sgl. Oc.: $45.00

William Penn Guest House—Historic New Castle. A charming, restored historic home, circa 1682, located across from the Courthouse on the Square. The house is decorated in antiques. Four cheerful guest rooms. Shared baths. One room with twin beds has private bath.

New Castle *

Rosenthal, Dr. Melvin
5 The Strand, 19720
(302) 322-8944, 322-0999

Amenities: 2,5,9,10,13,16
Breakfast: F.

Dbl. Oc.: $54.00 - $85.00
Sgl. Oc.: $49.00 - $85.00
Third Person: $10.00
Child: No charge

Jefferson House Bed And Breakfast—A charming 200-year-old riverfront hotel next to the park. Antique furnishings and air-conditioned. Located in the center of the historic district. In-room TV and outdoor Jacuzzi. Fully equipped efficiencies available. Call Chris at Cellar Gourmet for reservations.

1. No Smoking	5. Tennis Available	9. Credit Cards Accepted	13. Lunch Available	17. Shared Baths
2. No Pets	6. Golf Available	10. Personal Check Accepted	14. Conference Rooms Avail.	18. Afternoon Tea
3 Off Season Rates	7. Swimming Avail.	11. Reservations Necessary	15. Group Seminars Avail.	* Commisions given
4. Senior Citizen Rates	8. Skiing Available	12. Dinner Available	16. Private Baths	to Travel Agents

Rehoboth Beach

Vincent, Cindy & Kenny
41 Baltimore Ave., 19971
(302) 226-2535

Amenities: 1,2,3,4,5,6,7,8,9, 10,16,17
Breakfast: C. Plus

Dbl. Oc.: $49.00 - $119.00
Sgl. Oc.: $45.00 - $115.00
Third Person: $10.00 - $20.00

The Royal Rose Inn Bed And Breakfast—A charming and relaxing 1920s beach cottage with antiques and romantic rose theme. Scrumptious homemade breakfast. Air-conditioning. Large screened porch. Beach, shops and restaurants within walking distance. Centrally located. Open May-October. Midweek specials/weekend packages.

Wilmington *

Brill, Dot & Art
215 W. Crest Rd., 19803
(302) 764-0789, (800) 373-0781

Amenities: 1,2,5,6,7,9,10,11, 16
Breakfast: F.

Dbl. Oc.: $60.00 - $65.00
Sgl. Oc.: $50.00 - $55.00

A Small Wonder Bed And Breakfast Homestay—Awards for B&B hospitality and landscaping. Traditional suburban home with pool/spa, A/C, TV, menu choice. A suite with double bed and guest room with king-size bed. Near I-95. Visit DuPont mansions, Winterthur, Nemours, Longwood, Bellevue, Hagley and Wyeth Museums and New Castle.

1. No Smoking	5. Tennis Available	9. Credit Cards Accepted	13. Lunch Available	17. Shared Baths
2. No Pets	6. Golf Available	10. Personal Check Accepted	14. Conference Rooms Avail.	18. Afternoon Tea
3 Off Season Rates	7. Swimmming Avail.	11. Reservations Necessary	15. Group Seminars Avail.	* Commisions given
4. Senior Citizen Rates	8. Skiing Available	12. Dinner Available	16. Private Baths	to Travel Agents

76

DISTRICT OF COLUMBIA

Washington D.C.

Founded: Site Chosen — 1791
                Became Capitol — 1800

Washington D.C. is the capitol of the United States. It lies between Maryland and Virginia and it is the only American city or town that is not part of a state.

The District is mainly made up of government buildings and monuments. Millions of people are employed here for the government, but they live outside the District.

Visitors flock here year round, but especially in the springtime when the cherry blossoms along the Potomac River Basin are in bloom. They come because it is a beautiful city, but mainly to see their government in action.

Some of the most popular attractions are the Capitol Building, the House of Congress and Senate, The White House, Lincoln's and Jefferson's Memorial and the Washington Monument. There are also the Smithsonian buildings, Ford's Theater, the J.F.K. center for the Performing Arts and many, many other government buildings and museums to visit. Guided tours are available, and through your Congressman or Senator, admission passes can be obtained to watch Congress and the Senate when they are in session.

DISTRICT OF COLUMBIA

Washington

Armbruster, Janet
P.O. Box 12011, 20005
(202) 328-3510, Fax: (202) 332-3885

Amenities: 1,2,3,7,9,10,11,17
Breakfast: C.

Dbl. Oc.: $75.00 - $80.00
Sgl. Oc.: $65.00 - $70.00

Painted Lady of Capitol Hill—A beautifully restored Victorian retaining most of the original architectural details. The house is decorated with American antiques throughout and has the charm and detail of the Victorian era. One-and-one-half blocks from the subway and six blocks from the Capitol.

Washington

Babich, Mark
101 Fifth St., NE, 20002
(202) 547-1050

Amenities: 1,2,3,4,9,10,11, 14,15,17,18
Breakfast: C.

Dbl. Oc.: $73.65 - $84.75
Sgl. Oc.: $51.45 - $62.55
Third Person: $15.00

Capitol Hill Guest House—A Victorian row house located just three blocks behind the U.S. Supreme Court and U.S. Capitol in Capitol Hill historic district. Walk to monuments, museums, Folger Theatre and Union Station. Convenient to metro. Home to members of Congress staff, artists, scholars and lobbyists.

Washington *

Pieczenik, Roberta
2700 Cathedral Ave., NW, 20008
(202) 328-0860

Amenities: 2,3,4,9,10,14,15, 16,17,18
Breakfast: C. Plus

Dbl. Oc.: $50.00 - $100.00
Sgl. Oc.: $45.50 - $90.85
Third Person: $10.00

The Kalorama Guest House At Woodley Park—Charming turn-of-the-century home furnished with period pieces. Downtown convenience and nationally acclaimed hospitality. Walk to underground metro, buses, shops and restaurants. Ten minutes from all major attractions. Quiet residential neighborhood.

Washington *

Reed, Jacqueline
P.O. Box 12011, 20005
(202) 328-3510

Amenities: 1,2,3,9,11,16,17
Breakfast: C. Plus

Dbl. Oc.: $73.65 - $90.30
Sgl. Oc.: $62.55 - $79.20
Third Person: $15.00
Child: Under 2 yrs.- $5.00(crib)

The Reeds—A beautifully restored Victorian town home built in 1887. Decorated with Victorian and art nouveau furniture. Large garden area and Victorian porch available for guest's use. The house was once part of "Christmas at the Smithsonian" and noted in the Washington Post.

Washington *

Thompson, Nancy & Gene
1744 Lanier Pl., N.W., 20009
(202) 745-3600, (800) 578-6807

Amenities: 1,2,9,10,16,17
Breakfast: C. Plus

Dbl. Oc.: $55.00 - $70.00
Sgl. Oc.: $45.00 - $60.00
Third Person: $10.00
Child: Under 2 yrs. - no charge

Adams Inn—Offers a comfortable, friendly place to stay when visiting DC. Private or shared baths, air-conditioning, continental-plus breakfast, convenient to restaurants, transportation, shopping and sightseeing. Limited parking. Unique multi-cultural neighborhood.

1. No Smoking	5. Tennis Available	9. Credit Cards Accepted	13. Lunch Available	17. Shared Baths
2. No Pets	6. Golf Available	10. Personal Check Accepted	14. Conference Rooms Avail.	18. Afternoon Tea
3 Off Season Rates	7. Swimming Avail.	11. Reservations Necessary	15. Group Seminars Avail.	* Commisions given
4. Senior Citizen Rates	8. Skiing Available	12. Dinner Available	16. Private Baths	to Travel Agents

FLORIDA

The Sunshine State

Capitol: Tallahassee
Statehood: March 3, 1845: the 27th state
State Motto: In God We Trust
State Song: "Swanee River"
State Flower: Orange Blossom
State Tree: Sabal Palm

*Florida is one of the best known states for vacationing and retire-
ment. Its sunny climate beckons thousands of tourists and retirees
every year. Its beautiful beaches, orange and grapefruit groves, palm
and coconut trees blend to make it a vacationers paradise.*

*Walt Disney built his Disney World here and Cape Canaveral
boasts of Apollo II's lift-off on its way to man's first landing on the
moon.*

*St. Augustine, founded by a Spanish explorer in 1565, is the oldest
city in the United States.*

*Many of Florida's cities are located on canals or waterways, make
pleasure boating a way of life. Florida is often referred to as the Venice
of the U.S.*

FLORIDA

Amelia Island *

Caples, David
98 So. Fletcher Ave., 32034
(904) 277-4851

Amenities: 2,4,5,6,7,9,10,11,12,13,14,15,16
Breakfast: F.
Dbl. Oc.: $92.00 - $125.00
Sgl Oc.: $81.00 - $114.00
Third Person: $15.00
Child: Under 5 yrs. - no charge

Elizabeth Pointe Lodge—Oceanfront on Barrier Island. Charming rooms, soaking tubs and country breakfast. Newspaper and fresh flowers daily. Bike to nearby historic seaport. Wine every evening. Desserts and snacks always available. The getaway you deserve. Twenty rooms and suites.

Amelia Island *

Grable, Gary & Emily
584 So. Fletcher Ave., 32034
(800) 872-8531

Amenities: 2,4,5,6,7,9,10,11,16
Breakfast: C. Plus
Dbl. Oc.: $81.00
Sgl Oc.: $60.00
Third Person: $10.00
Child: $10.00

The 1735 House—Century-old charm on the beach on a small Barrier Island. Full suites with private bath, bedroom and living area. Spectacular beach view with access. Antiques, wicker and nautical furnishings. Freshly baked pastries and morning newspaper delivered to your private suite daily.

Amelia Island *

Warner, Karen & Bob
22 So. 3rd St., 32034
(904) 261-3300, (800) 258-3301

Amenities: 1,2,4,5,6,7,9,10, 12,13,14,16
Breakfast: F.

Dbl. Oc.: $75.00 - $130.00
Third Person: $10.00

Florida House Inn—Located on Amelia Island in the heart of the 50-block historic district. Built in 1857 as a tourist hotel, today's guests can enjoy the same large porches and 11 rooms, some with fireplaces, all with antiques, quilts and handmade rugs.

---

1. No Smoking	5. Tennis Available	9. Credit Cards Accepted	13. Lunch Available	17. Shared Baths
2. No Pets	6. Golf Available	10. Personal Check Accepted	14. Conference Rooms Avail.	18. Afternoon Tea
3 Off Season Rates	7. Swimmming Avail.	11. Reservations Necessary	15. Group Seminars Avail.	* Commisions given
4. Senior Citizen Rates	8. Skiing Available	12. Dinner Available	16. Private Baths	to Travel Agents

Big Pine Key *

Cornell, Joan
Long Beach Rd.
Rte. 1, Box 780A, 33043
(305) 872-3298

Amenities: 2,3,7,10,16
Breakfast: F.
Dbl. Oc.: $99.90 - $111.00

Barnacle Bed And Breakfast—Oceanside sandy beach in a quiet country setting. Looe Key Reef, Key Deer Refuge and Bahia Honda State Park nearby. Thirty miles to Key West. Bicycles, hot tub, masks and snorkels, tiki, hammocks available. Great laid-back relaxation. Couples only.

Big Pine Key

Threlkeld, Kathleen & Jon   **Amenities:** 2,3,5,6,7,10,11,16   **Dbl. Oc.:** $94.35
Long Beach Dr.   **Sgl. Oc.:** $94.35
P.O. Box 378, 33043   **Breakfast:** F.   **Third Person:** $16.65
(305) 872-2878

Bed & Breakfast On The Ocean — Casa Grande — A Spanish hacienda located on the Atlantic Ocean. All rooms have private baths, air-conditioning and small refrigerators. Lush garden patio and hot tub overlook a private beach. Nearby island excursions, reef trips, Key Deer and local restaurants.

Bradenton Beach *

Kern, Becky
1703 Gulf Dr., 34217
(813) 778-6858

Amenities: 1,2,3,7,9,10,11,16,17
Breakfast: F.
Dbl. Oc.: $71.50 - $93.50
Third Person: $10.00

Duncan House Bed And Breakfast—Located on beautiful Anna Maria Island is our pre-1910 Victorian home romantically decorated with antiques. Enjoy a longer stay in our suites equipped with kitchens. Full breakfast is a specialty of the house.

1. No Smoking	5. Tennis Available	9. Credit Cards Accepted	13. Lunch Available	17. Shared Baths
2. No Pets	6. Golf Available	10. Personal Check Accepted	14. Conference Rooms Avail.	18. Afternoon Tea
3 Off Season Rates	7. Swimmming Avail.	11. Reservations Necessary	15. Group Seminars Avail.	* Commisions given
4. Senior Citizen Rates	8. Skiing Available	12. Dinner Available	16. Private Baths	to Travel Agents

FLORIDA

Bushnell *

Fessler, Jan & Walt
Box 70, CR 476B, 33513
(904) 568-0909

Amenities: 1,3,4,9,10,12,16,17,18
Breakfast: C. Plus
Dbl. Oc.: $53.50 - $69.55
Sgl Oc.: $42.50
Child: Under 10 yrs. - no charge

Cypress House Bed And Breakfast—A large, new log home, set in 200 acres of trees and meadow. Enjoy relaxing under moss-hung oaks three miles off I-75, three miles north of Tampa. Canoeing, hiking, riding, antiquing nearby. Pool being built in mid 1993. Eclectic Americana decor, VCR in each guest room.

Casselberry *

Zacco, Bobbye
505 Queens Mirror Cr., 32707
(407) 695-7111

Amenities: 1,2,5,6,7,10,11,12, 13,16,17
Breakfast: F.
Dbl. Oc.: $55.00
Sgl. Oc.: $45.00
Third Person: $10.00
Child: Under 12 yrs. - no charge

Bobbye's Bed And Breakfast—Located on one acre of lakefront, 30 minues from Disneyworld, near Orlando. Discount golf package available. Sea World, MGM and Universal Studios a short drive away. Pool at your bedroom door. My home is your home! Friendly, warm and hospitable.

Cedar Key *

Sanders, Alison & Tom
Main St.
P.O. Box 460, 32625
(904) 543-5111

Amenities: 5,6,7,9,10,12,13,14,15,16,17,18
Breakfast: F.
Dbl. Oc.: $79.50 - $105.00
Sgl Oc.: $79.50 - $105.00
Third Person: $10.00
Child: $10.00

on the National Register of Historic Places

Historic Island Hotel—This 10-room, tabby-walled landmark island hotel pre-dates the Civil War. Rustic and authentic, with much of the original structure. It is in the National Register of Historic Places. It is like stepping back in time. Very romantic. Gourmet seafood restaurant and lounge.

1. No Smoking	5. Tennis Available	9. Credit Cards Accepted	13. Lunch Available	17. Shared Baths
2. No Pets	6. Golf Available	10. Personal Check Accepted	14. Conference Rooms Avail.	18. Afternoon Tea
3 Off Season Rates	7. Swimmming Avail.	11. Reservations Necessary	15. Group Seminars Avail.	* Commisions given
4. Senior Citizen Rates	8. Skiing Available	12. Dinner Available	16. Private Baths	to Travel Agents

Coleman

Martin, Jean
So. 301
P.O. Box 551, 33521
(904) PIT STOP

Amenities: 1,2,5,6,7,9,10,11,15,16
Breakfast: F.
Dbl. Oc.: $74.20
Sgl Oc.: $74.20
Third Person: $15.00

The Son's Shady Brook Bed And Breakfast—Offers a refreshing change. Modern, easy to find, 21 secluded wooded acres overlooking spring-fed creek. Picturesque setting with solitude and therapeutic tranquility. Sunny, warm hospitality. Comfortable accommodations, good food. Handicap accessible. Brochure.

Daytona Beach *

Fisher, Vinton
444-448 So. Beach St., 32114
(904) 252-4667

Amenities: 1,2,3,5,6,7,9,10, 12,13,14,15,16,18
Breakfast: C. Plus

Dbl. Oc.: $55.50 - $176.00
Sgl. Oc.: $55.00 - $170.50
Third Person: $11.00
Child: $11.00

Live Oak Inn And Restaurant—Gracious historic country inn overlooking marina and gardens. Best of both: river quiet and one mile to beach. 16 rooms, most with Jacuzzies. Special business and golf packages. Meeting rooms, massages, river cruises and weddings. AAA-3 diamond. Voted best for a rendezvous.

Daytona Beach *

Morgan, Becky Sue
3711 So. Atlantic Ave., 32127
(904) 767-3119

Amenities: 1,2,3,4,5,6,7,9,10, 11,13,16
Breakfast: F.

Dbl. Oc.: $107.50 - $162.50
Sgl. Oc.: $102.00 - $157.00
Third Person: $10.60
Child: Under 17 yrs. - $5.50

Captain's Quarters Inn—Daytona's first bed and breakfast inn. All ocean-front suites. Private balcony overlooks ocean. Heated pool. Family operated for 26 years. Old-fashioned coffee shop. Freshly baked bread each morning. Newspaper daily. Unique gift shop. Guest laundry.

1. No Smoking	5. Tennis Available	9. Credit Cards Accepted	13. Lunch Available	17. Shared Baths
2. No Pets	6. Golf Available	10. Personal Check Accepted	14. Conference Rooms Avail.	18. Afternoon Tea
3 Off Season Rates	7. Swimmming Avail.	11. Reservations Necessary	15. Group Seminars Avail.	* Commisions given
4. Senior Citizen Rates	8. Skiing Available	12. Dinner Available	16. Private Baths	to Travel Agents

FLORIDA

Fernandina Beach *

Fortenberry, Harriett
619 So. Fletcher Ave., 32034
(904) 277-2129

Amenities: 4,5,6,7,9,10,11,16
Breakfast: C.
Dbl. Oc.: $65.00 - $85.00
Sgl Oc.: $60.00 - $80.00
Third Person: $10.00
Child: Under 18 yrs. - no charge

The Phoenix' Nest—On Amelia Island in a Victorian seaport town. A seaside retreat in the B&B tradition. Wonderful ocean views. Four private, gracious, restful suites. Videos and bikes here. Golf, tennis, beach, horseback riding not far; 45 minutes to Jacksonville.

Fernandina Beach *

Kovacevich, Rita & John
804 Atlantic Ave., 32034
(904) 277-4300

Amenities: 1,2,3,4,9,10,14,15, 16
Breakfast: C. Plus

Dbl. Oc.: $75.60 - $118.80
Sgl. Oc.: $75.60 - $118.80
Third Person: $15.00

Hoyt House—Will open it's doors in the spring of 1993. Located in the historic district, this wonderful Victorian nine room B&B is within a mile and a half of the fine beaches of Amelia Island and a short walk to town for shopping, sightseeing and dining.

Florida City *

Newton, Mildred
40 N.W. 5th Ave., 33034
(305) 247-4413

Amenities: 3,6,7,16,17
Breakfast: F.

Dbl. Oc.: $56.25 - $67.50
Sgl. Oc.: $45.00 - $56.25
Third Person: $10.00
Child: Under 12 yrs. - no charge

Grandma Newton's Bed And Breakfast—Visit Grandma and the relaxed country atmosphere of her 1914 historic two-story renovated country home. Minutes from national parks, Florida Keys and Miami. Spacious rooms with air-conditioning insure a peaceful rest that sets your appetite for our huge country breakfast.

Gulf Breeze *

Swenson, Gladys & Swante
1251 Summit Lane, 32561
(904) 932-9697

Amenities: 1,2,6,7,10,11,16
Breakfast: F.

Dbl. Oc.: $60.00
Sgl. Oc.: $50.00
Third Person: $10.00
Child: $10.00

Summit Breeze B&B—Comfortable room and private bath in country-club setting. Just minutes to beautiful white sand beaches, charter boats for scuba diving and deep-sea fishing. Great golf courses, fine restaurants and historic tours. Northwest Florida's year-round vacation area.

1. No Smoking	5. Tennis Available	9. Credit Cards Accepted	13. Lunch Available	17. Shared Baths
2. No Pets	6. Golf Available	10. Personal Check Accepted	14. Conference Rooms Avail.	18. Afternoon Tea
3 Off Season Rates	7. Swimmming Avail.	11. Reservations Necessary	15. Group Seminars Avail.	* Commisions given
4. Senior Citizen Rates	8. Skiing Available	12. Dinner Available	16. Private Baths	to Travel Agents

FLORIDA

High Springs *

Justis, Leslie Ann & Rob
65 No. Main St., 32643
(904) 454-2900

Amenities: 1,2,7,9,10,12,13,
14,15,16
Breakfast: C.(weekdays),F.(weekends)

Dbl. Oc.: $85.32
Sgl. Oc.: $85.32
Third Person: $21.60

The Great Outdoors Inn—Just off I-75 in north Florida. Enjoy the solitude of six rooms on 40 acres. Each room has a private bath, refrigerator and coffee. Canoe and snorkel at area clear springs. Our cafe offers salads, pastas, hamburgers, seafood and vegetarian entrees.

Holmes Beach *

Davis, Frank H.
5626 Gulf Dr., 34217
(813) 778-5444

Amenities: 1,2,3,7,9,10,16
Breakfast: F.

Dbl. Oc.: $79.00 - $149.00

Harrington House B&B—Circa 1925, directly on the Gulf. The house features a living room with a 20-foot-high beamed ceiling and a fireplace. Some guest rooms have either four-poster, wicker or brass beds. Five rooms have French doors opening onto a deck overlooking the pool, Gulf and beautiful sunsets.

Key West *

Amsterdam, Edith & Albert
511 Caroline St., 33040
(305) 294-5349

Amenities: 3,4,5,6,7,9,10,11,14,16
Breakfast: C. Plus
Dbl. Oc.: $166.50 - $222.00
Sgl Oc.: $166.50 - $222.00
Third Person: $25.00
Child: Under 10 yrs. - no charge

Curry Mansion Inn—Victorian landmark mansion with a 15-room guest wing with private baths, air-conditioning, ceiling fans, wicker furnishings, patchwork quilts, heated pool and a private beach one block away. Daily cocktail party. Walk downtown to all attractions. Free parking.

---

1. No Smoking
2. No Pets
3. Off Season Rates
4. Senior Citizen Rates

5. Tennis Available
6. Golf Available
7. Swimmming Avail.
8. Skiing Available

9. Credit Cards Accepted
10. Personal Check Accepted
11. Reservations Necessary
12. Dinner Available

13. Lunch Available
14. Conference Rooms Avail.
15. Group Seminars Avail.
16. Private Baths

17. Shared Baths
18. Afternoon Tea
* Commisions given
to Travel Agents

FLORIDA

Key West *

Beres, Joe
525 Simonton St., 33040
(305) 294-6712, (800) 621-9405

Amenities: 2,3,7,9,11,16
Breakfast: C. Plus
Dbl. Oc.: $145.00 - $400.00
Sgl Oc.: $145.00 - $400.00
Third Person: $17.00

The Watson House—Circa 1860. A small, award-winning inn. Highest rating AB&BA and AAA. Distinctive, fully equipped guest suites/apartments in historic Preservation District. Spa, pool, decks and gardens. Private/adults only. Each unit has its own distinctive style. Brochure available.

Key West *

Carlson, Jody
415 William St., 33040
(305) 296-7274

Amenities: 2,3,5,6,7,9,10,11, 15,16,17
Breakfast: C.
Dbl. Oc.: 139.00 - 166.00
Sgl. Oc.: $85.00
Third Person: 10.00

The Popular House/Key West Bed And Breakfast—A 100-year-old Victorian located in old town. Eight rooms decorated in Caribbean style on three floors with 13 foot- high ceilings, hardwood floors, hunter fans and air-conditioning. Breakfast is complimentary and at your leisure. Within walking distance of everything.

Key West *

Geibelt, Fred
512 Simonton St., 33040
(305) 294-9227

Amenities: 2,3,7,9,11,15,16
Breakfast: C.
Dbl. Oc.: $61.05 - $194.25
Third Person: $16.65

Heron House—The most central location in historic district. Three blocks from beach. Spacious sundecks and tropical gardens offer quiet privacy.

1. No Smoking	5. Tennis Available	9. Credit Cards Accepted	13. Lunch Available	17. Shared Baths
2. No Pets	6. Golf Available	10. Personal Check Accepted	14. Conference Rooms Avail.	18. Afternoon Tea
3 Off Season Rates	7. Swimmming Avail.	11. Reservations Necessary	15. Group Seminars Avail.	* Commisions given
4. Senior Citizen Rates	8. Skiing Available	12. Dinner Available	16. Private Baths	to Travel Agents

Lake Wales *

Hinshaw, Vita & Carl
U.S. Hwy. 27 So. & CR. 17A
P.O. Box AC, 33859
(813) 676-6011, (800) 433-6011

Amenities: 3,7,9,10,12,13,14,15,16
Breakfast: F.
Dbl. Oc.: $114.45
Sgl Oc.: $103.55
Third Person: $13.08
Child: $13.08

Chalet Suzanne Country Inn And Restaurant—In National Register of Historic Places. Family owned and operated since 1931. Pastel-colored, European-style village overlooking lake in the heart of Florida's citrus country with 30 charming guest rooms, Mobil four-star restaurant lounge. Forty minutes from Disney World.

Loxahatchee

Thomas, Joanna
P.O. Box 1352, 33470
(407) 790-0052

Amenities: 3,5,6,7,10,11,16
Breakfast: C.

Dbl. Oc.: $65.00
Sgl. Oc.: $50.00

Khaki Campbell Bed And Breakfast—Charmingly furnished with English country antiques. Minutes from world-class polo and equestrian events, trap and skeet, sculling and beaches. Kitchen and laundry privileges. Terriers welcome. Guided tours of antique and equestrian districts available.

Marathon *

Hopp, Joan E.
5 Man-O-War Dr., 33050
(305) 743-4118,
FAX: (305) 743-9220

Amenities: 2,3,4,5,6,7,9,11, 16
Breakfast: F.

Dbl. Oc.: $49.95 - $72.15
Sgl. Oc.: $49.95 - $72.15

Hopp—Inn Guest House—Located in the heart of the Florida Keys. We are on the ocean. Charter fishing, scuba and snorkeling. All guest rooms with ocean view or ocean front. Each room has a private bath and a private entrance. Tropical setting in a quiet area. Children in one- or two-bedroom villas only.

Neptune Beach

Gerard, Lorene & Richard
1011 First St., 32266-6007
(904) 249-8582

Amenities: 2,10,16
Breakfast: C.

Dbl. Oc.: $60.00 - $80.00
Sgl. Oc.: $60.00 -$80.00

Steps from the beach on the Atlantic Ocean. Private and quiet. Home-like. Comfortable. Antique decor. Central air and heat. Kitchen, flowered patio, washer and dryer. Parking. Shopping malls, excellent restaurants and city parks nearby. Your home away from home.

1. No Smoking	5. Tennis Available	9. Credit Cards Accepted	13. Lunch Available	17. Shared Baths
2. No Pets	6. Golf Available	10. Personal Check Accepted	14. Conference Rooms Avail.	18. Afternoon Tea
3 Off Season Rates	7. Swimmming Avail.	11. Reservations Necessary	15. Group Seminars Avail.	* Commisions given
4. Senior Citizen Rates	8. Skiing Available	12. Dinner Available	16. Private Baths	to Travel Agents

FLORIDA

Orange Park *

Massee, Caleb
2143 Astor St.
P.O. Box 7059, 32073
(904) 264-6070,
Fax: (904) 264-7441

Amenities: 5,7,9,10,11,12,13, 14,16
Breakfast: C.

Dbl. Oc.: $65.00 - $85.00
Sgl. Oc.: $65.00 - $85.00
Third Person: $10.00

The Club Continental—Florida river-front inn, on the historic Palmolive estate. Superior suites, Jacuzzies, continental breakfast, tennis, marina privileges and fine dining. Informal socializing and live entertainment at the River House Pub.

Orlando *

Burkan, Eileen & Ted
3000 Barrymore Ct., 32835
(407) 292-2083

Amenities: 1,2,5,6,7,11,16
Breakfast: F.

Dbl. Oc.: $55.00
Sgl. Oc.: $50.00
Child: 8 - 16 yrs. - $15.00

Guest Suite Of Orlando—Modern private home. Separate three-room suite with TV and private bath, all on second floor. Convenient to airport, Disney World, MGM, Epcot, Universal Studio, Typhoon Lagoon, Sea World and Space Center. Discount shoppers paradise! Dining galore!

Orlando *

Freudenburg, Delores
532 Pinar Dr., 32825
(407) 277-4903

Amenities: 1,2,10,11,16
Breakfast: F.

Dbl. Oc.: $49,50
Sgl. Oc.: $38.50
Third Person: $5.50
Child: Under 3 yrs. - no charge

Rio Pinar House—A spacious nine-room home on the Rio Pinar Golf Course, near the East-West Expressway, Goldenrod exit. Convenient to the airport, downtown, Disney World and other attractions. Your hosts can recommend many nearby fine restaurants.

Orlando *

Meiner, Charles E.
211 No. Lucerne Circle, 32801
(407) 648-5188, (800) 444-5289

Amenities: 3,4,5,9,10,14,16
Breakfast: C.

Dbl. Oc.: $65.00 - $150.00
Sgl. Oc.: $65.00 - $150.00
Third Person: $10.00
Child: Under 6 yrs. - no charge

The Courtyard At Lake Lucerne—Consists of three buildings of distinctive styles: a classic Victorian home, 12 art-deco units and three Edwardian suites. All guest rooms are decorated in period furnishings and overlook a tropical courtyard praised as "an oasis in the heart of Orlando."

---

1. No Smoking	5. Tennis Available	9. Credit Cards Accepted	13. Lunch Available	17. Shared Baths
2. No Pets	6. Golf Available	10. Personal Check Accepted	14. Conference Rooms Avail.	18. Afternoon Tea
3 Off Season Rates	7. Swimmming Avail.	11. Reservations Necessary	15. Group Seminars Avail.	* Commisions given
4. Senior Citizen Rates	8. Skiing Available	12. Dinner Available	16. Private Baths	to Travel Agents

Orlando *

Perretti, Angi & Nick
10417 State Rd. 535, 32836
(800) 780-4830

Amenities: 1,2,4,5,6,7,9,10, 11,15,16
Breakfast: C. Plus

Dbl. Oc.: $71.50
Sgl. Oc.: $55.00
Third Person: $11.00
Child: Under 16 yrs. - $5.50

Perri House Bed And Breakfast—A secluded country estate inn nestled on 20 acres located in the "backyard" of the Walt Disney World Resort area of Orlando! OUTSTANDNG LOCATION. All that Disney has to offer is nly four minutes from your room. Family reunions our specialty. Call for brochure.

Palm Harbor *

Grimm, Vivian & David
126 Old Oak Circle
Oak Trail, 34683
(813) 785-2342

Amenities: 2,7,10,11,16,17
Breakfast: F.

Dbl. Oc.: $50.00
Sgl. Oc.: $35.00
Third Person: $10.00
Child: Under 6 yrs. - $5.00

Bed And Breakfast Of Tampa Bay—New, spacious art-deco-style home, 1-1/2 miles from the Gulf of Mexico. Located in historic Palm Harbor between St. Petersburg and Tarpon Springs, 80 minutes from Disneyworld, 25 minutes from Busch Gardens and Dali Museum. Near shopping, restaurants and public transportation.

Palmetto *

Kriessler, Bette
1102 Riverside Dr., 34221
(813) 723-1236

Amenities: 2,3,9,10,11,14 16,18
Breakfast: F.

Dbl. Oc.: $71.50 - $110.00
Sgl. Oc.: $71.50 - $110.00
Third Person: $16.50

Five Oaks Inn—A majestic waterfront home within walking distance of restaurants, town, marina, shops and churches. Near beaches and cultural area. Period decor, circa 1911. In historic register. Complimentary cocktail and relaxed atmosphere.

Pensacola *

Liechty, Jeanne & Neil
7830 Pine Forest Rd., 32526
(904) 944-4816

Amenities: 1,2,4,9,10,11,12, 13,16
Breakfast: F.

Dbl. Oc.: $86.11
Sgl. Oc.: $75.21
Third Person: $10.90
Child: Under 12 yrs. - $5.45

Liechty's Homestead Inn—This beautiful Victorian bed and breakfast inn combines the charm and grace of yesteryear with modern conveniences. Private baths, color TV, phones, two rooms with fireplaces and one with garden tub and skylight. Homemade desserts in the evening, full breakfast in the morning.

1. No Smoking	5. Tennis Available	9. Credit Cards Accepted	13. Lunch Available	17. Shared Baths
2. No Pets	6. Golf Available	10. Personal Check Accepted	14. Conference Rooms Avail.	18. Afternoon Tea
3 Off Season Rates	7. Swimmming Avail.	11. Reservations Necessary	15. Group Seminars Avail.	* Commisions given
4. Senior Citizen Rates	8. Skiing Available	12. Dinner Available	16. Private Baths	to Travel Agents

FLORIDA

Sanibel Island *

Slater, Patricia
863 E. Gulf Dr., 33957
(813) 472-2220, (800) 231-l045

Amenities: 2,3,5,6,7,9,10,11, 16
Breakfast: C.

Dbl. Oc.: $287.00
Third Person: $10.00

Sanibel's Song Of The Sea—Intimate, European-style seaside inn located directly on the Gulf of Mexico in southwest Florida. Newly renovated for 1992. Amenities include wine, fresh flowers and complimentary bicycle use. Shops, restauratns and wildlife refuge nearby. America's best shelling.

St. Augustine *

Burkley-Kovacik, Karen
70 Cuna St., 32084
(904) 829-2467

Amenities: 1,2,3,4,5,6,7,9,10, 11,16,18
Breakfast: F. or C. Plus

Dbl. Oc.: $65.40 - $114.45
Sgl. Oc.: $65.40 - $114.45
Third Person: $10.00

Carriage Way—A restored 1883 Victorian structure in the historic district. Includes cordials, cookies and use of bicycles. Romantic atmosphere with canopy, brass beds and four-poster beds. Honeymoon packages, breakfast in bed and picnic lunches available. Reservations strongly suggested.

St. Augustine *

Compton, Alice & Robert
115 Cordova St., 32084
904-826-0113

Amenities: 1,2,5,6,7,9,10,11, 12,13,16
Breakfast: F.

Dbl. Oc.: $65.40 - $114.45
Third Person: $10.00
Child: Under 6 yrs. - $5.00

Old City House Inn And Restaurant—Come and stay in one of St. Augustine's finest examples of colonial revival architecture and dine with us in our five- star restaurant. We are located in the heart of the oldest city within walking distance of all sights. Bicycles available. Wine served on the veranda.

St. Augustine

Constant, Mark
38 Marine St., 32084
(904) 824-2116

Amenities: 1,2,4,5,6,7,9,10, 11,16,18
Breakfast: C.

Dbl. Oc.: $59.95 - $92.65
Sgl. Oc.: $49.05 - $70.85
Third Person: $10.90
Child: Over 8 yrs. - $10.90

The Kenwood Inn—Built in 1865, this lovely Victorian building has been accommodating travelers since 1886. Located in the historic waterfront district of the nation's oldest city, The Kenwood Inn provides all the comforts of home featuring true Southern hospitality. AAA approved.

---

1. No Smoking	5. Tennis Available	9. Credit Cards Accepted	13. Lunch Available	17. Shared Baths
2. No Pets	6. Golf Available	10. Personal Check Accepted	14. Conference Rooms Avail.	18. Afternoon Tea
3 Off Season Rates	7. Swimmming Avail.	11. Reservations Necessary	15. Group Seminars Avail.	* Commisions given
4. Senior Citizen Rates	8. Skiing Available	12. Dinner Available	16. Private Baths	to Travel Agents

St. Augustine *

Finnegan, Joseph
279 St. George St., 32084
(904) 824-6068

Amenities: 1,2,7,9,10,11,16
Breakfast: C. Plus
Dbl. Oc.: $60.00 - $140.00
Third Person: $8.00

St. Francis Inn—Built in 1791 and located in the historic district. We offer the charm of yesterday and the comfort of today. Complimentary bicycles, admission to the oldest house, fireplaces, color cable TV, private parking and a variety of accommodations are here for you to enjoy.

St. Augustine *

Upchurch, Sandra
22 Avenida Menendez, 32084
(904 829-2915

Amenities: 2,5,6,7,9,10,16
Breakfast: F.

Dbl. Oc.: $65.00 - $115.00
Sgl. Oc.: $65.00 - $115.00
Third Person: $10.00

Casa De La Paz—Overlooking Matanzas Bay, this elegant Mediterranean-style inn graces St. Augustine's historic district. Each room is distinctive in style with imported linens. Enjoy the veranda views and Spanish courtyard. Gourmet breakfast and complimentary champagne.

St. Pete Beach Island *

Bernard, Mrs. Danie
8690 Gulf Blvd., 33706
(813) 360-1753

Amenities: 1,2,3,4,5,6,7,16, 17
Breakfast: C. Plus

Dbl. Oc.: $77.00 - $88.00
Sgl. Oc.: $60.00 - $72.00
Child: Under 3 yrs. - no charge

Swan Home—White sand Gulf beach nearby; fish off of dock; sun on deck; lounge in spa; kitchen and laundry use. Two day minimum, seventh day free. Three rooms; late checkouts; gorgeous sunsets; rental cars; bikes. Nightclub and sights nearby. Phone, TV, fridge and microwave in rooms.

St. Petersburg *

Powers, Antonia & Gordon
1719 Beach Dr., S.E., 33701
(813) 823-4955

Amenities: 1,2,5,6,7,9,10,11,16,18
Breakfast: C. Plus
Dbl. Oc.: $86.90
Sgl Oc.: $75.90

Bayboro House Bed And Breakfast—Award-winning Bayboro house extends to you a warm invitation to step back to a more tranquil time that used to be. Sit on the porch swing or rockers on our verandah cooled by the breeze off Old Tampa Bay. Sink your feet into the sand and stay awhile.

1. No Smoking	5. Tennis Available	9. Credit Cards Accepted	13. Lunch Available	17. Shared Baths
2. No Pets	6. Golf Available	10. Personal Check Accepted	14. Conference Rooms Avail.	18. Afternoon Tea
3 Off Season Rates	7. Swimmming Avail.	11. Reservations Necessary	15. Group Seminars Avail.	* Commisions given
4. Senior Citizen Rates	8. Skiing Available	12. Dinner Available	16. Private Baths	to Travel Agents

Stuart *

Bell, Jean
501 Akron Ave., 34994
(407) 220-9148

Amenities: 1,2,3,7,9,10,11, 16
Breakfast: F.

Dbl. Oc.: $85.00
Sgl. Oc.: $75.00
Third Person: $10.00

The Homeplace Bed And Breakfast Inn—Come retreat, relax and renew at our restored 1913 home. We offer charm and hospitality along with three bedrooms with private baths, creatively appointed with antiques. Pool and heated spa. Breakfasts feature home-baked, "old- Florida" recipes and fruit picked from our yard.

Stuart *

Elbert, JoAyne & John
310 Atlanta Ave., 34994
(407) 288-7289

Amenities: 1,2,3,5,6,7,10,11, 13,15,16
Breakfast: F.

Dbl. Oc.: $63.00 - $111.00
Sgl. Oc.: $53.00 - $101.00
Third Person: $10.00

HarborFront Bed And Breakfast—With spacious and unique accommodations, delightful dining and grounds overlooking the placid St. Lucie River, HarborFront offers you an escape into the leisurely pace of days gone by. Boating, fishing and sailing at your doorstep with beaches a few minutes away.

Tarpon Springs

Morrick, Cher & Ron
32 W. Tarpon Ave., 34689
(813) 938-9333

Amenities: 1,2,3,5,6,7,10,11, 16,17
Breakfast: C. Plus

Dbl. Oc.: $60.50 - $93.50
Sgl. Oc.: $49.50 - $82.50
Third Person: $15.00

Spring Bayou Inn—An elegant in-town Victorian home with modern conveniences. Walk to quaint village shops, sponge docks and restaurants. Stroll around the bayou. Golf, beaches, fishing and tennis are available nearby. Continental breakfast served in formal dining area.

Venice

McCormick, Susan & Chuck
519 S. Harbor Dr., 34285
(813) 484-1385

Amenities: 2,3,7,10,11,14,15, 16,17
Breakfast: C.

Dbl. Oc.: $49.00 - $87.00
Sgl. Oc.: $49.00 - $87.00
Third Person: $15.00

The Banyan House—A Mediterranean-style house built in 1926. Victorian living room, garden with swimming pool, hot tub, banyan tree and brick courtyard. Two bedrooms with shared baths; three efficiencies with private baths. Walking distance of beaches, shops and restaurants.

---

1. No Smoking	5. Tennis Available	9. Credit Cards Accepted	13. Lunch Available	17. Shared Baths
2. No Pets	6. Golf Available	10. Personal Check Accepted	14. Conference Rooms Avail.	18. Afternoon Tea
3 Off Season Rates	7. Swimming Avail.	11. Reservations Necessary	15. Group Seminars Avail.	* Commisions given
4. Senior Citizen Rates	8. Skiing Available	12. Dinner Available	16. Private Baths	to Travel Agents

West Palm Beach *

Keimel, Dennis
419 Thirty Second St.,
Old Northwood Historic District, 33407
(800) 736-4064

Amenities: 5,6,7,10,11,16
Breakfast: C.
Dbl. Oc.: $65.00 - $85.00
Sgl Oc.: $65.00

West Palm Beach Bed And Breakfast—An enchanting "Key-West" style cottage. Tropical pool area. Private baths. Centrally located in historic neighborhood one block from waterway. Minutes to beaches and Palm Beach. Bicycles and off-street parking. A relaxing place to kick off your sandals!

West Palm Beach *

Lesky, Bonnie
3215 Spruce Ave., 33407
(407) 863-1508

Amenities: 1,2,3,5,7,10,11,16, 17
Breakfast: C. Plus

Dbl. Oc.: $55.00 - $75.00
Sgl. Oc.: $50.00 - $70.00
Third Person: Under 10 yrs. - $10.00
Child: $10.00

Royal Palm House—This historic Dutch colonial home, built in 1924, is suitably located in the heart of the historic district. Charming, warm and hospitable, it is only two blocks from the intracoastal waterway. Enjoy our pool which is set amidst a lush tropical garden.

West Palm Beach *

Hill, Raleigh
501 30th St., 33407
(407) 863-5633

Amenities: 3,7,10,11,16
Breakfast: F.

Dbl. Oc.: $65.00 - $90.00
Sgl. Oc.: $65.00 - $90.00

Hibiscus House—Experience an elegant '20s Florida home! Large rooms. All with private baths - some with private terraces. Antiques galore! Tropical pool area - sunbathing decks. Full breakfast served by the pool or in the gazebo. Only five minutes to fabulous town of Palm Beach!

---

1. No Smoking	5. Tennis Available	9. Credit Cards Accepted	13. Lunch Available	17. Shared Baths
2. No Pets	6. Golf Available	10. Personal Check Accepted	14. Conference Rooms Avail.	18. Afternoon Tea
3 Off Season Rates	7. Swimming Avail.	11. Reservations Necessary	15. Group Seminars Avail.	* Commisions given
4. Senior Citizen Rates	8. Skiing Available	12. Dinner Available	16. Private Baths	to Travel Agents

GEORGIA

The Empire State of the South

Capitol: Atlanta
Statehood: January 2, 1788; the 4th state
State Motto: Wisdom, Justice and Moderation
State Song: "Georgia On My Mind"
State Bird: Brown Thrasher
State Flower: Cherokee Rose
State Tree: Live Oak

The state of Georgia is known for its natural beauty and it has many vacation resorts attracting visitors from all over the world. The climate is mild most of the time, but in the summer it tends to get quite warm and humid.

It is the largest east of the Mississippi and one of the leading growers of peaches. It is often called the Peach state.

The first Girl Scout troop in America was organized here by Juliette Low in 1912 and the first painless surgery was performed by Dr. Long in 1842, when he operated on a patient using ether as an anesthetic for the first time.

The capitol, Atlanta, represents the modern south. Almost two million people live here. It also was the home and the burial place of Dr. Martin Luther King.

Jimmy Carter, our 39th president, was born here.

Americus *

Morris, Troy
425 Timberlane Dr., 31709
(912) 924-4884

Amenities: 1,2,6,9,11,16
Breakfast: F.

Dbl. Oc.: $58.00
Sgl. Oc.: $48.00

The Morris Manor—Visit a stately Georgian colonial home in a quiet, rural setting at the edge of Americus. Here you will enjoy a wholesome atmosphere and Southern hospitality, including a bedtime snack, full breakfast and other amenities. Fresh fruit available in season.

Atlanta *

Amin, Mit
65 Sheridan Dr., NE, 30305
(800) 232-8520, (404) 233-8520,
(404) 233-8047

Amenities: 5,7,9,10,14,15,16
Breakfast: C.
Dbl. Oc.: $74.00 - $120.00
Sgl Oc.: $65.00 - $74.00
Third Person: $5.00
Child: Under 5 yrs. - no charge

Beverly Hills Inn—A charming city retreat in the heart of Buckhead. A European-style inn with antique furnishings and Oriental rugs. Play the piano in the parlor, read in the library or enjoy the vast choice of good restaurants within a short five-minute drive.

Atlanta *

Heartfield, Sandra
182 Elizabeth St., NE, 30307
(404) 523-8633

Amenities: 2,4,10,14,15,16
Breakfast: C.

Dbl. Oc.: $45.00
Sgl. Oc.: $35.00
Third Person: $10.00
Child: Under 8 yrs. - no charge

Heartfield Manor—A stately 1903 English Tudor, minutes from downtown. Experience a lovely Victorian neighborhood with the convenience of rapid transit to all parts of the city and airport. Walking distance of theatres, restaurants, pubs and shops. Rooms and suites available.

Atlanta *

Jones, Joan & Douglas
223 Ponce de Leon Ave., 30308
(404) 875-9449

Amenities: 1,3,9,10,14,15,16,
17,18
Breakfast: F. or C.

Dbl. Oc.: $75.00
Sgl. Oc.: $65.00
Third Person: $10.00
Child: Under 6 yrs. - $5.00

Woodruff Bed And Breakfast Inn—Southern charm and hospitality. Turn-of-the-century Victorian home decorated with fine antiques. Full Southern breakfast prepared by owner. Very convenient to fine restaurants and close to all cultural activities. Y'all come!

1. No Smoking	5. Tennis Available	9. Credit Cards Accepted	13. Lunch Available	17. Shared Baths
2. No Pets	6. Golf Available	10. Personal Check Accepted	14. Conference Rooms Avail.	18. Afternoon Tea
3 Off Season Rates	7. Swimmming Avail.	11. Reservations Necessary	15. Group Seminars Avail.	* Commisions given
4. Senior Citizen Rates	8. Skiing Available	12. Dinner Available	16. Private Baths	to Travel Agents

Augusta *

Upton, Herbert S.
836 Greene St., 30901
(706) 724-9774

Amenities: 1,2,4,9,11,14,15, 16
Breakfast: F.

Dbl. Oc.: $94.35
Sgl. Oc.: $94.35
Third Person: $10.00
Child: Under 2 yrs. - no charge

Oglethorpe Inn—Shaded by 100-year-old magnolias on Augusta's most beautiful street in the heart of the central business district and close to Riverwalk. 19 rooms carefully renovated with all modern conveniences. Many rooms with fireplaces and whirlpool tubs. Outdoor hot tub.

Blairsville *

Citrin, Georgia
2592 Collins Lane, 30512
(706) 379-1603

Amenities: 1,2,3,4,5,6,7,9,10, 14,15,16
Breakfast: F.

Dbl. Oc.: $85.00
Sgl. Oc.: $75.00
Third Person: Under 12 yrs. - $10.00

Souther Country Inn—English country manor rests on mountain overlooking breathtaking panorama. The sweet mountain people of this area will warm your heart. Miles of secluded mountain trails on property. Stocked lake. Outdoor activities and white-water rafting nearby. Seasonal fairs.

Brunswick *

Rose, Rachel
1108 Richmond St., 31520
(912) 267-6369

Amenities: 1,2,10,11,16,17, 18
Breakfast: F.

Dbl. Oc.: $65.00 - $95.00
Sgl. Oc.: $55.00
Third Person: $22.50
Child: Under 12 yrs. - $12.50

Rose Manor Guest House—A circa 1890, elegantly restored and gracefully furnished Victorian bungalow. Gateway to the Golden Isles at Hanover Square in historic Old Town. Nestled among old Southern trees laden with yards of Spanish moss surrounded by beautiful gardens. Charming ambience.

Clarkesville

Newman, Mary & Fred
108 N. Washington St.,
P.O. 392, 30523
(706) 754-9347

Amenities: 2,6,9,10,11,12,13, 14,15,16
Breakfast: F.

Dbl. Oc.: $83.25
Third Person: $15.00
Child: Over 10 yrs. - $15.00

The Charm House—A beautiful old Southern mansion with large, cheerfuly decorated rooms. Located in the foothills of the Blue Ridge Mountains. White-water rafting, hiking, horseback riding, golf and quaint shops. Fine dining available at the inn for guests - limited reservations.

1. No Smoking	5. Tennis Available	9. Credit Cards Accepted	13. Lunch Available	17. Shared Baths
2. No Pets	6. Golf Available	10. Personal Check Accepted	14. Conference Rooms Avail.	18. Afternoon Tea
3 Off Season Rates	7. Swimmming Avail.	11. Reservations Necessary	15. Group Seminars Avail.	* Commisions given
4. Senior Citizen Rates	8. Skiing Available	12. Dinner Available	16. Private Baths	to Travel Agents

Cleveland

Mauney, Sharon
Old Clarkesville Rd., Rt. 7, Box 7202, 30528
(706) 865-5738

Amenities: 1,2,6,9,11,16
Breakfast: F.
Dbl. Oc.: $84.00
Sgl Oc.: $56.00
Third Person: $17.00
Child: Under 3 yrs. - no charge

RuSharon Inn—Restored 1890s home in N. Georgia mountains furnished in antiques with fireplaces, TV and A/C. Southern breakfast served in your room or on the veranda. Near Cabbage Patch Kids®' birthplace, Alpine Helen hiking, lakes and waterfalls! Quiet, casual elegance in a garden setting.

Commerce *

Tomberlin, Dot & Tom
103 Homer St., 30529
(404) 335-3823

Amenities: 1,2,5,6,7,9,10,16, 17
Breakfast: F.

Dbl. Oc.: $59.00
Sgl. Oc.: $53.00
Third Person: $10.00

The Pittman House—Located in NE Georgia on U.S. Highway 441, three miles off I-85 at Exit 53, about halfway between Atlanta and Greenville, South Carolina. Discount mall, pottery, golf and water sports are located nearby. Antiques. Shoppers delight. Furnished in turn-of-the-century decor.

Dahlonega *

Middleton, David
Rte. 7, Box 150, 30533
(706) 864-5257, (800) 526-9754

Amenities: 1,2,9,10,14,15,16
Breakfast: F.

Dbl. Oc.: $71.50 - $137.50
Sgl. Oc.: $49.50 - $115.50
Third Person: $16.50

Mountain Top Lodge At Dahlonega—Enjoy antique-filled rooms in a beautiful mountain setting. Cathedral ceiling greatroom, spacious decks and heated outdoor spa. All rooms with privte bath, some have fireplaces and whirlpool tubs. Full country breakfast with homemade biscuits.

Ellijay

Handte, Mrs. June D.
75 Dalton St., 30546
(706) 635-2218

Amenities: 1,2,4,6,7,10,11,14,15,16,17,18
Breakfast: F.
Dbl. Oc.: $59.40 - $70.20
Sgl Oc.: $48.60 - $59.40

"Elderberry Inn" Bed And Breakfast—Historic home west of Downtown Square. Mountain view. Afternoon tea and desserts from 3:00 p.m. - 5:00 p.m. Antique and gift shop. Golf, fishing, hiking, horseback riding, white water. Advance reservations preferred. Y' all come!

1. No Smoking	5. Tennis Available	9. Credit Cards Accepted	13. Lunch Available	17. Shared Baths
2. No Pets	6. Golf Available	10. Personal Check Accepted	14. Conference Rooms Avail.	18. Afternoon Tea
3 Off Season Rates	7. Swimmming Avail.	11. Reservations Necessary	15. Group Seminars Avail.	* Commisions given
4. Senior Citizen Rates	8. Skiing Available	12. Dinner Available	16. Private Baths	to Travel Agents

GEORGIA

Fort Oglethorpe

Humphrey, Pam & Gilbert Ann
13 Barnhart Circle, 30742
(706) 858-0624

Amenities: 1,2,4,9,10,11,16
Breakfast: F.

Dbl. Oc.: $60.00 - $90.00
Sgl. Oc.: $60.00 - $90.00

Captain's Quarters Bed And Breakfast—Located adjacent to the Chickamauqa-Chattanooga National Military Park, Captain's Quarters was originally part of the military post which was Fort Oglethorpe. We are approximately 15 to 20 minutes from Lookout Mountain, Warehouse Row and the Chattanooga Choo Choo.

Hamilton *

Neuffer, Janice M.
P.O. Box 115, Hwy. 27, 31811
(706) 628-5659

Amenities: 1,2,3,5,6,7,10,
11,12,13,16
Breakfast: F.

Dbl. Oc.: $63.00 - $73.00
Sgl. Oc.: $58.00 - $68.00
Child: Under 6 - $3.00 - $5.00

Wedgwood Bed And Breakfast—Six miles south of Callaway Gardens. Make this spacious home yours while visiting the area. Little White House at Warm Springs is nearby. The 1850 home's decor is Wedgwood blue with white stenciling. The home radiates the warmth and hospitality of your hostess.

Helen *

Allen, Ms. Frankie
Chattahoochee, 30545
(404) 878-2388

Amenities: 3,6,7,9,10,11,16,
17
Breakfast: F.

Dbl. Oc.: $75.00
Sgl. Oc.: $60.00
Third Person: $15.00
Child: Under 12 yrs. - $10.00

Hilltop Haus—Contemporary split-level overlooks the Alpine town of Helen and the Chattahoochee River. Rich wood paneling and fireplaces create a homey atmosphere. Private efficiency with fireplace ideal for two to six guests. .04 of a mile from Alpine Helen. Afternoon coffee or tea with dessert.

Lakemont *

Pettys, N. William
Lake Rabun Rd.
P.O. Box 10, 30552
(404) 782-4946

Amenities: 2,4,5,6,7,8,9,10,
11,15,16,17,18
Breakfast: C. Plus

Dbl. Oc.: $54.50
Sgl. Oc.: $54.50
Third Person: $10.90
Child: Under 10 yrs. - no charge

Lake Rabun Hotel—Welcome to relaxation, hospitality and family-style comfort. Nestled in the heart of the Chattahoochee National Forest near the small community of Lakemont. Across the street is the lake it was named for. A peaceful, rustic hideaway. A local landmark reminiscent of times gone by.

Macon *

Jenkins, Phillip
353 College St., 31201
(912) 741-1842, (800) 336-1842

Amenities: 2,4,9,10,11,14,15,
16,18
Breakfast: C. Plus

Dbl. Oc.: $75.00 - $95.00
Sgl. Oc.: $65.00
Third Person: $10.00
Child: Under 12 yrs. - no charge

1842 INN—A 21-room historic inn located in beautiful historic district. A diamond award from AAA. This magnificent Greek Revival mansion has all the amenities of a grand hotel and the charm of an intimate fine home. Two blocks off I-75, exit 52 and the same from I-16.

1. No Smoking	5. Tennis Available	9. Credit Cards Accepted	13. Lunch Available	17. Shared Baths
2. No Pets	6. Golf Available	10. Personal Check Accepted	14. Conference Rooms Avail.	18. Afternoon Tea
3 Off Season Rates	7. Swimmming Avail.	11. Reservations Necessary	15. Group Seminars Avail.	* Commisions given
4. Senior Citizen Rates	8. Skiing Available	12. Dinner Available	16. Private Baths	to Travel Agents

GEORGIA

Madison

Rasch, Christian
250 No. Second St., 30650
(706) 342-4400

Amenities: 5,6,7,9,10,12,13, 15,16,17
Breakfast: F.

Dbl. Oc.: $55.00 - $77.00
Sgl. Oc.: $44.00 - $55.00
Third Person: $15.00

The Brady Inn—Charming Victorian cottages with period furniture located in the town that Sherman "refused to burn." One block from downtown square. Walking tour of antebellum homes available. Pleasant accommodations, local lore and Southern hospitality.

Sautee

Schwartz, Hamilton
Hwy. 255 N.
Rte. 1, Box 1476, 30571
(404) 878-3355

Amenities: 2,9,10,11,12,16
Breakfast: C.

Dbl. Oc.: $70.00
Sgl. Oc.: $40.00
Third Person: $17.00
Child: Under 17 yrs. - $11.00

The Stovall House—Relax in an attentively restored 1837 farmhouse on 26 acres in the mountains near Helen. Five guest rooms with private baths, period antiques, handmade curtains and stenciling. Award-winning restaurant. Dinner $15.00. It's a country experience.

Savannah *

Barnett, Anne
106 W. Jones St., 31401
(912) 234-6928

Amenities: 5,6,7,10,11,16
Breakfast: C.

Dbl. Oc.: $72.15
Sgl. Oc.: $72.15
Third Person: $38.85

Remshart-Brooks House—Enjoy the hospitality of this historic home. Features a terrace garden suite with bedroom, living room, bath and kitchen. Home-baked delicacies enhance the continental breakfast. Private front and back entrances. Off-street parking available. Please add 11% tax to prices listed.

Savannah *

McAlister, Robert
117 W. Gordon St., 31401
(912) 238-0518

Amenities: 3,9,10,16,17
Breakfast: F.

Dbl. Oc.: $48.00 - $90.00
Sgl. Oc.: $34.00 - $79.00
Third Person: $11.10s
Child: Under 5 yrs. - no charge

Bed And Breakfast Inn—An 1853 restored Federalist townhouse in historic district. Poster beds, rare porcelain, Oriental carpets, books, original art, antiques and traditional furnishings. A lovely walled garden. Quiet and convenient. Situated in a residential area.

Savannah *

Smith, Johnny B.
203 W. Charlton St., 31406
(912) 236-3620, (800) 348-9378

Amenities: 2,3,4,5,6,7,10,16, 17
Breakfast: C.

Dbl. Oc.: $88.00
Sgl. Oc.: $88.00
Third Person: $12.00
Child: Under 12 yrs. - no charge

Pulaski Square Inn—A historic townhouse built in 1853. Located in downtown Savannah within walking distance of the river and historic places of interest. Beautifully restored with original pine floors, marble mantels and chandeliers.

---

1. No Smoking	5. Tennis Available	9. Credit Cards Accepted	13. Lunch Available	17. Shared Baths
2. No Pets	6. Golf Available	10. Personal Check Accepted	14. Conference Rooms Avail.	18. Afternoon Tea
3 Off Season Rates	7. Swimmming Avail.	11. Reservations Necessary	15. Group Seminars Avail.	* Commisions given
4. Senior Citizen Rates	8. Skiing Available	12. Dinner Available	16. Private Baths	to Travel Agents

GEORGIA

Savannah *

Smith, Lee
5 W. Jones St., 31401
(912) 348-9378, (800) 236-3620

Amenities: 3,4,5,6,7,9,10,11, 14,15,16,18
Breakfast: C. Plus
Dbl. Oc.: $120.00
Sgl. Oc.: $95.00
Third Person: $10.00
Child: Under 10 yrs. - no charge

Eliza Thompson House—Nestled in a tranquil residential neighborhood in the heart of one of America's largest national historic districts is the Eliza Thompson House. Exquisite furnishings but the emphasis is on comfort. Spectacular gardens with fountains. Superb breakfast.

Savannah *

Steinhauser, Susan
14 W. Hull St., 31401
(912) 232-6622

Amenities: 2,4,5,6,7,9,10,11,15,16,18
Breakfast: C.
Dbl. Oc.: $85.00 - $175.00
Sgl Oc.: $85.00 - $175.00
Third Person: $10.00
Child: Under 12 yrs. - no charge

Foley House Inn—Circa 1896. Located in the heart of the historic district. Every room is an individual masterpiece. Antiques, Oriental rugs, fireplaces and many rooms with oversized jacuzzies. A delicate blend of traditional aristocracy and contemporary finesse. Evening cordial.

Savannah *

Sullivan, Virginia & Hal
102 W. Hall St., 31401
(912) 233-6800

Amenities: 2,5,6,7,9,14,16
Breakfast: C.
Dbl. Oc.: $94.00 - $161.00
Sgl. Oc.: $67.00 - $94.00
Third Person: $17.00
Child: Under 2 yrs. - no charge

The Forsyth Park Inn—An elegantly restored Victorian mansion in the historic district. Rooms feature wet bars, fireplaces and whirlpool tubs. Evening wine social hour.

Senoia *

Boal, Jan & Bobby
252 Seavy St.
Box 177, 30276-0177
(404) 599-3905

Amenities: 1,2,5,6,9,10,11,12, 13,14,15,16,18
Breakfast: F.
Dbl. Oc.: $84.80 - $106.00
Sgl. Oc.: $58.30 - $79.50
Third Person: $15.90
Child: Under 2 yrs. - no charge

The Veranda—Beautifully restored spacious Victorian rooms in a 1907 hotel in the National Register, 30 miles south of the Atlanta Airport. Freshly prepared Southern gourmet meals by reservation. Gift shop, kaleidoscopes, 1930 Wurlitzer piano-organ, antique collections. Air-conditioned.

1. No Smoking	5. Tennis Available	9. Credit Cards Accepted	13. Lunch Available	17. Shared Baths
2. No Pets	6. Golf Available	10. Personal Check Accepted	14. Conference Rooms Avail.	18. Afternoon Tea
3 Off Season Rates	7. Swimmming Avail.	11. Reservations Necessary	15. Group Seminars Avail.	* Commisions given
4. Senior Citizen Rates	8. Skiing Available	12. Dinner Available	16. Private Baths	to Travel Agents

Thomasville *

Walker, Anne-Marie
Rte. 3, Box 1010, 31792
(912) 377-9644

Amenities: 5,7,10,12,14,16
Breakfast: F.

Dbl. Oc.: $157.50
Sgl. Oc.: $120.75

Susina Plantation Inn—A Greek Revival antebellum plantation home listed in the National Register of Historic Places. Situated on 115 acres. Five-course gourmet dinner with wine and full breakfast is included in the rates.

Thomson *

Zieger, Maggie & Ralph
2316 Wire Rd., S.E., 30824
(706) 597-0220

Amenities: 2,6,9,10,11,16,17
Breakfast: C.

Dbl. Oc.: $49.95
Sgl. Oc.: $44.40

Four Chimneys, A Bed And Breakfast—Early 1800s country house with pine plank floors, walls and ceilings. Four-poster beds and fireplaces in the guest rooms. Large herb and flower garden. Area events include: steeplechase, hunts, Augusta Futurity and the Masters Golf Tournament. Seven miles to I-20.

Toccoa *

Ferguson, Joni & Don
130 W. Tugalo St., 30577
(706) 886-8411, (800) 533-7693

Amenities: 5,6,7,9,10,12,13,
14,15,16
Breakfast: C.

Dbl. Oc.: $55.00
Sgl. Oc.: $43.00
Third Person: $5.00
Child: $5.00

Simmons-Bond Inn—Victorian mansion on courthouse square. Home of lumber baron. Listed in the National Register. Beautiful, ornate oak interior. Comfortable, spacious rooms with private baths. Ideal for retreats and seminars. Great food, pub open evenings. Music fills the house.

1. No Smoking	5. Tennis Available	9. Credit Cards Accepted	13. Lunch Available	17. Shared Baths
2. No Pets	6. Golf Available	10. Personal Check Accepted	14. Conference Rooms Avail.	18. Afternoon Tea
3 Off Season Rates	7. Swimmming Avail.	11. Reservations Necessary	15. Group Seminars Avail.	* Commisions given
4. Senior Citizen Rates	8. Skiing Available	12. Dinner Available	16. Private Baths	to Travel Agents

HAWAII

The Aloha State

Capitol: Honolulu
Statehood: August 21, 1959; the 50th state
State Motto: The Life of the Lad is Perpetuated
in Righteousness
State Song: "Hawaii Ponoi"
State Bird: Nene (Hawaiian Goose)
State Flowers: Hibiscus
State Tree: Kukui

Hawaii is the only state that is completely set apart from the rest of the United States in North America. It consists of 132 beautiful islands, some larger than others, about 2,400 miles west of the United States.

These islands were first discovered by Captain Cook in 1778 and called the Sandwich Islands after the Earl of Sandwich. Inhabited then by only natives, the first white settlers were missionaries that came here in 1820. The Chinese and Japanese arrived later as laborers and workers for the plantations, but gradually entered the political and economic world here and today we have a happy mixture of many different peoples living and working together.

Hawaii's mild and beautiful climate beckons tourists from all over the world. Beautiful beaches have made swimming and surfing a way of life here.

Tourism and the pineapple and sugar industries from the leading source of income for this state.

HAWAII

Big Island of Hawaii *
Hawaii
Kaia, JoLoyce
P.O. Box 404, 96713
(808) 248-7725

Amenities: 1,2,7,10,11,16
Breakfast: C.

Dbl. Oc.: $50.00

Volcano Heart Chalet - Big Island of Hawaii—Near national park. Three keyed rooms. Private half-bathrooms. Shared kitchen and sitting room. No smoking - no alcohol. Two-night minimum.

Holualoa *
Durkee, Marilyn
P.O. BOx 596, 96725
(808) 322-9142

Amenities: 1,2,3,10,11,16,17
Breakfast: F.

Dbl. Oc.: $65.70 - $71.00
Sgl. Oc.: $49.50
Third Person: $15.00

Durkee's Coffeeland Bed And Breakfast—Seven miles south of Kailua-Kona; 1 5 minutes to beach, shops or snorkeling. Double and queen beds or garden apartment with private entrance. Sunset lanai with hot tub offers ocean view. Breakfast of homemade breads, home grown island fruits, jams and our own Kona coffee.

Kailua-Kona *
Berger, Lisa
75-5984 Alii Dr., 96740
(808) 329-3727

Amenities: 1,2,5,6,7,9,10,11,
16
Breakfast: C. Plus

Dbl. Oc.: $136.20 - $190.75
Sgl. Oc.: $136.20 - $190.75

Kailua Plantation House—A tropical haven for travelers seeking luxurious accommodations with the coziness of an ocean-front bed and breakfast inn. One mile from Kailua town; all rooms with private bath; on the water; hot tub and dip pool. Come and enjoy.

Keaau *
Peyton, Stephen E.
HCR 9558, 96749-9318
(808) 966-4600

Amenities: 2,11,16
Breakfast: C. Plus

Dbl. Oc.: $55.00
Sgl. Oc.: $50.00
Third Person: $10.00

Paradise Place Bed And Breakfast—Volcano, ocean and mountain views surround this quiet, rural hideaway. Kitchenette and private entrances to guest rooms overlooking tropical gardens. Centrally located to Hilo, active lava flows and Volcanos National Park. Relax in the" Aloha" spirit.

Pahoa-Kalapana *
Koob, Richard
Ocean Hwy. 137
"Red Rd.", 96778
(800)800-6886, (808) 965-7828

Amenities: 1,2,4,5,7,9,10,11,
12,13,14,15,16,17
Breakfast: C. & F.

Dbl. Oc.: $62.00 - $85.00
Sgl. Oc.: $52.00 - $85.00
Third Person: $15.00
Child: Under 5 yrs. - no charge

Kalani Honua By The Sea—A Hawaiian country getaway with fresh ocean breezes, comfy lodging, delicious cuisine, optional health and educational programs, Olympic pool, spa, tennis, horses, nearby national and state parks and secluded beaches. Color brochure. ALOHA!

1. No Smoking	5. Tennis Available	9. Credit Cards Accepted	13. Lunch Available	17. Shared Baths
2. No Pets	6. Golf Available	10. Personal Check Accepted	14. Conference Rooms Avail.	18. Afternoon Tea
3 Off Season Rates	7. Swimmming Avail.	11. Reservations Necessary	15. Group Seminars Avail.	* Commisions given
4. Senior Citizen Rates	8. Skiing Available	12. Dinner Available	16. Private Baths	to Travel Agents

HAWAII

Papaikou *

Miller, Sharon
P.O. Box 469, 96781
(808) 964-5250, (800) 245-5250

Amenities: 1,4,5,6,7,10,11,12,13,16,17
Breakfast: C. Plus
Dbl. Oc.: $50.00 - $71.00
Sgl Oc.: $50.00 - $71.00
Third Person: $10.00

Our Place Papaikou's Bed And Breakfast—Custom cedar home located four miles north of Hilo. Hawaiian-style common lanai open to each bedroom. Overlooks Kupue stream and tropical garden. Cathedral ceilings in the greatroom with library. Fireplace, grand piano and cable TV.

Volcano *

De Castro, Daniel
P.O. Box 7, 96785
(808) 985-8647

Amenities: 1,4,6,9,10,11,15, 16,18
Breakfast: C. Plus

Dbl. Oc.: $70.96
Sgl. Oc.: $70.96
Third Person: $16.38
Child: Under 5 yrs. - no charge

Lokahi Lodge Bed And Breakfast—Feel the healing power of this island in a truly enchanting place, just one mile from Volcanoes National Park and golf course. You have your own private bath and entrance that opens to a luxurious veranda overlooking a lush Ohia forest. Total peace and relaxation.

Volcano

Jeyte, Lorna & Albert
P.O. Box 116, 96785
(808) 967-7366

Amenities: 2,6,9,10,11,12,15,16
Breakfast: F.
Dbl. Oc.: $92.79 - $125.55
Sgl Oc.: $92.79 - $125.55
Third Person: $16.39
Child: Under 2 yrs. - no charge

Kilauea Lodge—A country inn one mile from Volcano's National Park. Pristine forest setting. Private bath, 12 rooms with six fireplaces. Area noted for family hikes, golf and heli-tours. The inn has excellent full-service dining with continental cuisine. Fresh, BIG ISLAND products.

---

1. No Smoking	5. Tennis Available	9. Credit Cards Accepted	13. Lunch Available	17. Shared Baths
2. No Pets	6. Golf Available	10. Personal Check Accepted	14. Conference Rooms Avail.	18. Afternoon Tea
3 Off Season Rates	7. Swimmming Avail.	11. Reservations Necessary	15. Group Seminars Avail.	* Commisions given
4. Senior Citizen Rates	8. Skiing Available	12. Dinner Available	16. Private Baths	to Travel Agents

Island of Kauai
Kapaa, Kauai *

Barker, Gordon
P.O. Box 740, 96746
(808) 822-3073, FAX: (800) 835-2845

Amenities: 5,6,7,9,10,11,16
Breakfast: C. Plus

Dbl. Oc.: $49.00 - $76.30
Sgl. Oc.: $38.15 - $65.40
Third Person: $11.00
Child: Under 12 yrs. - $5.50

Kay Barker's Bed And Breakfast—Located in a quiet rural area. Overlooks miles of pasture. Ten minutes from golf, tennis, beaches, restaurants and more. A large home with extensive library, TV room and Lanai to enjoy. Your host, Gordon, knows of the special places.

Kapaa

Ross, Leonora & Norm
6402 Kaahele St., 96746
(808) 822-7201, (800) 578-2194

Amenities: 1,2,11,16
Breakfast: C.

Dbl. Oc.: $82.00
Sgl. Oc.: $82.00

The Orchid Hut—A cozy, romantic cottage with kitchenette, mid-way between Kauai's north and south shores' recreational areas. A short drive to beach, golf, shopping and fine dining. Spectacular view of the Wailua River Canyon form the tea house. Quiet and private. Three day minimum.

Koloa*

Gooch, Katie
4160 Omao Rd., 96756
(808) 742-9089

Amenities: 1,10,16
Breakfast: C.

Dbl. Oc.: $76.00
Sgl. Oc.: $76.00
Third Person: $15.00
Child: $15.00

Katie's Kauai Bed And Breakfast—Enjoy the spirit of "Aloha" in charming apartment adjacent to host's home. Private entrance, bath, kitchenette and lanai. Centrally located between Kauai's spectacular north and west shores. Scenic, rural setting, 10 minutes to beaches, golf and tennis.

Koloa*

Seymour, Edee
3459 Lawai Loa Lane
Box 930, Lawai, Kauai, 96765 (mail)
(808) 332-9300

Amenities: 1,2,3,5,6,7,10,15, 16
Breakfast: C. Plus

Dbl. Oc.: $70.95 - $103.55
Sgl. Oc.: $59.00
Third Person: $10.00

Victoria Place—Spacious and sky-lit with jungle and ocean view. All bedrooms have private baths and open onto pool and garden. Near beaches, boutiques, golf and botanical garden. Barrier free. We pamper: flowers, popcorn, homemade muffins and "Aloha."

1. No Smoking	5. Tennis Available	9. Credit Cards Accepted	13. Lunch Available	17. Shared Baths
2. No Pets	6. Golf Available	10. Personal Check Accepted	14. Conference Rooms Avail.	18. Afternoon Tea
3 Off Season Rates	7. Swimmming Avail.	11. Reservations Necessary	15. Group Seminars Avail.	* Commisions given
4. Senior Citizen Rates	8. Skiing Available	12. Dinner Available	16. Private Baths	to Travel Agents

HAWAII

Poipu Beach*

Cichon, Dottie
2720 Hoonani Rd., 96756
(800) 552-0095, (808) 742-1146

Amenities: 1,2,4,5,6,7,9,10,11,14,15,16,18
Breakfast: C.
Dbl. Oc.: $98.49 - $136.79
Sgl Oc.: $93.02 - $131.32
Third Person: $16.41
Child: $16.41

Poipu Bed And Breakfast Inn—A romantic 1933 plantation house in sunny Poipu. All luxurious rooms have the charm of old Hawaii plus every modern amenity. TVs, VCRs, white wicker, pine antiques and the spirit of "Aloha." Walk to beach, shops, restaurants, etc. Family suite available - $54.70.

Island of Maui
Kula

Endres, Annette
210 Ahinahina Place, 96790
(808) 878-6096, (800) 241-6284

Amenities: 1,2,10,11,16
Breakfast: C. Plus

Dbl. Oc.: $81.75 - $98.10
Sgl. Oc.: $76.30 - $92.65
Third Person: $15.00

Ahinahina Farm Bed And Breakfast—Two cottages on two acres of citrus and flowers. Ocean and mountain views. Sunny, warm days, cool nights, rural and quiet. Near Haleakala National Park and only minutes from beaches. Highest quality accommodations. Up-country Maui's best place to stay.

Maui *

Kaia, JoLoyce
P.O. Box 404, Hana, 96713
(808) 248-7725

Amenities: 1,2,7,10,11,16
Breakfast: C.

Dbl. Oc.: $75.00
Child: $25.00

Kaia Ranch & Co.—Secluded flower farm, private studio, bath, kitchen. No smoking, no alcohol. Two night minimum.

Island of Molokai
Kaunakakai,*

Foster, Akiko & Glenn
Star Rte. Box 128, 96748
(808) 558-8236

Amenities: 1,2,4,10,11,16,17
Breakfast: C. Plus

Dbl. Oc.: $65.40
Sgl. Oc.: $65.40
Third Person: $65.40
Child: $65.40

"Kamalo Plantation"—Private cottage with kitchen and bath on acres of tropical botanical gardens beside ancient Hawaiian ruins and a lime orchard. Two rooms and shared bath in the main house. Aloha breakfast. Experience real Hawaiian living, plantation style.

1. No Smoking	5. Tennis Available	9. Credit Cards Accepted	13. Lunch Available	17. Shared Baths
2. No Pets	6. Golf Available	10. Personal Check Accepted	14. Conference Rooms Avail.	18. Afternoon Tea
3 Off Season Rates	7. Swimmming Avail.	11. Reservations Necessary	15. Group Seminars Avail.	* Commisions given
4. Senior Citizen Rates	8. Skiing Available	12. Dinner Available	16. Private Baths	to Travel Agents

HAWAII

Island of Oahu
Honolulu *

Bridges, Gene
3242 Kaohinani Dr., 96817
(800) 288-4666, Fax:(808) 595-2030

Amenities: 1,9,10,16
Breakfast: C.

Dbl. Oc.: $60.18
Sgl. Oc.: $54.71
Third Person: $10.94
Child: Under 5 yrs. - $5.47

Bed And Breakfast Honolulu—Centrally located in an area of fine homes. Twenty minutes to downtown Honolulu, Waikiki, airport and Windward Oahu. Located in lush, cool Nuuanu Valley, near Queen Emma Summer Palace. Private entrance. Queen beds. Room phones, TV, light cooking facilities.

Honolulu *

Cruthers, Shirley
521 Prospect St., 96813
(808) 521-6830

Amenities: 1,2,9,10,11,17
Breakfast: C. Plus

Dbl. Oc.: $84.00
Sgl. Oc.: $84.00

Prospect House—Located on the slopes of Punchbowl overlooking downtown Honolulu. Fully air-conditioned and centrally located. On-site parking. Hot tub, hammock and garden lanais for relaxing.

Honolulu *

Hookano-Holly, Lisa
2001 Vancouver Dr., 96822
(808) 947-6019

Amenities: 1,2,9,10,11,16,17
Breakfast: C.

Dbl. Oc.: $95.00 - $175.00
Sgl. Oc.: $95.00 - $175.00

Manoa Valley Inn—A beautiful historic country inn nestled on a lush half-acre with flowering Hawiian shade trees located two miles from Waikiki and downtown Honolulu. Historic accuracy is evidenced by every detail. Quiet moments and relaxing days. Unique!

*Kailua**

Epp, Doris
19 Kai Nani Pl., 96734
(808) 263-4848, FAX: (808) 261-6573

Amenities: 5,6,7,9,10,11,16
Breakfast: F

Dbl. Oc.: $95.00

Pacific Found—Ocean front white sand beach. Two-room suite, private entrance, sleeps up to four, cooking facilities, TV, large yard fronting two miles of ideal swimming beach. Residential area yet only 15 minutes drive to downtown Honolulu. Walk to bus and shopping. Weekly - $490.

1. No Smoking	5. Tennis Available	9. Credit Cards Accepted	13. Lunch Available	17. Shared Baths
2. No Pets	6. Golf Available	10. Personal Check Accepted	14. Conference Rooms Avail.	18. Afternoon Tea
3 Off Season Rates	7. Swimmming Avail.	11. Reservations Necessary	15. Group Seminars Avail.	* Commisions given
4. Senior Citizen Rates	8. Skiing Available	12. Dinner Available	16. Private Baths	to Travel Agents

HAWAII

Kailua

Martz, Jeanette & Bob
395 Auwinala Rd., 96734
(808) 261-0316

Amenities: 2,5,6,7,11,16
Breakfast: F.

Dbl. Oc.: $71.00 - $76.00
Sgl. Oc.: $71.00 - $76.00
Third Person: $15.00

Papaya Paradise—Just 20 miles from Waikiki and 1-1/2 hours from all attractions. Walk to Kailua Beach. Quiet and private, with 20X40 pool, jacuzzi and tropical gardens. Private entry, TV, air-conditioning and refrigerator. Beach towels, mats, chairs and coolers provided. 3 day minimum.

Kailua

Van Ryzin, Diane
172 Kuumele Pl., 96734
(808) 261-2227, (800) 642-5366

Amenities: 2,3,5,6,7,10,11,12, 13,16
Breakfast: F.

Dbl. Oc.: $60.00
Sgl. Oc.: $60.00
Third Person: $10.00

Akamai Bed And Breakfast—Hawaiian style: large private studio, fully equipped. Pool, garden, laundry facility. Quiet. Access to all Oahu. Write for free brochure.

---

1. No Smoking	5. Tennis Available	9. Credit Cards Accepted	13. Lunch Available	17. Shared Baths
2. No Pets	6. Golf Available	10. Personal Check Accepted	14. Conference Rooms Avail.	18. Afternoon Tea
3 Off Season Rates	7. Swimmming Avail.	11. Reservations Necessary	15. Group Seminars Avail.	* Commisions given
4. Senior Citizen Rates	8. Skiing Available	12. Dinner Available	16. Private Baths	to Travel Agents

IDAHO

The Gem State

Capitol: Boise
Statehood: July 3, 1890; the 43rd state
State Motto: It Is Forever
Sate Song: "Here We Have Idaho"
State Bird: Mountain Bluebird
State Flower: Syringa (Mock Orange)
State Tree: Western White Pine

Idaho is located in the Rocky Mountains with exciting scenery and enormous resources. Its natural wonders, such as Hells Canyon and the craters of the Moon National Monument, thrill visitors to this state every year.

Idaho is also a skier's paradise where ski areas and ski trails are considered among the best in the world.

This state is a leading producer of silver and phosphate. The Snake River and its many dams have made for rich farmlands. The Idaho potato is its number one farm product. More potatoes are grown here than in any other state in the union.

IDAHO

Ashton

Jessen, Nieca & Jack
Idaho Hwy. #20
P.O. Box 11, 83420
(208) 652-3356

Amenities: 1,2,6,7,8,10
Breakfast: F.
Dbl. Oc.: $45.00
Sgl Oc.: $35.00
Third Person: $10.50

Jessen's Bed And Breakfast—This B&B is 1-1/2 miles south of Ashton on Highway U.S. 20 with Yellowstone National Park to the north, Jackson Hole and The Great Tetons to the east. Our home is comfortable and hospitable.

Bonners Ferry *

Owsley, Artis
Rte. 4, Box 5090, 83805
(208) 267-2117

Amenities: 1,2,3,6,8,9,10,16
Breakfast: F.

Dbl. Oc.: $53.50 - $80.25
Sgl. Oc.: $53.50 - $80.25
Third Person: $10.70

Old Rose Inn—Conveniently located off Hwy. 95, just north of the golf course, 30 miles north of Sandpoint and Schweitzer Ski area. Enjoy local hiking, fishing, rafting, skiing and snowmobiling. Three beautifully decorated guest rooms. Comfortable and hospitable.

McCall

Shikrallah, Bonni & Bill
P.O. Box 1716
143 E. Lake St., 83638
(208) 634-4661

Amenities: 1,2,5,6,7,8,10,11, 14,15,17,18
Breakfast: F.

Dbl. Oc.: $69.55 - $74.90

1920 House Bed And Breakfast—"Historic home by Payette Lake, centrally located in year-round resort town. Spacious rooms, guest sitting room, complimentary sherry, family antiques, gracious decor and pampering hospitality. Room for sports equipment. Off-street parking. Perfect retreat. Deposit required.

Shoup *

Smith, Marsha & Aubrey
49 Salmon River Rd., 83469
(208) 394-2121

Amenities: 1,7,8,9,10,11,14, 15,16,17
Breakfast: F.

Dbl. Oc.: $37.45 - $57.78
Sgl. Oc.: $32.10 - $55.64
Third Person: $5.00
Child: Under 12 yrs. - $3.50

Smith House Bed And Breakfast—Situated on the Salmon River, 50 miles from Salmon, Idaho. Beautiful split-level log home with five warm and distinctively different guest rooms. Hot tub, orchard and library. Nearby fishing, float trips, hunting and skiing. Sample homemade wines. Gift shop. Weekly rates.

1. No Smoking	5. Tennis Available	9. Credit Cards Accepted	13. Lunch Available	17. Shared Baths
2. No Pets	6. Golf Available	10. Personal Check Accepted	14. Conference Rooms Avail.	18. Afternoon Tea
3 Off Season Rates	7. Swimmming Avail.	11. Reservations Necessary	15. Group Seminars Avail.	* Commisions given
4. Senior Citizen Rates	8. Skiing Available	12. Dinner Available	16. Private Baths	to Travel Agents

McCall

Schott, Barbara & Steve
201 Rio Vista
P.O. Box 4208, 83638
(208) 634-5349

Amenities: 1,5,6,7,8,9,10,11, 16,17
Breakfast: F.

Dbl. Oc.: $55.37
Sgl. Oc.: $44.30
Third Person: $15.00
Child: Under 4 yrs. - no charge

Northwest Passage Bed And Breakfast—Nestled among the tall ponderosa pines, the Northwest Passage has been an intergral part of McCall's history. Our four-season resort has something for everyone to enjoy. Two hours from Boise airport in the beautiful Rocky Mountains. Come enjoy the serenity.

Stanley

Leavell, Jeana & Bill
HC 64, Box 9934, 83278
(208) 774-3544

Amenities: 1,2,7,8,9,10,11,12,13,15,16
Breakfast: F.
Dbl. Oc.: $85.00 - $155.00
Sgl Oc.: $80.00 - $150.00
Third Person: $25.00
Child: Under 3 - no charge

Idaho Rocky Mountain Ranch—Secluded, quiet 1,000 acres guest and cattle ranch in the Sawtooth Mountains. Comfortable historic lodge and surrounding cabins with spectacular views. Fine dining, hot spring swimming pool, fishing, horseback riding and much more. Color brochure upon request.

1. No Smoking	5. Tennis Available	9. Credit Cards Accepted	13. Lunch Available	17. Shared Baths
2. No Pets	6. Golf Available	10. Personal Check Accepted	14. Conference Rooms Avail.	18. Afternoon Tea
3 Off Season Rates	7. Swimmming Avail.	11. Reservations Necessary	15. Group Seminars Avail.	* Commisions given
4. Senior Citizen Rates	8. Skiing Available	12. Dinner Available	16. Private Baths	to Travel Agents

ILLINOIS

The Land of Lincoln

Capitol: Springfield
Statehood: December 3, 1818; the 21st state
State Motto: State Sovereignty, National Union
State Song: "Illinois"
State Bird: Cardinal
State Flower: Native Violet
State Tree: White Oak

Illinois boasts of having more people than any other state in the Midwest and the second largest city in the United States, Chicago. Its deep and rich soil has made for large-scale farming and its mighty deposits of coal have brought great prosperity.

The steel frames necessary for the building of sky scrapers were invented here. It resulted in the erection of some of the tallest buildings in the world, including Chicago's own Sears Tower.

Chicago is the crossroads of the country. Trains and barges leave here with the products of the Midwest farms and take them from one coast to another, either by rail or waterways.

Historically, Illinois first won national attention when Abraham Lincoln debated Stephen Douglas on the subject of slavery. Although not born in the state, Lincoln's burial place in Springfield is a national shrine. Ulysses S. Grant's home in Galea is maintained as it was when he lived there. Built in 1856, it has been a state memorial since 1932.

Although our 40th president, Ronald Wilson Reagan, spent most of his life in California he was born in this state in Tampico on February 6, 1911.

The first successful railroad sleeping car was invented by George Pullman at Bloomington, Illinois in 1859. It pioneered a new way of travel for Americans.

ILLINOIS

Arcola

Arthur, Maxine & Warren
RR 2, Box 590, 61910
(217) 268-3352

Amenities: 1,2,6,7,10,11,16, 17
Breakfast: F.

Dbl. Oc.: $53.00
Sgl. Oc.: $42.50
Third Person: $10.00
Child: Over 10 yrs. - $10.00

Curly's Corner—This ranch-style farmhouse is located in a quiet Amish community. Hosts are dedicated to cordial hospitality and will gladly share information about the area. Enjoy clean, cool, comfortable bedrooms with king- and queen size beds. Breakfasts of homemade buscuits, jams, bacon and eggs.

Carlyle *

Cook, Vickie & Ron
1191 Franklin, 62231
(618) 594-8313

Amenities: 1,2,5,6,7,8,9,10, 11,12,16
Breakfast: F.

Dbl. Oc.: $60.00
Sgl. Oc.: $50.00

Country Haus Bed And Breakfast—1890s Eastlake home where country hospitality makes your stay memorable. A spa, library with TV and four comfortable guest rooms with private baths await you. One mile from Carlyle Lake, rated third best inland sailing lake. 55 miles east of St. Louis.

Chicago *

Sandoval, Elia
2022 No. Sheffield Ave., 60614
(312) 327-6546

Amenities: 2,3,10,16,17
Breakfast: C.

Dbl. Oc.: $60.00 - $75.00
Sgl. Oc.: $50.00 - $60.00

Bed And Breakfast Lincoln Park/Sheffield—Victorian building with renovated guest rooms; one one- bedroom suite and two two -bedroom apartments. Self-serve breakfast. Contemporary furnishings. Excellent public transportation. Many fine restaurants and shopping nearby. Walk to zoo, lake and DePaul University.

Du Quoin *

Morgan, Frances H.
104 So. Line St., 62832
(618) 542-6686

Amenities: 1,2,9,10,11,14,15, 16
Breakfast: F.

Dbl. Oc.: $65.40 - $87.20
Sgl. Oc.: $54.50 - $76.30
Third Person: $10.90
Child: Under 6 yrs. - no charge

Francie's Bed And Breakfast Inn—Restored 1908 orphanage. Sits on three acres in the center of town. Bicycles and yard games available. Within walking distance of shops and the beautiful 1,400-acre fairgrounds park. In-house gift shop. Monthly Sunday brunches. Murder-mystery weekends.

Galena

Dugan, Marjorie & Harry
113 S. Prospect, 61036
(815) 777-1387, (800) 373-0732

Amenities: 2,3,4,5,6,7,9,10, 11,16,17
Breakfast: F.

Dbl. Oc.: $70.85 - $87.20
Sgl. Oc.: $70.85
Child: $10.00

Grandview Guest Home—An 1870 brick traditional on "Quality Hill." Antiques and owners treasured items throughout the house. Beautiful gardens and great views. Private and shared baths. Two blocks from downtown.

1. No Smoking	5. Tennis Available	9. Credit Cards Accepted	13. Lunch Available	17. Shared Baths
2. No Pets	6. Golf Available	10. Personal Check Accepted	14. Conference Rooms Avail.	18. Afternoon Tea
3 Off Season Rates	7. Swimmming Avail.	11. Reservations Necessary	15.Group Seminars Avail.	* Commisions given
4. Senior Citizen Rates	8. Skiing Available	12. Dinner Available	16. Private Baths	to Travel Agents

ILLINOIS

Galena

Fallbacher, Sharon
208 Park Ave., 61036
(815) 777-1075, (800) 359-0743

Amenities: 1,2,3,4,9,10,11,16
Breakfast: C.Plus
Dbl. Oc.: $76.00
Sgl Oc.: $76.00
Third Person: $10.00

Park Avenue Guest House—An 1893 Queen Ann "Painted Lady." Screened porch and gardens with gazebo. Original woodwork, pocket doors, transoms with antique furniture and decor. Short stroll to historic Main Street shops and restaurants. Casino, riverboats, golf and skiing in area.

Galena *

Jensen, Flo & Roger
606 S. Prospect St., 61036
(815) 777-3883

Amenities: 1,2,3,4,9,10,11,17, 18
Breakfast: C.

Dbl. Oc.: $66.00
Sgl. Oc.: $55.00
Third Person: $10.00
Child: Under 12 yrs. - $5.00

Avery Guest House—Located within Galena's historic district. Close to antique shops, fine restaurants and historic buildings. Scenic view from our porch swing. Breakfast in sunny dining room with bay window. Golf, tennis, swimming, hiking and skiing. Mississippi River is nearby.

Galena

Lozeau, Pamela
513 Bouthillier, 61036
(815) 777-0557

Amenities: 2,3,9,10,12,16
Breakfast: C.
Dbl. Oc.: $71.00 - $136.50

Stillman's Country Inn—An 1858 Victorian mansion adjacent to General Grant's home. Features fine dining and weekend nightclub. All guest rooms have private baths.

Havana

Stephens, Shirley
112 N. Schrader St., 62644
(309) 543-3295

Amenities: 2,10,16,17
Breakfast: C.

Dbl. Oc.: $58.10
Sgl. Oc.: $36.97

The McNutt Guest House—Just steps from the scenic Illinois River. Restaurants, grocery stores and shops are within walking distance. A gracious and beautifully furnished eight-room home. Reserve a bedroom or the entire guest house which sleeps eight. Entire guest house - $132.05.

---

1. No Smoking	5. Tennis Available	9. Credit Cards Accepted	13. Lunch Available	17. Shared Baths
2. No Pets	6. Golf Available	10. Personal Check Accepted	14. Conference Rooms Avail.	18. Afternoon Tea
3 Off Season Rates	7. Swimmming Avail.	11. Reservations Necessary	15.Group Seminars Avail.	* Commisions given
4. Senior Citizen Rates	8. Skiing Available	12. Dinner Available	16. Private Baths	to Travel Agents

Lanark

Standish, Norman W.
540 W. Carroll St., 61046
(815) 493-2307, (800) 468-2307

Amenities: 1,2,6,8,9,10,11,16,17
Breakfast: Full
Dbl. Oc.: $60.00 - $71.00
Sgl Oc.: $60.00 - $71.00

Standish House—An adventure in early American history (1620). English and early American antiques with modern conveniences such as central air conditioning. Walking distance to shopping and restaurants. About 120 miles west of Chicago.

Metamora

Fischer, Philip
104 Walnut St.
P.O. Box 187, 61548
(309) 367-2831

Amenities: 1,2,4,10,11,17,18
Breakfast: C. & F.

Dbl. Oc.: $58.50
Sgl. Oc.: $58.50
Third Person: $10.00

Stevenson House Bed & Breakfast—Relax and enjoy this 1858 Federal style house in the National Register of Historic Places furnished with Victorian furniture. Previously the home of Adlai Stevenson, Vice President of the United States with President Grover Cleveland. Riverboat casino packages.

Mossville

Ramseyer, Holly & Dean
1416 E. Mossville Rd., 61552
(309) 579-2300

Amenities: 1,2,5,6,7,8,9,10,
11,16,17,18
Breakfast: C. Plus

Dbl. Oc.: $68.90 - $94.34
Sgl. Oc.: $53.00

Old Church House Inn—Nestled in central Illinois near the Rock Island bike trail, this 1869 colonial-style church welcomes you to the plush warmth of a Victorian era. Enjoy flower gardens, afternoon tea, queen featherbeds and pampering amenities in Peoria's finest B&B. Advance deposit required.

Naperville *

Harrison, Lynn
26 N. Eagle St., 60540
(708) 420-1117

Amenities: 1,2,3,4,5,6,7,8,9,
10,11,14,16,17,18
Breakfast: F. & C. Plus

Dbl. Oc.: $74.00 - $151.00
Sgl. Oc.: $53.50 - $129.00
Third Person: $10.00

Harrison House Bed And Breakfast—Circa 1911, 25 miles west of Chicago in historic Naperville. Walk to fantastic restaurants, shops and historic sites. Five antique-filled, air-conditioned guest rooms. One bath with Jacuzzi. Business or pleasure, come and be pampered.

1. No Smoking	5. Tennis Available	9. Credit Cards Accepted	13. Lunch Available	17. Shared Baths
2. No Pets	6. Golf Available	10. Personal Check Accepted	14. Conference Rooms Avail.	18. Afternoon Tea
3 Off Season Rates	7. Swimmming Avail.	11. Reservations Necessary	15.Group Seminars Avail.	* Commisions given
4. Senior Citizen Rates	8. Skiing Available	12. Dinner Available	16. Private Baths	to Travel Agents

ILLINOIS

Nauvoo

Starr, Marge
Box 291, RR 1, 62354
(217) 453-2771

Amenities: 1,2,6,7,9,10,16
17
Breakfast: F.

Dbl. Oc.: $65.00
Sgl. Oc.: $43.00
Third Person: $10.00

Mississippi Memories Bed And Breakfast—Gracious lodging on bank of the Mississippi River. Quiet, wooded area. Elegantly served full breakfast. Wildlife barges drifting by and geode hunting. A/C, piano and fireplaces. Two miles to riverboat gambling and restored Morman City of Nauvoo. Five guest rooms.

Peoria

Giles, Ruth
1506 W. Alta Rd., 61615
(309) 243-5977

Amenities: 10,11,17
Breakfast: C.

Dbl. Oc.: $30.00
Sgl. Oc.: $25.00
Child: Under 6 yrs. - $5.00

Ruth's Bed And Breakfast—Private home. Guest rooms with shared bath. Family atmosphere. Children welcome. Five acres to roam. Twenty minutes or less from city attractions. Family restaurants nearby.

St. Joseph

Vernon, Alice
R.R.# 2, Box 273, 61873
(217) 469-2402

Amenities: 2,5,7,10,11,12,13,
14,15,16,18
Breakfast: C. Plus

Dbl. Oc.: $45.00 - $75.00
Sgl. Oc.: $45.00

Home At Last—Pleasing blend of contemporary and antiques in decor and menu. On the edge of a small town within walking distance of shops and river, 15 minutes from University of Illinois. Herb garden, decks, wooded setting. Breakfast on antique linen and china. Herb baths, terry robes.

Sycamore

Petersen, Donna & Howard
Rte. 2, Quigly Rd., 60178
(815) 895-5386

Amenities: 5,6,7,10,11,16
Breakfast: C. Plus &
F.(weekends)

Dbl. Oc.: $45.00 - $60.00
Sgl. Oc.: $35.00 - $50.00
Third Person: $10.00

Country Charm Inn—Understated elegance is the hallmark of this three-story country farmhouse on a tree-topped knoll. Pit fireplace, 2,000-book library, mini petting zoo, trick-horse champion, breakfast on the cozy front porch. Howard and Donna are former AFS hosts and Donna is eldest of 14 children.

1. No Smoking	5. Tennis Available	9. Credit Cards Accepted	13. Lunch Available	17. Shared Baths
2. No Pets	6. Golf Available	10. Personal Check Accepted	14. Conference Rooms Avail.	18. Afternoon Tea
3 Off Season Rates	7. Swimmming Avail.	11. Reservations Necessary	15.Group Seminars Avail.	* Commisions given
4. Senior Citizen Rates	8. Skiing Available	12. Dinner Available	16. Private Baths	to Travel Agents

Urbana

Shurts, Denni & Bruce
710 W. Oregon St., 61801
(217) 367-8793, 328-5139

Amenities: 1,2,6,7,9,10,11,14,15,16,17
Breakfast: C. Plus
Dbl. Oc.: $83.25 - $166.50
Sgl Oc.: $83.25 - $166.50
Third Person: $37.50

Shurts House Bed And Breakfast—Built in 1909, it hosts 18 + rooms. It is brick English Tudor-style. It is furnished with rare odd and unusual furniture. Its hosts are friendly and the home is extremely comfortable. Our coffees are hand-blended and fresh-ground daily.

West Dundee *

Hejhal, Sarah
305 Oregon Ave., 60118
(708) 426-7777

Amenities: 1,2,3,4,6,8,9,10, 11,14,15,16,17,18
Breakfast: C. Plus
Dbl. Oc.: $63.00
Sgl. Oc.: $53.00
Third Person: $20.00

Iron hedge Inn—Romantic 28-room historic mansion near beautiful Fox River. European ambience. Floral Tiffany-style windows; oversize double whirlpools; luxury suites; library; verandas and a large gazebo. Perfect for wedding receptions, corporate seminars and retreats. Formal breakfast.

1. No Smoking	5. Tennis Available	9. Credit Cards Accepted	13. Lunch Available	17. Shared Baths
2. No Pets	6. Golf Available	10. Personal Check Accepted	14. Conference Rooms Avail.	18. Afternoon Tea
3 Off Season Rates	7. Swimmming Avail.	11. Reservations Necessary	15.Group Seminars Avail.	* Commisions given
4. Senior Citizen Rates	8. Skiing Available	12. Dinner Available	16. Private Baths	to Travel Agents

INDIANA

The Hoosier State

Capitol: Indianapolis
Statehood: December 11, 1816; the 9th state
State Motto: Crossroads of America
State Song: "On the Banks of the Wabash"
State Bird: Cardinal
State Flower: Peony
State Tree: Tulip Tree

Indiana is a great steel producing state. Gary is its major industrial city, close to Lake Michigan. It produces steel products for the automobile industry. Indiana has always had a penchant for cars and their capacity for speed. This goes back to the late 1800's. and the beginning of the Indianapolis races. These races continue even today, bringing thousands of racing enthusiasts here every Memorial Day to once again experience the thrill of the powerful racing machine.

Yet, Indiana has another side. In the southern hills of this state are those who live on quiet farms independent of everyone, content to do what strikes their fancy, from beekeeping to arts and crafts. This is a state that is very much Americana.

The Indianian likes to celebrate holidays, loves parades and picnics. He is neighborly and invites tourists to come and enjoy his state with him.

The weather most of the year is warm and enjoyable. Winter months get their share of the snow and cold.

INDIANA

Angola *

Goranson, Betty
1245 So. Golden Lake Rd.,
46703
(219) 665-2690

Amenities: 1,2,9,10,11,16,17
Breakfast: F.

Dbl. Oc.: $39.59 - $55.64
Sgl. Oc.: $28.89 - $44.94
Third Person: $10.07
Child: Under 3 yrs. - no charge

Sycamore Hill B&B—Two-story colonial pillared home. Built 29 years ago by a master craftsman. Tucked away amid rolling meadows and woods with walking trails. Picnic tables in a shady back yard are at your disposal. Swimming, golf and canoeing are close by. Six minute drive to state park.

Bluffton

Harris, Bonnie
411 W. Market St., 46714
(219) 824-4619

Amenities: 1,2,7,9,10,11,12,
13,14,15,16,18
Breakfast: F.

Dbl. Oc.: $57.75
Sgl. Oc.: $42.00
Third Person: $15.75

Wisteria Manor—Century-old Victorian mansion in historic area. Enjoy the six fireplaces, leaded - glass windows and ornate staircase. Furnished in period furniture with private garden and pool. Gracious hospitality and home-cooked meals. Walking distance of downtown.

Chesterton *

Wilk, Timothy
350 Indian Boundary Rd., 46304
(219) 926-5781

Amenities: 2,5,6,7,8,9,10,11,12,13,14,15,16,18
Breakfast: F.
Dbl. Oc.: $82.50 - $93.50
Sgl Oc.: $71.50 - $82.50
Third Person: $11.00
Child: $11.00

Gray Goose Inn—English country house on 100 wooded acres. Individually decorated rooms, private baths, fireplaces and suites. In- room phones, TV, walking trails, bikes and boats. Gateway to Dunes National Lakeshore. Near I-94, 80 and 90; 50 minutes to Chicago, three hours to Indianapolis.

Corydon *

Wiseman, Blaine H.
P.O. Box 95
Capitol and Chestnut Sts.,47112
(812) 738-2020, (812) 738-7430

Amenities: 1,2,5,6,7,9,10,11,
16
Breakfast: F.

Dbl. Oc.: $39.00 - $89.00
Sgl. Oc.: $39.00 - $69.00
Third Person: $15.00
Child: Under 12 yrs. - no charge

Kintner House Inn—First state capital building. Listed in National Register of Historic Places. Located in historic downtown Corydon. Unique shops, fine restaurants, antique malls and horse-drawn carriage rides. Excursion train, village blacksmith and art glass factory are within walking.

1. No Smoking	5. Tennis Available	9. Credit Cards Accepted	13. Lunch Available	17. Shared Baths
2. No Pets	6. Golf Available	10. Personal Check Accepted	14. Conference Rooms Avail.	18. Afternoon Tea
3 Off Season Rates	7. Swimmming Avail.	11. Reservations Necessary	15. Group Seminars Avail.	* Commisions given
4. Senior Citizen Rates	8. Skiing Available	12. Dinner Available	16. Private Baths	to Travel Agents

INDIANA

Fort Wayne *

Fiandt, Beverly
704 Rockhill St., 46802
1647 Fairhill Rd., 46808(mail)

Amenities: 1,2,4,11,14,16

Breakfast: F.

Dbl. Oc.: $58.00 - $68.00
Sgl. Oc.: $48.00 - $58.00
Third Person: $10.00

The Carole Lombard House—A comfortable home adjacent to downtown Fort Wayne in west central neighborhood. Located on teh 20 Mile River Greenway System (bikes available) close to museums, fort, sporting events, theatres, antiquing, geneology, parks and great restaurants. Exercise room.

Fort Wayne *

Smith, Dee
8214 Maysvill Rd., 46815
(219) 493-8814

Amenities: 1,2,3,4,10,11,16,18
Breakfast: F.
Dbl. Oc.: $40.00 - $70.00
Sgl. Oc.: $35.00 - $65.00
Third Person: $15.00

Maysville Manor—The warmth and beauty of the past with conveniences of the present. A 150-year-old, elegantly furnished Victorian home on one acre of beautifully landscaped grounds. Relax before a glowing fire, in a hot tub, or in the wicker fern room.

Huntington *

Gernand, Jean
326 So. Jefferson, 46750
(219) 356-4218, (219) 356-9215

Amenities: 1,2,10,12,13,14,15,16,17
Breakfast: F.
Dbl. Oc.: $42.00 - $52.50
Sgl Oc.: $36.75 - $42.00
Third Person: $5.25
Child: under 8 yrs. - $3.25

Purviance House Bed And Breakfast—An 1859 Italianate/Greek Revival listed in National Register of Historic Places. Lovingly restored and decorated. Comfy beds, TV, books, complimentary snacks; beverages. Near nature trails, lakes and golf. On SR 5 and U.S. 224, just off I-69 and US 24 near Ft. Wayne.

1. No Smoking	5. Tennis Available	9. Credit Cards Accepted	13. Lunch Available	17. Shared Baths
2. No Pets	6. Golf Available	10. Personal Check Accepted	14. Conference Rooms Avail.	18. Afternoon Tea
3 Off Season Rates	7. Swimming Avail.	11. Reservations Necessary	15. Group Seminars Avail.	* Commisions given
4. Senior Citizen Rates	8. Skiing Available	12. Dinner Available	16. Private Baths	to Travel Agents

Indianapolis *

Morris, Joan H.
7161 Edgewater Pl., 46240
(317) 257-2660

Amenities: 1,2,10,11,16,18
Breakfast: F.

Dbl. Oc.: $73.00 - $98.00
Sgl. Oc.: $67.00 - $75.00
Third Person: $20.00

The Nuthatch B&B—B&B home in a resort-like setting, minutes from downtown. A 1920s French country cottage with arched windows and leaded-glass doors. The Nutwatch overlooks scenic White River. Romantic hideaway. Exciting breakfasts. Rates change for 500 Mile Race and NCAA. Herb and flower garden.

Jasper

Roach, Gail
429 W. Haysville Rd., 47546
(812) 695-4500

Amenities: 1,11,16,17
Breakfast: C.

Dbl. Oc.: $45.00
Sgl. Oc.: $40.00
Third Person: $10.00
Child: Under 6 yrs. - $8.00

The Artist's Studio Bed And Breakfast—Spacious 1920s bungalow with oak floors and woodwork, period furniture and antiques. Home of watercolor artist Gail Roach. Close to antique shops, Archabbey, Patoka Lake, Holiday World and Lincoln Land. Local art on display. Enjoy the rolling hills of southern Indiana.

Ligonier

Blue, Doris & Ronald
508 So. Cavin St., 46767
(219) 894-3668

Amenities: 1,2,3,9,10,16,18
Breakfast: C.

Dbl. Oc.: $47.25 - $57.75
Sgl. Oc.: $42.00
Third Person: $20.00

Solomon Mier Manor Bed And Breakfast—This home is in the National Historic Register. Located in the center of Amish country. A Queen Anne classic completely furnished with antiques of the era. Enjoy the history of Ligonier and browse the antique shop. Relax and step back into history with us!

Middlebury *

Eash, Diane & Carl
205 So. Main St., 46540
(219) 825-9666

Amenities: 1,2,3,5,6,9,10,16
Breakfast: C. Plus

Dbl. Oc.: $68.25
Sgl. Oc.: $63.00
Third Person: $10.50
Child: $10.50

Varns Guest House—Circa 1898, this fourth-generation family home has been lovingly restored to feature five bedrooms with private baths. Located in the heart of Amish country. Enjoy many fine restaurants and quaint shops nearby. Relax on the porch swing as horse-drawn buggies clip along.

1. No Smoking	5. Tennis Available	9. Credit Cards Accepted	13. Lunch Available	17. Shared Baths
2. No Pets	6. Golf Available	10. Personal Check Accepted	14. Conference Rooms Avail.	18. Afternoon Tea
3 Off Season Rates	7. Swimmming Avail.	11. Reservations Necessary	15. Group Seminars Avail.	* Commisions given
4. Senior Citizen Rates	8. Skiing Available	12. Dinner Available	16. Private Baths	to Travel Agents

Middlebury

Swarm, Treva & Herb
Box 1191, 46540
(219) 825-5023

Amenities: 1,2,6,8,9,10,15,16, 17
Breakfast: F.

Dbl. Oc.: $49.95 - $65.00
Sgl. Oc.: $39.95
Third Person: $15.00

Bee Hive Bed And Breakfast—Located in an Amish community. Easy access to Indiana Turnpike. Snuggle under handmade quilts in a country home and wake up to the smell of muffins baking. Come prepared to relax and enjoy a quiet evening with a glass of iced tea.

Middlebury *

Yoder, Evelyn
504 So. Main
P.O. Box 1396, 46540
(219) 825-2378

Amenities: 1,2,3,7,9,10,11, 17
Breakfast: F.

Dbl. Oc.: $52.50
Sgl. Oc.: $42.00
Third Person: $15.75
Child: Under 12 yrs. - $10.50

Yoder's Zimmer Mit Fruhstuck Haus—The Yoders enjoy sharing their Amish-Mennonite heritage in their beautiful Crystal Valley home, located in the heart of Indiana's Amish country near the Shipshewana Flea Market. Their home is filled with various collections and antiques.

Nashville *

Shirley, Suanne
St. Rd. 135 N, R.R. 3
Box 62, 47448
(812) 988-4537

Amenities: 2,3,5,6,7,8,9,10, 11,17
Breakfast: C. Plus

Dbl. Oc.: $66.00 - $71.50
Sgl. Oc.: $55.00 - $60.50
Third Person: $16.50
Child: Under 10 yrs. - no charge

Plain And Fancy/Traveler's Accommodations And—Country Store Turn-of-the-century log home; protected natural environment. Walking distance of Brown County's renowned arts and shopping center. Nearby entertainment, golf, swimming, fishing, boating and skiing. A quiet weekend retreat.

Paoli

Cornwell, Terry
210 No. Gospel, 47454
(812) 723-4677

Amenities: 5,6,7,8,9,10,11,15, 16
Breakfast: F.

Dbl. Oc.: $68.25
Sgl. Oc.: $47.25

Baxton House Inn—Thomas Braxton, son of the original Quaker settlers, was a businessman who built this 1893 Victorian home. Oak, cherry, chestnut and maple woodwork are featured. The inn is furnished in antiques and highlighted with stained-glass windows.

1. No Smoking	5. Tennis Available	9. Credit Cards Accepted	13. Lunch Available	17. Shared Baths
2. No Pets	6. Golf Available	10. Personal Check Accepted	14. Conference Rooms Avail.	18. Afternoon Tea
3 Off Season Rates	7. Swimmming Avail.	11. Reservations Necessary	15. Group Seminars Avail.	* Commisions given
4. Senior Citizen Rates	8. Skiing Available	12. Dinner Available	16. Private Baths	to Travel Agents

INDIANA

Peru *

Henderson, Zoyla & Carm
54 N. Hood, 46970
(317) 472-7151

Amenities: 1,4,5,6,7,8,9,10, 11,14,15,16
Breakfast: F.

Dbl. Oc.: $60.00 - $68.00
Sgl. Oc.: $55.00 - $60.00
Third Person: $15.00
Child: Under 12 yrs. - $10.00

Rosewood Mansion - A Bed And Breakfast Inn—Only three blocks from the center of town, this 1862 mansion surrounds you in elegance with its grand staircase, oak-paneled library and oval dining room. The large guest rooms are decorated in antiques. Nearby are many sport activities and attractions such as the Air Force Museum.

Rockville

McCullough, Bob & Ann
514 N. College, 47872
(317) 569-5660

Amenities: 1,2,10,16,17
Breakfast: C. Plus

Dbl. Oc.: $49.50 - $60.50
Sgl. Oc.: $49.50 - $60.50
Third Person: $11.00
Child: $11.00

Suits Us" Bed And Breakfast—Located in the heart of scenic Parke Co. Enjoy our warm hospitality in a beautiful plantation-style home. We are located within 10 minutes of Turkey Run St. Park and Billie Creek Village. Each room equipped with a color TV. Free refreshments available.

Syracuse

Kennedy, Jean & Robert
11007 No. St. Rd. 13, 46567
(219) 457-4714

Amenities: 1,2,6,7,9,16,17
Breakfast: F.

Dbl. Oc.: $55.00 - $71.50
Sgl. Oc.: $46.75

Anchor Inn Bed And Breakfast—Centrally located between South Bend and Fort Wayne, in the heart of Indiana's lake country. Lake Wawasee, Amish area and antique shops nearby. Five guest rooms. Open year round.

1. No Smoking	5. Tennis Available	9. Credit Cards Accepted	13. Lunch Available	17. Shared Baths
2. No Pets	6. Golf Available	10. Personal Check Accepted	14. Conference Rooms Avail.	18. Afternoon Tea
3 Off Season Rates	7. Swimmming Avail.	11. Reservations Necessary	15. Group Seminars Avail.	* Commisions given
4. Senior Citizen Rates	8. Skiing Available	12. Dinner Available	16. Private Baths	to Travel Agents

IOWA

The Hawkeye State

Capitol: Des Moines
Statehood: December 28, 1846; the 29th state
State Motto: "Our Liberties We Prize and Our
　　　　　Rights We Will Maintain"
State Song: "The Song of Iowa"
State Bird: Eastern Goldfinch
State Flower: Wild Rose
State Tree: Oak

Iowa is one of the greatest farming states in the United States, sometimes called the "Corn State", or "The Land Where the Tall Corn Grows". Back in the mid-1800's many young people heeded the advice of Horace Greeley to " Go west, young man, go west", and they did. It was the beginning of a great love affair between man and the soil. Some of the most productive corn farms are here and some of the best-fed livestock.

Iowa has many lakes and streams that offer fine fishing and swimming, but the greatest excitement of the year is the annual Iowa State Fair. Farmers from all over Iowa gather together to show their personal farm prizes, from hogs to preserves, each one competing for the coveted Blue Ribbon.

Herbert Hoover, our 31st president, was born in West Branch, Iowa.

Amana Colonies

Janda, Sheila & Don
Main St. Homestead, 52236
(319) 622-3937

Amenities: 1,3,5,6,7,8,9,10,14,15,16
Breakfast: F.
Dbl. Oc.: $39.19 - $68.62
Sgl Oc.: $39.19 - $68.62
Third Person: $5.45
Child: Under 6yrs. - $3.27

Die Heimat Country Inn—Built in 1854, this charming inn is decorated with Amana walnut and cherry furniture, quilts and antiques. The inn is located in the famous Amana Colonies. Walnut canopy beds available. An ideal getaway with warm hospitality.

Atlantic *

Stensvad, Barbara
1409 Chestnut St., 50022
(712) 243-5652

Amenities: 1,2,5,6,7,9,12,16, 17
Breakfast: F.

Dbl. Oc.: $57.20 - $78.00
Sgl. Oc.: $46.80 - $67.60
Third Person: $10.00

Chestnut Charm Bed And Breakfast—Relax and relish your time in this enchanting 1898 Victorian manor with serene surroundings. Enjoy warm Iowa hospitality and exquisite gourmet meals. Five elegant guest rooms. Come, relax and be pampered in style!

Bentonsport *

McDermet, Sheral & Bill
Rte. 2, Box 237, Keosauqua, 52565
(319) 592-3133

Amenities: 1,2,3,6,7,9,10,11, 12,13,14,15,16,17
Breakfast: F.

Dbl. Oc.: $43.00 - $69.00
Sgl. Oc.: $33.00 - $58.00
Third Person: $10.00

Mason House Inn—Built to serve steamboat travelers in 1846 by Mormons on their famous trek to Utah. We think Abe Lincoln and Mark Twain slept here - we know you can. Antiques, blacksmith, potter, glass sculptor, artists and canoeing. Cookie jar in every room.

Calmar

Kruse, Lucille B.
103 N. St.
RR 1, Box 206, 52132
(319) 562-3851

Amenities: 1,2,5,6,7,8,9,10, 11,17
Breakfast: F.

Dbl. Oc.: $47.25
Sgl. Oc.: $42.00
Child: Under 5 yrs. - no charge

Calmar Guesthouse—Newly remodeled Victorian home; neat and clean; good food, warm hospitality. Near Luther College, Decorah, NICC Community College, world-famous Billy Clocks, Laura Ingalls museum, world's smallest church, Niagara and Spook Caves, Norweigian American Museum and many beautiful parks.

1. No Smoking	5. Tennis Available	9. Credit Cards Accepted	13. Lunch Available	17. Shared Baths
2. No Pets	6. Golf Available	10. Personal Check Accepted	14. Conference Rooms Avail.	18. Afternoon Tea
3 Off Season Rates	7. Swimmming Avail.	11. Reservations Necessary	15. Group Seminars Avail.	* Commisions given
4. Senior Citizen Rates	8. Skiing Available	12. Dinner Available	16. Private Baths	to Travel Agents

IOWA

Clayton *

Bonomolo, Karilyn
R.R. 2, Box 125A, 52049
(319) 964-2776

Amenities: 2,4,6,8,9,10,12,16,17
Breakfast: F.
Dbl. Oc.: $63.00
Sgl Oc: $31.50
Third Person: $5.25
Child: Under 12 yrs. - no charge

Claytonian Inn—Along the Mississippi River located on the Great River Road. Unsurpassed beauty surrounded by bluffs. Each suite has a river view. Full breakfast, complimentary wine, soda, hot tub, ample parking for boats and trailers. Cable TV in each room. Antiques. Parks nearby.

Colo *

Kash, Martha
620 W. St., 50056
(515) 377-2586

Amenities: 1,5,6,10,16,18
Breakfast: F.

Dbl. Oc.: $45.00
Sgl. Oc.: $40.00
Third Person: $10.00
Child: $10.00

Martha's Vineyard—Feel pampered like a visit to Gramma's house! Short drive from Ames (US #35). Experience gracious country living, homemade and home-grown foods featured. Wildlife area and gardens. Very quiet. Open April - October.

Council Bluffs

Smith, Dorothea
327 9th Ave., 51503
(712) 323-1649

Amenities: 1,2,5,6,7,9,10,14, 17
Breakfast: F.

Dbl. Oc.: $55.00
Sgl. Oc.: $50.00
Third Person: $5.00
Child: Under 5 yrs. - no charge

Robin's Nest Inn Bed And Breakfast—Located in historic area, boasts Italianate architecture, hand-stenciled decor, walking distance of Dodge House. Bicycling, stenciling, theatre packages with advanced notice. Innkeeper knowledgeable on local points of interest.

---

1. No Smoking	5. Tennis Available	9. Credit Cards Accepted	13. Lunch Available	17. Shared Baths
2. No Pets	6. Golf Available	10. Personal Check Accepted	14. Conference Rooms Avail.	18. Afternoon Tea
3 Off Season Rates	7. Swimmming Avail.	11. Reservations Necessary	15. Group Seminars Avail.	* Commisions given
4. Senior Citizen Rates	8. Skiing Available	12. Dinner Available	16. Private Baths	to Travel Agents

IOWA

Dubuque *

Delaney, Michelle
1492 Locust St., 52001
(319) 557-1492

Amenities: 1,2,3,9,10,11,14,16,17,18
Breakfast: F.
Dbl. Oc.: $44.80 - $106.40
Sgl Oc.: $44.80 - $76.30
Third Person: $16.800
Child: Under 10 yrs. - $11.20

The Richards House—An 1883 stick-style mansion. Original interior features over 80 stained-glass windows, seven varieties of woodwork, embossed wallcoverings and period furnishings. Working fireplaces and queen-size beds in guest rooms. Mid-week discounts.

Dubuque *

Oswald, Jan
199 Loras Blvd., 52001
(319) 556-0069

Amenities: 1,3,5,6,8,9,10,14, 15,16,17
Breakfast: F.

Dbl. Oc.: $76.00 - $106.00
Sgl. Oc.: $70.00 - $100.00

The Mandolin Inn—Tarry awhile amid Edwardian columns, beveled and stained-glass windows, parquet and mosaic floors. A perfect place to kindle and rekindle romance. Enjoy a sumptuous breakfast served to strains of Mozart in a magnificent dining room. Ideally located downtown.

Fort Madison *

Reinhard, Myrna
707 Avenue H. (Hwy. 61), 52627
(800) 441-2327, (319) 372-7074

Amenities: 1,2,3,4,6,9,10,11,14,15,16
Breakfast: C. Plus
Dbl. Oc.: $71.00 - $115.00
Sgl Oc.: $71.00 - $115.00
Third Person: $11.00
Child: Under 12 yrs. - no charge

Kingsley Inn—Yesterday's charm - today's luxury! Historic Victorian inn on the Mississippi River. Near 1808 fort, antiques, galleries, marina, parks, steam engine, 10 minutes to 1840s historic Nauvoo, IL. "Williamsburg of the Midwest." Whirlpool, phones, CATV, AC, special breakfast. Elevator.

1. No Smoking	5. Tennis Available	9. Credit Cards Accepted	13. Lunch Available	17. Shared Baths
2. No Pets	6. Golf Available	10. Personal Check Accepted	14. Conference Rooms Avail.	18. Afternoon Tea
3 Off Season Rates	7. Swimmming Avail.	11. Reservations Necessary	15. Group Seminars Avail.	* Commisions given
4. Senior Citizen Rates	8. Skiing Available	12. Dinner Available	16. Private Baths	to Travel Agents

Greenfield *

Wilson, Wendy
RR 1, Box 132, 50849
(515) 743-2031

Amenities: 1,7,10,11,16
Breakfast: F.

Dbl. Oc.: $68.00 - $79.00
Sgl. Oc.: $68.00 - $79.00
Third Person: $15.00
Child: Under 12 yrs. - no charge

The Wilson Home—A huge indoor pool and spacious guest rooms that open onto the beautiful pool decks make this country B&B truly unique. Excellent pheasant hunting packages available. Antiques close by located just 15 minutes off I-80 between Des Moines and Amana.

Iowa City *

Haverkamp, Dorothy & Clarence
619 N. Linn St., 52245
(319) 337-4363

Amenities: 1,2,10,17
Breakfast: F.

Dbl. Oc.: $32.50 - $43.50
Sgl. Oc.: $27.25 - $38.25
Third Person: $5.00
Child: Under 2 yrs. - no charge

Haverkamps' Linn Street Homestay—Large, comfortable 1908 Edwardian-style home filled with antiques and collections. Front porch/swing. One mile south off I-80, Exit 244. Close to University of Iowa campus. Short drive to Amana Colonies, Kalona, West Branch and Cedar Rapids.

Lake View *

Glines, Sandi & Jerry
306 5th St.
P.O. Box 292 (mail), 51450
(712) 657-2535

Amenities: 1,3,4,6,7,9,10,11,
12,13,16
Breakfast: C.

Dbl. Oc.: $45.00
Sgl. Oc.: $45.00
Third Person: $10.00
Child: Under 13 yrs. - no charge

Armstrong Inn—Just four blocks from Black Hawk Lake. Large Victorian home built in 1897 by founders of Lake View. Many antiques plus modern comforts. Sunbed on site. Restaurants, shops, fishing, boating, sailing, mini-golf, go-carts, dancing or just relaxing.

Leighton *

Vander Wilt, Iola
1345 Hwy. 163, 50143
(515) 626-3092

Amenities: 2,3,4,6,8,10,11,16,
18
Breakfast: F.

Dbl. Oc.: $35.00 - $45.00
Sgl. Oc.: $30.00 - $40.00
Third Person: $15.00
Child: Under 8 yrs. - $10.00

Heritage House B&B—Stately country home with three newly decorated guest rooms. TV, air-conditioning, family antiques and gourmet breakfast. Near tourist areas and central Iowa. Pheasant hunters welcome.

1. No Smoking	5. Tennis Available	9. Credit Cards Accepted	13. Lunch Available	17. Shared Baths
2. No Pets	6. Golf Available	10. Personal Check Accepted	14. Conference Rooms Avail.	18. Afternoon Tea
3. Off Season Rates	7. Swimmming Avail.	11. Reservations Necessary	15. Group Seminars Avail.	* Commisions given
4. Senior Citizen Rates	8. Skiing Available	12. Dinner Available	16. Private Baths	to Travel Agents

Marengo *

Walker, Loy
I-80, Exit 216
R.R. 1, Box 82, 52301
(319) 642-7787

Amenities: 1,5,6,7,10,11,12,15,16,17
Breakfast: F.
Dbl. Oc.: $54.50 - $65.40
Sgl Oc.: $43.60
Third Person: $16.35
Child: Under 12 yrs. - $10.90

Loy's Bed And Breakfast—Architecturally beautiful farm home on an operating grain and hog farm. Farm tour, recreation room, outdoor play equipment, gourmet breakfast and fireplace. Hunters welcome. Close to the Amana Colonies, Iowa City, Kalona and Cedar Rapids. Close to I-80.

Middle Amana

Hahn, Lynn
P.O. Box 124, 52307
(319) 622-3029

Amenities: 1,2,6,9,10,16
Breakfast: C.

Dbl. Oc.: $43.05
Sgl. Oc.: $38.15
Third Person: $5.45

Dusk To Dawn Bed And Breakfast Inn—Relax in an old Amana-style setting. Enjoy the comforts of a Jacuzzi, spacious deck,and greenhouse. Private baths, air-conditioning and television.

Missouri Valley *

Strub, Electa
RR 3, Box 129, 51555
(712) 642-2418

Amenities: 1,2,5,6,7,8,9,10, 12,13,14,15,17,18
Breakfast: F.

Dbl. Oc.: $66.00
Sgl. Oc.: $50.00
Child: Under 12 yrs. - $15.00

Apple Orchard Inn Bed And Breakfast—Turn a night away into an experience! Scenic Loess Hills, deck with a view and Jacuzzi. Enjoy Loess Hills, DeSoto Bend, golf, Pioneer Musuem, a walk in the orchard, pick an apple. Meals available. Home-grown wheat in fresh-baked bread with apple butter.

Nevada *

Page, Paula & Phil
1110 Ninth St., 50201
(515) 382-6444

Amenities: 1,2,9,10,11,17
Breakfast: F.

Dbl. Oc.: $63.60 - $79.50
Sgl. Oc.: $63.60 - $79.50

Queen Anne Bed And Breakfast—Victorian home built in 1878 listed in the National Register of Historic Places. Features include papier-mache ceilings, stained-glass windows and parquet floors. Close to Iowa State University at Ames and I-35. Forty minutes north of Des Moines.

1. No Smoking	5. Tennis Available	9. Credit Cards Accepted	13. Lunch Available	17. Shared Baths
2. No Pets	6. Golf Available	10. Personal Check Accepted	14. Conference Rooms Avail.	18. Afternoon Tea
3 Off Season Rates	7. Swimmming Avail.	11. Reservations Necessary	15. Group Seminars Avail.	* Commisions given
4. Senior Citizen Rates	8. Skiing Available	12. Dinner Available	16. Private Baths	to Travel Agents

IOWA

Newton *

Owen, Kay
629 1st. Ave. E., 50208
(515) 792-6833

Amenities: 1,9,10,12,16
Breakfast: F.
Dbl. Oc.: $60.50 - $137.50
Sgl Oc.: $60.50 - $137.50
Third Person: $15.00 - $25.00
Child: $20.00

LaCorsette Maison Inn—Bed and breakfast at its most gracious! Contemporary comforts blend with turn-of-the-century charm in a mission-style "le" mansion. Charming French bed chambers and beckoning hearths. Listed in National Register of Historic Places. Gourmet dining. Off I-80.

Spencer *

Nichols, Mary
Rte. One, Hwy. 71, So., 51301
(712) 262-1286

Amenities: 1,2,5,6,7,8,9,10, 11,12,13,16,18
Breakfast: F.

Dbl. Oc.: $57.75 - $68.25
Sgl. Oc.: $52.75 - $63.25
Third Person: $15.75
Child: Under 10 yrs. - no charge

Hannah Marie Country Inn—Lovingly restored. Time spent here comes gently. Three guest rooms, rocking chairs, porch swing. Country herb garden, air-conditioning. Croquet. Near Iowa's great lakes. Seen in: Midwest Living, Iowan, and Country Woman. "Best B&B in Iowa," 1990.

Walnut

Reddie, Sylvia
400 Central
P.O. Box 584, 51577
(712) 784-3722

Amenities: 1,2,9,10,12,13,17
Breakfast: F.

Dbl. Oc.: $42.00
Sgl. Oc.: $42.00
Third Person: $10.00

Antique City Inn Bed And Breakfast—Victorian home built in 1911 has been restored to its original state. Enjoy nostalgic experience of life, craftmanship of yesterday, quiet living and small-town hospitality. Stroll through antique shops and enjoy an unchanged atmosphere of yesterday.

1. No Smoking	5. Tennis Available	9. Credit Cards Accepted	13. Lunch Available	17. Shared Baths
2. No Pets	6. Golf Available	10. Personal Check Accepted	14. Conference Rooms Avail.	18. Afternoon Tea
3 Off Season Rates	7. Swimmming Avail.	11. Reservations Necessary	15. Group Seminars Avail.	* Commisions given
4. Senior Citizen Rates	8. Skiing Available	12. Dinner Available	16. Private Baths	to Travel Agents

KANSAS

The Sunflower State

Capitol: Topeka
Statehood: January 29, 1861; the 34th state
State Motto: "To The Stars Through Difficulties"
State Song: "Home On The Range"
State Bird: Western Meadow Lark
State Flower: Sunflower
State Tree: Cottonwood

Kansas is know as The Wheat State and The Breadbasket of America. It leads all other states in the production of wheat. The farmer is cowboy and rancher who grows cattle and grain at the same time. The wheat at harvest time stands so tall that it makes the land look like a huge sea of gold. It is a beautiful sight to see. In Kansas, wheat harvesting is the biggest part of farming. Machines roll through the fields, cutting and producing bushels of grain every minute.

Kansas is also nicknamed Cowboy Capitol of the World, suggesting Kansas' background as a cattle country. One of its most famous cities is Dodge. Visitors can see ruts made by wagons on the Santa Fe Trail. They can visit Pony Express stations and frontier forts, which were built to protect settlers from the Indians. Kansas is proud of its history and tries to keep a bit of it for all to enjoy.

Dwight D. Eisenhower's boyhood home is preserved at Abilene.

KANSAS

Columbus

Meriwether, Margaret
322 W. Pine, 66725
(316) 429-2812

Amenities: 1,2,5,6,7,9,10,16, 17
Breakfast: C.

Dbl. Oc.: $32.00 - $43.00
Sgl. Oc.: $27.00 - $38.00
Third Person: $5.00

Meriwether House Bed And Breakfast—Located in beautiful S.E. Kansas, just two hours from Kansas City, Tulsa and Springfield. A quiet cottage filled with antiques and goodies, all for sale. Interior decor shop located within. Excellent fishing area. Small-town "friendliness and peaceful comfort."

Concordia *

Thompson, Marvel Jean
508 W. 7th St., 66901
(913) 243-2192

Amenities: 1,2,5,6,7,9,10,14, 16,17
Breakfast: C.

Dbl. Oc.: $35.00 - $45.00
Sgl. Oc.: $35.00 - $45.00
Third Person: $5.00
Child: under 5 yrs. - no charge

Crystle's Bed And Breakfast—Hospitality and charm overflowing! A beautiful 1889 Victorian home on a tree-lined avenue. Discover historic Concordia. Theatres, restaurants and museums nearby.

Wakefield

Nuttall, Phyllis & Dick
201 Dogwood
P.O. Box 342, 67487
(913) 461-5732

Amenities: 5,6,7,10,11,12,17
Breakfast: F.

Dbl. Oc.: $35.00 - $45.00
Sgl. Oc.: $30.00 - $40.00
Third Person: $15.00
Child: under 10 yrs. - $10.00

The Rock House Bed'n Breakfast—Oak warmth. Built in 1914. Gift shop. Three blocks through park to Milford Lake. Across the street from public pool. Fenced patio. Near arboretum and antique shops. Share entire home and craft room. Brochure available.

Wichita

Eaton, Roberta
3910 E. Kellogg, 67218
(316) 689-8101

Amenities: 2,9,10,14,15,16
Breakfast: C.
Dbl. Oc.: $78.33 - $139.88
Sgl Oc.: $61.55 - $106.31
Third Person: $15.00
Child: $15.00

Max Paul...An Inn—Three English Tudor cottages that include 14 rooms furnished with European antiques, featherbeds and Cable/HBO. Some suites have fireplace, decks and "tub for two." Exercise room and spa opens onto garden. Centrally located for business, shopping, parks, and museums.

---

1. No Smoking
2. No Pets
3 Off Season Rates
4. Senior Citizen Rates

5. Tennis Available
6. Golf Available
7. Swimmming Avail.
8. Skiing Available

9. Credit Cards Accepted
10. Personal Check Accepted
11. Reservations Necessary
12. Dinner Available

13. Lunch Available
14. Conference Rooms Avail.
15. Group Seminars Avail.
16. Private Baths

17. Shared Baths
18. Afternoon Tea
* Commisions given
  to Travel Agents

KENTUCKY

The Blue Grass State

Capitol: Frankfort
Statehood: January 1, 1792; the 15th state
State Motto: "United We Stand, Divided We Fall"
State Song: "My Old Kentucky Home"
State Bird: Cardinal
State Flower: Goldenrod
State Tree: Kentucky Coffee Tree

Kentucky is a beautiful and diverse state. Lexington, the home of thoroughbred horses and horse farms, provides hundreds of people with work. Churchill Downes is one of Kentucky's biggest tourist attractions. During the horse racing season, people come from all over the world just for the thrill of seeing these beautiful horses compete against each other. This is Old Kentucky at its best!

Southwest Kentucky is an area of caves formed by huge underground deposits of limestone. One of the caves often visited by tourists is The Mammoth. It stretches out and runs underground like a suburban city's subway.

The eastern part of Kentucky is Appalachia, named for the Appalachian Mountains. Here people exist differently. Their employment depends almost entirely upon the mining of coal. This is the most important commodity in this region, and it brings good times and bad.

Tobacco growing and bourbon whiskey are also big business.

Kentucky has a steady influx of tourists because it is such a pretty and interesting state. It also claims to have mild and comfortable weather most of the time.

KENTUCKY

Bardstown *

McCoy, Fran
111 W. Stephen Foster Ave., 40004
(502) 348-3703

Amenities: 1,2,9,16
Breakfast: C. Plus

Dbl. Oc.: $70.00 - $77.00
Sgl. Oc.: $70.00 - $77.00
Third Person: $10.00

Jailer's Inn—Unique experience! Used as a jail until 1987. Completely renovated and decorated with heirlooms and antiques. All private baths. Located in center of Bardstown. Come spend time in our wonderful jail.

Bowling Green

Hunter, Ronna Lee
1415 Beddington Way, 42104
(502) 781-3861

Amenities: 1,2,10,11,16,17, 18
Breakfast: F. or C. Plus

Dbl. Oc.: $55.00
Sgl. Oc.: $44.00

Bowling Green Bed And Breakfast—Comfortable bedrooms in antique decor await you in a new, quiet neighborhood. Near I-65, Mammoth Cave, Western Kentucky University, restaurants, shopping and activities. Hosts enjoy travel, music, theater and coordinate foreign exchange program. Deck and patio to enjoy. TV. Library.

Bowling Green *

Livingston, Dr. & Mrs. David
5310 Morgantown Rd., 42101
(502) 843-4846

Amenities: 2,4,5,6,7,10,11,12, 13,15,16,17,18
Breakfast: F.

Dbl. Oc.: $49.50
Sgl. Oc.: $39.50
Third Person: $10.00
Child: Under 12 yrs. - $10.00

Alpine Lodge—Handsomely decorated with timely and traditional antiques suited to express all the comforts of home. There are 12 spacious rooms that can accommodate up to 19 guests visiting the area sights of Western Kentucky University, Mammoth Cave, Shakertown, Opryland and museum.

Carrollton

Gants, Judy & Bill
406 Highland Ave., 41008
(502) 732-4210

Amenities: 2,4,5,6,7,8,9,10, 11,16
Breakfast: F.

Dbl. Oc.: $65.50
Sgl. Oc.: $49.10
Third Person: $10.95
Child: Under 10 yrs. - $5.45

P.T. Baker House—Be a pampered guest at a beautifully restored and appointed century-old Victorian home in a charming historic district. Easy walk to antique and craft shops; two miles from state park; mid-way between Cincinnati and Louisville. A unique experience — an ideal getaway.

Covington *

Moorman, Bernard
215 Garrrd St., 41011
(606) 431-2118

Amenities: 4,9,10,14,15,16
Breakfast: F.

Dbl. Oc.:$68.00 - $110.00
Sgl. Oc.:$58.00 - $100.00
Third Person: $10.00
Child: Under 12 yrs.- $10.00

Log Cabin Bed And Breakfast—Neighborly, posh. quiet and comfortable. Located in the heart of Covington's Riverside historic district. A restful getaway. Set in an area of dooryard gardens and buildings that resemble England's Chelsea, overlooking the River Thames. A 15-minute walk to Cincinnati.

1. No Smoking	5. Tennis Available	9. Credit Cards Accepted	13. Lunch Available	17. Shared Baths
2. No Pets	6. Golf Available	10. Personal Check Accepted	14. Conference Rooms Avail.	18. Afternoon Tea
3 Off Season Rates	7. Swimmming Avail.	11. Reservations Necessary	15. Group Seminars Avail.	* Commisions given
4. Senior Citizen Rates	8. Skiing Available	12. Dinner Available	16. Private Baths	to Travel Agents

KENTUCKY

Georgetown

McKnight, Janis & Clay
350 N. Broadway, 40324
(502) 863-3514

Amenities: 5,10,16
Breakfast: C. Plus

Dbl. Oc.: $69.76
Sgl. Oc.: $69.76
Third Person: $15.00
Child: Under 12 yrs. - $10.00

Log Cabin Bed And Breakfast—Enjoy this Kentucky log cabin (circa 1809). Shake roof and chinked logs. Completely private. Two bedrooms, fireplace and fully equipped kitchen. Five miles to Kentucky Horse Park and 12 miles north of Lexington. Children welcome.

Georgetown *

Porter, Annette & Felice
201 S. Broadway, 40324
(502) 863-3163

Amenities: 9,10,11,16
Breakfast: F.

Dbl. Oc.: $70.85
Sgl. Oc.: $58.50
Third Person: $5.00
Child: Under 5 yrs. - no charge

Breckinridge House Bed And Breakfast—Historic Georgian home (1820). In Historic Register. Two suites available - each with bedroom, sitting room, kitchen and bath. Furnished with antiques. Kentucky horse park less than five miles away, fourteen miles north of Lexington.

Glasgow *

Carter, Henry
4107 Scottsville Rd., 42141
(502) 678-1000

Amenities: 1,2,4,7,9,10,15, 16
Breakfast: C.

Dbl. Oc.: $52.47 - $63.07
Sgl. Oc.: $52.47 - $63.07
Third Person: 5.30
Child: Under 6 yrs. - no charge

Four Seasons Country Inn—A luxurious inn built in 1989. All 17 rooms are furnished with antique reproductions and queen-size, four-poster beds, as well as modern amenities. Near Mammoth Cave, Barren River State Park and fine restaurants. Situated on three acres. Two miles from town on Highway 31-E.

Hazel *

Parks, Sheri & Max
P.O. Box 4, 42049
(502) 436-5858

Amenities: 3,5,6,7,9,10,11,12,13,16
Breakfast: F.
Dbl. Oc.: $100.00
Sgl Oc.: $75.00
Third Person: $10.00
Child: Under 6 yrs. - no charge

Outback Bed And Breakfast—Lakeside chalet country hideaway. Perfect for honeymooners, a weekend getaway or a week of serious fishing. Boat ramp, dock, picnic area, complete kitchen and a hot tub. A place you will never want to leave.

1. No Smoking	5. Tennis Available	9. Credit Cards Accepted	13. Lunch Available	17. Shared Baths
2. No Pets	6. Golf Available	10. Personal Check Accepted	14. Conference Rooms Avail.	18. Afternoon Tea
3 Off Season Rates	7. Swimmming Avail.	11. Reservations Necessary	15. Group Seminars Avail.	* Commisions given
4. Senior Citizen Rates	8. Skiing Available	12. Dinner Available	16. Private Baths	to Travel Agents

KENTUCKY

Louisville *

Lesher, Marianne
1359 So. Third St., 40208
(502) 635-1574

Amenities: 2,5,9,10,11,14,15, 16,17
Breakfast: C. Plus

Dbl. Oc.: $60.00 - $195.00
Sgl. Oc.: $55.00 - $155.00
Third Person: $10.00
Child: Under 12 yrs. - no charge

Old Louisville Inn—Wake up to the aroma of home-baked breads, muffins and popovers when you stay in one of our 11 guest rooms or suites. Centrally located between the airport and downtown. Consider us your "home-away-from-home." Specializing in historic neighborhood tours.

Louisville *

Ohlmann, Mary
1353 So. 4th St., 40208
(502) 636-0295

Amenities: 1,2,4,5,6,7,10,11, 12,15,17,18
Breakfast: F.

Dbl. Oc.: $75.00
Sgl. Oc.: $60.00

Rose Blossom—An 1884 18-room Victorian newly decorated and renovated. In the National Register. Located across from the park. Near downtown, the Ohio River, theatres, museums, tennis, carriage, trolley, boat rides, dining, race and golf courses, Univ. of Louisville campus. Beautiful gardens.

Louisville *

Roosa, Nan-Ellen & Stephen A.
1132 So. First St., 40203-2804
(502) 581-1914

Amenities: 2,3,16,17
Breakfast: C.

Dbl. Oc.: $69.00
Sgl. Oc.: $64.00
Third Person: $10.00
Child: Under 5 yrs. - $5.00

The Victorian Secret Bed And Breakfast—This stately 110-year-old Queen Anne brick mansion is restored to its original elegance. Centrally located between the airport and downtown. The spacious 14 rooms, original woodwork and 11 fireplaces will take you back 100 years in time. Easy access to I-65.

Louisville *

Stern, Jr., Walt
Bruce Johnson
1436 St. James Ct., 40208
(502) 636-1742

Amenities: 1,5,7,10,11,16
Breakfast: C. Plus

Dbl. Oc.: $78.00
Sgl. Oc.: $70.00
Third Person: $78.00

St. James Court B&B—Located in the heart of Old Louisville. Gas lights, majestic fountain and village green. An 1895 Georgian Revival. Bedroom, full kitchen, two baths, living room, full deck, piano and swimming pool. Wonderful preservation district. Two miles from Churchill Downs.

Middlesboro *

Richards, Susan
208 Arthur Heights, 40965
(606) 248-4299

Amenities:1,2,6,9,10,15,16,17
Breakfast: F.

Dbl. Oc.:$50.00
Sgl. Oc.:$45.00
Third Person: $16.38

The Riderunner —Nestled in the Cumberland Mountains of S.E. Kentucky, between Pine Mountain State Park and the National Park of Cumberland Gap. A Victorian house emphasizing a view and the peace of yesteryear. View the spectacular spring and fall mountain foliage from our 60-foot front porch.

---

1. No Smoking	5. Tennis Available	9. Credit Cards Accepted	13. Lunch Available	17. Shared Baths
2. No Pets	6. Golf Available	10. Personal Check Accepted	14. Conference Rooms Avail.	18. Afternoon Tea
3 Off Season Rates	7. Swimming Avail.	11. Reservations Necessary	15. Group Seminars Avail.	* Commisions given
4. Senior Citizen Rates	8. Skiing Available	12. Dinner Available	16. Private Baths	to Travel Agents

Morehead

Lake, Betty & Allen
910 Willow Dr., 40351
(606) 784-5421

Amenities: 1,2,10,11,17,18
Breakfast: F.

Dbl. Oc.: $48.00
Sgl. Oc.: $43.00

Appalachian House—A large, one-family home where five children have grown up and left. Our house is part museum and part home. It contains many collections. Betty is a potter. Allen is a wood carver. Both were teachers. Only one mile from I-64, off the Morehead exit.

Paducah

Harris, Beverly & David
201 Broadway, 42001
(502) 442-2698

Amenities: 1,2,3,9,10,14,15 17
Breakfast: C.

Dbl. Oc.: $47.70 - $68.90
Sgl. Oc.: $47.70
Third Person: $5.00

The Riderunner —Nestled in the Cumberland Mountains of S.E. Kentucky, between Pine Mountain State Park and the National Park of Cumberland Gap. A Victorian house emphasizing a view and the peace of yesteryear. View the spectacular spring and fall mountain foliage from our 60-foot front porch.

Versailles

Yawn, Marlin & Sylvia
31 Heritage Rd. (US 60), 40383
(606) 873-7843

Amenities: 1,2,9,10,16
Breakfast: F.

Dbl. Oc.: $68.90
Sgl. Oc.: $63.60
Third Person: $5.30

Shepherd Place—Make yourself comfortable in our pre-Civil War home. Enjoy the lovely scenery while sitting on the porch swing. You may want to look through the brochures in the parlor, or feed the ducks outside, or take a stroll to the barn to pet the resident ewes, Abigail and Victoria.

1. No Smoking	5. Tennis Available	9. Credit Cards Accepted	13. Lunch Available	17. Shared Baths
2. No Pets	6. Golf Available	10. Personal Check Accepted	14. Conference Rooms Avail.	18. Afternoon Tea
3 Off Season Rates	7. Swimmming Avail.	11. Reservations Necessary	15. Group Seminars Avail.	* Commisions given
4. Senior Citizen Rates	8. Skiing Available	12. Dinner Available	16. Private Baths	to Travel Agents

LOUISIANA

The Pelican State

Capitol: Baton Rouge
Statehood: April 30, 1812; the 18th state
State Motto:: "Union, Justice and Confidence"
State Song: "Song Of Louisiana"
State Bird: Brown Pelican
State Flower: Magnolia
State Tree: Bald Cypress

In 1803, the state of Louisiana was part of the Louisiana Purchase from France. The $15,000,000 sale doubled the size of the United States.

French and Spanish speaking people came and settled in New Orleans. Their descendents are referred to as Creoles. Later settlers arrived from Nova Scotia. Henry Wadsworth Longfellow wrote of this journey in his poem, "Evangeline". The Acadians settled in Lafayette City and retained most of their old customs. As a result of this mixture of nationalities and customs, Louisiana and especially the city of New Orleans, is a most colorful and interesting place to visit. Over 4,000,000 tourists come here each year.

The main attraction is the Mardi Gras in New Orleans and the French Quarter. The merrymaking of Carnival commences on Twelfth Night, approximately two weeks before the start of Lent, and it continues until Mardi Gras, the day before Lent starts.

Louisiana is located along the beautiful Gulf of Mexico, with the Mississippi River flowing along its eastern border and through the state to Baton Rouge and New Orleans.

Carencro *

McLemore, Joeann & Fred
825 Kidder Rd., 70520
(318) 896-6529

Amenities: 1,2,7,9,10,11,13,14,16
Breakfast: F.
Dbl. Oc.: $75.10
Sgl Oc.: $75.10
Third Person: $20.60

La Maison de Campagne, Lafayette—Landmark Victorian, "The Country House" is located in the heart of Cajun country, famous for its food, festivals and fun. Pastoral setting 15 minutes from downtown Lafayette. Warm, south Louisiana hospitality awaits you.

Monroe *

LaFrance, Kay & Cliff
185 Cordell Lane, 71202
(318) 325-1550

Amenities: 4,9,10,11,12,13, 16
Breakfast: F.

Dbl. Oc.: $75.00
Sgl. Oc.: $65.00
Third Person: $10.00
Child: Under 12 yrs. - $5.00

Boscobel Cottage—Built in 1820. Listed in the National Register of Historic Places. Stay in a chapel or garconniere and step back in time. Wonderful getaway! Lovely country setting on scenic Ouachita River.

Napoleonville *

Marshall, Millie & Keith
4250 Hwy. 308, 70390
(504) 369-7151

Amenities: 1,2,9,10,11,12,16
Breakfast: C. and F.
Dbl. Oc.: $165.00 (MAP)

Madewood Plantation House—National historic landmark. Greek Revival plantation house on 20 acres, 75 miles from New Orleans. Antiques, canopy beds, wine and cheese. Southern country dinner (family- style) by candlelight included in rate. One hour and 10 minutes to New Orleans Airport. No TV or phones in room.

New Iberia *

Fox, Emma
4018 Old Jeanerette Rd., 70560
(800) 336-7317, (318) 367-7045

Amenities: 1,5,7,10,16
Breakfast: C. Plus

Dbl. Oc.: $65.00 - $90.00
Sgl. Oc.: $60.00 - $85.00
Third Person: $5.00

Pourtos House—Luxurious Acadian plantation estate located on Bayou Teche. Landscaped grounds featuring strolling exotic birds. All guest rooms professionally decorated with each one having a private bath. Historic Acadian cabin, circa 1850, is available as a guest house. Splendid!

1. No Smoking	5. Tennis Available	9. Credit Cards Accepted	13. Lunch Available	17. Shared Baths
2. No Pets	6. Golf Available	10. Personal Check Accepted	14. Conference Rooms Avail.	18. Afternoon Tea
3 Off Season Rates	7. Swimmming Avail.	11. Reservations Necessary	15. Group Seminars Avail.	* Commisions given
4. Senior Citizen Rates	8. Skiing Available	12. Dinner Available	16. Private Baths	to Travel Agents

New Iberia *

Nereaux, Jr., Ernie	**Amenities:** 1,10,12,15,16	**Dbl. Oc.:** $80.00
442 E. Main, 70560	**Breakfast:** F.	**Sgl. Oc.:** $60.00
(318) 364-5922		**Third Person:** $45.00

Masion Marceline—Victorian townhouse, circa 1893. One guest suite with parlor, TV, private bath and Jacuzzi tub. Second bedroom has a queen bed with private bath. Continental breakfast served on the deck or in the library.

New Orleans

Brown, Sarah Margaret	**Amenities:** 1,2,3,4,9,11,16,	**Dbl. Oc.:** $55.00 - $65.00
3660 Gentilly Blvd., 70122	17	**Sgl. Oc.:** $50.00 - $60.00
(504) 947-3401	**Breakfast:** C.	

New Orleans B&B—Safe, convenient area of large 1930s homes on tree-lined boulevard. Off-street parking. On direct bus line to the French Quarter and downtown. Lovely bedroom with private bath; two-bedroom suite with bath; cozy garage apartment.

New Orleans *

Chauppette, Carol	**Amenities:** 2,3,9,10,11,16	**Dbl. Oc.:** $77.00 - $195.00
621 Esplanade, 70116	**Breakfast:** C.	**Sgl. Oc.:** $65.00 - $185.00
(504) 947-1161, (800) 367-5858		**Third Person:** $15.00
		Child: Under 12 yrs. - no charge

Lamothe House—Offers all the "old-South" enchantment one could wish for. Lavish 19th-century antiques. Complimentary Creole "little breakfast" served in an opulent dining room setting. The inn is located on a wide, tree-shaded esplanade street on the eastern boundary of the Quarter.

New Orleans *

Gagnon, Kimily & Gillis	**Amenities:** 2,9,11,16	**Dbl. Oc.:** $75.00
1930 Napolean Ave., 70115	**Breakfast:** C.	**Sgl. Oc.:** $65.00
(504) 897-3746		**Third Person:** $10.00

Beau LeJour—A grand turn-of-the-century mansion located uptown, convenient to the historic streetcar taking visitors to the French Quarter, Convention Center and Superdome. A tropical ambience lends a flavor found only in New Orleans.

New Orleans *

Guyton, Dr. Robert	**Amenities:** 2,3,9,16	**Dbl. Oc.:** $79.00 - $165.00
1003 Bourbon St., 70116	**Breakfast:** C.	**Sgl. Oc.:** $79.00 - $165.00
(504) 581-2678, (800) 331-7971		**Third Person:** $20.00

Lafitte Guest House—Elegant French manor house in the heart of the French Quarter, meticulously restored and furnished in fine antiques. All the comforts of home including air conditioning. Located in quiet residential section of Bourbon St. Complimentary wine and hors d'oeuvres.

1. No Smoking	5. Tennis Available	9. Credit Cards Accepted	13. Lunch Available	17. Shared Baths
2. No Pets	6. Golf Available	10. Personal Check Accepted	14. Conference Rooms Avail.	18. Afternoon Tea
3 Off Season Rates	7. Swimmming Avail.	11. Reservations Necessary	15. Group Seminars Avail.	* Commisions given
4. Senior Citizen Rates	8. Skiing Available	12. Dinner Available	16. Private Baths	to Travel Agents

New Orleans *

Hulin, Alma Fertitta
608 Kerlerec St., 70116
(504) 949-1196, (504) 271-0228

Amenities: 2,3,4,10,11,16
Breakfast: C.

Dbl. Oc.: $65.00 - $125.00
Sgl. Oc.: $65.00 - $125.00
Third Person: $15.00
Child: Under 8 yrs. - no charge

La Maison—Built in 1805 in the historic "Faubourg Marginy" area. It is within walking distance of the French Quarter and many restaurants. Each mini-suite has a double bed, sitting room, phone, color TV and courtyard. Parking is across the street.

New Orleans *

Prigmore, Maralee
2631 Prytania St., 70130
(504) 891-0457

Amenities: 3,9,10,11,14,16
Breakfast: C.

Dbl. Oc.: $75.00 - $175.00
Sgl. Oc.: $68.00 - $157.00

Sully Mansion—Queen Anne, circa 1890, located in the heart of the world-renowned Garden District. A blend of yesterday's antiques and today's comfortable furnishings. Ride the famous St. Charles streetcar to main attractions. Each room unique, 10-foot doors, 12-foot ceilings. A grand staircase.

New Orleans *

Salisbury, Beverly
719 Esplanada Ave., 70116
(504) 948-9328

Amenities: 3,9,10,11,16
Breakfast: C.
Dbl. Oc.: $75.00 - $85.00
Sgl Oc.: $65.00

Quarter Esplanada Guest House—An elegant old New Orleans home located on beautiful Esplanade Ave. Within walking distance oa all the favorite French Quarter nightspots. All rooms have modern kitchens and private baths.

Port Vincent *

Schmieder, Fran
16520 Airport Rd., Prairieville, 70769
(800) 532-2246

Amenities: 1,2,4,7,9,10,11,12, 16
Breakfast: F.

Dbl. Oc.: $100.00
Sgl. Oc.: $100.00

Tree House In The Park—Cajun cabin in the swamp high among the trees. Two bedrooms- private hot tubs on private decks, steps down to pool. Living room, dining room, kitchen area, fireplace for supper and breakfast. Ponds, footbridges and hammock. Fishing dock, float trip, cypress trees. Beautiful.

1. No Smoking	5. Tennis Available	9. Credit Cards Accepted	13. Lunch Available	17. Shared Baths
2. No Pets	6. Golf Available	10. Personal Check Accepted	14. Conference Rooms Avail.	18. Afternoon Tea
3 Off Season Rates	7. Swimmming Avail.	11. Reservations Necessary	15. Group Seminars Avail.	* Commisions given
4. Senior Citizen Rates	8. Skiing Available	12. Dinner Available	16. Private Baths	to Travel Agents

LOUISIANA

Shreveport

Harris, Vicki & Jimmy
2439 Fairfield Ave., 71104
(318) 424-2424

Amenities: 1,2,3,4,9,10,14,15,16
Breakfast: F.
Dbl. Oc.: $85.00 - $125.00

Twenty Four, Thirty Nine Fairfield Ave. B&B—This fabulous home offers Victorian elegance and Southern charm. Decorated in English antiques, down bedding and Amish quilts. Private whirlpool baths. Balconies overlook landscaped gardens with gazebo, park bench, Victorian swing, fountain and lampposts.

St. Francisville *

Butler, Anne
HC 69, Box 438(mail)
U.S.61, 70775
(504) 635-6312

Amenities: 7,10,16
Breakfast: C.
Dbl. Oc.: $75.00
Sgl Oc.: $75.00
Third Person: $10.00
Child: $10.00

Butler Greenwood—A 1796 plantation with extensive oak-shaded grounds and antebellum home. Filled with antiques. Two historic guest cottages on a peaceful pond, quiet and private. Located in the heart of Audubon's Happyland and English plantation country. Bird walks. Host tour included. Swimming pool.

St. Francisville *

Dittloff, Lyle
524 Royal St.
P.O. Box 1461, 70775
(504) 635-4791

Amenities: 2,6,10,12,16
Breakfast: C.

Dbl. Oc.: $82.50 - $104.50
Sgl. Oc.: $71.50
Third Person: $16.50
Child: Under 12 yrs. - $11.00

Barrow House—Circa 1809. Located on historic Royal Street in a neighborhood of antebellum homes. Rooms have period antiques. A cassette walking tour of the historic area is included. Visit seven nearby plantations. Enjoy rockers on the porch and acclaimed gourmet dinners. Golf nearby.

---

1. No Smoking	5. Tennis Available	9. Credit Cards Accepted	13. Lunch Available	17. Shared Baths
2. No Pets	6. Golf Available	10. Personal Check Accepted	14. Conference Rooms Avail.	18. Afternoon Tea
3 Off Season Rates	7. Swimmming Avail.	11. Reservations Necessary	15. Group Seminars Avail.	* Commisions given
4. Senior Citizen Rates	8. Skiing Available	12. Dinner Available	16. Private Baths	to Travel Agents

MAINE

The Pine Tree State

Capitol: Augusta
Statehood: March 15, 1820; the 23rd state
State Motto: "I Direct or I Guide"
State Song: "State of Maine Song"
State Bird: Chickadee
State Flower: White Pine Cone and Tassel
State Tree: White Pine

Of all the New England states, Maine is perhaps the largest and best known for its beautiful Atlantic coastline. Traveling along the rugged coast of Maine, a visitor can see and visit many lighthouses, fishing villages and beautiful sandy beaches.

For hundreds of years, the forest of Maine was the mainstay of its economy and it remains that way today. However, with the modernization of machinery, the business of logging has become much safer. Paper and paper products are Maine's big business.

Maine is also know for growing potatoes. It supplies 8% of the nation's harvest.

Visitors to Maine can enjoy real clambakes. The lobsters and clams for these clambakes are found right in the Maine waters.

Maine's weather for the most part is cool. This kind of weather attracts vacationers in the summer and skiers in the winter. It has become a big vacation area.

Bar Harbor *

Burns, Marian
69 Mt. Desert St., 04609
(207) 288-4263 (in Maine),
(800) 553-5109

Amenities: 2,6,7,9,10,11,15, 16,18
Breakfast: C.
Plus (buffet)

Dbl. Oc.: $97.00 - $160.00
Sgl. Oc.: $97.00 - $160.00
Third Person: $10.00

Mira Monte Inn—A 17-room Victorian in historic corridor. Two acres of exquisite grounds. Friendly, helpful staff. Antiques. Period furniture. King/queen beds, balconies, fireplaces. Walk to waterfront. Breakfast buffet includes eggs, homemade breads, oatmeal and fruit. Open May-Oct.

Bar Harbor

Noyes, Malcom
106 West St., 04609
(207) 288-3759

Amenities: 1,2,5,6,7,8,9,10, 11,15,16
Breakfast: C.

Dbl. Oc.: $74.90 - $160.50
Third Person: $20.00

Manor House Inn—An 1887 Victorian mansion furnished in authentic Victorian style. Several guest rooms have fireplaces and many overlook one acre of lawns and gardens. All the beauty and activities of Acadia National Park are at your doorstep. Walk to shops and restaurants.

Bar Harbor

O'Brien, Norah
39 Holland Ave., 04609
(207) 288-4563, (800) 338-4563

Amenities: 3,5,6,7,9,10,16
Breakfast: C. Plus

Dbl. Oc.: $98.00 - $148.00
Sgl. Oc.: $98.00 - $148.00
Third Person: $25.00

Castlemaine Inn—Victorian charm and gracious hospitality abounds in this fully restored 19th-century inn. Rooms feature queen-size canopy beds and fireplaces. Delightful continental breakfast served daily. Nestled on a quiet side street minutes from Acadia National Park and downtown.

Bar Harbor

Ochtera, Jean & Jack
74 Mt. Desert St., 04609
(207) 288-4970

Amenities: 1,2,3,5,6,7,9,10, 11,14,15,16,18
Breakfast: F.

Dbl. Oc.: $117.70 - $144.45

Holbrook House—An in-town 1876 Victorian summer home on the historic corridor. Within a five-minute walk to shops, restaurants and ocean. One mile to Acadia National Park. Twelve bedrooms, all with private baths. Ample on-premises parking and bicycle storage.

Bar Harbor

Schwartz, Susan & Barry
7 High St., 04609
(207) 288-4533

Amenities: 1,2,3,9,10,16,18
Breakfast: F.

Dbl. Oc.: $80.25 - $117.70
Third Person: $16.05

Hearthside B&B—We invite you to stay in our newly redecorated turn-of-the-century home. Our guest rooms feature a blend of Victorian and traditional pieces. All rooms have queen beds, some have fireplaces and private porches. Conveniently located on a quiet side street in town.

---

1. No Smoking	5. Tennis Available	9. Credit Cards Accepted	13. Lunch Available	17. Shared Baths
2. No Pets	6. Golf Available	10. Personal Check Accepted	14. Conference Rooms Avail.	18. Afternoon Tea
3 Off Season Rates	7. Swimming Avail.	11. Reservations Necessary	15. Group Seminars Avail.	* Commisions given
4. Senior Citizen Rates	8. Skiing Available	12. Dinner Available	16. Private Baths	to Travel Agents

MAINE

Bar Harbor

Suydam, Michele
12 Roberts Ave., 04609
(207) 288-2112

Amenities: 1,2,3,5,6,7,10,15, 16,17
Breakfast: C. Plus

Dbl. Oc.: $69.55 - $85.60

Canterbury Cottage—A Victorian cottage that has been tastefully restored to provide the comfort and modern conveniences of today. Located on a quiet street with a short walk to all shops, restaurants and harbor activities. A five-minute drive to Acadia National Park.

Bath *

Lansky, Gladys
60 Pearl St., 04530
(207) 443-1191

Amenities: 1,2,4,6,9,10,11, 17
Breakfast: C. Plus

Dbl. Oc.: $48.15
Sgl. Oc.: $48.15

Glad II—Come home to a B&B as it was meant to be. Nicholas, my four-legged concierge, will meet you at the door with one of his teddy bears and show you to your room. Beds are comfortable and breakfast is delicious. Why not stay longer and do your touring from here?

Bath

Messler, Elizabeth & Vincent
45 Pearl St., 04530
(207) 443-6069

Amenities: 1,2,3,5,6,7,8,9,10, 16,17
Breakfast: F.

Dbl. Oc.: $69.55 - $85.60
Sgl. Oc.: $64.20 - $80.25
Third Person: $15.00

Packard House—Classic Georgian home in historic district. Belonged to famous shipbuilder Benjamin F. Packard. Period furnishings; three guest rooms. Walk to restaurants and shops; Maritime Museum, beaches, musical theatre, galleries and L.L. Bean nearby. Enjoy the history of our city of ships.

Bath

Pollard, Sallie & Geo
No. Bath Rd.
RR 2, Box 85, 04530
(207) 443-4391

Amenities: 3,5,6,7,8,9,10,11, 14,15,16,17
Breakfast: F.

Dbl. Oc.: $60.00 - $80.00
Sgl. Oc.: $45.00 - $50.00
Third Person: $15.00 - $20.00
Child: Under 6 yrs. - $10.00

Fairhaven Inn—A 200-year-old home on the river, set amidst woods and fields. Fairhaven is truly "one of the best places to stay" (midcoast Maine). Three miles from the center on 24A. We are handy to all that the midcoast has to offer: beaches, museums, antiques and restaurants.

---

1. No Smoking	5. Tennis Available	9. Credit Cards Accepted	13. Lunch Available	17. Shared Baths
2. No Pets	6. Golf Available	10. Personal Check Accepted	14. Conference Rooms Avail.	18. Afternoon Tea
3 Off Season Rates	7. Swimmming Avail.	11. Reservations Necessary	15. Group Seminars Avail.	* Commisions given
4. Senior Citizen Rates	8. Skiing Available	12. Dinner Available	16. Private Baths	to Travel Agents

MAINE

Bath *

Valdaski, Michele
1024 Washington St., 04530
(207) 443-5202

Amenities: 5,6,7,9,11,12,15,16,17
Breakfast: F.
Dbl. Oc.: $72.80 - $95.00
Sgl Oc.: $67.80 - $82.00
Third Person: $20.00
Child: Under 14 yrs. - $10.00

1024 Washington—An elegant and romantic atmosphere in historic district. Two beautiful beaches, wildlife sanctuary and Maine Maritime Museum. Fine restaurants, art galleries and a short drive to L.L. Bean! Come and enjoy our fresh flowers, fireplaces and music. Where memories are made.

Belfast *

Heffentrager, Cathy & Carl
16 Pearl St., 04915
(207) 338-2304

Amenities: 1,2,5,6,7,8,10,11,15,16,18
Breakfast: F.
Dbl. Oc.: $58.85 - $90.95
Sgl Oc.: $53.50 - $85.60
Third Person: $10.70

The Jeweled Turret Inn—An exquisite turreted, columned and gabled Queen Anne Victorian in a lovely historic village. Period decor. Antiques, lace and beautiful woodwork. Unique fireplaces, verandas and peaceful gardens. Walk to shops, restaurants and the harbor. Activities galore!

Belfast *

Lightfoot, Phyllis & John
6 Northport Ave., 04915
(207) 338-4159

Amenities: 2,5,6,7,8,10,16, 18
Breakfast: F.
Dbl. Oc.: $64.20 - $85.60
Sgl. Oc.: $53.50 - $74.90
Third Person: $10.00

Frost House—A Victorian home four blocks from water. Walk to town. Tandem bike, harbor cruises, croquet and badminton. Music at breakfast. Cookies and milk at night. Gardens and arbor. Routes 7/10 off Highway 1. One hour to Bar Harbor and 20 minutes to Camden. Stained glass and wood interior.

Bethel *

Cardello, Penny & Joseph
Walker Mill (Rte. 26), 04217
(207) 824-7600

Amenities: 1,2,3,6,7,8,9,10, 12,13,17,18
Breakfast: F.
Dbl. Oc.: $70.00
Sgl. Oc.: $70.00
Third Person: $15.00

Abbott House—A 1773 New England Cape nestled in the western mountains. Arise to a country breakfast. Enjoy four seasons: canoe, hike, ski Sunday River, breathtaking fall foliage, stargaze in the hot tub, refresh yourself in the pool. In-house registered massage therapist.

1. No Smoking	5. Tennis Available	9. Credit Cards Accepted	13. Lunch Available	17. Shared Baths
2. No Pets	6. Golf Available	10. Personal Check Accepted	14. Conference Rooms Avail.	18. Afternoon Tea
3 Off Season Rates	7. Swimmming Avail.	11. Reservations Necessary	15. Group Seminars Avail.	* Commisions given
4. Senior Citizen Rates	8. Skiing Available	12. Dinner Available	16. Private Baths	to Travel Agents

Boothbay, East *

Morissette, Ellen & Paul
Murray Hill Rd., E. Boothbay
04544 (mail)
(207) 633-4551, (800) 451-5048

Amenities: 3,4,9,10,16,18
Breakfast: F.

Dbl. Oc.: $85.60 - $128.40
Third Person: $10.00
Child: Under 8 yrs. - $10.00

Five Gables Inn—A restored Victorian with unique decor in all 15 rooms with a view of the bay. Five with fireplaces. A full breakfast is served in the common room or on the porch. Swimming and boating across the street. Boothbay Harbor three miles away. Open May-October. AAA, three diamonds.

Boothbay Harbor

Brewer, Dorothy
57 Oak St., 04538
(207) 633-5565

Amenities: 1,2,3,9,10,17
Breakfast: F.

Dbl. Oc.: $53.50
Sgl. Oc.: $53.50

The Sleepy Lobsterman—Our 1865 home offers you three spacious rooms with double beds sharing a large full bath. A full breakfast is served in our sunny dining room. Relax in our comfortable living room which has cable TV. A five- minute walk to shops, restaurants and boat trips.

Boothbay Harbor *

Campbell, Diane
3 Eames Rd., 04538
(207) 633-7565

Amenities: 1,2,3,9,10,11,16,
18
Breakfast: F.

Dbl. Oc.: $85.00 - $100.00
Sgl. Oc.: $80.00 - $95.00
Third Person: $20.00

Anchor Watch Bed And Breakfast—On the prettiest shore in the harbor. Country decor with nautical theme. Private pier to watch sunsets, lobstermen at work and ducks. One hour to L.L. Bean, Pemaquid light, Wiscasset and antiques. Fine restaurants. Monhegan day trip, clambakes and dinner cruise. Short walk to town.

Boothbay Harbor

Piggott, Donna
64 Atlantic Ave.
(207) 633-5690

Amenities: 1,2,3,9,10,16,18
Breakfast: F.

Dbl. Oc.: $65.00 - $95.00
Sgl. Oc.: $65.00 - $95.00
Third Person: $15.00

Atlantic Ark Inn — A small and intimate bed and breakfast offering scenic harbor views, mohongany poster beds, private baths, period antiques, Oriental rugs, full gourmet breakfasts, fresh flowers, afternoon wine and a 5 minute walk to the village over an historic bridge.

1. No Smoking	5. Tennis Available	9. Credit Cards Accepted	13. Lunch Available	17. Shared Baths
2. No Pets	6. Golf Available	10. Personal Check Accepted	14. Conference Rooms Avail.	18. Afternoon Tea
3 Off Season Rates	7. Swimmming Avail.	11. Reservations Necessary	15. Group Seminars Avail.	* Commisions given
4. Senior Citizen Rates	8. Skiing Available	12. Dinner Available	16. Private Baths	to Travel Agents

MAINE

Boothbay Harbor *

Thomas, George
71 Townsend Ave., 04538
(207) 633-4300, (800) 722-4240

Amenities: 1,2,4,5,6,7,8,9,10,
11,12,13,14,15,16
Breakfast: C. Plus
Dbl. Oc.: $50.00 - $175.00
Sgl Oc.: $50.00 - $175.00
Third Person: $20.00
Child: Crib - $10.00

Harbour Towne Inn—The finest B&B on the waterfront. All private baths. Handsomely restored Victorian. Scenic outside decks. Harbor views. A luxurious penthouse sleeps six. Short stroll to all activities. Private parking. Open most of the year. Advance reservations recommended.

Bridgton *

Starets, Jane & Richard
37 Highland Rd., 04009
(207) 647-3733

Amenities: 1,2,3,5,6,7,8,9,10,
11,16,17
Breakfast: F.

Dbl. Oc.: $72.76 - $117.70
Sgl. Oc.: $67.41 - $72.11
Third Person: $25.00
Child: Under 12 yrs. - $15.00

The Noble House—A stately manor with private frontage on scenic Highland Lake. Canoe and footpedal boat for guests' use. Sumptuous full breakfast. Family suites. Whirlpool baths. Nearby hiking, swimming, antiques, summer theatre and romantic restaurants. Cross-country and downhill skiing.

Brunswick

Holbrook, Tom
7 South St., 04011
(207) 729-6959

Amenities: 1,2,9,10,17
Breakfast: C.

Dbl. Oc.: $53.50 - $58.85
Sgl. Oc.: $42.80 - $48.15
Third Person: $10.70

The Samuel Newman House—An 1821 Federal-style house with seven guest rooms furnished in comfortable antiques. Adjacent to Bowdoin College and 10 minutes from L.L. Bean in Freeport. Delicious home-baked pastries and muffins. Open year-round.

Brunswick

Packard, Elizabeth & Peter
Bethel Point Rd. 2387, 04011
(207) 725-1115

Amenities: 1,2,3,7,10,11,17
Breakfast: F.

Dbl. Oc.: $70.00
Sgl. Oc.: $60.00
Third Person: $15.00

Bethel Point Bed And Breakfast—Peaceful oceanside comfort in 150-year-old home. Perfect view of ocean birds, seals and lobster boats. An opportunity for shoreline walks to explore the local coast. An easy drive to area's features such as Bowdoin College, Popham Beach, L.L.Bean and local restaurants.

1. No Smoking	5. Tennis Available	9. Credit Cards Accepted	13. Lunch Available	17. Shared Baths
2. No Pets	6. Golf Available	10. Personal Check Accepted	14. Conference Rooms Avail.	18. Afternoon Tea
3 Off Season Rates	7. Swimming Avail.	11. Reservations Necessary	15. Group Seminars Avail.	* Commisions given
4. Senior Citizen Rates	8. Skiing Available	12. Dinner Available	16. Private Baths	to Travel Agents

Camden

Davis, Mary & Jon
6 High St., 04843
(207) 236-9656

Amenities: 1,2,3,5,6,7,8,9,10, 11,15,16,18
Breakfast: F.

Dbl. Oc.: $65.00 - $125.00
Sgl. Oc.: $60.00 - $100.00
Third Person: $10.00

Windward House—Enjoy the charm and comfort of our historic and beautifully restored Greek Revival home situated above picturesque Camden harbor. Guest rooms furnished with fine antiques and private baths. Enjoy our common rooms, gardens and gourmet breakfasts. Just steps to the harbor.

Camden*

Donner, Marie & Ray
The Other Rd.,Lincolnville,
04849 (mail)
(207) 236-3785, (800) 382-9817

Amenities: 1,2,3,5,6,7,8,9,10, 11,16,18
Breakfast: F.

Dbl. Oc.: $85.60 - $107.00
Sgl. Oc.: $78.11 - $99.51
Third Person: $15.00

The Victorian B&B—A century old Victorian home that has been restored to its original charm. Spacious rooms and period decor provide a quiet atmosphere in a unique country setting. Enjoy our views of the water or walk just 400 feet to the shore.

Camden *

Goodspeed, Don
60 Mountain St., 04843
(207) 236-8077

Amenities: 3,5,6,7,8,10,11,16, 17
Breakfast: C.

Dbl. Oc.: $72.00 - $85.00
Sgl. Oc.: $49.00
Third Person: $15.00
Child: $15.00

Goodspeed Guest House—An 1879 farmhouse with eight restored guest rooms. Antique clocks and furnishings throughout. Enjoy a continental breakfast on the sunny deck. A quiet location. Spacious grounds. Five blocks from the harbor.

Camden *

Schmoll, Jody ,   Hayden, Dennis
67 Elm St., 04843
(207) 236-3196, (800) 248-3196
FAX: (207) 236-6523

Amenities: 1,3,4,5,6,7,8,9,10, 12,13,14,15,16,18
Breakfast: F.
Dbl. Oc.: $90.95 - $133.75
Sgl Oc.: $90.95 - $133.75
Third Person: $20.00
Child: $20.00

Blue Harbor House, A Bed And Breakfast—A casual country inn located in the heart of Camden Village. Greet the morning with breakfast on the sunporch. Dinner - a gourmet presentation or Down East lobster bake. Carriage house suites provide the perfect setting for any occasion.

1. No Smoking
2. No Pets
3. Off Season Rates
4. Senior Citizen Rates
5. Tennis Available
6. Golf Available
7. Swimming Avail.
8. Skiing Available
9. Credit Cards Accepted
10. Personal Check Accepted
11. Reservations Necessary
12. Dinner Available
13. Lunch Available
14. Conference Rooms Avail.
15. Group Seminars Avail.
16. Private Baths
17. Shared Baths
18. Afternoon Tea
* Commisions given to Travel Agents

Camden *

Smith, Peter & Donny
Robson, Diana
22 High St., 04843
(207) 236-9636

Amenities: 1,2,3,5,6,7,8,9,10,11,15,16,17,18
Breakfast: F.
Dbl. Oc.: $75.00 - $99.00
Sgl Oc.: $65.00 - $89.00
Third Person: $16.00

The Camden Main Stay Inn—A comfortable bed, a hearty breakfast and a friendly innkeeper are found in this treasured old colonial home. Listed in the National Register of Historic Places. Located in Camden's historic district. The inn is a short five-minute walk from the harbor, shops and restaurants.

Capitol Island

Peckham, Kimberly
04538
(207) 633-2521

Amenities: 1,2,5,7,10,11,16, 17
Breakfast: C.

Dbl. Oc.: $69.55 - $123.05
Sgl. Oc.: $51.36
Third Person: $10.60

Albonegon Inn—Perched on the rocks near Boothbay Harbor, we offer a quiet place to relax and enjoy the sea, nearby islands and passing boats. Romantic, simple and peaceful.

Chamberlain

Hahler, M/M John J.
Rte. 32
Box 105, 04541
(207) 677-2386

Amenities: 2,5,6,7,10,16
Breakfast: C.

Dbl. Oc.: $66.00
Sgl. Oc.: $53.00
Third Person: $13.00

Ocean Reefs On Long Cove—Located on Long Cove, a non-resort atmosphere Four rooms. Two cabins. Watch waves break over the reef, lobstermen hauling traps and nature in its environment between tides. Nature trails, sightseeing boat and dining within two miles. Enjoy the coast from the rocks or the rockers.

Cherryfield

Conway, William
Park St.
P.O. Box 256, 04622
(207) 546-2780

Amenities: 1,2,5,6,7,10,15, 17
Breakfast: F.

Dbl. Oc.: $50.00
Sgl. Oc.: $45.00
Third Person: $10.00

Ricker House—A beautiful 1803, National Historic Register, home in a quaint, historic town on Narraguagus River. Centrally located for many activities in coastal Maine. Rugged shorelines, lakes and rivers. Great seafood restaurants. Your hosts can help you get the most out of your visit.

1. No Smoking	5. Tennis Available	9. Credit Cards Accepted	13. Lunch Available	17. Shared Baths
2. No Pets	6. Golf Available	10. Personal Check Accepted	14. Conference Rooms Avail.	18. Afternoon Tea
3 Off Season Rates	7. Swimmming Avail.	11. Reservations Necessary	15. Group Seminars Avail.	* Commisions given
4. Senior Citizen Rates	8. Skiing Available	12. Dinner Available	16. Private Baths	to Travel Agents

MAINE

Corea *

Canner, Barry
Travers, Robert
Crowley Island Rd., 04624
(207) 963-2689

Amenities: 1,2,3,6,7,10,14,16, 17
Breakfast: F.

Dbl. Oc.: $48.00 - $80.00
Sgl. Oc.: $48.00 - $80.00
Third Person: $15.00
Child: Over 10 yrs. - $15.00

The Black Duck On Corea House—Small, casually elegant on 12 acres overlooking an unspoiled lobstering harbor and open ocean. Furnished with art and antiques. Near Schoodic, the quiet part of Acadia, and other wildlife refuges. Watch eagles soar, hunt antiques, relax and read.

Damariscotta

Hovance, Joseph R.
Rte. 129
HCR 64, Box 045F, 04543
(207) 563-5941

Amenities: 1,2,9,10,11,16,17
Breakfast: C.

Dbl. Oc.: $53.00 - $69.20
Sgl. Oc.: $48.15 - $63.85
Third Person: $10.70 - $15.70
Child: Under 10 yrs. - $5.35

Brannon-Bunker Inn—An intimate and relaxing country B&B with river view. Mid-coast location. Seven rooms reflect the charm of yesterday with comforts of today. Private or shared baths. Selection of queen, double or twin beds. An antique shop in the inn! Nearby beach, lighthouse and fort shops.

Eastport

McInnis, Ruth
Todd's Head, 04631
(207) 853-2328

Amenities: 1,10,16,17
Breakfast: C.

Dbl. Oc.: $45.00 - $80.00
Sgl. Oc.: $35.00
Third Person: $10.00
Child: Under 8 yrs. - no charge

Todd House—A center-chimney Cape, circa 1775, on Todd's Head. A unique good-morning staircase. A spectacular view of Passamaquoddy Bay. A library of local history items. Deck and barbecue facilities. Children and well-behaved pets welcome. Some rooms with private baths. Kitchenettes.

Eliot

Raymond, Elaine
Rte. 101, 03903
(207) 439-0590

Amenities: 1,2,7,10,11,14, 16,17,18
Breakfast: F.

Dbl. Oc.: $53.50 - $64.20
Sgl. Oc.: $32.10 - $37.45
Third Person: $21.40

High Meadows B&B—Situated on the side of a hill. Colonial house built in 1736. We offer a quiet country atmosphere. All rooms are furnished with period antiques. Historic Portsmouth, NH, is nearby as well as the beaches. We are open April through October. Come and relax with us.

Freeport *

Bradley, Loretta & Alan
188 Main St., 04032
(207) 865-3289

Amenities: 1,2,6,7,9,11,16, 17
Breakfast: F.

Dbl. Oc.: $68.00 - $85.00
Sgl. Oc.: $58.00 - $75.00

Captain Josiah Mitchell House—Famous historic sea captain's home. Four-minute walk to L.L. Bean and 120 outlets. Luxurious antique furnishings, more like a museum than a house. Owners/hosts have lived here for over 25 years. Oriental rugs. Relax on covered veranda. Breakfast overlooking formal gardens.

1. No Smoking	5. Tennis Available	9. Credit Cards Accepted	13. Lunch Available	17. Shared Baths
2. No Pets	6. Golf Available	10. Personal Check Accepted	14. Conference Rooms Avail.	18. Afternoon Tea
3 Off Season Rates	7. Swimming Avail.	11. Reservations Necessary	15. Group Seminars Avail.	* Commisions given
4. Senior Citizen Rates	8. Skiing Available	12. Dinner Available	16. Private Baths	to Travel Agents

MAINE

Freeport

Hassett, Edward
181 Main St., 04032
(207) 865-1226

Amenities: 1,2,3,6,7,8,9,10, 16
Breakfast: F.

Dbl. Oc.: $101.65
Sgl. Oc.: $80.25
Third Person: $15.00

181 Main Street, Bed And Breakfast—Perfectly charming and comfortable classic New England Cape. Appointed in country antiques and period pieces. In-ground pool. Five-minute walk to L.L. Bean and Freeport's luxury outlets. Approved by AAA and American B&B Association.

Freeport *

Knudsen, Jr., Sigurd A.
RR 3, Box 269C, 04032
(207) 865-6566

Amenities: 1,2,6,7,8,9,10,11, 16
Breakfast: F.

Dbl. Oc.: $102.00 - $124.00
Sgl. Oc.: $87.00 - $109.00
Third Person: $15.00
Child: $15.00

The Bagley House—Peace, tranquility and history abound in this magnificent 1772 country home. Antiques, handmade quilts and fireplaces. Six acres of fields, woods and flowers. A warm welcome awaits you. Just minutes from downtown Freeport's famous shopping.

Freeport *

Ring, Gaila & Captain Thomas
25 Main St.
P.O. Box 146, So. Freeport,
04078 (mail)
(207) 865-6112

Amenities: 1,2,3,7,8,10,11,13, 16,17,18
Breakfast: F.

Dbl. Oc.: $69.55 - $133.75
Sgl. Oc.: $58.85 - $107.00
Third Person: $16.05
Child: $16.05

Atlantic Seal Bed And Breakfast—Lovely harbor views year-round. An 1850 Cape. Cozy rooms, antiques, old-fashioned parlor with fireplace. Guest rooms feature sea breezes, fresh flowers, thick towels, homemade quilts and down comforters. Five minutes to L.L. Bean and outlet stores. Resident dog and cat.

Freeport *

Ryan, Cynba & Shannon
5 Independence Dr., 04032
(207) 865-9295

Amenities: 1,3,4,5,6,7,8,9,10, 11,16,17,18
Breakfast: F.
Dbl. Oc.: $74.90 - $112.35
Sgl. Oc.: $64.20 - $101.65
Third Person: $15.00
Child: Under 8 yrs. - no charge

The Isaac Randall House Bed And Breakfast—A walk to L.L. Bean and outlets. Quiet setting on five acres with pond. Historic Federal farmhouse. Rooms with antiques. Close to Casco Bay beaches and sights. Second guest kitchen. Complimentary snacks. Warm hospitality. Wheelchair accessible. Children welcome. Open year-round.

---

1. No Smoking
2. No Pets
3 Off Season Rates
4. Senior Citizen Rates

5. Tennis Available
6. Golf Available
7. Swimmming Avail.
8. Skiing Available

9. Credit Cards Accepted
10. Personal Check Accepted
11. Reservations Necessary
12. Dinner Available

13. Lunch Available
14. Conference Rooms Avail.
15. Group Seminars Avail.
16. Private Baths

17. Shared Baths
18. Afternoon Tea
* Commisions given
to Travel Agents

MAINE

Great Chebeague Island *

Bowden, Jan & Dick
South Road
P.O. Box 492, 04017
(207) 846-5155

Amenities: 1,2,3,4,6,7,9,10, 11,12,13,14,15,16, 17

Breakfast: F.

Dbl. Oc.: $90.00 - $110.00
Sgl. Oc.: $75.00 - $95.00
Child: $20.00 (cot)

Chebeague Island Inn—An island getaway in a 20-room inn just a short boat ride from Portland. No phones or TV. Native lobster. Circa 1926, only inn on island. Full liquor license, bikes, 117-foot front porch with rockers. Family adventures. Weekly rates. Honeymoons.

Kennebunk

Ellenberger, Cathy
154 Port Rd., 04043
(207) 967-3824

Amenities: 2,3,4,5,6,7,9,10, 11,16,18

Breakfast: F.

Dbl. Oc.: $75.00 - $110.00
Sgl. Oc.: $55.00
Third Person: $50.00
Child: Under 13 yrs. - $15.00

Ellen Berger's Guest House And Bed And Breakfast—Located in the heart of the lower village. Two-bedroom suite with a fireplaced living room. Comfortable setting decorated with antiques. Walk to shops and harbor. One mile to the beach. Great breakfasts. Family accommodations in guest house. Gallery and antique shop on premises.

Kennebunk *

Foley, Maryellen & Tom
1917 Alewife Rd., 04043
(207) 985-2118

Amenities: 1,2,5,6,7,8,9,10, 16

Breakfast: C. Plus

Dbl. Oc.: $74.20
Sgl. Oc.: $74.20

The Alewife House—A 1756 farmhouse with six acres of rolling hills. Furnished throughout with antiques. Quiet country atmosphere, yet close to the ocean. Antique shop. Guaranteed reservation with MasterCard or VISA. Four miles north of Exit 3 off the Maine Turnpike. Open year-round.

Kennebunk

Kenny, Laurence
48 Beach Ave.
P.O. Box 1147, 04043
(207)967-3850

Amenities: 2,3,5,6,7,8,9,10,16
Breakfast: C. Plus
Dbl. Oc.: $83.00 - $151.00
Sgl Oc.: $83.00 - $151.00
Third Person: $26.75
Child: $26.75

Sundial Inn—Unique ocean-front inn with turn-of-the-century Victorian antiques. Each of the 34 rooms has a private bath, phone, color TV and air-conditioning. Several rooms also offer ocean views and whirlpool baths. Elevator and handicapped accessible.

1. No Smoking	5. Tennis Available	9. Credit Cards Accepted	13. Lunch Available	17. Shared Baths
2. No Pets	6. Golf Available	10. Personal Check Accepted	14. Conference Rooms Avail.	18. Afternoon Tea
3 Off Season Rates	7. Swimmming Avail.	11. Reservations Necessary	15. Group Seminars Avail.	* Commissions given
4. Senior Citizen Rates	8. Skiing Available	12. Dinner Available	16. Private Baths	to Travel Agents

Kennebunk

McAdams, Carolyn
57 Western Ave.
Lower Village, 04043
(207) 967-4069

Amenities: 1,2,3,5,6,7,8,10, 16
Breakfast: F.

Dbl. Oc.: $74.90 - $85.60
Sgl. Oc.: $64.20 - $74.90
Third Person: $15.00

Lake Brook B&B Guest House—A turn-of-the-century farmhouse with comfortable rockers, great breakfasts, beautiful flower gardens and charming accommodations. Lake Brook is 1/2 mile from Dock Square and downtown Kennebunkport and one mile from Kennebunk Beach. Come join us.

Kennebunk *

Yaeger, Murray
Bechelder, Mark
P.O. Box 1129, 04043
(207) 985-3770

Amenities: 2,9,10,11,15,16,18
Breakfast: F.
Dbl. Oc.: $80.00 - $120.00
Third Person: $20.00

Arundel Meadows Inn—A 165-year-old farmhouse with seven guest rooms. Decorated with art and antiques. Three rooms with fireplaces. Two suites. Private bathrooms. Gourmet breakfasts. Five miles to Kennebunkport and beaches. Two miles north of Kennebunk on Route 1. Write for brochure/reservations.

Kennebunkport *

Copeland, Carol & Lindsay
34 Maine St.
P.O. Box 500, 04046
(800) 950-2117, (207) 967-2117

Amenities: 2,3,5,6,7,9,10,14,15,16,18
Breakfast: F.
Dbl. Oc.: $134.00 - $193.00
Sgl Oc.: $129.00 - $188.00
Third Person: $16.00 - $21.00
Child: Under 12 yrs. - $0. - $9.

Maine Stay Inn And Cottages—"Exceptional warmth and hospitality" at this 1860 Victorian inn located in the historic district. Elegant inn rooms and delightful garden cottages. Sumptuous full breakfast. Easy walk to shops, galleries and harbor. Near beaches, golf and sailing.

1. No Smoking	5. Tennis Available	9. Credit Cards Accepted	13. Lunch Available	17. Shared Baths
2. No Pets	6. Golf Available	10. Personal Check Accepted	14. Conference Rooms Avail.	18. Afternoon Tea
3 Off Season Rates	7. Swimmming Avail.	11. Reservations Necessary	15. Group Seminars Avail.	* Commisions given
4. Senior Citizen Rates	8. Skiing Available	12. Dinner Available	16. Private Baths	to Travel Agents

Kennebunkport

Doane, Charles
Rte. 35, 04046
(207) 967-5766

Amenities: 1,2,3,9,10,11,16,17,18
Breakfast: F.
Dbl. Oc.: $80.25 - $96.30
Sgl Oc.: $80.25 - $96.30
Third Person: $16.05
Child: Under 12 yrs. - $16.05

English Meadows Inn—An 1860 Victorian farmhouse, operating as an inn for more than 80 years. Relax among the comforts of home amid works of nationally acclaimed artists and period antiques. There is also a large studio apartment and charming four-room cottage.

Kennebunkport *

Downs, Eva
South St.
P.O. Box 478A, 04046
(207) 967-5151

Amenities: 1,2,3,5,6,7,8,9,10,16,18
Breakfast: F.
Dbl. Oc.: $101.65 - $176.55
Sgl Oc.: $101.65
Third Person: $21.40
Child: Under 1 yr. - no charge

The Inn On South Street—Enjoy the comfortable elegance of this 19th-century Greek Revival home and the personal attention. Three spacious guest rooms and a luxurious suite, beautifully decorated with antiques. Located on a quiet street, yet close to restaurants, shops and the water.

Kennebunkport *

Kyle, Mary & Bill
South St.
P.O. Box 1333, 04046
(207) 967-2780

Amenities: 1,2,3,9,10,11,16,18
Breakfast: F.
Dbl. Oc.: $96.30
Sgl Oc.: $90.95
Third Person: $15.00
Child: Over 10 yrs. - $15.00

Kylemere House, 1818—A graciously appointed Federal seaport inn. A quiet haven in the historic district. Enjoy four spacious, warm and inviting rooms with private bath, friendly atmosphere, beautiful gardens and creative breakfast. Walking distance of restaurants, galleries, shops and water.

1. No Smoking	5. Tennis Available	9. Credit Cards Accepted	13. Lunch Available	17. Shared Baths
2. No Pets	6. Golf Available	10. Personal Check Accepted	14. Conference Rooms Avail.	18. Afternoon Tea
3 Off Season Rates	7. Swimmming Avail.	11. Reservations Necessary	15. Group Seminars Avail.	* Commisions given
4. Senior Citizen Rates	8. Skiing Available	12. Dinner Available	16. Private Baths	to Travel Agents

MAINE

Kennebunkport *

Perry, Carol & Ron
Locke St.
Box 646A, 04046
(207) 967-5632

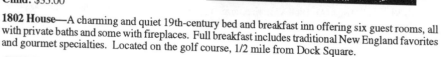

Amenities: 1,2,3,4,5,6,9,10,11,15,16
Breakfast: F.
Dbl. Oc.: $80.00 - $120.00
Third Person: $35.00
Child: $35.00

1802 House—A charming and quiet 19th-century bed and breakfast inn offering six guest rooms, all with private baths and some with fireplaces. Full breakfast includes traditional New England favorites and gourmet specialties. Located on the golf course, 1/2 mile from Dock Square.

Kennebunkport

Reid, Elizabeth & Charles
Ocean Ave.
P.O. Box 2578, 04046
(207) 967-3315

Amenities: 3,5,6,7,10,16
Breakfast: F.
Dbl. Oc.: $68.50 - $118.00
Sgl Oc.: $52.00 - $77.00
Third Person: $10.00 - $15.00
Child: Under 2 yrs. - no charge

The Green Heron Inn—A cozy, clean and comfortable inn located on scenic Ocean Avenue. Close to a small beach and within walking distance of Dock Square. The inn offers 10 guest rooms and one cottage, each with private bath, color TV and air-conditioning.

Kennebunkport

Sutter, Joan & David
41 Pier Rd.
RR 2, Box 1180, 04046
(207) 967-5564

Amenities: 1,2,3,5,6,7,8,9,10, 11,16
Breakfast: F.
Dbl. Oc.: $139.10 - $187.25
Third Person: $16.05

The Inn At Harbor Head—A century-old, shingled waterfront inn in the loveliest part of Kennebunkport —Cape Porpoise Harbor. Private baths; wind chimes; photographic breakfasts. Slow down, relax and unwind in the beautiful and uniquely furnished guest rooms. A smoke-free inn.

1. No Smoking	5. Tennis Available	9. Credit Cards Accepted	13. Lunch Available	17. Shared Baths
2. No Pets	6. Golf Available	10. Personal Check Accepted	14. Conference Rooms Avail.	18. Afternoon Tea
3 Off Season Rates	7. Swimmming Avail.	11. Reservations Necessary	15. Group Seminars Avail.	* Commisions given
4. Senior Citizen Rates	8. Skiing Available	12. Dinner Available	16. Private Baths	to Travel Agents

MAINE

Kennebunkport *

Tallagnon, Bonnie & Dennis
P.O. Box 1308
Corner of Pleasant & Green St., 04046
(207) 967-4454

Amenities: 1,2,3,4,5,6,7,8,9,10,14,15,16,18
Breakfast: F.
Dbl. Oc.: $74.90 - $144.45
Sgl Oc.: $69.55 - $133.75
Third Person: $21.40
Child: Under 8 yrs. - $21.40

The Captain Fairfield Inn—Beautiful, romantic sea captain's mansion in the picturesque historic district. Lovely gardens, graceful, quiet bedrooms, fireplaces, down comforters, gourmet coffees, delicious breakfasts. Living room with fireplace and library. Friendly, intimate and refreshing.

Kittery *

Lamandia, Peter
Boegenberger, Nancy
29 Wentworth St.,Scenic Rte. 103, 03904
(207) 439-1489

Amenities: 1,3,9,10,14,16,17
Breakfast: C. & F.
Dbl. Oc.: $48.15 - $101.65
Sgl Oc.: $37.45 - $96.30
Third Person: $16.05 - $26.75
Child: Under 18 - $5.35 - $16.05

Enchanted Nights Bed And Breakfast—Romantic and whimsical, the quaintness of a French country inn. Elegant breakfasts, lavish bedding, whirlpool tub for two! Cable TV! Pets welcome! One mile to charming, historic Portsmouth's dining and dancing; outlet malls, scenic ocean drives to lovely neighboring resorts.

Kittery

Rosol, Cevia & George
6 Water St., 03904
(207) 439-4040

Amenities: 1,2,3,5,6,7,9,10, 15,16,18
Breakfast: F.

Dbl. Oc.: $101.65
Sgl. Oc.: $90.95
Third Person: $16.05

Gundalow Inn—Victorian, six romantic rooms. Water views. Breakfast by the fire then stroll to historic Portsmouth's harbor, museums, theatres and restaurants. Roam our beaches. Shop the outlets. Sit and rock. Business and single travelers welcome. Recommended by the *New York Times*.

1. No Smoking	5. Tennis Available	9. Credit Cards Accepted	13. Lunch Available	17. Shared Baths
2. No Pets	6. Golf Available	10. Personal Check Accepted	14. Conference Rooms Avail.	18. Afternoon Tea
3 Off Season Rates	7. Swimmming Avail.	11. Reservations Necessary	15. Group Seminars Avail.	* Commisions given
4. Senior Citizen Rates	8. Skiing Available	12. Dinner Available	16. Private Baths	to Travel Agents

Little Deer Isle

Broadhead, Sophie
R.F.D. #1, Box 324, 04650
(207) 348-2540

Amenities: 2,5,6,7,10,16,17
Breakfast: F.

Dbl. Oc.: $75.00 - $85.00
Sgl. Oc.: $60.00 - $70.00
Third Person: $18.00
Child: Under 3 yrs. - no charge

Eggmoggin Inn—A small, secluded coastal inn in a beautiful location and a view of Eggmoggin Reach, which is world-famous for sailing. The area is still unspoiled. Come and relax with us and enjoy life as it should be lived.

Lubec

Childs, Lovetta
27 Summer St., 04652
(207) 733-2403

Amenities: 1,2,6,9,10,16,17,
18
Breakfast: F.

Dbl. Oc.: $69.55
Sgl. Oc.: $58.85
Third Person: $10.00
Child: Under 18 yrs. - $10.00

Peacock House—This historic home hosted Maine's most prominent people including Margaret C. Smith, several governors, Donald McMillen and Ed Muskey. Quiet ambience and friendly hosts are hallmarks of the inn. Fishing, hiking, whale watching or golf nearby.

Lubec

Elg, E.M.
37 Washington, 04652
(207) 733-2487

Amenities: 1,2,6,10,15,16,17
Breakfast: F.

Dbl. Oc.: $42.80 - $58.35
Sgl. Oc.: $42.80 - $58.35
Child: $10.00

Breakers By The Bay—Enjoy the breathtaking views of the sea from your own private deck. Rooms have handmade quilts and hand-crocheted tablecloths. Located close to International Bridge which leads to Campobello and Roosevelt's house. Enjoy the beauty of Quoddy Head State Park.

Naples *

Hincks, Irene & Maynard
Lake House Rd.
P.O. Box 806, 04055
(207) 693-6226,
(800) 437-0328 (outside ME)

Amenities: 1,2,3,6,7,8,9,10,11,15,16,18
Breakfast: C. Plus
Dbl. Oc.: $66.00 - $96.00 & up
Sgl Oc.: $59.40 - $86.40 & up
Third Person: $12.00
Child: Under 15 yrs. - no charge

Inn At Long Lake—A relaxing 16-room inn complete with TVs, private baths, air-conditioning and expanded continental breakfast in Naples, Maine. Mid-week discounts and special weekends available. Four-season activities and excellent area dining.

1. No Smoking	5. Tennis Available	9. Credit Cards Accepted	13. Lunch Available	17. Shared Baths
2. No Pets	6. Golf Available	10. Personal Check Accepted	14. Conference Rooms Avail.	18. Afternoon Tea
3 Off Season Rates	7. Swimmming Avail.	11. Reservations Necessary	15. Group Seminars Avail.	* Commisions given
4. Senior Citizen Rates	8. Skiing Available	12. Dinner Available	16. Private Baths	to Travel Agents

Naples *

Stetson, Arlene & David
Corner of Rtes 302 & 114
RR1, Box 501, 04055 (mail)
(207) 693-6365

Amenities: 3,4,5,6,7,8,9,10,
11,12,15,16,17,18
Breakfast: F.

Dbl. Oc.: $49.00 - $85.00
Sgl. Oc.: $39.00
Third Person: $10.00
Child: Under 12 yrs. - $5.00

The Augustus Bove House—Your home away from home - historic Hotel Naples restored for comfort and a relaxed atmosphere at affordable prices. Overlooks Long Lake. An easy walk to the water, shops, restaurants and recreation. Open all year. Off-season specials. Air-conditioning and TV.

New Harbor

Phinney Family, The
Northside Rd., Rte. 32
HC 61, Box 161, 04554 (mail)
(207) 677-3727

Amenities: 1,2,3,6,7,9,10,12,
16
Breakfast: F.

Dbl. Oc.: $95.00 - $125.00
Sgl. Oc.: $70.00
Third Person: $16.00
Child: Under 2 yrs. - no charge

The Gosnold Arms—On the historic Pemaquid peninsula. Attractive and comfortable rooms and cottages, most with water views. A glassed-in dining porch overlooks the harbor. Lobster pounds, boat trips, historic sites, shops and beach nearby. Congenial family atmosphere.

Newcastle

Markert, William
Glidden St., 04543
(207) 563-1309

Amenities: 1,2,5,6,7,8,9,10,
15,17
Breakfast: F.

Dbl. Oc.: $45.00 - $55.00
Third Person: $10.00

The Markert House—Four rooms with two shared baths in a 1900 Victorian on a hillside overlooking the Damariscotta River. Your host is an artist, photographer, gourmet cook and gardener. Reproduction Victorian veranda, antique furnishings and tasteful art.

Newcastle *

Sprague, Chris & Ted
River Rd., 04553
(207) 563-5685,
(800) 83-BUNNY

Amenities: 1,2,3,6,7,8,9,10,
11,12,16
Breakfast: F.

Dbl. Oc.: $80.00 - $120.00
Sgl. Oc.: $72.00 - $108.00

The Newcastle Inn—A country inn of distinction on the picturesque Damariscotta River. Romantic, pampering, relaxing and truly memorable cuisine. Food & Wine "exactly what a small coutnry inn should be, superb, delectable." Unwind, relax and enjoy the romance of our area.

Ogunquit *

Hartwell, James
118 Shore Rd., 03907
(207) 646-7210

Amenities: 2,5,6,7,9,10,11,15,
16,18
Breakfast: F.

Dbl. Oc.: $95.00 - $175.00
Sgl. Oc.: Priced accordingly

Hartwell House—This inn welcomes you in the tradition of fine European country inns, while offering authentic New England charm. Stroll the Marginal Way past picture-postcard seascapes and rock formations. Ogunquit Beach and Perkins Cove are both within a few steps.

1. No Smoking	5. Tennis Available	9. Credit Cards Accepted	13. Lunch Available	17. Shared Baths
2. No Pets	6. Golf Available	10. Personal Check Accepted	14. Conference Rooms Avail.	18. Afternoon Tea
3 Off Season Rates	7. Swimmming Avail.	11. Reservations Necessary	15. Group Seminars Avail.	* Commisions given
4. Senior Citizen Rates	8. Skiing Available	12. Dinner Available	16. Private Baths	to Travel Agents

Ogunquit

Sachon, Eeta
30 Bourne Lane
P.O. Box 1940, 03907
(207) 646-3891

Amenities: 2,3,9,10,11,16
Breakfast: C.

Dbl. Oc.: $80.25 - $134.55
Sgl. Oc.: $80.25 - $134.55
Third Person: $10.00

The Morning Dove Bed And Breakfast—An 1860s farmhouse furnished with antiques and European accents. A quiet and convenient location near shops, beaches and restaurants! Spectacular gardens. Owner is an interior designer.

Old Orchard Beach

Bolduc, Cyndi & Dan
20 Portland Ave.
P.O. Box 334, 04064
(207) 934-5295

Amenities: 1,2,3,9,16,17
Breakfast: C. Plus
Dbl. Oc.: $84.53
Sgl. Oc.: $63.13
Third Person: $10.00
Child: Under 12 yrs. - $5.00

The Atlantic Birches Inn—Located around the corner from downtown and a three-minute walk to Maine's largest white-sand beach. Five comfortable and uniquely decorated guest rooms. Enjoy a large, homemade continental breakfast and linger over coffee on the Birch-shaded front porch.

Pemaquid *

De Khan, Kristina
Rte. 130
HC 62, Box 178, 04558
(207) 677-2845

Amenities: 2,6,7,9,10,15,16, 17
Breakfast: F.

Dbl. Oc.: $60.00 - $70.00
Sgl. Oc.: $55.00 - $65.00
Third Person: $10.00

Little River Inn—Enjoy a relaxing coastal Maine vacation in one of Maine's most historic and scenic areas. Select a traditional room or one of our rustic gallery rooms. Delicious banquet breakfast. Minutes from the lighthouse, beach, archaeological digs, New Harbor, galleries and shops.

Rumford

Tucker, Joan
E. Bethel Rd.
Box 12, 04279
(207) 364-4986

Amenities: 2,6,7,8,10,13,17
Breakfast: F.

Dbl. Oc.: $53.50
Sgl. Oc.: $32.10
Third Person: $10.70
Child: Under 2 yrs. - no charge

The Last Resort Bed & Breakfast—A colonial Cape in Rumford Corner nestled in the foothills of western Maine. Country comfort, charm and good homecooking are our specialties. Skiing within minutes. Nearby are two state parks and golf course. Fishing, hiking and hunting are by the back door. Children welcome.

1. No Smoking	5. Tennis Available	9. Credit Cards Accepted	13. Lunch Available	17. Shared Baths
2. No Pets	6. Golf Available	10. Personal Check Accepted	14. Conference Rooms Avail.	18. Afternoon Tea
3 Off Season Rates	7. Swimming Avail.	11. Reservations Necessary	15. Group Seminars Avail.	* Commisions given
4. Senior Citizen Rates	8. Skiing Available	12. Dinner Available	16. Private Baths	to Travel Agents

Saco *

Barclay, John
Forester, Martha
121 North St., P.O. Box 228, 04072-0228
(207) 282-3829

Amenities: 1,2,5,6,7,9,10,16
Breakfast: F.
Dbl. Oc.: $65.00 - $85.00
Sgl Oc.: $65.00 - $85.00
Third Person: $15.00

Crown 'n' Anchor Inn—A Greek Revival (1827-1828) two-story house in the Federal-Adamesque style with a temple front in the National Register of Historic Places. Formerly the home of George Lincoln Goodale, founder of The Glass Flower collection at Harvard University. Fireplaces. Library. Near beaches.

Sorrento

Solet, Mary Ann
Rte. 185, Hc 32, Box 132, 04677
(207) 422-3564

Amenities: 1,2,3,4,5,6,7,9,10, 11,17
Breakfast: C. Plus
Dbl. Oc.: $55.00
Sgl. Oc.: $50.00
Third Person: $5.00

Bass Cove Farm Bed And Breakfast—Coastal farmhouse, water view. Queen-size beds. Parlor, exercise room, porch. Gardens. Area rich in history, nature, culture, antiques, galleries and shopping. Convenient to Bar Harbor and Acadia National Park. Easy drive to Bangor or Maritime Canada.

Southwest Harbor *

Brower, Gardiner
Clark Point Rd., 04679
(207) 244-5335

Amenities: 1,2,3,5,6,7,8,10, 11,16,17
Breakfast: F.
Dbl. Oc.: $58.85 - $123.05
Third Person: $16.05

Lindenwood Inn—A warm and friendly inn overlooking the harbor on the quiet side of Acadia National Park. Nearby sightseeing, hiking, boating, shops and restaurants. Relax in the parlor or play our harpsichord. Children over 12 years welcome. Open all year.

Southwest Harbor

Cervelli, Nancy & Tom
100 Main St., 04679
(207) 244-5302

Amenities: 1,2,3,4,6,7,8,9,10, 16,18
Breakfast: F.
Dbl. Oc.: $80.25 - $165.85
Sgl. Oc.: $74.90 - $155.15
Third Person: $16.05

The Kingsleigh Inn—Located in the heart of Acadia National Park. We offer gracious hospitality in a warm and cozy setting. All guest rooms are tastefully decorated, many having harbor views and all with private baths. Within walking distance to restaurants and shops. Open all year.

1. No Smoking	5. Tennis Available	9. Credit Cards Accepted	13. Lunch Available	17. Shared Baths
2. No Pets	6. Golf Available	10. Personal Check Accepted	14. Conference Rooms Avail.	18. Afternoon Tea
3 Off Season Rates	7. Swimmming Avail.	11. Reservations Necessary	15. Group Seminars Avail.	* Commisions given
4. Senior Citizen Rates	8. Skiing Available	12. Dinner Available	16. Private Baths	to Travel Agents

Southwest Harbor

Eden, Margaret A.
Main St., 04679
207-244-5388

Amenities: 1,2,3,6,7,8,10,16
Breakfast: F.

Dbl. Oc.: $96.30
Sgl. Oc.: $90.95

Harbour Woods Lodging—Quiet, intimate B&B. Comfortable furnishings accented by fresh flowers, keepsakes and candlelight. Large guest rooms with private baths, harbor or garden views. Full breakfast on fine china. At edge of the village surrounded by Acadia National Park. Lower off-season rates.

Southwest Harbor *

Gill, Ann
Clark Point Rd.
Box 1006, 04679
(207) 244-5180

Amenities: 1,2,3,5,6,7,10,11,
15,16,17,18
Breakfast: F.

Dbl. Oc.: $58.85
Sgl. Oc.: $48.15
Third Person: $20.00
Child: $20.00

The Island House—Relax in a gracious seacoast home on the quiet side of Mount Desert Island. A charming and private loft apartment across the street from the harbor. A five-minute walk to village and restaurant. A five-minute drive to Acadia National Park. Open April through October.

Southwest Harbor *

Hoke, Elizabeth & George
Clark Point Rd.
P.O. Box 30, 04679
(207) 244-9828

Amenities: 1,2,3,7,9,10,16
Breakfast: F.

Dbl. Oc.: $70.00 - $130.00
Third Person: $21.50

The Lambs Ear Inn—Please come and visit our stately old main house, built in 1857. Comfortable and serene, away from the hustle and bustle. Crisp, fresh linens, a sparkling harbor view and a breakfast to remember. Be a part of this special village surrounded by Acadia National Park.

Southwest Harbor

Strong, Prentice
Main St., Box 68, 04679
(207) 244-7102

Amenities: 1,2,3,5,6,7,8,10,
11,17
Breakfast: F.

Dbl. Oc.: $58.85
Sgl. Oc.: $48.15

Penury Hall—Guests are honorary family, but don't have to wash the dishes. Share our two cats and interest in art, antiques, gardening and sailing. The sauna will relax you after hiking or skiing. Scrumptious varied breakfasts. We play backgammon for blood! Reservations advised.

Swan's Island

Joyce, Jeanne
Main St., 04685
(207) 526-4116

Amenities: 1,10,15,17,18
Breakfast: F.

Dbl. Oc.: $48.15
Sgl. Oc.: $37.45
Third Person: $16.05
Child: Under 5 yrs. - $5.35

Jeannie's Place B&B—A 45-minute ferry ride from Bass Harbor. Breakfast includes fresh-baked bread and muffins plus eggs and bacon. Enjoy picnics, beachcombing and peaceful walks through forests and along the seashore. Two guest rooms overlook the ocean.

---

1. No Smoking	5. Tennis Available	9. Credit Cards Accepted	13. Lunch Available	17. Shared Baths
2. No Pets	6. Golf Available	10. Personal Check Accepted	14. Conference Rooms Avail.	18. Afternoon Tea
3 Off Season Rates	7. Swimmming Avail.	11. Reservations Necessary	15. Group Seminars Avail.	* Commisions given
4. Senior Citizen Rates	8. Skiing Available	12. Dinner Available	16. Private Baths	to Travel Agents

MAINE

York Beach

Billings, Evelyn & Gil
7 Cross St., 03910
(207) 363-6292 (summer),
  (413) 568-0758 (winter)

Amenities: 1,2,10,16,17
Breakfast: C.

Dbl. Oc.: $59.00 - $70.00
Sgl. Oc.: $48.00 - $59.00
Third Person: $10.00
Child: Under 12 yrs. - $5.00

Red Shutters—A cozy B&B for non-smokers. A quiet setting. Five-minute walk to beach, shops, dining and entertainment. "Your home while you're here." You'll awaken to the aroma of homemade muffins baking for your breakfast. Open June-August.

York Beach

Duffy, Danielle & Dan
8 S. Main St.(Route 1A), 03910
(207) 363-8952

Amenities: 1,2,3,4,5,6,7,10,
              11,17
Breakfast: C.

Dbl. Oc.: $63.00
Sgl. Oc.: $53.00
Child: Under 12 yrs. - $10.00

Homestead Inn B&B—Built in 1905.. Four large and quiet rooms with panoramic ocean view. Fireplaced living room. Sun deck. Breakfast served in barn-board dining room with ocean view. Walk to beach, lighthouse, shops and restaurants. Enjoy sunset serenity. Let us pamper you! Let the seashore happen.

York Beach

Jennings, Virginia
44 Freeman St., 03910
(207) 363-4087, (207) 384-3276

Amenities: 4,9,10,11,15,17
Breakfast: C.

Dbl. Oc.: $50.00 - $60.00
Sgl. Oc.: $40.00 - $50.00
Third Person: $10.00
Child: $5.00

The Candleshop Inn—Like a visit to Grandma's house — if Grandma lived in a quaint New England seaside village. An easy stroll to beach and town and an easy drive to nightlife and malls. Definitely not an impersonal motel! Return to a simple way of life. Come and join a new family!

York Beach

Stemska, Rita & Matthew
55 Ocean Ave., Ext., 03910
(207) 363-1447

Amenities: 1,2,3,4,9,16,17
Breakfast: F.

Dbl. Oc.: $80.25 - $160.50
Sgl. Oc.: $69.55

Rock Ledge Inn—Beautifully located on Maine's rock-bound coast overlooking the Atlantic Ocean. Warm hospitality, homemade gourmet breakfast, attractive rooms, one with Jacuzzi. Walk to sandy beach, gift shops, restaurants and famous Nubble Lighthouse. Short ride to Oqunquit and summer theatre.

1. No Smoking	5. Tennis Available	9. Credit Cards Accepted	13. Lunch Available	17. Shared Baths
2. No Pets	6. Golf Available	10. Personal Check Accepted	14. Conference Rooms Avail.	18. Afternoon Tea
3 Off Season Rates	7. Swimming Avail.	11. Reservations Necessary	15. Group Seminars Avail.	* Commisions given
4. Senior Citizen Rates	8. Skiing Available	12. Dinner Available	16. Private Baths	to Travel Agents

MAINE

York Harbor

Cook, Kathie & Wes
570 York St.
Box 445, 03911
(207) 363-7264

Amenities: 2,3,10,16,17,18
Breakfast: F.

Dbl. Oc.: $69.55
Sgl. Oc.: $58.85
Third Person: $10.00

Bell Buoy Bed And Breakfast—At the Bell Buoy, there are no strangers — only friends who have not met. Our Victorian home offers casual elegance in a quiet setting. You may walk to the nearby beaches, sit on the porch or curl up by the fireplace. Minutes from I-95 and outlet shopping.

York Harbor *

Dominguez, Garry
Rte. 1 A, 03911
(207) 363-5119

Amenities: 2,4,5,6,7,9,10,11,
12,13,14,15,16,17
Breakfast: C.

Dbl. Oc.: $95.23
Sgl. Oc.: $84.53
Third Person: $15.00
Child: Under 12 yrs. -
no charge

York Harbor Inn—A 1637 historic country inn with ocean-view lodging and dining. Charming rooms feature fireplaces, antiques, poster beds, private baths, phone, air-conditioning, Jacuzzi, boating, beach and mega-outlet mall shopping. AAA - 3 three diamond and Mobil rated.

1. No Smoking	5. Tennis Available	9. Credit Cards Accepted	13. Lunch Available	17. Shared Baths
2. No Pets	6. Golf Available	10. Personal Check Accepted	14. Conference Rooms Avail.	18. Afternoon Tea
3 Off Season Rates	7. Swimmming Avail.	11. Reservations Necessary	15. Group Seminars Avail.	* Commisions given
4. Senior Citizen Rates	8. Skiing Available	12. Dinner Available	16. Private Baths	to Travel Agents

MARYLAND

The Old Line State

Capitol: Annapolis
Statehood: April 28, 1788; the 7th state
State Motto: "Manly Deeds, Womanly Words"
State Song: "Maryland, My Maryland"
State Bird: Baltimore Oriole
State Flower: Black-Eyed Susan
State Tree: White Oak (Wye Oak)

Maryland was founded in 1634 by an Englishman named Calvert, who named it for Queen Henrietta Marie of England.

Francis Scott Keye wrote The Star Spangled Banner while watching the British bombard Fort McHenry during the War of 1812. He was inspired by the rockets and glare from the guns and his inspiration became the National Anthem.

Today, Maryland is the bedroom for hundreds of government workers in Washington, D.C. The Baltimore harbor is one of the busiest on the eastern seaboard. Much of our imports from Europe come through here.

The Chesapeake Bay divides Maryland almost in half. IN 1952, the world's first all-steel bridge over salt water was erected. Before this time, the people of each section of Maryland led entirely different lives, the country folk vs. the city folk.

Fishermen have wonderful fishing in the Chesapeake Bay. They are known all over the world for their oysters and clams.

The United States Naval Academy was established in Annapolis in 1845. It is a tourist attraction for hundreds of people every year.

MARYLAND

Annapolis *

Dennis, Karen
Donald Silawsky
145 Edgewater Dr., Edgewater(mail), 21037-1321
(410) 974-8152

Amenities: 1,2,7,10,11,16
Breakfast: C. Plus

Dbl. Oc.: $84.00 & $68.00

Riverwatch—Waterfront B&B offers luxurious accommodations and spectacular river views, just minutes from historic Annapolis. Queen/king beds, pool, hot tub, boat dock and waterfront balconies. Exquisite contemporary and Oriental decor.

Annapolis *

Ren, Lilith
161 Green St., 21401
(410) 268-9750

Amenities: 1,2,3,10,14,15,16, 17,18
Breakfast: C.

Dbl. Oc.: $78.25 - $110.25
Third Person: $25.00

Shaw's Fancy Bed And Breakfast—Elegant suites with queen beds and private baths. Relax on our porch swing or in our hot tub. Great romantic getaway. Let us pamper you! Special packages on request. Within walking distance of dozens of restuarants, shops, historic homes and the U.S. Naval Academy.

Annapolis *

Schrift, Jeanne & Claude
110 Prince George St., 21401
(410) 268-5555

Amenities: 1,2,9,10,14,15,16, 17
Breakfast: C.

Dbl. Oc.: $75.48 - $133.20
Sgl. Oc.: $64.38 - $122.10
Third Person: $11.10
Child: under 1 yr. - no charge

Gibson's Lodgings—Three houses in historic Annapolis — one 18th-century Georgian, one 19th-century stucco and a new house with a unique conference room — offer 21 guest rooms and suites, parlors and dining rooms. All are furnished in antiques. Parking. Walk to everything.

Annapolis *

Wolfrey, Don
One College Ave., 21401
(410) 263-6124

Amenities: 1,2,9,11,16
Breakfast: C. Plus

Dbl. Oc.: $160.00
Sgl. Oc.: $160.00
Third Person: $40.00

College House Suites—Elegant multi-room suites. AAA approved. Nestled between the U.S. Naval Academy and St. John's College. The "Anapolitan" has a fireplace and private entrance. The "Colonial" has orientals, antiques and views of the Academy. Breakfast - option. Two-night minimum.

Baltimore *

Bragaw, Paul
1601 Bolton St., 21217
(410) 728-1179, Fax: (410) 728-3379

Amenities: 1,2,9,10,11,15,16
Breakfast: C. Plus

Dbl. Oc.: $84.00 - $145.60
Sgl. Oc.: $72.80 - $95.20

Mr. Mole Bed And Breakfast—An 1870 row house on historic Bolton Hill with 14 ft. ceilings, marble fireplaces, antiques and concert grand piano. Suites, some with two bedrooms and sitting room. Phones and parking included. Near museums, John Hopkins U., Symphony and Inner Harbor. Handicap-access suite.

1. No Smoking	5. Tennis Available	9. Credit Cards Accepted	13. Lunch Available	17. Shared Baths
2. No Pets	6. Golf Available	10. Personal Check Accepted	14. Conference Rooms Avail.	18. Afternoon Tea
3 Off Season Rates	7. Swimmming Avail.	11. Reservations Necessary	15. Group Seminars Avail.	* Commisions given
4. Senior Citizen Rates	8. Skiing Available	12. Dinner Available	16. Private Baths	to Travel Agents

Baltimore *

Eiserman, Doreen
205 W. Madison St., 21201
(410) 728-6550

Amenities: 2,3,4,9,11,14,15
Breakfast: C.

Dbl. Oc.: $85.00 - $95.00
Sgl. Oc.: $85.00 - $95.00
Third Person: $10.00
Child: Under 12 yrs. - no charge

The Shirley Madison Inn—A Victorian mansion decorated with the elegance of a bygone era. A short walk to Inner Harbor and city's cultural corridor. Landscaped courtyard. Victorian and Edwardian antiques. Complimentary continental breakfast and evening sherry.

Baltimore *

Grater, Betsy
1428 Park Ave., 21217-4230
(410) 383-1274

Amenities: 1,2,9,10,11,16
Breakfast: F.

Dbl. Oc.: $84.00
Sgl. Oc.: $72.80
Third Person: $15.00

Betsy's B&B—A petite estate in a downtown Baltimore historic residential neighborhood. Four stories, center hall, large rooms, 12-foot ceilings, special achitectural features. Public transportation, parking, five minutes from Inner Harbor, baseball park and restaurants.

Baltimore *

Paulus, Lucie
2406 Kentucky Ave., 21213
(410) 467-1688

Amenities: 1,2,4,5,6,9,10,11,
16,17
Breakfast: F.

Dbl. Oc.: $65.00
Sgl. Oc.: $60.00
Third Person: $10.00
Child: $10.00

The Paulus Gasthaus—Located in a lovely residential area near Inner Harbor. A really different B&B. No valuable antiques, but quality accommodations, friendly, personal service and lots of Gemuetlichkeit. American- or German- style breakfast. Hostess/owner speaks fluent German. Cat in residence.

Bel Air

Fox, Dorothy & Howard
Tudor Hall, 21015
(410) 838-0466

Amenities: 2,7,10,11,14,15,16,
17
Breakfast: C.

Dbl. Oc.: $50.00
Sgl. Oc.: $50.00

Tudor Hall—Home of the Maryland Booths. An 18th-century Gothic Revival cottage built as a country retreat by Junius Brutus Booth (1796-1852). The birthplace of Thomas Edwin and John Wilkes Booth. Twenty minutes to downtown Harbor Place, Baltimore.

1. No Smoking	5. Tennis Available	9. Credit Cards Accepted	13. Lunch Available	17. Shared Baths
2. No Pets	6. Golf Available	10. Personal Check Accepted	14. Conference Rooms Avail.	18. Afternoon Tea
3 Off Season Rates	7. Swimmming Avail.	11. Reservations Necessary	15. Group Seminars Avail.	* Commisions given
4. Senior Citizen Rates	8. Skiing Available	12. Dinner Available	16. Private Baths	to Travel Agents

MARYLAND

Berlin

Jacques, Stephen
2 N. Main St., 21811
(410) 641-3589

Amenities: 2,5,6,9,10,11,12,13,15,16
Breakfast: C.
Dbl. Oc.: $60.00 - $130.00
Sgl Oc.: $60.00 - $130.00

Atlantic Hotel Inn And Restaurant—Built in 1895, this restored Victorian hotel is located in the heart of Berlin's historic district. Antique shops and museums are within walking distance. Eight miles from Ocean City and Assateague National Seashore. Four-star restaurant and piano lounge on the premises.

Chesapeak City *

Landry, Gavin — c/o Bohemia House
1236 Townspoint Rd., 21915
(410) 885-3024

Amenities: 3,6,7,9,10,11,12,13,14,15,16
Breakfast: F.
Dbl. Oc.: $89.00 - $160.00
Sgl Oc.: $89.00 - $160.00
Third Person: $10.00
Child: Under 12 yrs. - no charge

Bohemia House—Located just moments from two marinas, the house overlooks the Bohemia River and Chesapeake Bay. An equine motif and period antiques underscore the relaxing, peaceful location. Screened veranda with sitting area, cordials and petit- fours. Call us for special needs.

Chestertown

Brook, Mrs. Marge
8046 Quaker Neck Rd., 21620
(410) 778-5540

Amenities: 1,2,4,5,6,7,10,15, 16,18
Breakfast: F.

Dbl. Oc.: $70.00
Sgl. Oc.: $65.00
Third Person: $15.00
Child: $10.00 (if not in crib)

Radcliffe Cross—A pre-Revolutionary (circa 1725) brick house with many original features. We invite you to enjoy a delightful night's lodging and breakfast amidst the colonial charm of yesteryear. Weekend rates available.

Church Creek *

Slavin, Marlene & Lenny
2142 Lingers Rd., 21622
(410) 397-3033

Amenities: 4,6,7,9,10,11,12, 13,17
Breakfast: F.

Dbl. Oc.: $104.00
Sgl. Oc.: $83.20
Child: Under 5 yrs. - no charge

Loblolly Landings And Lodge—Country retreat on Maryland's eastern shore (170 acres with airstrip) near Blackwater Refuge. Birding, photo, nature trails, fishing, biking, sporting clays. Country club access with golf and swimming. Rustic, antique-filled lodge, 30'x30' greatroom with 90-ton stone fireplace.

1. No Smoking	5. Tennis Available	9. Credit Cards Accepted	13. Lunch Available	17. Shared Baths
2. No Pets	6. Golf Available	10. Personal Check Accepted	14. Conference Rooms Avail.	18. Afternoon Tea
3 Off Season Rates	7. Swimmming Avail.	11. Reservations Necessary	15. Group Seminars Avail.	* Commisions given
4. Senior Citizen Rates	8. Skiing Available	12. Dinner Available	16. Private Baths	to Travel Agents

MARYLAND

Ellicott City *

Osantowski, Margo
4344 Columbia Rd., 21042
(410) 461-4636

Amenities: 1,2,9,10,11,16,17
Breakfast: C. Plus
Dbl. Oc.: $70.00 - $90.00
Third Person: $20.00

The Wayside Inn—A Federal period restored stone farmhouse on two acres with pond. Antique and reproduction pieces. Minutes from historic Ellicott City, near Columbia for business travelers, convenient to Baltimore, Annapolis and Washington, DC. Gift certificates available.

Frederick *

Compton, Beverly & Ray
7945 Worman's Mill Rd., 21701
(301) 694-0440

Amenities: 1,2,5,6,9,10,14,16,17
Breakfast: C.
Dbl. Oc.: $75.00 - $90.00
Sgl Oc.: $65.00 - $80.00
Third Person: $15.00

"Spring Bank" — A B&B Inn—In National Register of Historic Places. The former home of a gentleman farmer/banker. Original 1880 details and period furnishings. Situated on 10 acres. Three miles north of Frederick's historic district. Nearby fine dining.

Frederick *

Mullican, Shirley & Dwight
9549 Liberty Rd., 21701
(301) 898-7128

Amenities: 1,2,5,6,7,10,16
Breakfast: C.

Dbl. Oc.: $85.00 - $95.00

Middle Plantation Inn—A rustic bed and breakfast on 256 acres built of stone and logs. Drive through horse country to the village of Mt. Pleasant. Located several miles east of Frederick. Furnished with antiques that have 19th-century ambience. Each room has a private bath, air-conditioning and TV.

Gaithersburg *

Danilowicz, Suzanne & Joe
18908 Chimney Pl., 20879
(301) 977-7377

Amenities: 1,2,5,6,7,10,14,15, 16,17
Breakfast: F.

Dbl. Oc.: $52.50
Sgl. Oc.: $42.00
Third Person: $15.00
Child: Under 10 yrs - no charge

Gaithersburg Hospitality Bed And Breakfast—Located in Montgomery Village. Nearby restaurants, shopping and recreation. This luxurious home is furnished with family pieces and has your comfort and pleasure in mind. It offers all amenities and is a 35-minute drive to Washington, D.C. via car or metro. Offers home cooking.

1. No Smoking	5. Tennis Available	9. Credit Cards Accepted	13. Lunch Available	17. Shared Baths
2. No Pets	6. Golf Available	10. Personal Check Accepted	14. Conference Rooms Avail.	18. Afternoon Tea
3 Off Season Rates	7. Swimming Avail.	11. Reservations Necessary	15. Group Seminars Avail.	* Commisions given
4. Senior Citizen Rates	8. Skiing Available	12. Dinner Available	16. Private Baths	to Travel Agents

MARYLAND

Hagerstown *

Day, Shirley & Don
20432 Beaver Creek Rd., 21740
(301) 797-4764

Amenities: 1,2,6,7,8,9,10,11,16,17,18
Breakfast: F.
Dbl. Oc.: $91.80
Sgl Oc.: $81.00
Third Person: $10.80

Beaver Creek House Bed And Breakfast—Comfort, relaxation and hospitality await you at this antique-filled Victorian home. Located in a beautiful country setting near I-70 and I-81. Nearby fine restaurants, recreation, historic sights and antiquing. Central air. Mid-week rates. Children 10 yrs. & up ok.

Hagerstown

Lehman, Irene
9738 Downsville Pike, 21740
(301) 582-1735

Amenities: 1,5,6,7,8,10,16, 17
Breakfast: F.

Dbl. Oc.: $54.00 - $81.00
Sgl. Oc.: $48.60 - $75.60
Third Person: $10.80
Child: $5.40 - $7.56

Lewrene Farm B&B—A colonial home on a 125-acre farm for tourists and families. Enjoy our hospitality, large living room, fireplace, piano, antiques and six bedrooms with either poster or canopy beds. Near Antietam battlefield, Harpers Ferry and C&O Canal. Quilts for sale. Fine restaurants

---

Havre de Grace *

McKee, Mary
301 So. Union Ave., 21078
(410) 939-5200

Amenities: 2,4,9,10,12,14,15,16
Breakfast: F.
Dbl. Oc.: $69.95 - $101.45
Sgl Oc.: $69.95 - $101.45
Third Person: $10.00

The Vandiver Inn—An 1886 Victorian surrounded by historic sites, museums, antiquing and marinas. Dining on weekends. Two blocks from Chesapeake Bay. Private baths. Air-conditioning. Catering available.

---

1. No Smoking	5. Tennis Available	9. Credit Cards Accepted	13. Lunch Available	17. Shared Baths
2. No Pets	6. Golf Available	10. Personal Check Accepted	14. Conference Rooms Avail.	18. Afternoon Tea
3 Off Season Rates	7. Swimmming Avail.	11. Reservations Necessary	15. Group Seminars Avail.	* Commisions given
4. Senior Citizen Rates	8. Skiing Available	12. Dinner Available	16. Private Baths	to Travel Agents

New Market

Rimel, Terry & Tom
9 W. Main St.
P.O. Box 299, 21774
(301) 865-5055

Amenities: 1,2,5,6,9,10,11,12, 13,16,17,18
Breakfast: F.

Dbl. Oc.: $78.75 - $126.50
Sgl. Oc.: $78.75 - $126.50

National Pike Inn—This Federal house (1800s) offers a special charm. Each guest room has its own special decor. Shop for antiques, dine in excellence, or just stroll the streets of this historic village. Many attractions nearby: wineries, parks and Frederick's bountiful sites.

New Market

Rossig, Jane
17 Main St.
Box 237, 21774
(301) 865-3318

Amenities: 2,5,8,
Breakfast: F.

Dbl. Oc.: $89.25
Sgl. Oc.: $78.75
Third Person: $10.00

Strawberry Inn—A professionally run B&B serving guests for the past 20 years. The restored 1837 Maryland farmhouse has five antique-furnished guest rooms. On the grounds is a restored log house with all the facilities for a small business meeting. Brochure. Children over seven only.

North East *

Demond, Lucia & Nick
102 Mill Lane, 29011
(410) 287-3532

Amenities: 1,2,9,10,11,17
Breakfast: F.

Dbl. Oc.: $57.75 - $68.25
Sgl. Oc.: $52.50 - $63.00
Third Person: $10.50

The Mill House—Circa 1710, in Maryland Historic Trust List of Historic Sites. We are on a tidal creek and furnished with antiques. The riverfront town has four antique shops and is t10 minutes from a designer factory outlet. Two miles south of I-95, exit 100. Brochure available.

Oakland *

Kight, Ed & Jana
208 N. 2nd St., 21550
(301) 334-9265

Amenities: 1,2,3,6,8,9,16,17
Breakfast: C. Plus

Dbl. Oc.: $54.00
Sgl. Oc.: $48.00
Third Person: $5.40

The Oak And Apple Bed And Breakfast—Colonial Revival on large lawn with mature trees in historic district. Columned front porch, living room with fireplace, cozy TV room. Breakfast served on the sunporch or by fireside in the dining room. Large lake, ski resorts, many parks and restaurants nearby.

1. No Smoking	5. Tennis Available	9. Credit Cards Accepted	13. Lunch Available	17. Shared Baths
2. No Pets	6. Golf Available	10. Personal Check Accepted	14. Conference Rooms Avail.	18. Afternoon Tea
3 Off Season Rates	7. Swimmming Avail.	11. Reservations Necessary	15. Group Seminars Avail.	* Commisions given
4. Senior Citizen Rates	8. Skiing Available	12. Dinner Available	16. Private Baths	to Travel Agents

Olney *

Polinger, Helen
16410 Batchellor's Forest Rd., 20832
(301) 774-7649

Amenities: 1,2,5,6,7,9,10,11,16,17
Breakfast: F.
Dbl. Oc.: $63.00 - $115.50
Sgl Oc.: $63.00 - $115.50
Third Person: $31.50

The Thoroughbred Bed And Breakfast—A beautiful 175-acre estate. Full breakfast, hot tub, swimming pool, pool table and piano. You may choose to stay in the main house, carriage house or quaint, renovated farmhouse. Two rooms have their own fireplaces and whirlpool tubs. 12 miles to DC. Six miles to Metrorail.

Salisbury *

Davenport, Flo
804 Spring Hill Rd., 21801
(410) 742-4887

Amenities: 1,2,4,9,10,17
Breakfast: C.

Dbl. Oc.: $64.80 - $70.20
Sgl. Oc.: $54.00

White Oak Inn—A warm, hospitable lakeside colonial home set on five acres of lush trees. Enjoy the wildlife and beautiful sunsets. A historic town of fine restaurants, antique shops, zoo, college and nearby beaches. Cruise the Wicomico River on the Paddle Queen.

Vienna *

Altergott, Harvey
111 Water St.
P.O. Box 98, 21869
(410) 376-3347

Amenities: 2,5,10,17,18
Breakfast: F.

Dbl. Oc.: $71.00 - $76.00
Sgl. Oc.: $65.00 - $70.00

The Tavern House—A colonial tavern on the Nanticoke River where special, full breakfasts are a social occasion. Glimpse into Michener's Chesapeake and enjoy the peace of a small town, the solitude of the marshes, biking over flat, rural roads or watching osprey in flight.

---

1. No Smoking	5. Tennis Available	9. Credit Cards Accepted	13. Lunch Available	17. Shared Baths
2. No Pets	6. Golf Available	10. Personal Check Accepted	14. Conference Rooms Avail.	18. Afternoon Tea
3 Off Season Rates	7. Swimmming Avail.	11. Reservations Necessary	15. Group Seminars Avail.	* Commisions given
4. Senior Citizen Rates	8. Skiing Available	12. Dinner Available	16. Private Baths	to Travel Agents

MASSACHUSETTS

The Bay State

Capitol: Boston
Statehood: February 6, 1788; the 6th state
State Motto: "By The Sword We Seek Peace,
               But Peace Only Under Liberty"
State Song: "All Hail To Massachusetts"
State Bird: Chickadee
State Flower: Mayflower
State Tree: American Elm

Much of the history of our country began in this state. The Pilgrims landed in Plymouth in 1620 and the Boston Tea Party took place in Boston Harbor on December 16, 1773. The historic ride of Paul Revere on April 19, 1775 is still reenacted each year and the battlefields of Lexington and Concord remain a great tourist attraction.

Massachusetts, a champion of education, boasts of having the oldest college in our country. Harvard College was established in 1636 in Cambridge and the first public library was started here when John Harvard gave his collection of books to the college.

The vacationer will find beautiful beaches from Newburyport on the north shore to Cape Cod on the south shore. The lovely Berkshire Hills in the western part of the state provide the stage for the Annual Berkshire Music Festival. Downtown Boston, especially Quincy Market, is a haven for entertainment, gourmet restaurants and lovely shops. Throughout the state, large industrial and technological companies are springing up because of the proximity to the educational facilities that are here.

Presidents John Adams, John Quincy Adams, John F. Kennedy and George Herbert Walker Bush were all born here.

MASSACHUSETTS

Alford

Miller, Lorraine & Daniel
35 Tremont Dr., 01230
(413) 528-1028

Amenities: 1,2,3,5,6,7,8,10, 11,16,17,18
Breakfast: F.

Dbl. Oc.: $80.00 - $95.00
Sgl. Oc.: $80.00 - $95.00
Third Person: $15.00

Hidden Acres — B&B In The Country—Away from the noises of the main road, yet minutes to area attractions and ski slopes. Quiet and peaceful setting. Treated like friends instead of guests. Breakfast in a large, sunny kitchen — "all you can eat." Become a part of our family of friends.

Amherst

Zieminski, Ann & Alan
599 Main St., 01002
(413) 253-5000

Amenities: 1,2,3,5,6,7,8,10,16
Breakfast: F.
Dbl. Oc.: $55.00 - $95.00
Sgl Oc.: $45.00 - $85.00
Third Person: $15.00
Child: $15.00

Allen House Bed And Breakfast Inn—Authentic antique-filled 1886 Victorian on three acres. Spacious bed chambers, private baths. Historic Preservation Award winner. Opposite Emily Dickinson's homestead. Located in a five- college area. Nearby historic Deerfield and Old Sturbridge Village.

Attleboro *

Logie, Caroline
18 French Farm Rd., 02703
(508)226-6365

Amenities: 1,2,3,4,6,7,9,10,16,17,18
Breakfast: F.
Dbl. Oc.: $55.00 - $70.00
Sgl Oc.: $45.00 - $60.00
Third Person: $10.00
Child: Under 6 yrs. - no charge

Emma C.'s Bed And Breakfast—Enjoy warmth and hospitality in this "country colonial" home. Guest rooms complete with antiques, quilts, fresh flowers, A/C and TVs. Enjoy sundeck by the pool in summer and wood stove in winter. Near train to Providence and Boston, 10 minutes to Wheaton College and Brown University.

1. No Smoking	5. Tennis Available	9. Credit Cards Accepted	13. Lunch Available	17. Shared Baths
2. No Pets	6. Golf Available	10. Personal Check Accepted	14. Conference Rooms Avail.	18. Afternoon Tea
3 Off Season Rates	7. Swimming Avail.	11. Reservations Necessary	15. Group Seminars Avail.	* Commisions given
4. Senior Citizen Rates	8. Skiing Available	12. Dinner Available	16. Private Baths	to Travel Agents

Boston

Butterworth, Susan
27 Brimmer St., 02108
(617) 523-7376

Amenities: 1,2,3,11,16
Breakfast: F.
Dbl. Oc.: $100.00 - $125.00
Sgl Oc.: $100.00 - $125.00
Third Person: $20.00
Child: $20.00

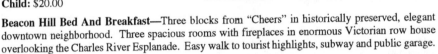

Beacon Hill Bed And Breakfast—Three blocks from "Cheers" in historically preserved, elegant downtown neighborhood. Three spacious rooms with fireplaces in enormous Victorian row house overlooking the Charles River Esplanade. Easy walk to tourist highlights, subway and public garage.

Boston *

Caldwell, Mary Lee
Box 158, 02133
(617) 479-6215

Amenities: 1,2,9,10,11,16
Breakfast: C. (F. on weekends)
Dbl. Oc.: $60.00 - $75.00
Sgl Oc.: $50.00 - $60.00
Third Person: $10.00

Quincy Adams Bed And Breakfast—An elegant Victorian home. Fireplaces, canopy bed and a jacuzzi spa. Downtown Boston and the Freedom Trail only 15 minutes away by subway or car. Located near restaurants, shops and the beach. Healthy and hearty breakfast served.

Boston *

Cote Dennis F.
82 Chandler St., 02116
(617) 482-0408

Amenities: 1,2,3,11,14,15,16
Breakfast: C. and F.
Dbl. Oc.: $110.00 - $120.00
Sgl Oc.: $105.00 - $115.00

82 Chandler Streer—Located in historic downtown off famous Copley Square, near the Hynes Convention Center. Beautifully restored 1863 red-brick townhouse. Finely furnished bedrooms with private bath and kitchenettes. Family-style breakfast served in penthouse kitchen. Easy walk to all city sites.

1. No Smoking	5. Tennis Available	9. Credit Cards Accepted	13. Lunch Available	17. Shared Baths
2. No Pets	6. Golf Available	10. Personal Check Accepted	14. Conference Rooms Avail.	18. Afternoon Tea
3 Off Season Rates	7. Swimmming Avail.	11. Reservations Necessary	15. Group Seminars Avail.	* Commisions given
4. Senior Citizen Rates	8. Skiing Available	12. Dinner Available	16. Private Baths	to Travel Agents

MASSACHUSETTS

Boston *

Hagopian Family , The
261 Newbury St., 02116
(617) 437-7666

Amenities: 2,3,9,16
Breakfast: C. and F.
Dbl. Oc.: $93.25
Sgl Oc.: $82.28
Third Person: $10.97
Child: Under 3 yrs. - no charge

Newbury Guest House—A 19th-century townhouse with 15 renovated rooms. Common parlor and outdoor patio on fashionable Newbury Street. Private baths. Parking available. Minutes from public transportation. Walking distance of entire city of Boston.

Boston *

Handler, Steven
248 Newbury St., 02116
(617) 266-7142

Amenities: 2,3,4,9,10,11,16
Breakfast: C.
Dbl. Oc.: $76.79
Sgl Oc.: $60.34
Third Person: $10.00

Beacon Inns And Guesthouses—Located in historic Back Bay offering guest rooms with private bath, kitchenette and air-conditioning. On the Green Line MBTA (public transit system) and Cambridge bus line. Welcome to Boston!

Boston *

Houghton, Mimi
106 Chestnut St., 02108
(617) 227-7866

Amenities: 10,11,14,15,16,17
Breakfast: F.

Dbl. Oc.: $85.00 - $100.00
Sgl. Oc.: $75.00 - $90.00
Child: Under 5 yrs. - no charge

Beacon Hill Accommodations—Close to "Cheers," Freedom Trail, fine shops and restaurants. Filled with antiques, books and paintings. Roof deck and central air-conditioning. Ideal for business or pleasure. Hostess is a native Bostonian — full of ideas for your stay.

---

1. No Smoking	5. Tennis Available	9. Credit Cards Accepted	13. Lunch Available	17. Shared Baths
2. No Pets	6. Golf Available	10. Personal Check Accepted	14. Conference Rooms Avail.	18. Afternoon Tea
3 Off Season Rates	7. Swimmming Avail.	11. Reservations Necessary	15. Group Seminars Avail.	* Commisions given
4. Senior Citizen Rates	8. Skiing Available	12. Dinner Available	16. Private Baths	to Travel Agents

Boston *

Rosenbaum, Thomas
26 Chandler, 02116
(800) 842-3450, (617) 482-3450

Amenities: 2,9,11,14,15,16
Breakfast: C.

Dbl. Oc.: $75.69 - $92.15
Sgl. Oc.: $64.72 - $81.18
Third Person: $10.97
Child: Under 12 yrs. - no charge

Chandler Inn—A small European-style hotel in the center of the city. The perfect option for the price-conscious traveler or tourist seeking a friendly sopt. Located between Copley and Park Square. We are within walking distance to most of Boston's historic sites as well as Amtrak, bus and subway.

Boston *

Terwilliger, Christine & Bob
23 Farrington Ave.
Allston Station (mail), 02134
(617)787-1860,(800)767-5337,0-800-896-040(from UK)

Amenities: 3,9,11,16,17
Breakfast: C. Plus

Dbl. Oc.: $50.00
Sgl. Oc.: $40.00
Third Person: $10.00

The Farrington Inn—A small European-style bed-and-breakfast inn, close to everything in downtown Boston. With comfort, convenience and hospitality, this is an economical choice in one of the most expensive cities in the world. On the Green Line of the subway system.

CAPE COD
*Barnstable**

Bain, Fay & Donald
3660 Rte. 6A,
P.O. Box 856, 02630
(508) 362-8044

Amenities: 2,3,5,6,7,9,10,15,16
Breakfast: F.
Dbl. Oc.: $109.70 - $181.01
Sgl Oc.: $109.70 - $181.01

Ashley Manor—A very special place. A secluded 1699 mansion in Cape Cod's historic area. Gracious, romantic and comfortable. Antiques and Oriental rugs. Beautifully appointed rooms and suites. All private baths. Fireplaces. New, private tennis court. Walk to beach and village.

1. No Smoking	5. Tennis Available	9. Credit Cards Accepted	13. Lunch Available	17. Shared Baths
2. No Pets	6. Golf Available	10. Personal Check Accepted	14. Conference Rooms Avail.	18. Afternoon Tea
3 Off Season Rates	7. Swimmming Avail.	11. Reservations Necessary	15. Group Seminars Avail.	* Commisions given
4. Senior Citizen Rates	8. Skiing Available	12. Dinner Available	16. Private Baths	to Travel Agents

MASSACHUSETTS

CAPE COD
Barnstable

Gedrin, Genny
61 Pine Lane,
Barnstable, 02630
(508) 362-8559

Amenities: 1,2,5,6,7,10,16
Breakfast: C.

Dbl. Oc.: $65.00 - $70.00
Sgl. Oc.: $60.00 - $65.00

Goss House—Located on the quiet north side of mid-Cape Cod. Three rooms with private baths. No children under 12. Open May 15 through October 31.

Barnstable Village

Chester, Evelyn
31 Powder Hill Rd.
P.O. Box 208, 02630
(508) 362-9356, Fax: (508) 362-9356

Amenities: 2,5,6,7,9,10,12,15,16,18
Breakfast: F.
Dbl. Oc.: $163.90 - $185.90
Sgl Oc.: $163.90 - $185.90

Cobb's Cove—A romantic, secluded, timbered colonial inn on a 1643 historic site. Centrally located on Cape Cod's quiet north side. Spacious rooms with gorgeous water views, whirlpool tubs and terrycloth robes. Superb breakfasts on flower- and bird-filled patio.

---

*Bourne Village**

Deasy, Terry & Paul
7 Coastal Way, 02532
(508) 759-6564

Amenities: 1,2,3,4,5,6,7,10,16,17
Breakfast: C. & F.
Dbl. Oc.: $60.00 - $75.00
Sgl Oc.: $50.00 - $65.00
Third Person: $15.00

Cape Cod Canalside Bed And Breakfast—"On Canal and bike path." Billion-dollar view of worldwide ships and fabulous yachts. New post-and-beam house. Separate private guest area. Fireplace, two cable TVs and kitchenette with microwave. Bikes, jog, fish, cookout, relax. Near Gulf Stream beaches. Open all year.

---

1. No Smoking	5. Tennis Available	9. Credit Cards Accepted	13. Lunch Available	17. Shared Baths
2. No Pets	6. Golf Available	10. Personal Check Accepted	14. Conference Rooms Avail.	18. Afternoon Tea
3 Off Season Rates	7. Swimmming Avail.	11. Reservations Necessary	15. Group Seminars Avail.	* Commisions given
4. Senior Citizen Rates	8. Skiing Available	12. Dinner Available	16. Private Baths	to Travel Agents

CAPE COD
Brewster *

DiCesare, Charles
1187 Main St., 02631
(508) 896-2223

Amenities: 1,2,3,5,6,7,9,10,11,16
Breakfast: F.
Dbl. Oc.: $86.00 - $119.00
Sgl Oc.: $72.00
Third Person: $30.00

Isaiah Clark House And Rose Cottage—Award-winning inn built in 1780, completely restored in 1986, with all the creature comforts. Set on five lush acres. Walk to beach and shops. Bike trail nearby. Country breakfast served on deck. Rated "Best of Outer Cape" - *Insiders Guide to Cape Cod.* Very hospitable hosts.

Brewster

Messina, Robert
716 Main St., 02631
(508) 896-3910, (800) 892-3910,
 Fax:(508) 896-4232

Amenities: 1,2,3,5,6,7,9,10,11,
 12,14,15,16,17,18
Breakfast: F.
Dbl. Oc.: $93.00 - $154.00
Sgl Oc.: $83.00 - $144.00

The Brewster Farmhouse Inn—Share the casual elegance of our 1850 farmhouse. Five impeccably furnished guest rooms, fireplaced gathering room, heated pool, spa, gardens and orchard. Walk to Cape Cod bay. Gourmet breakfast and afternoon tea. Unsurpassed services and amenities.

Brewster*

Rowan, Michele & Stephen
2553 Main St.
Box 1026, 02631
(508) 896-6114

Amenities: 1,2,3,5,6,7,9,10,
 11,14,15,16,17,18
Breakfast: F.

Dbl. Oc.: $44.00 - $94.00
Sgl. Oc.: $44.00 - $94.00
Third Person: $16.00
Child: $16.00

Old Sea Pines Inn—Lovely old turn-of-the-century mansion furnished with antiques. Front porch rockers, rooms with working fireplaces, 3-1/2 acres of privacy. Newly renovated and decorated. Noted for hospitality and service. Complimentary beverage on arrival. Near beautiful beaches.

---

1. No Smoking	5. Tennis Available	9. Credit Cards Accepted	13. Lunch Available	17. Shared Baths
2. No Pets	6. Golf Available	10. Personal Check Accepted	14. Conference Rooms Avail.	18. Afternoon Tea
3 Off Season Rates	7. Swimmming Avail.	11. Reservations Necessary	15. Group Seminars Avail.	* Commisions given
4. Senior Citizen Rates	8. Skiing Available	12. Dinner Available	16. Private Baths	to Travel Agents

CAPE COD
Centerville

Diehl, Joyce
497 Main St., 02632
(508) 771-5488

Amenities: 2,3,5,6,7,9,10,11, 16
Breakfast: F.

Dbl. Oc.: $85.00
Sgl. Oc.: $80.00

Copper Beach Inn—Built in 1830 and listed in The National Register of Historic Places, the inn features a parlor, common room and three bedrooms with private baths and A/C. Walk to Craigville Beach. Three miles to Hyannis and the ferry to Nantucket and Martha's Vineyard.

Chatham*

DeHan, Margaret
359 Main St., 02633
(800) 332-4667, (508) 945-9232

Amenities: 1,2,3,5,6,7,9,10, 11,16
Breakfast: C.

Dbl. Oc.: $90.00 - $160.00
Third Person: $20.00

Cranberry Inn At Chatham—A landmark village inn, located in the lovely seaside village of Chatham on Cape Cod. Newly renovated with modern amenities, including private baths, TV, phone and air-conditioning. Four-poster beds and antiques. Resident innkeepers are old-house enthusiasts.

Cotuit *

Goldstein, Lynn & Jerry
451 Main St., 02635
(508) 428-5228

Amenities: 1,2,3,5,6,7,9,10, 11,16,17
Breakfast: C. Plus

Dbl. Oc.: $75.00
Sgl. Oc.: $67.50
Third Person: $15.00

Salty Dog Inn—A circa 1850 restored Victorian house once owned by a cranberry farmer. Enjoy quaint Cotuit, a seaside village on Cape Cod. Warm-water ocean beach is nearby, which may be reached on a complimentary bike. Island boats are a short drive away. Convenient to dining and shopping.

Dennis*

Brophy, Marie
152 Whig St., 02638
(800) 736-0160, (508) 385-9928

Amenities: 2,3,5,6,7,9,10,11,15,16,17
Breakfast: C. Plus
Dbl. Oc.: $60.00 - $109.00
Sgl Oc.: $53.88 - $97.00
Third Person: $12.00
Child: Under 12 yrs. - no charge

Isaiah Hall B&B Inn—Come share the delight of Cape Cod's past. Enjoy the simple country pleasures of this lovely 1857 farmhouse. Relax in antique-filled guest and sitting rooms or in the quiet gardens. A leisurely walk to the beach or village with its restaurants, shops and playhouse.

---

1. No Smoking	5. Tennis Available	9. Credit Cards Accepted	13. Lunch Available	17. Shared Baths
2. No Pets	6. Golf Available	10. Personal Check Accepted	14. Conference Rooms Avail.	18. Afternoon Tea
3 Off Season Rates	7. Swimmming Avail.	11. Reservations Necessary	15. Group Seminars Avail.	* Commisions given
4. Senior Citizen Rates	8. Skiing Available	12. Dinner Available	16. Private Baths	to Travel Agents

CAPE COD
Dennis*

Jervant, Christina
946 Main St., 02638
(508) 385-6317

Amenities: 2,34,5,6,7,9,10,11,
16,17,18
Breakfast: C. Plus

Dbl. Oc.: $55.00 - $110.00
Sgl. Oc.: $55.00 - $110.00
Third Person: $15.00

The Four Chimneys Inn—Relaxing and comfortable, this charming Victorian home is located in Dennis Village, the geographical center of Cape Cod. Nine bright rooms, spacious common areas, lovely gardens and grounds. Lake views. Walk to beach, playhouse, shops and museums.

Dennisport*

Kelly, Gayle & Dan
152 Sea St., 02639
(508) 398-8470

Amenities: 2,3,9,10,17,18
Breakfast: F.

Dbl. Oc.: $60.34
Sgl. Oc.: $60.34
Third Person: $16.45
Child: Under 12 yrs. - $10.97

The Rose Petal Bed And Breakfast—An inviting 1872 home in a delightful seaside resort neighborhood. Superb full breakfast. Guest parlor, attractive yard, walk to sandy beach, shops, dining. In the heart of Cape Cod, enjoy diverse recreation, beautiful scenery and interesting history. Open all year.

Eastham*

Aitchison, Nan
3085 County Rd., 02642
(508) 255-1886

Amenities: 1,2,3,4,5,6,7,9,
10,11,12,14,15,16,18
Breakfast: F.
Dbl. Oc.: $65.00 - $110.00
Sgl Oc.: $65.00 - $110.00

The Over Look Inn, Cape Cod—A gracious Victorian manor located on the beautiful outer Cape. Victorian billiard room, library, parlor, porches, garden, ocean beach, bike trails, nature walks, whale watching, golf, windsurfing, antique and craft shops and fine restaurants. Scottish hospitality. Open year-round.

1. No Smoking	5. Tennis Available	9. Credit Cards Accepted	13. Lunch Available	17. Shared Baths
2. No Pets	6. Golf Available	10. Personal Check Accepted	14. Conference Rooms Avail.	18. Afternoon Tea
3 Off Season Rates	7. Swimmming Avail.	11. Reservations Necessary	15. Group Seminars Avail.	* Commisions given
4. Senior Citizen Rates	8. Skiing Available	12. Dinner Available	16. Private Baths	to Travel Agents

CAPE COD
Eastham*

Keith, Margaret
4885 Country Rd.
P.O. Box 238,
N. Eastham ,02651 (mail)
(508) 255-6632

Amenities: 2,3,4,5,6,7,9,10,
11,14,15,16,18
Breakfast: F.

Dbl. Oc.: $85.00 - $110.00
Sgl. Oc.: $70.00 - $100.00
Third Person: $15.00

Penny House Inn—Restored sea captain's house (1751). 10 guest rooms. In Cape Cod National Seashore area. Warm, relaxing, wide-plank floors, antiques, beamed ceilings, fireplaces and three public rooms. Theatres, galleries, restaurants nearby. Whale watching, hiking and bike trails.

East Orleans*

Anderson, Donna
186 Beach Rd.
P.O. Box 756, 02643
(508) 255-1312

Amenities: 2,3,5,7,9,10,15,16,17
Breakfast: C.
Dbl. Oc.: $54.85 - $109.70
Sgl Oc.: $54.85 - $109.70
Third Person: $21.94
Child: $21.94

Ship's Knee Inn—A 170-year-old restored sea captain's home that offers an intimate setting with only a three minute walk to beautiful sand-duned Nauset Beach. Tennis and swimming on premises. Open all year. Also 2-1/2 miles away on the town cove are heated cottages.

East Orleans *

Browne, Elizabeth
202 Main St.
Box 1501, 02643
(508) 255-8217

Amenities: 1,2,3,9,10,16
Breakfast: C.Plus

Dbl. Oc.: $71.31 - $104.22
Sgl. Oc.: $65.82 - $98.73
Third Person: $10.00
Child: Over 6 yrs. - $5.00

The Parsonage—A cozy, romantic inn tastefully decorated with country antiques, close to Nauset Beach. Studio apartment available. Bountiful breakfast served on patio or in dining room. Evening appetizer offered. Walk to restaurants and shops. Open year-round.

1. No Smoking	5. Tennis Available	9. Credit Cards Accepted	13. Lunch Available	17. Shared Baths
2. No Pets	6. Golf Available	10. Personal Check Accepted	14. Conference Rooms Avail.	18. Afternoon Tea
3 Off Season Rates	7. Swimmming Avail.	11. Reservations Necessary	15. Group Seminars Avail.	* Commisions given
4. Senior Citizen Rates	8. Skiing Available	12. Dinner Available	16. Private Baths	to Travel Agents

MASSACHUSETTS

CAPE COD

Fairhaven *

Reed, Kathleen
2 Oxford St., 02719
(508) 997-5512

Amenities: 1,2,5,6,7,9,10,11, 16
Breakfast: C.

Dbl. Oc.: $60.00 - $75.00
Sgl. Oc.: $55.00 - $70.00
Third Person: $10.00

Edgewater Bed And Breakfast—Historic house so close to water you'll think you're on a boat. Five rooms, all with private baths. Close to ferries to the islands, Cape Cod, Plymouth, Newport and New Bedford factory outlet shopping. Whale watching and swimming nearby. Year-round vacation area.

Falmouth

Lloyd, Caroline & Jim
27 Main St., 02540
(508) 548-3786,
(800) 682-0565

Amenities: 1,2,3,5,6,7,9,10,11,16,18
Breakfast: F.
Dbl. Oc.: $105.00 - $125.00
Sgl Oc.: $85.00 - $105.00

Mostly Hall Bed And Breakfast Inn—Romantic 1849 New Orleans-style home secluded from the road near historic village green. Close to beaches, ferries, shops and restaurants. Six large corner rooms with queen-size canopy beds. Air-conditioned. Bicycles, garden gazebo, widow's walk and wrap-around porch.

Falmouth

Long, Linda & Don
40 W. Main St., 02540
(508) 548-5621

Amenities: 1,2,3,5,6,7,9,10,11,16
Breakfast: F.
Dbl. Oc.: $75.00 - $110.00
Sgl Oc.: $65.00 - $100.00
Third Person: $15.00 - $20.00

Village Green Inn—Gracious 1804 colonial Victorian ideally located on historic village green. It offers four lovely guest rooms and a romantic two-room suite. Walk or bike to fine shops, restaurants and beach. Enjoy delightful gourmet breakfasts and seasonal refreshments.

---

1. No Smoking	5. Tennis Available	9. Credit Cards Accepted	13. Lunch Available	17. Shared Baths
2. No Pets	6. Golf Available	10. Personal Check Accepted	14. Conference Rooms Avail.	18. Afternoon Tea
3 Off Season Rates	7. Swimmming Avail.	11. Reservations Necessary	15. Group Seminars Avail.	* Commisions given
4. Senior Citizen Rates	8. Skiing Available	12. Dinner Available	16. Private Baths	to Travel Agents

MASSACHUSETTS

CAPE COD
Falmouth*

Peterson, AnnaMarie
226 Trotting Park, 02536
(508) 540-2962

Amenities: 1,3,4,5,10,16,18   **Dbl. Oc.:** $65.00

Breakfast: F.   **Sgl. Oc.:** $60.00

Bayberry Inn—Come to Cape Cod! Lovely and inexpensive rooms set in the woods. Children and pets welcome. Old-fashioned charm with modern comforts. One mile from shops and restaurants; two miles to beaches and island ferry. Open all year. Write for brochure.

Falmouth*

Sabo-Feller, Barbara
75 Locust St., 02540
(508) 540-1445

Amenities: 1,2,3,4,5,6,9,10,11,16
Breakfast: F.
Dbl. Oc.: $75.00 - $99.00
Sgl Oc.: $55.00 - $79.00
Third Person: $20.00

Captain Tom Lawrence House—A beautiful 1861 whaling captain's residence lovingly decorated with antiques. Spacious guest rooms, designer linens, private baths and fireplace. Warm, peaceful atmosphere. Delicious home-cooked breakfasts containing natural ingredients. Close to bikeway and ferries.

Harwich Port*

Ayer, Sara & Cal
74 Sisson Rd., 02646
(508) 432-9452

Amenities: 2,5,6,7,9,10,11,16   **Dbl. Oc.:** $65.00 - $70.00
Sgl. Oc.: $60.00 - $65.00

Breakfast: C.

The Coach House—Quiet and comfortable elegance in king and queen rooms. Ideally located for bike trail to national seashore, whale watching, fine beaches and day trips to the islands. Open May - October. Two-night minimum is requested. Brochure available.

Harwich Port*

Cunningham, Alyce & Wally   **Amenities:** 2,3,5,6,7,9,10,14,   **Dbl. Oc.:** $75.00 - $150.00
24 Pilgrim Rd., 02646   15,16   **Sgl. Oc.:** $75.00 - $150.00
(800) 432-4345, (508) 432-0810 **Breakfast:** F.   **Third Person:** $25.00
Child: Over 12 yrs. - $25.00

Dunscroft By-The-Sea Inn And Cottage—Beautiful and private mile-long beach on Nantucket Sound. Romantic, quiet and casual elegance. Designer linens, king/queen four posters and canopies. All private baths. Honeymoon cottage with fireplace. Walk to shops and restaurants.

1. No Smoking	5. Tennis Available	9. Credit Cards Accepted	13. Lunch Available	17. Shared Baths
2. No Pets	6. Golf Available	10. Personal Check Accepted	14. Conference Rooms Avail.	18. Afternoon Tea
3 Off Season Rates	7. Swimmming Avail.	11. Reservations Necessary	15. Group Seminars Avail.	* Commisions given
4. Senior Citizen Rates	8. Skiing Available	12. Dinner Available	16. Private Baths	to Travel Agents

CAPE COD
Harwich Port *

Kenney, Susan & Ed
85 Bank St., 02646
(800) 992-6550, (508) 432-1991

Amenities: 1,2,3,4,5,6,7,9,10,16
Breakfast: C.
Dbl. Oc.: $75.00 - $95.00
Sgl Oc.: $65.00 - $85.00
Third Person: No charge
Child: No charge

Captain's Quarters—Romantic 1850s Victorian with classic wrap-around porch. Charming guest rooms, private baths, queen brass beds, comfortable reading chairs. Delicious continental breakfasts. Walk to beach and town. Relaxed, friendly atmosphere. Lots to see and do.

Harwich, West *

Connell, Eileen & Jack
77 Main St., 02671
(508) 432-9628, (800) 356-9628

Amenities: 2,3,4,5,6,7,9,10, 12,13,14,15,16,18
Breakfast: F.
Dbl. Oc.: $82.27 - $109.70
Sgl. Oc.: $82.27 - $109.70
Third Person: $25.00
Child: $25.00

Cape Cod Sunny Pines B&B Inn—Irish hospitality in a Victorian ambience near the Cape's elbow. Pool, Jacuzzi, A/C, TV, refrigerator. Walk to beach. Day trip to Boston, Nantucket, Vineyard and Plymouth. Whale watching. Irish pub and full-service restaurant. Gourmet Irish breakfast by candlelight.

Harwich , West*

Denton, Deborah, Fred & Ricky
186 Belmont Rd.
P.O. Box 444, 02671
(800) 321-3155, (508) 432-7766

Amenities: 2,3,4,5,6,7,9,10, 11,16
Breakfast: F.
Dbl. Oc.: $75.00 - $130.00
Sgl. Oc.: $65.00 - $120.00
Third Person: $20.00
Child: $20.00

The Lion's Head Inn—A distinctive blend of the history of Cape Cod and amenities of a small resort. All guest suites have private bath, sitting area and antique country decor. Full gourmet breakfast served poolside or fireside. Quiet wooded setting. Walk to beach, fine dining and shopping. Great!

---

1. No Smoking	5. Tennis Available	9. Credit Cards Accepted	13. Lunch Available	17. Shared Baths
2. No Pets	6. Golf Available	10. Personal Check Accepted	14. Conference Rooms Avail.	18. Afternoon Tea
3 Off Season Rates	7. Swimmming Avail.	11. Reservations Necessary	15. Group Seminars Avail.	* Commisions given
4. Senior Citizen Rates	8. Skiing Available	12. Dinner Available	16. Private Baths	to Travel Agents

CAPE COD
Hyannis *

Battle, Patricia
397 Sea St., 02601
(508) 771-7213

Amenities: 2,3,9,10,11,16
Breakfast: C. Plus

Dbl. Oc.: $65.00 - $92.00
Sgl. Oc.: $60.00 - $80.00
Third Person: $10.00
Child: Under 12 yrs. - $10.00

Sea Breeze Inn—The inn is a quaint B&B, situated three minutes from the beach and just a 20-minute walk to the ferries for the islands and to downtown Hyannis. All of our rooms have private baths and are very nicely decorated. Some of our rooms have air-conditioning.

Hyannis

Whitehead, J.B.
Nelson, Lois M.
358 Sea St., 02601
(508) 775-8030

Amenities: 1,2,5,6,7,9,10,11,
16,17
Breakfast: F.

Dbl. Oc.: $76.79 - $98.73
Sgl. Oc.: $71.31 - $93.25
Third Person: $10.00

The Inn On Sea Street—A romantic, elegant Victorian inn just steps from the beach. Fireplace; large, quiet rooms; canopy beds; private baths; antiques; gourmet breakfast of homemade delights; fruit and cheese. Near island ferries and Kennedy compound. Warm and friendly atmosphere.

Orleans*

Standish, Dorothy C.
163 Beach Rd., Orleans, 02653
(508) 255-6654

Amenities: 2,3,4,9,10,11,16,
17
Breakfast: C. Plus

Dbl. Oc.: $32.00 - $95.00
Sgl. Oc.: $30.00 - $80.00
Third Person: $15.00
Child: Under 6 yrs. - no charge

The Farmhouse—Walk to Nauset Beach and Atlantic Ocean. Seashore setting. Open year-round. Antiques. Some rooms have ocean views. Breakfast on the deck. Close to golfing, fine restaurants, theatre, beaches and museums. Picnic tables available.

---

1. No Smoking	5. Tennis Available	9. Credit Cards Accepted	13. Lunch Available	17. Shared Baths
2. No Pets	6. Golf Available	10. Personal Check Accepted	14. Conference Rooms Avail.	18. Afternoon Tea
3 Off Season Rates	7. Swimmming Avail.	11. Reservations Necessary	15. Group Seminars Avail.	* Commisions given
4. Senior Citizen Rates	8. Skiing Available	12. Dinner Available	16. Private Baths	to Travel Agents

CAPE COD
Orleans

Terrell, Sandy & Charles
8 Academy Pl., PO Box 1407, Orleans, 02653
508-255-3181

Amenities: 1,2,3,9,10,11,16,17,18
Breakfast: C.
Dbl. Oc.: $60.34 - $82.28
Sgl Oc.: $60.34 - $82.28
Third Person: $16.46
Child: Over 6 yrs. welcome

Academy Place Bed And Breakfast—Antique Cape Cod home awaits you. Walk to restaurants and shops. Continental breakfast of juice, fruit, cereal, homemade muffins, breads and jams. Beaches two miles away. National Seashore 10 minutes away. Bike path nearby. Open Memorial Day to Columbus Day.

Provincetown

Paoletti, Leonard
156 Bradford St., 02657
(508) 487-2543

Amenities: 2,3,9,11,16
Breakfast: C.

Dbl. Oc.: $83.16 - $88.56
Sgl. Oc.: $83.16 - $88.56
Third Person: $21.60
Child: $21.60

Elephant Walk Inn—A romantic country inn near Provincetown's center. The spacious, elegantly furnished rooms all have private baths, color TVs, refrigerators and ceiling fans. Enjoy our large sun deck or lounge with your morning coffee. Free parking on the premises. Open April - October.

Provincetown

Schoolman, David
22 Commercial St., 02657
(508) 487-0706

Amenities: 2,3,5,6,7,10,11,16,17
Breakfast: C.
Dbl. Oc.: $74.00 - $210.00
Sgl. Oc.: $74.00 - $210.00
Third Person: $16.20
Child: Under 1 yr. - no charge

Land's End Inn—Overlooking all of Cape Cod Bay, Land's End offers Victorian comfort and quiet. Close to Provincetown and the National Seashore beaches. Guest rooms are homey and comfortable. Common rooms offer quiet socializing or contemplation. Beautiful views abound.

1. No Smoking	5. Tennis Available	9. Credit Cards Accepted	13. Lunch Available	17. Shared Baths
2. No Pets	6. Golf Available	10. Personal Check Accepted	14. Conference Rooms Avail.	18. Afternoon Tea
3 Off Season Rates	7. Swimmming Avail.	11. Reservations Necessary	15. Group Seminars Avail.	* Commisions given
4. Senior Citizen Rates	8. Skiing Available	12. Dinner Available	16. Private Baths	to Travel Agents

CAPE COD
*Sandwich**

Dickson, Elaine & Harry
152 Main St., 02563
(800) 388-CAPT, Fax: (508) 888-2940

Amenities: 1,2,3,4,5,6,7,9,
10,11,14,16,17
Breakfast: F.
Dbl. Oc.: $54.85 - $93.25
Sgl Oc.: $49.37 - $87.76
Third Person: $16.46

Captain Ezra Nye House—Stately 1829 Federal in the heart of Sandwich Village. Walk to museums, ocean, Heritage Plantation. Chosen one of "the top 50 inns in America" by *Inn Times*. Six rroms, one suite, private baths, working fireplaces.

*Sandwich**

Lemieux, Reale J.
1-3 Bay Beach Ln.
Box 151, 02563
(508) 888-8813

Amenities: 1,2,3,5,6,7,10,11,
16,18
Breakfast: C. Plus

Dbl. Oc.: $125.00 - $175.00
Sgl. Oc.: $125.00 - $150.00
Third Person: $25.00

Bay Beach Bed And Breakfast—New ocean-front contemporary home which overlooks the beach and Cape Cod Bay. Choose from three spacious guest suites with ocean views, private balconies and elegant furnishings. The honeymoon suite features a whirlpool bath. Each room offers a private bath, color TV and A/C.

*Sandwich**

Merrell, Kay & David
158 Main St., Sandwich, 02563
(508) 888-4991

Amenities: 1,2,3,4,5,6,7,9,10,16,17,18
Breakfast: F.
Dbl. Oc.: $54.00 - $82.00
Sgl Oc.: $43.00 - $71.00
Third Person: $10.00 - $15.00
Child: $10.00 - $15.00

The Summer House—An elegant circa 1835 B&B featured in Country Living Magazine. Located in historic Sandwich Village. Antiques, hand-stitched quilts, large, sunny rooms. English-style gardens. Walk to dining, shops, museums and beach. Bountiful breakfast, elegantly served. Afternoon tea.

---

1. No Smoking	5. Tennis Available	9. Credit Cards Accepted	13. Lunch Available	17. Shared Baths
2. No Pets	6. Golf Available	10. Personal Check Accepted	14. Conference Rooms Avail.	18. Afternoon Tea
3 Off Season Rates	7. Swimmming Avail.	11. Reservations Necessary	15. Group Seminars Avail.	* Commisions given
4. Senior Citizen Rates	8. Skiing Available	12. Dinner Available	16. Private Baths	to Travel Agents

CAPE COD
Truro Center
Williams, Stephen
Route 6-A, 02666
(508) 349-3358

Amenities: 2,3,5,6,7,10,11,15,17
Breakfast: C.
Dbl. Oc.: $55.00
Sgl Oc.: $50.00
Third Person: $10.00

Parker House—A warm, classic 1850 full Cape house with many antiques. Close to beaches and the charming narrow streets of Provincetown and Wellfleet. Open year-round with a limited occupancy. Nearby restaurants.

Yarmouth Port*
Perna, Malcolm
Rte. 6A, 277 Main St., 02675
((800) 999-3416,
(508) 362-4348

Amenities: 3,4,5,6,7,,8,9,10,
12,13,14,15,16,18
Breakfast: C.

Dbl. Oc.: $60.00 - $95.00
Sgl. Oc.: $50.00 - $85.00
Third Person: $20.00
Child: Under 2 yrs. - $5.00

The Colonial House Inn—Offers Old-World charm on the quiet side of Cape Cod, yet is minutes from shopping, golf, beaches and night life. We provide you with "the best of all worlds." Indoor pool, jacuzzi, TV, A/C, sun deck and handicapped accessibility. All prices include dinner. Mobil-3 star.

Yarmouth Port
Tilly, Sven
101 Main St., 02675
(508) 362-4496

Amenities: 2,3,5,6,7,10,16,
17
Breakfast: C. Plus

Dbl. Oc.: $55.00 - $85.00
Third Person: $10.00

Olde Captain's Inn—Old captain's inn on the Cape. Charming, restored 160-year-old inn located in historic district of the village. Walk to fine restaurants, antique shops. Whale watching nearby. Bike trails and nature walks. Third night free.

Yarmouth, South
Crowell, Mary & Walter
345 High Bank Rd. So.
Yarmouth, 02664
(508) 394-4182

Amenities: 2,3,6,10,11,16
Breakfast: C. Plus

Dbl. Oc.: $55.00 - $100.00
Third Person: $15.00
Child: $15.00

The Four Winds—A 1712 sea captain's homestead in historic So. Yarmouth. Near golf, beaches and bike trail. A 1712 carriage house sleeps six, with wood stove and kitchen. Available seasonally. Cottage sleeps three. Fireplace and kitchen. Suite with queen bed, sitting room, sleep sofa and wet bar.

---

1. No Smoking	5. Tennis Available	9. Credit Cards Accepted	13. Lunch Available	17. Shared Baths
2. No Pets	6. Golf Available	10. Personal Check Accepted	14. Conference Rooms Avail.	18. Afternoon Tea
3 Off Season Rates	7. Swimmming Avail.	11. Reservations Necessary	15. Group Seminars Avail.	* Commisions given
4. Senior Citizen Rates	8. Skiing Available	12. Dinner Available	16. Private Baths	to Travel Agents

Chelmsford *

Pinette, Lorraine C.
4 Westview Ave.
P.O. Box 4141, 01824
(508) 256-0074

Amenities: 1,5,6,7,8,10,15, 17
Breakfast: C.

Dbl. Oc.: $60.00
Sgl. Oc.: $50.00

Westview Landing—A large contemporary on a tranquil pond. Boating, fishing and swimming in summer. During winter, relish the spa and rest by the fireplace. Thirty miles northwest of Boston. Near Routes 495, 93, 128 and 3. Close to historic Lexington, Concord and Lowell; 15 miles south of Nashua N.H.,

Cohasset *

Tibbetts, Maggie
90 Howard Gleason Rd., 02025
(617) 383-9200

Amenities: 1,2,5,7,10,11,14, 15,16,18
Breakfast: C. Plus

Dbl. Oc.: $89.25 - $131.25
Sgl. Oc.: $89.25 - $131.25
Third Person: $25.00

Actor's Row—Rambling Cape on three acres of manicured lawns and gardens. Nineteen miles from Boston. Situated on the harbor. Ten working fireplaces, exquisite moldings, bedrooms overlooking the harbor or gorgeous pool. Tennis court and jacuzzi. Fine restaurants nearby.

Concord *

Mudry, Marilyn
462 Lexington Rd., 01742
(508) 369-5610

Amenities: 2,3,10,16,18
Breakfast: C. Plus
Dbl. Oc.: $85.00 - $150.00
Sgl Oc.: $75.00 - $110.00
Third Person: $20.00
Child: Under 12 yrs. - $10.00

Hawthorne Inn—An 1870 colonial filled with antiques, quilts and modern and ancient artworks. Situated on land once owned by Emerson, Alcott and Hawthorne. Close to authors' homes, Walden Pond and the Old North Bridge. Site of first Revolutionary battle. Spiritually rejuvenating. Welcome.

Concord *

Williams, Kate
1694 Main St., 01742
(508) 369-9119, (800) 292-1369

Amenities: 1,2,3,5,6,7,8,9,10, 11,14,15,16,18
Breakfast: C. Plus

Dbl. Oc.: $71.30 - $82.28
Sgl. Oc.: $65.82 - $76.80
Third Person: $10.00

The Colonel Roger Brown House—A historic colonial house. All rooms have private baths, air-conditioning and TV. Use of adjacent fitness club. Perfect location for local historic sights and Walden Pond. Easy drive or public transportation to Boston and Cambridge.

1. No Smoking	5. Tennis Available	9. Credit Cards Accepted	13. Lunch Available	17. Shared Baths
2. No Pets	6. Golf Available	10. Personal Check Accepted	14. Conference Rooms Avail.	18. Afternoon Tea
3 Off Season Rates	7. Swimmming Avail.	11. Reservations Necessary	15. Group Seminars Avail.	* Commisions given
4. Senior Citizen Rates	8. Skiing Available	12. Dinner Available	16. Private Baths	to Travel Agents

Deerfield *

Whitney, Phyllis
330 N. Main St., 01373
(413) 665-3829

Amenities: 7,10,16,17
Breakfast: F.

Dbl. Oc.: $65.00 - $110.00
Third Person: $15.00

Orchard Terrace Bed And Breakfast—Located just four miles from historic Deerfield and central to five colleges. A lovely Georgian colonial situated on 11 acres. Nearby family ski areas. Only 10 miles to N.E. Morgan-horse show grounds. For those seeking something unique while in the Pioneer Valley.

Dartmouth , South *

Scully, Meryl
631 Elm St.
Padanaram Village, 02748
(508) 996-4554

Amenities: 1,2,9,10,11,17,18
Breakfast: F.

Dbl. Oc.: $65.00
Sgl. Oc.: $55.00

The Little Red House—A charming gambrel colonial home overlooking a horse and cow pasture. Offers many country accents, antiques, a lovely living room with fireplace and a gazebo to enjoy in the backyard. It is close to the harbor, historic sites and major tourist areas.

Gloucester *

Swinson, Ginny & Hal
83 Riverview, 01930
(508) 281-1826

Amenities: 2,3,4,5,6,7,10,11,
14,15,17
Breakfast: C. Plus

Dbl. Oc.: $65.00 - $75.00
Sgl. Oc.: $60.00 - $70.00

Riverview—In historic Cape Ann on the Intercoastal Waterway. Enjoy boats and private beach from this renovated Victorian home. Nearby art colony, shopping, restaurants, great beaches and whale watching.

Great Barrington *

Burdsall, Priscilla & Richard
RD 3, Box 125, 01230
(413) 528-4092

Amenities: 1,2,3,5,6,7,8,9,
10,11,15,16,17,18
Breakfast: F.
Dbl. Oc.: $70.00 & up

Baldwin Hill Farm—A hilltop farm home with four bedrooms. Spectacular views, 450 acres for walks, hiking and biking. Maps and menus. Away from highway noise, but close to major routes. Easy access to summer, fall and winter attractions. Many excellent restaurants in area. Wildlife. Open all year.

1. No Smoking	5. Tennis Available	9. Credit Cards Accepted	13. Lunch Available	17. Shared Baths
2. No Pets	6. Golf Available	10. Personal Check Accepted	14. Conference Rooms Avail.	18. Afternoon Tea
3 Off Season Rates	7. Swimming Avail.	11. Reservations Necessary	15. Group Seminars Avail.	* Commisions given
4. Senior Citizen Rates	8. Skiing Available	12. Dinner Available	16. Private Baths	to Travel Agents

Great Barrington

DuFour, Paul A.
1 Newsboy
Monument Lane, 01230
(413) 528-2882

Amenities: 1,2,3,5,6,7,8,10, 11,17,18
Breakfast: F.

Dbl. Oc.: $65.82 - $93.25
Sgl. Oc.: $60.34 - $87.76

Littlejohn Manor—Savor Victorian charm dedicated to your comfort. Antiques enhance warmly furnished air-conditioned rooms. Near Tanglewood, Jacob's Pillow, fine dining and shops. Scenic views. Herb and flower gardens. Five miles to Butternut and Catamount skiing. Traditional full English breakfast.

Lanesboro *

Sullivan, Marianne & Dan
30 Old Cheshire Rd., 01237
(413) 442-0260

Amenities: 1,2,5,6,7,8,10,15, 17
Breakfast: F.

Dbl. Oc.: $75.00
Sgl. Oc.: $60.00
Third Person: $15.00
Child: Under 3 yrs. - no charge

The Tuckered Turkey—Beautiful Berkshire location! Enjoy the cultural attractions in Lenox and Williamstown. Five minutes to the new Berkshire Mall. A restored 1800s farmhouse. Three guest rooms cater to special occasions. Three acres of views of the Berkshire Hills.

Lee

Toole, Joseph
Main St., 01238
(800) 537-4321,
(413) 243-2221

Amenities: 1,2,3,9,10,11,12,13,14,16
Breakfast: C. Plus
Dbl. Oc.: $75.00 - $220.00
Third Person: $25.00

The Chambery Inn—1885 restoration masterpiece with 500-square-foot suites, king canopy beds, whirlpool baths, fireplaces, breakfast delivered to your suite, TV, air-conditioning, private baths and room service. Impeccable facilities. No smoking.

1. No Smoking	5. Tennis Available	9. Credit Cards Accepted	13. Lunch Available	17. Shared Baths
2. No Pets	6. Golf Available	10. Personal Check Accepted	14. Conference Rooms Avail.	18. Afternoon Tea
3 Off Season Rates	7. Swimmming Avail.	11. Reservations Necessary	15. Group Seminars Avail.	* Commisions given
4. Senior Citizen Rates	8. Skiing Available	12. Dinner Available	16. Private Baths	to Travel Agents

MASSACHUSETTS

Lenox *

Mears, Joan & Richard
5 Greenwood St., 01240
(413) 637-0975

Amenities: 2,3,8,9,10,11,16,18
Breakfast: F.
Dbl. Oc.: $80.00 - $190.00
Sgl Oc.: $80.00 - $100.00
Third Person: $25.00
Child: $25.00

Whistler's Inn—Featured in *New York Magazine's* "Great Escapes.", and Fodor's. English Tudor mansion built in 1820 that captures the warmth and elegance of a bygone era. Eight acres of woodland and gardens. Antiques. Large library. Music room. Central to the Berkshires. Gracious accommodations.

Lenox

Mekinda, Mario
141 Main St., 01240
(413) 637-0193

Amenities: 2,3,5,6,7,8,9,11, 15,16,18
Breakfast: F.

Dbl. Oc.: $95.00 - $185.00
Sgl. Oc.: $90.00 - $180.00
Third Person: $25.00

Garden Gables Inn—A 220-year-old charming and quiet inn, located in historic Lenox on five wooded acres dotted with gardens. Fireplaces, porches, whirlpool tubs, antiques, 72-foot-long swimming pool. All 14 rooms have private baths. Tanglewood one mile away, skiing five miles away.

Lenox

Miller, Anne & Joseph
15 Hawthorne St., 01240
(413) 637-3013

Amenities: 1,2,3,5,6,7,8,9,10, 16,18
Breakfast: C. Plus

Dbl. Oc.: $70.00 - $165.00
Sgl. Oc.: $70.00 - $165.00
Third Person: $20.00

Brook Farm Inn—There is poetry here. Country Victorian in shaded glen with 12 bedrooms. fireplaces, library and pool. Poetry readings on weekends. Near Tanglewood, shops and museums. Fall foliage, downhill and cross-country skiing. Relax and enjoy.

Lenox *

Rolland, David
197 Main St., 01240
(413) 637-0562

Amenities: 2,3,5,6,7,8,9,10, 11,12,14,15,16
Breakfast: C. Plus

Dbl. Oc.: $50.00 - $325.00
Sgl. Oc.: $50.00 - $325.00
Third Person: $75.00

Cornell Inn—Located in the heart of Lenox, we are a full-service 1880s Victorian inn and tavern with a romantic atmosphere. Antique decor, private baths, air-conditioning, fireplaces, Jacuzzi and sauna. Four modern luxury apartments. Convenient to all Berkshire attractions.

---

1. No Smoking	5. Tennis Available	9. Credit Cards Accepted	13. Lunch Available	17. Shared Baths
2. No Pets	6. Golf Available	10. Personal Check Accepted	14. Conference Rooms Avail.	18. Afternoon Tea
3 Off Season Rates	7. Swimming Avail.	11. Reservations Necessary	15. Group Seminars Avail.	* Commisions given
4. Senior Citizen Rates	8. Skiing Available	12. Dinner Available	16. Private Baths	to Travel Agents

193

MASSACHUSETTS

Lenox *

Wessel, Sonya & Michael
830 East St., 01240
(413) 442-2057

Amenities: 2,3,6,7,8,10,11,16,17
Breakfast: F.
Dbl. Oc.: $66.00 - $148.00
Third Person: $25.00
Child: Under 12 yrs. - $12.00

Summer Hill Farm—An historic country farmhouse on 20 acres. Horse barn, woods, fields, views across October Mountain. Seven comfortable bedrooms, two with fireplaces. Old Persian rugs. Antiques. Tanglewood, theatre, Jacobs Pillow Dance, shops, museums and restaurants nearby. Pleasant

Lexington *

Halewood, Carol
2 Larchmont Lane, 02173
(617) 862-5404

Amenities: 1,2,5,6,10,16,17
Breakfast: F.

Dbl. Oc.: $60.00
Sgl. Oc.: $50.00
Third Person: $10.00
Child: Under 12 yrs. - $10.00

Halewood House—A cozy Cape home within one mile of Lexington Center and I-95. Charming bedrooms with special touches, porch, patio and large, modern bath. Guest rooms separate from hostess' living area. Delightful breakfasts.

Marblehead

Conway, Peter
58 Washington St., 01945
(617) 631-2186

Amenities: 2,9,10,11,16,18
Breakfast: C.

Dbl. Oc.: $75.00 - $175.00
Third Person: $15.00

The Harbor Light Inn—Premier inn one block form the harbor, with rooms featuring air-conditioning, TV, private baths and working fireplaces. Two rooms have double jacuzzis and sun decks. Beautiful 18th-century period mahongany furniture. Located in Old Town, 14 miles from Boston.

Marblehead

Livingston, Susan
23 Gregory St., 01945
(617) 631-1032

Amenities: 1,2,3,5,7,10,11, 17
Breakfast: C.

Dbl. Oc.: $70.00 - $75.00
Sgl. Oc.: $60.00 - $65.00
Child: Under 10 yrs. - no charge

Harborside House—A handsome 1830 colonial overlooking picturesque harbor. Two guest rooms with shared bath. Period dining room. Sunny breakfast porch. Fireplaced living room. Third-story deck. Near historic sites, antique shops and gourmet restaurants. Home-baked goods. Fat cat.

1. No Smoking	5. Tennis Available	9. Credit Cards Accepted	13. Lunch Available	17. Shared Baths
2. No Pets	6. Golf Available	10. Personal Check Accepted	14. Conference Rooms Avail.	18. Afternoon Tea
3 Off Season Rates	7. Swimming Avail.	11. Reservations Necessary	15. Group Seminars Avail.	* Commisions given
4. Senior Citizen Rates	8. Skiing Available	12. Dinner Available	16. Private Baths	to Travel Agents

Marblehead *

Pabich, Diane & Richard
25 Spray Ave., 01945
(800) 446-2995, (508) 741-0680

Amenities: 2,7,9,10,14,15,16, 18
Breakfast: C.

Dbl. Oc.: $100.42 - $211.40
Sgl. Oc.: $100.42 - $211.40
Third Person: $23.55
Child: $23.55

Spray Cliff On The Ocean—A 1910 English Tudor summer home set high above the Atlantic. The inn provides a spacious and elegant atmosphere inside. The grounds include a brick terrace surrounded by lush flower gardens where eider ducks, cormorants and sea gulls abound. Spectacular views!

MARTHA'S VINEYARD
Edgartown*

Pieczenik, Roberta
Pease's Point Way
Box 2798, 02539
(508) 627-7289

Amenities: 2,3,9,10,13,15,16, 18
Breakfast: C. Plus

Dbl. Oc.: $95.00 - $195.00
Sgl. Oc.: $95.00 - 4195.00
Third Person: $20.00

Captain Dexter House Of Edgartown—Your perfect country inn! Built in 1840 and meticulously restored. Many rooms have fireplaces, canopy beds and antique chests. Large outdoor landscaped gardens. Delicious home-baked breakfast. Walk to town and harbor. Unmatched hospitality.

Edgartown*

Hall, Peggy
222 Upper Main St.
P.O. Box 1228, 02539
(508) 627-8137

Amenities: 2,3,5,6,7,9,10,11,16,17,18
Breakfast: C.
Dbl. Oc.: $88.00 - $138.00
Sgl Oc.: $88.00 - $138.00

The Arbor—Turn-of-the-century English country inn, located on the bicycle path in Edgartown, furnished with antiques and vintage furniture. Relax in the garden or have tea in the parlor. Stroll to the enchanting, bustling village with its wonderful shops and restaurants

Edgartown*

Hurley, Fred
129 Main St., 02539
(508) 627-9655, (800) 477-9655

Amenities: 3,9,10,11,16,17
Breakfast: C. Plus

Dbl. Oc.: $93.25 - $191.98
Third Person: $15.00

Ashley Inn—A romantic 1860s sea captain's home nestled among spacious lawns and apple trees. Conveniently located on historic Main Street, the inn is a leisurely stroll to shops, beaches and fine foods. We look forward to welcoming you to Martha's Vineyard.

1. No Smoking	5. Tennis Available	9. Credit Cards Accepted	13. Lunch Available	17. Shared Baths
2. No Pets	6. Golf Available	10. Personal Check Accepted	14. Conference Rooms Avail.	18. Afternoon Tea
3 Off Season Rates	7. Swimmming Avail.	11. Reservations Necessary	15. Group Seminars Avail.	* Commisions given
4. Senior Citizen Rates	8. Skiing Available	12. Dinner Available	16. Private Baths	to Travel Agents

MARTHA'S VINEYARD
Edgartown

Radford, Earle
56 N. Water St.
Box 1211, 02539
(508) 627-4794

Amenities: 2,3,5,6,7,10,11,16,17
Breakfast: F.
Dbl. Oc.: $60.34 - $159.07
Third Person: $20.00

The Edgartown Inn—A historic inn. Guests include Daniel Webster, Nathaniel Hawthorne and John Kennedy. One block off the harbor in the heart of the historic district and convenient to beaches, restaurants and shops. Famous for our full breakfasts with all homemade breads, cakes and waffles.

Edgartown*

Smith, Linda & Ben
104 Main St.
P.O. Box 128, 02539
(508) 627-8633

Amenities: 2,3,4,5,6,7,9,10,11,15,16,18
Breakfast: C. Plus
Dbl. Oc.: $65.00 - $205.00
Sgl Oc.: $58.50 _ $184.50
Third Person: $20.00
Child: $20.00

Point Way Inn—A New England seaport 15- room inn, serving a full continental breakfast and afternoon tea. All rooms have private baths, many with fireplaces and balconies. Use of our "inn" auto is available to our guests. Open all year.

Gayhead

LeBovit, Elise
Off State Rd., 02535
(508) 645-9018

Amenities: 3,7,9,10,11,14,16, 17
Breakfast: F.

Dbl. Oc.: $90.00 - $185.00
Sgl. Oc.: $75.00 - $170.00
Third Person: $15.00
Child: Under 12 yrs. - $8.00

Duck Inn—The Martha's Vineyard's sunset, ocean-view retreat with gourmet health breakfasts. Short walk to beach, cliffs, lighthouse, restaurants and shops. A 200-year-old farmhouse on 8-1/2 acres with fireplaces, decks, piano, hot tub and masseuse. A casual and eclectic antique setting.

1. No Smoking	5. Tennis Available	9. Credit Cards Accepted	13. Lunch Available	17. Shared Baths
2. No Pets	6. Golf Available	10. Personal Check Accepted	14. Conference Rooms Avail.	18. Afternoon Tea
3 Off Season Rates	7. Swimmming Avail.	11. Reservations Necessary	15. Group Seminars Avail.	* Commisions given
4. Senior Citizen Rates	8. Skiing Available	12. Dinner Available	16. Private Baths	to Travel Agents

MARTHA'S VINEYARD

Oak Bluffs*

Convery-Luce, Betsi
Seaview Ave.
Box 299BB, 02557
(508) 693-4187

Amenities: 2,3,7,9,10,11,14, 15,16,18

Breakfast: C.

Dbl. Oc.: $110.00 - $220.00

The Oak House—A historic Victorian governor's mansion, circa 1872, located on the beach. Ten elegant, theme rooms, each with private bath and most with balconies and ocean views. Discount off-season. Steps to ferry, beach, town and shuttle bus.

Oak Bluffs

Katsomakis, Lisa
222 Circuit Ave.
P.O. Box 1033, 02557
(508) 693-7928

Amenities: 3,5,6,7,9,10,15, 17

Breakfast: C.

Dbl. Oc.: $88.00
Sgl. Oc.: $78.00
Third Person: $15.00
Child: Under 5 yrs. - no charge

Tivoli Inn—Charming rooms and reasonable rates. Within walking distance of town, shops, restaurants, night life, beaches and ferries. Complimentary breakfast buffet. A great place with a clean and friendly atmosphere.

Oak Bluffs*

Zaiko, Pamela & Calvin
2 Pennacook Ave., Oak Bluffs, 02557
(508) 693-3955

Amenities: 2,3,5,6,7,9,10,11, 12,13,16

Breakfast: C.

Dbl. Oc.: $98.73 - $137.13
Sgl. Oc.: $88.73 - $127.13
Third Person: $15.00
Child: No charge

The Beach House—Located on the beautiful island of Martha's Vineyard. Directly across from a large beach. We offer queen-size brass beds, private baths and TV. Close to shops, restaurants, ferries, bike and moped rentals, tennis and golf, shuttle and tour buses.

Owen Park

Clarke, Mary & John
Box 1939, Owen Park, 02568
(508) 693-1646

Amenities: 5,6,7,9,10,11,14,15,16,17
Breakfast: C.
Dbl. Oc.: $99.00 - $160.00
Third Person: $15.00
Child: Under 5 yrs. - $15.00

Lothrop Merry House—A charming 18th-century home overlooking the harbor. One block from the ferry. Beautiful views. Private beach. Seven rooms, some with fireplaces. Private baths. Sunfish, canoe and sailing charters available.

---

1. No Smoking	5. Tennis Available	9. Credit Cards Accepted	13. Lunch Available	17. Shared Baths
2. No Pets	6. Golf Available	10. Personal Check Accepted	14. Conference Rooms Avail.	18. Afternoon Tea
3 Off Season Rates	7. Swimming Avail.	11. Reservations Necessary	15. Group Seminars Avail.	* Commisions given
4. Senior Citizen Rates	8. Skiing Available	12. Dinner Available	16. Private Baths	to Travel Agents

MARTHA'S VINEYARD
Vineyard Haven

Casaccio, Tenee & Jim
100 Main St., Box 2457, 02568
(508) 693-6564

Amenities: 2,9,10,11,15,16, 18
Breakfast: C.

Dbl. Oc.: $71.31 - $175.52
Third Person: $20.00

Captain Dexter House Of Vineyard Haven—Built in 1843 as the home of sea captain Rodolphas Dexter, this country colonial inn is elegantly furnished with period antiques, original fireplaces and canopy beds. Enjoy a delicious, home-baked continental breakfast. Walk to ferry, beach, shops and restaurants.

Vineyard Haven*

Stavens, Darlene
4 Crocker Ave.,
, 02568
(508) 693-1151

Amenities: 1,2,3,4,5,9,10,11, 16,18
Breakfast: C.

Dbl. Oc.: $109.70 - $169.55
Third Person: $15.00
Child: Under 12 yrs. - no charge

The Crocker House Inn—A charming Victorian inn with eight unique rooms and suites, all with private baths. Some feature private entrances with balconies and a fireplace. A homemade continental breakfast is served in a lovely common area. Close to ferry, shops and restaurants.

Mendon

Meddaugh, Diedre & Michael
166 Millville Road, 01756
(508) 634-8143

Amenities: 1,2,5,7,10,11,17
Breakfast: F.
Dbl. Oc.: $60.00
Sgl Oc.: $40.00
Third Person: $10.00
Child: $10.00

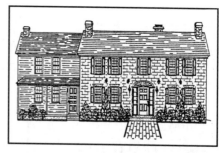

Arnold Taft House—Historic Federal brick home, circa 1800. Antiques, early American motif, three guest rooms, each with its own personality. Southwick Zoo, Willard Clock Museum, Purgatory Chasm, Bladstone Valley bike and canoe trips. Boston 37 miles, Providence 24 miles.

MASSACHUSETTS

Nantucket *

Amos, Shane
59 Easton St., 02554
(508) 228-0889

Amenities: 1,2,3,9,10,15,16, 18

Breakfast: C.

Dbl. Oc.: $142.61
Sgl. Oc.: $115.19
Third Person: $25.00

The Country Island Inn—Just minutes from town and beaches. Close to shopping and museums. Six comfortable rooms, all with private baths. A homemade breakfast every morning. Some bicycles and beach towels available for guests. A nice place to stay and relax while on a vacation.

Nantucket

Conway, Peter
26 No. Water St., 02554
(508) 228-0720

Amenities: 2,3,4,5,6,7,9,10, 11,16,17

Breakfast: C. Plus

Dbl. Oc.: $65.00 - $140.00
Sgl. Oc.: $40.00 - $55.00
Third Person: $15.00

The Carlisle House Inn—Built in 1765. Has been a quality inn for more than 100 years. Situated just off the center of town, the inn has been carefully restored. Hand-stenciled wallpaper, working fireplaces, inlaid pine paneling, wide-board floor, and rich Oriental carpets.

Nantucket *

Hammer-Yankow, Robin
5 Ash St., 02554
(508) 228-1987

Amenities: 1,2,3,5,6,7,9,10, 11,15,16

Breakfast: C.

Dbl. Oc.: $109.70 - $142.61
Third Person: $21.94

Cobblestone Inn—Circa 1725. Five rooms. All private baths. Located on a quiet street in town, just a few blocks from the ferry, shops, restaurants and museums. Enjoy our living room, sunporch or yard. Canopy beds. Non-smoking. Open year-round.

Nantucket *

Heron, Jean
Connick, Gerry
10 Cliff Rd., 02554
(508) 228-0530

Amenities: 1,2,3,5,6,7,11,15,16,17,18
Breakfast: C. Plus
Dbl. Oc.: $132.25 - $166.75
Sgl Oc.: $86.25 - $143.75
Third Person: $35.00
Child: $35.00

The Century House — B&B Inn—Gerry & Jean warmly welcome you to their cozy, comfortable inn. Residential historic district. Bountiful buffet breakfast. Happy hour setups and tea. Old fashioned veranda with rocking chairs and patio gardens. Short stroll to shops, galleries, museums, restaurants and beaches. Call today.

---

1. No Smoking	5. Tennis Available	9. Credit Cards Accepted	13. Lunch Available	17. Shared Baths
2. No Pets	6. Golf Available	10. Personal Check Accepted	14. Conference Rooms Avail.	18. Afternoon Tea
3 Off Season Rates	7. Swimmming Avail.	11. Reservations Necessary	15. Group Seminars Avail.	* Commisions given
4. Senior Citizen Rates	8. Skiing Available	12. Dinner Available	16. Private Baths	to Travel Agents

Nantucket

Mannix, Bernadette
38 Orange St., 02554
(508) 228-1912

Amenities: 3,5,6,7,9,10,
11,15,16,18
Breakfast: C.
Dbl. Oc.: $114.66 - $181.35

The Four Chimneys—Located in the heart of Nantucket Island's historic district. Four Chimneys is within a short walk from Main Street. Built in 1835, this beautiful sea captain's mansion has porches, fireplaces in five rooms, canopy beds and views of Nantucket Harbor and beyond.

Nantucket *

Parker, Ken
60 Union St., 02554
(508) 228-4886, (800) 228-4886

Amenities: 1,2,3,4,5,6,7,9,10,
11,12,13,14,15,16
Breakfast: C.
Dbl. Oc.: $110.00 - $130.00
Sgl Oc.: $100.00 - $120.00
Third Person: $15.00
Child: Under 12 yrs. - no charge

Tuckernuck Inn—In-town location near a beach. Panoramic harbor view, spacious lawn, very cozy rooms, oak post-and-beam dining room, wonderful breakfasts, common library. Recommended by Mobil Travel Guide and AAA. Innkeeper-owners on premises. Open all year round.

Nantucket *

Parker, Matthew
7 Sea St., 02554
(508) 228-3577

Amenities: 1,2,3,5,6,7,9,10,11,
12,13,15,16,18
Breakfast: C. Plus
Dbl. Oc.: $125.00 - $165.00
Sgl Oc.: $115.00 - $155.00
Third Person: $15.00

Seven Sea Street Inn—Enjoy our romantic post-and-beam inn, ideally located in historic Nantucket. We will serve you an elegant continental breakfast each morning. In the evening, watch the sunset from our windows, go for a walk, or relax in our jacuzzi bath. Your stay will exceed your expectations.

1. No Smoking	5. Tennis Available	9. Credit Cards Accepted	13. Lunch Available	17. Shared Baths
2. No Pets	6. Golf Available	10. Personal Check Accepted	14. Conference Rooms Avail.	18. Afternoon Tea
3 Off Season Rates	7. Swimming Avail.	11. Reservations Necessary	15. Group Seminars Avail.	* Commisions given
4. Senior Citizen Rates	8. Skiing Available	12. Dinner Available	16. Private Baths	to Travel Agents

Needham

Rainville, Susan
31 Fairfield St., 02192
(617) 444-5724

Amenities: 1,2,4,10,11,16,17
Breakfast: C. Plus

Dbl. Oc.: $55.00 - $60.00
Sgl. Oc.: $45.00 - $50.00

The Thistle Bed And Breakfast—Just 10 miles from Boston by car or commuter rail. Cape Cod-styled home located a few blocks from Rte. 95/128. Two clean bedrooms, one with twin beds and a guest living room are offered on a quiet, tree-lined street.

Peru

Halvorsen, Alice & Richard
E. Windsor Rd., 01235
(413) 655-8292

Amenities: 6,8,10,11,16,17
Breakfast: F.

Dbl. Oc.: $50.00 - $55.00

Chalet d'Alicia—This Swiss chalet-style home offers a private and casual atmosphere. Fresh, homemade breads and muffins round off a full country breakfast. Four resident cats and one dog make everyone welcome. Tanglewood, Jacob's Pillow, Williamstown theatre and skiing are nearby.

Petersham *

Day, Robert
No. Main St., 01366
(508) 724-8885

Amenities: 2,6,8,9,10,16
Breakfast: C.

Dbl. Oc.: $84.56
Sgl. Oc.: $63.42
Third Person: $15.86

Winterwood At Petersham—A 16-room Greek Revival mansion in the center of town. Five guest rooms, one is a two-room suite. All with private baths, most with fireplaces. In the National Register of Historic Places. Located in the center of the state.

Rockport

Kostka, Renate & Gunter
65 Eden Rd., 01966
(508) 546-2823

Amenities: 2,3,5,6,7,9,11,16
Breakfast: C.
Dbl. Oc.: $86.00 - $97.00
Sgl Oc.: $76.00 - $87.00
Third Person: $10.00
Child: Under 6 yrs. - no charge

Rocky Shores Inn And Cottages—Enjoy the panoramic views of Thacher Island and the open sea from this beautiful seaside inn. Rocky Shores is conveniently located between the picturesque harbor of Rockport and Gloucester and nearby beaches. A warm welcome awaits you for a great vacation.

1. No Smoking	5. Tennis Available	9. Credit Cards Accepted	13. Lunch Available	17. Shared Baths
2. No Pets	6. Golf Available	10. Personal Check Accepted	14. Conference Rooms Avail.	18. Afternoon Tea
3 Off Season Rates	7. Swimmming Avail.	11. Reservations Necessary	15. Group Seminars Avail.	* Commisions given
4. Senior Citizen Rates	8. Skiing Available	12. Dinner Available	16. Private Baths	to Travel Agents

Salem *

Kessler, Patricia
284 Lafayette St., 01970
(508) 744-4092, (800) 688-8689

Amenities: 2,3,5,6,7,9,16,17
Breakfast: C.

Dbl. Oc.: $81.18 - $93.25
Sgl. Oc.: $81.18 - $93.25
Third Person: $9.00
Child: Under 18 yrs. - $7.00

Coach House Inn—Return to the elegance of an earlier time. Built in 1879 by Captain E. Augustus Emmerton, a central figure in Salem's China trade. Guests enjoy cozy, comfortable rooms which retain the charm of this Victorian mansion. Private baths and off-street parking.

Salem *

Pabich, Diane & Richard
7 Summer St., 01970
(800) 446-2995, (508) 741-0680

Amenities: 9,10,12,13,14,15,16
Breakfast: C.
Dbl. Oc.: $93.25 - $137.13
Sgl Oc.: $93.25 - $137.13
Third Person: $16.46
Child: $16.46

The Salem Inn, built 1834   Salem, Massachusetts

The Salem Inn—History-making hospitality. An 1834 sea captain's home featuring spacious, comfortably appointed guest rooms with a blend of period detail and antique furnishings. Some working fireplaces. Jacuzzi suites and family suites. Ideal for families. On Salem's Heritage Trail, near museums.

Salem

Roberts, Ada May
16 Winter St., 01970
(508) 744-8304

Amenities: 1,2,3,9,16,18
Breakfast: C. Plus

Dbl. Oc.: $83.00 - $94.00

Amelia Payson Guest House—An 1845 Greek Revival. Rooms are furnised with period antiques and warmed by a personal touch. Located in the heart of historic Salem, walk to: Witch Museum, Maritime museums, waterfront dining, train to Boston and Gloucester. Brochure available.

Scituate *

Gilmour, Christine & Iain
18 Allen Pl., 02066
(617) 545-8221

Amenities: 1,2,3,9,10,11,16
Breakfast: F.

Dbl. Oc.: $79.00 - $109.00
Sgl. Oc.: $79.00 - $109.00

The Allen House—An ocean view, Victorian elegance and the warm welcome of English hosts in the heart of an unspoiled New England fishing town only one hour from Boston. Afternoon tea and quiet nights are preludes to a gourmet breakfast from your caterer-hosts who both cook.

---

1. No Smoking	5. Tennis Available	9. Credit Cards Accepted	13. Lunch Available	17. Shared Baths
2. No Pets	6. Golf Available	10. Personal Check Accepted	14. Conference Rooms Avail.	18. Afternoon Tea
3 Off Season Rates	7. Swimmming Avail.	11. Reservations Necessary	15. Group Seminars Avail.	* Commisions given
4. Senior Citizen Rates	8. Skiing Available	12. Dinner Available	16. Private Baths	to Travel Agents

MASSACHUSETTS

Seekonk *

Wyrsch, Marsha
32 Read St., 02771
(508) 399-7441

Amenities: 1,2,5,6,11,12,13, 16,18
Breakfast: C. Plus

Dbl. Oc.: $112.00
Sgl. Oc.: $80.00
Third Person: $20.00
Child: No charge - $10.00

The Read Homestead—Step back 150 years in time to rural America. Historic house set on rolling hills, offers private lodging in renovated in-law apartment. Enjoy skylights, high ceilings and full kitchen, 10 minutes to Providence, 30 minutes to ocean, 35 miles to Boston. Easy access to 95.

Sheffield

Ederer, June & Martin
Undermountain Rd
Rte. 41, P.O. Box 729, 01257
(413) 229-3363

Amenities: 1,2,3,5,6,7,8,9,10, 11,14,16
Breakfast: F.

Dbl. Oc.: $98.00 - $110.00
Sgl. Oc.: $88.00 - $100.00
Third Person: $25.00

Ramblewood Inn - A Unique Bed And Breakfast—Alpine hideaway among the pines, a lake and beautiful Mount Everett. A country inn with style, central air, gourmet breakfast and romantic room settings. Convenient to Tanglewood and all Berkshire cultural and natural attractions.

Sturbridge/Ware *

Skutnik, Margaret
14 Pleasant St., Ware, 01082
(413) 967-7847

Amenities: 1,2,3,4,5,7,10,11, 15,16,17,18
Breakfast: F.

Dbl. Oc.: $45.00 - $65.00
Sgl. Oc.: $40.00 - $50.00
Third Person: $15.00
Child: $15.00

1880 Inn B&B—Relax in yesterday's charm. Antiques, pumpkin hardwood floors, beamed ceilings and six fireplaces. Mid-point between historic Deerfield, Old Sturbridge, Boston and the Berkshires, 1/2 hour to Amherst and New Hampshire. Quabbin Reservoir with fishing and hiking.

Sudbury *

MacDonald, Irene & Stu
5 Checkerberry Circle, 01776
(508) 443-8660

Amenities: 1,2,10,11,17
Breakfast: F.

Dbl. Oc.: $65.00
Sgl. Oc.: $55.00

Checkerberry Corner Bed And Breakfast—Located in the heart of historic Minuteman country in a quiet residential neighborhood. Minutes from Concord, Lexington, Wayside Inn and easy access to Boston. Fine restaurants nearby. Three rooms - twin, double and queen. Full country breakfast.

Tyringham *

Rizzo, Lilja & Joseph
Main Rd.
Box 336, 01264
(413) 243-3008

Amenities: 2,3,4,5,6,7,8,9,10, 16,17,18
Breakfast: C.

Dbl. Oc.: $68.71 - $126.84
Sgl. Oc.: $68.71 - $126.84
Third Person: $10.00(Apt. only)
Child: Under 6 yrs. -$5.00(Apt.)

The Golden Goose—A warm, friendly B&B inn nestled between Stockbridge, Lenox and Becket. Antiques, fireplaces and homemade breakfasts. Six guest rooms plus charming studio apartment. Beautiful year-round. In the country, but close to Tanglewood, skiing and good restaurants.

1. No Smoking	5. Tennis Available	9. Credit Cards Accepted	13. Lunch Available	17. Shared Baths
2. No Pets	6. Golf Available	10. Personal Check Accepted	14. Conference Rooms Avail.	18. Afternoon Tea
3 Off Season Rates	7. Swimming Avail.	11. Reservations Necessary	15. Group Seminars Avail.	* Commisions given
4. Senior Citizen Rates	8. Skiing Available	12. Dinner Available	16. Private Baths	to Travel Agents

Wareham *

Murphy, Frances A.	**Amenities:** 1,2,5,6,7,8,9,10,	**Dbl. Oc.:** $45.00 - $55.00
257 High St., 02571	17,18	**Sgl. Oc.:** $45.00 - $55.00
(508) 295-0684	**Breakfast:** C.	**Third Person:** $10.00

Mulberry Bed And Breakfast—A circa 1840s home set on mulberry tree-shaded property in the historic area of Wareham. In this cozy, three-bedroom B&B, new friends enjoy a restful sleep, a hearty New England breakfast and hospitality. Close to historic Plymouth and New Bedford. Convenient to Cape Cod.

1. No Smoking	5. Tennis Available	9. Credit Cards Accepted	13. Lunch Available	17. Shared Baths
2. No Pets	6. Golf Available	10. Personal Check Accepted	14. Conference Rooms Avail.	18. Afternoon Tea
3 Off Season Rates	7. Swimmming Avail.	11. Reservations Necessary	15. Group Seminars Avail.	* Commisions given
4. Senior Citizen Rates	8. Skiing Available	12. Dinner Available	16. Private Baths	to Travel Agents

204

MICHIGAN

The Wolverine State

Capitol: Lansing
Statehood: January 26, 1837; the 26th state
State Motto: "If You Seek Pleasant Peninsula,
Look About You"
State Song: "Michigan, My Michigan"
State Bird: Robin
State Flower: Apple Blossom
State Tree: White Pine

Michigan is known for its long history of automobile manufacturing. Henry Ford built his first automobile here in 1896. The city of Detroit became the center of this industry and is called "The Automobile Capitol of the World."

To get automobiles to market, it was necessary to use the waterways that are readily available here. The Soo Canals at Sault Ste. Marie are the busiest ship canals in the western hemisphere. The railroads played a big part in this new industry too. In 1855, the first railroad in Michigan was the Erie and Kalamazoo, linking Michigan with Ohio.

The people of Michigan like to enjoy life. They are know for their delight in having tourists visit and, in fact, tourism is very beg here. The residents of Michigan use more of their lands for recreation than anything else.

MICHIGAN

Ann Arbor

Rosalik, Andre
Krys, Gloria
2759 Canterbury Rd., 48104
(313) 971-8110

Amenities: 2,10,11,16,17
Breakfast: F.

Dbl. Oc.: $58.30
Sgl. Oc.: $47.70

The Urban Retreat—A comfortable home on a quiet, tree-lined street. Minutes from downtown and the University of Michigan campus. Stroll in the adjacent 127-acre Country Farm Park. Pet the cats, watch the birds, smell the flowers and unwind. Two rooms available with antiques and period decor.

AuTrain

Krieg, Jenny & Jerry
Box 176, M28 W., 49806-0176
(906) 892-8300

Amenities: 1,2,7,8,9,15,16, 17
Breakfast: F.

Dbl. Oc.: $52.00 - $72.80
Sgl. Oc.: $41.60
Third Person: $15.60
Child: $15.60

Pinewood Lodge—Enjoy our log home set in Norway pine on Lake Superior, with a sand beach overlooking AuTrain Island. Eight guest rooms vary from antique to log furnishings. Cose by are Pictured Rocks National Lakeshore, Hiawatha National Forest and numerous waterfalls.

Cadillac

Suhs, Hermann
214 No. Mitchell St., 49601
(616) 775-9563

Amenities: 2,5,6,7,8,9,10,11, 12,13,14,15,16
Breakfast: C.

Dbl. Oc.: $85.00
Sgl. Oc.: $70.00
Third Person: $10.00

Hermann's European Inn—Every convenience is yours in an Old-World country setting atop a three-star European cafe and chefs deli. Hospitality unequaled. European flavor. Near lakes and skiing. Free parking, local phone calls, TVs and VCRs. Continental breakfast delivered to your door.

Coldwater

Schultz, Rebecca
215 E. Chicago St., 49036
(517) 279-8744

Amenities: 1,2,6,8,9,10,12,16,18
Breakfast: F.
Dbl. Oc.: $78.00 - $135.20
Sgl Oc.: $78.00 - $135.20
Third Person: $20.00

Chicago Pike Inn—"Lodging in Victorian elegance." Six beautifully restored rooms surrounded by peace and tranquility. Located in a national historic district. We take pride in our "knack" of making your stay a memorable one.

MICHIGAN

Douglas *

Charak, Susan
938 Center St.
P.O. Box 893, 49406
(616) 857-1246

Amenities: 1,2,3,5,6,7,8,9,10,11,16
Breakfast: C. Plus
Dbl. Oc.: $75.00 - $95.00
Third Person: $10.00

Sherwood Forest B And B—Beautiful Victorian-style home built in the 1890s. Five traditionally furnished rooms with queen-size beds and private baths. Jacuzzi and heated swimming pool, 1/2 block from Lake Michigan public beach. Skiing nearby. Woodsy surroundings provide a relaxing atmosphere.

Fennville *

Witt, Shirley & David
626 W. Main St., 49408
(616) 561-6425

Amenities: 1,2,5,6,7,8,9,10,11,16,18
Breakfast: F.
Dbl. Oc.: $79.50 - $132.50
Sgl Oc.: $53.00
Third Person: $15.00

The Kingsley House—An elegant Victorian built in 1886. Private bath. Family antiques. Honeymoon suite. Beautiful decor. Minutes to Saugatuck, Holland and the sandy beaches of Lake Michigan. Bicycles. Whirlpool baths. "Top-50 Inn in America." Boat cruises and carriage rides nearby. "A memorable experience.

Flint

Minore, Arletta
518 Avon St., 48503
(313) 232-6861

Amenities: 1,2,11,17
Breakfast: F.

Dbl. Oc.: $35.00
Sgl. Oc.: $30.00
Third Person: $10.00

Avon House—An 1880s enchanting Victorian home. Filled with beautiful warm woodwork, window benches and antiques. Enjoy the turn-of-the-century Steinway grand in the parlor and a homemade breakfast in the formal dining room. Walking distance of downtown, cultural center, college and museums.

---

1. No Smoking	5. Tennis Available	9. Credit Cards Accepted	13. Lunch Available	17. Shared Baths
2. No Pets	6. Golf Available	10. Personal Check Accepted	14. Conference Rooms Avail.	18. Afternoon Tea
3 Off Season Rates	7. Swimming Avail.	11. Reservations Necessary	15. Group Seminars Avail.	* Commisions given
4. Senior Citizen Rates	8. Skiing Available	12. Dinner Available	16. Private Baths	to Travel Agents

MICHIGAN

Frankenmuth

Hodge, Donna & Richard
327 Ardussi St., 48734
(517) 652-9019

Amenities: 1,10,17
Breakfast: C. Plus

Dbl. Oc.: $37.80
Sgl. Oc.: $27.80

Bed And Breakfast at The Pines—Our motto is "come as a stranger, leave as a friend." Enjoy the casual atmosphere of a ranch-style home with a secluded yard, surrounded by evergreen trees, in a quiet, residential area. Within walking distance of main tourist shops and famous restaurants.

Glen Arbor *

Olson, Jenny & Bill
6680 Western Ave. (M-109), 49636
(616) 334-4333

Amenities: 1,2,3,5,6,7,8,9,10,15,16,17
Breakfast: C.
Dbl. Oc.: $60.00 - $110.00
Sgl Oc.: $60.00 - $110.00
Third Person: $12.00

The Sylvan Inn—A luxuriously renovated historic landmark inn with 14 charming rooms and suites. Spa/sauna. Carefully preserved historic charm in the heart of Sleeping Bear Dunes National Lakeshore. Easy access to fine dining, shopping, swimming, biking, downhill and cross-country skiing.

Grand Haven

Meyer, Susan
20009 Breton, Spring Lake,
49456 (mail)
(616) 842-8409

Amenities: 2,3,7,8,9,10,11,14
15,16
Breakfast: F.

Dbl. Oc.: $95.40 - $79.50
Sgl. Oc.: $95.40 - $79.50
Third Person: $26.50
Child: $26.50

Seascape Bed And Breakfast—On a private Lake Michigan beach. Scenic lakefront rooms. Relax and enjoy the warm hospitality and "country living" ambience of our nautical lakeshore home. Panoramic view of Grand Haven harbor. Stroll or cross-country ski through dune preserve. Quiet residential setting.

---

1. No Smoking	5. Tennis Available	9. Credit Cards Accepted	13. Lunch Available	17. Shared Baths
2. No Pets	6. Golf Available	10. Personal Check Accepted	14. Conference Rooms Avail.	18. Afternoon Tea
3 Off Season Rates	7. Swimmming Avail.	11. Reservations Necessary	15. Group Seminars Avail.	* Commisions given
4. Senior Citizen Rates	8. Skiing Available	12. Dinner Available	16. Private Baths	to Travel Agents

Holland

Elenbaas, Pat & Bob
560 Central Ave., 49423
(616) 396-3664

Amenities: 1,5,6,7,8,9,10,14,16
Breakfast: F.
Dbl. Oc.: $65.00 - $130.00
Third Person: $15.00

The Dutch Colonial Inn—A gracious Dutch colonial home built in 1930. Award-winning B&B features lovely family heirlooms, antiques, 1930 furnishings. Elegant decor. Private baths with whirlpool tubs for two. Honeymoon suites. Close to Lake Michigan, Hope College and excellent shopping.

Jonesville *

Jamieson, Dorothy
Yarde, Joyce
202 Maumee St., 49250
(517) 849-9292

Amenities: 23,,6,8,9,10,14,15,
16,18
Breakfast: F.

Dbl. Oc.: $71.00
Sgl. Oc.: $66.00
Third Person: $5.00

The Munro House—An elegant 1834 home that was a station on the underground railroad. Its sweeping staircase, 12-foot ceilings, 10 fireplaces and numerous chandeliers present guests with a true taste of this bygone era. Enjoy golf, antiquing, biking and dinner at Billingsgate.

Mackinac Island *

Bacon, Jane
Box 192, Market St., 49757
(906) 847-6234

Amenities: 2,3,5,6,7,9,10,11,14,15,16
Breakfast: C. Plus
Dbl. Oc.: $101.92 - $171.60
Third Person: $20.80
Child: Under 5 yrs. - $8.32

Metivier Inn—Renovated historic home on Market Street. All ferry lines are within two blocks. Queen-size bed and private bath in all rooms. Deluxe continental breakfast served. Wicker-filled front porch. Cozy living room with fireplace. Enchanting and quaint island.

---

1. No Smoking	5. Tennis Available	9. Credit Cards Accepted	13. Lunch Available	17. Shared Baths
2. No Pets	6. Golf Available	10. Personal Check Accepted	14. Conference Rooms Avail.	18. Afternoon Tea
3 Off Season Rates	7. Swimming Avail.	11. Reservations Necessary	15. Group Seminars Avail.	* Commisions given
4. Senior Citizen Rates	8. Skiing Available	12. Dinner Available	16. Private Baths	to Travel Agents

Mackinac Island

Haan, Joy & Vernon
Haan, Nancy & Nicholas
P.O. Box 123, Huron St., 49757
(906) 847-6244, (414) 248-9244 (winter)

Amenities: 1,2,3,5,6,7,10,11, 16,17
Breakfast: C. Plus

Dbl. Oc.: $83.00 - $110.00
Sgl. Oc.: $83.00 - $110.00
Third Person: $10.00
Child: $10.00

Haan's 1830 Inn—Lovely greek Revival home with seven guest rooms beautifully furnished with antiques. Five rooms with private baths, two with shared. Fresh home-baked muffins and cakes served on long thresher's table in 1830s dining room. Three blocks from town. Three porches.

Michigamme *

Stabile, Linda & Frank
Box 97, Champion, 49855
(800) 358-0058

Amenities: 1,2,3,7,9,14,15,16,17
Breakfast: C. Plus
Dbl. Oc.: $133.00
Sgl Oc.: $133.00

Michigamme Lake Lodge—A grand lodge situated on Lake Michigamme, 30 miles west of Marquette. Built in 1934 on state and national sites. Nine rooms and a large grand room with a 2 1/2-story stone fireplace to gather in front of. Many outdoor activities: swimming, fishing, hiking, biking and boating.

Munising *

Carberry, Barbara
713 Prospect St., 49862
(906) 387-2542

Amenities: 1,2,3,5,6,7,8,11, 17
Breakfast: C. Plus

Dbl. Oc.: $52.00
Sgl. Oc.: $41.60
Child: Under 12 yrs. -$10.40

The Homestead Bed And Breakfast—Features: three bedrooms, two with double beds, one with twin beds and one with tub and shower. Large living room with TV. Quiet surroundings. Reservations. Activities for all seasons: fishing, hunting, scuba diving, snowmobiling and cross-country skiing.

Oscoda

Lorenz, Martha & Dennis
3124 N. US-23, 48750
(517) 739-9255

Amenities: 1,2,4,6,7,8,9,10, 11,16
Breakfast: C. Plus

Dbl. Oc.: $55.00 - $80.00
Sgl. Oc.: $50.00 - $75.00
Third Person: $5.00

Huron House—Spectacular sunrises! Located on beautiful Lake Huron. All rooms are uniquely decorated and have private baths and TVs. Air-conditioning. A cozy gathering/breakfast room and three large decks that overlook the lake. Relax in the hot tub, under the stars. See the river road scenic by-way.

1. No Smoking	5. Tennis Available	9. Credit Cards Accepted	13. Lunch Available	17. Shared Baths
2. No Pets	6. Golf Available	10. Personal Check Accepted	14. Conference Rooms Avail.	18. Afternoon Tea
3 Off Season Rates	7. Swimmming Avail.	11. Reservations Necessary	15. Group Seminars Avail.	* Commisions given
4. Senior Citizen Rates	8. Skiing Available	12. Dinner Available	16. Private Baths	to Travel Agents

MICHIGAN

Port Huron *

Secory, Lynne & Lew
Vicki & Ed Peterson
1229 7th St., 48060
(313) 984-1437

Amenities: 2,9,10,12,13,14,15,16,17
Breakfast: C.
Dbl. Oc.: $57.20 - $67.60

The Victorian Inn—Features fine dining and guest rooms in authentically restored Victorian elegance. One hour north of metropolitan Detroit, this fine inn features classically creative cuisine and gracious service. Extensive wine list. Pierpoint's Pub at lower level.

Romulus *

Laroy, Veronica
32285 Sibley Rd., 48174
(313)753-4586

Amenities: 1,4,10,11,17
Breakfast: F.

Dbl. Oc.: $45.00
Sgl. Oc.: $35.00
Third Person: $10.00
Child: $5.00

Country Lane Bed And Breakfast—Modern Cape Cod home on 20 acres near I-275. Full country breakfast. Large rooms with air-conditioning and TV. Near Detroit Metro Airport, 20 minutes to Detroit, Henry Ford Greenfield Village, Ann Arbor and Canada. Golfing, swimming, hiking and parks are nearby.

Saline *

Grossman, Shirley
9279 Macon Rd., 48176
(313) 429-9625

Amenities: 2,6,8,9,10,11,14,
15,17
Breakfast: F.

Dbl. Oc.: $53.00 - $68.00
Sgl. Oc.: $31.80 - $47.70
Third Person: $15.00
Child: $15.00

The Homestead Bed And Breakfast—An 1851 brick farmhouse. Comfort, country and Victorian elegance. Walk, relax or cross-country ski. Fifteen minutes to Ann Arbor and Ypsilanti. Forty minutes to Detroit or Toledo. Children over 10 welcome.

Saugatuck *

Indurante, Dan
Kott, Gary
132 Mason, 49453
(616) 857-8851

Amenities: 1,2,3,5,6,7,8,9,10,
16,17
Breakfast: C.

Dbl. Oc.: $58.30 - $84.80
Sgl. Oc.: $58.30 - $84.80
Third Person: $10.00
Child: Under 6 yrs. - no charge

The Red Dog Bed And Breakfast—A comfortable place to stay in the heart of Saugatuck, steps away from restaurants, shopping and year-round activities. Built in 1879. Seven guest rooms, five with private baths. Open all year. No minimum stay required. Come and enjoy our town, "The Cape Cod of the Midwest."

1. No Smoking	5. Tennis Available	9. Credit Cards Accepted	13. Lunch Available	17. Shared Baths
2. No Pets	6. Golf Available	10. Personal Check Accepted	14. Conference Rooms Avail.	18. Afternoon Tea
3 Off Season Rates	7. Swimmming Avail.	11. Reservations Necessary	15. Group Seminars Avail.	* Commisions given
4. Senior Citizen Rates	8. Skiing Available	12. Dinner Available	16. Private Baths	to Travel Agents

Saugatuck *

Lemons, Sherron & James
736 Pleasant St.
P.O. Box 876, 49453
(616) 857-1587

Amenities: 1,2,3,4,5,6,7,8,9,10,
        11,14,16,17,18
Breakfast: F. & C.Plus
Dbl. Oc.: $74.20 - $96.30
Sgl Oc.: $74.20 - $96.30
Third Person: $25.00
Child: Under 12 yrs. - $15.00

Beechwood Manor—Restored Victorian diplomat's home, built in 1874. French Gothic picket fence surrounds the estate. Shaker antiques, queen-size beds, 3-1/2 baths, 18-inch-wide pine floors from Vermont and pine woodwork. Also, three-bedroom fully furnished guest house. Both open all year.

Saugatuck *

Petty, Lynda & Joe
888 Holland St., 49453
(800) 321-4535

Amenities: 1,2,3,5,6,7,9,10,
        15,16
Breakfast: C. Plus

Dbl. Oc.: $79.50 - $169.60
Sgl. Oc.: $79.50 - $169.60
Third Person: $15.90
Child: $15.90

The Park House—Built in 1857, Park House is Saugatuck's oldest residence. Five guest rooms, two luxury suites, a family suite and two guest cottages await you. Fireplaces and jet tubs. New England charm, Midwest hospitality and Lake Michigan sunsets welcome you. Enjoy!

Saugatuck *

Simcik, Denise & Michael
900 E. Lake St.
P.O. Box 881, 49453
(616) 857-4346

Amenities: 1,2,3,5,6,7,8,9,10,
        11,12,13,14,16
Breakfast: C.

Dbl. Oc.: $44.00 - $99.64
Third Person: $10.00

Twin Gables Country Inn—Overlooking the lake, this state historic inn is totally air-conditioned and features 14 guest rooms with private baths. Furnished with antiques and country. Summer guests can enjoy our side-garden park with its outdoor pool. In winter, guests can use the indoor hot tub.

---

1. No Smoking	5. Tennis Available	9. Credit Cards Accepted	13. Lunch Available	17. Shared Baths
2. No Pets	6. Golf Available	10. Personal Check Accepted	14. Conference Rooms Avail.	18. Afternoon Tea
3 Off Season Rates	7. Swimmming Avail.	11. Reservations Necessary	15. Group Seminars Avail.	* Commisions given
4. Senior Citizen Rates	8. Skiing Available	12. Dinner Available	16. Private Baths	to Travel Agents

MICHIGAN

Sault Ste. Marie

Walker, Phyllis & Gregory
140 E. Water St., 49783
(906) 632-1900, (800) 236-1904

Amenities: 1,2,3,6,8,9,10,11,16
Breakfast: F.
Dbl. Oc.: $73.00 - $98.00
Sgl Oc.: $73.00 - $98.00

The Water Street Inn—A Victorian welcome awaits you at this restored 1900s Queen Anne home. Stained-glass windows, marble fireplaces, original woodwork and a wrap-around porch promise a special visit whatever the season. Walking distance to the locks and fine restaurants.

Suttons Bay *

Sutherland, Mary
613 St. Mary's Ave., 49682
(616) 271-4300

Amenities: 2,3,5,6,7,8,10,17
Breakfast: C. Plus

Dbl. Oc.: $65.00
Sgl. Oc.: $50.00
Third Person: $10.00

Open Windows Bed And Breakfast—This century-old home with fireplace is within walking distance of unique shops and restaurants. It is beautifully furnished with antiques and family memorabilia, complemented by flower gardens and a lovely front porch for viewing the bay.

1. No Smoking	5. Tennis Available	9. Credit Cards Accepted	13. Lunch Available	17. Shared Baths
2. No Pets	6. Golf Available	10. Personal Check Accepted	14. Conference Rooms Avail.	18. Afternoon Tea
3 Off Season Rates	7. Swimmming Avail.	11. Reservations Necessary	15. Group Seminars Avail.	* Commisions given
4. Senior Citizen Rates	8. Skiing Available	12. Dinner Available	16. Private Baths	to Travel Agents

MINNESOTA

The Gopher State

Capitol: St. Paul
Statehood: May 11, 1858; the 32nd state
State Motto: "The Star of the North"
State Song: "Hail! Minnesota"
State Bird: Common Loon
State Flower: Pink and White Lady's Slipper
State Tree: Norway Pine

Minnesota is the land of ten thousand lakes. Many of its cities and towns are named for lakes, falls or rapids. For every 20 acres of land, there is an acre of water. It is a popular playground for campers and canoers, with its many acres of wilderness along each lake site. Water skiing was developed here and the blue lakes attract swimmers, boaters and fishermen.

This state's million dairy cows make it a leading butter producing state. And with its flour mills it isn't hard to see how it got the name of "the bread and butter state."

The city of Duluth is its major port on Lake Superior. From here the grain and manufactured products of Minnesota are shipped to the Great Lakes cities and overseas.

The Mayo Clinic was established at Rochester in 1889 by Dr. William W. May and his two sons, William and Charles. It is one of the greatest medical research centers in the world.

MINNESOTA

Albert Lea *

Roemmich, Darrel & Linda
609 W. Fountain St., 56007
(507) 373-7602, (800) 252-6558

Amenities: 1,2,9
Breakfast: F.
Dbl. Oc.: $50.00 - $66.00
Sgl Oc.: $39.00 - $60.00
Third Person: $10.00
Child: Under 10 yrs. - $5.00

The Victorian Rose Inn—Beautiful Queen Anne-style home in the National Register of Historic Places. Spacious rooms, stained glass, restored antiques and a homey atmosphere. One block from the lake. Lovely city to visit any season. Golf, theatre and musuem nearby.

Burnsville *

Toombs, Mary
165 Timberland Dr., 55337
(612) 890-3874

Amenities: 1,2,10,11,16
Breakfast: C.

Dbl. Oc.: $75.00
Sgl. Oc.: $60.00
Third Person: $60.00
Child: Under 12 Yrs. - $10.00

Burnsville Guest House—Large deck, full bath, living room, kitchen, queen bed and hide-a-bed; 15 minutes from Mall of America, MN, 20 minutes from Valleyfair, 30 minutes from downtown Minneapolis and St. Paul. Near parks, hiking, golf, skiing, restaurants and shopping.

Dundas

Gery, Marie & Frank
107 First St., 55019
(507) 645-4644

Amenities: 1,2,5,6,8,9,10,11,
12,17,18
Breakfast: F.

Dbl. Oc.: $70.00
Sgl. Oc.: $50.00
Third Person: $15.00
Child: $15.00

Martin Oaks Bed And Breakfast—Restored 1869 home in National Register. Furnished with antiques. Candlelight breakfast. Storytelling. St. Olaf and Carleton Colleges. Good restaurants, shopping and antiques five minutes away. One hour from Minneapolis/St. Paul and Rochester. A time and place to slow down and relax.

Fergus Falls

Nlms, Judy & Dennis
R.R. 2, Box 187A, 56537
(218) 739-2915

Amenities: 1,3,4,5,6,7,8,10,
16,17,18
Breakfast: F.

Dbl. Oc.: $58.58 - $90.53
Sgl. Oc.: $58.85
Third Person: $15.00

Bakketopp Hus—A wooded lake setting where you can relax by the fire, on the deck or in the spa. Natural wood, patio windows and antiques create a feeling of tranquility. Nearby ski trails, golf, state park, antiques and restaurants. Spacious rooms. 10 minutes off I-94 at exit 50.

---

1. No Smoking	5. Tennis Available	9. Credit Cards Accepted	13. Lunch Available	17. Shared Baths
2. No Pets	6. Golf Available	10. Personal Check Accepted	14. Conference Rooms Avail.	18. Afternoon Tea
3 Off Season Rates	7. Swimming Avail.	11. Reservations Necessary	15. Group Seminars Avail.	* Commisions given
4. Senior Citizen Rates	8. Skiing Available	12. Dinner Available	16. Private Baths	to Travel Agents

MINNESOTA

Grand Marais *

Beattie, Mary & Scott
220 Gunflint Trail, 55604-9701
(218) 387-1276, (800) 542-1226

Amenities: 1,2,8,9,10,11,15, 16
Breakfast: F.

Dbl. Oc.: $75.00 - $90.00
Sgl. Oc.: $69.00 - $84.00
Third Person: $15.00

Pincushion Mountain Bed And Breakfast—Three miles from Grand Marais. A contemporary home sits on forested ridgeline overlooking north shore of Lake Superior 1,000 feet below. Four guest rooms. Country decor. Great hiking, mountain biking, cross-country ski trails at door-step. Lodge-to-lodge hiking. Free brochure.

Grand Marais *

Kerber, Viola & Jack
P.O. Box 963, 55604
(218) 387-1571

Amenities: 1,2,3,9,10,15,17
Breakfast: F.

Dbl. Oc.: $75.00 - $80.00
Sgl. Oc.: $72.00 - $77.00
Third Person: $15.00

The Superior Overlook B&B—A contemporary home with private area for guests. Three guest rooms, two bathrooms, sauna and family room. Grand Marais is located on the north shore of Lake Superior, 40 miles from the Canadian border. All winter and summer activities are nearby. Open all year.

Lutsen *

Lindgren, Shirley
Country Rd. 35
P.O. Box 56, 55612-0056
(218) 663-7450

Amenities: 2,4,5,6,8,9,10,11, 16
Breakfast: F.

Dbl. Oc.: $87.60 & up
Sgl. Oc.: $82.50 & up
Third Person: $15.00
Child: $15.00

Lindgren's Bed And Breakfast—Luxurious 1920s log home on walkable shores of Lake Superior. Dine overlooking the lake while enjoying the warmth from the roaring magnificent stone fireplace. Wildlife decor. Baby grand piano, sauna and whirlpool. Great golfing, hiking, biking, fall colors and skiing.

Minneapolis *

Griffin, Mari & Gatos
2321 Colfax Ave. So., 55405
(612) 377-5946

Amenities: 1,2,10,11,17
Breakfast: C.

Dbl. Oc.: $60.00 - $75.00
Sgl. Oc.: $50.00 - $60.00

Brasie House—A 1913 Craftsman home. Gracious hospitality near theatres, lakes, museums, unique shopping, restaurants and bus line. Antiques, fireplaces, resident cats. Let us make the most of your stay in the Twin Cities for business or pleasure.

Minneapolis *

Zosel, Nan
2304 Fremont Ave. So., 55405
(612) 377-5118

Amenities: 9,10,11,17
Breakfast: F.

Dbl. Oc.: $53.50
Sgl. Oc.: $48.15
Third Person: Under 12 yrs. -$5.35
Child: $5.35

Nan's Bed And Breakfast—An 1895 Victorian family home. Antique furniture. A short walk to theatres, restaurants, shopping and scenic lakeside walking paths. Friendly, outgoing hosts always have time to give directions to where you want to go. One block from bus stop. Maps available.

1. No Smoking	5. Tennis Available	9. Credit Cards Accepted	13. Lunch Available	17. Shared Baths
2. No Pets	6. Golf Available	10. Personal Check Accepted	14. Conference Rooms Avail.	18. Afternoon Tea
3 Off Season Rates	7. Swimmming Avail.	11. Reservations Necessary	15. Group Seminars Avail.	* Commisions given
4. Senior Citizen Rates	8. Skiing Available	12. Dinner Available	16. Private Baths	to Travel Agents

Morris *

Berget, Karen
410 E. 3rd St., 56267
(612) 589-4054

Amenities: 2,5,6,7,9,10,11, 17
Breakfast: F.

Dbl. Oc.: $37.28 - $42.60
Sgl. Oc.: $31.95 - $37.28
Third Person: $5.33

The American House—A Victorian home decorated with antiques and country charm. Ride our tandem bike on scenic trails. Within walking distance of area restaurants and shops. Located one block from the University of Minnesota - Morris campus.

North Branch *

Olson, Gloria & Lowell
15140 400th St., 55056
(612) 583-3326

Amenities: 1,3,4,8,10,11,14, 15,16,17
Breakfast: F.

Dbl. Oc.: $85.00 - $100.00
Sgl. Oc.: $75.00
Third Person: $20.00

Red Pine Log Bed And Breakfast—Uniquely designed and handcrafted by Lowell in 1985 on 30 acres. All exposed logs. Awesome 25-foot ceiling, log staircase, balconies and skylights. Suite-size rooms with queen beds. One hour to Twin Cities. Near cross-country skiing. Ceramics. Canoeing.

Spring Valley *

Chase, Jeannine & Bob
508 N. Huron Ave., 55975
(507) 346-2850

Amenities: 1,2,5,6,7,8,9,10, 11,16
Breakfast: F.

Dbl. Oc.: $79.88
Sgl. Oc.: $69.23
Third Person: $21.30
Child: Under 5 yrs. - no charge

Chase's—Second Empire 1879 mansion. In National Register of Historic Places. Farm-style breakfast. Near caves, hiking and biking trails, canoeing, trout fishing, birding, Amish area, state parks, Laura Ingalls Wilder sites and antique shops.

St. Paul

Conway, Mary & Miles
925 Goodrich Ave., 55105
(612) 227-8430

Amenities: 1,10,11,17
Breakfast: C.

Dbl. Oc.: $63.90
Sgl. Oc.: $53.25
Third Person: $21.30

The Garden Gate B&B—A large Victorian duplex in the heart of St. Paul's Victoria Crossing neighborhood. A short walk to Grand Avenue's shops and fine restaurants or historic Summit Avenue. Easy access to downtown, colleges, state capitol and airport. Transportation available upon request.

St. Paul

Gustafson, Donna
984 Ashland, 55104
(612) 227-4288

Amenities: 1,2,5,6,7,8,10,11, 15,16,17
Breakfast: C. Plus

Dbl. Oc.: $63.90 - $106.50
Sgl. Oc.: $58.58 - $101.18
Third Person: $20.00
Child: $20.00

Chatsworth B&B—A spacious lace-curtained Victorian home in a quiet neighborhood. Fifteen minutes from the airport and downtown Minneapolis. Ten minutes from downtown St. Paul. Walk to shopping areas and restaurants. Two whirlpool baths.

1. No Smoking	5. Tennis Available	9. Credit Cards Accepted	13. Lunch Available	17. Shared Baths
2. No Pets	6. Golf Available	10. Personal Check Accepted	14. Conference Rooms Avail.	18. Afternoon Tea
3 Off Season Rates	7. Swimmming Avail.	11. Reservations Necessary	15. Group Seminars Avail.	* Commisions given
4. Senior Citizen Rates	8. Skiing Available	12. Dinner Available	16. Private Baths	to Travel Agents

MISSISSIPPI

The Magnolia State

Capitol: Jackson
Statehood: December 10, 1817; the 20th state
State Motto: "By Valor and Arms"
State Song: "Go Mis-sis-sip-pi"
State Bird: Mockingbird
State Flower: Magnolia
State Tree: Magnolia

Once a land of quiet towns, Mississippi is fast becoming an urbanized state. Although the cotton growing industry is still an important industry here, more and more people are being employed in the lumber and manufacturing of wood product industries.

Because Mississippi has a warm climate with long summers and short winters, more tourists are vacationing here and finding it an enjoyable retreat. There are large, sunny beaches along the Gulf Coast and fine hotels. Costumed guides are available to show visitors through the handsome mansions and plantations. There is also excellent hunting and fishing, but most of all, genteel and wonderful southern hospitality.

MISSISSIPPI

Hernando *

McClanahan, Frances **Amenities:** 1,2,5,6,7,9,10,12, **Dbl. Oc.:** $75.00
785 Highway 51 So., 38632 14,16,18 **Sgl. Oc.:** $65.00
(601) 429-5864, (800) 882-1897 **Breakfast:** F. **Child:** Under 10 yrs. - $10.00

Sassafras Inn Bed And Breakfast—One of the South's enchanting settings. English Tudor home set on 1.5 lovely acres. Indoor pool, gardens and waterfalls, cabana room and sun patio, game room, billiards. Enjoy southern hospitality. Only 12 miles from Memphis and Graceland.

Kosciusko *

Garrett, Maggie
121 N. Wells St., 39090
(601) 289-5086, Fax: (601) 653-3108

Amenities: 1,2,4,5,6,9,10,11,12,13,14,16,17
Breakfast: F.
Dbl. Oc.: $80.25
Sgl Oc.: $64.20
Third Person: $10.70
Child: $10.70

The Redbud Inn—Owned by Rose Burge and Maggie Garrett, it is listed on the National Historic Register. A two-storied Queen Anne style house, travelers have been using it as a B&B since the 1890s. Restaurant and antique shop on premises. Mile marker 160, Natchez Trace Parkway.

Long Beach *

Mertz, Dr.& Mrs. Karl **Amenities:** 1,2,4,5,6,7,8,10, **Dbl. Oc.:** $53.90 - $75.90
7416 Red Creek Rd., 39560 11,15,16,18 **Sgl. Oc.:** $42.90 - $64.90
(800) 729-9670, (601) 452-3080 **Breakfast:** C. **Third Person:** $16.50
 Child: Under 6 yrs. - no charge

Red Creek Colonial Inn—A three-story, circa 1899, raised French cottage situated on 11 acres of live Oaks and Magnolias. Located less than two miles south of I-10, Long Beach Exit 28 and five miles north of Beach Hwy. 90. A 64-foot front porch. Antiques and six fireplaces. Nearby swimming and golf.

Lorman *

Hylander, Col. & Mrs. Walt **Amenities:** 2,7,9,10,16 **Dbl. Oc.:** $100.75
Rte. 552, 39096 **Breakfast:** F. **Sgl. Oc.:** $79.50
(601) 437-4215, (800) 533-5889 **Third Person:** $26.50
 Child: $26.50

Rosswood Plantation—A stately 1857 mansion on a working 100-acre plantation. Offers luxury, privacy, exquisite antiques, canopied beds, Civil War history, heated pool and spa and more. Ideal for honeymoons. In the National Register of Historic Places. AAA and three Diamonds rated. Near Natchez and Vicksburg.

1. No Smoking	5. Tennis Available	9. Credit Cards Accepted	13. Lunch Available	17. Shared Baths
2. No Pets	6. Golf Available	10. Personal Check Accepted	14. Conference Rooms Avail.	18. Afternoon Tea
3 Off Season Rates	7. Swimmming Avail.	11. Reservations Necessary	15. Group Seminars Avail.	* Commisions given
4. Senior Citizen Rates	8. Skiing Available	12. Dinner Available	16. Private Baths	to Travel Agents

MISSISSIPPI

Natchez *

Epperson, Durell
211 Clifton Ave., 39120
(601) 446-5730

Amenities: 2,10,15,16
Breakfast: F.

Dbl. Oc.: $75.00 - $110.00
Third Person: $20.00

Riverside—Overlooks the Mississippi River. Beautiful rooms with antiques. In the center of town. Private baths and tester beds. Antebellum house built in 1858. Listed in the National Register of Historic Places. TVs in guest rooms. Tour of the house included. Children over 12 welcome.

Pass Christian *

Bertucci, Shirley
1213 Tidewater Dr., # 399, 39571
(601) 255-1648

Amenities: 2,4,5,6,7,10,11,13,14,15,16
Breakfast: C.
Dbl. Oc.: $78.50
Sgl Oc.: $65.50

Tidewater Estates B&B—Located on 467 acres on the Bayou. Swimming, tennis, badminton and fishing. Gulf coast tour, historic and gambling. New Orleans 55 miles away. Main house is the B&B with two cottages containing two bedrooms each and garconiere. Seminars/receptions.

Port Gibson *

Lum, M/M William D.
1207 Church St., 39150
(601) 437-4350, (601) 437-5300,
(800) 729-0240

Amenities: 1,2,5,6,7,9,10,16,18
Breakfast: F.
Dbl. Oc.: $75.00 - $85.00
Sgl Oc.: $60.00 - $70.00
Third Person: $20.00

Oak Square—An antebellum mansion in the town General U.S. Grant said was "too beautiful to burn." Heirloom antiques. Canopy beds. In National Register of Historic Places. Located on U.S. Highway 61, between Natchez and Vicksburg, one mile off Natchez Trace Parkway.

MISSISSIPPI

Vicksburg *

Hudson, Julie
2200 Oak St., 39180
601)636-2800,
(800)862-1300 (USA)
(800)448-2820 (Mississippi)

Amenities: 1,3,4,5,6,7,9,10, 11,14,16,18

Breakfast: F.

Dbl. Oc.: $90.00 - $170.00
Sgl. Oc.: $80.00 - $160.00
Third Person: $20.00

Cedar Grove Mansion-Inn—Relive "Gone With The Wind" elegance in this 1840 antebellum mansion. Choose from 19 antique-filled rooms or suites on four acres of gardens, gazebos and fountains. Swimming pool, hot tub, roof garden overlooking the Mississippi River, afternoon tea and cocktails.

---

1. No Smoking	5. Tennis Available	9. Credit Cards Accepted	13. Lunch Available	17. Shared Baths
2. No Pets	6. Golf Available	10. Personal Check Accepted	14. Conference Rooms Avail.	18. Afternoon Tea
3 Off Season Rates	7. Swimmming Avail.	11. Reservations Necessary	15. Group Seminars Avail.	* Commisions given
4. Senior Citizen Rates	8. Skiing Available	12. Dinner Available	16. Private Baths	to Travel Agents

MISSOURI

Show Me State

Capitol: Jefferson City
Statehood: August 10, 1821; the 24th state
State Motto: "The Welfare Of The People Shall Be
   The Supreme Law"
State Song: "The Missouri Waltz"
State Bird: Bluebird
State Flower: Hawthorne
State Tree: Flowering Dogwood

Missouri is a state of yesterday's history and today's progress. Lewis and Clark started their trek to the Pacific Coast in 1804 from St. Louis, then called The Getaway to the West. The pony Express originated in St. Joseph in 1860 and traveled across the west to Sacramento, California, bringing mail for the first time from one coast to another. The ice cream cone, hot dog and iced tea were all introduced and made popular at the 1904 St. Louis World's Fair. Jesse James was born here as well as Samuel Clemens, who grew up to write about the adventures he and his friends had along the Mississippi River, and signed his name Mark Twain.

Today, the St. Louis Gateway Arch is the nation's tallest man-made monument and remains the symbol of St. Louis, The Gateway to the West. It is an important transportation city, with buying and selling of everything from cattle to antiques.

Tourism has become a very important part of Missouri's economy and the climate during most of the year is pleasant enough to bring visitors here, and in some cases, very often to stay.

President Truman was born and died here.

Branson *

Barber, Darlene & Ted
521 W. Atlantic, 65616
(417) 334-2280

Amenities: 1,2,7,9,10,11,16
Breakfast: F.

Dbl. Oc.: $75.41 - $96.95
Third Person: $10.78
Child: $10.78

Gaines Land Bed And Breakfast—A contemporary home within easy walking distance of downtown Branson. Exclusive use of large common room opening onto patio, hot tubs and swimming pool. Breakfast served in formal dining room or on deck overlooking pool and patio. Refreshments served on arrival.

Branson *

Coats, JoAnne & Bill
Indian Point Rd.
HCR 1, Box 1104, 65616
(417) 338-2978, (800) 289-4125

Amenities: 1,2,3,6,7,9,10,11,
15,16
Breakfast: F. or C.

Dbl. Oc.: $55.00 - $105.00
Sgl. Oc.: $50.00 - $100.00
Third Person: $10.00
Child: Under 3 yrs. - no charge

Josie's Bed And Breakfast—A peaceful getaway, 300 feet of lake front. Perfect for a honeymoon/anniversary. Veranda with panoramic view of clean Table Rock Lake. Contemporary design and tastefully decorated. A touch of lace, flowers, stain glass, huge stone fireplace, cathedral ceilings and private whirlpool.

Branson *

House, Gigi & Dick
HCR 5, Box 2368-2, 65616
(417) 334-6873

Amenities: 1,2,3,10,11,15,16
Breakfast: F.

Dbl. Oc.: $73.65
Sgl. Oc.: $68.39
Third Person: $10.53

The Brass Swan—Elegant contemporary in wooded area with a view of Lake Taneycomo, 1-1/2 easy access miles to Hwy. 76 and shows. Four spacious rooms with king and queen beds and sitting area and TVs. Two rooms have private entrances and decks. Game room, hot tub, kitchenette with beverages and popcorn.

Hannibal *

Andreotti, Donalene & Mike
213 So. 5th St., 63401
(314) 221-0445, (800) 874-5661

Amenities: 1,2,6,7,9,10,13,14,
15,16,18
Breakfast: F.

Dbl. Oc.: $65.00 - $90.00
Sgl. Oc.: $60.00
Third Person: $15.00

Fifth Street Mansion Bed And Breakfast—A historic 1858 mansion providing Victorian charm, antiques and period decor. Walk to Mark Twain's home, historic district, shops and restaurants.

Hannibal *

Feinberg, Irv
R.R. #1, Box 304, 63401
(314) 221-2789

Amenities: 1,2,5,6,7,9,10,11,
16,18
Breakfast: F.

Dbl. Oc.: $58.00 - $95.00
Sgl. Oc.: $58.00 - $95.00
Third Person: $15.00

Garth Woodside Mansion—Chosen "one of the 10 best inns in the Midwest," our 1871 Victorian country estate sits on 39 acres of meadows and woodlands. Enjoy pampered elegance in eight antique bedchambers with afternoon tea and nightshirts for you to wear. Come spoil yourself.

1. No Smoking	5. Tennis Available	9. Credit Cards Accepted	13. Lunch Available	17. Shared Baths
2. No Pets	6. Golf Available	10. Personal Check Accepted	14. Conference Rooms Avail.	18. Afternoon Tea
3 Off Season Rates	7. Swimmming Avail.	11. Reservations Necessary	15. Group Seminars Avail.	* Commisions given
4. Senior Citizen Rates	8. Skiing Available	12. Dinner Available	16. Private Baths	to Travel Agents

Hermann *

Birk, Gloria & Elmer
700 Goethe St., 65041
(314) 486-2911

Amenities: 1,2,9,10,11,15,16,17
Breakfast: F.
Dbl. Oc.: $51.21 - $83.49
Sgl Oc.: $41.21 - $73.49
Third Person: $20.00

Birk's Gasthaus—A 104-year-old Victorian mansion. Bed and breakfast every day except first two weekends a month, when you can be a detective and solve a murder mystery. Write or call for information. Seven private baths and two shared baths.

Hermann *

Sammons, Lavina
123 E. Third St., 65041
(314) 486-5560, (314) 486-3357

Amenities: 1,2,6,10,11,14,16
Breakfast: F.
Dbl. Oc.: $59.25 - $80.79
Sgl Oc.: $59.25 - $80.79
Third Person: $27.50
Child: Under 6 yrs. - no charge

Capt. Wohlt Inn—A charming facility in a 100-year-old river captain's home and two early 1800s settlers homes. Step back in nostalgic luxury where breakfast is an event. Lighted private parking. Private suites. Walking distance of many shops. Member of B&B of Missouri.

Jackson *

Wischmann, Patricia
203 Bellevue, 63755
(314) 243-7427

Amenities: 1,2,3,5,6,7,9,10, 12,14,15,16,17,18
Breakfast: F.

Dbl. Oc.: 75.00
Sgl. Oc.: $65.00
Third Person: $15.00
Child: Under 12 yrs. - $10.00

Trisha's Bed And Breakfast—Located four miles from Cape Girardeau on I-55. A late Victorian full of antiques and vintage clothes. Try on hats and chuckle over the lingerie collections. Breakfast is a delight - the hand-picked fruits and home-baked goodies are scrumptious! Discover small-town U.S.A. charm.

1. No Smoking	5. Tennis Available	9. Credit Cards Accepted	13. Lunch Available	17. Shared Baths
2. No Pets	6. Golf Available	10. Personal Check Accepted	14. Conference Rooms Avail.	18. Afternoon Tea
3 Off Season Rates	7. Swimmming Avail.	11. Reservations Necessary	15. Group Seminars Avail.	* Commisions given
4. Senior Citizen Rates	8. Skiing Available	12. Dinner Available	16. Private Baths	to Travel Agents

MISSOURI

Jamesport *

Richardson, Rebecca J.
P.O. Box 227, 64648
(816) 684-6664

Amenities: 3,9,10,11,12,13,14,
15,17
Breakfast: F.

Dbl. Oc.: $75.00
Sgl. Oc.: $75.00
Third Person: $15.00
Child: Under 6 yrs. - no charge

Richardson House Bed And Breakfast—An antique-filled house in Amish community. Perfect for family adventure or romantic retreat. You'll enjoy the whole house to yourself. Sleeps up to eight. Amish shops, tours, antiques, fishing, hunting, cable TV and air conditioning. Country cooking with prior arrangement.

Joplin *

Meeker, Bill & Marge
327 No. Jackson, 64801
(417) 624-1397

Amenities: 5,6,7,9,10,16,17,
18
Breakfast: F.

Dbl. Oc.: $40.00 - $60.00
Sgl. Oc.: $35.00 - $55.00
Third Person: $10.00
Child: Under 2 yrs. - no charge

Visages—Built in 1898, it is named for the faces on the exterior masonry walls and family portraits inside the inn. Its beauty is achieved through artistry and ingenuity, not money. Marge and Bill, retired teachers, enjoy serving a typical mid-American breakfast.

Kansas City *

Litchfield, Carolyn & Ed
217 E. 37th St., 64111
(816) 753-2667, FAX: (816) 753-2408

Amenities: 2,5,9,10,14,15,16
Breakfast: F.

Dbl. Oc.: $85.00 - $117.00
Sgl. Oc.: $85.00 - $117.00
Third Person: $10.00
Child: Under 1 yr. - no charge

Doanleigh Wallagh Inn—Located between the Plaza and Crown Center, the inn offers five rooms in a Georgian mansion built in 1907. Each room has a private bath, cable TV, phone and air conditioning. Internationally known for its comfort, elegance and romantic ambience.

Kansas City *

Mills, Pat & Ian
3605 Gillham Rd., 64111
(816) 753-1269

Amenities: 1,2,5,9,10,11,14,15,16
Breakfast: F.
Dbl. Oc.: $75.00
Sgl Oc.: $65.00

Milford House—A 100-year-old home situated in the heart of Kansas City, less than a mile from the Plaza, downtown and Crown Center. The house is listed in the National Register. Four guests rooms, each with private bath and television.

1. No Smoking	5. Tennis Available	9. Credit Cards Accepted	13. Lunch Available	17. Shared Baths
2. No Pets	6. Golf Available	10. Personal Check Accepted	14. Conference Rooms Avail.	18. Afternoon Tea
3 Off Season Rates	7. Swimmming Avail.	11. Reservations Necessary	15. Group Seminars Avail.	* Commisions given
4. Senior Citizen Rates	8. Skiing Available	12. Dinner Available	16. Private Baths	to Travel Agents

Kansas City *

Moehl, Susan
Penni Johnson
116 E. 46th St., 64112
(816) 531-7979

Amenities: 1,2,5,7,9,10,11,12,13,14,16
Breakfast: F.
Dbl. Oc.: $117.57 - $151.17
Sgl Oc.: $106.38 - $139.97

Southmoreland On The Plaza - An Urban Inn—Luxury urban inn located 1-1/2 blocks off renowned Country Club Plaza, in the cultural heart of Kansas City. Classic New England decor. Special amenities such as private decks, fireplaces and jacuzzi. Afternoon wine and cheese. Sports and dining privileges at nearby historic club.

Kansas City *

Talbot, Carolyn & John
2 E. 99th St., 64114
(816) 943-1212

Amenities: 2,7,10,11,15,16
Breakfast: F.

Dbl. Oc.: $85.00
Third Person: $20.00

Willow Creek Manor B&B—A '30s stone cottage with large lodge addition. Wood stove; big sleeping loft with king bed; master suite with king-size bed; third room with queen-size brass bed; large windows and two baths. 8x8 spa on big deck, chipping green, indoor racquetball and pool. Two acres.

Platte City *

Soper, Betty & Don
15880 Interurban Rd., 64079-9185
(816) 431-5556,
(816) 242-2776 (Reservations)

Amenities: 2,6,7,8,9,10,11,14,
15,16
Breakfast: C.

Dbl. Oc.: $66.10- $131.16
Sgl. Oc.: $60.86
Third Person: $7.48

Basswood Country Inn Resort—Now you can stay where the rich and famous relaxed and played in the 40s and 50s. Four king suites with mini kitchens, 1935 lakeside cottage, or the Truman, Bing Crosby or Rudy Vallee suites, all with two bedrooms and full kitchens. Bank fishing and pool. Minutes to Kansas City.

Springfield

Brown, Karol & Nancy
900 E. Walnut, 65806
(417) 864-6346

Amenities: 1,2,4,5,7,9,10,11,14,15,16
Breakfast: F.
Dbl. Oc.: $65.00 - $120.00
Sgl Oc.: $65.00 - $120.00
Third Person: $15.00

Walnut Street Inn—An award-winning 1894 showcase restoration. Eleven guest rooms with private baths, some with jacuzzis, in-room phones, European antiques, cozy fireplaces in five rooms. Historic district. Walk to restaurants, theatres and museums.

1. No Smoking	5. Tennis Available	9. Credit Cards Accepted	13. Lunch Available	17. Shared Baths
2. No Pets	6. Golf Available	10. Personal Check Accepted	14. Conference Rooms Avail.	18. Afternoon Tea
3 Off Season Rates	7. Swimmming Avail.	11. Reservations Necessary	15. Group Seminars Avail.	* Commisions given
4. Senior Citizen Rates	8. Skiing Available	12. Dinner Available	16. Private Baths	to Travel Agents

MISSOURI

Springfield *

Wells, Jef
1701 So. Fort, 65807
(417) 831-7242

Amenities: 1,2,9,10,13,14,16, 18
Breakfast: F.

Dbl. Oc.: $75.50 - $134.00
Sgl. Oc.: $75.50 - $134.00
Third Person: $10.00
Child: Over 9 yrs. - $10.00

Mansion At Elfindale—A romantic 19th-century getaway in the heart of the Ozarks. Beautiful grounds, individually decorated rooms - no two are alike. Not too far from the real world. Shopping nearby. Only 30 minutes from Branson, Missouri. Escape to our wonderland.

Ste. Genevieve *

Beckerman, Rob
1021 Market St., 63670
(314) 883-5881

Amenities: 2,5,6,7,9,10,16
Breakfast: F.

Dbl. Oc.: $51.20 - $61.90
Sgl. Oc.: $40.00 - $50.00
Third Person: $12.00
Child: Under 13 yrs. - $6.00

Steiger Haus—Situated in historic Ste. Genevieve (established in 1735) near restored French colonial tour homes. Steiger Haus (1880) features private suites, an indoor swimming pool and special murder-mystery weekends.

St. Louis

Ashdown, Lori
703 No. Kirkwood Rd., 63122
(314) 965-0066

Amenities: 1,2,5,6,9,10,11,14, 16
Breakfast: C. Plus

Dbl. Oc.: $55.00 - $70.00
Sgl. Oc.: $55.00 - $70.00
Third Person: $15.00

The Eastlake Inn—Located within strolling distance of the antique district and just minutes from downtown St. Louis. Quiet comfort and tasteful atmosphere, furnished with restored turn-of-the-century Charles Eastlake furniture. Several excellent restaurants nearby. Enjoy area parks.

St. Louis *

Doelling, Carol
4817 Towne So., 63128
(314) 894-6796

Amenities: 5,6,7,10,11,16,17, 18
Breakfast: F.

Dbl. Oc.: $40.00 - $55.00
Sgl. Oc.: $30.00 - $55.00
Child: Over 5 yrs. - $10.00

Doelling Haus—Features a country European decor and atmosphere, antique furniture and linens. European cuisine and homemade truffles are the house specialty. Minutes to St. Louis, shopping and fine dining. Rediscover "Old World hospitality."

1. No Smoking	5. Tennis Available	9. Credit Cards Accepted	13. Lunch Available	17. Shared Baths
2. No Pets	6. Golf Available	10. Personal Check Accepted	14. Conference Rooms Avail.	18. Afternoon Tea
3 Off Season Rates	7. Swimmming Avail.	11. Reservations Necessary	15. Group Seminars Avail.	* Commisions given
4. Senior Citizen Rates	8. Skiing Available	12. Dinner Available	16. Private Baths	to Travel Agents

MISSOURI

St. Louis *

Milligan, Sarah
2156 Lafayette Ave., 63104
(314) 772-4429

Amenities: 2,5,6,10,16,17
Breakfast: F.

Dbl. Oc.: $53.13 - $79.69
Sgl. Oc.: $47.81 - $58.44
Third Person: $15.00
Child: Under 15 yrs. - $10.00

Lafayette House—An 1876 Victorian mansion. "In the center of things to do in St. Louis." Children welcome. Private and shared baths. Third-floor suite with kitchen. Resident cats. Air conditioned. Bus to downtown. Restaurants nearby.

St. Louis *

Sundermeyer, Susan & Chuck
P.O. Box 8095, 63156
(314) 367-5870

Amenities: 1,2,9,10,11,16
Breakfast: F.
Dbl. Oc.: $68.72 - $84.58
Third Person: $15.00

Coachlight Bed And Breakfast—A turn-of-the-century brick home in the historic central west end. Within walking distance of unique shops, galleries, outdoor cafes and elegant mansions. Fine antiques, Laura Ashley fabrics, down comforters and generous, homemade breakfast.

St. Louis *

Winter, Sarah & Kendall
3522 Arsenal St., 63118
(314) 664-4399

Amenities: 1,2,5,6,7,9,10,14,
                15,16,18
Breakfast: C. Plus

Dbl. Oc.: $58.15 - $79.30
Sgl. Oc.: $50.75 - $63.44
Third Person: $17.00
Child: Under 2 yrs. - no charge

The Winter House B&B—A 10-room Victorian home with turret built in 1897. Near downtown, arch, Union Station, zoo, hospitals and colleges. Hand-squeezed orange juice and professional piano playing at breakfast. Pressed-tin ceiling in one bedroom. Suite available.

Warrensburg *

Wayne, Sandra & Bill
Route 3, Box 130 (Y Hwy.), 64093
(816) 747-5728, (800) 368-4944

Amenities: 1,2,9,10,11,12,13,
                15,17,18
Breakfast: F.

Dbl. Oc.: $47.00 - $55.00
Sgl. Oc.: $42.00 - $48.00
Third Person: $10.00 - $15.00

Cedarcroft Farm Bed And Breakfast—Historic 1867 farmhouse on 80 secluded acres one hour from Kansas City. Enjoy old-fashioned country hospitality, country quiet and all-you-can-eat country cooking. Explore western Missouri with private guide to antiquing and historic sites. Hosts are Civil War re-enactors.

---

1. No Smoking
2. No Pets
3 Off Season Rates
4. Senior Citizen Rates

5. Tennis Available
6. Golf Available
7. Swimming Avail.
8. Skiing Available

9. Credit Cards Accepted
10. Personal Check Accepted
11. Reservations Necessary
12. Dinner Available

13. Lunch Available
14. Conference Rooms Avail.
15. Group Seminars Avail.
16. Private Baths

17. Shared Baths
18. Afternoon Tea
* Commisions given
  to Travel Agents

Washington *

Davis, Kathy Chucky
3 Lafayette St., 63090
(314) 239-2417

Amenities: 1,2,3,10,11,16
Breakfast: F.
Dbl. Oc.: $80.00
Sgl Oc.: $70.00
Third Person: $10.00
Child: Under 3 yrs. - no charge

Washington House Bed And Breakfast—Built in 1837. An authentically restored inn on the Missouri River. It features river views, canopy beds, antique furnishings, complimentary wine and full breakfast. Only 50 minutes west of St. Louis, in the heart of the wine country.

1. No Smoking	5. Tennis Available	9. Credit Cards Accepted	13. Lunch Available	17. Shared Baths
2. No Pets	6. Golf Available	10. Personal Check Accepted	14. Conference Rooms Avail.	18. Afternoon Tea
3 Off Season Rates	7. Swimmming Avail.	11. Reservations Necessary	15. Group Seminars Avail.	* Commisions given
4. Senior Citizen Rates	8. Skiing Available	12. Dinner Available	16. Private Baths	to Travel Agents

MONTANA

The Treasure State

Capitol: Helena
Statehood: November 8, 1889; the 41st state
State Motto: "Gold And Silver"
State Song: "Montana
State Bird: Western Meadow Lark
State Flower: Bitterroot
State Tree: Ponderosa Pine

This is Big Sky Country, the land of mountain goats and grizzly bears. Montana is the fourth largest state in the union. The mountains, the old gold camps and the vast lonely distances still make a visitor fell close to the American frontier.

The beautiful and exciting Glacier National Park is visited by hundreds of tourists every year. Sportsmen from all over the world travel here to fish, hunt and enjoy the national forest, ranches and lodges.

Montana has its share of gold and silver mines as well as the largest deposit of copper in the world.

Bigfork *

Burggraf, Natalie & RJ
Rainbow Drive on Swan Lake, 59911
(406) 837-4608, (800) 525-3344

Amenities: 3,4,7,8,9,10,12,13,16,18
Breakfast: F.
Dbl. Oc.: $65.00 or $75.00
Third Person: $12.00
Child: Under 2 yrs. - $8.00

Burggraf's Country Lane BN'B.—True log home in heart of the Rocky Mountains. Seven acres on Swan Lake. Complimentary wine, fruit and cheese. Use of canoes. Fishing, picnic areas, jacuzzi tub, gourmet breakfast, breathtaking view, minutes from golfing, parks and hiking trails.

Bigfork*

Doohan, Margot & Tom
675 Ferndale Dr., 59911
(406) 837-6851

Amenities: 1,3,4,6,7,8,9,10, 11,14,15,16,17
Breakfast: F.

Dbl. Oc.: $65.00 - $85.00
Sgl. Oc.: $55.00 - $75.00
Third Person: $15.00
Child: Under 5 yrs. - no charge

O'Duachain Country Inn—Gracious three-level log home on five acres near Flathead, Swan Lakes and Glacier National Park. Pristine grounds with exotic birds and wildlife. Antique decor, hot tub and decks enhance the surroundings. Full breakfast is a gourmet delight. Luxury and serenity. Access to all N.W.

Bigfork *

Gustin, Carol
E. Lake Shore, 59911
(406) 982-3329

Amenities: 3,5,6,7,8,10,11,16, 18
Breakfast: C.(cabin), F.(rooms)

Dbl. Oc.: $75.00 - $115.00
Sgl. Oc.: $65.00 - $115.00
Third Person: $10.00
Child: $10.00(cabin)

Gustin Orchard Bed And Breakfast—Amidst tall mountain firs. Beautiful 9 acre cherry orchard with lake frontage. Choose from a restored, romantic, lakeside, one-room log cottage, bath, fireplace and kitchen, or a sprawling 1950s home with a very private room. Fireplace. Unforgettable views.

1. No Smoking	5. Tennis Available	9. Credit Cards Accepted	13. Lunch Available	17. Shared Baths
2. No Pets	6. Golf Available	10. Personal Check Accepted	14. Conference Rooms Avail.	18. Afternoon Tea
3 Off Season Rates	7. Swimmming Avail.	11. Reservations Necessary	15. Group Seminars Avail.	* Commisions given
4. Senior Citizen Rates	8. Skiing Available	12. Dinner Available	16. Private Baths	to Travel Agents

Bozeman *

Volz, Stephanie
202 Lindley Pl., 59715
(406) 587-8403

Amenities: 1,2,5,6,7,8,9,10,11,
12,13,14,15,16,18
Breakfast: F.
Dbl. Oc.: $75.00
Sgl Oc.: $65.00
Third Person: $15.00
Child: Under 5 yrs. - no charge

Lindley House—A unique and elegant inn featuring period wall coverings, antiques and local artwork. Friendly owners, Stephanie and daughter, Erin, provide for your comfort and personal needs. University town with much to offer. Numerous attractions, recreations and much wildlife.

Hamilton *

Reuthlinger, Ahn & Peter
163 Bowman Rd., 59840
(406) 363-4063

Amenities: 1,3,6,8,10,14,15,
16,17
Breakfast: F.

Dbl. Oc.: $45.00 - $50.00
Sgl. Oc.: $35.00
Third Person: $10.00

The Bavarian Farmhouse B&B—(1898) - 44 miles south of Missoula off scenic Highway 93. Five rooms, four baths, sink/vanity in each room. Mountain views. European-style comfort; privacy. Guest sitting room. Big trees; hammock; five acres; historic area; fishing; trail riding; river rafting available.

Helena

Uecker, Bobbi
328 No. Ewing, 59601
(406) 442-3309

Amenities: 1,2,9,10,14,16
Breakfast: F.

Dbl. Oc.: $65.00 - $95.00
Sgl. Oc.: $55.00 -$70.00
Third Person: $15.00

The Sanders - Helena's Bed And Breakfast—Offers elegant accommodations steeped in Helena's historic past. Seven guest rooms, each with private bath, phone and TV. Original antique furnishings. Gourmet breakfasts served in wainscotted dining room. Located in the heart of Helena, three blocks from downtown.

Laurel

Perey, Lynn
2231 Thiel Rd., 59044
(406) 628-7890

Amenities: 1,2,3,6,8,9,10,11,
16
Breakfast: F.

Dbl. Oc.: $62.57
Sgl. Oc.: $57.35
Third Person: $15.64

Riverside Bed And Breakfast—Enjoy a relaxing visit just 20 minutes from Billings via I-90. Fly fish the Yellowstone River from our backyard; golf Laurel's 18 hole course; ski nearby Red Lodge; or just relax in the hot tub. Direct access to Yellowstone Park and Big Sky. We'd love to meet you.

1. No Smoking	5. Tennis Available	9. Credit Cards Accepted	13. Lunch Available	17. Shared Baths
2. No Pets	6. Golf Available	10. Personal Check Accepted	14. Conference Rooms Avail.	18. Afternoon Tea
3 Off Season Rates	7. Swimmming Avail.	11. Reservations Necessary	15. Group Seminars Avail.	* Commisions given
4. Senior Citizen Rates	8. Skiing Available	12. Dinner Available	16. Private Baths	to Travel Agents

Loma *

Sorensen, Donald
HCR 67, Box 50, 59460
(800) 426-2926

Amenities: 1,2,3,9,10,17
Breakfast: F.

Dbl. Oc.: $85.00
Sgl. Oc.: $65.00
Third Person: $25.00

Virgelle Mercantile—Your ghost-town getaway! Enjoy restored rooms above a 1912 general store in Virgelle, a ghost town along the wild and scenic Missouri River. Shop for antiques downstairs, canoe the river, follow the Lewis-Clark Trail or just relax on the porch.

Polson

Lenz, Karen & Gerry
304 3rd Ave., E., 59860
(406)883-2723

Amenities: 1,2,3,5,6,7,10,17
Breakfast: C. or F.

Dbl. Oc.: $52.00
Sgl. Oc.: $47.50

Hawthorne House—Located in a small western Montana town of Polson just one block from Flathead Lake. Cozy home with lovely antiques and plate collections. National Bison Range and historic Mission Church close by. Glacier National Park is just two hours away.

Red Lodge *

Boggio, Carolyn & Elven
224 So. Platt Ave., 59068
(406) 446-3913

Amenities: 1,2,4,6,7,8,9,10,
16,17,18
Breakfast: C. Plus

Dbl. Oc.: $52.00 - $62.40
Sgl. Oc.: $46.80 - $52.00
Third Person: $10.40
Child: $10.40

Willows Inn—Warm and inviting atmosphere. A lovely Victorian minutes from skiing, golf and magnificent mountain scenery. Charming and romantic rooms. Movies, books, games and afternoon refreshments. Delicious home-baked pastries. Large and airy sundeck. Two-bedroom family cottage available.

Troy

Thompson, Mrs. Alex
15303 Bull Lake Rd., 59935
(406) 295-4228

Amenities: 2,7,8,10,17
Breakfast: F.

Dbl. Oc.: $51.28
Sgl. Oc.: $35.86
Third Person: $20.64
Child: Under 3 yrs. - no charge

Bull Lake Guest Ranch—Located mid-way on Highway 56. Beautiful Bull Lake on the west and Cabinet Wilderness on the east. Six modern, comfortable rooms with three shared baths. Primitive cabin sleeps six. Family style meals by day or week. Scenic trail rides.

Whitefish

Masters, Nancy
12 Dakota Ave., 59937
(406)862-9663

Amenities: 1,2,5,6,8,9,10,
11,17
Breakfast: F.

Dbl. Oc.: $46.80
Sgl. Oc.: $36.40
Child: Family rate - $104.00

The Edgewood—Near Glacier National Park and Big Mountain Ski Resort. Decorated with antiques and dolls from owner's collection. Sourdough waffles a breakfast specialty.

1. No Smoking	5. Tennis Available	9. Credit Cards Accepted	13. Lunch Available	17. Shared Baths
2. No Pets	6. Golf Available	10. Personal Check Accepted	14. Conference Rooms Avail.	18. Afternoon Tea
3 Off Season Rates	7. Swimmming Avail.	11. Reservations Necessary	15. Group Seminars Avail.	* Commisions given
4. Senior Citizen Rates	8. Skiing Available	12. Dinner Available	16. Private Baths	to Travel Agents

NEBRASKA

The Cornhusker State

Capitol: Lincoln
Statehood: March 1, 1867; the 37th state
State Motto "Equality Before The Law"
State Song: "Beautiful Nebraska"
State Bird: Western Meadow Lark
State Flower: Goldenrod
State Tree: Cottonwood

The name Nebraska comes from the Oto Indian word, "Nebrathka" meaning flat water. Nebraska was a flat area of vast land with very cold winters and extremely hot summers when the first pioneers arrived. They came to farm and evidence of their hard labor can be seen where hundreds of trees first planted for shade, still stand today. "D" Street in Lincoln is famous for the many huge Oak trees that remain a symbol of these first settlers.

Every year, thousands of visitors drive the Nebraska Highway that follows the Oregon and Mormon trails. Ruts left by the pioneer's covered wagons can be seen along the roadside. In Gothesburg the pony Express Station stands reminding us of where fresh supplies of horses were kept for the early mail carriers.

Omaha is the state's largest city and the center of trade and industry for eastern Nebraska and western Iowa. The capitol, Lincoln, is the second largest city in the state.

The leading crop is corn, but during WW II Nebraska farmers produced millions of tons of corn, oat, potatoes and wheat to meet the wartime shortage.

Nebraska is very proud of its well known sons & daughters: 38th President Gerald Ford, William Jennings Bryant, Willa Cather, Father Edward Flanagan, founder of Boys' Town and Buffalo Bill Cody whose frontier ranch home still stands at Scout Rest near North Platte.

NEBRASKA

Grand Island

Kehm, Norma
220 No. Wheeler, 68801
(308) 382-3568

Amenities: 1,2,10,16,17
Breakfast: F.

Dbl. Oc.: $50.00
Sgl. Oc.: $45.00
Third Person: $15.00
Child: Under 10 yrs. - $5.00

Downtown Bed And Breakfast Inn—Awaken to the smell of ginger muffins served in the dining room or out under the umbrellas. You will find a guest living room and eight large bedrooms tastefully decorated. Just a few steps away is a theatre and many antique shops.

Omaha

Jones, Donald
1617 So. 90th St., 68124
(402) 397-0721

Amenities: 6,10,11,16,17
Breakfast: C.

Dbl. Oc.: $25.00
Sgl. Oc.: $15.00
Third Person: $5.00

Private Residence—A large, comfortable home on one acre of land. Five minutes from I-80. Near large shopping centers and race tracks. Homemade cinnamon rolls for a delicious breakfast in the enclosed gazebo — weather permitting.

Paxton

Meyer, Gwen
Box 247, 69155
(308) 239-4265

Amenities: 1,2,3,9,10,14,16,17
Breakfast: F.
Dbl. Oc.: $50.00
Sgl Oc.: $30.00
Third Person: 10.00
Child: Under 12 yrs. - no charge

Gingerbread Inn—We invite you to enjoy warm hospitality and relax in a bygone era. Beautiful gazebo and private picnic grounds. Relax on porch swing. Awaken to the smell of a sumptuous, homemade breakfast. Gingerbread cookies are among the special touches.

1. No Smoking	5. Tennis Available	9. Credit Cards Accepted	13. Lunch Available	17. Shared Baths
2. No Pets	6. Golf Available	10. Personal Check Accepted	14. Conference Rooms Avail.	18. Afternoon Tea
3 Off Season Rates	7. Swimmming Avail.	11. Reservations Necessary	15. Group Seminars Avail.	* Commisions given
4. Senior Citizen Rates	8. Skiing Available	12. Dinner Available	16. Private Baths	to Travel Agents

NEVADA

The Silver State

Capitol: Carson City
Statehood: October 31, 1864; the 36th state
State Motto: "All For Our Country"
State Song: "Home Means Nevada"
State Bird: Mountain Bluebird
State Flower: Sagebrush
State Tree: Single Leaf Pinon

In this state, rich deposits of silver ore were discovered in 1859. Virginia City became the site of one of the largest bonanzas of silver ore discovered by Henry Comstock. The massive strike brought hundreds of prospectors rushing to Nevada to 'strike it rich'. Some did, but many others did not. Along with mining came ranching, but in early 1869 when mining became less lucrative, gambling was legalized and the beginning of the state's largest and fastest growing industries began, tourism.

Over twenty million people visit this state each year. They enjoy the night life and gambling of Las Vegas, Reno, Lake Tahoe and Virginia City, as well as the summer and winter sports.

Hoover Dam is another tourist attraction. Man-made and one of the highest concrete dams in the world, measuring 726 Ft. from base to crest.

East Ely *

Lindley, Jane & Norman
220 E. 11th St.
P.O. Box 151110, 89315-1110
(702) 289-8687

Amenities: 1,2,3,9,10,11,16
Breakfast: F.
Dbl. Oc.: $79.00
Sgl Oc.: $67.00
Third Person: $7.00

Steptoe Valley Inn—Elegant, romantic, five-room Ely City historic building with private balconies, library, veranda, rose garden and gazebo. Guests enjoy the nearby scenery, the "Ghost Train of old Ely" and the Great Basin National Park. Open June through September.

1. No Smoking	5. Tennis Available	9. Credit Cards Accepted	13. Lunch Available	17. Shared Baths
2. No Pets	6. Golf Available	10. Personal Check Accepted	14. Conference Rooms Avail.	18. Afternoon Tea
3 Off Season Rates	7. Swimmming Avail.	11. Reservations Necessary	15. Group Seminars Avail.	* Commisions given
4. Senior Citizen Rates	8. Skiing Available	12. Dinner Available	16. Private Baths	to Travel Agents

NEW HAMPSHIRE

The Granite State

Capitol: Concord
Statehood: June 21, 1788; the 9th state
State Motto: "Live Free Or Die"
State Song: "Old New Hampshire"
State Bird: Purple Finch
State Flower: Purple Lilac
State Tree: White Birch

The White Mountains make this New England state one of the most beautiful of all Mt. Washington, the tallest mountain in this range, is one of the most popular attractions for visitors. It brings great excitement to the winter skier and is a summer tourist delight. The mountain can be climbed either by foot, car or cog-railroad. In any case, it is not easy and not everyone makes it to the top.

New Hampshire was settled in 1633 and the people worked the land and quarries. Factories sprung up, but in the late '30s and early '40s, they either moved south or closed completely. People had to look elsewhere for an income. Tourism became that other income. Today, tourism is a major source of income for this state.

The taxes are very low here and the people wish to keep them this way. Because of this, more and more people are moving here.

Daniel Webster and our 14th President Franklin Pierce, were both born in New Hampshire.

Andover

Smith, Gillian & Ken
Main St., P.O. Box 162, 03216
(603) 735-5987

Amenities: 1,2,5,6,7,8,9, 10,16,18
Breakfast: F.

Dbl. Oc.: $81.00
Sgl. Oc.: $54.00
Third Person: $21.60

"The English House"—Built in 1906, now fully renovated. A year-round B&B. A comfortable sitting room, seven elegant bedrooms with private baths and a huge breakfast guarantee guests a memorable stay in a special English atmosphere.

Andover, East *

Sherman, M/M Bradford
Maple St.
P.O. Box 107, 03231
(603) 735-6426

Amenities: 1,2,3,4,5,6,7,8,9,10,11,16,17
Breakfast: F.
Dbl. Oc.: $54.00 - $70.00
Sgl Oc.: $43.00 - $54.00
Third Person: $16.00

Patchwork Inn—An 1805 village colonial on three acres. Cross-country and downhill skiing. Lake and mountain views. Walk to beach. Furnished with antiques, pewter and braided rugs. Three common rooms, all with fireplaces. Piano. Breakfast features family-made genuine honey and maple syrup.

Ashland *

Paterman, Betsy & Karol
43 Highland St.
P.O. Box 719, 03217-0819
(603) 968-3775, (800) 637-9599

Amenities: 1,2,3,5,6,7,8,9, 10,14,16
Breakfast: F.

Dbl. Oc.: $81.00
Sgl. Oc.: $81.00
Third Person: $10.80

Glynn House "Victorian" Inn—A romantic escape in the heart of the White Mountains and lakes region of New Hampshire. "Golden Pond" area. Gracious four-bedroom Victorian filled with antiques and Old-World hospitality. Jacuzzi bath and fireplace. Quaint New England town off I-93, Exit 24. Just two hours from Boston. Gourmet breakfast.

Bartlett *

Dindorf, Mark
Route 302, 03812-0327
(603) 374-2353, (800) 292-2353

Amenities: 3,4,6,7,8,9,10, 16,17,18
Breakfast: F.

Dbl. Oc.: $69.00 - $89.00
Sgl. Oc.: $42.00 - $48.00
Third Person: $29.00
Child: Under 12 yrs. - no charge

The Country Inn At Bartlett—A bed-and-breakfast inn for hikers, skiers and outdoor lovers in the White Mountains. Enjoy a hearty breakfast, relax by the fireside and unwind in the outdoor hot tub. Choose a room in the main inn or one of the cozy cottage rooms. We welcome you to New Hampshire's White Mountains.

---

1. No Smoking	5. Tennis Available	9. Credit Cards Accepted	13. Lunch Available	17. Shared Baths
2. No Pets	6. Golf Available	10. Personal Check Accepted	14. Conference Rooms Avail.	18. Afternoon Tea
3 Off Season Rates	7. Swimmming Avail.	11. Reservations Necessary	15. Group Seminars Avail.	* Commisions given
4. Senior Citizen Rates	8. Skiing Available	12. Dinner Available	16. Private Baths	to Travel Agents

Bethlehem *

Burns, Robert
Main St., 03574
(603) 869-3389

Amenities: 1,2,3,5,6,7,8,9,10, 15,16
Breakfast: F.
Dbl. Oc.: $70.00
Sgl. Oc.: $45.00
Third Person: $11.00

The Mulburn Inn—A sprawling summer estate built in 1913 as a family retreat known as the Ivie House on the Woolworth estate. We have seven spacious and elegant rooms, all with private baths. Minutes from Franconia Notch and Mt. Washington attractions. AAA rated. Open all year.

Bradford *

Mazol, Connie & Tom
Main St.
RR 1, Box 40, 03221
(603) 938-5309

Amenities: 3,4,5,6,7,8,9,10,11,12,14,15,16
Breakfast: F.
Dbl. Oc.: $63.00 - $74.00
Sgl Oc.: $48.00 - $56.00
Third Person: $14.00
Child: Under 5 yrs. - $7.00

The Bradford Inn—This historic hotel established in 1898. Is located in the southern lakes and mountains of New Hampshire. Offers the guest a variety of activities in all four seasons. Chef owned. Family operated. A small, intimate dining room serves a variety of tasty house specialties.

Campton *

Preston, Susan & Nicholas
Mad River Rd., 03223
(603) 726-4283

Amenities: 1,2,4,5,6,7,8,10, 11,12,16
Breakfast: F.
Dbl. Oc.: $64.00
Sgl. Oc.: $35.00
Third Person: $20.00
Child: Under 12 yrs. - $10.00

The Mountain Fare Inn—An 1845 farm-style home. Fresh and welcoming. White Mountain village. Flowers, foliage, biking, hiking and skiing. Two hours north of Boston. Perfect stop between Vermont and Maine. Reunions, small groups (20). Guided hikes. Bring your family to New Hampshire!

Centre Harbor

Lauterbach, Barbara
Old Meredith Rd., 03226
(603) 253-4334

Amenities: 1,3,5,6,7,8,10,11, 17
Breakfast: F.
Dbl. Oc.: $65.00
Sgl. Oc.: $60.00
Third Person: $15.00

Watch Hill—Within walking distance of the beach and shops. Historic Watch Hill offers warm, Yankee hospitality. A 1772 house on two acres overlooking Lake Winnipesaukee. Enjoy a full gourmet breakfast in a tasteful setting of English and American antiques.

1. No Smoking	5. Tennis Available	9. Credit Cards Accepted	13. Lunch Available	17. Shared Baths
2. No Pets	6. Golf Available	10. Personal Check Accepted	14. Conference Rooms Avail.	18. Afternoon Tea
3 Off Season Rates	7. Swimmming Avail.	11. Reservations Necessary	15. Group Seminars Avail.	* Commisions given
4. Senior Citizen Rates	8. Skiing Available	12. Dinner Available	16. Private Baths	to Travel Agents

Claremont

Albee, Debbie & Frank
25 Hillstead Rd., 03743-3399
(603) 543-0603, (800) 736-0603

Amenities: 1,2,5,6,7,8,10,15,16,17
Breakfast: F.
Dbl. Oc.: $70.20 - $102.60
Third Person: $16.20

Goddard Mansion B&B—A delightful 18-room 1905 mansion. Elegant, yet "homey." Eight unique guest rooms. Natural breakfast. Smoke-free! Mountain view. Peaceful and quiet. Musical host. Puzzles and games available. Great antiquing country. Nearby fine dining. Short drive to historic points of interest.

Conway *

Lein, Lynn, Bob, Amy & Frisky
148 Washington St.
P.O. Box 1649, 03818
(603) 447-3988

Amenities: 1,2,3,5,6,7,8,9,10,16,17,18
Breakfast: F.
Dbl. Oc.: $59.00 - $95.00
Sgl Oc.: $39.00 - $59.00
Third Person: $15.00
Child: Under 13 yrs. - $10.00

Mountain Valley Manner B&B—A friendly, restored country Victorian at the Kancamagus Highway in sight of two historic covered kissing bridges and Mt. Washington. Enjoy family-size, air-conditioned rooms, many antiques, pool, waterbed and cable TV. Near health club, restaurants, ski areas, hiking, golf and outlets.

Deering

Farrell, Jeanne & Ray
Farrell Hill Rd., 03244
(603) 529-7477

Amenities: 1,2,9,11,13,16
Breakfast: F.

Dbl. Oc.: $70.00
Sgl. Oc.: $60.00

Midwood Inn B&B—A 1794 colonial Cape on 100 acres, 30 minutes from Keene, Concord and Manchester. Amenities include hiking, cross-country skiing trails and fishing in a tranquil, country atmosphere. Ten minutes from two golf courses and 20 minutes from the ski area.

1. No Smoking	5. Tennis Available	9. Credit Cards Accepted	13. Lunch Available	17. Shared Baths
2. No Pets	6. Golf Available	10. Personal Check Accepted	14. Conference Rooms Avail.	18. Afternoon Tea
3 Off Season Rates	7. Swimmming Avail.	11. Reservations Necessary	15. Group Seminars Avail.	* Commisions given
4. Senior Citizen Rates	8. Skiing Available	12. Dinner Available	16. Private Baths	to Travel Agents

Eaton Center *

Spink, Jacqueline & Walter
Rte. 153, Box 12, 03832
(603) 447-2120, (800) 343-7336

Amenities: 1,2,3,5,6,7,8,9,10, 11,12,14,15,16
Breakfast: F.

Dbl. Oc.: $98.00 - $118.00
Sgl. Oc.: $68.00 - $73.00
Third Person: $37.00
Child: 2 - 12 yrs. - $25.00

The Inn At Crystal Lake—Be pampered in this 1884 Victorian inn in a quiet corner. Enjoy imaginative four-course multi-entree cuisine in metal-sculpture-enhanced, fireplaced dining room. Begin breakfast with Irish soda bread. Relax in our TV-den/library, cozy lounge or Victorian parlor.

Franconia

Kerivan, Kate
Easton Valley Rd.
P.O. Box 15, 03580
(603) 823-7775

Amenities: 1,2,3,8,9,10,11,15, 16,17,18
Breakfast: F.

Dbl. Oc.: $60.00 - $110.00
Sgl. Oc.: $50.00 - $75.00
Third Person: $20.00

Bungay Jar Bed And Breakfast—Set in Robert Frost's Easton Valley. Mountain views and private woodlands bounded by a river and national park. King-size suites, sauna, balconies, fireplace and country antiques throughout. Home built from an 18th-century barn. Hosts are avid hikers and skiers. Memorable!

Franconia *

Morris, Alec
1300 Easton Rd., 03580
(603) 823-5542, (800) 473-5299

Amenities: 1,2,3,5,6,7,8,9,10,12,13,14, 15,16,17,18
Breakfast: F.
Dbl. Oc.: $84.25
Sgl Oc.: $73.45
Third Person: $16.25
Child: Under 4 yrs. - no charge

Franconia Inn—White clapboards and green shutters. Breathtaking views of Franconia Notch. First class, full service, turn-of-the-century inn. Award-winning cuisine. Thirty-four rooms and suites. On-premis, fun includes: swimming, horseback riding, tennis, skiing and sleigh rides.

1. No Smoking	5. Tennis Available	9. Credit Cards Accepted	13. Lunch Available	17. Shared Baths
2. No Pets	6. Golf Available	10. Personal Check Accepted	14. Conference Rooms Avail.	18. Afternoon Tea
3 Off Season Rates	7. Swimmming Avail.	11. Reservations Necessary	15. Group Seminars Avail.	* Commisions given
4. Senior Citizen Rates	8. Skiing Available	12. Dinner Available	16. Private Baths	to Travel Agents

Franconia

Shannon, Brenda
351 Easton Valley Rd., 03580
(603) 823-7061

Amenities: 1,2,5,6,7,8,9,10,12,15,17
Breakfast: F.
Dbl. Oc.: $65.00
Sgl Oc.: $40.00
Third Person: $20.00
Child: $20.00

Blanche's B&B—An English-style B&B in a Victorian farmhouse restored to a former glory it probably never had. Rurally located in the Easton Valley, we look upon the Kinsman Ridge. Six miles from Franconia Notch. 100 percent cotton sheets on comfortable beds. Great home-cooked breakfasts.

Glen

Wroblewski, Sharon
Rte. 302, 03838
(800) 548-8007

Amenities: 1,2,3,5,6,7,8,9,10,
           11,12,13,14,15,16
Breakfast: F.
Dbl. Oc.: $135.00
Sgl Oc.: $75.00
Third Person: $25.00
Child: Under 12 pay their age.

The Bernerhof—A small, elegant hotel featuring antiqued deluxe rooms with spa tub. In the foothills of the White Mountains. Participate in our renown "A Taste of the Mountains Cooking School" or enjoy our chef's creative cuisine in our lovely dining rooms.

Greenfield *

Mangini, Vic
Forest Rd.
Box 400, 03047
(603) 547-6327

Amenities: 2,4,5,6,7,8,9,10,
11,12,13,14,15,16,
17,18
Breakfast: F.

Dbl. Oc.: $49.00 - $99.00
Sgl. Oc.: $49.00 - $99.00
Third Person: $20.00
Child: No charge under 1 yr.

Greenfield Inn—Mr. & Mrs. Bob Hope visited twice! A romantic Victorian mansion only 90 minutes from Boston in a small mountain valley town. A full breakfast party with crystal, china and Mozart. Vacation apartment available for honeymooners and anniversary retreats. Romantic restaurants nearby.

---

1. No Smoking
2. No Pets
3 Off Season Rates
4. Senior Citizen Rates

5. Tennis Available
6. Golf Available
7. Swimming Avail.
8. Skiing Available

9. Credit Cards Accepted
10. Personal Check Accepted
11. Reservations Necessary
12. Dinner Available

13. Lunch Available
14. Conference Rooms Avail.
15. Group Seminars Avail.
16. Private Baths

17. Shared Baths
18. Afternoon Tea
* Commisions given
   to Travel Agents

Hampton Beach *

Roy, Matthew
473 Ocean Blvd., 03842
(603) 926-7893

Amenities: 2,3,6,7,9,12,17
Breakfast: C. Plus

Dbl. Oc.: $75.00
Sgl. Oc.: $75.00
Third Person: $5.00
Child: $5.00

Roy Family Bed And Breakfast—The Roys would like to share their home with you during your visit to the seacoast. Six rooms to choose from. On-site parking. Two sun decks, TV room, formal living and dining rooms. Across the street from the ocean. Ask about our mid-summer lobster special. Reserve early.

Holderness *

Webb, Bonnie & Bill
Rte. 3, 03245
(603) 968-7269

Amenities: 1,2,3,5,6,7,8,9,10, 16
Breakfast: F.

Dbl. Oc.: $105.00
Sgl. Oc.: $70.00
Third Person: $25.00

The Inn On Golden Pond—An impressive colonial home built in 1879. Nine bright and cheerful rooms and suites. Located in the beautiful lakes region. Across the road is Squam Lake, the setting for the film "On Golden Pond." Open year-round.

Intervale

Davies, Eileen
Franke, Dean
Rte. 16, 03845
(603) 356-2224

Amenities: 2,9,10,11,16,17
Breakfast: C.

Dbl. Oc.: $51.84 - $99.36
Sgl. Oc.: $43.20
Third Person: $16.20
Child: $16.20

Wildflowers Guest House—Filled with Victorian antiques and located 1-1/2 miles from North Conway Village, our small B&B inn specializes in your comfort and convenience. We look forward to sharing our home with you here in the heart of the Mt. Washington Valley.

Jackson *

Crocker, Robin
Rte. 16A, Box 359, 03846
(603) 383-6666

Amenities: 2,3,5,6,7,8,9,10,16,17
Breakfast: C. Plus and F.
Dbl. Oc.: $50.00 - $100.00
Third Person: $5.00 - $20.00

The Village House—A colonial inn serving guests for over 100 years. The comforts of a large inn with the personality of a small B&B. Pool, jacuzzi, tennis and porch. In winter: cross-country from our front door, downhill nearby. Relax in our four-season spa. Warm hospitality. Affordable.

1. No Smoking	5. Tennis Available	9. Credit Cards Accepted	13. Lunch Available	17. Shared Baths
2. No Pets	6. Golf Available	10. Personal Check Accepted	14. Conference Rooms Avail.	18. Afternoon Tea
3 Off Season Rates	7. Swimmming Avail.	11. Reservations Necessary	15. Group Seminars Avail.	* Commisions given
4. Senior Citizen Rates	8. Skiing Available	12. Dinner Available	16. Private Baths	to Travel Agents

Jackson *

Cyr, Nancy & Robert
Dinsmore Rd., 03846
(603) 383-8071

Amenities: 1,2,3,7,8,9,10,11, 16

Breakfast: F.

Dbl. Oc.: $171.10 - $253.70
Sgl. Oc.: $119.71 - $177.59
Third Person: $51.33 - $76.11

Nestlenook Resort—Elegant 65-acre Victorian resort. Seven rooms with private baths, two-person jacuzzis, fireplaces and parlor stoves. Nestled in the heart of the White Mountains. Year-round sleigh rides. Charming New England village with gourmet dining. A resort that should not be missed!!

Jackson *

Levine Family, The
Rte. 16,
Pinkham Notch, 03846
(800) 537-9276, (603) 383-6822

Amenities: 3,4,5,6,7,8,9,10,12,
13,14,16,17,18
Breakfast: F. (C. — off-season)
Dbl. Oc.: $75.00 - $125.00
Sgl Oc.: $70.00 - $120.00
Third Person: $25.00
Child: Under 18 yrs. -meals only charge

Dana Place Inn—A century-old inn at base of Mt. Washington on 10 acres along Ellis River. Cozy rooms, fine dining, pub, indoor pool, jacuzzi, tennis, hiking, fishing and cross-country skiing on-site. Alpine skiing, golf and attractions nearby. Special package plans available. Children welcome.

Jackson *

Tradwell, Lori
Thornhill Rd., 03846
(603) 383-4321

Amenities: 2,3,5,6,7,8,9,10,
11,16,18

Breakfast: F.

Dbl. Oc.: $92.00
Sgl. Oc.: $92.00
Third Person: $39.00
Child: Under 13 yrs. - $12.00

Inn At Jackson—Enjoy the pleasures of the White Mountains with a cozy atmosphere, in our 1902 country inn. We offer spacious rooms with fireplaces and private baths. We serve a hearty breakfast by the fire or on the glassed-in veranda. Hiking, golf, cross-country trails, views at our door.

1. No Smoking	5. Tennis Available	9. Credit Cards Accepted	13. Lunch Available	17. Shared Baths
2. No Pets	6. Golf Available	10. Personal Check Accepted	14. Conference Rooms Avail.	18. Afternoon Tea
3 Off Season Rates	7. Swimming Avail.	11. Reservations Necessary	15. Group Seminars Avail.	* Commisions given
4. Senior Citizen Rates	8. Skiing Available	12. Dinner Available	16. Private Baths	to Travel Agents

Jefferson *

Brown, Gregory W.
RFD 1, Box 68A, 03583
(603) 586-7998

Amenities: 1,2,3,5,6,7,8,9,10,11,14,16,18
Breakfast: F.
Dbl. Oc.: $52.00 - $80.00
Sgl Oc.: $48.00 - $72.00
Third Person: $12.00
Child: $8.00

The Jefferson Inn—Near Mt. Washington, 360-degree mountain views, wrap-around porch with rockers, acres of fields. Swimming pond. Near five golf courses. Superb hiking from the inn. Family suites, 13 rooms with private baths. Nearby cross-country and downhill skiing. Skating rink. Summer theatre.

Laconia

Damato, Diane
R-1, Box 335, 03246
(603) 524-0087

Amenities: 1,2,5,6,7,10,11,16

Breakfast: F.

Dbl. Oc.: $70.20 - $81.00
Sgl. Oc.: $64.80 - $75.60
Third Person: $15.00

Ferry Point House—Gracious country Victorian located on picturesque Lake Winnisquam. Enjoy mountain views from our 60-foot veranda and lake-front gazebo, or swim and boat in pristine waters. Inside you will find five tastefully decorated rooms with private baths. Hospitality plus!

Lincoln

Deppe, Loretta & William
Pollard Rd.
P.O. Box 562, 03251
(603) 745-8517

Amenities: 1,2,5,6,7,8,9,10,11,17
Breakfast: F.
Dbl. Oc.: $59.40
Sgl Oc.: $37.80
Third Person: $16.20
Child: $16.20

The Red Sleigh—Family-run inn with mountain views from each window, just off the scenic Kancamagus Highway. One mile to Loon Mountain ski area, Waterville and Cannon. Many summer attractions and superb fall foliage. Nearby shopping, dining and theatre. Barbecue facilities available.

---

1. No Smoking	5. Tennis Available	9. Credit Cards Accepted	13. Lunch Available	17. Shared Baths
2. No Pets	6. Golf Available	10. Personal Check Accepted	14. Conference Rooms Avail.	18. Afternoon Tea
3 Off Season Rates	7. Swimmming Avail.	11. Reservations Necessary	15. Group Seminars Avail.	* Commisions given
4. Senior Citizen Rates	8. Skiing Available	12. Dinner Available	16. Private Baths	to Travel Agents

Littleton *

Fisher-Motheu, Catherine & John
247 W. Main St., 03561
(603) 444-2661

Amenities: 1,2,3,5,6,7,8,9,10, 12,16,17
Breakfast: F.

Dbl. Oc.: $48.60 - $81.00
Sgl. Oc.: $43.20
Child: $10.00 - $15.00

Beal House Inn—1833 charm in 13 antique-filled guest rooms, nine with private baths. Fireside breakfast gatherings before White Mountain adventure. Robust European fare in our jazzy little evening dining room. Antiques and local art for sale. Three hours from Boston, MA and Montreal. Welcome!

New Ipswich *

Bankuti, Ginny & Steve
Porter Hill Rd.
P.O. Box 208, 03071
(603) 878-3711

Amenities: 1,2,8,9,10,15,16, 18
Breakfast: F.

Dbl. Oc.: $70.20
Sgl. Oc.: $48.60
Child: 8-18 yrs. - $16.20

The Inn At New Ipswich—A graceful 1790 home surrounded by stone walls and fruit trees. Six spacious guest rooms. Leisurely hearth-side breakfasts. Only minutes to numerous antique shops, ski areas and hiking trails. Come and relax, read by the fire, rock on the porch. Enjoy the quiet.

New London *

Rich, Margaret & Grant
125 Pleasant St., 03257
(603) 526-6271

Amenities: 1,2,3,5,6,7,8,9,10, 11,12,14,15,16
Breakfast: F.

Dbl. Oc.: $90.00 - $108.00
Sgl. Oc.: $60.00 - $78.00
Third Person: $30.00
Child: $30.00

Pleasant Lake Inn—Nestled off the shore of Pleasant Lake. Restored Victorian farmhouse with 11 bedrooms, fireplace, antiques, mountain views, lovely gardens, quiet atmosphere. Guests may enjoy hiking trails and nature undisturbed by modern times. Three star Mobil and AAA rated.

Newport

Tatem, Judi & Dick
HCR 63, Box 3, 03773
(603) 863-3583, (800) 367-2364

Amenities: 2,5,6,7,8,9,10,11, 12,13,
Breakfast: F.

Dbl. Oc.: $91.80 - $189.00
Sgl. Oc.: $70.20 - $189.00
Third Person: $21.60

The Inn At Coit Mountain—Something more than a bed and breakfast. "Ohhh" is the best way to describe the library, with its oak paneling and granite fireplace. Sheer elegance! Breakfast is country-style or gourmet, as you wish.

1. No Smoking	5. Tennis Available	9. Credit Cards Accepted	13. Lunch Available	17. Shared Baths
2. No Pets	6. Golf Available	10. Personal Check Accepted	14. Conference Rooms Avail.	18. Afternoon Tea
3 Off Season Rates	7. Swimmming Avail.	11. Reservations Necessary	15. Group Seminars Avail.	* Commisions given
4. Senior Citizen Rates	8. Skiing Available	12. Dinner Available	16. Private Baths	to Travel Agents

NEW HAMPSHIRE

North Conway *

Begley, Ann & Hugh
P.O. Box 1817
Mt. Surprise Rd., 03860
(800) 258-2625, (603) 356-2625

Amenities: 2,3,6,7,8,10,16,17
Breakfast: F.
Dbl. Oc.: $65.00 - $98.00
Sgl Oc.: $45.00 - $75.00
Third Person: $18.00
Child: Under 5 yrs. - no charge

The Buttonwood Inn—Built in 1820, our Cape Cod-style inn is tucked away on the mountain where it's quiet and secluded yet only two miles to town and one mile to downhill skiing. Nine antique-furnished guest rooms. Hiking and 65 km. of groomed cross-country trails from our door.

North Conway

Halpin, Valerie & Dave
River Rd., 03860
(603) 356-2831

Amenities: 1,2,5,6,7,8,9,10, 16,17
Breakfast: F.

Dbl. Oc.: $63.72 - $91.80
Sgl. Oc.: $48.60 - $81.00
Third Person: $16.05
Child: Under 12 - $1.00 per year

Nereledge Inn—Comfortable and casual. Nine guest rooms (some private baths). English-style pub with darts and draft beer. Close to all activities: hiking, climbing, skiing and fishing. Walk to river for swimming or to village for shops, dining and theatre. Small groups and families welcome.

North Conway *

Helfand, Judy & Dennis
Kearsarge Rd.
P.O. Box 1194, 03860
(603) 356-2044, (800) 356-3596

Amenities: 2,3,5,6,7,8,9,10,12,13,16
Breakfast: F.
Dbl. Oc.: $60.00 - $110.00
Sgl Oc.: $55.00 - $95.00
Third Person: $15.00 - $27.00
Child: Under 12 yrs. - $10.00

Cranmore Mt. Lodge—A small country inn with resort facilities. Main inn has quaint rooms with private baths. "Barn loft" offers new rooms with private baths, air-conditioning and color TV. Forty-bed dorm available for groups.

---

1. No Smoking	5. Tennis Available	9. Credit Cards Accepted	13. Lunch Available	17. Shared Baths
2. No Pets	6. Golf Available	10. Personal Check Accepted	14. Conference Rooms Avail.	18. Afternoon Tea
3 Off Season Rates	7. Swimming Avail.	11. Reservations Necessary	15. Group Seminars Avail.	* Commisions given
4. Senior Citizen Rates	8. Skiing Available	12. Dinner Available	16. Private Baths	to Travel Agents

NEW HAMPSHIRE

North Conway *

Jackson, Claire
Kearsage Rd., 03860
(603) 356-9041

Amenities: 2,4,5,6,7,8,9,10,12,15,16,18
Breakfast: F.
Dbl. Oc.: $98.00
Sgl Oc.: $88.00
Third Person: $44.00
Child: Under 12 yrs. - $22.00

Peacock Inn—Recapture romance in our intimate, classic country inn nestled in the heart of the scenic White Mountains, near the quaint village of North Conway. Mountain views. Country breakfast. Package plans available. Superior accommodations and service. AAA - 3 Diamonds.

North Conway

Rattay, Peter
Rte. 16, 03860-1937
(800) 525-9100

Amenities: 2,3,5,7,8,9,12,14,15,16
Breakfast: F.
Dbl. Oc.: $60.50
Sgl. Oc.: $56.15
Third Person: $15.10
Child: Under 6 yrs. - no charge

Stonehurst Manor—In the White Mountains. We offer the best view, the best food, the most in-room fireplaces, a huge jacuzzi and pool. Walking and ski touring from our door. We are highly recommended by *Bon Appetit*. Open year-round. Call for "best buy" packages.

North Conway

Whitley, Farley
River Rd., 03860
(603) 356-6788

Amenities: 5,6,7,8,10,14,17
Breakfast: C.

Dbl. Oc.: 49.00 - $55.00
Sgl. Oc.: $40.00
Third Person: $10.00

The Center Chimney — 1787—A cozy, affordable B&B in a quiet, woodsy setting. Just off Main St. Saco River swimming, canoeing and fishing. Five- minute walk to free cross-country skiing and ice skating, shops, restaurants and summer theatre. Package plans available.

Northwood *

Cody, David
Goose Pond Rd.
RFD 1, Box 3205 , 03261 (mail)
(603) 942-5596

Amenities: 1,7,8,10,17,18
Breakfast: F.

Dbl. Oc.: $65.00
Sgl. Oc.: $65.00
Third Person: $65.00

Wild Goose Farm—A restored antique, pre-Revolutionary farm. Period furnishings. Canopy beds. Fireplaces. Enjoy this quiet, sylvan setting, serenity and sherry. Beach and canoeing on secluded pond. Full breakfast with homemade bread, jams and jellies. French also spoken.

1. No Smoking	5. Tennis Available	9. Credit Cards Accepted	13. Lunch Available	17. Shared Baths
2. No Pets	6. Golf Available	10. Personal Check Accepted	14. Conference Rooms Avail.	18. Afternoon Tea
3 Off Season Rates	7. Swimmming Avail.	11. Reservations Necessary	15. Group Seminars Avail.	* Commisions given
4. Senior Citizen Rates	8. Skiing Available	12. Dinner Available	16. Private Baths	to Travel Agents

NEW HAMPSHIRE

Plymouth

Durham, Maria & Harry
RR 4, Box 1955, 03264
(603) 536-4476

Amenities: 2,3,5,6,7,8,9,10,
16,18
Breakfast: F.

Dbl. Oc.: $75.00 - $95.00
Sgl. Oc.: $75.00 - $95.00
Third Person: $20.00

Crab Apple Inn—The inn is a 1835 brick building of Federal design that was built by John Adams and featured on the cover of *Discover The Back Roads Of New England.* It is beautifully furnished. It includes six fireplaces and is filled with New England charm and hospitality.

Portsmouth

O'Donnell, Sarah Glover
314 Court St., 03801
(603) 436-7242

Amenities: 1,2,3,5,6,7,8,9,10,
16
Breakfast: F.

Dbl. Oc.: $80.00 - $100.00
Sgl. Oc.: $65.00 - $85.00
Third Person: $20.00
Child: Over 11 yrs. - $20.00

The Inn At Strawbery Banke—A quiet, relaxing colonial inn with seven comfortable rooms with private baths. In the heart of historic Portsmouth. A few short blocks from a working port, quaint shops, waterfront parks, historic homes, harbor cruises, great restaurants and dockside eateries.

Rindge

Linares, Carmen
Multer, Robert, 03461
(603) 899-5167, 899-5166

Amenities: 1,2,5,6,7,8,10,16,
17
Breakfast: F.

Dbl. Oc.: $65.00
Sgl. Oc.: $55.00

Grassy Pond House—An 1831 homestead nestled among 150 forested acres overlooking water and gardens with a screened gazebo. Convenient to main roads, restaurants, antique shops, auctions, summer theatre and craft fairs. Hike Grand Monadnock.

Rochester *

Ejarque, Herman & Anthony
78 Wakefield St., 03867
(603) 332-0107

Amenities: 1,2,5,9,10,12,
13,14,15,16,17
Breakfast: F.
Dbl. Oc.: $60.00 - $85.00
Sgl Oc.: $45.00 - $60.00
Third Person: $15.00

The Governor's Inn—Relax in comfort at the elegant estate of a former New Hampshire governor. Located between coastline, lakes region and downtown. Floral gardens, clay tennis court, river-front lawn. Sunny, spacious rooms with air-conditioning. Telephones. Unique.

1. No Smoking	5. Tennis Available	9. Credit Cards Accepted	13. Lunch Available	17. Shared Baths
2. No Pets	6. Golf Available	10. Personal Check Accepted	14. Conference Rooms Avail.	18. Afternoon Tea
3 Off Season Rates	7. Swimming Avail.	11. Reservations Necessary	15. Group Seminars Avail.	* Commisions given
4. Senior Citizen Rates	8. Skiing Available	12. Dinner Available	16. Private Baths	to Travel Agents

Rye
Marineau, Janice & Norman
1413 Ocean Blvd., 03870
(603) 431-1413

Amenities: 1,2,5,6,7,10,11,16,
17
Breakfast: F.

Dbl. Oc.: $86.40
Sgl. Oc.: $75.60
Third Person: $20.00

Rock Ledge Manor Bed And Breakfast—A gracious and traditional seaside manor home. Its excellent location offers an ocean view from all rooms. Formal rooms. Rooms with either private or shared baths. Ideally located to all New Hampshire and southern Maine seacoast activities.

Snowville *
Cutrone, Trudy,
Peter & Frank
03849
(800) 447-4345

Amenities: 2,3,5,6,7,8,9,10,
11,12,14,15,16,18
Breakfast: F.

Dbl. Oc.: $90.00
Sgl. Oc.: $65.00
Third Person: $35.00
Child: 7 - 12 yrs. - $20.00

Snowvillage Inn—One of the most peaceful places on earth. Magnificent views of Mt. Washington. X-C ski, sauna, tennis, hiking. Walk to private Crystal Lake. Gourmet food, wine, romantic candlelight dining. Hearty breakfasts. 18 rooms with fireplaces. See the view, hear the quiet, feel the romance!

Sugar Hill
Hern, Meri & Mike
Sugar Hill Rd., 03585
(603) 823-5695

Amenities: 5,6,7,8,9,10,11,12,
16,18
Breakfast: F.

Dbl. Oc.: $60.00 - $110.00
Sgl. Oc.: $50.00 - $75.00
Third Person: $15.00 - $20.00
Child: $15.00-$20.00
(4 yrs. & up)

The Hilltop Inn—An 1895 Victorian, filled with antiques, in the heart of the Franconia Notch Mts. Peaceful and homey with beautiful sunset views. Lovely views and quiet strolls. Large country breakfast and afternoon snacks. English flannel sheets and handmade quilts. Fine dining by candlelight and wood fire.

Sunapee
Pedrero, Laraine
26 Seven Hearths Lane, 03782
(603) 763-5657

Amenities: 3,5,6,7,8,9,10,11,
12,14,15,16
Breakfast: F.

Dbl. Oc.: $125.00
Third Person: $25.00
Child: Under 4 yrs. - no charge

Seven Hearths Inn—At the center of a year-round resort area, within minutes of Sunapee Harbor and its marina and state park's beach and ski area. Some of our rooms have fireplaces and all of our rooms are air-conditioned. On-site pool and liquor license.

Sutton Mills *
Forand, Margaret & Norman
Grist Mill Rd.
RR 1, Box 151, 03221
(603) 927-4765

Amenities: 1,2,5,6,7,8,10,12,
15,17,18
Breakfast: F.

Dbl. Oc.: $48.60
Sgl. Oc.: $37.80
Third Person: $10.80
Child: $10.80

The Village House At Sutton Mills, NH—Newly restored 1857 country Victorian, tastefully decorated with antiques and old quilts. Overlooks quaint New England village. Nearby shopping, antiques and restaurants. Stroll down lane to yesteryear and the general store. Snowmobile and cross-country skiing right on premises.

---

1. No Smoking	5. Tennis Available	9. Credit Cards Accepted	13. Lunch Available	17. Shared Baths
2. No Pets	6. Golf Available	10. Personal Check Accepted	14. Conference Rooms Avail.	18. Afternoon Tea
3 Off Season Rates	7. Swimmming Avail.	11. Reservations Necessary	15. Group Seminars Avail.	* Commisions given
4. Senior Citizen Rates	8. Skiing Available	12. Dinner Available	16. Private Baths	to Travel Agents

NEW HAMPSHIRE

Tamworth *

Erickson, Karen
Rte. 113A
& Hemenway Rd., 03886
(603) 323-7337

Amenities: 1,5,6,7,8,10,16,17
Breakfast: F.
Dbl. Oc.: $60.00 - $85.00
Sgl Oc.: $60.00 - $85.00

Whispering Pines Bed And Breakfast—Woodland setting, tall sheltering pines, relaxing quiet. Between the White Mountains and Winnipesaukee Lakes region, close to Mt. Washingtn Valley. Summer theatre, swimming, hiking, fishing, cross-country and downhill skiing, sled-dog races and outlet shopping.

Warner

Baese, Deb & Marlon
Main St., RFD 1, Box 11, 03278
(603) 456-3494

Amenities: 1,5,6,8,10,16,17
Breakfast: F.

Dbl. Oc.: $43.20
Sgl. Oc.: $43.20
Third Person: $5.00

Jacob's Ladder Bed And Breakfast—Conveniently located between I-89, Exits 8 and 9 at the heart of a quaint New England village. Four ski areas within 20 miles with cross-country and snowmobile trails on site. Early 1800s home on four acres furnished with antiques. Nearby lakes, crafts, shopping and antiques.

Wentworth *

Kauk, Marie
East Side & Buffalo Rd., 03282
(603) 764-5896

Amenities: 1,2,7,8,9,10,11,14,16,18
Breakfast: C. Plus
Dbl. Oc.: $64.80
Sgl Oc.: $64.80
Third Person: $10.80
Child: Under 12 yrs. - $5.40

Hilltop Acres—A peaceful country retreat in the White Mtns. Rooms with private baths, housekeeping cottages with fireplaces and screened-in porch. Pine-paneled recreation room with piano. Fireplaces, games. Cable TV. Hiking, swimming, boating and skiing nearby. Antiques. Fine dining.

---

1. No Smoking
2. No Pets
3 Off Season Rates
4. Senior Citizen Rates

5. Tennis Available
6. Golf Available
7. Swimmming Avail.
8. Skiing Available

9. Credit Cards Accepted
10. Personal Check Accepted
11. Reservations Necessary
12. Dinner Available

'13. Lunch Available
14. Conference Rooms Avail.
15. Group Seminars Avail.
16. Private Baths

17. Shared Baths
18. Afternoon Tea
* Commisions given
   to Travel Agents

Wentworth*

LaBrie, Don
Rte 25 & Atwell Hill Rd.
P.O. Box 147, 03282
(603) 764-9600, (800) 338-9986

Amenities: 1,9,10,16,17

Breakfast: F.

Dbl. Oc.: $65.00 - $70.00
Sgl. Oc.: $65.00 $70.00
Third Person: $10.00
Child: Under 8 yrs. -$5.00

Mountain Laurel Inn—Step back into the 19th century when you visit this 1840 colonial. Your romantically appointed room with king-size bed is distinctive and comfortable. Your leisurely breakfast in our dining room will energize you for your day's activities in New Hampshire.

Winnisquam *

Kern, Kate & Kent
P.O. Box 327, 03289
(800) 722-6870

Amenities: 1,2,3,5,6,7,8,9,10
12,13,16,17,18

Breakfast: F.

Dbl. Oc.: $59.40 - $70.20
Sgl. Oc.: $54.00 - $64.80
Third Person: $16.20(limited)

Tall Pines Inn—Features outstanding views and four seasons recreational use of 12 mile long Lake Winnisquam and the White Mountains. Short walk to beach and marina with boat rentals. Bright, clean and comfortable rooms. Full "all you can eat" country breakfasts and seasonal treats.

Woodstock, No.

Brisson, Diane
Crete, Brian
RR#1, Box 72,
No. Main St., 03262
(603) 745-2711, (800) 241-2711

Amenities: 2,3,6,8,9,10,12,16

Breakfast: F.

Dbl. Oc.: $60.00 - $90.00
Sgl. Oc.: $50.00
Third Person: $15.00

Three Rivers House—Olde Yanke hospitality since 1875. Newly renovated rooms, each with private bath and TV. Suites available, some with jacuzzis and fireplaces. Hike, bike, ski, shop or just relax and enjoy our spectacular views. You can do it all, any season, in the White Mountains.

Woodstock, No. *

Yarnell, Rosanna & Michael
Rtes. 3 & 112, 03262
(603) 745-3890

Amenities: 2,3,7,8,9,10,16,17,
18

Breakfast: F.

Dbl. Oc.: $43.20 - $91.80
Sgl. Oc.: $32.40 - $81.00
Third Person: $10.80 - $16.20
Child: Under 6 yrs. - no charge

Wilderness Inn—An intimate country inn built in 1912. Six guest rooms/suites with private or shared baths and a cottage overlooking Lost River. Gourmet breakfast served on front porch. Five miles from Franconia Notch State Park in the midst of the White Mountains National Forest.

1. No Smoking	5. Tennis Available	9. Credit Cards Accepted	13. Lunch Available	17. Shared Baths
2. No Pets	6. Golf Available	10. Personal Check Accepted	14. Conference Rooms Avail.	18. Afternoon Tea
3 Off Season Rates	7. Swimmming Avail.	11. Reservations Necessary	15. Group Seminars Avail.	* Commisions given
4. Senior Citizen Rates	8. Skiing Available	12. Dinner Available	16. Private Baths	to Travel Agents

NEW JERSEY

The Garden State

Capitol: Trenton
Statehood: December 18,1787: the 3rd state
State Motto: "Liberty and Prosperity"
State Bird: Eastern Goldfinch
State Flower: Purple Violet
State Tree: Red Oak

New Jersey is a state of hundreds of thousands of people. Most of these people live in the northern industrial area around Newark. They are hard working and are involved in just about every kind of manufacturing there is in America. Sixty of the largest companies we have in the United States have plants in New Jersey.

The New Jersey Turnpike is the busiest turnpike in the country, bringing people in and out of this state on their way either north, south, east or west.

There are many historic places to visit in New Jersey, and also some very beautiful beaches along the Atlantic coast. Vacationers love this state. Atlantic City and the boardwalk has been a tremendous tourist attraction for years.

Organized baseball was first played in Hoboken, New Jersey in 1846 and Grover Cleveland was born in Cadwell in 1837.

Avon-By-The-Sea *

Curley, Kathleen & Jim
109 Sylvania Ave., 07717
(908) 988-6326

Amenities: 1,2,3,4,5,6,7,9,14,15,16,17
Breakfast: C.
Dbl. Oc.: $65.00 - $105.00
Sgl Oc.: $55.00 - $100.00
Third Person: $20.00

The Avon Manor—A gracious turn-of-the-century home where you will always find a warm and friendly welcome for your special seaside getaways. Relax in the serenity and the romance of yesteryear amid many antiques. Enjoy ocean breezes on a full wrap-around veranda. Air conditioned. Open all year.

Bay Head *

Conover, Beverly
646 Main Ave., 08742
(908) 892-4664

Amenities: 1,2,3,5,6,7,9,10, 14,15,16,18
Breakfast: F.

Dbl. Oc.: $65.00 - $165.00
Sgl. Oc.: $65.00 - $155.00
Third Person: $30.00

Conover's Bay Head Inn—New Jersey shore's finest antique-filled B&B. Special touches for a memorable stay. A short walk to the ocean, shops and restaurants. A view from every window! All private baths. Tea served in winter. Full breakfast served.

Bay Head *

Haurie, Donald
200 Main Ave., 08742
(908) 892-9844

Amenities: 1,2,3,5,6,7,9,10, 14,15,16
Breakfast: F.

Dbl. Oc.: $125.00 - $175.00

Bay Head Gables—"An inn for all seasons" is a 1914 architectural splendor. Located in a country village by the sea, it is 75 miles from New York City and Philadelphia. Decorated to please the most discriminating tastes. Some rooms have decks and ocean or lake views.

1. No Smoking	5. Tennis Available	9. Credit Cards Accepted	13. Lunch Available	17. Shared Baths
2. No Pets	6. Golf Available	10. Personal Check Accepted	14. Conference Rooms Avail.	18. Afternoon Tea
3 Off Season Rates	7. Swimmming Avail.	11. Reservations Necessary	15. Group Seminars Avail.	* Commisions given
4. Senior Citizen Rates	8. Skiing Available	12. Dinner Available	16. Private Baths	to Travel Agents

Cape May

Burow, Greg
609 Hughes St., 08204
(609) 884-7293

Amenities: 1,2,3,5,6,7,9,10,11,16,18
Breakfast: F.
Dbl. Oc.: $125.00 - $165.00
Sgl Oc.: $125.00 - $165.00
Third Person: $15.00
Child: $15.00

The Wooden Rabbit—Located on the prettiest street in Cape May, in the heart of the historic district, surrounded by Victorian cottages. Decor is country. All rooms have private baths, air conditioning and TV. Two blocks to shops and fine food. Children welcome.

Cape May

Carroll, Sue & Tom
635 Columbia Ave., 08204
(609) 884-8690

Amenities: 1,2,3,7,10,11,15, 16,18
Breakfast: F.

Dbl. Oc.: $95.00 - $175.00
Sgl. Oc.: $85.00 - $165.00
Third Person: $20.00

Mainstay Inn And Cottage—"The jewel of them all has got to be the Mainstay" — *Washington Post.* Twelve large, antique-filled rooms. This former gentlemen's gambling club offers history, romance and hospitality. Nearby shops, restaurants, historic attractions and beaches.

Cape May

Dunwoody, John
719 Columbia Ave., 08204
(609) 884-8075

Amenities: 2,3,9,10,11,16,17,18
Breakfast: F.
Dbl. Oc.: $75.00 - $136.00
Sgl Oc.: $70.00 - $131.00

The Brass Bed Inn—We invite you to share our lovingly restored Victorian! Historic area. Two blocks to ocean beach. Beautiful antique brass beds, bountiful breakfasts. Billowy curtains. Wonderful year-round veranda. Tea by the fire, cozy rooms to relax and romance. Just perfect.

---

1. No Smoking	5. Tennis Available	9. Credit Cards Accepted	13. Lunch Available	17. Shared Baths
2. No Pets	6. Golf Available	10. Personal Check Accepted	14. Conference Rooms Avail.	18. Afternoon Tea
3 Off Season Rates	7. Swimmming Avail.	11. Reservations Necessary	15. Group Seminars Avail.	* Commisions given
4. Senior Citizen Rates	8. Skiing Available	12. Dinner Available	16. Private Baths	to Travel Agents

NEW JERSEY

Cape May
Echevarria, Joan & Fred
28 Gurney St., 08204
(609) 884-0211

Amenities: 3,16,17,18
Breakfast: F.

Dbl. Oc.: $92.00 - $150.00
Sgl. Oc.: $82.00
Third Person: $17.00

Gingerbread House—An 1869 elegantly restored inn boasting period antiques, original water colors and Fred's fine craftsmanship. Enjoy ocean breezes on the porch or classical music in the parlor. 1/2 block from the beach and within walking distance to restaurants and all activities.

Cape May *
Emerson, Kate
12 Jackson St., 08204
(609) 884-1371

Amenities: 1,2,3,5,7,9,10,11,16,17,18
Breakfast: F.
Dbl. Oc.: $102.00 - $139.00
Sgl Oc.: $98.00 - $134.00
Third Person: $25.00
Child: $25.00

Abigail Adams' Bed And Breakfast By The Sea—A delightful country style inn located on historic Jackson St. and just steps from the beach. Ocean view rooms are decorated in antiques, "cheery" chintzes and handmade quilts. Cozy fireplaces in the winter and ocean breezes in the summer welcome you here.

Cape May *
Kulkowitz, Mark
19 Jackson St., 08204
(609) 884-9619

Amenities: 2,3,5,6,7,9,10,11,12,
            13,14,15,16
Breakfast: F.
Dbl. Oc.: $58.85 - $128.40
Sgl Oc.: $48.15 - $118.40
Third Person: $21.40
Child: Under 5 yrs. - $13.91

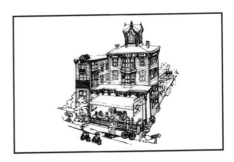

Carroll Villa Bed And Breakfast—Our 110-year-old Victorian hotel is 1/2 block from a dip in the ocean and a Victorian mall. Modestly priced rooms include full breakfast. Roll out of bed and come downstairs to our nationally acclaimed restaurant for one of the best breakfasts of your life—or dinner!

1. No Smoking	5. Tennis Available	9. Credit Cards Accepted	13. Lunch Available	17. Shared Baths
2. No Pets	6. Golf Available	10. Personal Check Accepted	14. Conference Rooms Avail.	18. Afternoon Tea
3 Off Season Rates	7. Swimmming Avail.	11. Reservations Necessary	15. Group Seminars Avail.	* Commisions given
4. Senior Citizen Rates	8. Skiing Available	12. Dinner Available	16. Private Baths	to Travel Agents

NEW JERSEY

Cape May

LeDuc, Anne
301 Howard St., 08204
(609) 884-8409

Amenities: 2,5,6,7,9,10,11,
12
Breakfast: F.

Dbl. Oc.: $90.00 - $151.00
Sgl. Oc.: $60.00 - $73.00
Third Person: $28.00
Child: Under 14 yrs. - $3 - $15

Chalfonte Hotel—A traditional Victorian summer hotel with sweeping verandas, rocking chairs and down-home southern cooking. Breakfast and dinner included in daily rate. Separate dining room for children under seven. Entertainment includes Kine Edward Bar, concerts and theatre.

Cape May

Miller, Sandy & Owen
24 Jackson St., 08204
(609) 884-3368

Amenities: 1,2,3,5,6,7,9,10,
11,16,18
Breakfast: F.

Dbl. Oc.: $80.00 - $140.00
Sgl. Oc.: $70.00 - $130.00
Third Person: $20.00 - $25.00

Windward House—Elegant Edwardian inn 1/2 block from the ocean and mall. Eight antique-filled rooms with queen beds, private baths and air conditioning. Three sun and shade porches. Cozy parlor fireplace. Vintage clothing and other collectibles on display. Free parking, beach tags and bicycles.

Cape May

Rein, Barry
1513 Beach Dr., 08204
(609) 884-2228

Amenities: 1,2,3,7,10,11,14,16,18
Breakfast: F.
Dbl. Oc.: $118.00 - $177.00
Sgl Oc.: $108.00 - $167.00
Third Person: $50.00

Colvmns By The Sea—Elegant turn-of-the-century, ocean-front mansion in landmark Victorian village. Decorated with antiques, all guest rooms have private baths. Gourmet breakfast, high tea and evening snacks. Hot tub. Free bikes and beach badges. Great for history buffs, birders or to relax.

Cape May

Schmidt, Lorraine
29 Ocean St., 08204
(609) 884-4428

Amenities: 1,3,5,6,7,9,11,14,
15,16,18
Breakfast: F.

Dbl. Oc.: $90.00 - $200.00
Sgl. Oc.: $80.00 - $190.00

The Humphrey Hughes House—Located in the primary historic district. Five houses from the beach. Circa 1903. Stained-glass windows mark each landing of the staircase and intricately carved chestnut columns add to the atmosphere in this 30-room mansion. Beautifully decorated in Victorian style.

---

1. No Smoking	5. Tennis Available	9. Credit Cards Accepted	13. Lunch Available	17. Shared Baths
2. No Pets	6. Golf Available	10. Personal Check Accepted	14. Conference Rooms Avail.	18. Afternoon Tea
3 Off Season Rates	7. Swimmming Avail.	11. Reservations Necessary	15. Group Seminars Avail.	* Commisions given
4. Senior Citizen Rates	8. Skiing Available	12. Dinner Available	16. Private Baths	to Travel Agents

Cape May *

Smith, Frank
619 Hughes St., 08204
(800) 321-DOVE

Amenities: 1,2,3,5,6,7,10,16,18
Breakfast: F.
Dbl. Oc.: $133.00
Third Person: $25.00

White Dove Cottage—Elegant 1866 bed and breakfast inn located in the center of the historic district on a tree-lined, gas-lit street. Rooms and suites have A/C and private baths. Private parking. Close to beach, tours, theatre and shops. A memorable occasion, a delightful retreat. Open all year.

Cape May *

Tice, Rita & John
30 Gurney St., 08204
(609) 884-1012

Amenities: 1,2,3,10,11,14,15, 16,17
Breakfast: C.

Dbl. Oc.: $80.00 - $130.00
Sgl. Oc.: $70.00 - $120.00
Third Person: $15.00

John Wesley Inn—Located in the historic district only 1/2 block from the beach and shopping. It has been restored to the original splendor of 1869. Step back in time. Free brochure available. Air-conditioned apartments. Beach tags and free parking.

Cape May *

Wood, Edwin
808 Washington St., 08204
(609) 884-7123

Amenities: 1,2,3,5,6,7,10, 11,16
Breakfast: C. Plus

Dbl. Oc.: $75.00 - $105.00
Sgl. Oc.: $75.00 - $105.00
Third Person: $15.00

Woodleigh House—Nestled in Cape May's historic district, within easy walking distance of everything and surrounded by comfortable porches, gardens and a courtyard. Woodleigh House B&B is an attractively inviting example of "country Victorian" - informal but charmingly hosted.

Clinton

Schlegel, Terry
66 Leigh St., 08809
(908) 735-4311

Amenities: 1,2,9,10,16
Breakfast: C. Plus

Dbl. Oc.: $79.50
Sgl. Oc.: $68.90
Third Person: $10.00
Child: Under 12 yrs. - $5.00

Leigh Way B&B—A warm welcome awaits you in this charming Victorian home furnished with a wonderful mix of the old and the new. Enjoy the old-fashioned porches, spacious living room, lovely dining room and tastefully decorated bedrooms. Air-conditioning. Call for reservations.

1. No Smoking	5. Tennis Available	9. Credit Cards Accepted	13. Lunch Available	17. Shared Baths
2. No Pets	6. Golf Available	10. Personal Check Accepted	14. Conference Rooms Avail.	18. Afternoon Tea
3 Off Season Rates	7. Swimming Avail.	11. Reservations Necessary	15. Group Seminars Avail.	* Commisions given
4. Senior Citizen Rates	8. Skiing Available	12. Dinner Available	16. Private Baths	to Travel Agents

Denville

Bergins, Alex
11 Sunset Trail, 07834
(201) 625-5129

Amenities: 1,2,5,7,10,14,15, 16
Breakfast: F

Dbl. Oc.: $55.00
Sgl. Oc.: $50.00
Child: $10.00

Lakeside B&B—One mile from I-80 between New York City and Pennsylvania. Private guest quarters with a stunning view of the bay. Double bed in guest room plus a family room with a color TV. Swimming, boating, fishing, ice skating on the lake.

Flemington *

Studer, Judith
96 Broad St., 08822
(908) 782-8234

Amenities: 1,2,4,5,6,9,10,11, 14,15,16,17,18
Breakfast: C.

Dbl. Oc.: $63.00 - $100.70
Third Person: $20.00

Jerica Hill - A Bed And Breakfast Inn—Welcome to this gracious Victorian country home in the historic town center. Spacious, sunny guest rooms, living room with fireplace, wicker-filled screened porch. Champagne hot-air-ballon flights. Winery tours. Wonderful escape weekends. Corporate travelers welcome!

Flemington

Venosa, Pam
162 Main St., 08822
(908) 788-0247

Amenities: 1,2,6,7,9,10,11,14, 16
Breakfast: C. Plus

Dbl. Oc.: $85.60 - $112.35
Third Person: $15.00

The Cabbage Rose Inn—Romantic Victorian in historic district. Luxurious guest rooms with private baths, telephones, A/C; one with fireplace. Steps from outlet shops, galleries and restaurants; minutes from Bucks County, PA; one hour from New York City. "Romance and roses" Package. AAA rated.

Frenchtown *

Johnson, Clark F.
12 Bridge St., 08825
(800) 382-0375

Amenities: 1,2,3,4,7,9,10,16
Breakfast: F.
Dbl. Oc.: $90.00 - $120.00
Third Person: $15.00

The Hunterdon House—Comfort, elegance and gracious hospitality await you in Frenchtown in this stately Civil War-era stone Italianate mansion. Seven distinctively charming guest rooms, each with its own private bath. The mansion creates the warmth and romance of the wealthy Victorians.

---

1. No Smoking	5. Tennis Available	9. Credit Cards Accepted	13. Lunch Available	17. Shared Baths
2. No Pets	6. Golf Available	10. Personal Check Accepted	14. Conference Rooms Avail.	18. Afternoon Tea
3 Off Season Rates	7. Swimmming Avail.	11. Reservations Necessary	15. Group Seminars Avail.	* Commisions given
4. Senior Citizen Rates	8. Skiing Available	12. Dinner Available	16. Private Baths	to Travel Agents

Long Valley

Kadosh, Mrs. Iris
143 W. Mill Rd., 07853
(908) 876-3519

Amenities: 2,7,11,16,17
Breakfast: F.

Dbl. Oc.: $65.00
Sgl. Oc.: $65.00
Third Person: $65.00

The Neighbor House—A warm, hospitable, high-style colonial farmhouse on 3.5 acres. Wonderful restaurants, antiques, shops in both historic Cheter and Oldwick. Outlet shopping in Flemington. Canoeing and fishing on nearby private six-acre lake. Horseback riding lessons available.

Lyndhurst *

Pezzolla, Evelyn & Frank
410 Riverside Ave., 07071
(201) 438-9457

Amenities: 1,2,4,5,9,10,11, 17
Breakfast: C.

Dbl. Oc.: $58.30
Sgl. Oc.: $53.00

Jeremiah J. Yereance House—This tiny house has cobblestone walks, a front yard and a wisteria arbor with benches. This provides a cool, shady, restful seating area across from a riverside park with walking and jogging paths, bicycle trails, picnicking and tennis. Located 20 minutes from New York City.

Manahawkin

Carney, Maureen
190 N. Main St., 08050
(609) 597-6350

Amenities: 1,2,3,6,7,10,11,14, 16,17,18
Breakfast: C. and F.

Dbl. Oc.: $53.50 - $74.20
Sgl. Oc.: $42.80 - $68.90
Third Person: $10.00

The Goose N Berry Inn—An 1800s historic home comfortably furnished with period antiques. Tree-shaded porches overlook the wooded acreage. Nearby are ocean beaches, boating, canoeing, preserve, antiquing and crafts. Thirty minutes to Atlantic City. Exit 63 on the Garden State Parkway.

Ocean City

Hand, Donna & Daniel
519 5th St., 08226
(609) 399-2829

Amenities: 1,2,3,5,6,7,9,10,11,16,17
Breakfast: F.
Dbl. Oc.: $60.00 - $75.00
Sgl Oc.: $50.00 - $65.00
Third Person: $10.00

New Brighton Inn—Magnificently restored 1880 Queen Anne Victorian. Large, open porch with rockers and swing. All rooms furnished with antiques. Three blocks from beach, boardwalk and tennis courts. Wonderful restaurants and shops nearby. Elegant, charming and definitely romantic.

1. No Smoking	5. Tennis Available	9. Credit Cards Accepted	13. Lunch Available	17. Shared Baths
2. No Pets	6. Golf Available	10. Personal Check Accepted	14. Conference Rooms Avail.	18. Afternoon Tea
3 Off Season Rates	7. Swimmming Avail.	11. Reservations Necessary	15. Group Seminars Avail.	* Commisions given
4. Senior Citizen Rates	8. Skiing Available	12. Dinner Available	16. Private Baths	to Travel Agents

NEW JERSEY

Ocean City *

Hydock, Patty & Steve
1020 Central Ave., 08226
(609) 398-1698

Amenities: 2,3,5,6,7,9,10,16, 17
Breakfast: F.

Dbl. Oc.: $55.00 - $85.00
Sgl. Oc.: $45.00 - $65.00
Third Person: $10.00

The Enterprise Bed And Breakfast Inn—Breakfast is the focus of your stay offering luscious quiche, eggs benedict casseroles or stratas. Turn-of-the-century ambience. A little bit of country at the shore. Certificate of appreciation, exclusive for our guests, includes discounts at area stores and restaurants.

Ocean City

Loeper, Marj & John
401 Wesley Ave., 08226
(609) 399-6071

Amenities: 1,2,5,6,7,9,10,11,14,16,18
Breakfast: F.
Dbl. Oc.: $80.25 - $149.80
Sgl Oc.: $80.25 - $149.80
Third Person: $16.05

Northwood Inn (Bed And Breakfast)—An elegantly restored 1894 Victorian. A 1991 Beautification Award winner. Nine distinctively decorated guest rooms, fully stocked library, central air conditioning. Walk to beach, boardwalk, shops and restaurants. Eight miles south of Atlantic City. Open year-round.

Ocean City *

Nunan, Virginia
5447 Central Ave., 08226
(609) 399-0477

Amenities: 2,4,5,6,7,9,10,11, 13,14,15,16
Breakfast: C.(winter) and F.(summer)

Dbl. Oc.: $85.86 - $174.90
Third Person: $18.50
Child: $10.00

Top O The Waves, Inc.—Relax on your own beach-front deck. Enjoy the outstanding ocean view in comfort, warm hospitality and high standards of innkeeping. Walk on the beach or ride bikes on the boardwalk. Go antiquing, shopping, fishing or sailing. Visit the wineries. Play tennis or golf. Come and enjoy.

NEW JERSEY

Ocean Grove *

Chernik, Doris
26 Webb Ave., 07756
(908) 774-3084 (summer),
 (212) 751-9577 (winter)

Amenities: 1,2,4,5,7,10,11,15,17
Breakfast: C. Plus
Dbl. Oc.: $37.00 - $52.00
Sgl Oc.: $31.00 - $44.00
Child: Under 12 yrs. - $10.00

Cordova—Century-old Victorian B&B in historic Ocean Grove. Old World charm. Listed in *New Jersey Magazine* as one of the seven best places on the New Jersey shore. Three porches. Guest kitchen. BBQ. Picnic tables. Ideal for family reunions. Weekly wine/cheese parties. 50s music events.

Ocean Grove *

Klein, Lisa
19 Broadway, 07756
(908) 775-3232

Amenities: 1,2,7,9,11,15,16
Breakfast: C. Plus

Dbl. Oc.: $63.60
Sgl. Oc.: $31.20

The Innkeeper—Spectacular ocean views from porch and most rooms. Town in National Historic Register. Everything from antiquing and deep-sea fishing to horseback riding is close by, plus discounts at New Jersey's fine seafood or steak restaurants.

Pittstown *

Bowers, Dina W.
Perryville Rd.
R.D. #3. Box 223, 08867
(908) 735-7675

Amenities: 1,2,6,7,10,11,12, 13,17
Breakfast: F.

Dbl. Oc.: $31.80
Sgl. Oc.: $31.80
Child: Under 10 yrs. - $15.90

Seven Springs Farm Bed 'N' Breakfast—Enjoy your five senses: the smell of freshly mown hay, the sound of farm animals, the taste of country cooking, the feel of snug flannel and down, and the sight of lovely country vistas on a working farm. History, sport, garden, arts and shopping buffs need apply.

Point Pleasant Beach

Shaughnessy, Joanne & Mark
18 Forman Ave., 08742
(908) 899-8208

Amenities: 2,7,9,17
Breakfast: C.

Dbl. Oc.: $48.00 - $64.00
Sgl. Oc.: $37.00 - $48.00
Third Person: $10.00
Child: Under 12 - $5.00

Century House—A 100-year-old Queen Anne on quiet residential street. Three houses from the beach and boardwalk amusements. Mid-way between New York City and Atlantic City. Public transportation available to both. Fine dining. Party fishing boats. Antique shops within walking distance.

---

1. No Smoking	5. Tennis Available	9. Credit Cards Accepted	13. Lunch Available	17. Shared Baths
2. No Pets	6. Golf Available	10. Personal Check Accepted	14. Conference Rooms Avail.	18. Afternoon Tea
3 Off Season Rates	7. Swimmming Avail.	11. Reservations Necessary	15. Group Seminars Avail.	* Commisions given
4. Senior Citizen Rates	8. Skiing Available	12. Dinner Available	16. Private Baths	to Travel Agents

Princeton

Innkeeper
203 Raymond Rd., 08540
(908) 329-3821

Amenities: 1,2,5,7,10,11,12,13,17,18
Breakfast: F.
Dbl. Oc.: $55.00 - $75.00
Sgl Oc.: $45.00 - $65.00
Child: Under 10 yrs. - $10.00

Red Maple Farm—Charming and gracious 1740 Historic Register colonial farm on a two- acre country retreat minutes from Princeton University and Rte. 1 businesses. Wonderful breakfasts, swimming pool. Tea time on smokehouse patio or by the fire. One hour to New York, Philadelphia and Bucks County.

Salem *

Innkeeper
100 Tide-Mill Rd., 08079
(609) 935-2798

Amenities: 2,10,11,14,17
Breakfast: F.

Dbl. Oc.: $55.00 - $65.00
Sgl. Oc.: $50.00 - $60.00
Third Person: $20.00
Child: $20.00

Tide-Mill Farm—Tide Mill Farm outside of historic Salem (1675). An 1845 Greek Revival with three guest rooms located about 1 1/2 hours from Atlantic City and 15 minutes from Delaware Memorial Bridge and New Jersey Turnpike. 53 waterfront acres with fishing, crabbing and trails.

Spring Lake

Kirby, Carol J. & John R.
19 Tuttle Ave., 07762
(908) 449-9031

Amenities: 1,2,3,5,6,7,9,10,
                11,14,15,16,18
Breakfast: C. Plus
Dbl. Oc.: $126.00
Sgl Oc.: $126.00

Sea Crest By The Sea—Escape to the romantic refuge of a luxurious inn by the sea. We will pamper you with hospitality that is friendly yet unobtrusive. A lovingly restored 1885 Victorian inn for ladies and gentlemen on a seaside holiday.

---

1. No Smoking	5. Tennis Available	9. Credit Cards Accepted	13. Lunch Available	17. Shared Baths
2. No Pets	6. Golf Available	10. Personal Check Accepted	14. Conference Rooms Avail.	18. Afternoon Tea
3 Off Season Rates	7. Swimmming Avail.	11. Reservations Necessary	15. Group Seminars Avail.	* Commisions given
4. Senior Citizen Rates	8. Skiing Available	12. Dinner Available	16. Private Baths	to Travel Agents

Stanhope *

Williams, Paula
Mulay, Joe
P.O. Box 791,
110 Main St., 07874
(201) 347-6369

Amenities: 1,2,4,5,6,7,8,9,10, 11,14,15,16

Breakfast: F.

Dbl. Oc.: $68.90 - $100.70
Sgl. Oc.: $63.60 - $100.40
Third Person: $21.20
Child: Over 12 yrs. - $21.20

Whistling Swan Inn—Northwestern NJ"s finest Victorian B&B. One mile off Rte. 80 at Rte. 206. One hour west of New York City. Two hours from Philadelphia. Near antiquing, Waterloo Village, wineries, shopping, parks, lakes, winter sports and the International Trade Center. Many restaurants.

Woodbine

Thurlow, Annette M.
Cape May County
1336 Rte. 47, 08270
(609) 861-5847

Amenities: 1,2,7,9,10,11,15, 16,17

Breakfast: F.

Dbl. Oc.: $75.00 - $95.00
Third Person: $20.00
Child: Over 12 yrs. - $20.00

Henry Ludlam Inn—Romantic, lakeside, country B&B, circa 1740. Featuring bedrooms with working fireplaces. Four-course gourmet breakfast features our famous stuffed French toast and peach melba by the fire with candlelight. Picnic baskets available. Featured in many magazines. "Award-winning" B&B.

---

1. No Smoking	5. Tennis Available	9. Credit Cards Accepted	13. Lunch Available	17. Shared Baths
2. No Pets	6. Golf Available	10. Personal Check Accepted	14. Conference Rooms Avail.	18. Afternoon Tea
3 Off Season Rates	7. Swimmming Avail.	11. Reservations Necessary	15. Group Seminars Avail.	* Commisions given
4. Senior Citizen Rates	8. Skiing Available	12. Dinner Available	16. Private Baths	to Travel Agents

NEW MEXICO

The Land of Enchantment

Capitol: Santa Fe
Statehood: January 6, 1912; the 47th state
State Motto: "It Grows As It Goes"
State Song: "Of Fair New Mexico"
State Bird: Road Runner
State Flower: Yucca Flower
State Tree: Pinon or Nut Pine

New Mexico is a warm and scenic country. Its magnificent scenery attracts visitors from everywhere. The days are mild and sometimes quite warm, but the evenings are cool and delightful.

Lovers of history can visit Indian ruins, frontier forts and Spanish missions. They can see homes and shops still made from dried adobe bricks. Mexican food is still the most popular food here and fine jewelry is sold along the streets by vendors at bargain prices. Taos has the highest pueblo building in the southwest.

The Palace of Governors, the oldest government building in the United States, is here as well as the most interesting Carlsbad Caverns.

NEW MEXICO

Albuquerque

Cosgrove, Mary & John
327 Arizona S.E., 87108
(505) 256-9462

Amenities: 1,3,5,6,7,8,9,10,11,13,16
Breakfast: C.
Dbl. Oc.: $75.00
Sgl Oc.: $65.00
Third Person: $10.00

The Sandcastle—Large rooms. Comfortable common room. Private garage is $5.00 a night when available. Off-street parking available. Close to Sandia, Kirkland Air Force Base, fairgrounds, University of New Mexico and restaurants. Youngsters 12 and over welcome.

Cedar Crest *

O'Neil, Elaine
P.O. Box 444, 87008
(505) 281-2467, (800) 821-3092

Amenities: 1,2,8,10,16,17
Breakfast: F.

Dbl. Oc.: $66.00 - $83.00
Sgl. Oc.: $66.00 - $83.00
Third Person: $10.00
Child: $10.00

Elaine's, A Bed And Breakfast—Charm, elegance and hospitality in a beautiful three-story log home nestled in the evergreen forests of Sandia peaks. Vacationers can enjoy all the attractions of Santa Fe and Albuquerque plus the historic sites, galleries and shops along the historic Turquoise Trail.

Chama *

Cole, Sara
311 Terrace Ave., 87520
(505) 756-2908

Amenities: 1,2,8,9,10,12,13,
15,16,17,18
Breakfast: F.

Dbl. Oc.: $74.50
Sgl. Oc.: $48.50
Third Person: $16.50
Child: Under 18 yrs. - $11.00

Jones House Bed And Breakfast Inn—Historic steam railroad is across the street from this Tudor-style B&B. Train packages include all meals and train ticket. Winter sports, bird watching, hiking and fishing nearby. Friendly, comfortable atmosphere.

Chimayo *

Becker, Christiane
Box 142, 87522
(505) 351-4805, (800) 643-7201 (reservations)

Amenities: 1,2,8,9,10,12,16,18
Breakfast: F.
Dbl. Oc.: $68.90 - $127.20
Sgl Oc.: $60.00 - $115.00
Third Person: $15.00
Child: Under 4 yrs. - no charge

Casa Escondida—On six acres of land, Casa Escondida (the hidden house) is an intimate, serene home in the Spanish colonial adobe style of New Mexico. Six rooms (private baths), fireplaces, antiques, bucolic scenery, endless skies, a cozy atmosphere makes Casa Escondida truly special.

1. No Smoking	5. Tennis Available	9. Credit Cards Accepted	13. Lunch Available	17. Shared Baths
2. No Pets	6. Golf Available	10. Personal Check Accepted	14. Conference Rooms Avail.	18. Afternoon Tea
3 Off Season Rates	7. Swimmming Avail.	11. Reservations Necessary	15. Group Seminars Avail.	* Commisions given
4. Senior Citizen Rates	8. Skiing Available	12. Dinner Available	16. Private Baths	to Travel Agents

NEW MEXICO

Corrales

Briault, Mary
58 Perea Rd.
P.O. Box 1361, 87048
(505) 897-4422

Amenities: 3,9,10,11,16
Breakfast: F.

Dbl. Oc.: $68.98
Sgl. Oc.: $58.36
Third Person: $20.00
Child: Under 13 yrs. - $10.00

Corrales Inn Bed And Breakfast—Between Albuquerque and Santa Fe, a rural oasis of six gracious rooms with baths surrounding a courtyard with fountain and hot tub. Fireplaces, library, superior beds, good cooking. General rating: excellent.

Espanola *

Hoemann, Yolanda
Rte. 1, Box 368A, 87532
(505) 753-5368

Amenities: 1,2,7,8,10,11,16, 18
Breakfast: F.

Dbl. Oc.: $80.00
Sgl. Oc.: $80.00

The Inn Of La Mesilla—In this new home, a retired doctor and his wife offer two private guest rooms, each with private bath, king- or queen- size bed and beautiful views of the surrounding area. Guests are invited to join the hosts from 4 - 6 p.m. for the doctor's salmon mousse or caviar pie.

Espanola *

Sopanen-Vigil, Eileen
P.O. Box 92, 87532
(505) 753-2035

Amenities: 1,2,9,10,11,12,13, 16
Breakfast: F.

Dbl. Oc.: $79.50 - $100.70
Sgl. Oc.: $79.50 - $100.70
Third Person: $21.20

Casa del Rio—On the Chama River, high in the pink cliffs of northern New Mexico is a traditional adobe bed and breakfast. Furnished with local handmade crafts and furniture. Come stay with us. We're in the heart of it all, 35 minutes to Santa Fe or Taos.

Farmington *

Ohlson, Diana
3151 W. Main, 87401
(505) 325-8219

Amenities: 1,2,9,11,12,16
Breakfast: C. Plus

Dbl. Oc.: $65.00
Sgl. Oc.: $55.00
Third Person: $10.00

Silver River Adobe Inn—A newly built adobe in traditional New Mexican style, sitting on the cliff side of the San Jaun and La Plata Rivers. Located near Chaco Canyon, Aztec, Salmon Ruins, Mesa Verde, Canyon de Chelly and the Navajo, Ute, Hopi and Apache reservations. A Navajo rug gallery to enjoy.

---

1. No Smoking	5. Tennis Available	9. Credit Cards Accepted	13. Lunch Available	17. Shared Baths
2. No Pets	6. Golf Available	10. Personal Check Accepted	14. Conference Rooms Avail.	18. Afternoon Tea
3 Off Season Rates	7. Swimmming Avail.	11. Reservations Necessary	15. Group Seminars Avail.	* Commisions given
4. Senior Citizen Rates	8. Skiing Available	12. Dinner Available	16. Private Baths	to Travel Agents

NEW MEXICO

Placitas *

Butler, Rhea & Robert
Star Rte., Box 501, 87043
(505) 867-5586

Amenities: 1,3,4,6,8,10,11,16
Breakfast: C.
Dbl. Oc.: $68.50 - $99.75
Sgl Oc.: $68.50 - $99.75
Third Person: $11.00
Child: Under 12 yrs. - $6.00

Kensington House—A charming, unique New Mexican B&B located on a spectacular high mesa within minutes of Santa Fe, Albuquerque and several Indian Pueblos. Sandia and Jemez Mountain Ranges and the southwestern charm are all part of the magic! A beautiful and peaceful stay.

Santa Fe *

Alford, David
617 Don Gaspar, 87501
(505) 986-8664

Amenities: 1,2,10,11,12,13, 16
Breakfast: C. Plus

Dbl. Oc.: $110.00 - $225.00
Sgl. Oc.: $95.00 - $210.00
Third Person: $15.00
Child: Under 2 yrs. - no charge

The Don Gaspar Compound—A short walk from the plaza. The compound was built in the historic district in 1912. The main house and five suites overlook the walled gardens and fountain. An oasis in the high desert. Enjoy the compound's hospitality, New Mexico style.

Santa Fe *

Allen, Thom
MacGregor, Quida
220 W. Manhattan, 87501
(505) 988-1177

Amenities: 1,3,10,11,14,16,17,18
Breakfast: F.
Dbl. Oc.: $70.00 - $145.00
Sgl Oc.: $65.00 - $145.00
Third Person: $15.00
Child: 4 - 12 yrs. - $5.00

El Paradero—A 14-room adobe inn located four blocks south of the Plaza. Built between 1800 and 1820, the building reflects the history of the city. Tea time, outstanding breakfasts, southwestern decor. All create a relaxed, unique stay in this beautiful city.

1. No Smoking	5. Tennis Available	9. Credit Cards Accepted	13. Lunch Available	17. Shared Baths
2. No Pets	6. Golf Available	10. Personal Check Accepted	14. Conference Rooms Avail.	18. Afternoon Tea
3 Off Season Rates	7. Swimming Avail.	11. Reservations Necessary	15. Group Seminars Avail.	* Commisions given
4. Senior Citizen Rates	8. Skiing Available	12. Dinner Available	16. Private Baths	to Travel Agents

Santa Fe *

Ambrose, Trisha
652 Canyon Rd., 87501
(505) 988-5888

Amenities: 1,2,3,9,10,11,16
Breakfast: C. Plus

Dbl. Oc.: $95.00 - $145.00
Sgl. Oc.: $85.00 - $125.00
Child: Under 12 yrs. - no charge

Canyon Road Casitas—A small, luxurious inn located on Santa Fe's historic Canyon Road. A restored adobe with the finest southwestern decor and amenities. Accommodations in queen feather beds, private baths, quilts, guest robes and private garden. An award-winning inn.

Santa Fe

Dunshee, Susan
986 Acequia Madre, 87501
(505) 982-0988

Amenities: 1,2,9,10,11,16
Breakfast: F.

Dbl. Oc.: $99.11
Sgl. Oc.: $88.11
Third Person: $16.51

Dunshee's—A romantic adobe getaway in the historic zone. Your suite includes a private entrance, living room and bedroom with Kiva fireplaces, antiques, folk art, fresh flowers, homemade cookies, refrigerator, private bath and patio. Great breakfasts.

Santa Fe *

Harbour, Pat
202 Chapelle, 87501
(505) 983-3133

Amenities: 2,9,10,11,16
Breakfast: F.

Dbl. Oc.: $95.51 - $127.35
Sgl. Oc.: $90.21 - $106.25

Adobe Adobe Bed And Breakfast Inn—Three blocks from the plaza. A historic adobe restored into an intimate inn. Decorated with flair and authentic southwest charm. Two main-house guest rooms and a detached casita with large patio. Complimentary sherry, fruit, cookies and hearty gourmet breakfast.

Santa Fe *

McFerrin, Lela
215 Washington Ave., 87501
(505) 989-7737

Amenities: 2,5,6,7,8,9,10,11,
16,17,18
Breakfast: C. Plus

Dbl. Oc.: $80.00 - $150.00
Sgl. Oc.: $80.00 - $150.00
Third Person: $15.00
Child: Over 10 yrs. - $15.00

Territorial Inn—Elegant 100-year-old home one block from historic plaza. Ten rooms, hot tub, fireplaces, rose garden, private parking and personal service.

---

1. No Smoking	5. Tennis Available	9. Credit Cards Accepted	13. Lunch Available	17. Shared Baths
2. No Pets	6. Golf Available	10. Personal Check Accepted	14. Conference Rooms Avail.	18. Afternoon Tea
3 Off Season Rates	7. Swimmming Avail.	11. Reservations Necessary	15. Group Seminars Avail.	* Commisions given
4. Senior Citizen Rates	8. Skiing Available	12. Dinner Available	16. Private Baths	to Travel Agents

NEW MEXICO

Santa Fe *

Schneider, Mary Jo
529 E. Palace Ave., 87501
(505) 986-1431

Amenities: 1,3,5,6,7,8,9,10, 16,17,18

Breakfast: C.

Dbl. Oc.: $71.58 - $154.18
Sgl. Oc.: $71.58 - $154.18
Third Person: Over 6 yrs. - $16.52
Child: $16.52

Alexander's Inn—For a cozy stay in Santa Fe, nestle in a bed and breakfast featuring the best of American country charm. Built in 1903, the inn has been newly renovated to offer modern comfort along with the romance and charm of earlier and simpler times.

Santa Fe *

Vargas, Jule & Paul
1431 El Camino Real
P.O. Box 307, Algodones, 87001
(505) 867-9115, (800)732-2194 (outside New Mexico)

Amenities: 1,2,3,6,8,9,11,16
Breakfast: F.

Dbl. Oc.: $75.00 - $98.00
Third Person: $10.00

Hacienda Vargas—Historic hacienda minutes from Santa Fe and Albuquerque. Beautifully decorated and refurbished. All rooms have kiva fireplaces, private entrances and bathrooms. Many amenities: hot tubs, jacuzzi and BBQ area. Many outdoor activities: snow skiing, horseback riding, fishing, etc.

Santa Fe *

Walter, Martin
122 Grant Ave., 87501
(505) 983-6678

Amenities: 1,2,5,7,8,9,10,11, 13,14,15,16,17

Breakfast: F.

Dbl. Oc.: $70.00 - $135.00
Sgl. Oc.: $70.00 - $75.00
Third Person: $20.00
Child: Over 7 yrs. - $20.00

Grant Corner Inn—A delightful bed-and-breakfast hotel in a restored colonial home two blocks from Santa Fe's historic plaza. Restaurant serving gourmet breakfast to the public.

Taos *

Cheek, Mildred & Don
P.O. Box 2326, 87571
(505) 776-2913

Amenities: 1,2,5,6,7,8,9,10,11,16
Breakfast: F.
Dbl. Oc.: $81.94 - $131.10
Sgl Oc.: $81.94 - $131.10
Third Person: $15.00

Stewart House Gallery And Inn—Amidst high desert sagebrush mesas and mountains, you will find our artist-built B&B and gallery. Warm hospitality, great food, scenic drives and activities beckon. Pamper yourself in the historic art colony of Taos. Visit 1,000-year-old Taos Pueblo.

1. No Smoking	5. Tennis Available	9. Credit Cards Accepted	13. Lunch Available	17. Shared Baths
2. No Pets	6. Golf Available	10. Personal Check Accepted	14. Conference Rooms Avail.	18. Afternoon Tea
3 Off Season Rates	7. Swimming Avail.	11. Reservations Necessary	15. Group Seminars Avail.	* Commisions given
4. Senior Citizen Rates	8. Skiing Available	12. Dinner Available	16. Private Baths	to Travel Agents

NEW MEXICO

Taos *

Framan, Judie & Elliot
132 Frontier Rd.
P.O. Box 584, 87571
(505) 758-4446, (800) 532-2041,
Fax:(505) 758-0497

Amenities: 1,2,5,6,7,8,9,10,
11,14,15,16
Breakfast: F.

Dbl. Oc.: $70.00 - $105.00
Sgl. Oc.: $65.00 - $100.00
Third Person: $25.00
Child: $15.00

American Artists Gallery House—A charming southwestern hacienda filled with artwork. Fireplaces, hot tub and gardens. Magnificent view of mountains. Minutes from plaza, galleries and Ski Valley. No smoking, please. Six guest rooms.

Taos *

Hockett, Mary
Hwy. 150
P.O. Box 1468, El Prado, 87529
(505) 776-2422

Amenities: 1,2,5,6,7,8,9,10,
11,14,15,16,18
Breakfast: F.

Dbl. Oc.: $92.11 - $173.40
Third Person: $10.00

Salsa Del Salto Bed And Breakfast Inn—A world-class bed-and-breakfast inn. This sophisticated southwestern home offers a pool, hot tub and private tennis court. Elegant rooms, private baths, king-size beds and gourmet breakfast. Located between Taos and the famous Taos Ski Valley.

Taos *

Landon, Marcine & John
P.O. Box 177
109 Mabel Dodge Lane, 87571
(505) 758-0287

Amenities: 1,2,8,10,11,16,17,
18
Breakfast: F.

Dbl. Oc.: $60.64 - $126.79
Sgl. Oc.: $49.62 - $99.23
Third Person: $22.05
Child: Under 3 yrs. - $10.68

Hacienda Del Sol—Chosen by *USA Weekend* as one of the 10-most-romantic inns. A circa 1800 adobe in a country setting, yet in town. Fireplaces, views, hand-crafted furniture and original art. One room has a jacuzzi and one a steam room! Large, outdoor hot tub. Generous breakfast.

Truchas

Curtiss, Frank
P.O. Box 338, 87578
(505) 689-2374

Amenities: 1,2,8,9,10,12,17
Breakfast: F.

Dbl. Oc.: $55.00
Sgl. Oc.: $40.00
Third Person: $25.00
Child: Under 10 yrs. - $10.00

Rancho Arriba—A European-style B&B. A small, working farm located on a Spanish colonial land grant. We have a spectacular view, rural location and an informal atmosphere. Rooms are located in the adobe hacienda and breakfast is cooked on a wood-burning stove.

---

1. No Smoking	5. Tennis Available	9. Credit Cards Accepted	13. Lunch Available	17. Shared Baths
2. No Pets	6. Golf Available	10. Personal Check Accepted	14. Conference Rooms Avail.	18. Afternoon Tea
3 Off Season Rates	7. Swimmming Avail.	11. Reservations Necessary	15. Group Seminars Avail.	* Commisions given
4. Senior Citizen Rates	8. Skiing Available	12. Dinner Available	16. Private Baths	to Travel Agents

NEW YORK

The Empire State

Capitol: Albany
Statehood: July 26, 1788; the 11th state
State Motto: "Ever Upward"
State Song: "I Love New York"
State Bird: Bluebird
State Flower: Rose
State Tree: Sugar Maple

New York is a mecca for tourists. It offers something for everyone. Commercially, it is the greatest manufacturing state in the United States and it far out-ranks all other states in foreign trade and whole-sale and retail trade.

Besides everything else, it is the nation's center for transportation, banking and finance.

It is a farming state as well. Some of the finest fruits and vegetables are grown here.

Tourists can find just about any kind of recreation in this state, from the quiet and beauty of its mountains and streams, to the Big Apple - New York City, the largest city in the state. New York City offers skyscrapers, the United Nations Building, Statue of Liberty, New York Stock Exchange and numerous choices of theatres and sports.

Four presidents have been born in this state; Martin Van Buren, Millard Fillmore, Theodore Roosevelt and Franklin D. Roosevelt.

NEW YORK

Addison

Peters, Maryann & William
37 Maple St., 14801
(607) 359-4650

Amenities: 1,2,6,10,11,16,17, 18
Breakfast: F.

Dbl. Oc.: Up to $81.75
Sgl. Oc.: Up to $70.85

Addison Rose Bed And Breakfast—Step into "Victorian elegance in the heart of the country" in this restored, antique-furnished painted lady. Located in the quaint village of Addison, just minutes from Corning and Finger Lake attractions.

Albany *

Stofelano, Mary Ellen & Stephen
115 Philip St., 12202
(518) 465-2038

Amenities: 1,4,9,10,12,13,14, 15,16
Breakfast: F.

Dbl. Oc.: $105.00 - $145.00
Sgl. Oc.: $95.00 - $135.00
Child: Under 12 yrs. - $10.00

Mansion Hill Inn—An urban inn located around the corner from the New York States Governor's executive mansion. Built in 1861 for Daniel D. Brown, an Albany brushmaker. In most recent decades, the inn served as one of the south end's most popular taverns. In 1992, our restaurant was rated ****.

Albany *

Tricarico, Janice
531 Western Ave., 12203
(518) 482-1574

Amenities: 1,2,3,10,14,17
Breakfast: C.

Dbl. Oc.: $64.00
Sgl. Oc.: $49.00
Third Person: $15.00

Pine Haven Bed And Breakfast—A century-old, gracious Victorian located one mile from downtown. Within walking distance of restaurants, theatre and shopping. Furnished in antiques, iron and brass beds for a Victorian ambience in the heart of Albany. A half hour to Saratoga and 45 minutes to the Adirondacks.

Amenia *

Flaherty, James
Leedsville Rd.
Box 26, 12501
(914) 373-9681

Amenities: 2,5,6,7,8,9,10,11, 12,13,14,15,16
Breakfast: F. (C. - Sundays)

Dbl. Oc.: $575.00 - $790.00

Troutbeck—Dazzling English manor with four-star cuisine. Year-round pools on 442 acres. *Country Inns of New York* said: "Troutbeck must be considered one of the finest inns in the world." Rates cover from 5 p.m. Friday to 2 p.m. Sunday per couple, Six meals and all spirits. Conference center.

(Historic) Auburn *

Fitzpatrick, Patricia
102 South St., 13021
(315) 255-0196

Amenities: 3,4,5,6,7,8,9,10, 11,13,14,15,16,17, 18
Breakfast: F.

Dbl. Oc.: $90.95
Sgl. Oc.: $58.85
Third Person: $8.00
Child: Under 7 yrs. - no charge

The Irish Rose, A Victorian Bed And Breakfast—Large Queen Anne B&B. Immaculate. Outdoor 20' by 40' pool. Five beautifully decorated bedrooms. Historic registered B&B. Open year-round. Special off-season rates. Close to all attractions: skiing, wineries, canoeing. Special rates for whole house. AAA - 2 diamond award.

1. No Smoking	5. Tennis Available	9. Credit Cards Accepted	13. Lunch Available	17. Shared Baths
2. No Pets	6. Golf Available	10. Personal Check Accepted	14. Conference Rooms Avail.	18. Afternoon Tea
3 Off Season Rates	7. Swimmming Avail.	11. Reservations Necessary	15. Group Seminars Avail.	* Commisions given
4. Senior Citizen Rates	8. Skiing Available	12. Dinner Available	16. Private Baths	to Travel Agents

NEW YORK

Averill Park *

Tomlinson, Thelma
Rte. 3, Box 301, 12018
(518) 766-5035

Amenities: 1,2,6,7,8,9,10,11,
17,18
Breakfast: F.

Dbl. Oc.: $58.85
Sgl. Oc.: $48.15

Ananas Hus Bed And Breakfast—A hillside ranch home on 30 acres in West Stephentown. Early American decor. Panoramic views of the Hudson River Valley. Beauty and tranquility. Near Jiminy Peak and Brodie ski areas, theatres and other cultural activities in western Massachusetts and New York.

Berlin *

Evans, Edith
Rte. 22, 12022
(518) 658-2334, (800) 845-4886

Amenities: 5,6,7,8,9,10,12,13,
15,16
Breakfast: F.

Dbl. Oc.: $65.00 - $85.00
Sgl. Oc.: $55.00 - $70.00
Third Person: $12.00
Child: Under 6 yrs. - no charge

The Sedgwick Inn—A historic 1791 inn located in scenic Tacinic Valley. Beautifully furnished with antiques. Close to Williamstown Theatre, Tanglewood and other Berkshire attractions. Near downhill and cross-country skiing. Renowned restaurant. Small motel unit behind main house, 30 miles from Albany.

Bolton Landing

Richards, Anita
6883 Lakeshore Dr., 12814-0186
(518) 644-2492

Amenities: 2,3,5,6,7,8,10,16,
17
Breakfast: F.

Dbl. Oc.: $48.00 - $70.00
Sgl. Oc.: $37.00 - $70.00
Third Person: $11.00

Hilltop Cottage B&B—A renovated caretaker cottage near Lake George in the eastern Adirondacks. Walk to restaurants and beach. One room with private bath, two rooms share a bath. Guest cabin available. Full breakfast on screen porch. Helpful hosts with an at-home atmosphere. Smoking limited.

Branchport (New York Finger Lakes Area.)

Lewis, Linda
453 W. Lake Rd., 14418
(607) 868-4603

Amenities: 1,2,5,6,7,8,10,15,16,17
Breakfast: F.
Dbl. Oc.: $65.20 - $103.55
Sgl Oc.: $60.20 - $98.55
Third Person: $20.00
Child: $20.00

Gone With The Wind On Keuka Lake—The name paints the picture. A 1887 stone Victorian on 14 acres overlooking our quiet lake cove with picnic gazebo. Capture total relaxation and peace of mind enjoying solarium hot-tub, fireplaces, delectable breakfasts, cheerful rooms, private beach with dock and walking trails.

1. No Smoking	5. Tennis Available	9. Credit Cards Accepted	13. Lunch Available	17. Shared Baths
2. No Pets	6. Golf Available	10. Personal Check Accepted	14. Conference Rooms Avail.	18. Afternoon Tea
3 Off Season Rates	7. Swimmming Avail.	11. Reservations Necessary	15. Group Seminars Avail.	* Commisions given
4. Senior Citizen Rates	8. Skiing Available	12. Dinner Available	16. Private Baths	to Travel Agents

Branchport *(New York Finger Lakes Area.)*

Olmstead, Martha
470 West Lake Rd.,
Rte. 54A, 14418
(607) 868-4686

Amenities: 1,2,7,10,11,16,17
Breakfast: F.

Dbl. Oc.: $65.00 - $90.00
Sgl. Oc.: $65.00 - $90.00

Four Seasons—Century-old, remodeled farmhouse and vineyard property. Country atmosphere with expansive lawns, trees and creek. Four guest rooms, living room with fireplace. Porch and decks. Secure bike storage. Six nearby wineries. Convenient lake-front restaurant.

Brooklyn

Paolella, Liana
113 Prospect Park W., 11215
(718) 499-6115

Amenities: 1,2,5,9,10,14,15,
16,17
Breakfast: F.

Dbl. Oc.: $100.00 - $175.00
Sgl. Oc.: $100.00 - $175.00
Third Person: $35.00
Child: Under 3 yrs. - no charge

Bed And Breakfast On The Park—Just two miles from downtown Manhattan, a short walk from Brooklyn Museum and Botanical Garden. This 1892 Victorian mansion with views of New York City and Prospect Park has been converted to an urban B&B offering a European atmosphere and generous hospitality.

Cambridge *

Sullivan, Terry
R.R. 2, Little Colfax Farm Rd., 12816
(518) 677-5280

Amenities: 1,2,4,5,6,7,8,9,
10,11,14,16,17
Breakfast: F.
Dbl. Oc.: $160.50
Sgl Oc.: $160.50
Third Person: $160.50

Little Colfax Bed And Breakfast—Gorgeous 600-acre country estate to hike or ski. Views of three states. Pool, spa, fitness center, pond to fish, tanning bed, VHS library, dog kennel and more! Visit outlets, historic sites, colleges, fish Battenkill, attend SPAC or relax!

Canandaigua *

Freese, Elizabeth
4761 Rte. 364, Rushville, NY, 14544
(716) 554-6973

Amenities: 1,2,3,5,6,7,8,9,10,
17
Breakfast: F.

Dbl. Oc.: $58.85
Sgl. Oc.: $42.80
Third Person: $16.05
Child: Under 3 yrs. - no charge

Lakeview Farm Bed And Breakfast—A country home on 170 acres overlooking Canandaigua Lake. Two antique-furnished bedrooms with shared bath and upstairs sitting room. Enjoy views from lounge/dining area. Pond and beautiful ravine nearby. Public beach, restaurants, concert area and lake attractions. A/C.

1. No Smoking	5. Tennis Available	9. Credit Cards Accepted	13. Lunch Available	17. Shared Baths
2. No Pets	6. Golf Available	10. Personal Check Accepted	14. Conference Rooms Avail.	18. Afternoon Tea
3 Off Season Rates	7. Swimmming Avail.	11. Reservations Necessary	15. Group Seminars Avail.	* Commisions given
4. Senior Citizen Rates	8. Skiing Available	12. Dinner Available	16. Private Baths	to Travel Agents

Cazenovia *

Barr, James Grey
5 Albany St.
U.S. Rte. 20, 13035
(315) 655-3431

Amenities: 2,3,4,5,6,7,8,9,10, 11,12,14,15,16,17
Breakfast: C.

Dbl. Oc.: $80.65
Sgl. Oc.: $69.55
Third Person: $15.00
Child: Under 12 yrs. - no charge

Brae Loch Inn—Situated across from beautiful Cazenovia Lake. Two blocks from center of the village that features fine shops and restaurants. Antiquing and sightseeing nearby; golf and swimming priviledges. Downhill and cross-country skiing abound in winter.

Chappaqua

Crabtree, Dick & John
11 Kittle Rd., 10514
(914) 666-8044

Amenities: 9,10,12,13,16
Breakfast: C.

Dbl. Oc.: $92.45
Sgl. Oc.: $81.55
Third Person: $10.00

Crabtree's Kittle House—Built in 1790, Crabtree's Kittle House maintains a distinctive blend of country style and comfort. Not to be missed are the dinner specialties of the house including crisp roast duckling and the freshest seafood available.

Cherry Plain *

Rubin, Helane & Bob
Mattison Hollow
P.O. Box 92, 12040
(518) 658-2946

Amenities: 1,2,5,6,7,8,10,11, 12,16
Breakfast: F.

Dbl. Oc.: $120.25
Sgl. Oc.: $120.25
Third Person: $49.13

Mattison Hollow—Located on the state border of Massachusetts, Vermont and New York. Situated in the Berkshires. Furnished with antiques. Secluded 1790 country home, minutes from Tanglewood, Williamstown, skiing, hiking, pond, trout brook. Dinner is included in the above listed rates.

Chestertown *

Taylor, Sharon
Friends Lake Rd., 12817
(518) 494-4751

Amenities: 2,3,7,8,9,10,11,12, 14,15,16
Breakfast: F.

Dbl. Oc.: $65.00 -$140.00
Third Person: $22.00
Child: Under 12 yrs. - $22.00

Friends Lake Inn—A fully restored 19th-century country inn. Award-winning gourmet dining and wine list. 16 guest rooms with private baths, some with hot tubs or lake views. Outdoor hot tub, cross-country skiing trails, skiing and mountain biking rentals. Beach. Small boats, 20 minutes from Lake George and Gore Mountain.

Chichester

Parsons, Nancy & Albert
6 Park Rd., 12416
(914) 688-5433

Amenities: 1,2,7,8,10,11,17
Breakfast: F.

Dbl. Oc.: $60.00
Sgl. Oc.: $45.00
Child: Under 3 yrs. - no charge

Maplewood Bed And Breakfast—A lovely colonial home on a quiet country lane in the heart of the Catskill Mountains. Only 12 miles to Hunter or Belleayre for skiing. Near fishing, tubing, hiking and antiquing. Twenty minutes to Woodstock. Each spacious room has a beautiful view.

1. No Smoking	5. Tennis Available	9. Credit Cards Accepted	13. Lunch Available	17. Shared Baths
2. No Pets	6. Golf Available	10. Personal Check Accepted	14. Conference Rooms Avail.	18. Afternoon Tea
3 Off Season Rates	7. Swimmming Avail.	11. Reservations Necessary	15. Group Seminars Avail.	* Commisions given
4. Senior Citizen Rates	8. Skiing Available	12. Dinner Available	16. Private Baths	to Travel Agents

NEW YORK

Clinton

Bohling, Gary
7 Campus Rd.
Box 247, 13323
(315) 853-3016

Amenities: 4,5,6,7,8,9,10,11, **Dbl. Oc.:** $85.80
12,13,14,15,16,17 **Sgl. Oc.:** $74.80
Breakfast: F. **Child:** $16.50

The Westward Mansion—Come and experience a touch of luxury. This beautiful estate is nestled just off the Hamilton College campus. A large, cheerful common room with a working fireplace, a greenhouse and color TV with VCR is a favorite gathering spot.

Colden

Georgi, Shash
7233 Lower E. Hill Rd., 14033
(716) 652-0427

Amenities: 1,2,7,8,10,11,17 **Dbl. Oc.:** $64.80
Breakfast: F. **Sgl. Oc.:** $54.00
Child: $10.80

Back Of The Beyond—Charming country mini-estate in ski area of west New York. Separate chalet, 1-1/2 baths, piano, pool table, fireplace, furnished kitchen, living room. Organic gardens; antique gift shop; X-country skiing; pond on property. We serve a full country breakfast. Lawn games. Board games.

Cooperstown *

Grimes, Joan & Jack
RD #2, Box 514, 13326
(607) 547-9700

Amenities: 1,2,5,6,7,8,10,11, **Dbl. Oc.:** $55.00 - $80.00
15,16 **Sgl. Oc.:** $41.25 - $60.00
Breakfast: F. **Third Person:** $15.00
Child: Under 2 yrs. - no charge

The Inn At Brook Willow—This pastoral retreat is just a skip over a creek that winds its way to the inn. Guests are welcomed into a Victorian home and reborn barn furnished with fine antiques. Before going to the Hall of Fame in the morning, you will enjoy a bountiful meal.

Cooperstown *

Wolff, Margaret & Jim
P.O. Box 1048, 13326-1048
(607) 547-2501

Amenities: 1,2,5,6,7,8,
10,11,15,16,17
Breakfast: F.
Dbl. Oc.: $60.00
Sgl Oc.: $50.00
Third Person: $10.00
Child: Under 5 yrs. - no charge

Litco Farms Bed And Breakfast.—Three miles from Cooperstown. Well suited to families and couples. Enjoy our 20x40-foot pool and 70 acres with nature trails. Warm hospitality and marvelous breakfasts will make your visit with us memorable. Shop at Heartworks, our on-site quilt shop.

1. No Smoking	5. Tennis Available	9. Credit Cards Accepted	13. Lunch Available	17. Shared Baths
2. No Pets	6. Golf Available	10. Personal Check Accepted	14. Conference Rooms Avail.	18. Afternoon Tea
3 Off Season Rates	7. Swimmming Avail.	11. Reservations Necessary	15. Group Seminars Avail.	* Commisions given
4. Senior Citizen Rates	8. Skiing Available	12. Dinner Available	16. Private Baths	to Travel Agents

Corning

DePumpo, Mary
188 Delevan Ave., 14830
(607) 962-2347

Amenities: 1,6,7,8,10,16,17, 18
Breakfast: F.

Dbl. Oc.: $70.85 - $81.75
Sgl. Oc.: $54.50 - $70.85
Third Person: $16.35
Child: Under 12 yrs. - $16.35

The Delevan House—A southern colonial home overlooking Corning. Quiet surroundings, outstanding accommodations. Warm hospitality. Complimentary cool drink and full breakfast. Free pick-up from airport.

Corning

Donahue, Kathy & Joe
69 E. First St., 14830
(607) 962-6355

Amenities: 1,2,9,10,16,17
Breakfast: F.
Dbl. Oc.: $70.85
Sgl Oc.: $55.00
Third Person: $21.80
Child: Under 5 yrs. - no charge

"1865" White Birch Bed And Breakfast—Imagine a friendly and warm atmosphere in an 1865 Victorian setting. Cozy rooms await our guests with both private and shared baths. Awake to the tantalizing aromas of a full breakfast. Walk to local exhibits and glass center, fine dining and Market Street.

Croton-on-Hudson *

Notarius, Barbara
49 Van Wyck St., 10520
(914) 271-6737

Amenities: 1,7,9,10,11,14,15, 16,17
Breakfast: F.

Dbl. Oc.: $65.00 - $250.00
Sgl. Oc.: $50.00 - $100.75
Third Person: $25.00
Child: Under 18 yrs. - $15.00

The Alexander Hamilton House—An 1889 Victorian B&B with lots of antiques. In-ground pool. A/C. Fireplaces. Close to West Point, many historic Hudson Valley houses. One hour to New York City. Bridal chamber has jacuzzi, king bed, skylights and entertainment center. Corporate apartment available with kitchen.

1. No Smoking	5. Tennis Available	9. Credit Cards Accepted	13. Lunch Available	17. Shared Baths
2. No Pets	6. Golf Available	10. Personal Check Accepted	14. Conference Rooms Avail.	18. Afternoon Tea
3 Off Season Rates	7. Swimmming Avail.	11. Reservations Necessary	15. Group Seminars Avail.	* Commisions given
4. Senior Citizen Rates	8. Skiing Available	12. Dinner Available	16. Private Baths	to Travel Agents

NEW YORK

Cuba *

Lyon, Ted
Ammering, David
28 Genessee Pkwy., 14727-1130
(716) 968-3335

Amenities: 1,2,4,5,6,7,8,
　　　　9,10,11,16,18
Breakfast: C. Plus
Dbl. Oc.: $64.80 - $70.20
Sgl Oc.: $64.80 - $70.20

Rocking Duck Inn—An 1852 village estate on four acres located in the beautiful Allegheny foothills of New York's southern tier. Four attractively appointed guest rooms, rural charm, fireplaces and antiques create a relaxing ambience. Arts and crafts, hiking, foliage, antiques and museums nearby.

Davenport

Hodge, William
Wohlrab, Stewart
Main St., 13750
(607) 278-5068, (800) 273-1746 (New York state)

Amenities: 2,7,8,9,10,11,12,
　　　　14,15,16,17
Breakfast: C. Plus

Dbl. Oc.: $40.28 - $48.76
Sgl. Oc.: $20.14 - $36.04
Third Person: $10.60
Child: Under 8 yrs. - 1/2 rate

The Davenport Inn—A historic tavern built about 1819. Close to Oneonta, Cooperstown and Scotch Valley. AAA dining room and gift shop. Private and shared baths. Five rooms and apartment available. Full breakfast served Sundays in the summer and fall.

Dolgeville *

Naizby, Adrianna
44 Stewart, 13329
(315) 429-3249

Amenities: 6,7,8,9,10,16,17
Breakfast: F.

Dbl. Oc.: $55.00
Sgl. Oc.: $42.80
Third Person: $15.00
Child: Under 5 yrs. - $10.00

Adrianna Bed And Breakfast—Located off Thruway, Exit 29 A. Cozy residence in charming village, featuring eclectic blend of antique and contemporary furnishings. Convenient to Saratoga, Cooperstown, Utica, historic sights and diamond mines. Air conditioning.

Downsville

Adams, Nancy & Harry
Main St.
Rte. 206, 13755
(607) 363-2757

Amenities: 1,2,4,6,7,10,12,13,
　　　　17,18
Breakfast: F.

Dbl. Oc.: $50.00
Sgl. Oc.: $35.00
Third Person: $10.00
Child: Under 6 yrs. - $5.00

Adams' Farm House Inn—Come, enjoy our country hospitality. We will pamper you with our hearty breakfast, afternoon sweets and an evening drink, friendly conversation and information about the local Catskill area. Lots of fishing and antiquing nearby. Beautiful farmhouse. Canoeing, horseback riding and hunting.

---

1. No Smoking	5. Tennis Available	9. Credit Cards Accepted	13. Lunch Available	17. Shared Baths
2. No Pets	6. Golf Available	10. Personal Check Accepted	14. Conference Rooms Avail.	18. Afternoon Tea
3 Off Season Rates	7. Swimmming Avail.	11. Reservations Necessary	15. Group Seminars Avail.	* Commisions given
4. Senior Citizen Rates	8. Skiing Available	12. Dinner Available	16. Private Baths	to Travel Agents

Elizabethtown *

Murphy, Sandra
Thomas, Winifred
Roscoe Rd., RR 1, Box 69, 12932
(518) 873-9125

Amenities: 1,2,6,7,8,9,10,12, 13,14,16,18
Breakfast: F.

Dbl. Oc.: $70.00 - $80.00
Sgl. Oc.: $60.00
Third Person: $10.00
Child: $10.00

Stony Water Bed And Breakfast—Robert Frost often visited Stony Water in the '30s and '40s when his good friend and literary critic Louis Untermeyer was owner. Walk, swim and relax on 87 wooded acres. Enjoy Adirondack comfort and tranquility two miles from Elizabethtown and 25 miles from Lake Placid.

Fair Haven *

Brown, Sara
Stafford St., Box 378, 13064
(315) 947-5817

Amenities: 1,2,3,5,6,7,9,10, 13,17
Breakfast: C.

Dbl. Oc.: $60.00
Sgl. Oc.: $37.45
Child: Under 12 yrs. - $10.00

Brown's Village Inn—A country home offering old-fashioned hospitality in a warm and friendly atmosphere. Located in a quiet area within walking distance of shops and restaurants. Two miles to beach and Renaissance Faire. Antique shop on property.

Fleischmanns *

Palmer, Jeanne, Miller, Larry
Main St., Box D-4, 12430
(914) 254-4884

Amenities: 3,5,6,7,8,9,10, 11,15,16,17,18
Breakfast: F.
Dbl. Oc.: $42.00 - $90.00
Sgl Oc.: $27.00 - $74.00
Third Person: $10.00
Child: $10.00

River Run—Country village Victorian at the edge of the Catskill Forest. Ten inviting rooms, parlor, front porch and riverside picnic area. Skiing, hiking, fishing, golf, auction, theatre, restaurants within minutes. Children and pets welcome! New York City bus stops right in town.

Franklin

Millen, Barbara & Frank
135 Main St.
P.O. Box 896, 13775
(607) 829-8333

Amenities: 6,9,11,17
Breakfast: F.

Dbl. Oc.: $37.10
Sgl. Oc.: $26.50
Third Person: $10.60
Child: Under 5 yrs. - no charge

Franklin Manor Guest House—Quiet country village on main highway between New York City and upstate New York, close to Oneonta Colleges, SUCO and Hartwick. Established in 1982. Golf course, swimming and boat dock within 10 minutes radius. Local hunting, fishing, camping and hiking.

1. No Smoking	5. Tennis Available	9. Credit Cards Accepted	13. Lunch Available	17. Shared Baths
2. No Pets	6. Golf Available	10. Personal Check Accepted	14. Conference Rooms Avail.	18. Afternoon Tea
3 Off Season Rates	7. Swimmming Avail.	11. Reservations Necessary	15. Group Seminars Avail.	* Commisions given
4. Senior Citizen Rates	8. Skiing Available	12. Dinner Available	16. Private Baths	to Travel Agents

NEW YORK

Fulton *

Rice, Joyce
R.D. #1, Box 176, 13069
(315) 593-3699

Amenities: 1,2,6,9,10,15,16
Breakfast: F.

Dbl. Oc.: $64.20 - $90.00
Sgl. Oc.: $53.50 - $69.75
Third Person: $16.00

Battle Island Inn—A pre-Civil War farm estate, restored and furnished with period antiques. Golf and cross-country skiing across the road. Rooms include TV, phone, private bath and desk. Full breakfast served in our elegant 1840s dining room. Sit on one of four porches or stroll through the gardens.

Geneva

Schickel, Jr., Norbert H.
1001 Lochland Rd., 14456
(800) 3Geneva, (315) 789-7190

Amenities: 2,3,5,6,7,8,9,
      10,12,13,14,15,16
Breakfast: C.
Dbl. Oc.: $92.00 - $399.00
Sgl Oc.: $82.00 - $389.00
Third Person: $52.00
Child: $17.00 - $29.00

Geneva On The Lake—An elegant, small resort in New York's Finger Lakes wine district. Enjoy luxurious suites overlooking Seneca Lake. Furnished terrace, formal gardens, pool and sailing. A romantic winter escape. Candlelight dining with live musical entertainment. AAA - four Diamond for 10 years.

Gowanda

Lay, Phyllis
R.D.1, Box 543, 14070
(716) 532-2168

Amenities: 5,6,7,8,10,17
Breakfast: F.

Dbl. Oc.: $45.00
Sgl. Oc.: $35.00
Third Person: $10.00
Child: Under 10 yrs. - $5.00

The Teepee—Located on the Cattaraugus Indian Reservation. Light, bright rooms. Seneca Indian artifacts. Tours of Indian Reservation and Amish country. Indian pow-wow and fall festival featuring Indian food and crafts. Hot-air ballooon rides can be arranged.

Groton

Gleason, Irene
307 Old Stage Rd., 13073
(607) 898-4676 (evenings)

Amenities: 1,10,17
Breakfast: F.

Dbl. Oc.: $44.00
Sgl. Oc.: $44.00

Gleason B&B—Working crop farm just minutes from Cornell or Cortland. An 1880 farmhouse with shaded backyard. Golf, swimming, skiing and state parks are all nearby. Five minutes to restaurants. Come share our home while visiting the Finger Lakes.

1. No Smoking	5. Tennis Available	9. Credit Cards Accepted	13. Lunch Available	17. Shared Baths
2. No Pets	6. Golf Available	10. Personal Check Accepted	14. Conference Rooms Avail.	18. Afternoon Tea
3 Off Season Rates	7. Swimmming Avail.	11. Reservations Necessary	15. Group Seminars Avail.	* Commisions given
4. Senior Citizen Rates	8. Skiing Available	12. Dinner Available	16. Private Baths	to Travel Agents

Groton *

Salerno, Doris
210 Old Perville Rd., 13073
(607) 898-5786

Amenities: 1,2,4,5,6,8,10,11,16,17
Breakfast: F.
Dbl. Oc.: $60.00 - $65.00
Sgl Oc.: $50.00
Third Person: $20.00
Child: Under 3 years - $10.00

Austin Manor Bed And Breakfast—Enjoy the elegance of the past and the comfort of the present in a restored Victorian. Set on 185 acres of woods and fields, down a quiet country road. Lace curtains, patchwork quilts and three sitting rooms for your leisure time. Close to both Ithaca and Cortland.

Hamlin *

Hollink, Shirley
Krempasky, James
1960 Redman Rd., 14464-9635
(716) 964-7528

Amenities: 1,10,17,18
Breakfast: F.

Dbl. Oc.: $65.00
Sgl. Oc.: $50.00
Third Person: $18.00

Sandy Creek Manor House—A 1910 English Tudor placed on six wooded acres, perennial gardens and a stroll away from Sandy Creek. Amish quilts, feather pillows and an antique player piano take you back to quieter times. Three air-conditioned rooms with full breakfasts available.

Hammondsport

Carl, Linda & Walter
17 Sheather St.
P.O. Box 366, 14840
(607) 569-2440, (607) 569-3629

Amenities: 1,2,5,6,7,9,11,15,
16,17,18
Breakfast: F.

Dbl. Oc.: $62.00
Sgl. Oc.: $51.00

J.S. Hubbs Bed And Breakfast—Come and relax in our family home. This historic Greek Revival (ink bottle) house was built in 1840 and has been in our family for almost 100 years. We offer a suite, single and double rooms with two private baths and three halfs. One-half block from Lake Keuka.

---

1. No Smoking	5. Tennis Available	9. Credit Cards Accepted	13. Lunch Available	17. Shared Baths
2. No Pets	6. Golf Available	10. Personal Check Accepted	14. Conference Rooms Avail.	18. Afternoon Tea
3 Off Season Rates	7. Swimmming Avail.	11. Reservations Necessary	15. Group Seminars Avail.	* Commisions given
4. Senior Citizen Rates	8. Skiing Available	12. Dinner Available	16. Private Baths	to Travel Agents

Hammondsport *

Laufersweiler, Ellen & Bucky
11 William St., 14840
(607) 569-3402, (607) 569-3483

Amenities: 1,2,3,5,6,7,8,10,15,16
Breakfast: F.
Dbl. Oc.: $81.75 - $92.65
Sgl Oc.: $76.75 - $87.65
Third Person: $16.35

The Blushing Rose B&B—The Blushing Rose B&B extends an invitation to relax in a restored country home with the comfort of today. Four rooms with private baths. Copious breakfasts. Nearby historic village, wineries, museums and Corning. Quietly romantic ruffles and lace.

Hampton Bays *

Lambur, Ute
Box 106, 11946
(516) 728-3560

Amenities: 2,3,5,6,7,10,11, 16
Breakfast: F.

Dbl. Oc.: $75.00 - $95.00
Sgl. Oc.: $70.00 - $90.00
Third Person: $20.00

House On The Water—Eighty miles east of NY City, seven miles to Southampton and two miles to ocean beaches. Two-acre garden on bay. Terrace, lounges and kitchen privileges. Bicycles, windsurfer and pedal boat. Quiet location. Rooms with private bath, TV, water view and private entrance.

Hancock

Toth, Adele & Jim
RD 1, Box 232B, Walton (mail), 13856
(607) 865-7254

Amenities: 1,2,4,6,7,8,11,16, 17
Breakfast: C. Plus

Dbl. Oc.: $47.70 - $63.60
Sgl. Oc.: $37.10
Third Person: $15.90
Child: Under 2 yrs. - free crib

Sunrise Inn Bed And Breakfast—A 19-th century farmhouse with two cozy guest rooms. Cabin, woodstove, gazebo and antique shop. Trout creek for guests to enjoy in a peaceful, country setting. Family pets in residence. 135 miles northwest of New York City. Fine local dining.

Hempstead (on Garden City line) *

Duvall, Wendy
237 Cathedral Ave., 11550
(516) 292-9219

Amenities: 1,2,6,10,11,12,16
Breakfast: F.

Dbl. Oc.: $$64.80 - $92.25
Sgl. Oc.: $$64.80 - $92.25
Third Person: $$15.00
Child: Under 6 yrs. - $10.00

Country LIfe B&B—Gracious old Dutch colonial nestled in trees. Fine restaurants and shops within a walk. Period decor. Restored antiques. Selected for two house tours. Air-conditioning and color TV. Soda, coffee and tea. Near airports, train to New York City and Long Island.

1. No Smoking	5. Tennis Available	9. Credit Cards Accepted	13. Lunch Available	17. Shared Baths
2. No Pets	6. Golf Available	10. Personal Check Accepted	14. Conference Rooms Avail.	18. Afternoon Tea
3. Off Season Rates	7. Swimming Avail.	11. Reservations Necessary	15. Group Seminars Avail.	* Commisions given
4. Senior Citizen Rates	8. Skiing Available	12. Dinner Available	16. Private Baths	to Travel Agents

Herkimer *

Mielcarski, Barbara
611 W. German St., 13350
(315) 866-2770

Amenities: 1,2,5,6,8,9,10,16, 17
Breakfast: F.

Dbl. Oc.: $58.00
Sgl. Oc.: $45.00
Third Person: $10.00

Bellinger Woods B&B—This circa 1860 Victorian home was built as a wedding present. Has been carefully restored and furnished with antiques and traditional pieces. Three second-floor guest rooms. Common sitting room with TV. Located 1/2- mile from I-90, Exit 30, New York Thruway.

Hillsdale *

Breen, Linda
Rte. 23, 12529
(518) 325-7100

Amenities: 3,4,5,7,8,9,10,11, 12,13,14,15,16
Breakfast: F.

Dbl. Oc.: $95.00 - $150.00
Sgl. Oc.: $85.00 - $140.00
Third Person: $10.00

Linden-Valley—Located at the base of Catamount ski area. Seven rooms, all with private baths and one two-bedroom suite with fireplace available. Rooms have private terraces overlooking ponds and five acres of manicured lawns and flower gardens. Two tennis courts.

Hobart

Barber, Joyce
R.D.#1, Box 191, 13788
(607) 538-9338

Amenities: 1,2,5,6,7,8,9,10,16
Breakfast: F.

Dbl. Oc.: $60.00
Sgl. Oc.: $50.00
Child: $10.00

Breezy Acres Farm Bed And Breakfast—Our guests return again and again because of the friendly atmosphere and great breakfasts. Immaculate and beautifully decorated guest rooms. All private baths. Jacuzzi, fireplaces and gift shop. On 300 wooded acres. Close to skiing, hunting and fishing. Country hospitality.

Homer

Stone, Connie
80 So. Main, 13077
(607) 749-3548

Amenities: 1,5,7,8,10,11,12, 13,16
Breakfast: F.

Dbl. Oc.: $45.00 - $55.00
Sgl. Oc.: $35.00 - $45.00
Third Person: $8.00
Child: Under 5 yrs. - no charge

David Harum House—Located in the old Homer Village historic district. It is just 4/10 of a mile from I-81, exit 12. Choose from an elegant queen or charming double room, both with private baths. Special family arrangements available. Antiques and TV.

Ithaca

Grunberg, Wanda
P.O. Box 581, 14851
(607) 589-4771,(800) 274-4771

Amenities: 3,4,8,9,10,11,16, 18
Breakfast: F.

Dbl. Oc.: $60.50 - $71.50
Sgl. Oc.: $44.00 - $66.00
Third Person: $15.00
Child: Under 3 yrs. - no charge

Log Country Inn—The rustic charm of a log house at the edge of a 7,000-acre state forest. Modern accommodations provided in the spirit of international hospitality. Quiet and peaceful. We are convenient to Cornell, Ithaca College, state parks and trails. Enjoy country hospitality.

1. No Smoking	5. Tennis Available	9. Credit Cards Accepted	13. Lunch Available	17. Shared Baths
2. No Pets	6. Golf Available	10. Personal Check Accepted	14. Conference Rooms Avail.	18. Afternoon Tea
3 Off Season Rates	7. Swimming Avail.	11. Reservations Necessary	15. Group Seminars Avail.	* Commisions given
4. Senior Citizen Rates	8. Skiing Available	12. Dinner Available	16. Private Baths	to Travel Agents

NEW YORK

Ithaca Area *

Brownell, Beatrice
178 No. Main St., Spencer, 14883
(607) 589-6073

Amenities: 1,2,3,4,8,10,17
Breakfast: C. or F.

Dbl. Oc.: $55.00 - $70.00
Sgl. Oc.: $25.00 - $35.00
Third Person: $15.00

A Slice Of Home—Gracious hospitality and country atmosphere with a hearty breakfast on weekends. Cross-country skiing. Located in the heart of the Finger Lakes, 20 minutes south of Ithaca via Route 34/96 and 30 minutes to Owego and Route 17.

Jamesville *

Mentz, Nancy & Alex
3740 Eager Rd., 13078
(315) 492-3517

Amenities: 1,2,4,8,10,12,13, 17
Breakfast: C.

Dbl. Oc.: $55.00
Sgl. Oc.: $40.00
Third Person: $5.00
Child: Under 5 yrs. - $5.00

High Meadows B&B—Enjoy country hospitality at High Meadows B&B. High in the hills, 12 miles south of Syracuse, New York. A plant-filled solarium, fireplace and magnificent view. Whatever your pleaseure. A home-made continental breakfast awaits you. We are here to serve you.

Kent

Ward, Ashley & Bonnie
14846 Rte. 18, 14477
(716) 682-3037

Amenities: 1,2,3,11,16
Breakfast: C. Plus

Dbl. Oc.: $46.00
Sgl. Oc.: $35.00
Child: Under 12 yrs. - $11.56

Ward's Bed And Breakfast—Experience a most exclusive lodging choice. One of the area's first, finest and friendliest B&Bs. Weekly and nightly rates. A 19th-century modern farmhouse, park-like lawn, cookout facilities. 5 minutes to local fishing hot spot with King Salmon, Coho Salmon, trout and steelhead.

Lake Placid

Billerman, Gail & Bill
59 Sentinel Rd., 12946
(518) 523-3419

Amenities: 2,3,10,17
Breakfast: C. Plus

Dbl. Oc.: $45.00 - $65.00
Sgl. Oc.: $30.00
Third Person: $10.00
Child: Under 10 yrs. - no charge

Blackberry Inn—A large colonial situated one mile from the center of the village, close to all recreational and sightseeing activities. Newly redecorated rooms and a home-baked breakfast await our guests.

Lake Placid *

Blazer, Cathy
3 Highland Pl., 12946
(518) 523-2377

Amenities: 1,2,3,5,6,7,8,9,10, 16,18
Breakfast: F.

Dbl. Oc.: $70.00
Sgl. Oc.: $60.00
Third Person: $15.00
Child: Under 16 yrs.- $10.00

Highland House Inn—Located on a hill in a lovely residential section of Lake Placid, a five- minute walk from Main St., Mirror Lake and Olympic Center. Lovely Adirondack decor. All private baths. Full, hot, hearty breakfast served on the garden porch during summer. Many little extras. Hot tub spa!

---

1. No Smoking	5. Tennis Available	9. Credit Cards Accepted	13. Lunch Available	17. Shared Baths
2. No Pets	6. Golf Available	10. Personal Check Accepted	14. Conference Rooms Avail.	18. Afternoon Tea
3 Off Season Rates	7. Swimmming Avail.	11. Reservations Necessary	15. Group Seminars Avail.	* Commisions given
4. Senior Citizen Rates	8. Skiing Available	12. Dinner Available	16. Private Baths	to Travel Agents

Lake Placid

Hoffman, Carol
31 Sentinel Rd., 12946
(518) 523-9350

Amenities: 1,2,9,10,16,17
Breakfast: C.

Dbl. Oc.: $42.80 - $105.93
Child: $7.49

Spruce Lodge Bed And Breakfast—A family-run lodge, close to all area activities. Located within the limits of Lake Placid, in the heart of the beautiful Adirondack Mountains.

Lake Placid *

Johnson, Carol & Roy
15 Interlaken Ave., 12946
(518) 523-3180

Amenities: 1,3,4,5,6,7,8,9,10,
12,15,16,18
Breakfast: F.

Dbl. Oc.: $100.00 - $160.00
Sgl. Oc.: $80.00
Third Person: $40.00

Interlaken Inn And Restaurant—A Victorian inn in the heart of Lake Placid featuring a gourmet restaurant, 12 uniquely decorated rooms and carriage house. The inn has tin ceilings, a cozy fireplace in the living room. Lots of lace and charm. Nearby, you can enjoy golf, skiing and more. Rates include a five-course dinner.

LeRoy

Choquet, Warren M.
7856 Griswold Circle, 14482
(716) 768-2340

Amenities: 2,6,9,10,15,16
Breakfast: C.

Dbl. Oc.: $48.00 - $59.00
Sgl. Oc.: $38.00
Third Person: $11.00

Edson House—Many nearby places to explore: Letchworth State Park (the Grand Canyon of the East); Niagara Falls; Genesee Country Museum; Sonnenberg Gardens in Canandaigua; museums and activities in Rochester; horse racing in Batavia and Hamlin Beach State Park. Private baths.

Mohawk *

Hill, Mary Ann & Jim
RD #1, Box 80, Rte. #28, 13407
(315) 866-1306

Amenities: 1,2,3,5,6,8,9,10,
11,16
Breakfast: F.

Dbl. Oc.: $64.20
Sgl. Oc.: $64.20
Third Person: $10.70
Child: $10.70

Country Hills Bed And Breakfast—An 1860s farmhouse sitting amidst rolling lawns and private woods. Cozy bedroom suites, each with private bath, kitchen, TV, A/C and separate entrance. Upstate New York, off I-90 near Baseball Hall of Fame, Russian Monastery, diamond digging and historic sites. Children welcome.

1. No Smoking	5. Tennis Available	9. Credit Cards Accepted	13. Lunch Available	17. Shared Baths
2. No Pets	6. Golf Available	10. Personal Check Accepted	14. Conference Rooms Avail.	18. Afternoon Tea
3 Off Season Rates	7. Swimmming Avail.	11. Reservations Necessary	15. Group Seminars Avail.	* Commisions given
4. Senior Citizen Rates	8. Skiing Available	12. Dinner Available	16. Private Baths	to Travel Agents

Mt. Tremper

Caselli, Lou
Lascala, Peter
Corner of Rt. 212 & Wittenberg Rd.
P.O. Box 51, 12457
(914) 688-5329

Amenities: 1,2,5,7,8,9,10,16,17
Breakfast: F.
Dbl. Oc.: $65.20 - $97.30
Sgl Oc.: $65.20 - $97.30

Mt. Tremper Inn—Victorian ambience plus museum antiques await you in this 1850, 23-room mansion. Large parlor with fireplace, game/reading room and classical music. Near Woodstock and all ski slopes. No children/pets. Romantic. Elegant. Seen in the *New York Times* and many other feature articles.

Newfane *

Hoy, Peg & Bill
2516 Lockport Olcott Rd., 14108
(716) 778-9843

Amenities: 1,10,11,17,18
Breakfast: C. Plus

Dbl. Oc.: $40.00
Sgl. Oc.: $30.00
Third Person: $15.00
Child: Under 5 yrs. - no charge

Creekside Bed And Breakfast—Large country home. Four large and sunny bedrooms with shared baths. Large patio overlooking the creek for your enjoyment. Non-smoking rooms. Twenty miles from Niagara Falls, thirty miles to Buffalo with theatres, zoo and galleries.

New Lebanon *

Arthur, Michele & Michael
Rt. 22 & Churchill Rd.
P.O. Box 252, 12125
(518) 766-5852

Amenities: 1,3,10,16,17
Breakfast: F.

Dbl. Oc.: $80.00
Sgl. Oc.: $70.00
Third Person: $10.00
Child: $10.00

Churchill House Bed And Breakfast—Historic 1795 colonial on 18 acres. Enjoy the relaxing wrap-around porch with its beautiful view of the Berkshires. Furnished with antiques and feather beds. Fireplace in the guest living room. Minutes to Tanglewood, Shaker Villages, skiing, theatre and shops.

New Paltz *

Maloney, Kathleen
54 Old Ford Rd., 12561
(914) 255-5678

Amenities: 1,2,7,8,10,11,17
Breakfast: F.

Dbl. Oc.: $50.00
Sgl. Oc.: $40.00
Third Person: $10.00
Child: $10.00

"Nana's"—Charming country home. Hiking trails, skiing, horses, swimming, etc. Two rooms with shared bath. Choice of breakfast menu. Children welcome.

1. No Smoking	5. Tennis Available	9. Credit Cards Accepted	13. Lunch Available	17. Shared Baths
2. No Pets	6. Golf Available	10. Personal Check Accepted	14. Conference Rooms Avail.	18. Afternoon Tea
3 Off Season Rates	7. Swimming Avail.	11. Reservations Necessary	15. Group Seminars Avail.	* Commissions given
4. Senior Citizen Rates	8. Skiing Available	12. Dinner Available	16. Private Baths	to Travel Agents

New Rochelle *
Mayetta, Marilou
44 Rose Hill Ave., 10804
(914) 632-6464

Amenities: 10,11,14,17
Breakfast: C. Plus

Dbl. Oc.: $69.75
Sgl. Oc.: $48.25
Third Person: $15.00
Child: Under 6 yrs. - no charge

Rose Hill Guest House—Lovely Tudor residence 1/2 mile from the Hutchinson Pkwy., 30 minutes to New York City or lower Connecticut and 28- minute train ride from New Rochelle station. Enjoy breakfast in the country French dining room or the flower- filled patio. Hostess is a Life Master bridge player.

Parish
House, Frank
RD 2, County Rte. 38, 13131
(315) 625-7665

Amenities: 4,5,6,7,8,10,11, 17
Breakfast: C.

Dbl. Oc.: $42.80
Sgl. Oc.: $31.20
Third Person: $10.70
Child: Under 13 yrs. - no charge

Springbrook Farm Bed And Breakfast—An apartment-like facility with four bedrooms. Each room has a double and a single bed. There is a fully equipped kitchen/lounge. A hot tub/spa is available. Beautiful country just 1-1/2 miles off Interstate 81 and 30 miles from Syracuse, Watertown and Oswego.

Penn Yan
Worth, Evelyn
351 Elm St., 14527
(315) 536-4591

Amenities: 1,2,5,6,7,9,10,16, 17
Breakfast: F.

Dbl. Oc.: $75.00
Sgl. Oc.: $65.00
Third Person: $15.00

Wagener Estate Bed And Breakfast—Casual elegance, hospitality, in a historic home (1790) on four scenic acres. Relax on the veranda in the white wicker. Central to New York's Finger Lakes, wineries, summer sports and antiquing.

Pine City (Elmira/Corning) *
Knapp, William
1016 Sagetown Rd., 14871
(607) 732-0213

Amenities: 1,2,9,10,11,16
Breakfast: F.

Dbl. Oc.: $61.00 - $105.00
Sgl. Oc.: $55.00
Third Person: $5.00
Child: Under 12 yrs. - no charge

Rufus Tanner House—An 1864 Greek Revival farmhouse. Four rooms, one with jacuzzi, one with queen-size bed. Home-made syrup from our trees. Dwarf orchard. In the country yet only 12 minutes from Elmira and 20 minutes from Corning. Mark Twain Museum and Finger Lakes nearby. Great antiquing! Weekend packages.

Pittstown
Towne, Margaret
RD 2, Box 82, 12185
(518) 663-8369, (518) 686) 7331

Amenities: 1,6,7,8,10,14,15, 16,17,18
Breakfast: F.

Dbl. Oc.: $45.00
Sgl. Oc.: $35.00
Child: No charge

Maggie Towne's B&B—Located just off Route 7. Lovely old colonial. Lawns and trees welcome playing children. Twenty miles to historic Bennington, Vermont. Thirty miles to Saratoga. No smoking, please. Enjoy a glass of wine on porch or by the fireplace. Free crib.

1. No Smoking	5. Tennis Available	9. Credit Cards Accepted	13. Lunch Available	17. Shared Baths
2. No Pets	6. Golf Available	10. Personal Check Accepted	14. Conference Rooms Avail.	18. Afternoon Tea
3 Off Season Rates	7. Swimming Avail.	11. Reservations Necessary	15. Group Seminars Avail.	* Commisions given
4. Senior Citizen Rates	8. Skiing Available	12. Dinner Available	16. Private Baths	to Travel Agents

Port Jefferson *

Burk, Kathleen
415 W. Broadway/Route 25A, 11777
(516) 474-1111

Amenities: 2,3,4,7,9,10,11,16,17,18
Breakfast: C.
Dbl. Oc.: $58.00 - $125.00
Sgl Oc: $58.00 - $125.00
Third Person: $10.00

Compass Rose Bed And Breakfast—An old home dating from the 1820's in a historic ship-building village known for its quaint shops and fine dining. It offers rooms and suites with a colonial atmosphere. Cable TV and CAC. Wine and cheese are served every evening in the rose parlor.

Queensbury

Crislip, Joyce & Ned
Ridge Rd.
RD #1, Box 57, 12804
(518) 793-6869

Amenities: 1,5,6,7,8,9,10,11, 16
Breakfast: F.

Dbl. Oc.: $58.85 - $80.25
Sgl. Oc.: $48.15 - $69.55
Child: $10.00

Crislip's Bed And Breakfast—Minutes from Saratoga and Lake George. Spacious accommodations in landmark Federal home. Four-poster beds. Antiques. Once the home of Queensbury's first doctor, who used it as a training center. Great location to see Adirondacks in spring, summer, fall and winter.

Queensbury *

Rudolph, Carolyn
Ridge Rd.
9L - RR#1, Box 70, 12804
(518) 793-4923

Amenities: 1,2,3,7,9,10,11,16
Breakfast: F.
Dbl. Oc.: $69.55 - $80.25
Sgl Oc: $69.55 - $80.25
Third Person: $10.00

Sanford's Ridge Bed And Breakfast—Convenient to historic, cultural and recreational activities, with informal gardens and panoramic Adirondack mountain views. Restored 1790s colonial offers spacious guest rooms furnished with antiques, private baths. Hearty country breakfasts and warm hospitality.

1. No Smoking	5. Tennis Available	9. Credit Cards Accepted	13. Lunch Available	17. Shared Baths
2. No Pets	6. Golf Available	10. Personal Check Accepted	14. Conference Rooms Avail.	18. Afternoon Tea
3 Off Season Rates	7. Swimming Avail.	11. Reservations Necessary	15. Group Seminars Avail.	* Commisions given
4. Senior Citizen Rates	8. Skiing Available	12. Dinner Available	16. Private Baths	to Travel Agents

Rhinebeck *

Kohler, Judy
31 Center St., 12572
(914) 876-8345

Amenities: 1,2,5,6,7,8,9,10,
14,15,16,18
Breakfast: F.

Dbl. Oc.: $196.44 - $280.63
Third Person: $44.90

Village Victorian Inn—Recapture the romance of a Victorian fantasy filled with antiques and laces Quiet elegance with superb accommodations and sumptuous breakfasts. Antiquing, historic mansions and fine dining close by. Just 1-1/2 hours from Manhattan. Come let us pamper you.

Richfield Springs

Watson, Karen & Bruce
23 Prospect St.
Rt. 28 Box 1863, 13439
(315) 858-1870

Amenities: 1,2,3,4,5,6,7,9,10,
14,16
Breakfast: F.

Dbl. Oc.: $59.50
Sgl. Oc.: $31.50
Third Person: $10.90
Child: Under 3 yrs. - no charge

Country Spread Bed And Breakfast—Convenient to Cooperstown and many central New York state attractions. Enjoy warm and casual hospitality in our country - decorated home. Families welcome. Delicious samplings from Karen's kitchen await. Inspected and approved by American B&B Assoc. - three crowns.

Rochester *

Whited, Cynthia
1883 Penfield Rd., Penfield (mail), 14526
(716) 385-3266

Amenities: 2,5,6,7,9,10,11,16
Breakfast: F.
Dbl. Oc.: $83.25 - $105.45
Sgl Oc.: $66.00 - $88.80
Third Person: $16.65

Strawberry Castle—Step back to Victoriana in this classic Italianate mansion. Three acres of lawn, marshland and gardens, private pool and patio are yours. Rooms and suites with private baths in a safe suburban setting. Minutes from fine restaurants and downtown. Make this trip special!

Roscoe

Kinne, Debra & George
Old Rte. 17, 12776
(607) 498-5220

Amenities: 1,2,3,5,6,7,9,10,
11,16,18
Breakfast: C.

Dbl. Oc.: $54.50
Sgl. Oc.: $43.60
Third Person: $10.00
Child: Under 5 yrs. - no charge

Baxter House B&B—Rural country setting. Fishing on the famous Beaverkill River in Trout-Town, USA. Walk to Junction Pool. Circa 1890 house. All rooms have TVs. Fine restaurants and shops within walking distance. Nearby golf, swimming, covered bridge and Catskill Fly Fishing

1. No Smoking	5. Tennis Available	9. Credit Cards Accepted	13. Lunch Available	17. Shared Baths
2. No Pets	6. Golf Available	10. Personal Check Accepted	14. Conference Rooms Avail.	18. Afternoon Tea
3 Off Season Rates	7. Swimmming Avail.	11. Reservations Necessary	15. Group Seminars Avail.	* Commisions given
4. Senior Citizen Rates	8. Skiing Available	12. Dinner Available	16. Private Baths	to Travel Agents

Saratoga Springs *

Benton, Kate
149 Union Ave., 12866
(518) 583-1173

Amenities: 1,2,3,4,5,6,7,8,10,14,15,16,18
Breakfast: F.
Dbl. Oc.: $81.00 - $97.20
Sgl Oc.: $75.60 - $91.80
Third Person: $20.00

Six Sisters Bed And Breakfast—Elegant 1880 Victorian ideally located. Luxurious, immaculate rooms/suites with king beds, air-conditioning. Gourmet breakfast included. Antique furnishings, Orientals. Polished hardwoods. Special packages with mineral baths. SPAC, June home of the NYC opera. Open all year.

Saratoga Springs *

Collins-Breslin, Andrea
200 Wall St., Schuylerville,, 12871
(518) 695-3693

Amenities: 1,2,3,5,6,7,8,9,
  10,11,16,17,18
Breakfast: F.
Dbl. Oc.: $60.00 - $130.00
Sgl Oc.: $60.00 - $130.00
Third Person: $20.00

The Inn On Bacon Hill Bed And Breakfast—Peaceful alternative, 10 minutes from Saratoga Springs. An 1862 Victorian in quiet rural setting. Enjoy beautiful gardens and gazebo or relax in comfortable guest parlor with extensive library. Baby grand piano adorns Victorian parlor suite. Innkeeping courses available.

Saratoga Springs

Melvin, Stephanie & Bob
102 Lincoln Ave.
Box 944, 12866
(518) 587-7613

Amenities: 1,2,3,4,5,6,7,8,9,
  10,14,16,18
Breakfast: C. Plus
Dbl. Oc.: $81.00 - $108.00

The Westchester House—Gracious in-town, Queen Anne Victorian inn. Combines Old-World ambience with up-to-date comforts. Enjoy old-fashioned gardens, piano, extensive library and wrap-around porch. Walk to track, museums, shops and restaurants. Near spa. More than a bed and breakfast.

1. No Smoking	5. Tennis Available	9. Credit Cards Accepted	13. Lunch Available	17. Shared Baths
2. No Pets	6. Golf Available	10. Personal Check Accepted	14. Conference Rooms Avail.	18. Afternoon Tea
3 Off Season Rates	7. Swimmming Avail.	11. Reservations Necessary	15. Group Seminars Avail.	* Commisions given
4. Senior Citizen Rates	8. Skiing Available	12. Dinner Available	16. Private Baths	to Travel Agents

NEW YORK

Saratoga Springs

Siefker, Gregg
Parker, Sheila
365 Broadway, 12866
(518) 587-4688

Amenities: 9,10,16
Breakfast: C.

Dbl. Oc.: $75.00
Sgl. Oc.: $75.00

Adelphi Hotel—A small Victorian hotel with the charm of a country inn. The Adelphi is located in the historic section of Saratoga. All rooms are lavishly decorated and furnished with antiques. Restaurants and shopping within walking distance.

Severance

Wildman, Helen
Sawmill Rd.
P.O. Box 125, 12872
(518) 532-7734

Amenities: 1,5,6,7,10,11,16, 17
Breakfast: F.

Dbl. Oc.: $55.00 - $65.00
Sgl. Oc.: $35.00
Third Person: $15.00
Child: Under 2 yrs. - no charge

The Bed House B&B—Adirondack farmhouse one mile east of Exit 28 on I-87. Located on bank of Paradox Brook with 150 acres of land on Paradox Lake. Sand beach, boating, tennis, fishing, sailing on property. Four miles from Schroon Lake, 16 miles from Fort Ticonderoga and ferry to Vermont.

Skaneateles

Samuels, Elaine
4987 Kingston Rd.,
Elbridge, 13060 (mail)
(315) 689-2082

Amenities: 1,3,5,6,7,8,10,11, 17
Breakfast: C. Plus

Dbl. Oc.: $53.50
Sgl. Oc.: $42.80
Third Person: $10.70
Child: Over 10 yrs. - $10.70

Cozy Cottage Guest House—Country ranch. Clean, cozy, comfortable. Seven minutes to Skaneateles, 15 minutes to Auburn, 20 minutes to Syracuse. Orchards, berries and flowers abound. Near Lake Cruise, antiques, shops, state fair, skiing, museums, golf, university, arts and crafts. Friendly and casual hostess.

Southold *

Mooney-Getoff, Mary
1475 Waterview Dr., 11971
(516) 765-3356

Amenities: 1,4,5,6,7,16,17, 18
Breakfast: F.

Dbl. Oc.: $75.00 - $80.00
Sgl. Oc.: $55.00 - $60.00
Child: 6 - 12yrs. - $20.00

Goose Creek Guesthouse—A spacious pre-Civil War farmhouse on the creek. Surrounded by six wooded acres. We are a resort area near ferries to Montauk via Shelter Island and the ferry to New London.

---

1. No Smoking	5. Tennis Available	9. Credit Cards Accepted	13. Lunch Available	17. Shared Baths
2. No Pets	6. Golf Available	10. Personal Check Accepted	14. Conference Rooms Avail.	18. Afternoon Tea
3 Off Season Rates	7. Swimmming Avail.	11. Reservations Necessary	15. Group Seminars Avail.	* Commisions given
4. Senior Citizen Rates	8. Skiing Available	12. Dinner Available	16. Private Baths	to Travel Agents

Stanfordville *

Kohler, Judy
Shelley Hill Rd., 12581
(914) 266-8093

Amenities: 1,2,6,7,8,9,10,14, 15,16,18
Breakfast: F.

Dbl. Oc.: $196.44 - $392.88
Third Person: $44.90

Lakehouse Inn On Golden Pond—An enchanting lake-front sanctuary in the Hudson River Valley. Swimming, boating and fishing. Suites with jacuzzi tubs for two, wood-burning fireplaces, private decks and stunning views of the lake and woods. Gourmet breakfasts and afternoon appetizers.

Stony Brook

Roberts, Mrs. Nelson
1 Lilacs Dr., 11790-1416
(516) 751-0928

Amenities: 2,5,6,7,10,11,16
Breakfast: C.
Dbl. Oc.: $65.00
Sgl Oc.: $55.00

Twin Oaks—Just one mile from the Long Island Railroad and the State University. Restaurants and shops within walking distance. Museums and theatre nearby. Walk to beach. Quiet area. Private entrance. Air conditioned, telephone and television.

Syracuse *

Edwardsen, Lori & Scott
Two Main St., Camillus,13031(mail)
(315) 672-9276

Amenities: 2,5,6,7,8,9,10,12, 13,14,16
Breakfast: C.

Dbl. Oc.: $67.00 - $140.00
Sgl. Oc.: $67.00 - $140.00

Green Gate Inn—Beautifully restored Victorian inn located in the Finger Lakes region. Six charming guest rooms complete with jacuzzis or saunas. Fine dining in casual elegance. Village setting minutes from Syracuse and area attractions.

Syracuse *

Gero, Bernard
1402 James St., 13203
(315) 476-6541

Amenities: 1,2,3,5,6,8,10,14, 15,16,17,18
Breakfast: F.

Dbl. Oc.: $56,00

Benedict House—The house was designed by Ward Wellington, the leading architect of the arts-and-craft movement at the turn of the century. Spacious rooms, two to five miles from major highways, Syracuse University, LeMoyne College, malls, etc. Air- conditioned guest rooms with TVs.

1. No Smoking	5. Tennis Available	9. Credit Cards Accepted	13. Lunch Available	17. Shared Baths
2. No Pets	6. Golf Available	10. Personal Check Accepted	14. Conference Rooms Avail.	18. Afternoon Tea
3 Off Season Rates	7. Swimmming Avail.	11. Reservations Necessary	15. Group Seminars Avail.	* Commisions given
4. Senior Citizen Rates	8. Skiing Available	12. Dinner Available	16. Private Baths	to Travel Agents

Utica *

Kilgore, Shirley & Roy
16 Derbyshire Pl., 13501-4706
(315) 732-6720, (800) 446-1456

Amenities: 1,2,4,9,10,11,16,
17
Breakfast: F.

Dbl. Oc.: $49.05 - $65.40
Sgl. Oc.: $38.15 - $54.50
Third Person: $16.35

The Iris Stonehouse Bed And Breakfast—City charm, close to everything. Stone Tudor with lead glass windows. Central air. guest sitting room with fireplace, TV, games, reading and relaxing. Full breakfast from menu. Transportation available at local airport and Syracuse airport, train or bus.

Vernon *

Degni, Rosabel
RD #1, Box 325, 13476
(315) 829-2440

Amenities: 2,3,4,10,12,16,18
Breakfast: F.

Dbl. Oc.: $70.85
Sgl. Oc.: $59.95
Third Person: $21.80
Child: $21.80

Lavender Inn—This 1799 Federal-style home offers rest for the weary traveler. Set on five acres of perennial and annual gardens, this inn offers comfort and privacy with a full, hearty breakfast to start the day. Attractions include antiques, historic sites and seasonal leisure.

Warrensburg *

Carrington, Florence & Ken
2 Hudson St., 12885
(518) 623-2449

Amenities: 5,6,7,8,9,10,11,12,
13,14,15,16,18
Breakfast: F.

Dbl. Oc.: $95.00
Sgl. Oc.: $75.00
Third Person: $20.00

The Merrill Magee House—A historic house in the heart of an Adirondack village known for antiquing and year-round outdoor recreation. Luxurious rooms. Fine dining. Cozy pub. Secluded garden. Outdoor pool and jacuzzi. Five-person family suite available - $150.00.

Warrensburg *

Parisi, Stephen
HCR #1
227 Hickory Hill Rd., 12885
(518) 623-2207

Amenities: 2,10,11,16,17
Breakfast: F.

Dbl. Oc.: $55.64
Sgl. Oc.: $44.94
Third Person: $13.91

Country Road Lodge—Quiet, idyllic setting in a clearing along the Hudson River at the end of a country road. No traffic or TV. Near Lake George and garage-sale country. Hiking trails. Great for bird watchers. Full meal. Winter weekend and spring and summer birding packages.

1. No Smoking	5. Tennis Available	9. Credit Cards Accepted	13. Lunch Available	17. Shared Baths
2. No Pets	6. Golf Available	10. Personal Check Accepted	14. Conference Rooms Avail.	18. Afternoon Tea
3 Off Season Rates	7. Swimming Avail.	11. Reservations Necessary	15. Group Seminars Avail.	* Commisions given
4. Senior Citizen Rates	8. Skiing Available	12. Dinner Available	16. Private Baths	to Travel Agents

NEW YORK

Westhampton Beach *

Collins, Elsie
2 Seafield Lane, 11978
(800) 346-3290, (516) 288-1559

Amenities: 1,2,3,5,6,7,9,10,
11,14,15,16,18
Breakfast: F.
Dbl. Oc.: $108.00 - $216.00
Third Person: $64.80
Child: Under 5 yrs. - no charge

1880 House—A hidden 100-year-old bed and breakfast country retreat that is the perfect place for a romantic hideaway, a weekend of privacy or just a change of pace from city life. The Seafield estate includes a short brick walk to the ocean beach and outstanding restaurants.

Wevertown *

Cole, Douglas
Rte. 28, Glenn-Dillon Rd.
P.O. Box A, 12886
(518) 251-2194, (800) 950-2194

Amenities: 3,5,6,7,8,9,10,11,
12,16
Breakfast: F.

Dbl. Oc.: $50.00 - $75.00
Sgl. Oc.: $25.00 - $37.50

Mountainaire Adventures—Located in Adirondack Park near Saratoga, Lake George and Gore Mountain ski area. Complimentary hot drink, sauna and hot tub. Beer and wine served. Ski, raft, canoe, fish and hike. Bike rentals, clinics and guided trips. Fun and relaxation for the whole family. Chalet rental.

Windham *

Seidel, Lorraine
Rte. 23 W.
P.O. Box 700, 12496
(518) 734-4079

Amenities: 2,5,6,7,8,9,10,11,
14,15,16,17
Breakfast: F.

Dbl. Oc.: Up to $80.25
Sgl. Oc.: Up to $80.25
Third Person: $15.00

Country Suite Bed And Breakfast—Gracious Victorian farmhouse furnished with family heirlooms. Fireplace in parlor. Fine restaurants nearby. Two miles from ski Windham in the Catskill mountains. Antiquing and hiking. A note worthy luxury.

---

1. No Smoking
2. No Pets
3 Off Season Rates
4. Senior Citizen Rates

5. Tennis Available
6. Golf Available
7. Swimmming Avail.
8. Skiing Available

9. Credit Cards Accepted
10. Personal Check Accepted
11. Reservations Necessary
12. Dinner Available

13. Lunch Available
14. Conference Rooms Avail.
15. Group Seminars Avail.
16. Private Baths

17. Shared Baths
18. Afternoon Tea
* Commisions given
to Travel Agents

NORTH CAROLINA

The Tar Heel State

Capitol: Raleigh
Statehood: November 21, 1789; the 12 state
State Motto: "To Be, Rather Than To Seem"
State Song: "The Old North State"
State Bird: Cardinal
State Flower: Flowering Dogwood
State Tree: Pine

The brown gold of the ripe tobacco leaf has made North Carolina prosperous and the leading grower of tobacco in our country. Nothing is more exciting to the tobacco farmer than to take his product to town and listen to the auctioneer canting his tobacco prices.

Another prosperous industry in the state is furniture. From the early settlers' own pine trees and pioneering style, came perfect pieces of furniture and the beginning of what became another prosperous industry for North Carolina.

Situated along the Atlantic seacoast, tourists can enjoy swimming as well as visiting the beautiful gardens, historical battlefields and gracious southern mansions.

The first airplane flight by the Wright Brothers took place at Kitty Hawk and both presidents Andrew Johnson and James Polk were born in this state.

NORTH CAROLINA

Asheville *

Adams, Milli & Edward
217 Patton Mtn. Rd., 28804
(704) 252-9219

Amenities: 1,2,9,10,16,18
Breakfast: F.

Dbl. Oc.: $84.80 - $100.70
Sgl. Oc.: $74.20 - $90.10
Third Person: $15.90

Cairn Brae—A mountain retreat nestled on four wooded acres above Asheville. Wooded trails, beautiful views, gracious hospitality, scenic terrace, quiet and secluded. Only minutes from downtown. Children over five welcome.

Asheville *

Colby, Ann & Everett
230 Pearson Dr., 28801
(704) 253-5644, (800) 982-2118

Amenities: 1,2,5,6,7,8,9,10,
11,16,18
Breakfast: F.

Dbl. Oc.: $79.50 - $100.70
Third Person: $20.00

The Colby House—An elegant and charming Dutch Tudor in the Montford historic district. Each guest room has unique decor with queen beds and private baths. There are beautiful gardens, an outdoor porch and inviting fireplaces. Truly a special place.

Asheville

Faber, Helen & Fred
100 Reynolds Heights, 28804
(704) 254-0496

Amenities: 2,7,10,16,17,18
Breakfast: C. Plus
Dbl. Oc.: $50.00 - $95.00
Sgl Oc.: $45.00 - $85.00
Third Person: $17.00
Child: Over 6 yrs. - $17.00

The Old Reynold Mansion—A bed and breakfast in a circa 1855 antebellum mansion. Beautifully restored with furnishings from a bygone era. A country setting amidst acres of trees and mountains. Wood-burning fireplaces. Verandas. Pool. Listed in the National Register of Historic Places.

Asheville *

Fain, Karin & Sam
177 Cumberland Ave., 28801
(704) 254-3608

Amenities: 1,2,5,6,9,10,16
Breakfast: F.

Dbl. Oc.: $81.75 - $92.65
Sgl. Oc.: $70.85
Third Person: $21.80
Child: Under 13 yrs. - $10.90

Carolina Bed And Breakfast—A warm and comfortable turn-of-the-century home conveniently located in the historic Montford district. Charming guest rooms with antiques and collectibles. Seven fireplaces, two porches and acres of beautiful gardens. Truly a home-away-from-home.

1. No Smoking	5. Tennis Available	9. Credit Cards Accepted	13. Lunch Available	17. Shared Baths
2. No Pets	6. Golf Available	10. Personal Check Accepted	14. Conference Rooms Avail.	18. Afternoon Tea
3 Off Season Rates	7. Swimming Avail.	11. Reservations Necessary	15. Group Seminars Avail.	* Commisions given
4. Senior Citizen Rates	8. Skiing Available	12. Dinner Available	16. Private Baths	to Travel Agents

NORTH CAROLINA

Asheville *
Hotch, Ripley
296 Montford Ave., 28801
(704) 254-9569

Amenities: 1,2,6,7,8,9,10,11, 16,18
Breakfast: F.
Dbl. Oc.: $100.00 - $120.00

The Inn On Montford—A turn-of-the-century arts-and-crafts-style house in the heart of the historic district. An airy and light-filled setting for the owners' collection of fine antiques, Oriental rugs and porcelain. Whirlpool baths, fireplaces and full breakfast.

Asheville
McEwan, Barbara
674 Biltmore Ave., 28803
(704) 252-1389, (800) 252-0310

Amenities: 1,2,3,9,10,16,17, 18
Breakfast: C. Plus
Dbl. Oc.: $82.00 - $130.00
Sgl. Oc.: $76.00 - $125.00
Third Person: $15.00

Cedar Crest Victorian Inn—An 1890 Queen Anne mansion listed in the National Register of Historic Places. Lavish interior, carved-oak paneling and authentic period decor. Gardens, croquet, fireplaces, suites, even breakfast in bed! 1/4 mile from the Biltmore House. Opulence to nourish the senses.

Asheville *
Michel, Susan
87 Richmond Hill Dr., 28806
(704) 252-7313

Amenities: 1,2,9,11,12,13,14, 15,16
Breakfast: F.
Dbl. Oc.: $104.00 - $256.00
Sgl. Oc.: $104.00 - $256.00
Third Person: $15.00

Richmond Hill Inn—Enjoy the charm and luxury of a century-old Victorian estate with spectacular mountain views. There are 21 elegant guest rooms, each with a private bath and many with fireplaces. Savor American and nouvelle cuisine in our gourmet restaurant.

Asheville *
Spradley, Karen & Andy
53 Saint Dunstans Rd., 28803
(704) 253-3525

Amenities: 1,3,9,10,11,13,16
Breakfast: F.
Dbl. Oc.: $84.80 - $100.70
Sgl. Oc.: $68.90
Third Person: $15.90
Child: Under 5 yrs. - no charge

Corner Oak Manor—This lovely English Tudor home is surrounded by oak, maple and pine trees. It is decorated with antiques, weavings and many fine hand-crafted items. The outdoor jacuzzi, fireplace, baby grand piano and full gourmet breakfast.

Asheville
Turcot, Marge
119 Dodge St., 28803
(704) 274-1604

Amenities: 2,5,6,7,9,10,11,16, 17
Breakfast: C.
Dbl. Oc.: $50.00 - $70.00
Sgl. Oc.: $45.00 - $65.00
Third Person: $5.00
Child: Under 2 yrs. - no charge

Reed House—A comfortable 1892 Queen Anne Victorian near the Biltmore estate. A working fireplace in every room. Breakfast on the porch. Relaxing rocking chairs everywhere. Children welcome. Listed in the National Register of Historic Places. The Reed House is a local historic property.

1. No Smoking	5. Tennis Available	9. Credit Cards Accepted	13. Lunch Available	17. Shared Baths
2. No Pets	6. Golf Available	10. Personal Check Accepted	14. Conference Rooms Avail.	18. Afternoon Tea
3 Off Season Rates	7. Swimming Avail.	11. Reservations Necessary	15. Group Seminars Avail.	* Commisions given
4. Senior Citizen Rates	8. Skiing Available	12. Dinner Available	16. Private Baths	to Travel Agents

NORTH CAROLINA

Asheville *

Vogel, Lynn, Marion & Rick
100 & 116 Flint St., 28801
(704) 253-6723

Amenities: 2,9,10,16
Breakfast: F.

Dbl. Oc.: $87.20
Sgl. Oc.: $70.85

Flint Street Inns—Two lovely old family homes offering the best in bed and breakfast accommodations. Charming guest rooms, some with fireplaces and all with air-conditioning. The inns are within a comfortable walking distance of shops and restaurants. A full southern-style breakfast is served.

Asheville *

Young, Maryanne
Poole, Susan
62 Cumberland Circle, 28801
(704) 254-2244

Amenities: 1,2,5,7,9,10,16,
18
Breakfast: F.

Dbl. Oc.: $81.75 - $109.00
Sgl. Oc.: $76.30 - $103.55
Third Person: $16.35
Child: Over 11 yrs. - $16.35

Applewood Manor—A turn-of-the-century colonial revival home on two secluded acres in the historic district. Furnished with antiques, fine linens and lace. Most rooms have balconies and fireplaces. Come and romance yourselves with a stay.

Asheville (Weaverville)

Gibson, Mary Lou & Paul
26 Brown St., 28787
(704) 658-3899

Amenities: 1,2,6,8,9,10,15,
16
Breakfast: F.

Dbl. Oc.: $65.40
Sgl. Oc.: $54.50
Third Person: $10.90
Child: Under 2 yrs. - no charge

Dry Ridge Inn—A historic farmhouse 10 minutes north of Asheville. Large guest rooms with country antiques and handmade quilts. Gift shop features local arts and crafts. Friendly, small-town atmosphere. Close to shopping, attractions and the Blue Ridge Parkway.

Balsam

Kellam, Jennifer & Steven
Valley Rd., 28707
(704) 456-6528

Amenities: 1,2,6,8,10,11,
12,13,16,17
Breakfast: C.
Dbl. Oc.: $57.00
Sgl Oc.: $57.00
Third Person: $10.00
Child: Under 8 yrs. - $7.00

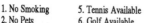

Balsam Lodge Bed And Breakfast—One mile from Blue Ridge Parkway. The house and restored train depot retain the charm of yesteryear. Restaurants and shops close by. Maggie Valley and Biltmore are among the local attractions. Scrumptious continental breakfast starts the day.

1. No Smoking	5. Tennis Available	9. Credit Cards Accepted	13. Lunch Available	17. Shared Baths
2. No Pets	6. Golf Available	10. Personal Check Accepted	14. Conference Rooms Avail.	18. Afternoon Tea
3 Off Season Rates	7. Swimmming Avail.	11. Reservations Necessary	15. Group Seminars Avail.	* Commisions given
4. Senior Citizen Rates	8. Skiing Available	12. Dinner Available	16. Private Baths	to Travel Agents

NORTH CAROLINA

Balsam *

Teasley, Merrily
P.O. Box 40
Balsam Mountain Inn Rd., 28707
(704) 456-9498

Amenities: 2,3,4,9,10,12,13,14,15,16
Breakfast: F.
Dbl. Oc.: $87.20
Sgl Oc: $81.90
Third Person: $16.35
Child: Under 2 yrs. - no charge

Balsam Mountain Inn—Magical enchantment awaits you at historic Balsam Mountain Inn, secreted away between three of the Blue Ridge's loftiest peaks. Rest, read, ramble, romp and revel in the easy-going hospitality of our southern mountain. Plump pillows and thick comforters inspire dreams.

Beaufort *

Johnson, Sue & Joe
116 Queen St., 28516
(919) 728-6733

Amenities: 1,2,3,9,10,16
Breakfast: C. Plus

Dbl. Oc.: $88.00 - $120.00
Sgl. Oc.: $78.00 - $110.00
Third Person: $15.00

Pecan Tree Inn—Antique-filled, recently renovated 1866 Victorian home featuring seven beautiful air-conditioned guest rooms. Located in the heart of the historic district, 1/2 block from the waterfront. Beaufort retains the charm and tranquility of the past. Offers many attractions.

Beaufort *

Kwaak, William
305 Front St., 28516
(919) 728-7036

Amenities: 1,2,3,4,5,6,7,10,
11,14,15,16
Breakfast: F.

Dbl. Oc.: $90.00 - $150.00
Sgl. Oc.: $45.00
Third Person: $15.00

The Cedars Inn—Circa 1768. This former home of a shipbuilder stands among a grove of ancient cedars in this historic seaport town on the outer banks of North Carolina. Many sights and activities are available to the traveler.

Beaufort

Ross, Kay & Philip
217 Turner St., 28516
(919) 728-4300

Amenities: 1,2,3,4,5,6,7,9,
10,16
Breakfast: C. Plus

Dbl. Oc.: $85.69
Sgl. Oc.: $85.69301
Third Person: $12.00

Delamar Inn—Located in the historic town of Beaufort, The inn, built in 1866, offers three antique-furnished guest rooms. Stroll to the harbor, shops and museum. A short drive to the beach, Fort Macon or the outer banks ferry. The inn is on Beaufort's '92 Historic Homes Tour.

1. No Smoking	5. Tennis Available	9. Credit Cards Accepted	13. Lunch Available	17. Shared Baths
2. No Pets	6. Golf Available	10. Personal Check Accepted	14. Conference Rooms Avail.	18. Afternoon Tea
3 Off Season Rates	7. Swimmming Avail.	11. Reservations Necessary	15. Group Seminars Avail.	* Commisions given
4. Senior Citizen Rates	8. Skiing Available	12. Dinner Available	16. Private Baths	to Travel Agents

Beech Mountain

Archer, Bonny & Joe
Rte. 2, Box 56-A, 28604
(704) 898-9004

Amenities: 2,3,5,6,7,8,9,12, 15,16
Breakfast: F.

Dbl. Oc.: $74.20 - $132.50
Sgl. Oc.: $74.20 - $132.50
Third Person: $8.48
Child: $8.48

Archers Inn—Perched on the side of Beech Mountain overlooking the surrounding mountains and valley. Fourteen guest rooms, all with fireplaces and either a porch or a deck. Eleven rooms have a long-range view, one a private hot tub. Common area hot tub in summer. Post and beam construction.

Belhaven

Smith, Axson
600 E. Main St., 27810
(919) 943-2151,
(800) 346-2151 (in N. Carolina)

Amenities: 2,4,5,7,9,10,11,12,14,15,16
Breakfast: C.
Dbl. Oc.: $47.70 - $79.50
Sgl Oc.: $47.70 - $79.50
Third Person: $10.60
Child: Under 6 yrs. - no charge

River Forest Manor Country Inn—Built in 1897 and operated as a country inn since 1947. World-famous buffet smorgasbord with over 65 dishes each night. All rooms have a Victorian decor with modern facilities. Come and enjoy our fine food, pool and jacuzzi. Located on the waterfront.

Black Mountain *

Colbert, June Bergeron
718 W. Old Hwy. 70, 28711
(704) 669-6528, (800) 735-6128

Amenities: 1,2,5,6,10,16
Breakfast: F.
Dbl. Oc.: $65.40 - $76.30
Sgl Oc.: $65.40 - $76.30
Third Person: $10.90

Black Mountain Inn—Turn-of-the-century mountain home nestled on three acres, a restful retreat for body and soul. Small and intimate, Black Mountain Inn embraces its guests with long-forgotten hospitality and charm. Full breakfast buffet.

---

1. No Smoking	5. Tennis Available	9. Credit Cards Accepted	13. Lunch Available	17. Shared Baths
2. No Pets	6. Golf Available	10. Personal Check Accepted	14. Conference Rooms Avail.	18. Afternoon Tea
3 Off Season Rates	7. Swimmming Avail.	11. Reservations Necessary	15. Group Seminars Avail.	* Commisions given
4. Senior Citizen Rates	8. Skiing Available	12. Dinner Available	16. Private Baths	to Travel Agents

Black Mountain *

Headley, Wilhelmina K.
North Fork Rd.
Rte. 1, Box 269, 27040
(704) 669-6762

Amenities: 1,2,5,6,7,10,16
Breakfast: F.

Dbl. Oc.: $48.60 - $64.80
Sgl. Oc.: $43.20 - $54.00
Third Person: $10.00
Child: $10.00

Bed And Breakfast Over Yonder—Secluded on 18 acres of mountainside with views of highest peaks in the East. Wildflower gardens surround breakfast porch. Near Biltmore estate, B.R. Parkway, antique shops, hiking trails, gem mining and white-water rafting.

Boone *

Probinsky, Dr. Jean
209 Meadowview Dr., 28607
(704) 262-3670

Amenities: 1,5,6,7,8,9,10,11,
15,17
Breakfast: C. Plus

Dbl. Oc.: $50.00 - $75.00
Sgl. Oc.: $40.00
Third Person: $10.00

Grandma Jean's Bed And Breakfast—Old-fashioned, country-style southern hospitalty in charming 65-year-old country farmhouse, yet within town limits. Minutes to most scenic attractions and restaurants. In the heart of Blue Ridge Mountains and Parkway, near Grandfather Mountain and Tweetsie Railroad. Great location.

Brevard

Ong, Lyn
412 W. Probart St., 28712
(704) 884-9349

Amenities: 1,2,3,9,11,16,17,
18
Breakfast: F.

Dbl. Oc.: $51.23 - $62.13
Sgl. Oc.: $44.69 - $54.50
Child: Over 12 yrs. - $10.90

The Red House—Built in 1851, this B&B has been lovingly restored and furnished with family antiques. Come by and relax on our porch in the mountains.

Charlotte *

Armstrong, Bill
1122 E. Morehead, 28204
(704) 376-3357

Amenities: 2,3,4,9,10,14,15,
16
Breakfast: C.

Dbl. Oc.: $70.00 - $95.00
Sgl. Oc.: $70.00 - $95.00
Third Person: $10.00
Child: Under 10 yrs. - no charge

Morehead Inn—A southern estate endowed with quiet elegance. Spacious public areas with intimate fireplaces. Luxurious private rooms furnished with English and American antiques. Just minutes from uptown Charlotte in historic Dillworth.

1. No Smoking	5. Tennis Available	9. Credit Cards Accepted	13. Lunch Available	17. Shared Baths
2. No Pets	6. Golf Available	10. Personal Check Accepted	14. Conference Rooms Avail.	18. Afternoon Tea
3 Off Season Rates	7. Swimmming Avail.	11. Reservations Necessary	15. Group Seminars Avail.	* Commisions given
4. Senior Citizen Rates	8. Skiing Available	12. Dinner Available	16. Private Baths	to Travel Agents

Charlotte *

Dyer, Janet & Rob
6221 Amos Smith Rd., 28214
(704) 399-6299

Amenities: 1,2,3,5,6,7,9,10,16
Breakfast: F.
Dbl. Oc.: $50.00 - $80.00
Sgl Oc: $50.00 - $80.00

Still Waters—A log house on two wooded acres featuring deck, garden, a boat ramp, slips, sport court and gazebo. Full breakfast served on glassed-in porch. Good access to I-85, I-77 and Billy Graham Parkway. Just 20 minutes from downtown and 10 minutes from the airport.

Charlotte *

Mastny, Joan
2145 E. 5th St., 28204
(704) 358-1368

Amenities: 1,2,9,10,11,16
Breakfast: C. Plus

Dbl. Oc.: $64.96 - $87.36
Sgl. Oc.: $61.60 - $78.40

The Elizabeth Bed And Breakfast—A 1927 home in Charlotte's second-oldest suburb. Both the garden room and the guest cottage feature antiques, decorator linens, telephone, air-conditioning and private courtyard entrances. Restaurants and shops within walking distance.

Charlotte

McElhinney, Mary & Jim
10533 Fairway Ridge Rd., 28277
(704) 846-0783

Amenities: 2,9,10,16
Breakfast: C.

Dbl. Oc.: $65.00
Sgl. Oc.: $55.00
Third Person: $10.00
Child: Under 2 yrs. - no charge

McElhinney House—Welcomes American and international guests. French-, German and Italian speaking host. Quiet residential area. Close to arboretum, fine restaurants, museums and hospitals. Minutes from three golf courses. Lounge, cable TV and barbeque included. Convenient to I-77 and I-85.

Clyde *

Livengood, Donna
120 Ferguson Ridge, 28721
(704) 627-6111

Amenities: 1,2,5,6,7,9,10,11, 16
Breakfast: F.

Dbl. Oc.: $98.10 - $152.60
Sgl. Oc.: $88.29 - $93.20
Third Person: $20.00

Windsong: A Mountain Inn—For a romantic interlude, a secluded contemporary log inn with breathtaking views of the Smoky Mountains. Large, bright rooms, fireplaces, tubs for two. Billiards, swimming, tennis, hiking. Llama trekking. Closed January. Also new two- bedroom deluxe log guest house available.

1. No Smoking	5. Tennis Available	9. Credit Cards Accepted	13. Lunch Available	17. Shared Baths
2. No Pets	6. Golf Available	10. Personal Check Accepted	14. Conference Rooms Avail.	18. Afternoon Tea
3 Off Season Rates	7. Swimmming Avail.	11. Reservations Necessary	15. Group Seminars Avail.	* Commisions given
4. Senior Citizen Rates	8. Skiing Available	12. Dinner Available	16. Private Baths	to Travel Agents

Durham *

Ryan, Barbara
106 Mason Rd., 27712
(919) 477-8430

Amenities: 1,2,5,6,7,9,10,14, 15,16,17,18
Breakfast: F.

Dbl. Oc.: $72.15 - $137.00
Sgl. Oc.: $66.60 - $133.20
Third Person: $10.80
Child: $5.00

Arrowhead Inn—A restored 1775 manor, carriage house and log cabin on four rural acres. Six private baths and two shared baths. Home baking and preserving. Close to Duke University, historic attractions, Life and Science Museum, Treyburn, hiking, sports activities. Seven miles to I-85.

Edentown

Dunne, Margaret & Kenneth
108 So. Granville St., 27932
(919) 482-5296

Amenities: 1,2,5,6,10,11,16
Breakfast: F.

Dbl. Oc.: $103.55
Sgl. Oc.: $76.30

Granville Queen Inn—Romantic getaway in historic district of two-century town undamaged by Civil and Revolutionary Wars. Nine themed rooms with garden, tubs, patios and fireplaces. Five- course gourmet breakfast. Not suitable for children. Town and restaurants within walking distance. Evening wine.

Franklin *

Allen, Dodie
238 E. Hickory Knoll Rd., 28734
(704) 524-9666

Amenities: 3,10,16
Breakfast: F.

Dbl. Oc.: $59.95 - $70.85
Sgl. Oc.: $59.95 - $70.85
Third Person: $10.90
Child: Under 12 yrs. - $8.72

Hickory Knoll Lodge—Located high and secluded in the Great Smoky Mountains. Enjoy hiking in pristine woodlands, fishing for trout on premises or relaxing on our big front porch. King- and queen-sized beds with jacuzzi baths in over-sized rooms. Year-round.

Franklin *

Oehser, Mary
190 Georgia Rd., 28734
(704) 369-8985

Amenities: 10,16,17
Breakfast: F.

Dbl. Oc.: $54.50 - $69.80
Sgl. Oc.: $48.60
Third Person: $10.00
Child: 3 - 6 yrs. - $5.00

Buttonwood Inn—A small mountain inn with a cozy country feeling filled with antiques, quilts and collectibles. Enjoy a country to gourmet breakfast before gem mining, hiking, golfing, shopping or just relaxing on the deck. Your comfort and satisfaction is this inn's pleasure.

Grassy Creek

Winston, Gayle
Rt. 1, Box 121-A, 28631
(919) 982-2109

Amenities: 6,7,8,9,10,11,12, 13,14,15,16
Breakfast: F.

Dbl. Oc.: $81.75 & $103.55
Sgl. Oc.: $65.40 & $87.20
Third Person: $16.35

River House—Located on the north fork of the scenic New River in Ashe County. Nine rooms for overnight guests. Situated on 2/3 mile of river front, 125 acres, hiking trails, beautiful views, rocking chairs and porches. Open year round. Superb cuisine in full service restuarant.

1. No Smoking	5. Tennis Available	9. Credit Cards Accepted	13. Lunch Available	17. Shared Baths
2. No Pets	6. Golf Available	10. Personal Check Accepted	14. Conference Rooms Avail.	18. Afternoon Tea
3 Off Season Rates	7. Swimmming Avail.	11. Reservations Necessary	15. Group Seminars Avail.	* Commisions given
4. Senior Citizen Rates	8. Skiing Available	12. Dinner Available	16. Private Baths	to Travel Agents

NORTH CAROLINA

Greensboro *

Green, JoAnne
205 No. Park Dr., 27401
(919) 274-6350, (800) 535-9363

Amenities: 2,3,5,6,7,9,10,11, 16,18
Breakfast: C. Plus

Dbl. Oc.: $59.40 - $81.00
Sgl. Oc.: $43.60 - $54.00
Third Person: $10.80

Greenwood—A 1905 home in the central historic district. Lovingly restored. Five guest rooms, guest kitchen, TV room and pool. Elegant decor with paintings and wood carvings from around the world. Park at our front door. Homemade breakfast features fresh squeezed-orange juice.

Henderson *

Cornell, Jean & Dick
Rte. 3, Box 610, 27536
(919) 438-2421

Amenities: 1,2,6,7,9,10,11, 16
Breakfast: F.

Dbl. Oc.: $92.05
Sgl. Oc.: $81.45

La Grange Plantation Inn—Nationally registered 18th-century plantation house on Kerr Lake. Near Virginia border. Award-winning restoration recognized by the National Trust for Historic Preservation. Five elegantly decorated and furnished rooms with private baths. Five miles from I-85.

Hendersonville *

Pacilio, Vicki & Dennis
755 No. Main St., 28792
(704) 697-7778,
(800) 225-4700, Fax: (704)697-8664

Amenities: 2,3,5,9,10,11,15, 16
Breakfast: F.

Dbl. Oc.: $63.00 - $89.00
Sgl. Oc.: $55.00 - $79.00
Third Person: $10.00
Child: Under 6 yrs. - no charge

Claddagh Inn At Hendersonville—A classic revival Victorian inn in the National Register and AAA approved. Fourteen guest rooms with private baths, TV, phone and air-conditioning. Within walking distance to shopping and restaurants in historic downtown Hendersonville. Open year-round.

Hertford

Harnisch, Jenny
103 So. Church St., 27944
(919) 426-5809

Amenities: 1,2,9,10,16
Breakfast: F.

Dbl. Oc.: $47.70
Sgl. Oc.: $37.10
Third Person: $10.60

Gingerbread Inn And Bakery, Inc.—On Business 17, 65 miles south of Norfolk. Restored early 1900 home with large rooms, king and queen beds, central air-conditioning, HBO, TV. Free to our guests, are gingerbread-boy souvenirs. Try our continental pastries.

Highlands

Alley, Donna & Chris
Rte.1, Box 22B, 28741
(704) 526-2060

Amenities: 1,2,3,9,10,11,16, 18
Breakfast: F.

Dbl. Oc.: $70.00 - $85.00
Sgl. Oc.: $60.00
Third Person: $10.00

Colonial Pines Inn—A charming country inn on two acres. Large porch with views. Cozy parlor with fireplace and grand piano. Homemade breads are a specialty. Close to great shopping, dining and waterfalls. Separate guest house with fireplace and view. Open all year.

---

1. No Smoking
2. No Pets
3 Off Season Rates
4. Senior Citizen Rates

5. Tennis Available
6. Golf Available
7. Swimming Avail.
8. Skiing Available

9. Credit Cards Accepted
10. Personal Check Accepted
11. Reservations Necessary
12. Dinner Available

13. Lunch Available
14. Conference Rooms Avail.
15. Group Seminars Avail.
16. Private Baths

17. Shared Baths
18. Afternoon Tea
* Commisions given
to Travel Agents

Highlands

Hernandez, Juanita
Rte. 2, Box 649N., Hwy. E.-64, 28741
(704) 526-4536

Amenities: 1,2,3,5,6,7,8,10, 11,16
Breakfast: F.

Dbl. Oc.: $68.00
Sgl. Oc.: $58.00
Third Person: $10.00

The Guest House—A lovely mountain chalet B&B nestled in tranquility. Tasteful decor, greatroom with fireplace and a panoramic view. Known for serving superb breakfasts! Just moments from town and all amenities: shopping, hiking, sports and fine dining. Perfect in any season.

Kill Devil Hills *

Combs, Phyllis
500 N. Virginia Dare Trail, 27948
(919) 441-6127

Amenities: 1,2,3,4,5,6,7,9,10, 11,16
Breakfast: C.

Dbl. Oc.: $75.00
Sgl. Oc.: $75.00

Ye Olde Cherokee Inn—Great for honeymoons and special occasions of the heart. Big pink beach house, 500 feet from the ocean. Beautiful sunrises and sunsets. Great food, history and sports. Enjoy the treat of a featherbed by request. Play, read, relax, the choice is yours. Nags Head beach. Cherokee.

Lake Junaluska

Cato, Wilma & Ben
207 Atkins Loop, 28745
(704) 456-6486

Amenities: 2,5,6,7,10,11,12, 16,17
Breakfast: F.

Dbl. Oc.: $66.00
Sgl. Oc.: $44.00
Third Person: $15.00
Child: 6 - 12 yrs. - $10.00

Providence Lodge—Rustic with period furniture, good beds, claw-foot tubs and big porches. Delicious family-style meals feature the best in country cooking. Nearby are the Blue Ridge Parkway, Great Smoky Mountains, Cherokee Indian Reservation and the Biltmore Estate in Asheville.

Lake Waccamaw

Garrell, Dot & Max
404 Lake Shore Dr.
P.O. Box 218, 28450
(919) 646-4744

Amenities: 7,10,16,17
Breakfast: F.

Dbl. Oc.: $52.50
Sgl. Oc.: $47.25
Child: Under 6 yrs. - $5.25

Bed And Breakfast By The Lake—Spend a night with us on tranquil Lake Waccamaw. The quiet beauty and peaceful surroundings will long be remembered. Here you will awaken to the unmistakable smell of frying bacon and perking coffee. A full southern breakfast tops off your stay.

Mars Hill *

Wessel, Yvette
121 So. Main St., 28754
(704) 689-5722

Amenities: 1,2,5,6,7,8,9,10, 16,17
Breakfast: F.

Dbl. Oc.: $42.40 - $53.00
Sgl. Oc.: $42.40 - $53.00
Third Person: $10.00
Child: Under 12 yrs. - no charge

Baird House—An 85-year-old brick charmer in garden setting. Furnished with fine antiques. Elegant yet homey. Tiny college town 18 miles north of Asheville.

1. No Smoking	5. Tennis Available	9. Credit Cards Accepted	13. Lunch Available	17. Shared Baths
2. No Pets	6. Golf Available	10. Personal Check Accepted	14. Conference Rooms Avail.	18. Afternoon Tea
3 Off Season Rates	7. Swimmming Avail.	11. Reservations Necessary	15. Group Seminars Avail.	* Commisions given
4. Senior Citizen Rates	8. Skiing Available	12. Dinner Available	16. Private Baths	to Travel Agents

NORTH CAROLINA

Mount Airy *

Haxton, Ellen & Manford
2893 W. Pine St., 27030
(919) 789-5034

Amenities: 2,4,5,6,7,8,9,10, 11,12,13,14,15,16
Breakfast: C. & F.

Dbl. Oc.: $60.00 - $100.00
Sgl. Oc.: $50.00
Third Person: $10.00
Child: $10.00

Pine Ridge Inn—A 1949 mansion, two miles east of I-79 and Hwy. 89. Private bedroom suites with private baths. Swimming pool. Large indoor hot tub. Exercise room. Wine and cheese served.

Murphy *

DeLong, Kate & Bob
500 Valley River Ave., 28906
(704) 837-9567, (800) 824-6189

Amenities: 2,3,4,5,6,7,9,10,11,15,16
Breakfast: F.
Dbl. Oc.: $70.85
Sgl Oc.: $53.41
Third Person: $10.00
Child: Under 16 yrs. - no charge

Huntington Hall—Awake to the aroma of a sumptuous breakfast sizzling on the stove. Feel the cool mountain breeze. Relax and unwind in our circa 1881 English country home. See a play, raft a river, hike a trail. Murder mystery weekends, white-water rafting packages.

Nags Head *

Lawrence, Alan
6720 So. Virginia Dare Tr., 27959
(919) 441-2340,
(800) 368-9390

Amenities: 1,2,3,5,6,7,9,10, 12,13,14,15,16,18
Breakfast: C. Plus

Dbl. Oc.: $110.00 - $253.00
Sgl. Oc.: $110.00 - $253.00
Third Person: $33.00
Child: Under 12 yrs. - $22.00

First Colony Inn—Experience southern hospitality at North Carolina outer banks' only historic B&B inn; 26 antique-filled rooms. Two stories of wrap-around verandas overlooking the ocean and sound. Private beach, jacuzzis, kitchenettes, king- size beds, TVs and cozy library. Near historic areas.

New Bern *

Hansen, Diane & A.E.
215 Pollock St., 28560
(919) 636-3810

Amenities: 1,2,9,10,16
Breakfast: F.

Dbl. Oc.: $87.20
Sgl. Oc.: $59.95
Third Person: $21.80
Child: $21.80

Harmony House Inn—Comfortable elegance in the historic district near Tryon Palace, restaurants and shops. Spacious Greek Revival inn, circa 1850, decorated with antiques, local reproductions and family history. Complimentary soft drinks and juices. Guest parlor. Porch with swings.

1. No Smoking	5. Tennis Available	9. Credit Cards Accepted	13. Lunch Available	17. Shared Baths
2. No Pets	6. Golf Available	10. Personal Check Accepted	14. Conference Rooms Avail.	18. Afternoon Tea
3 Off Season Rates	7. Swimmming Avail.	11. Reservations Necessary	15. Group Seminars Avail.	* Commisions given
4. Senior Citizen Rates	8. Skiing Available	12. Dinner Available	16. Private Baths	to Travel Agents

Ocean Isle Beach *

Pope, Miller
310 E. First St., 28469
(800) 334-3581

Amenities: 1,2,3,4,5,6,7,9,14,16
Breakfast: C.
Dbl. Oc.: $89.38 - $184.21
Sgl Oc.: $89.38 - $131.89
Third Person: $15.00
Child: Under 19 yrs. - no charge

The Winds-Clarion Carriage House Inn—Oceanfront on seven- mile island beach surrounded by palm trees and lush subtropical gardens just 20 miles from Myrtle Beach, SC. Rooms and suites with kitchens, seaside balconies, daily housekeeping, whirlpool, sauna and beach volleyball. Bicycle and sailboat rentals. Heated pool.

Old Fort *

Aldridge, Debbie & Chuck
W. Main St.
P.O. Box 1116, 28762
(704) 668-9384

Amenities: 1,2,5,6,7,8,10,16
Breakfast: C. Plus

Dbl. Oc.: $54.50
Sgl. Oc.: $49.05
Third Person: $5.45
Child: Under 12 yrs. -
no charge

The Inn At Old Fort—An 1880s Victorian cottage furnished with antiques. Large front porch for rocking, terraced lawn for croquet, back deck and flower gardens on 3-1/2 acres overlooking historic Blue Ridge town. Near Asheville and Blue Ridge Parkway.

Salisbury *

Webster, Gerry
220 So. Ellis St., 28144
(704) 633-6841

Amenities: 1,2,5,6,9,10,16
Breakfast: C. Plus

Dbl. Oc.: $54.50 - $59.95
Sgl. Oc.: $49.00 - $54.50
Third Person: $16.35

The 1868 Stewart-Marsh House—Federal-style home in the historic district. Screened porch with wicker furniture, cozy library, spacious guest rooms and antiques. Friendly, southern hospitality. Historic sites, shopping and restaurants within walking distance. Tours of the historic district available.

Saluda

Hough, Ken
P.O. Box 725, 28773
(704) 749-5471

Amenities: 1,2,5,6,7,9,10,11,
12,14,15,16
Breakfast: F.

Dbl. Oc.: $108.55
Sgl. Oc.: $97.65
Third Person: $16.35

The Orchard Inn—A truly memorable dining experience on the glassed-in porch with breathtaking views of the Southern Blue Ridge. This turn-of-the-century country house has a touch of plantation elegance with large fireplace, antiques, folk art, masses of books and fresh flowers.

1. No Smoking	5. Tennis Available	9. Credit Cards Accepted	13. Lunch Available	17. Shared Baths
2. No Pets	6. Golf Available	10. Personal Check Accepted	14. Conference Rooms Avail.	18. Afternoon Tea
3 Off Season Rates	7. Swimmming Avail.	11. Reservations Necessary	15. Group Seminars Avail.	* Commisions given
4. Senior Citizen Rates	8. Skiing Available	12. Dinner Available	16. Private Baths	to Travel Agents

NORTH CAROLINA

Sparta

Turbiville, Mimi R.
Star Rte. 1
Box 48, 28675
(919) 372-8490

Amenities: 2,6,10,16
Breakfast: F.

Dbl. Oc.: $53.00
Sgl. Oc.: $37.10
Third Person: $10.00
Child: $10.00

Turby-Villa—Mimi lives in a large contemporary brick home two miles out in the country, near public golf courses and New River canoeing. Set on 20 pastoral acres at the end of a long private drive. Each guest room has a private bath. Breakfast is served on a glassed-in porch.

Spruce Pine *

Ansley, Bill
101 Pine Ave., 28777
(704) 765-6993

Amenities: 1,2,3,4,5,6,7,8,9,
10,11,16,18
Breakfast: F.

Dbl. Oc.: $59.95 - $76.30
Sgl. Oc.: $49.05 - $65.40
Third Person: $10.90
Child: Under 12 yrs. -
no charge

Richmond Inn—A half-century-old, "country-elegant" estate home nestled in the hills above town. Nearby are spectacular hiking trails, gem mining, skiing and crafts. Exit MM 331 off the Blue Ridge Parkway. We specialize in making our guests comfortable.

Spruce Pine

Stevens, Margaret & John P.
110 Henry Lane, 28777
(704) 765-4917

Amenities: 2,3,5,6,7,8,9,10,
16,18
Breakfast: F.

Dbl. Oc.: $70.85
Sgl. Oc.: $60.00
Third Person: $13.00
Child: Under 3 yrs. - no charge

The Fairway Inn—Three miles from Blue Ridge Parkway. Beautiful country home. Six rooms with private baths. Lovely view overlooking golf course. (Public) gourmet breakfast. Wine and cheese in the afternoon. Early-morning coffee. Big front porch.

Tarboro *

Miller, Patsy & Tom
304 E. Park Ave., 27886
(919) 826-1314

Amenities: 2,5,9,10,16
Breakfast: F. or C. Plus

Dbl. Oc.: $68.90
Sgl. Oc.: $61.48
Third Person: $21.20
Child: Under 12 yrs. - $21.20

Little Warren Bed And Breakfast—Large, gracious, Edwardian home. Family owned and operated. Located on town common in quiet, historic district. Easy access from I-95. Enjoy wide porch in summer and warm fire in winter. Antiques available.

---

1. No Smoking	5. Tennis Available	9. Credit Cards Accepted	13. Lunch Available	17. Shared Baths
2. No Pets	6. Golf Available	10. Personal Check Accepted	14. Conference Rooms Avail.	18. Afternoon Tea
3 Off Season Rates	7. Swimmming Avail.	11. Reservations Necessary	15. Group Seminars Avail.	* Commisions given
4. Senior Citizen Rates	8. Skiing Available	12. Dinner Available	16. Private Baths	to Travel Agents

Tryon *

Wainwright, Jennifer & Jeremy
200 Pine Crest Land, 28782
(800) 633-3001

Amenities: 2,5,6,7,9,10,12,14,15,16
Breakfast: C.
Dbl. Oc.: $75.00 - $150.00
Sgl Oc.: $65.00 - $140.00
Child: Under 13 yrs. - $35.50

Pine Crest Inn—A Classic experience: country inn in foothills of Blue Ridge Mountains. Crisp mountain air, wide vernadas, romantic fireplaces, gourmet dining, causual elegance.

Tryon *

Weingartner, Anneliese & Ray
Howard Gap Rd.
P.O. Box 366, 28782
(704) 859-9114

Amenities: 2,5,6,7,9,10,12, 16
Breakfast: F.

Dbl. Oc.: $68.90 - $90.10
Sgl. Oc.: $53.00 - $68.90
Third Person: $10.60
Child: $7.95

Stone Hedge Inn—Beautiful old estate on 28 acres at the base of the Blue Ridge Mountains. Some fireplaces, some kitchens. Restaurant guests enjoy continental cuisine while viewing a mountainside setting through picture windows. Rooms are decorated with antiques.

Valle Crucis *

Schwab, "Chip" & Roland
Hwy. 194,
Box 713, 28691
(704) 963-5581

Amenities: 1,2,9,10,11,16
Breakfast: F.

Dbl. Oc.: $101.00 - $144.00
Sgl. Oc.: $101.00 - $144.00
Third Person: $26.50

The Inn At The Taylor House—Bed and breakfast in an elegantly restored farmhouse. Located in the peaceful rural surroundings of Valle Crucis, North Carolina.

---

1. No Smoking	5. Tennis Available	9. Credit Cards Accepted	13. Lunch Available	17. Shared Baths
2. No Pets	6. Golf Available	10. Personal Check Accepted	14. Conference Rooms Avail.	18. Afternoon Tea
3 Off Season Rates	7. Swimmming Avail.	11. Reservations Necessary	15. Group Seminars Avail.	* Commisions given
4. Senior Citizen Rates	8. Skiing Available	12. Dinner Available	16. Private Baths	to Travel Agents

Washington *

Hervey, Jeanne & Lawrence
400 E. Main St., 27889
(919) 946-7184

Amenities: 1,2,5,9,10,16
Breakfast: F.
Dbl. Oc.: $58.30 - $68.90
Sgl Oc.: $47.70 - $58.30
Third Person: $10.00

Pamlico House—Turn-of-the-century colonial revival home in the historic district. Large wrap-around porch, parlor, large formal dining room and elegant guest rooms. Air-conditioning and TV in each room. Telephone available. Located on historic Ablemarle tour route.

Waynesville

Sylvester, Lynn & Chris
409 So. Haywood St., 28786
(704) 456-9831

Amenities: 1,2,6,8,10,17
Breakfast: C. Plus

Dbl. Oc.: $50.00
Sgl. Oc.: $45.00
Third Person: $10.00
Child: $10.00

Haywood Street House Bed And Breakfast—Located one block off Main Street, this historic home, built in 1906, has a charming and cozy atmosphere with its beautiful wood interiors and elegant antiques. A large porch with rockers offers wonderful mountain views. Open year-round.

Wilmington *

Ackiss, Catherine
410 Orange St., 28401
(919) 251-0863. (800) 476-0723

Amenities: 1,2,3,4,5,6,9,10,
11,14,15,16,18
Breakfast: F.

Dbl. Oc.: $65.00
Sgl. Oc.: $55.00
Third Person: $15.00
Child: Over 4 yrs. - by age

Catherine's Inn On Orange—Experience the warm, gracious hospitality of our restored 1875 home. Charming rooms, private baths, furnished with reproductions. Relax by our pool and, after a tasty breakfast, enjoy nearby antique shops, galleries, museums and tours.

Wilmington

Anderson, Connie
520 Orange St., 28401
(919) 343-8128

Amenities: 1,5,6,7,10,11,16
Breakfast: F.

Dbl. Oc.: $70.85
Sgl. Oc.: $54.50
Third Person: $10.00
Child: Under 2 yrs. - no charge

Anderson Guest House—An 1851 Italianate townhouse overlooking private garden. Furnished with antiques and ceiling fans. Working fireplaces. Drinks upon arrival. A gourmet breakfast is served in the elegant dining room or on the porches. Walk to many sites and fine restaurants.

1. No Smoking	5. Tennis Available	9. Credit Cards Accepted	13. Lunch Available	17. Shared Baths
2. No Pets	6. Golf Available	10. Personal Check Accepted	14. Conference Rooms Avail.	18. Afternoon Tea
3 Off Season Rates	7. Swimmming Avail.	11. Reservations Necessary	15. Group Seminars Avail.	* Commisions given
4. Senior Citizen Rates	8. Skiing Available	12. Dinner Available	16. Private Baths	to Travel Agents

NORTH CAROLINA

Wilmington

Benson, Kathleen
311 Cottage Lane, 28401
(919) 763-0511

Amenities: 1,2,6,10,16
Breakfast: C.

Dbl. Oc.: $69.70
Sgl. Oc.: $64.70
Child: Under 12 yrs. - no charge

The Wine House—Luxurious accommodations in the heart of the historic district. Enjoy the charm of the brick-walled courtyard and the privacy of the separate guest house accommodations. Each room features a queen bed, fireplace, ceiling fan, wet bar, refrigerator and private bath.

Wilmington

Jarrett, Jo Anne
1704 Market St., 28403
(919) 763-5442, (800) 242-5442

Amenities: 1,2,5,6,7,9,10,16
Breakfast: F.

Dbl. Oc.: $70.00 - $85.00
Sgl. Oc.: $60.00

Market Street Bed And Breakfast—Circa 1917. Listed in the National Register of Historic Places, this Georgian house is furnished with antiques and reproductions. Our guests have breakfast in the dining room. Central heat and air-conditioning. Located on US 17 and 74. There is off-street parking.

Wilmington *

Smith, Sharon
412 So. Third St., 28401
(919) 762-8562

Amenities: 1,2,9,10,16,18
Breakfast: F.

Dbl. Oc.: $82.00 - $100.00
Sgl. Oc.: $75.00 - $95.00

The Worth House—Elegantly restored Victorian inn located in historic Wilmington. Spacious bedrooms all with private baths and fireplaces. Complimentary beverages and newspaper. Gourmet breakfast served in the privacy of your room, dining room or gardens.

Wilson *

Spitz, Betty & Fred
600 W. Nash St., 27893-3045
(919) 243-4447,
Reservations:(800) 258-2058

Amenities: 2,5,6,7,9,10,14,15,
16
Breakfast: F.

Dbl. Oc.: $65.40 - $76.30
Sgl. Oc.: $54.50 - $65.40

Miss Betty's Bed And Breakfast Inn—Located in the historic section, the inn, with its two beautifully restored historic homes, recaptures the elegance and style of an era gone by. Wilson, the "antique capital," is strategically located mid-way on the East Coast's main north-south route, I-95.

---

1. No Smoking	5. Tennis Available	9. Credit Cards Accepted	13. Lunch Available	17. Shared Baths
2. No Pets	6. Golf Available	10. Personal Check Accepted	14. Conference Rooms Avail.	18. Afternoon Tea
3 Off Season Rates	7. Swimmming Avail.	11. Reservations Necessary	15. Group Seminars Avail.	* Commisions given
4. Senior Citizen Rates	8. Skiing Available	12. Dinner Available	16. Private Baths	to Travel Agents

Winston-Salem *

Garrison, Barbara
927 W. 5th St., 27101
(919) 722-9045

Amenities: 1,2,3,4,9,10,16,17, 18
Breakfast: F.

Dbl. Oc.: $47.70 - $68.90
Sgl. Oc.: $42.40 - $53.00

Mickle House B&B—Quaint, soft-yellow Victorian cottage (1892). A gracious welcome, lovely antiques, restful canopy/poster beds and evening dessert await you. Fully restored. Easy access to historic district. Five minutes to Old Salem, the medical center and downtown. Walk to fine restaurants and parks.

Winston-Salem *

Kirley, Shelley
612 Summit St., 27101
(919) 724-1074

Amenities: 2,3,5,6,10,16,17, 18
Breakfast: F.

Dbl. Oc.: $53.00 - $100.70
Sgl. Oc.: $53.00 - $90.10
Third Person: $10.00
Child: Over 12 yrs. - $10.00

Lady Anne's Victorian Bed And Breakfast—Historic Victorian home, circa 1890. Walking distance of downtown, fine restaurants and parks. Near historic Old Salem. Elegant antiques and Oriental rugs. Phones, cable TV, VCR, stereo and refrigerator. Evening dessert tray. Private entrance, porch and parlor for guests.

Winston-Salem *

Land, Ken
Summit and W. 5th, 27101
(919) 777-1887

Amenities: 2,5,6,7,9,10,12,13, 16,18
Breakfast: F.

Dbl. Oc.: $98.56 - $133.28
Sgl. Oc.: $87.36

Colonel Ludlow Inn—An 1887 historic property. In your room: Victorian antiques, art and books, two-person jacuzzi with bubble bath and candle, stereo system with tapes, TV/VCR with free movies, phone, microwave, refrigerator and coffee maker. Walk to gourmet restaurants, cafes, shops and park.

---

1. No Smoking
2. No Pets
3 Off Season Rates
4. Senior Citizen Rates

5. Tennis Available
6. Golf Available
7. Swimming Avail.
8. Skiing Available

9. Credit Cards Accepted
10. Personal Check Accepted
11. Reservations Necessary
12. Dinner Available

13. Lunch Available
14. Conference Rooms Avail.
15. Group Seminars Avail.
16. Private Baths

17. Shared Baths
18. Afternoon Tea
* Commisions given to Travel Agents

NORTH DAKOTA

The Flickertail State

Capitol: Bismark
Statehood: November 2, 1889, the 39th state
State Motto: "Liberty and Union, Now and Forever, One
    and Inseparable"
State Song: "North Dakota Hymn"
State Bird: Western Meadow Lark
State Flower: Wild Prairie Rose
State Tree: American Elm

North Dakota was named for the Sioux Indians who once lived here and called themselves Dakota or Lakota, meaning allies or friend.

This northern state is mainly a farming state today. Few people settled here before 1870 because it was so difficult to get to and fear of Indians on the trails. In 1872, the North Pacific R.R. built a line to Fargo, the largest city in the state, and in 1873 the railroad was brought into Bismarck. With the coming of this new means of transportation, North Dakota started to become populated and farming began to prosper.

There is a variety of recreational activities for the traveler here. The beautiful autumn days attract the hunter and fisherman to the many streams and lakes. Winter sports prevail throughout the snowy days of winter and the summer offers many local shows depicting the folklore of the past. Theodore Roosevelt National Park and the beautiful scenic buttes of the badlands are here and bring tourists form all over the world.

The Strategic Air Command (SAC) bases are near Grand Forks and Minot.

NORTH DAKOTA

Dickinson

Scott, Joyce
1561 1st Ave., E., 58601
(701) 227-1524

Amenities: 5,6,7,10,14,16,
17,18

Breakfast: F.

Dbl. Oc.: $43.60
Sgl. Oc.: $26.25
Third Person: $26.25
Child: Under 16 yrs. - $10.90

Joyce's Home Away From Home Bed And Breakfast—A warm, hospitable, modern white brick ranch-style home with Spanish arches decorating the front. We are located only minutes from a shopping mall and eating places. We are only minutes from exit 13, on I-94. Our home has 5,000- square feet of living spaces. Coffee is always on.

Jamestown *

Oxtsby, Ethel
RR 3, Box 71, 58401
(701) 251-1372

Amenities: 1,2,8,10,12,13
14,15,17

Breakfast: F.

Dbl. Oc.: $52.50
Sgl. Oc.: $42.00

Country Charm Bed And Breakfast—An 1897 country home decorated with antiques, collectibles and handcrafted quilts. Peaceful park-like setting. The greatroom, sun porch and the deck provide space for relaxation. World's largest buffalo and frontier village is nearby.

Luverne

Wold, Joanne & Jim
RR 3, Box 50, 58056
(701) 769-2275

Amenities: 1,5,6,7,8,10,11,
12, 13, 16,17

Breakfast: F.

Dbl. Oc.:$52.50-
Sgl. Oc.: $42.00

Volden Farm B&B—Welcome you warmly to Volden Farm. Prairie, space, sky,hills, grasses, woods are here or your use. This place offers old-world ambience as well as good food and conversation, comfortable beds and careful attention to detail. If you come once, you'll come again.

New Salem*

Nagel, Beth & Fred
Rt. 2, Box 87, 58563
(701) 843-7236

Amenities: 10,16,17
Breakfast: F.

Dbl. Oc.: $36.75
Sgl. Oc.: $26.25

Prairie View Bed And Breakfast—Nestled in Poplar trees, this log home offers a warm country flavor with its wide open view and exquisite Finnish workmanship. On the historic prairies of North Dakota, this B&B room has a fireplace, wetbar, TV, VCR and private entrance. Additional rooms available. Near nationally known fossil site.

---

1. No Smoking	5. Tennis Available	9. Credit Cards Accepted	13. Lunch Available	17. Shared Baths
2. No Pets	6. Golf Available	10. Personal Check Accepted	14. Conference Rooms Avail.	18. Afternoon Tea
3 Off Season Rates	7. Swimmming Avail.	11. Reservations Necessary	15. Group Seminars Avail.	* Commisions given
4. Senior Citizen Rates	8. Skiing Available	12. Dinner Available	16. Private Baths	to Travel Agents

OHIO

The Buckeye State

Capitol: Columbus
Statehood: March 1, 1803; the 17th state
State Motto: "With God, All Things Are Possible"
State Song: "Beautiful Ohio"
State Bird: Cardinal
State Flower: Scarlet Carnation
State Tree: Buckeye

Ohio took its name from the Iroquois Indian word meaning something great. Ohio is great and it has a mixture of great people with different living habits settled in pockets up and down this state. You can get the feeling your are in New England, West Virginia or Iowa depending upon what section of the state you happen to visit.

Johnny Chapman, the original Johnny Appleseed, walked through Ohio sewing his apple seeds so that the frontier families might have fresh fruit. His orchards can still be found, but a modern Ohio has replaced his frontier land.

The state of Ohio is proud of her contribution to the space program. John Glenn, the first astronaut to orbit the world and Neil Armstrong, the first astronaut to walk on the moon, both came from this state. Seven presidents were also born in Ohio; Grant, Hayes, Garfield, Harrison, McKinley, Taft and Harding.

OHIO

Akron

Pinnick, Jeanne
601 Copley Rd., 44320
(216) 535-1952

Amenities: 1,5,6,7,8,10,16,
17
Breakfast: F.

Dbl. Oc.: $35.00
Sgl. Oc.: $30.00
Third Person: $6.00
Child: $6.00

Portage House—A gracious Tudor home built in 1918 in the historic park-like setting of Akron. Jeanne and her late husband, Harry, a retired physics professor at nearby University of Akron, opened the B&B in 1982. Refreshments offered on arrival - including warm bread if just baked!

Albany *

Hutchins, Sarah
9 Clinton St., 45710
(614) 698-6311

Amenities: 2,5,6,7,10,11,17,18
Breakfast: C. Plus
Dbl. Oc.: $50.00 - $75.00
Sgl Oc.: $35.00 - $45.00
Third Person: $10.00

The Albany House—Enjoy today's comfort in yesterday's atmosphere. You will find antiques, quilts, family heirlooms in this 150-year-old house. Swim in our indoor pool. Super continental breakfast includes fruit, homemade breads, gourmet coffee and tea. Ten minutes to Ohio University. Resident cat.

Ashtabula

Goode, Pat & Paul
1084 Walnut Blvd., 44004
(216) 964-8449

Amenities: 1,2,5,6,10,16,17
Breakfast: F.

Dbl. Oc.: $45.00 - $50.00
Sgl. Oc.: $35.00 - $40.00
Third Person: $10.00

Michael Cahill B&B—A restored 1887 Victorian home with period furnishings. Nine-room house features four guest rooms, three large parlors and a convenience kitchen. Located on Lake Erie. Walk to Walnut Beach, marine museum, restaurant and shopping on historic Bridge St., 10 minutes from I-90.

---

1. No Smoking	5. Tennis Available	9. Credit Cards Accepted	13. Lunch Available	17. Shared Baths
2. No Pets	6. Golf Available	10. Personal Check Accepted	14. Conference Rooms Avail.	18. Afternoon Tea
3 Off Season Rates	7. Swimmming Avail.	11. Reservations Necessary	15. Group Seminars Avail.	* Commisions given
4. Senior Citizen Rates	8. Skiing Available	12. Dinner Available	16. Private Baths	to Travel Agents

OHIO

Atwater

Paolino, Joyce & Fritz
6374 Waterloo Rd., 44201
216-947-3932

Amenities: 1,2,10,11,17,18
Breakfast: F.
Dbl. Oc.: $50.00 - $60.00
Sgl Oc.: $50.00 - $60.00
Third Person: No charge
Child: No charge

The Buckeye Lady Bed And Breakfast Home—Time stands still at this Victorian country home, circa 1900. Emerald, sapphire and amethyst guest rooms with antiques, refrigerators and air-conditioning. Library and a parlor await you. Sounds of trains recall earlier times. Activities nearby. A home-away-from-home.

Bellefontaine

Musser, Sandra
3985 St., Rte. 47 W., 43311
(513) 592-4290

Amenities: 1,2,5,6,7,8,10,11, 12,13,15,17,18
Breakfast: F.

Dbl. Oc.: $53.00
Sgl. Oc.: $37.10
Third Person: $15.00

Whitmore House—Relax in a Victorian setting, enjoy gourmet snacks/dinner in dining room, deck or gazebo. Stroll amongst four acres of lawn and gardens. Peaceful paradise. Local tourist activities available.

Birmingham

Walker, Joan
15307 St., Rte. 113
P.O. Box 152, 44816
(216) 965-5503

Amenities: 1,2,3,7,10,11,16, 17
Breakfast: F.

Dbl. Oc.: $60.00
Sgl. Oc.: $45.00
Third Person: $15.00

The House Of Seven Hearths—Circa 1832 brick Federal in National Historic Register. Lovely setting on seven acres with an in-ground pool. Casual and friendly atmosphere with a hearty breakfast. Forty miles from Cleveland; 25 miles from Cedar Point; six miles from Lake Erie.

Bryan

Roberts-Cline, Martha
215 N. Walnut St., 43506
(419) 636-2873

Amenities: 1,2,10,11,16,17
Breakfast: F.

Dbl. Oc.: $45.00
Sgl. Oc.: $40.00
Third Person: $5.00
Child: Under 5 yrs. - no charge

The Elegant Inn Bed And Breakfast—Within walking distance of the historic courthouse square with its fine restaurants and shops. Large, comfortable rooms make relaxing irresistible.

---

1. No Smoking	5. Tennis Available	9. Credit Cards Accepted	13. Lunch Available	17. Shared Baths
2. No Pets	6. Golf Available	10. Personal Check Accepted	14. Conference Rooms Avail.	18. Afternoon Tea
3 Off Season Rates	7. Swimmming Avail.	11. Reservations Necessary	15. Group Seminars Avail.	* Commisions given
4. Senior Citizen Rates	8. Skiing Available	12. Dinner Available	16. Private Baths	to Travel Agents

OHIO

Cincinnati

Hackney, Gary
408 Boal St., 45210
(513) 421-4408

Amenities: 1,2,9,10,11,14,16, 17
Breakfast: F.

Dbl. Oc.: $69.00 - $79.00
Sgl. Oc.: $69.00 - $79.00
Third Person: $15.00

Prospect Hill Bed And Breakfast—This elegantly restored 1867 Italiante townhouse is nestled into a wooded hillside with spectacular views of downtown. Rooms offer wood-burning fireplaces, bathrobes, sofas and period antiques. Within walking distance of the Ohio River and downtown Cincinnati.

Cincinnati *

Kartisek, Jill
Carmichael, Kris
312 Milton St., 45210
(513) 651-4220

Amenities: 10,11,16,18
Breakfast: C. Plus

Dbl. Oc.: $69.00
Sgl. Oc.: $69.00
Third Person: $10.00

Auburn Suite Bed And Breakfast—Spacious 1850s historic home, with a B&B suite, in downtown Cincinnati. Enjoy a charming bedroom, bath, living room and fully equipped kitchen. Elegantly presented homemade breakfast treats with stocked refrigerator. Walking distance of downtown shops, pubs and river walk. Join us.

Circleville *

Maxwell, Sue & Jim
610 So. Court St., 43113
(614) 477-3986

Amenities: 1,2,4,6,7,9,10,11,16,18
Breakfast: F.
Dbl. Oc.: $55.00 - $85.00
Sgl Oc.: $45.00 - $75.00
Third Person: $10.00
Child: Over 8 yrs. - $10.00

Castle Inn - Circleville, Ohio

Castle Inn—Arches, battlements, towers and plenty of stained glass bedeck this castle-like mansion affording romantic honeymoons, anniversaries and getaways. Victorian antiques. Great "antique" town. Enjoy our collection of "castle" toys, games, puzzles and books. "Whodunits."

Danville

Martin, Yvonne & Ian
29683 Walhonding Rd., 43014
(614) 599-6107

Amenities: 1,2,3,6,9,10,11,12, 14,15,16
Breakfast: C. & F. (on weekends)

Dbl. Oc.: $75.95 - $141.05
Sgl. Oc.: $54.25 - $130.20
Third Person: $27.13
Child: $16.28

The White Oak Inn—A true "country" inn located in an expansive private/public wooded area that ensures privacy. Antique furnishings; large fireplaced common room; 50' front porch; screen house; three fireplaced rooms. Near Amish country, historic Ohio- Erie Canal village, antiquing

1. No Smoking	5. Tennis Available	9. Credit Cards Accepted	13. Lunch Available	17. Shared Baths
2. No Pets	6. Golf Available	10. Personal Check Accepted	14. Conference Rooms Avail.	18. Afternoon Tea
3 Off Season Rates	7. Swimmming Avail.	11. Reservations Necessary	15. Group Seminars Avail.	* Commisions given
4. Senior Citizen Rates	8. Skiing Available	12. Dinner Available	16. Private Baths	to Travel Agents

East Fultonham

Graham, Dawn & Jim
7320 Old Town Rd., 43735
(614) 849-2728

Amenities: 2,5,6,7,9,10,11,12, 13,17

Breakfast: F.

Dbl. Oc.: $42.40
Sgl. Oc.: $37.10
Third Person: $10.60
Child: Under 10 years - $5.30

Hill View Acres—Located 10 miles southwest of Zanesville, off U.S. 22W. Large, spacious home on 21 acres with pond. Enjoy the pool, year-round spa or relax in family room by fireplace. Country cooking a specialty. Area popular for antiquing, pottery and outdoor activities.

Geneva-On-The-Lake

Haffa, Grace & Earle
5162 Old Lake Rd., 44041
(216) 466-8013

Amenities: 1,5,6,7,15,17

Breakfast: C.

Dbl. Oc.: $39.00
Sgl. Oc.: $39.00
Third Person: $16.00

Westlake House—Renovated home with wash lavatories and ceiling fans in rooms. Double beds. See sunrise and sunset on Lake Erie. Two-minute walk to beach. Swing on front porch or pitch horseshoes in backyard.

Geneva-On-The-Lake *

Otto, C. Joyce
5653 Lake Rd., 44041
(216) 466-8668

Amenities: 4,7,8,9,10,11,12, 13,15,16,17

Breakfast: F.

Dbl. Oc.: $45.37
Sgl. Oc.: $36.16
Third Person: $9.01
Child: Under 3 yrs. - $7.42

Otto Court B&B.—Family-run business located on two acres of lake front property. Besides a 19-room hotel, there are eight cottages by the week or daily off-season. Small game room on premises as well as horseshoes, volleyball, picnic tables and beach with bonfire. Open year-round.

Gloucester

Zimmerman, Sylvia
Rte 3, Box 433, 45732
(614) 767-4185

Amenities: 1,6,7,10,11,12,16

Breakfast: F.

Dbl. Oc.: $45.00
Sgl. Oc.: $25.00
Third Person: $5.00
Child: Under 5 yrs. - $5.00

County Line Farm B&B—Fourteen miles from Athens. Quiet 1863 home on 130 acres. Milk a cow, feed a calf, collect and eat an egg for breakfast. Unusual place for out-of-the-way people. Enjoy good company, a poodle dog and very homemade meals. Walk forgotten roads or sit by the fire.

Grand Rapids

Delvin, Nancy & John
24070 Front St., 43522
(419) 832-MILL

Amenities: 1,2,3,10,11,16

Breakfast: F.

Dbl. Oc.: $68.90 - $90.10
Sgl. Oc.: $68.90 - $90.10
Third Person: $15.00

The Mill House—Originally a steam-driven mill built in 1900, converted and tastefully renovated. Three double suites, all on the first floor. Beautiful gardens along the canal and Maumee River. Walking distance of many craft and antique shops. Hiking trails along the canal towpaths.

1. No Smoking	5. Tennis Available	9. Credit Cards Accepted	13. Lunch Available	17. Shared Baths
2. No Pets	6. Golf Available	10. Personal Check Accepted	14. Conference Rooms Avail.	18. Afternoon Tea
3 Off Season Rates	7. Swimmming Avail.	11. Reservations Necessary	15. Group Seminars Avail.	* Commisions given
4. Senior Citizen Rates	8. Skiing Available	12. Dinner Available	16. Private Baths	to Travel Agents

OHIO

Johnstown

Bosveld, Jennifer & Jim
60 N. Main St., 43031
(614) 967-6060

Amenities: 1,2,5,6,10,11,14,
15,17
Breakfast: F.

Dbl. Oc.: $55.00
Sgl. Oc.: $55.00

Pudding House Bed And Breakfast For Writers—Create your way to a new you in this writers, therapists, teachers retreat for all. Fireplace, large front porch with jumbo rockers, swing, desks, library office and supplies in busy village near antiques, nature and colleges. Resume and career consulting available.

Louisville *

Shurilla, Mary
1320 E. Main St., 44641
(216) 875-1021

Amenities: 1,2,6,10,16
Breakfast: F.

Dbl. Oc.: $50.00
Sgl. Oc.: $40.00
Third Person: $10.00
Child: Under 6 years - $5.00

The Mainstay—A century-old, 12-room Victorian home with richly carved oak woodwork, antiques, gracious hospitality and only minutes from Canton Pro Football Hall of Fame. Upon arrival, complimentary fruit and cheese. Six a.m. coffee served to room.

Marietta

Schwaner, Alexander
524 Second St., 45750
(614) 376-9000

Amenities: 1,2,10,11,16
Breakfast: C.

Dbl. Oc.: $95.00 - $125.00
Sgl. Oc.: $75.00
Third Person: $5.00
Child: Under 12 yrs. -no charge

Larchmont B&B—A southern colonial mansion built in 1824 in historic Marietta, Ohio. High ceilings and spacious rooms, a Vernada with a view of the beautiful flower garden with fountain. Near museums and tours. Air-conditioning. The elegance of yesteryear. Quiet and peaceful.

Marion

Rimbach, Mary-Louisa
245 St. James St.,
43302
(614) 382-2402

Amenities: 2,5,6,9,10,11,16
Breakfast: F.
Dbl. Oc.: $55.00 - $65.00
Sgl Oc.: $55.00 - $65.00

Olde Towne Manor—Elegant stone home nestled on beautiful acre of land on a quiet street in Marion's historic district. A stroll will take you to the home of President Harding. Awarded 1990 Marion's beautifications most attractive building.

1. No Smoking	5. Tennis Available	9. Credit Cards Accepted	13. Lunch Available	17. Shared Baths
2. No Pets	6. Golf Available	10. Personal Check Accepted	14. Conference Rooms Avail.	18. Afternoon Tea
3 Off Season Rates	7. Swimmming Avail.	11. Reservations Necessary	15. Group Seminars Avail.	* Commisions given
4. Senior Citizen Rates	8. Skiing Available	12. Dinner Available	16. Private Baths	to Travel Agents

OHIO

Millersburg

Kaufman, Alma
175 W. Adams St., 44654
(216) 674-0766

Amenities: 1,2,3,6,10,11,17
Breakfast: F.

Dbl. Oc.: $45.00 & up
Sgl. Oc.: $35.00 & up
Child: Under 2 yrs. - no charge

Adams St. Bed And Breakfast—Small, homey B&B in world's largest Amish community. Shared bath. Browse in library, walk to shops or sit on porch. Formerly Amish owner happy to share information. Gourmet breakfast. Air-conditioning. Resident cat welcomes guests.

Monroeville *

Seaman, John
3057 Sand Hill Rd.
3508 State Rte., 113 W., 44847
(419) 465-2633

Amenities: 3,4,9,10,11,15,16, 17
Breakfast: F.

Dbl. Oc.: $45.00
Sgl. Oc.: $35.00
Child: Under 12 yrs. - no charge

Heymann House—Home to seven generations of the Heymann family. Even today, as a bed and breakfast, Heymann House is owned and operated by a descendant of the Heymann family. A restored Victorian home in a peaceful, pastoral setting.

Mt. Vernon

Meharry, Ron
304 N. Mulberry St., 43050
(614) 397-9594

Amenities: 1,2,5,6,7,9,10,11, 17,18
Breakfast: F.

Dbl. Oc.: $54.00
Sgl. Oc.: $44.00
Third Person: $5.00
Child: Over 5 yrs. - $5.00

The Stauffer House—Circa 1862 brick Victorian located in Old Merchants Square just two blocks from old downtown shops and restaurants. Period decor and antiques, this tastefully decorated home has a true feeling of what once was. Air-conditioned. Visit historic Mt. Vernon, Ohio.

Old Washington *

Wilson, Ruth
225 Old National Rd.
P.O. Box 115, 43768
(614) 489-5970

Amenities: 2,7,10,11,17
Breakfast: C.

Dbl. Oc.: $40.00 - $45.00
Sgl. Oc.: $38.00
Third Person: $20.00
Child: Under 10 years - $10.00

Zane Trace B&B—Exit 186 off I-70. Brick Victorian built in 1859. Spacious, quiet rooms. Five miles from Salt Fork State Park, 20 miles east of Zane Grey Museum. Antique parlor, lovely staircase, high ceilings, exquisite woodwork, large porch. Off-street parking. Small village seven miles east of Cambridge. In ground pool.

---

1. No Smoking	5. Tennis Available	9. Credit Cards Accepted	13. Lunch Available	17. Shared Baths
2. No Pets	6. Golf Available	10. Personal Check Accepted	14. Conference Rooms Avail.	18. Afternoon Tea
3 Off Season Rates	7. Swimmming Avail.	11. Reservations Necessary	15. Group Seminars Avail.	* Commisions given
4. Senior Citizen Rates	8. Skiing Available	12. Dinner Available	16. Private Baths	to Travel Agents

OHIO

Pickerington

Wagley, Judy & Rob
27 W. Columbus St., 43147
(614) 837-0932

Amenities: 1,2,5,6,9,10, 11,16
Breakfast: F.

Dbl. Oc.: $60.00 - $65.00
Sgl Oc.: $55.00 - $60.00
Third Person: $5.00
Child: $5.00

Central House—Formerly the Central Hotel, 1860-1938. Totally renovated. Looks like early photographs. Victorian antiques. On "old village" street with quaint shops. All rooms have top-quality mattresses. Park, tennis courts and playground behind the inn. Famous for giant cinnamon rolls!

Poland *

Meloy, Ginny & Steve
500 So. Main St., 44514
(216) 757-4688

Amenities: 2,5,6,9,10,11,14, 16
Breakfast: C.

Dbl. Oc.: $50.00
Sgl. Oc.: $45.00
Third Person: $5.00
Child: Under 2 yrs. - no charge

The Inn At The Green—Classic 1876 Victorian townhouse on village green of preserved Western Reserve Village. Great restaurants nearby. Antiques, Oriental rugs, parlor greeting room, sun porch, five working fireplaces, patio and garden. Seven miles southeast of Youngstown.

Powell

McCann, Patsy
10701 Riverside Dr., 43065
(614) 761-0863

Amenities: 1,4,6,11
Breakfast: F.

Dbl. Oc.: $45.00
Sgl. Oc.: $45.00
Third Person: $45.00

Patsy's Bed And Breakfast—Country cottage with airy room and queen-size bed, 25 minutes from downtown Columbus. Near the Sciota River, Columbus Zoo, golf and antique shops. Country breakfast.

Put-In-Bay

Barnhill, Barbara
910 State Rte. 357, 43456
(419) 285-6181

Amenities: 1,2,3,7,10,11,16, 17
Breakfast: F.

Dbl. Oc.: $70.00 - $85.00
Sgl. Oc.: $70.00 - $85.00

The Vineyard B&B—Situated on the east end of this charming island in Lake Erie, located on 20 acres that includs a six-acre vineyard and private beach. A 130-year-old Victorain home full of family antiques. Three large bedrooms, one with private bath. Bikes available.

---

1. No Smoking
2. No Pets
3 Off Season Rates
4. Senior Citizen Rates
5. Tennis Available
6. Golf Available
7. Swimmming Avail.
8. Skiing Available
9. Credit Cards Accepted
10. Personal Check Accepted
11. Reservations Necessary
12. Dinner Available
13. Lunch Available
14. Conference Rooms Avail.
15. Group Seminars Avail.
16. Private Baths
17. Shared Baths
18. Afternoon Tea
* Commisions given to Travel Agents

OHIO

Ripley

Kittle, Patricia & Glenn
201 No. Second St., 45167
(513) 392-4918

Amenities: 1,2,5,6,10,16,17, 18
Breakfast: F.

Dbl. Oc.: $60.00 - $75.00
Sgl. Oc.: $60.00

Baird House Bed And Breakfast Boutique—If you enjoy casual country relaxing times away from the scurry of the city, then you will love it here near the Ohio River. In National Register. Circa 1825. Porches, swings, shops, dining within walking distance. Museums. Fifty miles east of Cincinnati.

Sandusky

Hahn, Susan
210 W. Adam St., 44870
(419) 625-1285

Amenities: 2,3,10,11,16
Breakfast: F. or C. Plus

Dbl. Oc.: $68.00
Sgl. Oc.: $65.00

The Cottage Rose Bed And Breakfast—A gracious reminder of another time - decor is original draperies and wall coverings. High Victorian. Very private. In downtown Sandusky across from the historic gardens. Walking distance to all ferries. From an era of satin gowns. The smell of the roses linger.

So. Bloomingville

Holt, Barbara & Brad
24830 State Rte. 56, 43152
(614) 332-6084

Amenities: 2,10,11,17
Breakfast: F.

Dbl. Oc.: $35.00
Sgl. Oc.: $30.00
Third Person: $10.00
Child: Under 10 yrs. - $5.00

Steep Woods—New log home nestled on a wooded hillside in the beautiful Hocking Hills, 60 miles southeast of Columbus. Nearby is the Hocking State Park with its famous recessed caves, waterfalls and unusual rock formations. Available in the area are swimming, hiking and more.

Tipp City

Nordquist, Thomas
1900 W. State
Rte. 571, 45371
(513) 667-2957

Amenities: 1,2,4,5,6,7,9,15, 16,17
Breakfast: F.

Dbl. Oc.: $68.90
Sgl. Oc.: $53.00
Third Person: $15.00

Willow Tree Inn—A restored 1830 Federal-style manor house. Original outbuildings on site. Quiet and relaxing atmosphere. Decorated with antique furnishings. Four working fireplaces. Located 15 minutes north of Dayton. Close to airport. Take Exit 68 off I-75.

1. No Smoking	5. Tennis Available	9. Credit Cards Accepted	13. Lunch Available	17. Shared Baths
2. No Pets	6. Golf Available	10. Personal Check Accepted	14. Conference Rooms Avail.	18. Afternoon Tea
3 Off Season Rates	7. Swimmming Avail.	11. Reservations Necessary	15. Group Seminars Avail.	* Commisions given
4. Senior Citizen Rates	8. Skiing Available	12. Dinner Available	16. Private Baths	to Travel Agents

Troy

Smith, F. June
434 So. Market St., 45373
(513) 335-1181

Amenities: 2,4,5,6,7,9,10,14,16
Breakfast: F.
Dbl. Oc.: $65.00
Sgl Oc.: $45.00
Third Person: $10.00
Child: Under 12 yrs. - $5.00

H.W. Allen Villa Bed And Breakfast—An 1874 Victorian mansion furnished with antiques throughout. In-room private bath, king and queen beds, A/C, TV, phone and snack bar. Just north of Dayton, near wineries, ATA trapshoot, international air show, hamvention, antique shops, Air Force Museum and Troy's June Strawberry Festival.

Westerville

Savage, Sally & Tom
93 W. College Ave., 43081
(614) 882-2678

Amenities: 1,4,10,11,16,17, 18
Breakfast: C. Plus

Dbl. Oc.: $42.50 - $53.00
Sgl. Oc.: $37.00
Third Person: $15.00
Child: Under 8 yrs. - no charge

Cornelia's Corner Bed And Breakfast—Restored Victorian home (1850s) on Otterbein College campus. Walk to antique shops and eateries in uptown area. Our piano, porch, parlor and patio offer guests entertainment. Near gardens, parks, historic homes, Columbus Zoo, shopping malls and airport.

1. No Smoking	5. Tennis Available	9. Credit Cards Accepted	13. Lunch Available	17. Shared Baths
2. No Pets	6. Golf Available	10. Personal Check Accepted	14. Conference Rooms Avail.	18. Afternoon Tea
3 Off Season Rates	7. Swimmming Avail.	11. Reservations Necessary	15. Group Seminars Avail.	* Commisions given
4. Senior Citizen Rates	8. Skiing Available	12. Dinner Available	16. Private Baths	to Travel Agents

OKLAHOMA

The Sooner State

Capitol: Oklahoma City
Stathood: November 16, 1907; the 46th state
State Motto: "Labor Conquers All Things"
State Bird: Scissor-Tailed Flycatcher
State Flower: Mistletoe
State Tree: Redbud

Oklahoma was the last of the Indian territories in America. In 1893, the U.S. government opened it up to the white man for settlement. The name Oklahoma was derived fromtwo Indian words: "okla" for people and "home" for red. Some Indians have chosen to remain in the Ozark Hills and still speak Cherokee.

With the coming of irrigation, the land is now productive. However, for years the farmers had a difficult time. During the drought of the 1930s, this state suffered from the worst dry spell in years and those who managed to stay alive pushed on with what little they had left to live in California. John Steinbeck wrote of them in his best seller, The Grapes of Wrath.

Natural gas and oil are the largest industries today in Oklahoma. It is one of the leading states in oil production.

Oklahoma's most famous personality was Will Rogers. He was a great American humorist and had much to say about many things. On this country, he is well remembered for saying "There ought to be a law against anybody going to Europe until they have seen the things we have here."

OKLAHOMA

Kingston

Little, L.V. & Bobbie
999 No. Marshall
P.O. Box 491, 73439
(405) 564-3602

Amenities: 5,6,9,10,11,16
Breakfast: F.
Dbl. Oc.: $65.00
Sgl Oc.: $45.00

The Sun Ray Ranch—The southwest comes alive at the Sun Ray Ranch situated on a working ranch in Kingston, OK. The ranch is located four miles from Lake Texoma, one of the region's best fishing holes, known for its stripers. Enjoy fishing, antiques or help with ranch chores.

Oklahoma City

Wright, Claudia
1841 NW 15th, 73106
(405) 521-0011

Amenities: 2,9,10,12,15,16
Breakfast: C.

Dbl. Oc.: $48.00 - $100.00
Sgl. Oc.: $43.00
Third Person: $20.00

Grandison Inn—Circa 1896. Brick and shingled three-story house surrounded by fruit trees, grapevine, lovely gardens and gazebo. Original stained glass and brass chandeliers. Country Victorian decor. Three fireplaces, parlor and third-floor suite, close to downtown Interstates 35 and 40.

OREGON

The Beaver State

Capitol: Salem
Statehood: February 14, 1859; the 33rd state
State Motto: "The Union"
State Song: "Oregon, My Oregon"
State Bird: Western Meadow Lark
State Flower: Oregon Grape
State Tree: Douglas Fir

Oregon is noted for its mountains and coastal scenery. It is our most northwestern state and forest covers almost half of it. It receives a tremendous amount of rain, which results in these forests and the beautiful green everywhere. Oregon leads the nation in lumber and in wood products. Much of this is exported, but most is used right here at home. The freezing and packing of home-grown fruits and the vast salmon, shrimp, crab and tuna industry are the main source of income for Oregon.

Vacationers love t visit this state. Millions come here every year to visit the beautiful parks and enjoy the excitement of camping in them. Mt. Hood is Oregon's majestic mountain and a vacationer's paradise. It is perfect for the skier, hiker and climber.

OREGON

Ashland *

Huntley, Barbara & Bill
1313 Clay St., 97520
(503) 488-1590

Amenities: 1,2,3,5,6,7,8,9,10, 11,16
Breakfast: F.

Dbl. Oc.: $67.00 - $155.00
Sgl. Oc.: $62.00 - $150.00
Third Person: $30.00

Country Willows Inn B&B—Quiet, relaxing hideaway on five white-fenced acres. Trees, lawns, spa and pool. Cozy den with fireplace. Seven rooms, private baths, air-conditioning. Full breakfast. Romantic barn suite with fireplace and deck. Six minutes to Shakespeare Theatre.

Ashland *

Reinhardt, Carmen & Joe
159 N. Main St., 97520
(503) 488-2901

Amenities: 1,2,3,5,6,7,8,9,10, 16,18
Breakfast: F.

Dbl. Oc.: $55.00 - $110.00
Sgl. Oc.: $50.00 - $105.00
Third Person: $15.00 - $30.00

Cowslip's Belle Bed And Breakfast—Teddy bears and chocolate truffles, cozy down comforters and scrumptious breakfasts. Beautiful 1913 Craftsman home and carriage house nestled in Ashland's historic district. Three blocks to theatres, shops and restaurants. Four rooms. Private entrances and baths. Air-conditioned.

Ashland *

Roddy, Francoise & Lester
333 N. Main St., 97520
(503) 488-1598, (800) 435-8260

Amenities: 1,2,3,9,10,11,16
Breakfast: F.

Dbl. Oc.: $94.20 - $110.10
Sgl. Oc.: $89.20 - $105.10
Third Person: $35.00
Child: Over 12 yrs. - $35.00

The Woods House Bed And Breakfast Inn—This 1908 Craftsman, surrounded by flowering gardens, welcomes guests to the quiet, country elegance of its six spacious rooms. "This is a home to return to." Four blocks to theatres, restaurants and shops. Golf, hike, bike, river rafting nearby. Ski Mt. Ashland, 15 miles away.

Ashland *

Sargent, Leslie & Bruce
2200 Buckhorn Springs Rd., 97520
(503) 488-2200

Amenities: 1,2,3,6,8,9,10,11, 12,13,14,15,16,17
Breakfast: F.

Dbl. Oc.: $55.00 - $125.00
Sgl. Oc.: $55.00 - $100.00
Third Person: $15.00
Child: Under 8 yrs. - no charge

Buckhorn Springs—Enjoy modern-day comfort amidst the charms of yesteryear in this century-old mineral springs resort. Newly restored lodge with period decorated guest rooms, cabins, restaurant and large organic garden. Listed in the National Register. Secluded wooded valley 12 miles to town.

1. No Smoking	5. Tennis Available	9. Credit Cards Accepted	13. Lunch Available	17. Shared Baths
2. No Pets	6. Golf Available	10. Personal Check Accepted	14. Conference Rooms Avail.	18. Afternoon Tea
3 Off Season Rates	7. Swimmming Avail.	11. Reservations Necessary	15. Group Seminars Avail.	* Commisions given
4. Senior Citizen Rates	8. Skiing Available	12. Dinner Available	16. Private Baths	to Travel Agents

OREGON

Ashland *

Shanafelt, Elaine & Gerald
550 Mt. Ashland Rd., 97520
(503) 482-8707

Amenities: 1,2,3,8,9,10,11,12, 14,16
Breakfast: F.

Dbl. Oc.: $85.00 - $135.00
Sgl. Oc.: $80.00 - $130.00
Third Person: $20.00
Child: Over 10 yrs. - $20.00

Mt. Ashland Inn—Located on a mountain ridge in southern Oregon. This beautifully handcrafted log inn commands spectacular views. The rock fireplace, stained glass, handcarvings, antiques and finely crafted furniture creates an atmosphere of comfortable elegance. Hiking and skiing.

Ashland *

Treon, Donna & Francis
1819 Colestin Rd., 97520
(503) 482-0746

Amenities: 1,2,4,7,8,10,11 17
Breakfast: F.

Dbl. Oc.: $70.00
Sgl. Oc.: $65.00
Third Person: $15.00
Child: Under 3 yrs. - $10.00

Treon's Country Homestay—A peaceful B&B. nestled in the tall pine forest south of Ashland. A pond for swimming and boating, recreation room with pool table, living room with fireplace, guest kitchen, queen and twin rooms. Handmade quilts. Families welcome! Hiking, biking. Cross country skiing.

Astoria, *

Westling, Nola
3391 Irving Ave., 97103
(503) 325-8153

Amenities: 1,2,3,9,10,11,16
Breakfast: F.

Dbl. Oc.: $74.90 - $90.95
Sgl. Oc.: $69.55 - $85.60
Third Person: $10.00
Child: Under 5 yrs. - $5.00

Astoria Inn Bed And Breakfast—Relax and be pampered in the comfort of our 1890 Victorian farmhouse. Lovely river views. Quiet location. Two minutes from downtown. Music, movies, TV available. Restored antiques blend beautifully with country French decor.

Bandon

Jennings, David
370-1st St., 97411
(503) 347-9632

Amenities: 1,2,3,6,9,12,13 16
Breakfast: F.

Dbl. Oc.: $63.60 - $95.40
Sgl. Oc.: $63.60 - $95.40
Third Person: $5.00
Child: Under 16 yrs. - no charge

Sea Star Guesthouse—A uniquely designed coastal getaway in historic old town Bandon located right on the harbor with an incredible view of the harbor and beachland. Sleeping rooms and suites. Superb meals available in Sea Star's small, charming bistro.

---

1. No Smoking	5. Tennis Available	9. Credit Cards Accepted	13. Lunch Available	17. Shared Baths
2. No Pets	6. Golf Available	10. Personal Check Accepted	14. Conference Rooms Avail.	18. Afternoon Tea
3 Off Season Rates	7. Swimming Avail.	11. Reservations Necessary	15. Group Seminars Avail.	* Commisions given
4. Senior Citizen Rates	8. Skiing Available	12. Dinner Available	16. Private Baths	to Travel Agents

OREGON

Bend *

Bateman, Lorene
29 N.W. Greeley, 97701
(503) 382-4374

Amenities: 1,2,6,8,9,10,16
Breakfast: F.

Dbl. Oc.: $69.55 - $80.25
Sgl. Oc.: $58.85
Third Person: $15.00
Child: Over 12 yrs. - no charge

Farewell Bend Bed And Breakfast—Restored 70-year-old Dutch colonial house. Four blocks from downtown shopping, restaurants and Drake Park on the Deschutes River. In winter, ski Mount Bachelor; in summer golf and enjoy White River rafting. Complimentary wine or sherry. King beds, down comforters and terry robes.

Brookings *

Brugger, Sandra
21202 High Prairie Rd., 97415
(503) 469-8128

Amenities: 1,2,7,9,10,11,12, 13,15,16,17
Breakfast: F.

Dbl. Oc.: $85.00
Sgl. Oc.: $75.00

Chetco River Inn—Relax in the peaceful seclusion of 35 forested acres bordered on three sides by the beautiful Chetco River. The inn is small and the number of guests is limited. Full country breakfast, lovely views, warm beds and all the conveniences in an inn using alternate energy. Fish, swim and hike.

Corvallis *

May, Carol
27183 Bundy Rd., 97333
(503) 847-5992, (800) 821-4129

Amenities: 3,4,5,7,9,10,11,14,15,16,17,18
Breakfast: F.
Dbl. Oc.: $55.00 - $75.00
Third Person: $10.00

Shady Maple Farm Bed And Breakfast—A 1912 farmhouse offers cozy, casual elegance on 48 peaceful acres. River, tennis court, flower gardens, picnic area and barbeque. Hearty breakfast served on patio or fireside with views of grazing sheep and cattle. Great place for a relaxing vacation.

Elmira

McGillivray, Evelyn R.
88680 Evers Rd., 97437
(503) 935-3564

Amenities: 1,2,9,10,11,16
Breakfast: F.

Dbl. Oc.: $62.40 - $73.00
Sgl. Oc.: $52.40 - $63.00
Third Person: $25.90
Child: Under 16 yrs. - $20.60

McGillivray's Log Home Bed And Breakfast—This 1982 log home has the best of yesterday with the comforts of today. King beds, private baths and central air. Breakfast is usually prepared on the antique wood-burning cookstove. Fourteen miles west of Eugene, Oregon, on the way to the Pacific.

1. No Smoking	5. Tennis Available	9. Credit Cards Accepted	13. Lunch Available	17. Shared Baths
2. No Pets	6. Golf Available	10. Personal Check Accepted	14. Conference Rooms Avail.	18. Afternoon Tea
3 Off Season Rates	7. Swimmming Avail.	11. Reservations Necessary	15. Group Seminars Avail.	* Commisions given
4. Senior Citizen Rates	8. Skiing Available	12. Dinner Available	16. Private Baths	to Travel Agents

OREGON

Eugene *

Brod, Barbara & Henri
988 Lawrence at Tenth, 97401
(503) 683-3160

Amenities: 9,10,12,14,15,16
Breakfast: F.

Dbl. Oc.: $60.00 - $83.00
Sgl. Oc.: $55.00 - $78.00
Third Person: $10.00

The Lyon And The Lambe Inn—An elegant home in a quiet neighborhood, only two blocks from the city center. Whirlpool bath, full gourmet breakfast, congenial hosts. Large, light guest rooms. Library. Living room with fireplace. Phones in rooms. Airport pick-up. A notable inn.

Eugene *

Getty, Jacki & Bob
640 Audel, 97404
(503) 688-6344 (voice or TDD)

Amenities: 1,2,7,9,10,16,18
Breakfast: F.

Dbl. Oc.: $57.70
Sgl. Oc.: $52.70
Third Person: $15.60
Child: Under 2 yrs. - $5.00

Getty's Emerald Garden Bed And Breakfast—An architecturally interesting home in a country-like setting. Large landscaped gardens with fruit, berries and vegetables. Near most activities. Bikes. Bike paths. Piano, TV/VCR. Books. Park with pool. Sauna. Hot tubs. You and your party are our only guests. Children welcome.

Eugene *

Kjaer, Eunice
814 Lorane Hwy., 97405
(503) 343-3234

Amenities: 2,3,4,10,11,14,16,
17,18
Breakfast: F.

Dbl. Oc.: $68.75
Sgl. Oc.: $42.00
Third Person: $10.00
Child: Under 2 yrs. - $5.00

Kjear's House In The Woods—A 1910 Craftsman home in peaceful wooded setting with abundant wildlife. Near hiking and biking trails. Perfect spot to relax. Breakfasts catered to special needs. Antiques include square grand piano, Oriental carpets. College town offers many cultural opportunities.

Eugene

Larson, Maryellen
1583 Fircrest, 97403
(503) 342-7375

Amenities: 1,2,3,4,5,6,7,8,9,
10,11,12,13,14,15,
16
Breakfast: F.

Dbl. Oc.: $88.15
Sgl. Oc.: $66.65
Third Person: $10.00
Child: $10.00

Maryellen's Guest House—Guests enjoy all the comforts of home: queen beds, reading and sitting areas. Overlooks Douglas fir and Oregon grape. Walk through nearby beautiful Hendricks Park. Close to University of Oregon. You will enjoy personal attention to every detail.

---

1. No Smoking	5. Tennis Available	9. Credit Cards Accepted	13. Lunch Available	17. Shared Baths
2. No Pets	6. Golf Available	10. Personal Check Accepted	14. Conference Rooms Avail.	18. Afternoon Tea
3 Off Season Rates	7. Swimmming Avail.	11. Reservations Necessary	15. Group Seminars Avail.	* Commisions given
4. Senior Citizen Rates	8. Skiing Available	12. Dinner Available	16. Private Baths	to Travel Agents

Florence

Booth, Kay & Doug
394 Oak St.
P.O. Box 2799, 97439
(503) 997-4000

Amenities: 1,2,6,9,10,16,17
Breakfast: F.
Dbl. Oc.: $54.00 - $82.00
Sgl Oc.: $49.00 - $77.00
Third Person: $25.00

Oak Street Bed And Breakfast—You will feel instantly at home in our Victorian country home. Very quiet, end of street location, large Fir trees on sand dune. Walk to unique shops, watch fishing boats unload at the docks on the Siuslaw River in old-town Florence.

Grants Pass *

Clark, Maureen & Gerry
612 NW 3rd St., 97526
(503) 476-5564, (800) 344-2820

Amenities: 1,2,3,9,10,15,16
Breakfast: F.

Dbl. Oc.: $64.00 - $85.00
Sgl. Oc.: $52.00 - $73.00
Third Person: $12.00
Child: Under 6 yrs. - no charge

Clemens House Bed And Breakfast Inn—Lovely historic home in flower-garden setting. Antiques and period furnishings, comfortable queen- or twin-size beds and air-conditioning. Best breakfast in town, special diets met with notice. Five minutes from I-5 and Rogue River. See the area by air, land or river. Brochure.

Grants Pass *

Head, Barbara
1304 N.W. Lawnridge, 97526
(503) 476-8518

Amenities: 1,2,3,10,16,17,18
Breakfast: F.
Dbl. Oc.: $47.70 - $68.90
Sgl Oc.: $42.40 - $63.60

Lawnridge House—Since 1984, guests have enjoyed this oak-shaded 1909 Craftsman with its large, quiet rooms, comfortable antique furniture, king and queen canopy beds, beamed ceilings, TV, VCR and air-conditioning. Hearty northwest breakfasts, special dietary requests are OK.

1. No Smoking	5. Tennis Available	9. Credit Cards Accepted	13. Lunch Available	17. Shared Baths
2. No Pets	6. Golf Available	10. Personal Check Accepted	14. Conference Rooms Avail.	18. Afternoon Tea
3 Off Season Rates	7. Swimmming Avail.	11. Reservations Necessary	15. Group Seminars Avail.	* Commisions given
4. Senior Citizen Rates	8. Skiing Available	12. Dinner Available	16. Private Baths	to Travel Agents

OREGON

Halfway *

Olson, Mary Ellen
Rte. 1, Box 91, 97834
(503) 742-2990

Amenities: 1,2,4,8,9,10,11,12, 15,17,18
Breakfast: F.

Dbl. Oc.: $50.00 - $65.00
Sgl. Oc.: $35.00 - $45.00
Third Person: $25.00
Child: No charge - $12.50

Birch Leaf Farm Bed And Breakfast—Historic country house featuring sweeping views from the verandas, pristine cross-country snowfields; raft or hike the Snake River, the Wallowas Mountains, or the National Recreation Area. Five bedrooms and bunkhouse. Birding. Ponds and orchards on 42 acres. Horses available.

Jacksonville *

Evans, Jerry
175 E. California, 97530
(503) 899-1900

Amenities: 1,2,9,10,12,13,16
Breakfast: F.

Dbl. Oc.: $80.00 - $175.00
Sgl. Oc.: $60.00 - $155.00
Third Person: $10.00
Child: $10.00

Jacksonville Inn—Built in 1861, this historic inn has eight air-conditioned rooms that are furnished with restored antiques. Luxurious honeymoon cottage. The award-winning restaurant is recommended by AAA and is open for breakfast, lunch, dinner and Sunday brunch. Over 700 wines.

Jacksonville *

Winsley, Charlotte & George
540 E. California St.
P.O. Box 128, (mail), 97530
(503) 899-1868

Amenities: 1,2,3,5,6,7,8,10, 11,15,16,17
Breakfast: F.

Dbl. Oc.: $75.00 - $90.00
Sgl. Oc.: $75.00 - $90.00
Third Person: $20.00

Reames House, 1868—Listed in the National Register of Historic Places. The perfect place to enjoy Jacksonville's music festivals, Ashland's Shakespeare, rafting, hiking, fishing and skiing. Victorian elegance, lace twining roses and potpourri. Four guest rooms. Spacious garden setting.

Lafayette

Ross, Ronald
675 Hwy. 99 W., 97127
(503) 864-3740

Amenities: 1,2,6,10,16,18
Breakfast: C. and F.

Dbl. Oc.: $55.00 - $65.00
Sgl. Oc.: $55.00 - $65.00
Third Person: $10.00

Kelty Estate Bed And Breakfast—Built in 1872, this early colonial-style home is in the National Register of Historic Places. Located in the heart of the Oregon wine country, across the street from the Lafayette Antique Mall. Nearby are the Yamhill County Museum and wineries. One hour to the coast or mountains.

---

1. No Smoking	5. Tennis Available	9. Credit Cards Accepted	13. Lunch Available	17. Shared Baths
2. No Pets	6. Golf Available	10. Personal Check Accepted	14. Conference Rooms Avail.	18. Afternoon Tea
3 Off Season Rates	7. Swimmming Avail.	11. Reservations Necessary	15. Group Seminars Avail.	* Commisions given
4. Senior Citizen Rates	8. Skiing Available	12. Dinner Available	16. Private Baths	to Travel Agents

OREGON

Lincoln City *

Brey, Milton
3725 N.W. Keel, 97367
(503) 994-7123

Amenities: 2,3,9,10,16,17
Breakfast: F.

Dbl. Oc.: $64.20 - $80.25
Sgl. Oc.: $58.85
Third Person: $16.05

Brey House Ocean View Bed And Breakfast—The ocean awaits you just across the street. This large Cape Cod house has all the makings of a great vacation. Restaurants and shopping within walking distance. Close to deep-sea fishing and crabbing. Whale watching and storm watching.

McMinnville *

Steiger, Doris & Lynn
360 Wilson St., 97128
(503) 472-0821, 472-0238

Amenities: 1,2,6,9,10,14,16
Breakfast: F.
Dbl. Oc.: $65.00 - $85.00
Sgl Oc.: $60.00 - $80.00
Third Person: $15.00

Steiger Haus Bed And Breakfast—An architecturally delightful classic inn with old-European country character and a lovely wooded garden setting. *The Inn Times 1991,* " # 2 B&B in America." Regional winery tours and NW Oregon day trips inspire countless return visits. Walk to downtown restaurants.

Newport

Garrard, Bette & Bob
4920 N.W. Woody Way, 97365
(503) 265-6158, 265-7779

Amenities: 1,2,3,6,9,10,11, 16,18
Breakfast: F.

Dbl. Oc.: $65.00 - $100.00
Sgl. Oc.: $60.00 - $95.00

Ocean House—Breath-taking coastal get-a-way. Gardens with decks, beach trail to tide pools, early a.m. coffee, walks to the lighthouse, smashing storms, breakfast in the sunroom, evenings by the fire. Near Newports many attractions. Unforgettable all seasons.

Portland

Laughlin, Milli
5758 N.E. Emerson, 97218-2406
(503) 282-7892

Amenities: 1,17
Breakfast: F.

Dbl. Oc.: $40.00 - $45.00
Sgl. Oc.: $35.00 - $40.00

Hostess House—Warmth and hospitality in a contemporary setting. Breakfast is served in the dining room overlooking a deep terraced yard. Large deck for sitting, reading or writing. A quiet residence adjacent to public transportation. Near main highway, arteries and airport.

1. No Smoking	5. Tennis Available	9. Credit Cards Accepted	13. Lunch Available	17. Shared Baths
2. No Pets	6. Golf Available	10. Personal Check Accepted	14. Conference Rooms Avail.	18. Afternoon Tea
3 Off Season Rates	7. Swimmming Avail.	11. Reservations Necessary	15. Group Seminars Avail.	* Commisions given
4. Senior Citizen Rates	8. Skiing Available	12. Dinner Available	16. Private Baths	to Travel Agents

OREGON

Portland*

Sauter, Mary
4314 N. Mississippi Ave., 97217
(503) 284-5893

Amenities: 1,2,3,9,10,11,12,
16,17,18
Breakfast: F.

Dbl. Oc.: $42.70 - $134.95
Sgl. Oc.: $31.80
Third Person: $16.35

The John Palmer House Bed And Breakfast Inn—This historic family-run inn comes complete with a pioneer granny, resident musicians, CCA-trained chef, hot tub, computer, warm hospitality, humor, weekend dinners and high tea.

Port Oxford

Mitchell, Brenda & Alan
444 Jackson St., 97465
(503) 332-2855

Amenities: 1,2,5,6,9,10,16
Breakfast: F.

Dbl. Oc.: $65.00 - $75.00
Sgl. Oc.: $65.00 - $75.00
Third Person: $10.00
Child: Under 12 yrs. - no charge

Home By The Sea Bed And Breakfast—Dramatic ocean views; direct beach access; a very short walk to restaurants and the town's harbor. Two rooms with queen-size Oregon myrtlewood beds; laundry privileges; phone jacks; cable TV. Macintosh spoken.

Yachats

Morgan, Baerbel & Smuel
444 Jackson St., 97465
(503) 332-2855

Amenities: 1,2,6,7,9,10,11,16
Breakfast: F.

Dbl. Oc.: $69.00 - $145.00
Sgl. Oc.: $69.00 - $145.00
Third Person: $12.00

Serenity Bed and Breakfast—Wholesome retreat nestled in lush valley. Gentle place to relax after countryside, forest and tidepool explorations. Minutes from Cape Perpetua and Sea Lion caves. Elegant European comfort with private two-person jacuzzi tubs. Yachats is gem on central Oregon coastline.

---

1. No Smoking	5. Tennis Available	9. Credit Cards Accepted	13. Lunch Available	17. Shared Baths
2. No Pets	6. Golf Available	10. Personal Check Accepted	14. Conference Rooms Avail.	18. Afternoon Tea
3 Off Season Rates	7. Swimmming Avail.	11. Reservations Necessary	15. Group Seminars Avail.	* Commisions given
4. Senior Citizen Rates	8. Skiing Available	12. Dinner Available	16. Private Baths	to Travel Agents

PENNSYLVANIA

The Keystone State

Capitol: Harrisburg
Statehood: December 12, 1787: the 2nd state
State Motto: "Virtue, Liberty and Independence"
State Bird: Ruffed Grouse
State Flower: Mountain Laurel
State Tree: Hemlock

Pennsylvania is enjoyed by tourists because it offers such a variety of things to see and so. It is the land where liberty began, the land of chocolate candy, steel mills and the beginning of Little League baseball.

One of the major attractions for tourists is the Liberty Bell in Philadelphia. This bell is a reminder to all Americans that here is where our Constitution was adopted and signed, giving all of us the right to private enterprise and initiative and the right to live and worship as we wish.

The steel mills in Pittsburgh, the beautiful Amish farms in Reading and Lancaster, the lively homes and cooking of the Pennsylvania Dutch throughout the heart of this state, is representative of what our forefathers visualized.

Pennsylvania offers scenic beauty and many historical attractions, from Valley Forge to the Gettysburg battlefields.

One of the oldest universities in our country is Pennsylvania University.

James Buchanan, our 15th president, was born here in 1791.

PENNSYLVANIA

Adamstown *

Berman, Wanda
62 W. Main St., 19501
(215) 484-0800, (800) 594-4808

Amenities: 1,2,5,6,7,9,10,14,16,18
Breakfast: C. Plus
Dbl. Oc.: $68.90 - $100.70
Sgl Oc.: $62.00 - $90.60

Adamstown Inn—Experience the simple elegance of a Victorian B&B with leaded glass-doors, chestnut woodwork and Oriental rugs. The inn is located in a small town brimming with antique shops and minutes from outlet shopping. Two rooms feature two-person jacuzzis. Highly recommended.

Annville *

Hess, Jeannette
Box 692, RD 2
Jonestown Rd., 17003
(717) 865-3259

Amenities: 1,2,3,4,5,6,7,9,10, 11,14,16
Breakfast: F.

Dbl. Oc.: $50.00 - $70.00
Sgl. Oc.: $40.00 - $60.00
Third Person: $10.00
Child: 3 - 12 yrs. - $5.00

Swatara Creek Inn—An 1860 Victorian mansion near Hershey. Rooms have queen canopy beds and private baths. Sitting room, dining room and gift shop. Handicap accessible. Also near Renaissance Faire, Amish, Gettysburg and outlets.

Atglen

Stoltzfus, Hanna & Harold
RD #1, Box 69, 19310
(215) 593-5656

Amenities: 2,6,10,11,12,16, 17,18
Breakfast: F.

Dbl. Oc.: $40.00
Sgl. Oc.: $40.00
Third Person: $40.00
Child: Under 4 yrs. - no charge

Glen Run Valley View Farm—Experience country in a warm and friendly atmosphere near Amish country, Hershey chocolate plant, Longwood Gardens, antique shops, Gettysburg farmer's market and outlets.

Avella *

Tudor, Marcy
RD 1, Box 250, 15312
(412) 587-3763

Amenities: 1,2,7,9,10,16
Breakfast: F.

Dbl. Oc.: $64.00
Sgl. Oc.: $59.00
Third Person: $11.00
Child: $11.00

Weatherbury Farm—Far from the maddening crowd, nestled amidst 100 acres on working farm. The perfect getaway from everyday pressures. Spectacular views. Meadows and gardens. Guest rooms in 1860s farmhouse are lovingly furnished with country charm. Convenient to Pittsburgh and Wheeling.

1. No Smoking	5. Tennis Available	9. Credit Cards Accepted	13. Lunch Available	17. Shared Baths
2. No Pets	6. Golf Available	10. Personal Check Accepted	14. Conference Rooms Avail.	18. Afternoon Tea
3 Off Season Rates	7. Swimmming Avail.	11. Reservations Necessary	15. Group Seminars Avail.	* Commisions given
4. Senior Citizen Rates	8. Skiing Available	12. Dinner Available	16. Private Baths	to Travel Agents

Bird-In-Hand *

Davis, Sally & Ed
2658 Old Philadelphia Pike
P.O. Box 270, 17505
(717) 393-4233

Amenities: 2,4,5,6,9,10,11,14, 16
Breakfast: C.

Dbl. Oc.: $65.72
Sgl. Oc.: $65.72
Third Person: $10.60

Greystone Manor Bed And Breakfast—Located in the center of the Amish country on two grassy acres. Rooms are in a French Victorian mansion and carriage house. Quilt and craft shop on premises. Farmers markets, outlets, Strasburg Railroad and other attractions are nearby.

Boalsburg

Scott, Mark
126 E. Main St., 16827
(814) 466-6290

Amenities: 1,2,5,6,9,10,11,16
Breakfast: F.

Dbl. Oc.: $84.80 - $106.00
Sgl. Oc.: $68.90

Springfield House B&B—An 1880s Victorian offering three standard rooms, an efficiency apartment and a special services unit for physical and special needs. Just three miles from Penn State campus. Area attractions include skiing, golf, hiking, sport fishing. Wheelchair accessible.

Boyertown *

Groff, Richard
R.D. 4, Box 337
So. Benfield Rd., 19512
(215) 845-8845

Amenities: 5,6,8,10,11,12,13, 16
Breakfast: F.

Dbl. Oc.: $80.00
Sgl. Oc.: $70.00
Third Person: $18.00

The Enchanted Cottage—Complete privacy awaits you in this romantic retreat nestled in the woods. Nearby are historic sites, the Amish country, flea markets, antiques and outlet shoping. Fresh flowers, gourmet meals, open fire, kitchenette and free wine and cheese. Informal but gracious.

Boyertown

Tuttle, Loren & David W.
RD 3, Box 341
Covered Bridge Rd., 19512
(215) 689-4814

Amenities: 1,10,16
Breakfast: C. Plus

Dbl. Oc.: $65.00
Sgl. Oc.: $65.00
Third Person: $10.00

The Little House—You will be the only guests in a totally restored 1790 stone guest house on a 125-acre Oley Valley farm in a national registered rural district, yet only 12 miles to the Reading outlets. Antique markets, country auctions, fine restaurants nearby. Complete kitchen.

Brackney *

Strnatka, Nancy & Dan
Tripp Lake Rd.
RD 1, Box 68, 18812
(800) 435-3362

Amenities: 1,2,6,7,8,9,10,12, 15,16
Breakfast: F.

Dbl. Oc.: $65.00 - $75.00
Sgl. Oc.: $60.00 - $70.00
Third Person: $15.00
Child: $15.00

Indian Mountain Inn—Country inn sequestered in 3,500+ acres of wilderness. Authentic country inn cuisine. Murder mystery and other theme weekends, hiking, cross-country skiing. Beautiful vistas, hot tub, ice skating, trout fishing and more.

1. No Smoking	5. Tennis Available	9. Credit Cards Accepted	13. Lunch Available	17. Shared Baths
2. No Pets	6. Golf Available	10. Personal Check Accepted	14. Conference Rooms Avail.	18. Afternoon Tea
3 Off Season Rates	7. Swimmming Avail.	11. Reservations Necessary	15. Group Seminars Avail.	* Commisions given
4. Senior Citizen Rates	8. Skiing Available	12. Dinner Available	16. Private Baths	to Travel Agents

PENNSYLVANIA

Brogue *

Marino, Sharon
Rte. 1, P.O. Box 742, 17309
(717) 927-9646

Amenities: 9,10,11,15
Breakfast: F.

Dbl. Oc.: $95.00
Sgl. Oc.: $95.00
Child: Under 12 yrs. - $25.00

The Miller House—This 19th-century home has three bedrooms, living room, dining room and furnished kitchen. Ideal for couples, families, business people or small seminars. Quiet with 120 acres of wooded mountains. Activities include trout fishing, horseback riding, antiquing and shopping.

Canadensis *

Dornich, Charlotte & Dick
Rte. 447, 18325
(717) 595-2532

Amenities: 5,6,7,8,9,10,11,12,
15,16
Breakfast: F.

Dbl. Oc.: $167.04
Sgl. Oc.: $92.80
Child: $35.00

Pine Knob Inn—Step back into yesteryear. This 1840s inn is furnished with antiques and collectibles. Enjoy gourmet dining at its best. Guests gather on the veranda in summer or by the fireplace in our spacious living room in winter. Dinner and breakfast is included in the rates.

Canadensis

Pickett, Esther & William
Rte. 447 & Seese Hill Rd.,
18325-007
(717) 595-7115

Amenities: 2,5,6,7,8,10,11,16,
17
Breakfast: C. Plus

Dbl. Oc.: $37.10 - $53.00
Third Person: $15.00

Dreamy Acres—Located in the heart of the Pocono Mountain vacationland on three acres with a stream flowing into a small pond. The lodge is 500 feet back from the highway, giving it a pleasing, quiet atmosphere. B&B from May 1 through October 31. Close to stores, churches and recreation.

Carlisle *

Fitting, Jeanne
1880 McClures Gap Rd., 17013
(717) 249-1455

Amenities: 1,2,6,10,11,12,16,
17
Breakfast: F.

Dbl. Oc.: $45.00 - $55.00
Sgl. Oc.: $40.00 - $50.00

Alwayspring Farm—Quiet, small farm in rural setting. Ten minutes to Carlisle, Dickinson College, U.S. War College and antique shops. Central air. Ten minutes to Pennsylvania Turnpike. Easy day trips to Gettysburg, Harrisburg, Hershey Park and Washington, DC.

Carlisle

Line, Joan & Robert
2070 Ritner Hwy., 17013
(717) 243-1281

Amenities: 2,6,10,11,16,17
Breakfast: F.

Dbl. Oc.: $55.00 - $65.00
Sgl. Oc.: $45.00
Third Person: $15.00
Child: $15.00

Line Limousin Farmhouse B&B—An 1864 large brick and stone farmhouse on 100 acres. Our cows are from Limoges, France. Two rooms, private bath. King beds. Use of golf driving range, player piano and picnic tables. Near Dickinson College. Two miles to Exit 12 of I-81. Two or more nights reduced rates.

1. No Smoking	5. Tennis Available	9. Credit Cards Accepted	13. Lunch Available	17. Shared Baths
2. No Pets	6. Golf Available	10. Personal Check Accepted	14. Conference Rooms Avail.	18. Afternoon Tea
3 Off Season Rates	7. Swimmming Avail.	11. Reservations Necessary	15. Group Seminars Avail.	* Commisions given
4. Senior Citizen Rates	8. Skiing Available	12. Dinner Available	16. Private Baths	to Travel Agents

PENNSYLVANIA

Christiana

Metzler, Minnie & Bob
107 Noble Rd., 17509
(215) 593-5535

Amenities: 1,2,6,10,17
Breakfast: F.

Dbl. Oc.: $40.00
Sgl. Oc.: $30.00
Third Person: $16.00
Child: Under 12 yrs. - $9.00

Winding Glen Farm Guest Home—A dairy farm situated in a beautiful valley. Guests stay in the 250-year-old stone farmhouse. Watch the cows being milked or take a walk to the covered bridge. Many Amish farms and shops nearby. Also handmade quilts for sale.

Clarion

Miller, Judy & Bill
77 So. Seventh Ave., 16214
(814) 226-4996

Amenities: 1,2,6,9,10,16,17
Breakfast: C. Plus

Dbl. Oc.: $63.60
Sgl. Oc.: $63.60

The Clarion House Bed And Breakfast—Our beautiful turn-of-the-century home is located in the small university town of Clarion with easy access to university activities, shopping, restaurants, golfing, hiking and river sports. Tasteful decor, memorable breakfasts and warm hospitality.

Clearfield *

Durant, Peggy & Tim
216 So. Front St., 16830
(814) 765-4805, 765-1711

Amenities: 1,2,4,9,10,16,17,
18
Breakfast: C. Plus

Dbl. Oc.: $48.00
Sgl. Oc.: $37.00
Third Person: $11.00
Child: Under 7 yrs. - no charge

The Victorian Loft—An 1894 home on river transports visitors to a more graceful era. Gingerbread, stained glass, magnificent cherry woodwork, whirlpool, weaving and spinning demos. Design studio featured in *Threads Magazine*. Hosts are country lawyer and fiber artist. PA exit 19, I-80.

Cooksburg *

O'Day, Ellen
Cook Forest — River Rd., 16217
(800) 648-6743

Amenities: 2,3,4,7,9,11,12,13,15,16
Breakfast: C.
Dbl. Oc.: $67.00 - $109.00

Clarion River Lodge—A small, romantic country inn on the gentle Clarion River adjacent to Cook Forest Park. Fine dining and spirits. Only 20 rooms. Air conditioning, TV and queen or king beds. Great hiking, canoeing, biking, X-C skiing. Open year-round.

1. No Smoking	5. Tennis Available	9. Credit Cards Accepted	13. Lunch Available	17. Shared Baths
2. No Pets	6. Golf Available	10. Personal Check Accepted	14. Conference Rooms Avail.	18. Afternoon Tea
3 Off Season Rates	7. Swimmming Avail.	11. Reservations Necessary	15. Group Seminars Avail.	* Commisions given
4. Senior Citizen Rates	8. Skiing Available	12. Dinner Available	16. Private Baths	to Travel Agents

PENNSYLVANIA

Cresco

Swingle, Katherine G.
RD 2, Box 1051, 18326
(717) 676-4225

Amenities: 2,5,6,7,8,10,17
Breakfast: C.

Dbl. Oc.: $30.00
Sgl. Oc.: $25.00
Third Person: $10.00
Child: Under 5 yrs. - $5.00

LaAnna Guest House—A Victorian home furnished with antiques of the Empire and Victorian periods. Spacious rooms, quiet village, lovely walks, waterfalls, mountain views and privacy Close to large Pocono resorts.

Dallas *

Rowland, Jeanette & Clifford
RR 1, Box 349, 18612-9604
(717) 639-3245 (anytime),
(800) 950-9130 (Noon-4 p.m.)

Amenities: 1,2,8,9,10,11,14,15,16,18
Breakfast: F.
Dbl. Oc.: $54.00 - $74.00
Sgl. Oc.: $54.00 - $74.00
Third Person: No charge
Child: No charge

Ponda Rowland Bed And Breakfast Inn—Mountain farm overlooking private wilderness sanctuary, ponds and farm animals. Canoeing, hiking, ice skating on premises. Large stone fireplace, beamed ceilings, country antique collections. Montage ski area, golfing, hunting, fishing, racetrack and antiquing nearby.

Downingtown

Reigel, Joan & Earl
1417 Highland Ave., 19335
(215) 269-8207

Amenities: 1,2,10,11,16,17
Breakfast: C.

Dbl. Oc.: $69.00 - $95.00
Sgl. Oc.: $79.00 - $105.00

Bradford Hills B&B—Our 17-room Victorian home for 20 years was built in 1890. The surrounding eight, mostly wooded, acres provide homes for a wide variety of animals and birds. Nice views. Pleasant walks. Four rooms. One with private bath. Three rooms share two baths, powder room and sitting room.

Eagles Mere *

Dougherty, Dennis
Allegheny Ave.
P.O. Box 314, 17731
(717) 525-3394

Amenities: 1,2,3,4,5,6,7,8,10,
11,15,16,18
Breakfast: F.

Dbl. Oc.: $68.90
Sgl. Oc.: $58.30
Third Person: $15.90
Child: Over 12 Yrs. - $10.60

Shacy Lane Bed And Breakfast—A picturesque mountain-top resort close to excellent hiking, swimming, golf and skiing. Located in a quiet Victorian town high in the endless mountains. This charming seven bedroom inn offers all the conveniences and amenities of a home-away from-home. Mystery weekends. AAA approved.

---

1. No Smoking	5. Tennis Available	9. Credit Cards Accepted	13. Lunch Available	17. Shared Baths
2. No Pets	6. Golf Available	10. Personal Check Accepted	14. Conference Rooms Avail.	18. Afternoon Tea
3 Off Season Rates	7. Swimming Avail.	11. Reservations Necessary	15. Group Seminars Avail.	* Commisions given
4. Senior Citizen Rates	8. Skiing Available	12. Dinner Available	16. Private Baths	to Travel Agents

PENNSYLVANIA

Eagles Mere

Wilkinson III, Joseph C.
Box 2, Eagle Mere Ave., 17731
(717) 525-3245

Amenities: 2,3,5,6,7,8,9,10,
11,16,17,18
Breakfast: F.

Dbl. Oc.: $60.00 - $110.00
Sgl. Oc.: $45.00 - $80.00
Third Person: $25.00
Child: Under 6 yrs. - $10.00

The Flora Villa Inne—Elegant three story, 19th-century Victorian. Located in the center of the village. Access to private lake, country club with exceptional 18-hole golf course. Entire inn recently restored. Antiques, fireplace, wonderful porch. Perennial gardens. Six rooms, 4-1/2 baths.

Elizabethville *

Facinelli, Beth & Jim
30 W. Main St., 17023
(717) 362-3476, Fax: (717) 362-4571

Amenities: 1,2,6,7,9,10,15,16
Breakfast: C.

Dbl. Oc.: $63.60
Sgl. Oc.: $58.30
Third Person: $5.30

The Inn At Elizabethville—A comfortable 12-room house furnished in arts and crafts/Mission Oaks style. Located on Route 209 in south central Pennsylvania. Seven rooms with private baths. Fax, phone and copy service on site. Conference room seating 16 available for seminars, meetings and small dinners.

Emlenton

Burns, Cynthia
109 River Ave., 16373
(412) 867-2261

Amenities: 1,2,6,9,10,17
Breakfast: C.

Dbl. Oc.: $42.40
Sgl. Oc.: $42.40
Third Person: $10.60

The Barnard House Bed And Breakfast—A cozy retreat nestled along the banks of the Allegheny River. The many porches and all five bedrooms offer scenic views of the peaceful river. Antique shops, golfing (on the nation's oldest golf course) — all within five minutes.

Ephrata *

Donecker, H. William
318-324 No. State St., 17522
(717) 733-8696

Amenities: 2,6,9,10,11,12, 13,14,15,16
Breakfast: C. Plus
Dbl. Oc.: $59.00 - $175.00
Sgl Oc.: $51.00 - $167.00
Third Person: $10.60
Child: Under 3 yrs. - $8.00

The Guesthouse And 1777 House At Doneckers—Country elegance, suites, jacuzzis and fireplaces. Complimentary breakfast. Near Doneckers Restaurant, fashion stores, art/craft/quilt galleries and farmers' market. Historic Lancaster County. Amish farmlands and antiques.

---

1. No Smoking
2. No Pets
3. Off Season Rates
4. Senior Citizen Rates

5. Tennis Available
6. Golf Available
7. Swimming Avail.
8. Skiing Available

9. Credit Cards Accepted
10. Personal Check Accepted
11. Reservations Necessary
12. Dinner Available

13. Lunch Available
14. Conference Rooms Avail.
15. Group Seminars Avail.
16. Private Baths

17. Shared Baths
18. Afternoon Tea
* Commisions given
to Travel Agents

PENNSYLVANIA

Ephrata

Graybill, Dorothy
900 W. Main St., 17522
(717) 733-6094

Amenities: 1,5,6,7,9,10,12,15,18
Breakfast: F.
Dbl. Oc.: $65.00 - $115.00
Sgl Oc.: $55.00 - $105.00
Third Person: $35.00
Child: Under 12 yrs. - $20.00

Historic Smithton Country Inn—A smiling, welcoming inn. Every room has a fireplace, a four-poster or canopy bed, leather-upholstered furniture, books, reading lamps and optional featherbeds. Antiques, handmade things, chamber music, candles and quilts contribute to make a very romantic setting.

Ephrata

Hackman, Kathryn
140 Hackman Rd., 17522
(717) 733-3498

Amenities: 1,2,9,10,16,17
Breakfast: C. Plus

Dbl. Oc.: $63.60 - $74.20
Sgl. Oc.: $53.00 - $63.60

Hackman's Country Inn - B&B — Historic 1857 farmhouse on 90 acres in Lancaster County. Stenciled rooms with patchwork quilts. Breakfast by the walk-in fireplace. Shaded lawns and porch provide a peaceful retreat on summer days. Tour Amish farm country. Shop antique malls. Fine restaurants nearby.

Erwinna

Faure, Barbara
763 River Rd., 18920
(215) 294-9595

Amenities: 1,2,7,9,10,11,12,16
Breakfast: C.
Dbl. Oc.: $110.00 - $135.00

Golden Pheasant Inn—Elegant 1857 fieldstone inn situated between the Delaware River and the Pennsylvania Canal. Six spacious guest rooms featuring four-poster queen-size beds. Country French cuisine served in three romantic dining rooms. The greenhouse overlooks the canal and is candlelit for dinner.

1. No Smoking	5. Tennis Available	9. Credit Cards Accepted	13. Lunch Available	17. Shared Baths
2. No Pets	6. Golf Available	10. Personal Check Accepted	14. Conference Rooms Avail.	18. Afternoon Tea
3 Off Season Rates	7. Swimmming Avail.	11. Reservations Necessary	15. Group Seminars Avail.	* Commisions given
4. Senior Citizen Rates	8. Skiing Available	12. Dinner Available	16. Private Baths	to Travel Agents

PENNSYLVANIA

Erwinna *

Strouse, Ronald
River Rd., 18920
(215) 294-9100

Amenities: 2,3,9,10,11,12,14, 15,16,18
Breakfast: C. Plus
Dbl. Oc.: $86.40 - $167.40
Sgl. Oc.: $59.40 - $81.00

Evermay-on-the-Delaware—Located in rural Bucks County on 25 acres of gardens and meadows. The country hotel, in the National Register of Historic Places, offers lodging, including breakfast and afternoon tea. An elegant dinner is served Friday, Saturday, Sunday and holidays.

Exton

Guanbeck, Kerry E.
146 So. Whitford Rd., 19341
(215) 524-1830

Amenities: 1,2,6,9,12,13,14,15,16
Breakfast: C. Plus
Dbl. Oc.: $55.45 - $129.70
Sgl Oc.: $55.45 - $129.70
Third Person: $15.00

Duling-Kurtz House And Country Inn—A cozy parlor will welcome you. Each room has been comfortably furnished with beautiful period reproductions! All baths are private. Experience old-style candlelight dining in intimate rooms of our lovely stone house. Located near historic sites and museums.

Gap *

Golish, Tara
6051 Old Philadelphia Pike
(Rte. 340), 17527
(717) 442-3139

Amenities: 1,2,9,16,17
Breakfast: F.
Dbl. Oc.: $63.60 - $79.50
Sgl. Oc.: $63.60 - $79.50

Fassitt Mansion Bed And Breakfast—Located in the rolling hills of Pennsylvania Dutch country. Our restored 1845 country home combines Old-World charm with all the modern conveniences. If you bring your bicycle, we have maps for tours ranging from five to 50 miles.

1. No Smoking	5. Tennis Available	9. Credit Cards Accepted	13. Lunch Available	17. Shared Baths
2. No Pets	6. Golf Available	10. Personal Check Accepted	14. Conference Rooms Avail.	18. Afternoon Tea
3 Off Season Rates	7. Swimmming Avail.	11. Reservations Necessary	15. Group Seminars Avail.	* Commisions given
4. Senior Citizen Rates	8. Skiing Available	12. Dinner Available	16. Private Baths	to Travel Agents

Gettysburg *

Agard, Mimi
44 York St., 17325
(717) 337-3423

Amenities: 1,2,5,6,7,8,9,10,
  11,15,16,17,18
Breakfast: F.
Dbl. Oc.: $70.00 - $120.00
Sgl Oc.: $65.00 - $85.00
Third Person: $10.00

The Brafferton Inn—The first house built in Gettysburg's historic district. Hand painted stencils and primitive antiques amidst large living room, atrium, and sitting room. Flower garden. Significant Civil War history. Sumptuous breakfast served in muraled dining room.

Gettysburg *

Hormel, Monna
315 Broadway, Hanover, 17331 (mail)
(800) 553-7009

Amenities: 2,5,6,7,8,9,10,14,16,18
Breakfast: F.
Dbl. Oc.: $74.20 - $132.50
Sgl Oc.: $74.20 - $132.50

Beechmont Inn—An elegant 1834 Federal inn with seven rooms, all private baths, fireplaces, whirlpool, A/C, gourmet breakfast and afternoon tea. Antiquing, Lake Marburg and outlets nearby. Close to Hershey and the Lancaster Amish. Weekend packages available. Mobil and AAA aproved.

Gettysburg

Martin, Doris
231 Hanover St., 17325
(717) 337-3888

Amenities: 1,2,3,5,6,7,8,9,10
  11,16,17,18
Breakfast: F.

Dbl. Oc.:$62.50 - $79.50
Sgl. Oc.: $58.30 - $73.15
Third Person: $15.90
Child: Under 12 yrs. - $10.60

Keystone Inn— A large late Victorian brick inn. The interior includes lots of natural wood and flowered wall paper. The guest rooms have a reading nook, writing desk and are air-conditioned. Soft pastels and ruffles create a warm welcome. Near battlefield, antiques, Amish and outlets.

1. No Smoking	5. Tennis Available	9. Credit Cards Accepted	13. Lunch Available	17. Shared Baths
2. No Pets	6. Golf Available	10. Personal Check Accepted	14. Conference Rooms Avail.	18. Afternoon Tea
3 Off Season Rates	7. Swimming Avail.	11. Reservations Necessary	15. Group Seminars Avail.	* Commisions given
4. Senior Citizen Rates	8. Skiing Available	12. Dinner Available	16. Private Baths	to Travel Agents

PENNSYLVANIA

Gettysburg

Martin, Mary
96 Hickory Bridge Rd.,
Orrtanna, PA, 17353 (mail)
(717) 642-5261

Amenities: 1,2,6,8,9,10,12,15, 16
Breakfast: F.

Dbl. Oc.: $$75.00 - $89.00
Sgl. Oc.: $50.00 - $65.00

Hickory Bridge Farm—Only eight miles west of Gettysburg. Unique country dining and bed and breakfast. Farm-style dinners served in a Pennsylvania barn. Country cottages in a quiet wooded setting by a stream. Full breakfast served at restored 1750 farmhouse. Owned and operated for 15 years.

Gettysburg *

Skradski, Maribeth & Frank
218 Carlisle Str., 17325
(717) 337-1711,
Fax: (717) 334-6228

Amenities: 1,2,3,5,6,7,8,9,10, 11,14,15,16,18
Breakfast: F.

Dbl. Oc.:$87.98 - $98.58
Sgl. Oc.: $82.65 - $93.28

The Old Appleford Inn—Return in time to this 1867 Italianate mansion now known as the Old Appleford Inn. Twelve guest bedrooms, all with private baths, are decorated with period antiques. Centrally located to all attractions, we offer numerous amenities. "For the discriminating traveler."

Greenville

Ochs, Diane & Tom
32 Eagle St., 16125
(412) 588-8887

Amenities: 2,6,10,11,16,17
Breakfast: C. Plus

Dbl. Oc.: $42.40 - $63.60
Sgl. Oc.: $37.10 - $53.00
Third Person: $10.60

Phillips House 1890—A 100-year-old restored Victorian home in western Pennsylvania, mid-way between Erie and Pittsburgh. Near I-80 and I-79. Greenville is the home of Theil College. The surrounding Lakeland area offers many outdoor activities. Antiques, quilts and comfort.

Hawley *

Lazan, Judith & Sheldon
528 Academy St., 18428
(717) 226-3430

Amenities: 2,9,16,17,18
Breakfast: F.
Dbl. Oc.: $65.00 - $75.00
Sgl. Oc.: $40.00
Third Person: $30.00

Academy Street Bed And Breakfast—Outstanding historic 1863 Victorian built by Civil War captain. Near largest and most beautiful recreational lake in state with all activities. Convenient to I-84. Antique-furnished rooms by hostess Judith, an avid cook. Gourmet buffet breakfast. Large, airy A/C rooms.

---

1. No Smoking	5. Tennis Available	9. Credit Cards Accepted	13. Lunch Available	17. Shared Baths
2. No Pets	6. Golf Available	10. Personal Check Accepted	14. Conference Rooms Avail.	18. Afternoon Tea
3 Off Season Rates	7. Swimmming Avail.	11. Reservations Necessary	15. Group Seminars Avail.	* Commisions given
4. Senior Citizen Rates	8. Skiing Available	12. Dinner Available	16. Private Baths	to Travel Agents

PENNSYLVANIA

Hershey *

Long Family, The
50 Northeast Dr., 17033
(717) 533-2603

Amenities: 1,2,3,5,6,7,9,10, 11,15,16,17
Breakfast: F.

Dbl. Oc.: $54.00
Sgl. Oc.: $54.00
Third Person: $5.00
Child: Under 2 yrs. - no charge

Pinehurst Inn B&B—A country setting within walking distance of Hershey attractions. Twelve guest rooms, large dining room and living room with fireplace. Wonderful for family reunions or small seminars. Less than an hour's drive to Gettysburg and the Pennsylvania Dutch county of Lancaster.

Intercourse

Schoen, Robin & Sterling
313 Osceola Mill Rd.,
Gordonville, 17529 (mail)
(717) 768-3758

Amenities: 1,2,10,11,16,17
Breakfast: F.

Dbl. Oc.: $100.00
Sgl. Oc.: $75.00

Osceola Mill House—Located in scenic Lancaster County surrounded by old-order Amish farms in a quaint historic setting. The 1766 inn is decorated with period antiques and reproductions. We have been told that breakfast alone is worth the trip.

Kennett Square *

Hicks, Anne
201 E. St. Rd. (Rte. 926), 19348
(215) 444-3903

Amenities: 2,7,10,11,13,15,16,17,18
Breakfast: F.
Dbl. Oc.: $79.50
Sgl Oc.: $58.30
Third Person: $20.00
Child: Under 6 yrs. - $10.00

Meadow Spring Farm—An 1836 farmhouse on working farm. Seven guest rooms, four with private baths, furnished with family antiques, dolls and country crafts. Nearby: Longwood Gardens, Winterthur Museum and Brandywine Museum. Featured in *Country Inn Magazine, Washington Post* and *New York Times*.

Kinzers

Groff, Charles
35 So. Kinzer Rd., 17535
(717) 442-4901

Amenities: 1,3,10,17
Breakfast: C.

Dbl. Oc.: $29.68
Sgl. Oc.: $29.68
Third Person: $3.00
Child: Under 4 yrs. - $3.00

Sycamore Haven Farm—A dairy farm 15 miles east of Lancaster, 1/4 mile off Rte. 30 in Pennsylvania Dutch country. There is a balcony with swing and chairs. Forty dairy cows are milked morning and evening. You may watch. Children will enjoy kittens and a pet sheep will enjoy your attention.

1. No Smoking	5. Tennis Available	9. Credit Cards Accepted	13. Lunch Available	17. Shared Baths
2. No Pets	6. Golf Available	10. Personal Check Accepted	14. Conference Rooms Avail.	18. Afternoon Tea
3 Off Season Rates	7. Swimmming Avail.	11. Reservations Necessary	15. Group Seminars Avail.	* Commisions given
4. Senior Citizen Rates	8. Skiing Available	12. Dinner Available	16. Private Baths	to Travel Agents

Lahaska *

Jamison, Earl
Rtes. 202 and Street Rd., Box 218,
Peddlers Village, 18931
(215) 794-4004

Amenities: 1,2,4,5,6,9,10,11, 12,13,14,15,16
Breakfast: C. Plus

Dbl. Oc.: $95.00
Sgl. Oc.: $95.00
Third Person: $15.00
Child: Under 1 yr. - no charge

The Golden Plough Inn—Luxurious rooms and suites with private baths, refrigerators, TV, fireplaces, jacuzzis; in 18th-century shopping village with 70 shops and restaurants. Nearby are antiques, museums and historic sites. Five miles from New Hope. Seasonal packages available.

Lampeter *

Mason, Richard
837 Village Rd.
P.O. Box 294, 17537
(717) 464-0707

Amenities: 1,2,3,5,6,7,9,10, 11,12,13,14,16,18
Breakfast: F.

Dbl. Oc.: $73.14 - $104.94
Sgl. Oc.: $62.54
Third Person: $21.20
Child: 9 - 13 yrs. - $15.90

Walkabout Inn—Restored Mennonite home. Elegant antique decorated rooms. English garden, village setting. Candlelight five course breakfast. Specials include Amish dinner, tour, quilt auctions. Romantic honeymoon/anniversary suites. Canopy beds. All rooms with private baths and cable TV. AAA.

Lancaster

Flatley, Sue & Jack
1105 E. King, 17602
(717) 293-1723

Amenities: 1,2,9,10,16,17
Breakfast: F.

Dbl. Oc.: $63.60 - $74.20
Third Person: $10.00
Child: $10.00

O'Flaherty's Dingeldein House—Come and make our home your home. Enjoy genuine warmth and hospitality in the homey atmosphere of the Dingeldein House. Our Dutch colonial home is traditionally appointed for your comfort for a restful stay in beautiful Lancaster County. Our breakfast will make your day.

Lancaster *

Giersch, Carol & Bill
1400 E. King St., 17602
(717) 396-8928

Amenities: 1,2,16,17
Breakfast: F.

Dbl. Oc.: $53.00 - $74.20
Sgl. Oc.: $46.00 - $53.00
Third Person: $15.00
Child: Under 10 yrs. - $5.50

New Life Homestead Bed And Breakfast—A stately 1912 brick home in center of Amish and historic area. The feeling of visiting your auntie, spoiling guests with flowers, fruit and candy. Air conditioning. Hearty breakfasts and evening treats. Tours arranged. Videos on Amish. Rest in the gardens. Mennonite family.

---

1. No Smoking
2. No Pets
3 Off Season Rates
4. Senior Citizen Rates
5. Tennis Available
6. Golf Available
7. Swimming Avail.
8. Skiing Available
9. Credit Cards Accepted
10. Personal Check Accepted
11. Reservations Necessary
12. Dinner Available
13. Lunch Available
14. Conference Rooms Avail.
15. Group Seminars Avail.
16. Private Baths
17. Shared Baths
18. Afternoon Tea
* Commisions given
to Travel Agents

Lancaster *

Hartung, Brant
2014 Old Philadelphia Pike, 17602
(717) 299-5305

Amenities: 2,5,6,7,8,10,11,15,16,17
Breakfast: C.
Dbl. Oc.: $63.60 - $95.40
Sgl Oc.: $63.60 - $95.40
Third Person: $10.00
Child: Under 2 yrs. - no charge

Witmer's Tavern — Historic 1725 Inn—Lancaster's only remaining authentic pre-Revolutionary inn still lodging travelers. Fireplaces, fresh flowers and antique quilts in each romantic room. In National Register of Historic Places. Intercourse, Bird-in-Hand villages, market, auctions, Pennsylvania Dutch farms next door.

Lancaster

Kepiro, Lori & Robert
184 E. Brook Rd.
Rte. 896, Smoketown, 17576
(717) 393-6927

Amenities: 1,2,3,5,6,7,9,16
Breakfast: C.

Dbl. Oc.: $29.68 - $51.94
Sgl. Oc.: $25.44 - $46.64
Third Person: $5.00
Child: Under 12 yrs. - no charge

Homestead Lodging—Family-operated lodge with a homey atmosphere in clean country rooms. Adjacent to an Amish farm. Wonderful restaurants, quilt shops, farmer's markets, craft and antique shops. Also many museums and shopping outlets. Tours available. Refrigerators in room.

Lancaster

Mitrani, Jacqueline & Stephen
2129 Main St. (Churchtown), 17555
(215) 445-6713

Amenities: 1,2,5,6,7,11,16, 17
Breakfast: C., (F.weekends)

Dbl. Oc.: $58.00 & $68.00
Sgl. Oc.: $48.00 & $55.00
Third Person: $10.60

The Foreman House Bed And Breakfast—Located in Amish country in Lancaster County, surrounded by beautiful farmlands. Quilts and antiques in area to purchase. An elegant old home in a quaint village. Furnished with heirlooms and local art. Many repeat guests. Gregarious hosts.

Lancaster *

Owens, Karen & Jim
1049 E. King St., 17603
(717) 397-1017

Amenities: 1,2,3,5,6,7
Breakfast: F.

Dbl. Oc.: $80.00 - $120.00
Sgl. Oc.: $80.00 - $120.00
Third Person: $30.

The King's Cottage—Escape to an elegant, award-winning National Register inn near Amish farms. King/queen beds, private baths, full breakfast, afternoon tea, air conditioning and fireplaces. Antiques, crafts, quilt shopping and historic sites. Amish dinner available. AAA, Mobil listed — excellent.

1. No Smoking	5. Tennis Available	9. Credit Cards Accepted	13. Lunch Available	17. Shared Baths
2. No Pets	6. Golf Available	10. Personal Check Accepted	14. Conference Rooms Avail.	18. Afternoon Tea
3 Off Season Rates	7. Swimming Avail.	11. Reservations Necessary	15. Group Seminars Avail.	* Commisions given
4. Senior Citizen Rates	8. Skiing Available	12. Dinner Available	16. Private Baths	to Travel Agents

Lancaster

Simpson, David
2574 Lincoln Hwy. E.
(Rte. 30 E.), Ronks (mail), 17572
(717) 299-6005

Amenities: 1,2,9,10,17
Breakfast: F.

Dbl. Oc.: $55.00 - $65.00
Sgl. Oc.: $55.00 - $65.00
Third Person: $12.00

Candlelite Inn Bed And Breakfast—Surrounded by Amish farmlands. This 1920s brick farmhouse offers four clean, quiet rooms, sitting room with TV, central air/heat, phone and country breakfast. It is close to all attractions. There is also an antiques and collectibles shop on the premises.

Lancaster *

Smith, Stuart
Rte. 23, Churchtown (location)
2100 Main St., Narvon (mail), 17555
(215) 445-7794

Amenities: 2,5,6,7,9,10,11,
       12,14,15,16,17
Breakfast: F.
Dbl. Oc.: $49.00 - $95.00
Sgl Oc.: $49.00 - $95.00
Third Person: $20.00
Child: Over 12 yrs. - $20.00

Churchtown Inn B&B—National Historic Register stone mansion, circa 1735, in heart of Pennsylvania Dutch country. Dinner with an Amish family arranged. Musical innkeeper. Special-event weekends (murder mysteries, concerts, Victorian Ball, etc.) Tourist attractions, antique markets. Outlets. Evening tea.

Lancaster

Zook, Mary K.
1687 Lincoln Hwy. E., 17602
(717) 392-9412

Amenities: 1,2,3,10,11,12,16
Breakfast: F.
Dbl. Oc.: $45.00 - $65.00
Sgl Oc.: $43.00 - $60.00
Third Person: $10.00
Child: Under 6 mo. - no charge

Lincoln Haus Inn Bed And Breakfast—Air-conditioning. Built in 1915 with distinctive hip roofs. Stained glass entryway accented with antique furniture and rugs. Being Amish, I will give you information first hand as we eat a good, hearty, family-style breakfast. Close to bus, train, Amish and historic areas.

1. No Smoking	5. Tennis Available	9. Credit Cards Accepted	13. Lunch Available	17. Shared Baths
2. No Pets	6. Golf Available	10. Personal Check Accepted	14. Conference Rooms Avail.	18. Afternoon Tea
3 Off Season Rates	7. Swimmming Avail.	11. Reservations Necessary	15. Group Seminars Avail.	* Commisions given
4. Senior Citizen Rates	8. Skiing Available	12. Dinner Available	16. Private Baths	to Travel Agents

Leola

Parmer, Jean W.
111 Turtle Hill Rd., 17540
(717) 656-6163

Amenities: 1,2,10,17,18
Breakfast: F.

Dbl. Oc.: $50.00
Sgl. Oc.: $30.00
Third Person: $10.00
Child: Under 5 yrs. - $5.00

Turtle Hill Bed And Breakfast—Very scenic, one mile off Routes 222 and 272. Overlooks Conestoga River near an old mill — photographer's paradise. Rural area. Neighboring Amish farms.

Lititz *

Mosimann, Debrah & Warner
500 Blantz Rd., 17543
(717) 627-3358

Amenities: 1,2,3,9,10,11,15, 16,18
Breakfast: F.

Dbl. Oc.: $70.00 - $117.00
Third Person: $15.00
Child: Under 2 yrs. - no charge

Swiss Woods Bed And Breakfast—Nestled on the edge of the wood overlooking a lake, this inn is convenient to Hershey and Lancaster. Private baths (two jacuzzis), queen beds and patios or balconies adjoining each room. Breakfast served in our sunny common room features Swiss and local fare.

Lumberville *

Nessler, Harry
River Rd., 18933
(215) 297-5661

Amenities: 2,7,10,14,16
Breakfast: F.

Dbl. Oc.: $78.50 - $111.00
Sgl. Oc.: $73.10
Third Person: $10.60

1740 House—Situated in the most charming section of Bucks County, this B&B inn offers guests 24 early-American rooms, each with private bath and either terrace or balcony overlooking the Delaware River.

Manheim *

Avella, Alice
140 So. Charlotte St., 17545
(717) 664-4168

Amenities: 1,2,4,5,6,7,9,10, 11,16,18
Breakfast: F.

Dbl. Oc.: $85.00 - $106.00
Sgl. Oc.: $85.00 - $106.00
Third Person: $20.00

Manheim Manor Bed And Breakfast Inn And Gift Shop—An 1856 Victorian B&B in National Register. Antique furnishings, lace curtains, Oriental carpets, TV in rooms, Compact refrigerator, bedside cordials and mints. Bountiful breakfast. Minutes from fine restaurants and Renaissance Faire. Six rooms, private baths. Amish Country

Manheim

Herr, Barry
2256 Huber Dr., 17545
(717) 653-9852

Amenities: 1,2,3,6,9,10,11,16, 17
Breakfast: C. Plus

Dbl. Oc.: $74.20 - $100.70
Sgl. Oc.: $74.20 - $100.70
Third Person: $15.00

Herr Farmhouse Inn—Fully restored 1750 stone farmhouse on 26 scenic acres. All original woodwork. Six functional fireplaces. Central air-conditioning. Take a step into yesteryear amidst colonial antiques, reproductions and local quilts. Antiquing and historic attractions nearby.

1. No Smoking	5. Tennis Available	9. Credit Cards Accepted	13. Lunch Available	17. Shared Baths
2. No Pets	6. Golf Available	10. Personal Check Accepted	14. Conference Rooms Avail.	18. Afternoon Tea
3 Off Season Rates	7. Swimmming Avail.	11. Reservations Necessary	15. Group Seminars Avail.	* Commisions given
4. Senior Citizen Rates	8. Skiing Available	12. Dinner Available	16. Private Baths	to Travel Agents

PENNSYLVANIA

Mansfield

Crossen, Sylvia S. & Stuart
131 So. Main, 16933
(717) 662-7008

Amenities: 1,2,4,5,6,7,8,9,10, 12,13,15,16,17
Breakfast: F.

Dbl. Oc.: $44.52 - $63.60
Sgl. Oc.: $40.28 - $63.60
Third Person: $12.00
Child: Under 3 yrs. - $3.00

Crossroads Bed And Breakfast—A 1926 Georgian-style B&B four plus bedrooms. Situated in small college community in the scenic mountain region of northern Pennsylvania. Nearby museums, hiking, boating and sightseeing. Lounge, game/card room available. Whirlpool tub, TV and air conditioning.

Mertztown

Dimick, Elsa
RD #2, Box 26, 19539
(215) 682-6197

Amenities: 1,2,5,7,8,9,10,11, 14,16,17,18
Breakfast: F.

Dbl. Oc.: $74.20 - $79.50
Sgl. Oc.: $63.60 - $68.90
Third Person: $30.00
Child: Under 10 yrs. - no charge

Longswamp Bed And Breakfast—A historic house set in lush Berks County farmland, near the Amish and minutes from a ski area. Great hiking, biking and antiquing. Fine restaurants nearby. Superb breakfast served in old summer kitchen. Six rooms in main house, three rooms in the cottage and one barn suite.

Middletown

Killian, Donna & Lee
475 Roundtop Rd., 17057
(717) 944-2148

Amenities: 1,2,10,11,17
Breakfast: C. or F.

Dbl. Oc.: $47.70
Sgl. Oc.: $47.70
Third Person: $5.30
Child: Under 10 yrs. - no charge

The Gathering Place—A country home situated amid nine wooded acres. Relax in front of 2-story fireplace, take a walk in the woods or watch the wildlife while enjoying refreshments on the deck. Visit Hershey Park or take a tour of Lancaster County's Amish country.

Milford

Schneider, Stewart
RD 2, Box 9285, 18337
(717) 296-6322

Amenities: 1,2,7,8,9,10,11,12, 16,17
Breakfast: F.

Dbl. Oc.: $60.00 - $100.00
Sgl. Oc.: $60.00 - $85.00

Black Walnut B&B Inn—A Tudor-style stone house with historic marble fireplace, 12 charming bedrooms with antique and brass beds. A 160-acre quiet and peaceful estate. Conveniently located near horseback riding, antiquing, golfing, skiing, rafting and canoeing on the Delaware River.

Millersburg

Wingard, Suzanne & Donald
312 Market St., 17061
(717) 692-3511

Amenities: 1,2,5,6,9,10,11,16, 17
Breakfast: C. Plus

Dbl. Oc.: $63.60
Sgl. Oc.: $58.30

Victorian Manor Inn—Located on Route 147 midway between Harrisburg and Sunbury. The restored second Empire house, furnished with period antiques, is a step back to a by-gone era. Two blocks from historic Ferry and Riverfront Park. Unique shops closeby.

1. No Smoking	5. Tennis Available	9. Credit Cards Accepted	13. Lunch Available	17. Shared Baths
2. No Pets	6. Golf Available	10. Personal Check Accepted	14. Conference Rooms Avail.	18. Afternoon Tea
3 Off Season Rates	7. Swimmming Avail.	11. Reservations Necessary	15. Group Seminars Avail.	* Commisions given
4. Senior Citizen Rates	8. Skiing Available	12. Dinner Available	16. Private Baths	to Travel Agents

Millville

Swanson, Bette
R.R. 2, Box 93H, 17846
(717) 458-4681, (717) 458-6654

Amenities: 1,2,10,11,17,18
Breakfast: F.
Dbl. Oc.: $51.94
Sgl Oc.: $34.98
Third Person: $14.00
Child: Under 6 yrs. - no charge

Log Home Bed And Breakfast—Two lovely bedrooms; always a snack; endless tea and coffee; recipes available. Steel erection spoken here. Super views; 10 miles from Route 80; near Geisinger Medical Center. New log home. Golden retriever in residence. All on nine acres.

Montoursville *

Mesaris, Harold
RD 1, Box 11A, 17754
(717) 433-4340

Amenities: 5,6,7,8,10,14, 16,17
Breakfast: C. Plus

Dbl. Oc.: $53.00
Sgl. Oc.: $53.00
Third Person: $21.20

The Carriage House At Stonegate—Provides 1,400 square feet of privacy for guests on two floors with two bedrooms. Located in the middle of an all-season recreational area, minutes north of I-180 and 15 minutes north of I-80 on an 1800s-era farm.

Montrose *

Rose, Candace & Frederick
26 So. Main St., 18801
(717) 278-1124

Amenities: 5,6,8,9,10,12,13, 15,16,17
Breakfast: F.

Dbl. Oc.: $35.00 - $60.00
Sgl. Oc.: $35.00 - $60.00
Third Person: $10.00 - $15.00
Child: Under 10 yrs. - $5.00

The Montrose House—Open year-round. Chef owned-and-operated. Within walking distance of shops and stately homes. Set in the Endless Mountains, the inn is a favorite with sports enthusiasts and vacationers. Fine dining and cozy rooms in an early American setting.

Mount Joy

Landis, Darlene & Lester
2285 Bull Moose Rd., 17552
(717) 367-5167

Amenities: 1,2,9,10,11,17
Breakfast: C. Plus

Dbl. Oc.: $58.30
Sgl. Oc.: $47.70

The Country Stay Bed And Breakfast—Enjoy the elegance of an 1880 Victorian farm home with yesteryear's charm. Serene colorful setting. Treasure a memorable stay from the warmth of beautifully decorated rooms and country hospitality. Breakfast - delicious home-baked pastry and fresh fruit.

---

1. No Smoking	5. Tennis Available	9. Credit Cards Accepted	13. Lunch Available	17. Shared Baths
2. No Pets	6. Golf Available	10. Personal Check Accepted	14. Conference Rooms Avail.	18. Afternoon Tea
3 Off Season Rates	7. Swimmming Avail.	11. Reservations Necessary	15. Group Seminars Avail.	* Commisions given
4. Senior Citizen Rates	8. Skiing Available	12. Dinner Available	16. Private Baths	to Travel Agents

PENNSYLVANIA

Mount Joy

Swarr, Gladys
305 Longenecker Rd., 17552
(717) 653-4655

Amenities: 1,2,5,6,9,10,11,16

Breakfast: C. Plus

Dbl. Oc.: $58.30 - $63.60
Sgl. Oc.: $47.70 - $58.30
Third Person: $20.00
Child: Under 12 yrs. - $8.00

Cedar Hill Farm—Host born in this 1817 stone farmhouse that sits in a quiet area overlooking a stream. Each air-conditioned room has a private bath. Honeymoon suite boasts private balcony. Near Amish farms and Hershey. Good restaurants, markets, antiquing and historic sites. Gift certificates.

Muncy *

Smith, Marie Louise & David
307 So. Main St., 17756
(717) 546-8949

Amenities: 1,2,5,7,8,9,10,11,16
Breakfast: F.
Dbl. Oc.: $47.70 - $74.20
Sgl Oc.: $37.10 - $58.30
Third Person: $10.00
Child: Under 10 yrs. - $10.00

The Bodine House—Restored, Federal townhouse built circa 1805. Featured in December, 1991, edition of *Colonial Homes Magazine*. Listed in National Register of Historic Places. Furnished with period antques and reproductions. Three blocks from town center with shops, theatre and fine dining.

New Bloomfield

Ulsh, Carol & David
41 W. Main St., 17068
(717) 582-2914

Amenities: 1,2,5,6,7,8,10,11,
16,17
Breakfast: F.

Dbl. Oc.: $58.30
Sgl. Oc.: $42.40
Third Person: $26.50

The Tressler House Bed And Breakfast—Relax in the spacious Federal-period home tastefully decorated with antiques. Small-town location. Nearby rural attractions and historic points. Close to Harrisburg, Hershey and Carlisle for added interests.

New Hope *

Butkus, Ellen & Richard
677 Durham Rd.
Rte. 413, Wrightstown, 18940
(215) 598-3100

Amenities: 1,2,4,5,6,7,9,10,
11,14,15,16
Breakfast: F.

Dbl. Oc.: $91.80 - $135.00
Third Person: $21.60

Hollileif Bed And Breakfast Establishment—Escape to country elegance. Six miles from New Hope, shopping and history. Experience 18th-century warmth in an antique-furnished farmhouse on 5-1/2 rolling acres. Romantic ambience, gourmet breakfasts, central A/C and fireplaces. Mid-week and extended-stay rates available.

1. No Smoking	5. Tennis Available	9. Credit Cards Accepted	13. Lunch Available	17. Shared Baths
2. No Pets	6. Golf Available	10. Personal Check Accepted	14. Conference Rooms Avail.	18. Afternoon Tea
3 Off Season Rates	7. Swimmming Avail.	11. Reservations Necessary	15. Group Seminars Avail.	* Commisions given
4. Senior Citizen Rates	8. Skiing Available	12. Dinner Available	16. Private Baths	to Travel Agents

New Hope *

Glassman, Carl
111 W. Bridge St., 18938
(215) 862-2570

Amenities: 1,2,3,5,7,8,9,10,14,15,16,17,18
Breakfast: C. Plus
Dbl. Oc.: $68.90 - $169.60
Sgl Oc.: $63.60 - $159.00
Third Person: $22.00
Child: $22.00 (if crib provided)

Wedgwood Inn Of New Hope—Voted 1989 "Inn of the Year" by *Inn Guidebook* readers. This Victorian painted lady sits on two acres and is steps from the village center. Innkeepers Nadine and Carl Glassman speak French, Dutch, Spanish and Hebrew. AAA and Mobil rated. Five fireplaces, A/C and turn-down service.

New Hope *

Luccard, Amy
6987 Upper York Rd., 18938
(215) 862-3136

Amenities: 4,5,7,9,10,11,14, 15,16
Breakfast: F.

Dbl. Oc.: $102.60 - $162.00
Sgl. Oc.: $92.60 - $152.00
Third Person: $17.00
Child: Under 2 yrs. - no charge

Holly Hedge B&B—Warm, relaxing atmosphere on old country estate. Minutes to Bucks County's antiques, dining, shopping and Delaware River activities. Fireplaces in guest rooms; all with private baths. Catering available on premise for large or small parties, conferences, retreats and seminars.

N. Wales *

Kratz, Terry
1005 Horsham Rd., 19454
(215) 362-7500

Amenities: 2,5,6,7,9,10,11,12, 14,15,16
Breakfast: F.

Dbl. Oc.: $102.60 - $151.20
Sgl. Oc.: $91.80 - $140.40
Third Person: $15.00

Joseph Ambler Inn—The 1734 estate sits on 12 acres in Montgomeryville. The inn features 28 delightful guest rooms and an outstanding colonial restaurant in our Pennsylvania fieldstone barn. Private baths, TVs, telephones and air-conditioning in every room.

Numidia *

Batdorf, Judy & Ray
P.O. Box 97, Main St., 17858
(717) 799-0264

Amenities: 1,2,6,8,10,17
Breakfast: F.

Dbl. Oc.: $53.00
Sgl. Oc.: $48.00

Fair Haven Bed And Breakfast—Charming older home in picturesque country village. Near mountains, hunting and fishing. Lovingly furnished with antiques, reproductions made by the host and crafts made by the hostess. Near Bloomsburg University and Geisinger Medical Center.

1. No Smoking	5. Tennis Available	9. Credit Cards Accepted	13. Lunch Available	17. Shared Baths
2. No Pets	6. Golf Available	10. Personal Check Accepted	14. Conference Rooms Avail.	18. Afternoon Tea
3 Off Season Rates	7. Swimmming Avail.	11. Reservations Necessary	15. Group Seminars Avail.	* Commisions given
4. Senior Citizen Rates	8. Skiing Available	12. Dinner Available	16. Private Baths	to Travel Agents

PENNSYLVANIA

Oxford

Hershey, Arlene
15225 Limestone Rd., 19363
(215) 932-9257

Amenities: 1,2,5,6,7,8,10,11, 16,17
Breakfast: F.
Dbl. Oc.: $45.00
Sgl. Oc.: $30.00
Third Person: $10.00
Child: Under 12 yrs. - $5.00

Log House B&B—Chester County. Clean, quiet, cozy and comfortable nook in wooded farm area, away from city and traffic noises. Rooms air conditioned, family room with TV and radio. Children are welcome. Mid-way between Lancaster (Amish) country, Philadelphia and Wilmington. Open all year. Try it.

Palmyra

Eckert, Flo
409 So. Lingle Ave., 17078
(717) 838-4120, 838-8282

Amenities: 1,2,5,6,7,9,10,11, 16,18
Breakfast: F.
Dbl. Oc.: $68.90
Sgl. Oc.: $58.30

The Hen-Apple B&B—Just five minutes from downtown Hershey. Circa 1825 farmhouse has six bedrooms with private baths, air-conditioning and private parking. There are plenty of places to relax in this cozy, old-fashioned country home. Close to restaurants and attractions.

Paradise

Rohrer, Marion
505 Paradise Lane, 17562
(717) 687-7479

Amenities: 1,2,6,10,11,16,17
Breakfast: C.
Dbl. Oc.: $45.00 - $60.00
Sgl Oc.: $40.00 - $55.00
Third Person: $10.00
Child: Under 5 yrs. - $4.00

Maple Lane Guest House—Situated on a 200-acre farm in the heart of Amish country. Four guest rooms with antiques, quilts, needlework, stenciling, canopy and poster beds. Forty-mile view. Good food and attractions here in Lancaster County Dutch country.

Philadelphia *

Bompard, Terry
235 Chestnut St., 19106
(215) 922-4443

Amenities: 1,2,4,9,11,14,15, 16,18
Breakfast: C. Plus
Dbl. Oc.: $162.40
Sgl. Oc.: $151.20
Third Person: $10.00

Independence Park Inn—Located in America's most historic square mile only two blocks from Independence Mall, Liberty Bell, Betsy Ross' house and Penn's Landing. The inn is surrounded by Philadelphia's finest restaurants and theatres. Our 36 room inn is ideal for visitors coming to the city.

1. No Smoking	5. Tennis Available	9. Credit Cards Accepted	13. Lunch Available	17. Shared Baths
2. No Pets	6. Golf Available	10. Personal Check Accepted	14. Conference Rooms Avail.	18. Afternoon Tea
3 Off Season Rates	7. Swimmming Avail.	11. Reservations Necessary	15. Group Seminars Avail.	* Commisions given
4. Senior Citizen Rates	8. Skiing Available	12. Dinner Available	16. Private Baths	to Travel Agents

PENNSYLVANIA

Philadelphia *

Rhule, Raymond
416 Bain Bridge St., 19147
(215) 627-7266

Amenities: 1,2,3,9,10,11,16, 18

Breakfast: C. Plus

Dbl. Oc.: $78.40 - $117.60
Sgl. Oc.: $56.00
Third Person: $11.20

Shippen Way Inn—Restored 18th-century inn, family run, in historic downtown. Nine rooms with private baths, one with fireplace. Afternoon wine and cheese. Near South Street, within walking distance of shops, restaurants and theatre. Six blocks south of Independence National Park.

Pittsburgh

Fennell, Allison & Rich
Delaney, Nancy, Jim & Doug
5516 Maple Height Rd., 15232
(412) 683-6501

Amenities: 1,2,9,10,11,16,17, 18

Breakfast: C. Plus

Dbl. Oc.: $99.90 - $166.50
Sgl. Oc.: $99.90 - $166.50

The Shadyside Bed And Breakfast—An elegant English Jacobean manor house with antique furnishings and designer linens. Our finest guest rooms include private or shared bathroom, use of library, billiard room, large porch, dining room and guest kitchen. Restaurants and shops within walking distance.

Pocono Mountains

Robinson, Barb & Dick
RD 1, Box 630, Canadensis, 18325
(717) 595-3152

Amenities: 1,4,5,6,7,8,10,11, 15,16,17

Breakfast: F.

Dbl. Oc.: $45.00
Sgl. Oc.: $30.00
Third Person: $12.50

Nearbrook—A 1930s charming home surrounded by roses, rock gardens, woods and a stream. Breakfast is served on the porch. Hiking trails and points of interest are mapped out. A contagious informality encourages guests to use the piano, games, wooden trains and sleds. Art lessons arranged.

Reading

Staron, Norma
118 So. 5th St., 19602
(215) 374-6608

Amenities: 9,10,11,16,17
Breakfast: F.

Dbl. Oc.: $63.60 - $74.20
Sgl. Oc.: $53.00 - $63.60
Third Person: $10.60

Hunter House—Elegant 1846 restoration with spacious rooms/suites. TV, air-conditioning. Furnishings and friendly atmosphere create a sheltered urban experience in this historic area. Fine restaurants, outlet centers and commercial hubs nearby. Business travelers welcome.

---

1. No Smoking	5. Tennis Available	9. Credit Cards Accepted	13. Lunch Available	17. Shared Baths
2. No Pets	6. Golf Available	10. Personal Check Accepted	14. Conference Rooms Avail.	18. Afternoon Tea
3 Off Season Rates	7. Swimmming Avail.	11. Reservations Necessary	15. Group Seminars Avail.	* Commisions given
4. Senior Citizen Rates	8. Skiing Available	12. Dinner Available	16. Private Baths	to Travel Agents

Ridgway

Shoemaker, Lois
Montmorenci Rd., Box 17, 15853
(814) 776-2539

Amenities: 1,2,6,7,10,11,16,17,18
Breakfast: C. or F.
Dbl. Oc.: $40.00
Sgl Oc.: $40.00
Third Person: $10.00
Child: Under 6 yrs. - $10.00

Faircroft Bed And Breakfast—Two miles from Route 219. A warm, comfortable and quiet homestead on 75 acres of farmland. Next door to Allegheny National Forest. Area famous for scenery, outdoor recreation, good food, relaxation and fresh air. Antique decor. Young, middle-aged professional owners.

Schellsburg *

Lau, Martha A.
R.D. 1, Box 196, 15559
(814) 733-4093

Amenities: 1,2,5,6,7,8,9,10,16,18
Breakfast: F.
Dbl. Oc.: $55.00 - $75.00
Sgl Oc.: $45.00 - $65.00
Third Person: $15.00

Bedford's Covered Bridge Inn—Historic inn beside a covered bridge in a picturebook setting. Hiking, skiing, biking, swimming, fishing, horseback riding on premesis or at adjacent Shawnee State Park. Old Bedfored village, 14 covered bridges, antiquing and many historic points of interest nearby.

Scottdale

Horsch, Ruth A. & James E.
Rte. 1, Box 634, 15683-9567
(412) 887-5404

Amenities: 1,5,6,7,8,9,10, 11,17,18
Breakfast: F.

Dbl. Oc.: $53.00
Sgl. Oc.: $42.40
Third Person: $21.20
Child: Under 5 yrs. - $5.30

Pine Wood Acres—A country getaway located in the Laurel Highlands of western Pennsylvania. A country home. Four acres of woods, wildflowers, perennials and herbs. Ten miles from I-70 and the Pennslyvania Turnpike exits at New Stanton. Near Wright's Fallingwater, resorts, rafting, hiking and antiques.

1. No Smoking	5. Tennis Available	9. Credit Cards Accepted	13. Lunch Available	17. Shared Baths
2. No Pets	6. Golf Available	10. Personal Check Accepted	14. Conference Rooms Avail.	18. Afternoon Tea
3 Off Season Rates	7. Swimming Avail.	11. Reservations Necessary	15. Group Seminars Avail.	* Commisions given
4. Senior Citizen Rates	8. Skiing Available	12. Dinner Available	16. Private Baths	to Travel Agents

PENNSYLVANIA

Selinsqrove

Thomson, Marilyn & Kent
350 So. Market St., 17870
(717) 374-2929

Amenities: 1,2,5,6,7,9,10,16, 18

Breakfast: F.

Dbl. Oc.: $55.65 - $66.25
Sgl. Oc.: $45.05 - $55.65
Third Person: $10.60
Child: Under 12 yrs. - no charge

The Blue Lion Inn—Experience a night in an authentic plantation home over 150 years old. Antiques, gourmet breakfasts and warm hospitality add to the atmosphere. A few blocks from Susquehanna University; convenient to Bucknell University in Lewisburg. "Your Home Away From Home."

Shawnee On Delaware

Cox, Jane & Jim
River Rd.
Box 265, 18356
(717) 421-2139

Amenities: 2,6,7,8,10,14,16, 17,18

Breakfast: F.

Dbl. Oc.: $68.90 - $79.50
Sgl. Oc.: $58.30
Third Person: $58.30

Eagle Rock Lodge In The Poconos—Awake to a hearty breakfast served on a wicker-furnished porch overlooking the Delaware. This old country inn nestled on 10-1/2 acres includes seven guest rooms and lots of lounging space. Close to all activities, sports, theatre and fine dining. Borders Water Gap National Park.

Slippery Rock *

McKnight, Sandra & Gary
152 Applewood Lane, 16057
(412) 794-1844

Amenities: 1,2,4,5,6,8,9,10, 12,13,16

Breakfast: F.

Dbl. Oc.: $73.14 - $121.90
Sgl. Oc.: $58.30 - $85.86
Third Person: $15.90
Child: $10.60

Applebutter Inn—A charming 1844 farmhouse restoration with 11- room addition. Restored woodwork, antique furnishings, canopied beds and gas log fireplaces provide yesterday's charm with the comforts of today. State parks, tennis, golf and bicycling.

Somerset *

Jones, Janet
RD 6, Box 250, 15501
(814) 443-4978

Amenities: 3,5,6,7,8,9,10,16, 17

Breakfast: F.

Dbl. Oc.: 84.80
Sgl. Oc.: $63.60
Third Person: $10.00
Child: Under 18 yrs.- no charge

Glades Pike Inn—Since 1842, this inn has welcomed visitors to the scenic Laurel Mountains. This charming B&B once served as a stagecoach stop along Glades Pike, now Rte. 31. Situated in the center of a 200-acre dairy farm. Wood burning fireplaces. Near falling water, skiing and five parks.

1. No Smoking	5. Tennis Available	9. Credit Cards Accepted	13. Lunch Available	17. Shared Baths
2. No Pets	6. Golf Available	10. Personal Check Accepted	14. Conference Rooms Avail.	18. Afternoon Tea
3 Off Season Rates	7. Swimmming Avail.	11. Reservations Necessary	15. Group Seminars Avail.	* Commisions given
4. Senior Citizen Rates	8. Skiing Available	12. Dinner Available	16. Private Baths	to Travel Agents

Somerset

Russell, Phyllis L.
802 Tayman Ave., 15501
(814) 445-7767, (800) 528-5629

Amenities: 1,2,3,4,5,6,8,9,10,11,16
Breakfast: C. Plus
Dbl. Oc.: $125.00
Sgl Oc: $75.00
Third Person: $10.00

The V.I.P. House—The house for V.I.P. "very important people." We welcome you with champagne and fresh flowers. Bridal suite with whirlpool tub, two suites with private baths, refrigerator, microwave and private decks. Suites will sleep up to four persons.

St. Thomas

Rice, Joan
10111 Lincoln Way W., (Rte. 30), 17252
(717) 369-4224

Amenities: 1,2,6,8,10,11,16, 17,18
Breakfast: F.

Dbl. Oc.: $68.90
Sgl. Oc.: $58.30
Third Person: $15.90

Rice's White House Inn—Unique 1790 restored country inn in National Register of Historic Places. Beautiful view. Rooms are furnished with antiques. Hiking, fishing, X-country skiing available on the property. Ski slope is 20 minutes away. A lovely, quiet place to rest and relax. Ski package available.

Starlight *

McMahon, Judy & Jack
Box 27, 18461
(717) 798-2519

Amenities: 2,5,6,7,8,9,10,11, 12,13,14,15,16,17
Breakfast: F.

Dbl. Oc.: $79.50 - $106.00
Sgl. Oc.: $54.06 - $68.90
Third Person: $30.74
Child: 7-12 yrs. - $30.74

The Inn At Starlight Lake—Since 1909, this classic country inn has offered a lovely lake with year-round activities, from swimming to skiing. Twenty-six charming rooms and outstanding cuisine, all within a congenial, informal setting. Winding roads and quaint river towns complete the scene.

Starrucca

Nethercott, Virginia & Roland
Main St., 18462
(717) 727-2211

Amenities: 2,6,8,9,10,16
Breakfast: C. Plus

Dbl. Oc.: $74.20
Third Person: $15.00
Child: Under 1 yr. - no charge

Nethercott Inn—An 1893 Victorian home located in a quiet village in the Endless Mountains. Nearby hunting, cross-country and downhill skiing. Period decor. Furnished with antiques. Smoking limited.

1. No Smoking	5. Tennis Available	9. Credit Cards Accepted	13. Lunch Available	17. Shared Baths
2. No Pets	6. Golf Available	10. Personal Check Accepted	14. Conference Rooms Avail.	18. Afternoon Tea
3 Off Season Rates	7. Swimming Avail.	11. Reservations Necessary	15. Group Seminars Avail.	* Commisions given
4. Senior Citizen Rates	8. Skiing Available	12. Dinner Available	16. Private Baths	to Travel Agents

Strasburg

Joy, Debby
958 Eisenberger Rd., 17579
(717) 687-8585

Amenities: 1,2,3,10,16
Breakfast: F.

Dbl. Oc.: $47.70 - $63.60
Third Person: $10.00
Child: 4 - 12 yrs. - $5.00

The Decoy B&B—Former Amish home, with spectacular views, set in rural location. Bicycle tours arranged. Hostess is a quilter and knows where to find fabrics and frames. King and queen beds available. Family reunions welcome.

Strasburg

Settle, Pat & John
101 W. Main, 17579
(717) 687-8800

Amenities: 1,2,3,5,6,7,9,10, 16,17
Breakfast: C. Plus

Dbl. Oc.: $38.00 - $48.00
Sgl. Oc.: $32.00 - $43.00
Third Person: $10.00

PJ's—The serene Amish countryside of Lancaster County surrounds this lovely guest home, built in 1824. Your hosts, Pat and John, are long-time residents whose knowledge of this area can help you plan a fun-filled vacation. Call for more information.

Thompson

Stark, Douglas
Main St., Rte. 171
RD 2, Box 36, 18465
(717) 727-2625

Amenities: 5,6,7,8,9,10,12,13, 14,15,16,17,18
Breakfast: F.

Dbl. Oc.: $40.00
Sgl. Oc.: $30.00
Third Person: $15.00

Jefferson Inn—Warm country atmosphere. Built in 1871 with a full-menu restaurant. Enjoy one of the most reasonable inns in northeast Pennsylvania. Rolling hills, lots of snow trails, skiing, hunting or just taking it easy.

Titusville *

Rogalski, Charmaine
430 E. Main St., 16354
(814) 827-1592

Amenities: 2,6,8,10,16
Breakfast: C.

Dbl. Oc.: $58.30
Sgl. Oc.: $47.70
Third Person: $5.00
Child: Under 16 yrs. - no charge

McMullen House Bed And Breakfast—Situated in the picturesque Oil Creek Valley. Minutes away from Drake Well Park, the world's first oil well. Also, the Oil Creek and Titusville Railroad can take you for a ride "through the valley that changed the world."

---

1. No Smoking
2. No Pets
3 Off Season Rates
4. Senior Citizen Rates

5. Tennis Available
6. Golf Available
7. Swimmming Avail.
8. Skiing Available

9. Credit Cards Accepted
10. Personal Check Accepted
11. Reservations Necessary
12. Dinner Available

13. Lunch Available
14. Conference Rooms Avail.
15. Group Seminars Avail.
16. Private Baths

17. Shared Baths
18. Afternoon Tea
* Commisions given
to Travel Agents

PENNSYLVANIA

Trucksville

Troup, Kay
247 Post Rd., 18708-1833
(717) 696-4602

Amenities: 1,2,10,11,16,18
Breakfast: F.
Dbl. Oc.: $55.00
Sgl Oc.: $55.00

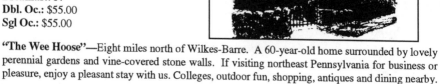

"The Wee Hoose"—Eight miles north of Wilkes-Barre. A 60-year-old home surrounded by lovely perennial gardens and vine-covered stone walls. If visiting northeast Pennsylvania for business or pleasure, enjoy a pleasant stay with us. Colleges, outdoor fun, shopping, antiques and dining nearby.

Wellsboro *

Kaltenbach, Lee
Stony Fork Rd. (Kelsey St.)
R.D. #6, Box 106A, 16901
(717) 724-4954

Amenities: 1,2,3,5,6,7,8,9,10,12,
　　　　　13,14,15,16,17,18
Breakfast: F.
Dbl. Oc.: $63.00 - $109.50
Sgl Oc.: $37.50
Third Person: $26.50
Child: $10.00

Kaltenbach's Bed And Breakfast—A spacious and attractive home on 72 acres. Two miles from Wellsboro. Turn left on Stony Fork Road. A warm, hospitable, small, family-run inn with 10 large rooms and fireplace. Pennsylvania Grand Canyon golf package.

West Chester *

Rupp, Winifred O.M.
409 So. Church St., 19382
(215) 692-4896

Amenities: 1,2,7,10,11,17
Breakfast: F.

Dbl. Oc.: $68.90
Sgl. Oc.: $63.60
Third Person: $15.00

The Crooked Windsor—A charming Victorian home centrally located in West Chester. Completely furnished with fine antiques. Tea and refreshments for those who so desire. Pool and garden available in-season. Drive 20 minutes to Brandywine Valley museums.

1. No Smoking	5. Tennis Available	9. Credit Cards Accepted	13. Lunch Available	17. Shared Baths
2. No Pets	6. Golf Available	10. Personal Check Accepted	14. Conference Rooms Avail.	18. Afternoon Tea
3 Off Season Rates	7. Swimmming Avail.	11. Reservations Necessary	15. Group Seminars Avail.	* Commisions given
4. Senior Citizen Rates	8. Skiing Available	12. Dinner Available	16. Private Baths	to Travel Agents

Wrightsville

Healey, Amelia & Roger
Rte. 2, Box 237 T, 17368
(717) 252-4643, (800) 722-6395

Amenities: 1,2,6,7,8,9,10,11, 12,13,16
Breakfast: F.

Dbl. Oc.: $63.60 - $74.20
Third Person: $20.00
Child: Under 2 yrs. - no charge

1854 House—Large restored brick farmhouse on 23 acres between Lancaster and York. Antique furnishings. Near Pennsylvania Dutch, Hershey, Carlisle and Gettysburg. Enjoy the 1800s with modern conveniences, A/C and whirlpool tubs. Full breakfast and welcome beverage.

York *

King Family, The
30 So. Beaver St., 17401
(717) 854-3411

Amenities: 1,2,3,6,8,9,10,14,16,17,18
Breakfast: F.
Dbl. Oc.: $63.80 - $84.80
Sgl. Oc.: $58.30
Third Person: $5.30

Smyser-Bair House—A magnificent Italianate townhouse in the historic district, with three antique-filled guest rooms and a two-room suite. Enjoy our warm hospitality and player piano. Walk to farmer's markets, historic sites and antique shops. Near Lancaster and Gettysburg. Air-conditioning.

York

LaRowe, Lojan
Kreutz Creek Rd.
R.D. 24, Box 1042, 17406
(717) 757-5384

Amenities: 1,2,3,4,7,8,10,15, 16,18
Breakfast: C. and F.

Dbl. Oc.: $75.00
Sgl. Oc.: $65.00
Third Person: $10.00

Cottage At Twin Brook Farm—A 200-year-old colonial farm nestled between three wooded ridges. Provides 55 acres of picturesque privacy. Brooks, ponds, woods, trails, fields and pastures. Member of National Trust For Historic Preservation. York, Lancaster and Gettysburg are nearby.

1. No Smoking	5. Tennis Available	9. Credit Cards Accepted	13. Lunch Available	17. Shared Baths
2. No Pets	6. Golf Available	10. Personal Check Accepted	14. Conference Rooms Avail.	18. Afternoon Tea
3 Off Season Rates	7. Swimmming Avail.	11. Reservations Necessary	15. Group Seminars Avail.	* Commisions given
4. Senior Citizen Rates	8. Skiing Available	12. Dinner Available	16. Private Baths	to Travel Agents

RHODE ISLAND

Little Rhody

Capitol: Providence
Statehood: May 29, 1790; the 13th state
State Motto: "Hope"
State Song: "Rhode Island"
State Bird: Rhode Island Red
State Flower: Violet
State Tree: Red Maple

Rhode Island is the smallest of the fifty states. Only 1,214 square miles, it lies on beautiful Narragansett Bay, just a little way out on the Atlantic Ocean.

It is quite a resort state. Thousands of visitors come here every year. The beaches afford plenty of swimming and boating.

In Newport, the tourist can take the Cliff Walk by the most beautiful mansions in the world, or see the America's Cup Sailboat Race off the coast of Newport.

Jewelry and silver seem to be the prime source of income for this state, along with tourism. The people of Rhode Island are very proud of their state and love to have others come to see it. They make wonderful hosts.

RHODE ISLAND

Block Island *

Abrams, Joan
1 Spring St., 02807
(401) 466-2421, (401) 466-2063

Amenities: 9,10,11,12,16,18

Breakfast: F.

Dbl. Oc.: $80.00 - $300.00
Third Person: $25.00

Hotel Manisses—Gracious Victorian rooms with private bath, telephone and some with jacuzzis. An elegant dining room and garden terrace serving dinner. Dinner reservations recommended. Outdoor deck with canopy. Nearby shops and beaches. Open all year.

Block Island

Butler, Barbara & Kevin
Water St., 02807
(401) 466-2212,
(914) 967-4144 (off season)

Amenities: 2,3,7,9,10,16,17,18
Breakfast: C.
Dbl. Oc.: $95.00 - $145.00

Inn At Old Harbour—Magnificent gingerbread Victorian built in 1882 with commanding views of the Atlantic Ocean and the island's quaint Water Street. The inn has 10 newly renovated individually decorated guest rooms, most with private bath. Walking distance to all shops, restaurants and beach.

Block Island

Connolly, Violette M. & Joseph V.
Spring St., 02807
(401) 466-2653

Amenities: 5,7,9,10,11,12,15, 16,17

Breakfast: F.

Dbl. Oc.: $53.50 - $128.40
Sgl. Oc.: $37.45 - $80.25

The White House—A gracious island mansion. Presidential autograph collection on display. French Provincial antiques throughout. Spectacular ocean views from the rooms. Limo service to the ferry and airport. Close to beaches and restaurants.

Block Island *

Rose, Judith
Roslyn Rd., 02807
(401) 466-2021

Amenities: 2,3,5,7,9,11,16, 17

Breakfast: C. Plus

Dbl. Oc.: $105.00 - $180.00
Sgl. Oc.: $105.00 - $180.00
Third Person: $29.00
Child: Over 12 yrs. - $29.00

Rose Farm Inn—Nestled in sea and country setting near beaches, town and ferries. Ocean views, antique furnishings, king/queen beds, some with canopies. Bordering stone walls and flower gardens reminiscent of an earlier time. Light buffet breakfast served on great stone porch.

1. No Smoking	5. Tennis Available	9. Credit Cards Accepted	13. Lunch Available	17. Shared Baths
2. No Pets	6. Golf Available	10. Personal Check Accepted	14. Conference Rooms Avail.	18. Afternoon Tea
3 Off Season Rates	7. Swimmming Avail.	11. Reservations Necessary	15. Group Seminars Avail.	* Commisions given
4. Senior Citizen Rates	8. Skiing Available	12. Dinner Available	16. Private Baths	to Travel Agents

RHODE ISLAND

Bristol *

Rose, Mary & Michael
154 High St., 02809
(401) 253-4222

Amenities: 1,2,3,4,10,11,14, 15,16,18
Breakfast: C. Plus

Dbl. Oc.: $95.00 - $105.00
Third Person: $15.00
Child: $15.00
(Over 12 yrs. welcome.)

Williams Grant Inn—In the heart of the historic waterfront district, this stately home, built in 1808, welcomes its guests with a showcase of beautiful antiques and original folk art. Walk to shops, restaurants and museums. Scenic bike path close by. Central to Newport and Providence.

Middletown (Newport) *

Lindsey, Anne
6 James St., 02840
(401) 846-9386

Amenities: 1,2,3,9,10,16,17
Breakfast: C. Plus

Dbl. Oc.: $44.80 - $89.00
Sgl. Oc.: $44.80
Third Person: $20.00
Child: $10.00

Lindsey's Guest House—Enjoy your stay, short or long, in our large 1955 split-level home in a quiet residential neighborhood with large yard, deck and off-street parking. Two beaches and restaurants only a 1/2 mile away. Five-minute drive to famous mansions and downtown Newport's special events.

Narragansett

Panzeri, Sandra & William
59 Kingstown Rd., 02882
(401) 789-7971

Amenities: 1,2,3,5,6,7,10,16,17
Breakfast: F.
Dbl. Oc.: $50.00 - $65.00
Sgl Oc.: $40.00 - $55.00
Third Person: $10.70

The 1900 House—A restored Victorian located in the heart of Narragansett Pier. Walk to the beach, shops or fine dining. A brief ride will take you to the Newport mansions, the Block Island Ferry, University of Rhode Island, Mystic Seaport and the Foxwood Casino.

Narragansett

Snee, Mildred
191 Ocean Rd., 02882
(401) 783-9494

Amenities: 2,10,11,17
Breakfast: F.

Dbl. Oc.: $64.20
Sgl. Oc.: $48.15

The House Of Snee—Within easy walking distance of the beach, movies, restaurants and shops. Facing the open Atlantic, The House of Snee is a turn-of-the-century Dutch colonial with a cozy front porch. Newport and Block Island are nearby.

1. No Smoking	5. Tennis Available	9. Credit Cards Accepted	13. Lunch Available	17. Shared Baths
2. No Pets	6. Golf Available	10. Personal Check Accepted	14. Conference Rooms Avail.	18. Afternoon Tea
3 Off Season Rates	7. Swimmming Avail.	11. Reservations Necessary	15. Group Seminars Avail.	* Commisions given
4. Senior Citizen Rates	8. Skiing Available	12. Dinner Available	16. Private Baths	to Travel Agents

RHODE ISLAND

Newport *

Bayuk, Pam & Bruce
123 Spring St., 02840
(800) 525-8373

Amenities: 1,2,3,5,6,7,9,10, 11,14,15,16,17,18
Breakfast: C.

Dbl. Oc.: $84.00 - $140.00
Sgl. Oc.: $84.00 - $140.00
Third Person: $15.00

The Pilgrim House Inn—Lovely restored Victorian inn located in the heart of the historic district. Shops and restaurants within easy walking distance. Mansions close by. Homemade continental breakfast served on rooftop deck overlooking scenic Newport Harbor. A/C. Parking. Children over 12 welcome. Come see.

Newport

Brandeis, Paul
29 Pelham St., 02840
(401) 846-3324

Amenities: 1,5,6,7,9,10,11,15, 16,17
Breakfast: F.

Dbl. Oc.: $65.00 - $150.00
Third Person: $20.00

Inn Of Jonathan Bowen—An elegant inn on a gas-lit historic hill. Located in the heart of activity. One-half block to the harbor. Renovated in 1987. Eclectic antique decor. Luxurious rooms. Safe, off-street parking. Walk everywhere. Famed mansions. Gourmet breakfast. Getaway plans.

Newport *

Burke, Helen
Halidon Ave., 02840
(401) 847-8318

Amenities: 2,3,4,7,9,10,11,14, 15,16,17
Breakfast: C. Plus

Dbl. Oc.: $75.00 - $150.00
Sgl. Oc.: $65.00 - $125.00
Third Person: $30.00

Halidon Hill Guest House—Modern and spacious rooms with ample on-site parking. A 10-minute walk to Hammersmith Farm and the beach. Convenient to shopping areas, local restaurants, mansions and yacht club. Call for reservations.

Newport

Droual, Margot
96 Pelham St., 02840
(401) 847-4400

Amenities: 2,3,9,10,11,16,17
Breakfast: C. and F.

Dbl. Oc.: $56.00 - $140.00
Third Person: $10.00
Child: Under 12 yrs. - no charge

La Forge Cottage—Classic Victorian makes this B&B one of the most pleasant inns around. On historic hill close to beaches and downtown. Private bath, TV, phone, A/C and refrigerator. Breakfast served to you in your room prepared by our own French chef. German and French spoken.

---

1. No Smoking	5. Tennis Available	9. Credit Cards Accepted	13. Lunch Available	17. Shared Baths
2. No Pets	6. Golf Available	10. Personal Check Accepted	14. Conference Rooms Avail.	18. Afternoon Tea
3 Off Season Rates	7. Swimmming Avail.	11. Reservations Necessary	15. Group Seminars Avail.	* Commisions given
4. Senior Citizen Rates	8. Skiing Available	12. Dinner Available	16. Private Baths	to Travel Agents

RHODE ISLAND

Newport *

Farrick, Rick
36 Elm St., 02840
(401) 846-9031

Amenities: 1,2,3,4,10,11,16
Breakfast: C.
Dbl. Oc.: $75.00 - $125.00
Sgl Oc.: $75.00 - $95.00

Elm Street Inn—This warm, elegant inn is situated in the historic Point section where you can stroll down gas-lit streets. This turn-of-the-century inn is located one block from the waterfront and within walking distance of all shops and restaurants.

Newport *

Latimore, Parvin
353 Spring St., 02840
(401) 847-4767

Amenities: 2,3,4,9,10,11,16, 17
Breakfast: F.

Dbl. Oc.: $84.00 - $145.00
Sgl. Oc.: $84.00 - $145.00
Third Person: $25.00
Child: Over 12 yrs. - $25.00

Spring Street Inn—A charming Victorian home two blocks from the harbor. Walk to all Newport highlights. All rooms with private baths. Harbor-view suite with balcony for two to four people. Generous home-cooked breakfast. On-site parking. Open year-round. VISA/MasterCard accepted.

Newport

Moy, Maggie & Terry
12 Clay St., 02840
(401) 849-6865

Amenities: 1,2,3,4,5,9,10,11, 14,15,16
Breakfast: F.

Dbl. Oc.: $100.00 - $165.00
Third Person: $15.00

Ivy Lodge—Step back in time and stay in one of Newport's famous cottages in the heart of the mansion area. Only three blocks from the Cliff Walk. Gracious and romantic. Each room is individually decorated and hand-stenciled. Relax and unwind on our wicker-filled porch.

---

1. No Smoking
2. No Pets
3 Off Season Rates
4. Senior Citizen Rates
5. Tennis Available
6. Golf Available
7. Swimmming Avail.
8. Skiing Available
9. Credit Cards Accepted
10. Personal Check Accepted
11. Reservations Necessary
12. Dinner Available
13. Lunch Available
14. Conference Rooms Avail.
15. Group Seminars Avail.
16. Private Baths
17. Shared Baths
18. Afternoon Tea
* Commisions given to Travel Agents

Newport *

Rogers, Rita & Sam
39 Clarke St., 02840
(401) 847-0640

Amenities: 2,3,5,6,7,9,10,11,16,17
Breakfast: C. Plus
Dbl. Oc.: $84.00 - $112.00
Sgl Oc.: $84.00 - $112.00

The Melville House—Seven rooms furnished in colonial style in the heart of the historic district. One block from Brick Market and the wharfs. Stay at a colonial inn built circa 1750. In the National Register of Historic Places. Off-street parking. Complimentary sherry. Homemade breakfast.

Newport *

Weintraub, Amy
23 Brinley St., 02840
(401) 849-7645

Amenities: 2,3,7,9,10,16
Breakfast: C.

Dbl. Oc.: $145.60
Sgl. Oc.: $128.80
Third Person: $15.00

Brinley Victorian Inn—A haven in historic Newport. Romantic antique decor, including faux finishes, lots of lace and fresh flowers. This award-winning inn is known for its friendly service and high standard of cleanliness. Park and walk to beaches and historic sites. AAA approved. Mobil rated.

Newport/Middletown *

Canning, Polly
349 Valley Rd., Rte. 214, 02840
(401) 847-2160

Amenities: 1,2,3,6,7,11,
15,16,17
Breakfast: F.

Dbl. Oc.: $82.25
Sgl. Oc.: $64.20

Polly's Place—A quiet retreat two minutes from Newport Harbor and beaches. Lovely large, clean rooms with homey atmosphere and delicious home-baked goodies. Polly also has a three-room apartment available by the week or longer. She is a native and a realtor. Helpful information offered.

Providence *

Hopton, Frank
43 Jewett St., 02908
(401) 785-1235

Amenities: 1,2,3,4,9,10,
11,16,18
Breakfast: F.

Dbl. Oc.: $84.00
Sgl. Oc.: $77.28
Third Person: $10.00
Child: Under 12 yrs. - no charge

State House Inn Bed And Breakfast—A country bed and breakfast located five minutes from downtown Providence. A 102-year-old building with a fascinating history. Newly renovated and restored. King- and queen-sized beds, private baths and a full breakfast included in rate.

---

1. No Smoking	5. Tennis Available	9. Credit Cards Accepted	13. Lunch Available	17. Shared Baths
2. No Pets	6. Golf Available	10. Personal Check Accepted	14. Conference Rooms Avail.	18. Afternoon Tea
3 Off Season Rates	7. Swimmming Avail.	11. Reservations Necessary	15. Group Seminars Avail.	* Commisions given
4. Senior Citizen Rates	8. Skiing Available	12. Dinner Available	16. Private Baths	to Travel Agents

RHODE ISLAND

Providence *

Parker, Yvonne
P.O. Box 2441, 02906
(401) 421-7194

Amenities: 1,9,10,11,17
Breakfast: C.

Dbl. Oc.: $64.20
Sgl. Oc.: $48.15
Third Person: $15.00

Lansing House Bed And Breakfast—Convenient to Brown University, Rhode Island School of Design and downtown commuter train to Boston. Listed in a city-wide survey of historic resources. The hostess, a former newspaper and TV journalist who now writes fiction, has lived in Paris, Japan and many areas of the U.S.

Westerly *

Madison, Ellen L.
330 Woody Hill Rd., 02891
(401) 322-0452

Amenities: 1,2,3,5,6,7,10,16,
17
Breakfast: F.

Dbl. Oc.: $72.70
Sgl. Oc.: $61.60
Third Person: $10.00

Woody Hill Guest House—Retreat from your busy routine and entrench yourself in the peace and quiet of this antique-filled country home. Two miles from superb ocean beaches. In-ground pool, gardens and porch swing. Near Mystic Seaport, Ledyard Casino and Newport.

Wyoming *

Sohl, Charles R.
64 Kingstown Rd., 02898
(401) 539-2680

Amenities: 1,2,3,6,7,9,10,16,
17
Breakfast: F.

Dbl. Oc.: $59.00
Sgl. Oc.: $53.00
Third Person: $16.00

The Cookie Jar Bed And Breakfast—The heart of our home, the living room, was built in 1732 by slaves as a blacksmith shop. The original ceiling, hand hewn-beams and granite walls remain today. Located on the remaining three acres of the original plantation. A perfect environment for rest and relaxation.

1. No Smoking	5. Tennis Available	9. Credit Cards Accepted	13. Lunch Available	17. Shared Baths
2. No Pets	6. Golf Available	10. Personal Check Accepted	14. Conference Rooms Avail.	18. Afternoon Tea
3 Off Season Rates	7. Swimmming Avail.	11. Reservations Necessary	15. Group Seminars Avail.	* Commisions given
4. Senior Citizen Rates	8. Skiing Available	12. Dinner Available	16. Private Baths	to Travel Agents

SOUTH CAROLINA

The Palmetto State

Capitol: Columbia
Statehood: May 23, 1788; the 8th state
State Motto: "Prepared in Mind and Resources,
    While I Breathe, I Hope"
State Song: "Carolina Wren"
State Bird: Carolina Wren
State Flower: Carolina Jessamine
State Tree: Palmetto

South Carolina is a great state to visit, and for those who live there, it is a great place to call home. It stretches from the beautiful Appalachian foothills to the spacious and popular Atlantic Coast beaches.

It is home for more than three million energetic and resourceful people. These people share a common bond, whether they live in the larger municipalities of the Palmetto State or in its growing small towns and rural communities. That common bond is a commitment to preserving a quality of life which is their heritage and building upon it by encouraging businesses and industries to grow and prosper here.

South Carolina is a most gracious state and invites visitors to come and enjoy its beautiful beaches and flower gardens and fish and hung in its well-stocked fields and streams.

SOUTH CAROLINA

Anderson

Ryter, Myrna
1109 So. Main St., 29621
(803) 225-1109

Amenities: 2,5,6,7,9,10,12, 14,15,16
Breakfast: C.

Dbl. Oc.: $65.00
Sgl. Oc.: $52.00
Third Person: $10.00

Evergreen Inn—A luxuriously restored mansion listed in Register of Historic Places. Specialty suites for a romantic getaway. Within walking distance of downtown antique shops and 20 minutes to Lake Hartwell. Next door to an award-winning, Swiss-owned restaurant in an elegant mansion.

Beaufort *

Harrison, Stephen
1009 Craven St., 29902
(803) 524-9030

Amenities: 1,2,5,6,7,9,10,11, 12,13,14,15,16,18
Breakfast: F.

Dbl. Oc.: $85.60 - $192.60
Sgl. Oc.: $85.60 - $192.60
Third Person: $21.40

The Rhett House Inn—Nestled in historic Beaufort, this is an authentic B&B inn that beautifully re-creates the feeling of the "old" South. All guest rooms have been created for your comfort and convenience. All guest rooms have private baths and some have fireplaces.

Beaufort *

Roe, Eugene L.
601 Bay St., 29902
(803) 524-7720

Amenities: 2,3,5,6,7,9,10,11, 14,16
Breakfast: F.

Dbl. Oc.: $80.00 - $95.00
Sgl. Oc.: $75.00 - $80.00
Third Person: $15.00

Bay Street Inn—On the water, within the historic district. Historic planters home, site of filming of the movie "Prince Of Tides." All rooms with bath, air-conditioning, fireplaces and river view. Off-street parking, gardens, antiques and art. A true glimpse of the antebellum South.

Charleston *

Bishop, Linda
116 Broad St., 29401
(803) 723-7999, (800) 476-9741

Amenities: 1,2,3,4,5,6,9,15, 16,18
Breakfast: C.

Dbl. Oc.: $129.60 - $210.60
Sgl. Oc.: $113.40 - $183.60
Third Person: $15.00
Child: Under 12 yrs. - no charge

John Rutledge House Inn—Located in the historic district. Built in 1763 by John Rutledge, a signer of the U.S. Constitution. Nightly turn-down, continental breakfast and newspaper delivered to your room. Wine served in the ballroom. AAA - Four Diamond and Historical Homes of America approved.

Charleston *

Chapman, Benjamin
30 King St., 29401
(803) 577-2633

Amenities: 1,2,3,9,10,11,16, 17
Breakfast: C. & C. Plus

Dbl. Oc.: $45.00 - $88.00
Sgl. Oc.: $45.00 - $88.00
Third Person: $20.00

The Hayne House—A fantasy realized nestled in the heart of the historic district. Treasure of art, antiques, good books and no TV. Back porch smoking. Sherry in the parlor. Charming Charleston garden. Joggling board, morning doves, oldest B&B in the city. One block from Battery Park.

---

1. No Smoking	5. Tennis Available	9. Credit Cards Accepted	13. Lunch Available	17. Shared Baths
2. No Pets	6. Golf Available	10. Personal Check Accepted	14. Conference Rooms Avail.	18. Afternoon Tea
3 Off Season Rates	7. Swimmming Avail.	11. Reservations Necessary	15. Group Seminars Avail.	* Commisions given
4. Senior Citizen Rates	8. Skiing Available	12. Dinner Available	16. Private Baths	to Travel Agents

Charleston *

Craven, Joye & Paul
27 State St., 29401
(803) 722-4243

Amenities: 1,2,3,10,11,16
Breakfast: C. Plus
Dbl. Oc.: $95.00 - $125.00
Sgl Oc.: $95.00 - $125.00
Third Person: $15.00
Child: $15.00

27 State Street Bed And Breakfast—Circa 1800 carriage house suites furnished with antiques and reproductions. Located in the French Quarter and within the original walled city. Amenities include morning newspaper, fresh fruit and flowers, bicycles and parking. Air-conditioned. Near restaurants and points of interest.

Charleston *

Evans, Lois
126 Tradd St., 29401
(803)577-6362

Amenities: 2,3,5,6,7,9,10,11, 16,17
Breakfast: F.

Dbl. Oc.: $100.00 - $150.00
Sgl. Oc.: $100.00 - $150.00

The Kitchen House—Restored 18th-century dwelling located in the heart of the historic district. Fireplaces, antiques, patio, herb garden, breakfast, sherry. Featured in *Colonial Homes Magazine* and the *New York Times*. Concierge service. Southern hospitality.

Charleston

Hancock, Aubrey
138 Wentworth St., 29401
(803) 577-7709

Amenities: 1,2,3,9,10,11,16
Breakfast: F.

Dbl. Oc.: $100.00
Sgl. Oc.: $100.00
Third Person: $15.00

Villa De La Fontaine Bed And Breakfast—A classic revival porticoed mansion built in 1838. Restored and furnished with museum-quality furniture. Located in the heart of the historic area. Operated by a retired interior designer. Formal gardens, terrace, fountain and gazebo. Cottage on premise. Parking.

Charleston *

Howard, Laura
198 King St., 29401
(803) 723-7000, (800) 845-6119

Amenities: 1,2,3,4,5,6,9,14, 15,16,18
Breakfast: C. and F.

Dbl. Oc.: $108.00 - $162.00
Sgl. Oc.: $91.80 - $145.80
Third Person: $16.20
Child: Under 12 yrs. - no charge

Kings Courtyard Inn—Located in the heart of antique and historic districts. An 1853 restored inn. Rates include continental breakfast, newspaper and evening turn-down with brandy and chocolate. Sherry upon arrival. Free on-site parking. Historic Hotels of America, AAA - Four Diamond award.

1. No Smoking	5. Tennis Available	9. Credit Cards Accepted	13. Lunch Available	17. Shared Baths
2. No Pets	6. Golf Available	10. Personal Check Accepted	14. Conference Rooms Avail.	18. Afternoon Tea
3 Off Season Rates	7. Swimmming Avail.	11. Reservations Necessary	15. Group Seminars Avail.	* Commissions given
4. Senior Citizen Rates	8. Skiing Available	12. Dinner Available	16. Private Baths	to Travel Agents

SOUTH CAROLINA

Charleston

Smith, B.J.
114 Rutledge Ave., 29401
(803) 722-7551

Amenities: 1,2,3,5,7,9,10,16,17,18
Breakfast: C.
Dbl. Oc.: 55.00 - 90.00
Third Person: $5.00
Child: Under 12 yrs. - no charge

Rutledge Victorian Inn And Guest House—Very authentic old Charleston house in the historic district. Quaint but elegant. Large gingerbread porch. Inside: decorative fireplaces, hardwood floors, 10-foot oak doors and windows and antiques. Atmosphere casual. Refreshment table. Parking. Across from old museum park.

Charleston

Smith, B.J.
32 George St., 29401
(803) 723-9339

Amenities: 1,2,3,5,6,7,9,10, 16,18
Breakfast: C.

Dbl. Oc.: $50.00 - $85.00
Third Person: $5.00
Child: Under 12 - no charge

King George IV Inn And Guests—A 200-year-old (circa 1790s) Charleston historic house, the Freneau House, located in the historic district. Federal- style home: lovely decorative fireplaces, 10-foot ceilings, six- foot windows; wide-planked hardwood floors. Five- minute walk to the Market. Parking.

Charleston

Spell, David
40 Rutledge Ave., 29401
(803) 722-0973

Amenities: 1,2,5,6,7,10, 11,16
Breakfast: C.

Dbl. Oc.: $95.00
Sgl. Oc.: $95.00
Third Person: $15.00

Belvedere Guest House—Offers hospitable accommodations in a gracious mansion overlooking Colonial Lake. Located in the historic district of downtown Charleston at the corner of Rutledge Avenue and Queen Street.

Charleston

Spell, Jean & Pete
2 Meeting St., 29401
(803) 723-7322

Amenities: 1,2,3,10,11,16,18
Breakfast: C.

Dbl. Oc.: $85.00 - $155.00
Third Person: $20.00

Two Meeting Street Inn—Located in the historic district. Charleston's most renowned and elegant inn where guests enjoy the entire inn. No children under eight years. Located across from Battery Park on waterfront.

---

1. No Smoking	5. Tennis Available	9. Credit Cards Accepted	13. Lunch Available	17. Shared Baths
2. No Pets	6. Golf Available	10. Personal Check Accepted	14. Conference Rooms Avail.	18. Afternoon Tea
3 Off Season Rates	7. Swimmming Avail.	11. Reservations Necessary	15. Group Seminars Avail.	* Commisions given
4. Senior Citizen Rates	8. Skiing Available	12. Dinner Available	16. Private Baths	to Travel Agents

SOUTH CAROLINA

Charleston *

Weed, Diane Deardurff
105 Tradd St., 29401-2422
(803) 577-0682

Amenities: 1,2,3,5,6,7,10,11, 16,18

Breakfast: C. Plus

Dbl. Oc.: $75.00 - $90.00
Sgl. Oc.: $75.00 - $90.00
Third Person: $25.00
Child: Under 2 yrs. - $25.00

Country Victorian Bed And Breakfast—Private entrances, antique iron and brass beds, old quilts and antique oak and wicker furniture. Located in the historic area within walking distance of everything. Relax on piazza of this historic home and watch carriages pass by. Enjoy bicycles, free parking and many extras.

Columbia *

Vance, Dan
2003 Greene St., 29205
(803) 765-0440, (800) 622-3382

Amenities: 1,2,4,6,9,11,14, 15,16

Breakfast: C.

Dbl. Oc.: $94.16
Sgl. Oc.: $83.46
Third Person: $10.70
Child: Under 12 yrs. - no charge

Claussen's Inn—A historic restored inn. Adjacent to the University of South Carolina campus. Convenient to shopping, dining and downtown. Rates include continental breakfast, turn-down service with chocolates and brandy. Complimentary wine and sherry. AAA - Four Diamond award.

Dillon

Lannoo, Pam & Jim
601 E. Main St., Hwy. 9, 29536
(803) 774-0679

Amenities: 1,2,3,9,10,14,15, 16,17

Breakfast: F.

Dbl. Oc.: $50.00
Sgl. Oc.: $40.00
Third Person: $10.00
Child: $10.00

Magnolia Inn Bed And Breakfast—Easy access from I-95. Southern hospitality and beautiful decor grace this century-old Southern colonial home. Antiques and reproductions. One hour to Grand Strand beaches. Golfing nearby. Picnic lunches available. Full home-cooked breakfasts. Rest and relax.

Georgetown *

Shaw, Mary
8 Cypress Court, 29440
(803) 546-9663

Amenities: 5,6,7,10,16,18
Breakfast: F.

Dbl. Oc.: $50.00
Sgl. Oc.: $45.00 - $50.00
Third Person: $10.00

The Shaw House—Our colonial-style home sits on a bluff overlooking a beautiful marsh; bird watcher's paradise. Spacious rooms, private baths, many antiques throughout, rocking chairs, swing and hammock on front porch. Walking distance of town and great restaurants. Southern breakfast served.

---

1. No Smoking	5. Tennis Available	9. Credit Cards Accepted	13. Lunch Available	17. Shared Baths
2. No Pets	6. Golf Available	10. Personal Check Accepted	14. Conference Rooms Avail.	18. Afternoon Tea
3 Off Season Rates	7. Swimmming Avail.	11. Reservations Necessary	15. Group Seminars Avail.	* Commisions given
4. Senior Citizen Rates	8. Skiing Available	12. Dinner Available	16. Private Baths	to Travel Agents

SOUTH CAROLINA

Georgetown *

Wiley, Patricia & John
630 Highmarket St., 29440
(803) 546-4821

Amenities: 1,2,3,4,5,6,9,10
         11,14,15,16,18
Breakfast: F.
Dbl. Oc.: $65.00 - $139.00
Sgl Oc.: $60.00 - $134.00
Third Person: $25.00

1790 House—Meticulously restored 200-year-old plantation-style inn located in the heart of the historic district. Spacious, luxurious rooms. Beautiful, separate cottage with jacuzzi tub. Central air/heat. Fireplaces. Lovely gardens. Walk to shops, restaurants and historic sites. Golfers' paradise.

Leesville

Wright, Annabelle & Jack
244 W. Church St., 29070
(803) 532-2763

Amenities: 2,4,6,7,9,10,11,
        16
Breakfast: C.

Dbl. Oc.: $50.00 - $55.00
Sgl. Oc.: $45.00 - $50.00
Third Person: $10.00
Child: Under 12 yrs. - no charge

Able House Inn—A chateau estate 10 miles from I-20 on Route 1, 30 minutes from Columbia. Surrounded by pecan, pine and pink dogwood trees. Five charming guest rooms, imported antiques, air-conditioning, TV and stereo. Fresh popcorn and soda in the evenings. Closely supervised children welcome.

Myrtle Beach *

Ficarra, Ellen & Cos
407 No. 71 Ave., 29577
(803) 449-5268

Amenities: 1,2,3,5,6,7,9,16
Breakfast: C. Plus

Dbl. Oc.: $70.45
Sgl. Oc.: $65.11
Third Person: $10.70
Child: $10.70

Serendipity, An Inn—An award-winning, Mission-style inn open year-round. All rooms have A/C, color TV, private baths and refrigerators; 300 yards to ocean beach. Pool, Jacuzzi and gas grill. Near 77 golf courses, tennis, fishing, restaurants, shopping and theatres. Maid service - squeaky clean!

Rock Hill *

Peterson, Melba & Jerry
600 E. Main St., 29730
(803) 366-1161

Amenities: 1,2,6,9,10,11,14,
        16,18
Breakfast: C.

Dbl. Oc.: $59.00 - $79.00
Sgl. Oc.: $59.00 - $79.00

East Main Guest House... A Bed And Breakfast Inn—This extensively renovated home now contains three guest rooms with modern baths. The honeymoon suite has a canopy bed, fireplace and a whirlpool tub. The east room has a fireplace and a queen-size bed. The garden room has twin beds. Wine and cheese are served in the parlor.

1. No Smoking	5. Tennis Available	9. Credit Cards Accepted	13. Lunch Available	17. Shared Baths
2. No Pets	6. Golf Available	10. Personal Check Accepted	14. Conference Rooms Avail.	18. Afternoon Tea
3 Off Season Rates	7. Swimmming Avail.	11. Reservations Necessary	15. Group Seminars Avail.	* Commisions given
4. Senior Citizen Rates	8. Skiing Available	12. Dinner Available	16. Private Baths	to Travel Agents

Sumter

Carnes, Merilyn & Bob
6 Park Ave., 29150
(803) 773-2903

Amenities: 2,5,6,9,10,11,
16,17
Breakfast: C.

Dbl. Oc.: $55.00
Sgl. Oc.: $40.00
Third Person: No charge
Child: No charge

Sumter Bed And Breakfast—Charming 1896 home facing a quiet park in the historic district. Large front porch, four guest rooms, HBO and a library with ancient artifacts. Tours, tennis, 15 golf courses available. Breakfast: fresh juice, fruit, home-baked pastries and homemade granola.

1. No Smoking	5. Tennis Available	9. Credit Cards Accepted	13. Lunch Available	17. Shared Baths
2. No Pets	6. Golf Available	10. Personal Check Accepted	14. Conference Rooms Avail.	18. Afternoon Tea
3 Off Season Rates	7. Swimmming Avail.	11. Reservations Necessary	15. Group Seminars Avail.	* Commisions given
4. Senior Citizen Rates	8. Skiing Available	12. Dinner Available	16. Private Baths	to Travel Agents

SOUTH DAKOTA

The Sunshine State

Capitol: Pierre
Statehood: November 2, 1889; the 40th state
State Motto: "Under God the People Rule"
State Song: "Hail South Dakota"
State Bird: Ring-Necked Pheasant
State Flower: American Pasqueflower
State Tree: Black Hills Spruce

South Dakota is a land of rare beauty and unusual landscapes. It has fertile crop-growing land, canyons, the strange Badlands and the enchanting Black Hills.

The wild west look is still here. Buffaloes can be seen roaming Custer's State Park in herds.

South Dakota is visited by hundreds of tourists every year. Probably one of the most popular attractions is Mt. Rushmore. Here in 1928, Gutzon Borglum began a memorial to freedom and to the spirit of the American people. It took him and his small group of men 14 years to complete this task, but when he finished, the sculptured and carved faces of four of our greatest presidents, George Washington, Abraham Lincoln, Thomas Jefferson and Theodore Roosevelt, were enshrined here forever.

SOUTH DAKOTA

Chamberlain *

Cable, Alta & Frank
HC 69, Box 82A, 57325
(605) 734-6084

Amenities: 3,6,7,10,11,16,17
Breakfast: F.

Dbl. Oc.: $42.50 - $47.50
Sgl. Oc.: $37.00
Third Person: $10.00
Child: Under 3 yrs. - no charge

Riverview Ridge—Country peace and quiet with a beautiful view of the Missouri River. Two miles north of downtown Chamberlain on Highway 50. Big Bend Dam, St. Joseph's Indian School, Akta Lakota, Old West and Wildlife Museums, Golden Buffalo Casino all nearby.

Custer *

Seaman, Carole & Mill
35 Centennial Dr., 57730
(605) 673-3333

Amenities: 1,2,3,4,5,6,7,8,10, 11,16,17,18
Breakfast: F.

Dbl. Oc.: $48.00 - $80.00
Sgl. Oc.: $43.00 - $64.00
Third Person: $11.00

Custer Mansion Bed And Breakfast—An 1891 historic Victorian Gothic on one acre. Charmingly restored. Offers Western hospitality and home-cooking in a unique setting of the beautiful Black Hills. Nearby biking, hiking, trout fishing and hunting. Near Custer State Park, Mount Rushmore and restaurants.

Hill City

Nash, Evelyn
HC 87, Box 75B, 57745
(605) 574-2316

Amenities: 1,2,10,11,16,17
Breakfast: C. Plus

Dbl. Oc.: $45.00
Sgl. Oc.: $35.00
Child: Under 12 yrs. - $10.00

Peaceful Valley Bed And Breakfast—Located in the heart of the Black Hills. Centrally located to Mount Rushmore, Crazy Horse Mountain, Custer State Park, Hill City's 1880 train, Black Hills Playhouse, Hot Springs Momouth site, Spearfish Passion Play. Quiet, country living.

Jamestown *

Oxtsby, Ethel
R.R. 3, Box 71, 58401
(701) 251-1372

Amenities: 1,8,10,11,17
Breakfast: F.

Dbl. Oc.: $50.00
Sgl. Oc.: $40.00

Country Charm Bed And Breakfast—Built on the prairie in 1897. The entire home is tastefully decorated in country style with many collections and antiques. Hearts and sheep stenciled on the walls lead you to your choice of three charming guest rooms with shared baths. The comforts of the guests are treasured. Escape your hectic life style and enjoy the tranquility.

---

1. No Smoking	5. Tennis Available	9. Credit Cards Accepted	13. Lunch Available	17. Shared Baths
2. No Pets	6. Golf Available	10. Personal Check Accepted	14. Conference Rooms Avail.	18. Afternoon Tea
3 Off Season Rates	7. Swimmming Avail.	11. Reservations Necessary	15. Group Seminars Avail.	* Commisions given
4. Senior Citizen Rates	8. Skiing Available	12. Dinner Available	16. Private Baths	to Travel Agents

SOUTH DAKOTA

Lead *

Ackerman, LaVonne
HC37, Box 1214, 57754
(605) 584-2473

Amenities: 1,8,9,10,11,12,16, 17,18
Breakfast: F.

Dbl. Oc.: $68.00 - $78.00
Sgl. Oc.: $52.00
Third Person: $21.00
Child: Under 6 yrs. - no charge

Deer Mountain Bed And Breakfast—Unique log home featuring Western hospitality. Skiing available five minutes away. Located a few miles from historic Deadwood gambling town. Enjoy the spa; play a game of pool; relax by the fireside. Mt. Rushmore, hunting, fishing, rodeos all close by.

Owanka

Reeves, Judy & Wes
R.R., Exit 90, 57767
(605) 798-5405

Amenities: 1,11,12,13,15,16, 18
Breakfast: C.

Dbl. Oc.: $40.00
Sgl. Oc.: $30.00
Third Person: $10.00
Child: Under 8 yrs. - no charge

Country Bed And Breakfast—Just 30 miles from Black Hills, home of Mount Rushmore and 30 miles from The Badlands. Located in a quiet area and a great place to relax. Small family farm on 40 acres with access to kitchen. Horseback riding available. See the trail that covered wagons crossed to Deadwood.

Rapid City

Kuhnhauser, Audry & Hank
RR 8, Box 2400, 57702
(605) 342-7788

Amenities: 1,2,10,11,16
Breakfast: F.

Dbl. Oc.: $78.00 - $85.00

Audrie's Cranbury Corner B&B And Abend Haus Cottage — "The Black Hills Inn-Place." Our country home and five acre estate is surrounded by miles of National Forest. Each quiet, comfortable room, suite or cottage has private entrances, hot tubs, cable TVs and refrigerators. Free trout fishing, biking and hiking on property.

---

1. No Smoking	5. Tennis Available	9. Credit Cards Accepted	13. Lunch Available	17. Shared Baths
2. No Pets	6. Golf Available	10. Personal Check Accepted	14. Conference Rooms Avail.	18. Afternoon Tea
3 Off Season Rates	7. Swimmming Avail.	11. Reservations Necessary	15. Group Seminars Avail.	* Commisions given
4. Senior Citizen Rates	8. Skiing Available	12. Dinner Available	16. Private Baths	to Travel Agents

TENNESSEE

The Volunteer State

Capitol: Nashville
Statehood: June 1, 1796; the 16th state
State Motto: "Agriculture and Commerce"
State Song: "Rocky Top Tennessee"
State Bird: Mockingbird
State Flower: Iris
State Tree: Tulip Poplar

Tennessee is a state of varied industries. In the east there are the coal mines; in the middle of the state, the farmers raise cattle and tobacco; and in the west there are large cotton plantations. But regardless, there is one thing everyone here enjoys and that is Country Music, as played at the Grand Ole Opry in Nashville.

There is a lot of Civil War history here and beautiful scenic drives. However, the majority of visitors that come to Tennessee come first to see the Grand Ole Opry.

Three presidents were born and lived here: Andrew Jackson, James Polk and Andrew Johnson.

Cleveland

Brown, Beverlee
215 20th St., N.E., 37311
(615) 476-8029, (615) 479-5311

Amenities: 1,2,4,5,6,7,9,11, 16,17,18
Breakfast: F.

Dbl. Oc.: $75.00
Sgl. Oc.: $65.00

Brown Manor—A deluxe manor with special attention to personal service. In the heart of a quaint town on I-75. Chattanooga is 30 miles away. White-water rafting is 16 miles away. Glidder-Port is 20 miles away. National Forest - 10 miles away. Walking tours and biking. Privacy and pampering.

Cleveland *

Chadwick, Winnie A.
2766 Michigan Ave. Rd., NE, 37312
(615) 339-2407

Amenities: 2,4,5,6,7,9,10,11, 12,13,15,16,17
Breakfast: F.

Dbl. Oc.: $42.00 - $47.00
Sgl. Oc.: $30.00
Third Person: $30.00
Child: Under 5 yrs. - no charge

Chadwick House—A charming family home set on three acres of woodland. Just five miles from I-75 and four miles from Cleveland. Irish host is world traveler. Nearby white-water rafting, Cherokee National Forest, Ruby Falls, The Lost Sea and good restaurants. A great place to relax and unwind.

Dandridge

Franklin, Lucy & Hood
140 Mill Dale Rd., 37725
(615) 397-3470

Amenities: 2,5,6,7,8,10,15, 16,18
Breakfast: F.

Dbl. Oc.: $70.04
Sgl. Oc.: $53.87
Third Person: $10.77
Child: Under 10 yrs. - no charge

Mill Dale Farm—A hospitable working farmhouse one mile off I-40. Breakfast prepared with home-cured hams, breads, jams and jellies. Built and owned since 1843. The antique-filled antebellum home is centrally located for visits to mountains, lakes, arts, Gatlinburg and Pigeon Forge.

Dandridge *

Price, Mary
743 Garrett Rd., 37725
(615) 397-7327

Amenities: 2,5,6,7,8,9,10,11, 16,17,18
Breakfast: F.

Dbl. Oc.: $70.04
Sgl. Oc.: $53.88

Sugarfork Lodge Bed And Breakfast—This unique B&B is situated in a tranquil setting on the shores of Douglas Lake, 3.8 miles from I-40. There are three guest rooms, a fireplace and guest kitchen. Enjoy a hearty breakfast, relax by the lake or sit on the deck. Near mountains, outlet malls, Dollywood and Gatlinburg.

1. No Smoking	5. Tennis Available	9. Credit Cards Accepted	13. Lunch Available	17. Shared Baths
2. No Pets	6. Golf Available	10. Personal Check Accepted	14. Conference Rooms Avail.	18. Afternoon Tea
3 Off Season Rates	7. Swimmming Avail.	11. Reservations Necessary	15. Group Seminars Avail.	* Commisions given
4. Senior Citizen Rates	8. Skiing Available	12. Dinner Available	16. Private Baths	to Travel Agents

Gatlinburg

Burns, Connie & John
2140 Tudor Mountain Rd., 37738
(615) 436-4668

Amenities: 1,2,9,10,12,14,
15,16
Breakfast: F.

Dbl. Oc.: $105.00 - $250.00
Sgl. Oc.: $95.00 - $125.00
Third Person: $20.00
Child: $20.00

Buckhorn Inn—A truly unique country inn offering peaceful seclusion with the feeling and tradition of early Gatlinburg. Established in 1938. Buckhorn Inn was built on a hillside facing the magnificent views of the Smokies and includes 40 acres of woodlands, meadows and quiet walkways.

Gatlinburg

Butcher, Gloria
1520 Garrett Lane, 37738
(615) 436-9457

Amenities: 1,2,3,5,6,7,8,9,10,
11,14,16,17
Breakfast: F.
Dbl. Oc.: $74.87 & up

Butcher House Bed And Breakfast—In the mountains. Cradled 2,800 feet above the city, this B&B offers a commanding view of the Smokies. Elegant cedar, glass and stone chalet, graced by Victorian, French and Queen Anne antiques. High AAA, ABBA - A+.

Gatlinburg *

Mellor, Lee
1120 Tanrac Trail, 37738
(615) 436-5432

Amenities: 1,2,3,9,11,15,16,18
Breakfast: F.
Dbl. Oc.: $95.00 - $115.00
Sgl Oc.: $95.00 - $115.00
Third Person: $20.00

The Colonel's Lady—Re-creates the elegance and charm of an English country inn. Secluded in its own lush mountain top grounds, it's still convenient to local attractions. Panoramic views of the Great Smoky Mountains, fireplaces, hot tubs and whirlpool spas.

---

1. No Smoking	5. Tennis Available	9. Credit Cards Accepted	13. Lunch Available	17. Shared Baths
2. No Pets	6. Golf Available	10. Personal Check Accepted	14. Conference Rooms Avail.	18. Afternoon Tea
3 Off Season Rates	7. Swimming Avail.	11. Reservations Necessary	15. Group Seminars Avail.	* Commisions given
4. Senior Citizen Rates	8. Skiing Available	12. Dinner Available	16. Private Baths	to Travel Agents

TENNESSEE

Gatlinburg *

Wolcott, Virginia
3944 Castle Rd., 37738
(615) 430-5000, (800) 248-2923

Amenities: 2,3,5,6,7,8,9,10, 11,15,16
Breakfast: F.

Dbl. Oc.: $96.57
Sgl. Oc.: $96.57
Third Person: $16.28

7th Heaven Log Inn—On the 7th green of the golf resort across the road from Smoky Mountains National Park. Game room, fireplace, pool tables, guest kitchen, TV and VCR. Log gazebo and jacuzzi. Close to Dollywood, craft, antique and outlet stores. Luxurious with magnificent views. Group specials.

Kodak *

Hickman, Hilda
734 Pollard Rd., 37764
(615) 933-3512, (800) 676-3512

Amenities: 1,2,6,9,10,11, 16,18
Breakfast: F.

Dbl. Oc.: $65.00
Sgl. Oc.: $50.00
Third Person: $10.00

Grandma's House—On a quiet country lane at the base of the Great Smoky Mountains. Two miles off I-40 at Exit 407 near Pigeon Forge— Gatlinburg area. Two-story, colonial-style house. Decor is antiques and country. Three guest rooms, all with private baths. Hosts are native east Tennesseans.

Maryville

Sherrod, Lucy
212 High St., 37801
(615) 981-2966

Amenities: 2,9,10,12,13,16
Breakfast: F.

Dbl. Oc.: $66.30
Sgl. Oc.: $66.30
Third Person: $11.05
Child: Under 10 yrs. - no charge

The High Court Inn—Located only 25 minutes form the Smoky Mountains National Park. Three luxurious bedrooms, each with a private bath, are located on the second floor. Each room has its own bath with old-fashioned clawfoot tubs you will enjoy as a guest.

Memphis

Long, Samantha
217 N. Waldran, 38105
(901) 527-7174

Amenities: 1,2,4,10,16
Breakfast: F.

Dbl. Oc.: $65.00 - $85.00
Third Person: $10.00

The Lowenstein-Long House—The house was built at the turn of the century and was restored in 1984. It is centrally located and convenient to many attractions. The house has beautiful mahogany woodwork and impressive plaster moldings. A great example of Victorian architecture.

Monteagle*

Adams, Wendy & David
Monteagle Assembly, 37356
(615) 924-2669

Amenities: 1,2,3,4,5,6,7,9,10 11,12,14,15,16
Breakfast: C. Plus

Dbl. Oc.: $60.00 - $100.00
Child: Under 6 yrs. - no charge

Adams Edgeworth Inn — Fine lodging since 1896 in this beautiful historic country inn in the National Historic District near the University of the South, Sewanee. English country decor, fine antiques, handmade quilts and renown art collections. 200 feet of porches. Hiking, views and waterfalls nerby.

---

1. No Smoking	5. Tennis Available	9. Credit Cards Accepted	13. Lunch Available	17. Shared Baths
2. No Pets	6. Golf Available	10. Personal Check Accepted	14. Conference Rooms Avail.	18. Afternoon Tea
3 Off Season Rates	7. Swimmming Avail.	11. Reservations Necessary	15. Group Seminars Avail.	* Commisions given
4. Senior Citizen Rates	8. Skiing Available	12. Dinner Available	16. Private Baths	to Travel Agents

Murfreesboro

Deaton, Barbara & Robert
435 E. Main St., 37130
(615) 893-6030

Amenities: 2,3,10,11,16,17
Breakfast: C.

Dbl. Oc.: $50.00
Sgl. Oc.: $35.00
Third Person: $5.00
Child: Under 12 yrs. - no charge

Clardy's Guest House—A Victorian home in the historic district, furnished with antiques. House features 8'x8' stained glass, ornate woodwork and fireplaces. Just two miles from I-24 and 30 miles southeast of Nashville. Good antique shopping, touring and dining area.

Pigeon Forge *

Hilton, Norma & Jack
2654 Valley Heights Dr., 37863
(615) 428-9765

Amenities: 1,2,4,5,6,7,8,9,10, 12,13,14,15,16,18
Breakfast: F.

Dbl. Oc.: $87.49
Sgl. Oc.: $76.42
Third Person: $16.61
Child: Under 12 yrs. - $11.08

Hilton's Bluff Bed And Breakfast Inn—Romantic hilltop hideaway minutes from the Great Smoky Mountains National Park, Dollywood. Outlet shopping. Den with majestic stone fireplace, gameroom. Covered decks with rockers, king-size beds. Two— person, heart-shaped jacuzzis. Perfect for honeymoons or retreats. Elegant!

Pigeon Forge *

Trombley, Yvonne
2720 Colonial Dr., 37863
(615) 428-0370,
(800) 377-1469 (PA only)

Amenities: 1,2,3,5,6,7,8,9,10, 11,14,15,16,18
Breakfast: F.

Dbl. Oc.: $79.00 - $120.00
Sgl. Oc.: $69.00 - $99.00
Third Person: $12.50
Child: $10.00

Day Dreams Country Inn—Enjoy a down-home country atmosphere. Our log home, situated on three acres, offers beautiful trees, gardens and a stream to sit and relax by. Within walking distance you'll find outlet malls, Dollywood, the rest of Pigeon Forge and the Great Smoky Mountains.

Rugby

Jones, Bill
Hwy. 52, P.O. Box 5252, 37733
(615) 628-5252

Amenities: 1,2,6,7,9,10,11,12, 14,15,16,17,18
Breakfast: F.

Dbl. Oc.: $97.00 & up
Sgl. Oc.: $78.00 & up
Third Person: $30.00

Grey Gables Bed 'N' Breakfast—Cumberland Plateau - An 1880 historic English colony. A blend of Victorian English and Tennessee country. Dinner and country breakfast included in rate. White wicker or country rockers, croquet, horseshoes and canoe rental. Shuttle access to golf, swiming, hiking and cycling.

Rugby

Stagg, Barbara
Hwy. 52, 37733
(615) 628-2430

Amenities: 1,2,6,7,9,10,11,12, 13,14,15,16,17,18
Breakfast: F.

Dbl. Oc.: $58.00 - $68.00
Sgl. Oc.: $48.00 - $58.00
Third Person: $8.00

Newbury House At Historic Rugby—Built in 1880. Restored and furnished with antiques. Listed in the Register of Historic Places. A tranquil village near national and state parks. Historic cottages also available. Historic building tours, craft commissary and Victorian bookshop. Century-old walking trails to adjacent river.

1. No Smoking	5. Tennis Available	9. Credit Cards Accepted	13. Lunch Available	17. Shared Baths
2. No Pets	6. Golf Available	10. Personal Check Accepted	14. Conference Rooms Avail.	18. Afternoon Tea
3 Off Season Rates	7. Swimmming Avail.	11. Reservations Necessary	15. Group Seminars Avail.	* Commisions given
4. Senior Citizen Rates	8. Skiing Available	12. Dinner Available	16. Private Baths	to Travel Agents

Savannah

Ross, John
504 Main St.
P.O. Box 398, 38372
(901) 925-3974

Amenities: 1,2,9,10,11,16,17
Breakfast: C. Plus
Dbl. Oc.: $85.00
Sgl Oc.: $62.00

Ross House Bed And Breakfast—A 1908 neoclassical brick home in National Register Historic Districts. Large shaded lawn in town center with woods behind. Furnished with original antiques amd paintings. Large library. Near Cherry Mansion and Tennessee River. Ten miles to Shiloh and Pickwick Lake.

Sevierville *

McFarland, Cathey & Gary
2803 Old Country Way, 37862
(615) 428-4858

Amenities: 1,2,3,6,8,9,10,11, 16,17
Breakfast: F.
Dbl. Oc.: $65.00 - $97.00
Sgl. Oc.: $54.00 - $87.00

Milk And Honey Country Hideaway—Close to Gatlinburg, Pigeon Forge, outlet malls and Great Smoky Mountain National Park. Large front porch, rockers, cozy rooms and hearty breakfasts. Warm hospitality in a quiet, country setting.

Townsend

Hind, James
220 Winterberry Lane, 37882
(615) 448-6751

Amenities: 1,2,6,10,11,14,16
Breakfast: F.
Dbl. Oc.: $95.00 - $122.00
Sgl Oc.: $95.00 - $122.00
Third Person: $25.00

Richmont Inn—Barn beautifully furnished with 18th-century English antiques, French paintings. Luxury rooms, sitting areas, king-size beds, fireplaces, spa tubs, balconies. Breathtaking mountain views! French breakfast, evening candlelight dessert. Ten minutes to Great Smokies Park.

1. No Smoking	5. Tennis Available	9. Credit Cards Accepted	13. Lunch Available	17. Shared Baths
2. No Pets	6. Golf Available	10. Personal Check Accepted	14. Conference Rooms Avail.	18. Afternoon Tea
3 Off Season Rates	7. Swimmming Avail.	11. Reservations Necessary	15. Group Seminars Avail.	* Commisions given
4. Senior Citizen Rates	8. Skiing Available	12. Dinner Available	16. Private Baths	to Travel Agents

TEXAS

The Lone Star State

Capitol: Austin
Statehood: December 29, 1845; the 28th state
State Motto: "Friendship"
State Song: "Texas, Our Texas"
State Bird: Mockingbird
State Flower: Bluebonnet
State Tree: Pecan

Texas is second in size to Alaska. It is so big that when it entered the union, Congress gave it the right to divide into five state, but it preferred to remain one and BIG. It is called the Lone Star State because of the one lone star on its flag.

Many colorful people from history have come from Texas, including Davy Crockett, Jim Bowie and one of our more modernday heroes, President Lyndon B. Johnson.

Texas has many millionaires because of the great oil strikes there over the years. There is also much cattle and great cattle farms. The King Ranch is perhaps the largest cattle-raising ranch in the world.

The cities of Houston, Dallas, San Antonio and Fort Worth are exciting places for the tourist to visit.

TEXAS

Abilene

Bolin, Ginny & Sam
508 Mulberry, 79601
(915) 675-5855

Amenities: 1,2,9,10,17
Breakfast: F.

Dbl. Oc.: $45.00 - $57.00
Sgl. Oc.: $34.00 - $45.00
Third Person: $12.00

Bolin's Prairie House Bed And Breakfast—A 1902 home with high ceilings and hardwood floors decorated with a combination of antiques and modern conveniences. Enjoy the porch swing and the fireside. Breakfast of egg dishes, fruit and fresh bread served on a lace-covered table with blue-and-white china.

Austin *

Boyd, Grace
1006 E. 50th, 78751
(512) 452-1004

Amenities: 1,2,9,10,16
Breakfast: F.

Dbl. Oc.: $55.37
Sgl. Oc.: $44.07
Third Person: $11.30
Child: Under 12 yrs. - no charge

Bac Griesbach - Bed And Breakfast—Family hospitality awaits the traveler in this European-style B&B. We have seven cozy bedrooms, five with a private bathroom. Enjoy our full German-style breakfast. Located close to the airport. Minutes drive to the lake, downtown and campus area.

Austin *

Danley, Nancy & Roger
613 W. 32nd St., 78705
(512) 451-6744

Amenities: 1,2,3,10,11,16
Breakfast: F.

Dbl. Oc.: $67.80 - $96.05
Sgl. Oc.: $50.85 - $79.10
Third Person: $16.95
Child: Over 7 yrs. - $16.95

McCallum House—Just 10 blocks from University of Texas-Austin; 20 blocks from downtown. This historic Victorian has five rooms and suites, all with private baths, color TV, extension phones, sitting areas and kitchens. Four have private porches. Owner/occupant innkeepers. Discount three nights or more.

Austin *

Griesbach, Gerald
1006 E. 50th St., 78751
(512) 452-1004

Amenities: 1,2,5,6,7,9,10,11,
12,14,15,16
Breakfast: F.

Dbl. Oc.: $59.00

Bad Griesbach—European-style bed and breakfast.

Austin

Jackson, Kay
1200 W. 22-1/2 St., 78705
(512) 477-9639

Amenities: 1,2,4,5,9,10,11,16,
17
Breakfast: F.

Dbl. Oc.: $59.00 - $69.00
Sgl. Oc.: $50.00 - $60.00
Third Person: $15.00

The Wild Flower Inn—A lovely 50-year-old home located on a tree-lined street. The inn is seven blocks west of the University of Texas campus and just a few minutes from the state capitol complex. Convenient to the LBJ Presidential Library. Close to hiking and biking trails and tennis courts.

1. No Smoking	5. Tennis Available	9. Credit Cards Accepted	13. Lunch Available	17. Shared Baths
2. No Pets	6. Golf Available	10. Personal Check Accepted	14. Conference Rooms Avail.	18. Afternoon Tea
3 Off Season Rates	7. Swimmming Avail.	11. Reservations Necessary	15. Group Seminars Avail.	* Commissions given
4. Senior Citizen Rates	8. Skiing Available	12. Dinner Available	16. Private Baths	to Travel Agents

TEXAS

Austin *
Southard, Rejina & Jerry
908 Blanco, 78703
(512) 474-4731

Amenities: 1,3,9,10,14,15,16
Breakfast: C.

Dbl. Oc.: $59.00 - $129.00
Sgl. Oc.: $49.00 - $119.00

Southard House—Located in downtown Austin, a lovely 1890s Greek Revival inn. Enjoy our beautifully antique-decorated rooms. All have private baths and phones, some have clawfoot tubs and fireplaces. Two-block stroll to excellent restaurants, antiques and unusual gift shops.

Austin
Thurmond, Peninnah
10817 Ranch Rd. 2222,
78730-1102
(512) 338-1817

Amenities: 5,6,7,9,10,11,16
Breakfast: F.

Dbl. Oc.: $64.20
Sgl. Oc.: $64.20
Third Person: $32.10

Peaceful Hill Bed And Breakfast—Deer watch you come... to country inn: ranch land; rolling hills; 15 minutes west of Austin; 10 minutes to Lake Travis; Grand St.; one fireplace; rock on the porch; view of city skyline; hammock built for two. Peaceful is the name and peaceful is the game. Deer watch you go.....

Canyon *
Money, Tammy
8th St., 79015
(806) 655-7636

Amenities: 1,5,6,9,10,16,17,
18
Breakfast: F.

Dbl. Oc.: $58.30 - $100.70
Sgl. Oc.: $58.30
Third Person: $10.00
Child: Under 3 yrs. - no charge

Country Home Bed And Breakfast—Welcome to country relaxation, lovely west Texas sunsets, bountiful breakfasts including sausage quiche and baked French toast, antique decor, quilts and whirlpool bath in master suite. Close to Palo, Duro Canyon, Panhandle Plains Museum, "TEXAS" drama and West Texas State University.

Fort Worth *
Hancock, Susan & Mark
109-1/2 W. Exchange, 76106
(817) 626-1522

Amenities: 1,2,9,10,14,15,16,17
Breakfast: F.
Dbl. Oc.: 76.84 - $141.25
Sgl Oc.: 76.84 - $141.25
Third Person: $11.30

Miss Molly's Hotel Bed And Breakfast—Discover the living history of the cowboys and cattle along the red-brick streets of this 10-block historic district. In the middle of it all is Miss Molly's Hotel, once a prim-and-proper hotel and later a popular bordello. Each of eight guest rooms is furnished in Old West antiques..

1. No Smoking	5. Tennis Available	9. Credit Cards Accepted	13. Lunch Available	17. Shared Baths
2. No Pets	6. Golf Available	10. Personal Check Accepted	14. Conference Rooms Avail.	18. Afternoon Tea
3 Off Season Rates	7. Swimmming Avail.	11. Reservations Necessary	15. Group Seminars Avail.	* Commisions given
4. Senior Citizen Rates	8. Skiing Available	12. Dinner Available	16. Private Baths	to Travel Agents

TEXAS

Fredericksburg

Kothe, Naomi
HC 10, Box 53A, 78624
(210) 669-2471

Amenities: 2,5,6,7,10,11,16
Breakfast: F.

Dbl. Oc.: $68.90
Sgl. Oc.: $68.90
Third Person: $10.60
Child: $10.60

J Bar K Ranch Bed And Breakfast—A large historic German rock home with antique furnishings on a Texas hill-country ranch. Full country breakfast. Just 15 minutes from Fredericksburg with its German heritage and architecture. Real Texas hospitality. Excellent restaurants and shops.

Galveston *

Mafrige, Nancy & Don
511 - 17th St., 77550
(409) 762-3235

Amenities: 2,3,9,10,14,15, 16,17
Breakfast: C.

Dbl. Oc.: $85.31 - $102.36
Sgl. Oc.: $62.56 - $85.31
Third Person: $22.75

The Victorian Inn—Italianate villa home, circa 1899. Easy walk to historic Strand area where there is shopping, galleries, museums and restaurants. Spacious guest rooms with king-size beds, antiques and balconies. All this among magnolia and palm trees. Great for family reunions and weddings.

Galveston *

O'Donnell, Nonette
1627 Sealy Ave., 77550
(409) 765-4396, (800) 662-9647

Amenities: 2,3,4,5,6,7,9,10,11,16
Breakfast: F.
Dbl. Oc.: $164.00 - $220.00
Sgl Oc.: $140.00 - $195.00
Third Person: $17.00

Trube Castle Inn—Experience the grandeur of Galveston's "guilded age" in "the most fantastic of the Victorian houses in Texas." This meticulously restored 1890 replica of the Danish Royal Castle offers luxury suites amidst museum-quality antiques. Near all island attractions.

Galveston Island

Hanemann, Helen L.
1805 Broadway, 77550
(409) 763-0194, (800) 654-9380

Amenities: 2,5,6,7,9,10,11,15,16,17,18
Breakfast: F.
Dbl. Oc.: $164.21 - $175.54
Sgl Oc.: $164.21 - $175.54
Third Person: Half price

The Gilded Thistle—Enter into a wonderland of fanciful ambience, down-home elegance, superb service and bountiful amenities. Enjoy the memorable experience of choosing "one of the best guest residences Texas has to offer." - *Texas Monthly Press.*

1. No Smoking	5. Tennis Available	9. Credit Cards Accepted	13. Lunch Available	17. Shared Baths
2. No Pets	6. Golf Available	10. Personal Check Accepted	14. Conference Rooms Avail.	18. Afternoon Tea
3 Off Season Rates	7. Swimmming Avail.	11. Reservations Necessary	15. Group Seminars Avail.	* Commisions given
4. Senior Citizen Rates	8. Skiing Available	12. Dinner Available	16. Private Baths	to Travel Agents

TEXAS

Houston *

Swanson, Marguerite
921 Heights Blvd., 77008
(713) 868-4654

Amenities: 1,2,9,10,12,14, 15,16
Breakfast: F.

Dbl. Oc.: $60.00 - $85.00
Sgl. Oc.: $50.00 - $60.00
Third Person: $10.00
Child: Under 12 yrs. - $10.00

Durham House—A faithfully restored Victorian in the National Register of Historic Places. Antique furnishings, player piano, gazebo and porch swing. Just 10 minutes from downtown. Weddings and murder-mystery dinner parties. Elegant. Open all year.

San Antonio *

Cross, Alma & Steven
621 Pierce St., 78208
(512) 223-9426

Amenities: 2,5,6,7,9,13,14,15, 16,17
Breakfast: C. and F.

Dbl. Oc.: $45.20 - $66.67
Sgl. Oc.: $40.68 - $50.85
Third Person: $10.00
Child: No charge - $6.00

Bullis House Inn—Lovely historic Texas mansion minutes from downtown. Large columns, chandeliers, fireplaces and veranda. Eight rooms. Free parking. Located off I-35 next to historic Fort Sam Houston. Meeting facilities. Special weekday and honeymoon packages available. A Texas landmark.

San Antonio

Daubert, Grace & Bob
300 W. French Pl., 78212
(800) 880-4580

Amenities: 1,2,3,4,5,6,7,9,10, 11,12,13,14,15,16, 18
Breakfast: F.

Dbl. Oc.: $75.00
Sgl. Oc.: $75.00
Third Person: Suite - $110.00

Falling Pines B&B—Historic restoration near the Alamo, river walking and downtown businesses. Three-story mansion constructed of brick and limestone. Entry level has paneling, oak floors and Oriental rugs. Second level has designer guest rooms. Third level is a unique suite. On a park-like acre.

San Antonio *

Magatagan, Sharrie & Patrick
209 Washington, 78204
(512) 223-2353

Amenities: 1,2,4,6,9,10,11,14,15,16
Breakfast: C. Plus
Dbl. Oc.: $141.25
Sgl Oc.: $141.25
Third Person: $30.00

The Oge' House On The Riverwalk—Elegant romantic historic mansion filled with antiques on 1-1/2 acres. Nine bedrooms, all private baths, phones, TVs, air-conditioning. Nine fireplaces. Grand verandas. Quiet ambience. Dining, convention center, Alamo and trolley steps away. Weekday rates available.

1. No Smoking	5. Tennis Available	9. Credit Cards Accepted	13. Lunch Available	17. Shared Baths
2. No Pets	6. Golf Available	10. Personal Check Accepted	14. Conference Rooms Avail.	18. Afternoon Tea
3 Off Season Rates	7. Swimmming Avail.	11. Reservations Necessary	15. Group Seminars Avail.	* Commisions given
4. Senior Citizen Rates	8. Skiing Available	12. Dinner Available	16. Private Baths	to Travel Agents

San Antonio *

Rodriquez, Carmela
921 Matagorda, 78210
(800) 373-3137

Amenities: 1,2,9,10,11,16,17
Breakfast: C.

Dbl. Oc.: $62.15 - $90.40
Sgl. Oc.: $50.85 - $79.10
Third Person: $10.00

Naegelin Bed And Breakfast—A 1910 historic landmark colonial home in downtown area. Rich woodwork throughout the home. Four spacious bedrooms carefully furnished with antiques. Six blocks from the Alamo, Riverwalk and other downtown attractions.

San Antonio *

Schwartz, Betty Jo & Don
222 E. Guenther St., 78204
(201) 229-1449

Amenities: 1,2,9,16
Breakfast: C. Plus
Dbl. Oc.: $80.00 - $120.00

Beckmann Inn And Carriage House—Charming Victorian inn located in the heart of San Antonio in the King William historic district. Rooms are colorfully decorated with antiques and Victorian queen-size beds. Ride the trolley or take the Riverwalk to Mexican markets, Alamo, restaurants and more festivities.

Tyler

Mirsky, Mary
417 So. College, 75702
(903) 592-5181

Amenities: 1,2,9,10,11,16,17
Breakfast: C. Plus

Dbl. Oc.: $84.75
Sgl. Oc.: $67.80
Third Person: $16.95

Mary's Attic B&B—What could be more fun than staying in a restored 1926, two-bedroom, two-bath bungalow furnished with antiques? Brick streets. Close to shops and the Azalea Trails. Enjoy my homemade rolls. Three bedrooms with one-bath annex apartment fully furnished with kichenette available.

Tyler *

Powell, Rebecca & Bert
415 So. Vine, 75702
(903) 592-2221

Amenities: 1,2,5,6,9,10,16
Breakfast: F.

Dbl. Oc.: $84.49
Sgl. Oc.: $73.20
Third Person: $11.30
Child: $11.30

Rosevine Inn, Bed And Breakfast—Located in the historic "brick-street area" of Tyler. Near many shops. Enjoy our courtyard and outdoor hot tub. Refreshments are served on arrival and a delectable breakfast in the morning. The innkeepers enjoy visiting with their guests and acting as tour guides.

1. No Smoking	5. Tennis Available	9. Credit Cards Accepted	13. Lunch Available	17. Shared Baths
2. No Pets	6. Golf Available	10. Personal Check Accepted	14. Conference Rooms Avail.	18. Afternoon Tea
3 Off Season Rates	7. Swimmming Avail.	11. Reservations Necessary	15. Group Seminars Avail.	* Commisions given
4. Senior Citizen Rates	8. Skiing Available	12. Dinner Available	16. Private Baths	to Travel Agents

Uvalde *

Durr, Carolyn & Ben
1149 Pearsall Hwy.
P.O. Box 1829, 78802
(512) 278-8550

Amenities: 1,2,9,10,11,14,15, 16,17,18
Breakfast: C. Plus

Dbl. Oc.: $79.00
Sgl. Oc.: $55.00
Third Person: $15.00
Child: Under 1yr. - no charge

Casa De Leona—Spanish hacienda on the Leona River at old Fort Inge; 17 acres of wilderness for walking, hiking, bird watching, arrowhead hunting, fishing and relaxing. Sun deck, fountains and gazebo on the river. Good for art workshops or conferences for small groups.

Winnsboro *

Hubbell, Jan
307 W. Elm, 75494
(903) 342-5629

Amenities: 1,2,4,5,6,7,8,9,10, 11,12,16
Breakfast: F.

Dbl. Oc.: $65.00 - $150.00
Sgl. Oc.: $65.00 - $150.00
Third Person: $15.00
Child: Under 6 yrs. - no charge

Thee Hubbell House—Southern hospitality at its best. A 100-year-old colonial with five rooms, all with private baths. Texas historic marker. Candlelight dining by reservation. Five antique shopping malls; six golf courses; eight lakes; 90 miles east of Dallas in beautiful east Texas.

---

1. No Smoking
2. No Pets
3 Off Season Rates
4. Senior Citizen Rates

5. Tennis Available
6. Golf Available
7. Swimmming Avail.
8. Skiing Available

9. Credit Cards Accepted
10. Personal Check Accepted
11. Reservations Necessary
12. Dinner Available

13. Lunch Available
14. Conference Rooms Avail.
15. Group Seminars Avail.
16. Private Baths

17. Shared Baths
18. Afternoon Tea
* Commisions given to Travel Agents

UTAH

The Beehive State

Capitol: Salt Lake City
Statehood: January 4, 1896; the 45th state
State Motto: "Industry"
State Song: "Utah, We Love Thee"
State Bird: Sea Gull
State Flower: Sego Lily
State Tree: Blue Spruce

Utah was settled in 1847 by the Mormon pioneers, led by Brighham Young. They were industrious people and came to the west to live where they could express their religious beliefs as they wanted. Today most of the people of Utah live along the Wasatch Mountain area. Salt Lake City is a modern city with wide streets and tree-lined sidewalks. It has an open and very clean look. Tourists are attracted here from all over the country to hear the magnificent Mormon Chapel Singers and to see the Mormon church buildings.

Oil and copper have been the main occupation of the people of Utah for many years, but tourism has become a major source of income in the past 10 years. There are several National Parks here, including Bryce Canyon and Zion National Park.

UTAH

Kanab *

Barden, Aprile & Ronald
30 N. 200 W., 84741
(801) 644-5952

Amenities: 1,2,6,9,16
Breakfast: F.

Dbl. Oc.: $44.00
Sgl. Oc.: $44.00

Miss Sophie's Bed And Breakfast—A restored 1800s home with an in-town location. Guest rooms have antiques and private baths. Kanab, hub to parks, is called "Little Hollywood" for its movie past. Nice weather. Open May to October.

Moab *

Medford, Marcia
1275 E. San Jaun Dr., 84532
(801) 259-5793

Amenities: 1,2,4,9,10,16,17
Breakfast: C. Plus

Dbl. Oc.: $45.00 - $70.00
Sgl. Oc.: $35.00 - $60.00
Third Person: $10.00

Desert Chalet Bed And Breakfast—Large log home in quiet neighborhood near town. Large deck and barbeque area. Outdoor jacuzzi. Guests have full use of kitchen and laundry facilities. Safe storage for bicycles and kayaks, etc. Group and weekly rates available.

Moab *

Stucki, Marge & Richard
185 N. 300 E., 84532
(801) 259-2974

Amenities: 1,2,3,4,9,10,16
Breakfast: F.

Dbl. Oc.: $53.28 - $75.48
Sgl. Oc.: $53.28
Third Person: $13.32

Sunflower Hill Bed And Breakfast Inn—Warm hospitality in a delightfully appointed country inn. Deluxe rooms and suites, with private baths and TV. Antiques. Great breakfast buffet with home baking. Guest dining room. Spacious yard with shade trees, flower gardens, patios and hot tub. Quiet. AAA.

Nephi *

Gliske, Dorothy & Robert
110 So. Main St.
P.O. Box 73, 84648
(801) 623-2047

Amenities: 1,2,3,6,9,10,11,12, 13,16,18
Breakfast: F.

Dbl. Oc.: $50.00 - $75.00
Sgl. Oc.: $45.00 - $70.00
Third Person: $10.60
Child: $10.60

Whitmore Mansion—Victorian elegance and warm, personal service combine in reflecting the charm of bygone days. Original European oak woodwork, hand-crocheted rugs and afghans and antique furnishings add to your enjoyment. Private baths and queen beds. No smoking.

1. No Smoking	5. Tennis Available	9. Credit Cards Accepted	13. Lunch Available	17. Shared Baths
2. No Pets	6. Golf Available	10. Personal Check Accepted	14. Conference Rooms Avail.	18. Afternoon Tea
3 Off Season Rates	7. Swimmming Avail.	11. Reservations Necessary	15. Group Seminars Avail.	* Commisions given
4. Senior Citizen Rates	8. Skiing Available	12. Dinner Available	16. Private Baths	to Travel Agents

Park City *

Daniels, Hugh
615 Woodside Ave., 84060-2639
(801) 645-8068, (800) 648-8068

Amenities: 1,2,3,5,6,7,8,9,10, 11,14,15,16

Breakfast: F.

Dbl. Oc.: $49.62 - $198.45
Sgl. Oc.: $49.62 - $192.94
Third Person: $16.54 - $22.05
Child: Under 13 yrs. - $11.03

The Old Miners' Lodge - A Bed And Breakfast Inn—Originally built in 1893 in the national historic district of Park City. This area is known for its magnificent skiing and golf. Ten guest rooms, including three suites. Thirty miles east of Salt Lake City. No smoking. Outdoor hot tub and many amenities.

Salt Lake City *

Lind, Susan
6151 So. 900 E., 84121
(801) 268-8762

Amenities: 1,2,3,5,7,8,9,10, 16

Breakfast: C. Plus

Dbl. Oc.: $50.00 - $80.00
Sgl. Oc.: $50.00 - $80.00
Third Person: $50.00 - $80.00

The Spruces Bed And Breakfast—Situated on a quarter-horse operation of seven acres. The Spruces is a renovated farmhouse. From its windows, colts, pheasant and quail are often seen. While The Spruces has a definite country feel, it is close to good shopping, ski resorts, restaurants and downtown Salt Lake.

St. George

Curtis, Donna
217 No. 100 W., 84770
(801) 628-3737

Amenities: 1,2,5,6,7,9,10,14, 16

Breakfast: F.

Dbl. Oc.: $49.05 - $109.00
Sgl. Oc.: $49.05 - $109.00
Third Person: $10.00
Child: $10.00

Seven Wives Inn—Two side-by-side pioneer homes, one built in 1873 and the other built in 1883. Both are in the historic district of St. George and are on the city's walking tour. Both are furnished in antiques and include original hand-grained massive woodwork. Swimming pool.

1. No Smoking	5. Tennis Available	9. Credit Cards Accepted	13. Lunch Available	17. Shared Baths
2. No Pets	6. Golf Available	10. Personal Check Accepted	14. Conference Rooms Avail.	18. Afternoon Tea
3 Off Season Rates	7. Swimming Avail.	11. Reservations Necessary	15. Group Seminars Avail.	* Commisions given
4. Senior Citizen Rates	8. Skiing Available	12. Dinner Available	16. Private Baths	to Travel Agents

VERMONT

The Green Mountain State

Capitol: Montpelier
Statehood: March 4, 1791; the 14th state
State Motto: "Vermont, Freedom and Unity"
State Song: "Hail Vermont"
State Bird: Hermit Thrush
State Flower: Red Clover
State Tree: Sugar Maple

Vermont is called The Green Mountain State because of its beautiful and overwhelming Green Mountains. It is a state that receives much snow and their longest season is winter. However, the other seasons, although shorter in length, are just as beautiful because of the colorful foliage and magnificent scenery.

Vermont is the only New England state that does not have a coastline, but its lovely lakes and recreational facilities more than make up for the lack of a seashore. Swimming and boating in the summer and the best of skiing in the winter makes Vermont a tourist paradise.

The tapping of their own maple trees brings the Vermonters the sugar to make maple sugar products for which they are so well known.

Presidents Chester A. Arthur and Calvin Coolidge were both born here.

Alburg *

Schallert, Sr., Patrick J.
Blue Rock Rd.
Rte. 2, Box 149-B, 05440
(802) 796-3736 (VT),
(800) 348-0843(Canada & USA)

Amenities: 1,2,5,6,7,8,9,10, 11,12,14,16,18
Breakfast: F.

Dbl. Oc.: $54.00 - $70.20
Sgl. Oc.: $54.00 - $70.20
Third Person: $10.00
Child: Over 6 yrs. - $10.00

Thomas Mott Homestead Bed And Breakfast—An 1838 restored farmhouse with four guest rooms. One hour to Montreal Island, Burlington and Jay. Northwest Vermont near border. Off Hwy. 78, two miles east of #2. Ben & Jerry's ice cream company. Lawn games, canoes, horseshoes, bikes, X-country and sno-springers. Vast living room overlooks lake.

Arlington *

Ellis, Sandee & Bob
Historic Rte. 7A, 05250
(802) 375-6532, (800) 443-9442

Amenities: 1,3,5,8,9,10,11, 12,14,16
Breakfast: C. Plus

Dbl. Oc.: $70.20 - $172.80
Third Person: $20.00
Child: $20.00

Arlington Inn—Enjoy old-fashioned country hospitality in our 1848 Greek Revival mansion. Savor award-winning cuisine by romantic candlelight. Relax by a roaring fire or rock away the hours on the front porch.

Arlington *

Hardy, Joanne & George
RR #2, Box 2015, 05250
(802) 375-2269, (800) 882-2545

Amenities: 1,2,4,5,6,7,8,9,10,12, 14,15,16,17,18
Breakfast: F.
Dbl. Oc.: $70.00 - $108.00
Sgl Oc.: $45.00 - $65.00
Third Person: $22.00
Child: 6 - 12 yrs. - $16.00

Hill Farm Inn—One of Vermont's original farm vacation inns. Located in two renovated farmhouses built in 1790 and 1830. Quiet, comfortable and relaxed atmosphere. Delicious country cooking. Home-grown vegetables and homemade jam to take home. Splendid mountain views.

1. No Smoking	5. Tennis Available	9. Credit Cards Accepted	13. Lunch Available	17. Shared Baths
2. No Pets	6. Golf Available	10. Personal Check Accepted	14. Conference Rooms Avail.	18. Afternoon Tea
3 Off Season Rates	7. Swimmming Avail.	11. Reservations Necessary	15. Group Seminars Avail.	* Commisions given
4. Senior Citizen Rates	8. Skiing Available	12. Dinner Available	16. Private Baths	to Travel Agents

VERMONT

Arlington

Kenny, Mathilda
Sandgate Rd.
Box 2480, 05250
(802) 375-2272

Amenities: 5,6,7,10,11,12, 16,17
Breakfast: F.

Dbl. Oc.: $50.00 - $60.00
Sgl. Oc.: $25.00 - $30.00
Third Person: $20.00
Child: Under 12 yrs. - $15.00

The Evergreen Inn—An old-fashioned country inn nestled in the Green River Valley off the beaten path. Casual and relaxed atmosphere. Beautiful scenery. Family-owned-and-operated for 52 years. Home cooking and baking.

Arlington

Masterson, Woody
Battenkill Rd.
Box 3260, 05250
(802) 375-6372

Amenities: 1,2,7,8,9,10,11,1 15,16,17,18
Breakfast: F.

Dbl. Oc.: $65.00
Sgl. Oc.: $40.00
Third Person: $20.00
Child: Under 10 yrs. - $10.00

Shenandoah Farm—Experience New England in this lovingly restored 1820 colonial overlooking the Battenkill River. Wonderful Americana year-round. Full "farm-fresh" breakfast is served daily.

Arlington *

McAllister, Kathleen & Al
Manor House of Arlington, 05250
(802) 375-6784

Amenities: 1,2,3,4,5,6,7,8,9, 10,11,14,16,17,18
Breakfast: F.

Dbl. Oc.: $48.60 - $97.20
Sgl. Oc.: $37.80 - $70.20
Third Person: $10.80 - $21.60
Child: Under 17 yrs. - no charge

Arlington Manor House—Charming unusual private colonial. Vermont hospitality. Five guest rooms and two bedrooms with fireplaces, terrace and char-grill. Walk to gourmet dining, Rockwell Museum, fishing, canoeing, tubing. Eight golf courses. Antiques and buy-and-sell swap consignment shop. Bike, hike.

Bellows Falls *

Champagne, Helene
RD 1, Box 328, 05101
(802) 463-9008

Amenities: 1,2,3,4,5,6,7,8,9, 10,15,16,17,18
Breakfast: F.

Dbl. Oc.: $62.64 - $75.60
Sgl. Oc.: $48.60 - $54.00
Third Person: $21.40
Child: Under 12 yrs. - no charge

Blue Haven Guest House—An 1830 schoolhouse turned guest house. Canopy beds, hand-painted chests abound. Rustic common room boasts original oil paintings, stone fireplace. A lovingly appointed Christian home, truly peaceful. Two miles to highway, town and train ride. Ideal for group gatherings.

---

1. No Smoking	5. Tennis Available	9. Credit Cards Accepted	13. Lunch Available	17. Shared Baths
2. No Pets	6. Golf Available	10. Personal Check Accepted	14. Conference Rooms Avail.	18. Afternoon Tea
3 Off Season Rates	7. Swimmming Avail.	11. Reservations Necessary	15. Group Seminars Avail.	* Commisions given
4. Senior Citizen Rates	8. Skiing Available	12. Dinner Available	16. Private Baths	to Travel Agents

VERMONT

Belmont

Gorman, Mary
Box 62, 05730
(802) 259-2903, (800) 352-7439

Amenities: 1,2,3,5,6,7,8,9,10,
11,16
Breakfast: C. Plus

Dbl. Oc.: $64.80 (average rate)
Sgl. Oc.: $51.30 (average rate)
Third Person: $10.00
Child: $10.00

The Leslie Place—Peacefully set on 100 acres near Weston. This original farmhouse is close to major ski areas, restaurants, theatre and shops. A welcome retreat in a picturesque setting offering B&B and separate group accommodations. Brochure available.

Bethel *

Wolf, Lyle
RD 2, Box 60, 05032
(802) 234-9474

Amenities: 6,7,8,9,10,15,
16,17
Breakfast: C.

Dbl. Oc.: $50.00 - $95.00
Sgl. Oc.: $35.00 - $80.00
Third Person: $15.00
Child: $15.00

Greenhurst Inn—In the National Register of Historic Places. A Victorian mansion on the White River in the center of Vermont, with the elegance of another age. On Route 107, three miles west of I-89 in a quiet and rural setting. Mid-way between Boston and Montreal.

Brandon *

Milot, Norman
31 Franklin St., 05733
(802) 247-0098

Amenities: 1,2,3,4,6,8,9,11,12,16,17,18
Breakfast: F.
Dbl. Oc.: $54.00 - $86.40
Sgl Oc.: $48.60 - $64.80

Rosebelle's Victorian Inn—Mid-point between Rutland and Middlebury. Relax in the garden, play croquet or read a book. Hiking, biking and cross country skiing. Shelburn Museum, Morgan Horse Farm, antiques or shopping are nearby. Ici on parle Francais. Listed on the National Register.

Brandon

Reuschle, Winifred
RR1, Box 1023, 05733-9704
(802) 247-3042

Amenities: 1,5,6,7,8,10,11,
16
Breakfast: F.

Dbl. Oc.: $54.00
Sgl. Oc.: $54.00
Third Person: $10.80
Child: Under 1 yr. - no charge

HIVUE Bed And Breakfast Tree Farm—Country hospitality, 76 acres of wildlife. Tree farm, trout stream, a nature's paradise, 3-1/2 miles south of Brandon in south central Vermont.

1. No Smoking	5. Tennis Available	9. Credit Cards Accepted	13. Lunch Available	17. Shared Baths
2. No Pets	6. Golf Available	10. Personal Check Accepted	14. Conference Rooms Avail.	18. Afternoon Tea
3 Off Season Rates	7. Swimmming Avail.	11. Reservations Necessary	15. Group Seminars Avail.	* Commisions given
4. Senior Citizen Rates	8. Skiing Available	12. Dinner Available	16. Private Baths	to Travel Agents

VERMONT

Brookfield *

Simpson, Pat & Peter
P.O. Box 494, 05036
(802) 276-3412, (800) 243-3412

Amenities: 1,2,4,5,6,7,8,10, 12,14,15,16,17
Breakfast: F.

Dbl. Oc.: $84.00 - $100.00
Sgl. Oc.: $62.00 - $75.00
Third Person: $20.00

Green Trails Country Inn—By the famous floating bridge. A cozy and informal country inn — "like going home to Grandma's." Decorated with quilts and antiques. Featured on the "Today" show. "The epitome of a country inn."

Cabot *

Lloyd, Daniel
P.O. Box 187, 05647
(802) 563-2819

Amenities: 1,2,10,11,12,16,17
Breakfast: F.
Dbl. Oc.: $50.00 - $60.00
Sgl Oc.: $35.00

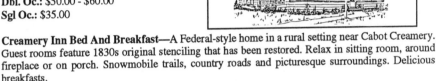

Creamery Inn Bed And Breakfast—A Federal-style home in a rural setting near Cabot Creamery. Guest rooms feature 1830s original stenciling that has been restored. Relax in sitting room, around fireplace or on porch. Snowmobile trails, country roads and picturesque surroundings. Delicious breakfasts.

Chelsea

Papa, Mary Lee & James
8 Main St., 05038
(802) 685-3031, (800) 441-6908

Amenities: 1,2,5,6,7,8,9,10,12,16
Breakfast: F.
Dbl. Oc.: $86.40 - $102.60
Third Person: $15.00

Shire Inn—Chelsea is Vermont's quintessential small village and we're Vermont's finest small village inn. An 1832 brick Federal home. Gourmet dining. Four rooms with working fireplaces. All rooms have private baths. Scenery abounds.

Chester *

Bowman, Jean
Green Mountain Turnpike, 05143
(802) 875-2674

Amenities: 1,2,3,9,10,16,18
Breakfast: F.

Dbl. Oc.: $82.60
Sgl. Oc.: $51.95
Third Person: $15.00

Henry Farm Inn—Nestled on 50 acres of land alongside a sparkling river. The Henry Farm provides peace and tranquility in a natural setting. The inn has retained the charm of its earlier days when it served as a stagecoach stop and tavern.

1. No Smoking	5. Tennis Available	9. Credit Cards Accepted	13. Lunch Available	17. Shared Baths
2. No Pets	6. Golf Available	10. Personal Check Accepted	14. Conference Rooms Avail.	18. Afternoon Tea
3 Off Season Rates	7. Swimmming Avail.	11. Reservations Necessary	15. Group Seminars Avail.	* Commisions given
4. Senior Citizen Rates	8. Skiing Available	12. Dinner Available	16. Private Baths	to Travel Agents

VERMONT

Chester *

Strohmeyer, Janet & Don	**Amenities:** 2,3,4,5,6,7,8,9,10,	**Dbl. Oc.:** $60.00 - $90.00
Rte. 11 W., 05143	11,12,13,15,16	**Sgl. Oc.:** $40.00 - $60.00
(802) 875-2525	**Breakfast:** F.	**Third Person:** $12.00
		Child: Under 8 yrs. - $6.00

The Stone Hearth Inn—A lovely and informal country inn built in 1810. Ten restored guest rooms, all with private baths. Library and living room, pub and large recreation room. Near major ski areas and quaint villages. Perfect for families. Dinner $15.00 - $20.00 (with advance notice).

Chester

Thomas, Georgette	**Amenities:** 1,5,6,7,8,9,10,16	**Dbl. Oc.:** $75.00 - $95.00
Main St., #32, 05143	**Breakfast:** F.	**Sgl. Oc.:** $55.00 - $65.00
(802) 875-2412		**Third Person:** $20.00
		Child: Under 14 yrs. - $10.00

The Hugging Bear Inn And Shoppe—A lovely Victorian, circa 1850. Six rooms with a teddy bear in every bed. Three family rooms, toys, TV and VCR. Nearby ski, tennis and golf areas. Children of all ages welcome. A magical place to stay. Two friendly cats in residence.

Chester *

Wrobel, Seiglainde & Steve	**Amenities:** 1,2,6,8,10,11,16,	**Dbl. Oc.:** $64.00 - $75.00
Grafton St., 05143	17,18	**Sgl. Oc.:** $54.00 - $64.00
(802) 875-3438	**Breakfast:** F.	**Third Person:** $15.00

"Second Wind" Bed And Breakfast—Small, cozy Victorian farmhouse; non-smoking environment. Music, fresh flowers and smiles greet you. A sumptuous candlelight breakfast second to none will delight you. Skiing, golf, horseback riding and wonderful restaurants all nearby.

Cuttingsville

Husselman, Grace & Samuel	**Amenities:** 1,2,5,6,7,8,11,15,	**Dbl. Oc.:** $54.00 - $64.80
Lincoln Hill Rd.,	16,17,18	**Sgl. Oc.:** $43.20
Shrewsbury (mail), 05738	**Breakfast:** F.	**Third Person:** $21.60
(802) 492-3485		**Child:**Under 5 yrs. - $16.20

Buckmaster Inn (Bed And Breakfast)—A circa 1801 inn standing on a knoll overlooking a picturesque red barn and valley scene. Its center hall, grand staircase, wide-pine floors and antiques grace the home. Spacious rooms and porches. Beautifully landscaped. Fireplaces and library/lounge area. Rural mountains.

---

1. No Smoking	5. Tennis Available	9. Credit Cards Accepted	13. Lunch Available	17. Shared Baths
2. No Pets	6. Golf Available	10. Personal Check Accepted	14. Conference Rooms Avail.	18. Afternoon Tea
3 Off Season Rates	7. Swimmming Avail.	11. Reservations Necessary	15. Group Seminars Avail.	* Commisions given
4. Senior Citizen Rates	8. Skiing Available	12. Dinner Available	16. Private Baths	to Travel Agents

VERMONT

Cuttingsville

Smith, Donna & William
Lincoln Hill
Box 120, 05738
(802) 492-3367

Amenities: 2,5,6,7,8,10,11,16, 17,18
Breakfast: F.

Dbl. Oc.: $50.00
Sgl. Oc.: $25.00
Third Person: $10.00
Child: Under 12 yrs. - $5.00

Maple Crest Farm—Located in the heart of the Green Mountains in the Rutland area. An 1808 farmhouse lovingly preserved for five generations; 27 rooms with beautiful views. Downhill and cross-country skiing and hiking. Central location to historic sites. Two-day minimum; 22 years as a B&B.

Danby *

Dansereau, Lois & Paul
So. Main St., 05739
(802) 293-5567

Amenities: 2,6,7,8,9,10,12, 16,17
Breakfast: F.

Dbl. Oc.: $63.48 - $92.02
Sgl. Oc.: $58.32 - $74.52
Third Person: $16.00
Child: Under 10 yrs. - no charge

Silas Griffith Inn—Built in 1891 by Vermont's first millionaire; 17 antique-filled guest rooms. Spectacular mountain views. Near the Appalachian Trail, hiking, biking, antiquing, skiing and pool. Village location. Comfortable and homey. Large living room and library with fireplace.

Danby

Edson, Anharad & Chip
Main St., P.O. Box 221, 05739
(802) 293-5099

Amenities: 2,3,5,6,7,8,9,10, 16,18
Breakfast: F.

Dbl. Oc.: 81.00
Sgl. Oc.: 54.00
Third Person: $15.00

The Quails Nest Bed And Breakfast—Nestled among the Green Mountains in a quiet Vermont village. Quiet and old-fashioned country fun in a circa 1835 antique-filled inn. Nearby skiing, hiking, swimming, fishing, country auctions, horseback riding, bicycling, canoeing, shopping and our own country folk-art barn.

Derby Line

Moreau, Phyllis & Tom
46 Main St., 05830
(802) 873-3604

Amenities: 1,2,9,10,16,18
Breakfast: F.

Dbl. Oc.: $55.00 - $65.00
Sgl. Oc.: $45.00 - $55.00
Third Person: $10.00
Child: $10.00

Derby Village Inn—Located at the Canadian border in an elegant Greek Revival mansion, furnished with restored antiques. Sleigh rides, skiing, antiques, golf, fishing and hiking. The village is nearby and home to an international library and opera house.

East Burke *

Pastore, Marilyn & John
Darling Hill Rd.
P.O. Box 355, 05832
(802) 626-9924

Amenities: 1,2,3,8,9,10,11,14, 15,16,18
Breakfast: F.

Dbl. Oc.: $108.00
Sgl. Oc.: $90.00
Third Person: $15.00
Child: Under 12 yrs. - no charge

Mountain View Creamery—Romantic B&B on historic 440-acre farm estate in beautiful northeast kingdom. Elegant brick creamery restored as country manor. Private baths. Breathtaking views of serene meadows and forest trails. Favorite of Vermont bicyclists and foliage viewers. Near Burke Mountain.

1. No Smoking	5. Tennis Available	9. Credit Cards Accepted	13. Lunch Available	17. Shared Baths
2. No Pets	6. Golf Available	10. Personal Check Accepted	14. Conference Rooms Avail.	18. Afternoon Tea
3 Off Season Rates	7. Swimmming Avail.	11. Reservations Necessary	15. Group Seminars Avail.	* Commisions given
4. Senior Citizen Rates	8. Skiing Available	12. Dinner Available	16. Private Baths	to Travel Agents

VERMONT

Enosburg Falls

Spoonire, Susan
RR 1, Box 850, 05450
(802) 933-2522

Amenities: 6,7,8,10,12,13,16, 17
Breakfast: F.

Dbl. Oc.: $54.00 - $64.80
Sgl. Oc.: $37.80 - $43.20
Third Person: $10.00
Child: Under 2 yrs. - no charge

Berkson Farms—Homey 150-year-old farmhouse on a working dairy farm. Relax on 600 acres surrounded by a variety of animals, nature and warm hospitality. Picnic, hike and bike in the warmer months; sled and cross-country ski in the winter. Enjoy hearty home-style meals. Close to Canada and skiing.

Fairlee *

Wright, Sharon & Scott
So. Main St., 05045
(802) 333-4326, (800) 666-1946

Amenities: 1,4,5,6,7,8,9,10, 16,17
Breakfast: C.

Dbl. Oc.: $47.52 - $69.12
Sgl. Oc.: $41.04 - $62.64
Third Person: $6.00
Child: $6.00

Silver Maple Lodge And Cottages—A historic B&B country inn. Convenient to restaurants and two lakes. Canoeing, fishing, golf and tennis nearby. Hot-air ballon, inn-to-inn packages available. Two cottages with kitchenettes, one with fireplace. AAA approved. Color brochure available.

Grafton

Chiffriller, Jr., Thomas F.
Pickle St., 05146
(802) 843-2515

Amenities: 1,2,3,5,6,7,8,10, 16,18
Breakfast: C. Plus

Dbl. Oc.: $70.00 - $80.00
Sgl. Oc.: $59.40
Third Person: $20.00

Farmhouse 'Round The Bend—An 1846 farmhouse with a warm, country atmosphere. Open, sunny porch and scrumptious breakfast. Five-minute walk to the most picturesque village in Vermont. Hiking, biking, fishing, tennis and golf nearby. Antique shops and museums. Catering.

Hardwick

Gaillard, Ruth
24 Highland Ave., 05843
(802) 472-5484

Amenities: 1,2,5,7,8,9,10,18
Breakfast: F

Dbl. Oc.: $70.00
Sgl. Oc.: $45.00
Third Person: $20.00
Child: Under 10 yrs. - $15.00

Somerset House Bed And Breakfast—Comfortable, elegant 1894 home on quiet maple-lined street. Short walk to village center. Four cozy bedrooms. Relax in the sitting room or enjoy a rocker on the porch overlooking the garden. In Vermont's Northeast Kingdom for lakes, mountains, skiing and biking.

Hyde Park *

Pugliese, Richard
Fitch Hill Rd., RFD, Box 1879, 05655
(802) 888-5941

Amenities: 1,2,3,6,8,9,10,11, 12,14,17,18
Breakfast: F.

Dbl. Oc.: $55.00 - $60.00
Sgl. Oc.: $50.00
Third Person: $10.00

Fitch Hill Inn—Affordable, friendly elegance, mountain-view setting on five acres near Stowe, Smugglers and Jay ski areas. Near all kinds of outdoor recreational activities. Spectacular views. Many fine restaurants nearby. Cross-country ski trails on premises. AAA rated.

1. No Smoking	5. Tennis Available	9. Credit Cards Accepted	13. Lunch Available	17. Shared Baths
2. No Pets	6. Golf Available	10. Personal Check Accepted	14. Conference Rooms Avail.	18. Afternoon Tea
3 Off Season Rates	7. Swimmming Avail.	11. Reservations Necessary	15. Group Seminars Avail.	* Commisions given
4. Senior Citizen Rates	8. Skiing Available	12. Dinner Available	16. Private Baths	to Travel Agents

VERMONT

Hyde Park *

Wheelwright, Maureen & George
Box 146, 05655
(802) 888-5894,
Fax: (802) 888-2466

Amenities: 1,2,5,6,7,8,9,10, 11,12,16,17,18

Breakfast: F.

Dbl. Oc.: $84.24
Sgl. Oc.: $54.00

Hyde Park House—Gracious accommodations in an 1830 antique-filled house renovated to offer such amenities as jacuzzi, sauna, guest parlor, cable TV and dining room. Extensive library and beautiful perennial garden. Hostess is a J.P. who enjoys marrying people. Vermont's #1.

Isle La Motte

Infante, Katherine & Mark
Box 32, Old Quarry Rd., 05463
(802) 928-3200

Amenities: 2,3,5,6,7,9,10,11, 12,13,16,17

Breakfast: C.

Dbl. Oc.: $64.80
Sgl. Oc.: $48.60
Third Person: $5.40

Ruthcliffe Lodge And Restaurant—Secluded island getaway on beautiful Lake Champlain. All rooms facing the lake with private baths. Family-owned since 1951. Swimming, biking, fishing, canoeing are at your front door. Golf and tennis nearby. Full-service restaurant. Dockage available. One hour to Montreal.

Jeffersonville *

Mann, Kelley
Rte. 108 So., 05464
(800) 937-6266

Amenities: 1,2,4,5,6,7,8,9,10, 16,17

Breakfast: F.

Dbl. Oc.: $65.00
Sgl. Oc.: $54.00
Third Person: $10.00

Manns View Inn—Built in the mid-1800s. A large white colonial with a Victorian flair set on 10 beautiful acres on a plateau at the base of Mt. Mansfield. Completely restored. Furnished with antiques. Parlor, sun-lit library with a bay window. Full country breakfast. Quiet and personalized.

Jericho *

Royce, Blanche
RD #2, Box 35, Underhill, 05481 (mail)
(802) 899-2234

Amenities: 1,2,3,5,6,7,8,9,10,11,15,16,18
Breakfast: F.
Dbl. Oc.: $60.00 - $70.00
Sgl Oc.: $50.00 - $60.00
Third Person: $10.00

Sinclair Towers B&B Inn—An elegant, yet comfortable, fully restored 1890 Victorian landmark. Close to Burlington, ski areas, hiking trails, bike routes and fine restaurants. Six air-conditioned rooms, parlor, living room with fireplace, barbecue area and handicap bath.

1. No Smoking	5. Tennis Available	9. Credit Cards Accepted	13. Lunch Available	17. Shared Baths
2. No Pets	6. Golf Available	10. Personal Check Accepted	14. Conference Rooms Avail.	18. Afternoon Tea
3 Off Season Rates	7. Swimming Avail.	11. Reservations Necessary	15. Group Seminars Avail.	* Commisions given
4. Senior Citizen Rates	8. Skiing Available	12. Dinner Available	16. Private Baths	to Travel Agents

VERMONT

Johnson

Speer, Ella May & Erwin
RR 2, Box 623, 05656
(802) 635-7354

Amenities: 1,2,5,6,7,8,9,10, 11,12,13,17
Breakfast: F.

Dbl. Oc.: $50.00
Sgl. Oc.: $40.00
Third Person: $10.00
Child: $10.00

The Homestead Bed And Breakfast—The quiet beauty of Vermont's countryside surrounds the circa 1830 brick colonial farmhouse. A hearty breakfast starts guests on their way to enjoying the many activities offered in the area: canoeing, hiking, fishing, biking, antiquing and skiing.

Killington *

Karlhuber, Jeanne & Manfred
Miller Brook Rd., 05751
(802) 422-3407

Amenities: 2,3,4,5,6,7,8,9,10, 16
Breakfast: C. Plus

Dbl. Oc.: $70.00 - $115.64
Sgl. Oc.: $53.00 - $115.64
Third Person: $29.00
Child: Under 12 yrs. - $10 - $15

Snowed Inn—A cordial, homey atmosphere. Modern rooms with private baths and color cable TV. Fieldstone fireplace, book-lined lounge, outdoor hot tub. Breakfast in our greenhouse room. Walk to restaurants, shops and nightspots, yet enjoy a private wooded setting.

Killington

MacKenzie, Vickie
RR 1, Box 2848, 05751
(802) 422-3731

Amenities: 2,3,4,6,7,8,9,11, 12,13,15,16
Breakfast: F.

Dbl. Oc.: $66.00 - $148.00
Sgl. Oc.: $61.00 - $120.00
Third Person: $5.00 - $34.00
Child: Under 12 yrs. - $25.00

Cascades Lodge—Set in the heart of Killington with spectacular mountain views. Large and comfortable rooms with private bath, phone and cable TV. Fireplaced lounge, sauna, whirlpool and heated indoor pool. Walk to ski slopes and golf. A great getaway area for all seasons. AAA - 3 Diamonds.

Killington *

The McGrath Family
Rte. 4, Box 267, 05751
(802) 775-7181

Amenities: 2,3,4,5,6,8,9, 11,12,13,15,16
Breakfast: F.

Dbl. Oc.: $56.00 - $214.00
Sgl. Oc.: $46.00 - $120.00
Third Person: $17.00 - $62.00
Child: Under 12 yrs. - 1/2 price

The Inn At Long Run—Historic country inn next to famous Long Trail and Appalachian Trail. Cozy, immaculate rooms. Fireplaced suites. Hot tub. Irish pub with live music on weekends. Weekend rates include all meals. Restaurant offers full, delicious candlelight dinners as well as a pub menu.

VERMONT

Ludlow *

Bentzinger, Carolyn
13 Pleasant St., 05149
(802) 228-4846

Amenities: 1,2,3,4,5,6,7,8,9,10,11,12,16
Breakfast: F.
Dbl. Oc.: $117.00 - $155.00
Sgl Oc.: $95.00 - $135.00

The Andrie Rose Inn—Gracious C.1829 village inn at the base of Okemo Mountain ski resort. Ten beautiful guest rooms with whirlpool tubs and sky lights. Fireside hors'doeuvres and endless amenities. Romantic, luxurious suites with fireplaces, whirlpools, canopy beds, TV and stereo available.

Ludlow *

Combes, Ruth & Bill
RFD #1, Box 275, 05149
(802) 228-8799

Amenities: 3,5,6,7,8,9,10,11, 12,16
Breakfast: F.

Dbl. Oc.: $105.80
Sgl. Oc.: $76.95
Third Person: $25.85
Child: $25.85

The Combes Family Inn—A family inn in a secluded setting on a country back road. Surrounded by acres of meadows. The inn was an operating dairy farm for over 100 years. It has a warm and casual ambience. Bring your family home to ours. Homey and comfortable rooms. Great food.

Ludlow

DelMastro, Cheryl & Rick
100 Main St., 05149
(802) 228-5585

Amenities: 2,3,5,6,7,8,9,10, 12,15,16,17
Breakfast: F.

Dbl. Oc.: $85.00 - $125.00
Sgl. Oc.: $70.00 - $110.00
Third Person: $15.00
Child: $15.00

Black River Inn—Charming 1835 country inn, at base of Okemo Mountain. Ten antique-furnished guest rooms, eight with private baths; down comforters, fluffy towels. Full country breakfast, fireside cocktails, candlelight dinners available. Vermont hospitality at its best.

Ludlow

Tofferi, Jill & Robert
1 Elm, 05149
(802) 228-3548

Amenities: 1,2,3,5,6,7,8,9,10,11,17
Breakfast: C.
Dbl. Oc.: $55.00 - $95.00
Sgl Oc.: $55.00 - $95.00
Third Person: $10.00

Fletcher Manor—Built in 1837, bordered by the Black River. Views of Okemo Mountain and boasting lovely manicured acres. We're uniquely located in the heart of Ludlow. Antiques fill our home. Handmade quilts, a baby grand in the music room, a fireplace in the parlor.

1. No Smoking	5. Tennis Available	9. Credit Cards Accepted	13. Lunch Available	17. Shared Baths
2. No Pets	6. Golf Available	10. Personal Check Accepted	14. Conference Rooms Avail.	18. Afternoon Tea
3 Off Season Rates	7. Swimming Avail.	11. Reservations Necessary	15. Group Seminars Avail.	* Commisions given
4. Senior Citizen Rates	8. Skiing Available	12. Dinner Available	16. Private Baths	to Travel Agents

VERMONT

Manchester *

Eichorn, Patricia & Robert
Highland Ave., 05255
(802) 362-4565

Amenities: 1,2,3,5,6,7,8,9,10, 16,17,18
Breakfast: F.

Dbl. Oc.: $112.86
Sgl. Oc.: $83.16
Third Person: $23.76
Child: Under 12 yrs. - $11.88

Manchester Highlands Inn—Graceful Queen Ann Victorian on hilltop above Manchester. Gourmet breakfast, afternoon snacks. Rooms feature feather beds, down comforters. Pool, pub and game room. Minutes to skiing, golf, hiking, biking, restaurants and shops. Relax, renew and return.

Manchester *

Lee, Jr., James J.
West Rd., 05254
(802) 362-2761

Amenities: 2,5,6,7,8,9,10,11, 12,16,18
Breakfast: F.

Dbl. Oc.: $128.00
Sgl. Oc.: $110.00
Third Person: $25.00

Birch Hill Inn—A quiet country inn away from busy village streets expressing warm hospitality. Enjoy each season with panoramic views, cross-country skiing, swimming and our own private trout pond. Dinner available some evenings. Member of Independent Innkeepers Association.

Middlebury *

Cole, Linda
R.D.#3, Box 2460, 05753
(802) 388-6429

Amenities: 1,2,5,6,7,8,9,10, 11,16
Breakfast: C. Plus

Dbl. Oc.: $86.40
Sgl. Oc.: $81.00
Third Person: $16.20

Brookside Meadows Country Bed And Breakfast—Located in a country setting with spacious lawns and perennial gardens. All private baths. Two- bedroom suite available. Near Middlebury College. Shelburne Museum a short drive. Excellent restaurants. Two-night minimum stay on weekends.

Montpelier, East *

Potter, Cheryl
Cherry Tree Hill Rd., 05651
(802) 223-0549

Amenities: 1,2,3,7,8,10,14,15, 16,17
Breakfast: F.

Dbl. Oc.: $64.75 - $81.10
Sgl. Oc.: $48.60
Third Person: $21.50

Cherry Tree Hill Bed And Breakfast—A meticulously restored Dutch-roof farmhouse offering panoramic mountain views. Three miles from the state capital. Luxurious accommodations amid 55 acres of fields and meadows. Heated pool, jacuzzi, fieldstone fireplace, solarium and poolside guest house with full kitchen.

Newport

Winfield, Carol L.
7 Herrick St., 05855
(802) 334-6624

Amenities: 1,5,6,7,8,10,11, 16
Breakfast: F.

Dbl. Oc.: $54.00
Third Person: $21.60
Child: Under 5 yrs. - $10.80

Mrs. Winfield's Non-Smokers' Bed And Breakfast—Amiable felicity in Newport, VT for graceful indoor-outdoor living. Near all seasonal sports or long nature walks. Breakfast on the sun deck or in front of the fireplace - it's up to you and the weather. Quality farm-fresh breakfasts. Cable TV.

1. No Smoking	5. Tennis Available	9. Credit Cards Accepted	13. Lunch Available	17. Shared Baths
2. No Pets	6. Golf Available	10. Personal Check Accepted	14. Conference Rooms Avail.	18. Afternoon Tea
3 Off Season Rates	7. Swimmming Avail.	11. Reservations Necessary	15. Group Seminars Avail.	* Commisions given
4. Senior Citizen Rates	8. Skiing Available	12. Dinner Available	16. Private Baths	to Travel Agents

VERMONT

Northfield

Rogler, Debra & Jim
Carrie Howe Rd., Roxbury, 05669
(802) 485-8961

Amenities: 1,6,7,8,10,16,17, 18
Breakfast: C. Plus

Dbl. Oc.: $59.40 - $70.20
Sgl. Oc.: $43.20
Third Person: $16.20
Child: Under 5 yrs. - no charge

Inn At Johnnycake Flats—Our small inn is located in a valley known to the local people as Johnnycake Flats. A restored stagecoach stop, circa 1800. Guest rooms are thoughtfully decorated with family antiques, quilts and Shaker baskets. Enjoy cross- country skiing, trout fishing and a country way of life.

Northfield

Stalb, Aglaia & Alan
27 Highland Ave., 05663
(802) 485-8558

Amenities: 1,2,3,5,6,7,8,9,10, 11,12,13,14,15,16, 17,18
Breakfast: F.

Dbl. Oc.: $92.00
Sgl. Oc.: $60.00
Third Person: $48.00

The Northfield Inn—Luxurious Victorian country inn. Elegant but casual dining. A romantic interlude of Victorian antiques, European feather beds, magnificent panoramic views set on a sun-bathed hillside with golden sunsets. Victorian comfort and congeniality. A Romantic getaway.

North Troy *

Mead, Camilla & Jay
RR 2, Box 300, E. Hill Rd., 05859
(802) 988-4300

Amenities: 1,2,5,6,7,8,9,10, 11,16,17
Breakfast: C. Plus

Dbl. Oc.: $46.00 - $57.00
Sgl. Oc.: $38.00
Third Person: $22.00

Rose Apple Acres Farm—A 1910 farmhouse. Three large guest rooms with panoramic mountain views on 52 acres of fields, woods, ponds and gardens. Friendly farm animals include horses, sheep and family pets. Bikers and hikers welcome. Four hours north of Boston and two hours southeast of Montreal.

Orwell *

Korda, Joan
Rte. 22A
P.O. Box 36, 05760
(802) 948-2727

Amenities: 1,2,4,8,10,12,13,14,15,16,17,18
Breakfast: F.
Dbl. Oc.: $85.00 - $150.00
Sgl Oc.: $50.00 - $75.00
Third Person: $25.00 - $35.00
Child: Under 12 yrs. - $15 - $25

Historic Brookside Farms—An 1843 Greek Revival mansion that adjoins a 1789 farmhouse on 300 scenic acres. Hike and cross-country ski through our forest. Canoe and fish in our lake. Cozy up to crackling fireplaces. Savor candlelight dining. Period antiques and country rarities in our shop.

1. No Smoking	5. Tennis Available	9. Credit Cards Accepted	13. Lunch Available	17. Shared Baths
2. No Pets	6. Golf Available	10. Personal Check Accepted	14. Conference Rooms Avail.	18. Afternoon Tea
3 Off Season Rates	7. Swimming Avail.	11. Reservations Necessary	15. Group Seminars Avail.	* Commisions given
4. Senior Citizen Rates	8. Skiing Available	12. Dinner Available	16. Private Baths	to Travel Agents

Pittsfield *

Morris, Barbara
Budasi, Vikki
Rte. 100, Box 675, 05762
(802) 746-8943

Amenities: 2,3,5,6,7,8,9,10, 12,16
Breakfast: F.

Dbl. Oc.: $75.00 - $115.00
Sgl. Oc.: $65.00 - $100.00
Third Person: $30.00
Child: Under 5 yrs. - no charge

The Inn At Pittsfield—Nestled in the Green Mountains, this classic inn's central location puts you minutes away from all Vermont has to offer. Nine rooms with private baths, living room, dining room and tavern, recently renovated in a country motif. Wonderful meals prepared from "scratch."

Plainfield

Yankee, Joani & Glenn
RD #2, Box 1000, 05667
(802) 454-7191

Amenities: 1,3,5,6,7,8,10,11, 17,18
Breakfast: F.

Dbl. Oc.: $40.00 - $55.00
Sgl. Oc.: $30.00 - $40.00
Third Person: $10.00
Child: Under 6 yrs. - no charge

Yankees' Northview Bed And Breakfast—Off quiet country road in historic Calais. Antiques, heirloom quilts, bouquets and sitting room with fireplace. Breakfast on garden patio with mountain views. Nearby museums, antiques and quaking bog. Year-round recreation. Nine miles to the capital and quarries.

Proctorsville

Button, Delores & Charles
Box 247, Main St., 05153
(802) 226-7770, (800) 232-7077

Amenities: 3,6,7,8,9,10,12, 16
Breakfast: F.

Dbl. Oc.: $97.20
Sgl. Oc.: $48.60

Okemo Lantern Lodge—Victorian country inn. Original butternut woodwork, stained-glass windows and antiques. Hearty country breakfasts, superb New England and continental cuisine. Ten attractive and individually decorated rooms, each with its own bath. Pete and Dody Button, innnkeepers.

Putney *

Miller, Jeffrey
RD 2, Box 510, 05346

Amenities: 1,3,9,16,17
Breakfast: F.

Dbl. Oc.: $52.00 - $85.00
Sgl. Oc.: $42.00 - $75.00
Third Person: $15.00

Mapleton Farm Bed And Breakfast—An 1803 Vermont farmhouse is a step back in time. Decorated with antiques and old country furnishings, situated on 25 beautiful acres. It's the perfect place to unwind. Convenient to Brattleboro and Putney's fine shops and restaurants.

Reading *

Taylor, Joan & Bill
Rte. 106, 05062
(802) 484-9192

Amenities: 5,6,7,8,10,11,17, 18
Breakfast: C. Plus

Dbl. Oc.: $60.00
Sgl. Oc.: $45.00
Third Person: $30.00
Child: Under 10 yrs. - $20.00

1797 House—A charming 18th-century home set on 25 acres with apple trees and a stream. South of Woodstock, where antiquing and shopping abound. Alpine and cross-country skiing. Two large rooms share bath. Livingroom with fireplace, sitting room and dining room. Relax in a rural Vermont setting.

1. No Smoking	5. Tennis Available	9. Credit Cards Accepted	13. Lunch Available	17. Shared Baths
2. No Pets	6. Golf Available	10. Personal Check Accepted	14. Conference Rooms Avail.	18. Afternoon Tea
3 Off Season Rates	7. Swimmming Avail.	11. Reservations Necessary	15. Group Seminars Avail.	* Commisions given
4. Senior Citizen Rates	8. Skiing Available	12. Dinner Available	16. Private Baths	to Travel Agents

VERMONT

Richmond

Bower, Hedwig
P.O. Box 22, 05477
(802) 434-2632

Amenities: 1,10,17
Breakfast: F.

Dbl. Oc.: $54.00
Sgl. Oc.: $38.00
Third Person: $15.00
Child: Under 10 yrs. - $10.00

Mama Bower's Bed And Breakfast—We offer a friendly, homey atmosphere and a hearty breakfast to a maximum of five people in three guest rooms (one room has twin beds) with shared bath in our 150-year-old, beautifully renovated home, located in the center of Richmond Village. Children welcome.

Royalton

Curley, Jean & Gary
Rte. 14, RR 1, Box 108F, 05068
(802) 763-8437

Amenities: 2,9,10,12,15,17
Breakfast: F.

Dbl. Oc.: $54.00
Sgl. Oc.: $37.80 (weekdays)
Third Person: $10.80

Fox Stand Inn—A brick building built in 1818 on the banks of the White River. Located one mile off Interstate 89 (Exit 3). Restaurant and tavern are open to the public. Five guest rooms are available. River swimming, tubing and fishing on premises. Nearby skiing.

St. Johnsbury

Newell, Molly & Joe
RFD #2, Box 153, 05819
(802) 748-9902

Amenities: 2,6,7,8,9,10,11, 17
Breakfast: C. Plus

Dbl. Oc.: $54.00
Sgl. Oc.: $44.00

Broadview Farm Bed And Breakfast—Four rooms with 2 shared baths in Historic National Register 1800s country manor. 300 plus acres offering country walks, views of Green/White Mountains and cross-country skiing. Working maple sugar house - mail order mail syrup. Ski packages. Apartment - $120.00.

Starksboro

Messer, Patricia
P.O. Box 22, 05487
(802) 453-2008

Amenities: 1,2,4,6,7,8,10,11, 14,16,17,18
Breakfast: C. Plus

Dbl. Oc.: $64.20 - $74.90
Sgl. Oc.: $32.40 - $37.80
Child: Under 12 yrs. - 1/2 price

Millhouse Bed And Breakfast—An elegant and historic Vermont country home near the great falls of Lewis Creek. Within 25 miles of ski resorts, golf courses and Lake Champlain. Apres ski room with fireplace. Homemade and regional specialties. Handicap accessible.

Stockbridge *

Hughes, Jan
Rte. 100N, 05772
(802) 746-8165

Amenities: 2,3,6,7,8,9,10,11, 16,17,18
Breakfast: F.

Dbl. Oc.: $54.00 - $97.20
Sgl. Oc.: $43.20 - $64.80
Third Person: $10.80
Child: $10.80

The Stockbridge Inn Bed And Breakfast—Nestled near the banks of the White River, close to major ski areas and golf. This large Victorian home is a historic landmark. Rooms are furnished with an Old-World atmosphere to ensure your comfort. Relax and enjoy. Our home is your home.

1. No Smoking	5. Tennis Available	9. Credit Cards Accepted	13. Lunch Available	17. Shared Baths
2. No Pets	6. Golf Available	10. Personal Check Accepted	14. Conference Rooms Avail.	18. Afternoon Tea
3 Off Season Rates	7. Swimming Avail.	11. Reservations Necessary	15. Group Seminars Avail.	* Commisions given
4. Senior Citizen Rates	8. Skiing Available	12. Dinner Available	16. Private Baths	to Travel Agents

VERMONT

Stowe *

Aldrich, Mindy, Andy & Dustin
717 Maple St., 05672
(802) 253-2229, (800) 729-2980

Amenities: 1,2,3,5,6,7,8,9,10, 14,15,16,18

Breakfast: F.

Dbl. Oc.: $85.00 & up
Sgl. Oc.: $75.00 & up
Third Person: $30.00
Child: $30.00

The Inn At The Brass Lantern—A traditional B&B inn. Award-winning restored1800 farmhouse. Features antiques, quilts, fireplaces and air conditioning. Mountain views. Many activity packages available. An intimate inn in the heart of Stowe featured in national publications. Three Diamond and Mobil rated.

Stowe *

Baas, Jr., Dee & John
180 Edson Hill,, 05672
(802) 253-8376

Amenities: 3,5,6,7,8,10,11,16, 17,18

Breakfast: F. or C. Plus

Dbl. Oc.: $52.00 - $60.00
Sgl. Oc.: $42.00 - $45.00
Third Person: $6.00 - $10.00
Child: Under 3 yrs. - $5.00

Baas' Gastehaus—Member of American Bed & Breakfast. A "B&B" in the traditional sense. Private three-acre retirement estate. Pastoral setting in prestigious area. Early American. Antiques. Twin and double beds. Minutes to Mt. Mansfield, recreation path, hiking and best cross-country areas.

Stowe *

Francis, Linda & Christopher
Mountain Rd., 05672
(802) 253-7558

Amenities: 3,5,6,7,8,9,10,11,
        12,13,15,16,18
Breakfast: F.
Dbl. Oc.: $100.00 & up
Sgl Oc.: $100.00 & up
Third Person: $25.00

Ye Olde England Inne—Classic English luxury. Laura Ashley rooms and cottages, four-poster beds, fireplaces and jacuzzis. Elegant and romantic gourmet dining by candlelight in Copperfields. Mr. Pickwick's Polo Pub internationally acclaimed for traditional English fare - 120 beers and ales. AAA/ Mobile.

Stowe *

Heiss, Gertrude & Dietmar
3430 Mtn. Rd., 05672
(802) 253-7336

Amenities: 3,4,5,6,7,8,9,10, 11,12,16

Breakfast: C. or F.

Dbl. Oc.: $68.00 - $95.00
Sgl. Oc.: $45.00 - $65.00
Third Person: $18.00
Child: Under 12 yrs. - $10.00

Andersen Lodge - An Austrian Inn—Charming Tyrolean-style inn located between Stowe and Mt. Mansfield. Rooms with TV, private bath and air-conditioning. Heated pool. Five-mile recreation path. Hiking trails. Lovely golf course. Guests can relax in our sauna or jacuzzi.

1. No Smoking	5. Tennis Available	9. Credit Cards Accepted	13. Lunch Available	17. Shared Baths
2. No Pets	6. Golf Available	10. Personal Check Accepted	14. Conference Rooms Avail.	18. Afternoon Tea
3 Off Season Rates	7. Swimmming Avail.	11. Reservations Necessary	15. Group Seminars Avail.	* Commisions given
4. Senior Citizen Rates	8. Skiing Available	12. Dinner Available	16. Private Baths	to Travel Agents

VERMONT

Stowe *

Heyer, Mrs. Larry
Rte. #108, 05672
(802) 253-4050

Amenities: 5,6,7,8,10,16,17
Breakfast: C.

Dbl. Oc.: $40.00 - $60.00
Sgl. Oc.: $30.00 - $45.00
Third Person: $15.00
Child: Under 8 yrs. - no charge

Ski Inn—A Vermont country inn noted for good food and conversation. The warmth and informality of an old-fashioned ski lodge where guests enjoy themselves and each other. Full breakfast and dinner are available to guests during the ski season.

Stowe *

Hildebrand, Kay
452 Cottage Club Rd., 05672
(802) 253-7603, (800) 753-7603

Amenities: 3,5,6,7,8,9,10,16, 18
Breakfast: F.

Dbl. Oc.: $72.00
Sgl. Oc.: $47.00
Third Person: $15.00
Child: $15.00

Timberholm Inn—A delightful country inn in a quiet wooded setting. We have 10 individually decorated rooms with antiques and private baths. Spacious common room with large fieldstone fireplace. Game room with cable TV and shuffleboard. Deck overlooks mountains. Outdoor hot tub. Air-conditioning.

Stowe *

Horman, Christel
4583 Mountain Rd., 05672
(802) 253-4846,
(800) 821-7891 (reservations)

Amenities: 2,3,5,6,7,8,9,10, 11,16
Breakfast: F.

Dbl. Oc.: $66.96 - $105.84
Sgl. Oc.: $50.00 (not on holidays)
Third Person: $21.50 - $25.00

Guest House Christel Horman—A European B&B with eight large, comfortable double rooms. Guest living room on first floor. TV and VCR can be watched while sitting by the hearthstone fireplace. 1-1/2 miles to cross-country and downhill skiing. Recreation path close by. Swimming pool, trout brook and BBQ.

Stowe *

Kerr, Sam
199 Edson Hill Rd., 05672
(800) 426-6697, (802) 253-7354

Amenities: 2,3,5,7,9,10, 16,17
Breakfast: F.

Dbl. Oc.: $55.00 - $65.00
Third Person: $15.00
Child: Under 3 yrs. - $5.00

Logwood Inn—Halfway between Stowe and Mt. Mansfield, just off the main road. Large, quiet living room. Fieldstone fireplace, TV room, swimming pool, tennis. Five private wooded acres with spacious lawns and flowers. Near biking, shopping and restaurants.

1. No Smoking	5. Tennis Available	9. Credit Cards Accepted	13. Lunch Available	17. Shared Baths
2. No Pets	6. Golf Available	10. Personal Check Accepted	14. Conference Rooms Avail.	18. Afternoon Tea
3 Off Season Rates	7. Swimmming Avail.	11. Reservations Necessary	15. Group Seminars Avail.	* Commisions given
4. Senior Citizen Rates	8. Skiing Available	12. Dinner Available	16. Private Baths	to Travel Agents

Stowe *

Wimberly, Deborah & Jim
2309 Mountain Rd., 05672
(802) 253-4277,
(800) 3-BUTTER

Amenities: 1,2,3,5,6,7,8,9, 16,18
Breakfast: F.

Dbl. Oc.: $102.60 - $140.40

Butternut Inn At Stowe—An award-winning, non-smoking, adults-preferred country inn. Antiques. Eight acres, landscaped grounds, gardens, pool. Mountain views. Written up as one of the better B&B inns of the Northeast. Sleigh rides. Ice skating. Skiing. Honeymoon anniversary packages. Hospitality at its finest.

Townshend *

Messenger, Sarah
Box 112, 05353
(802) 365-4086

Amenities: 1,3,4,10,13,16
Breakfast: F.

Dbl. Oc.: $81.00
Sgl. Oc.: $70.20
Third Person: $10.80
Child: $10.80

Boardman House—Combines modern comfort (all bedrooms have private baths) with the relaxed Vermont charm of a 19th-century farmhouse on a village green. Minutes from downhill and cross-country skiing, hiking, canoeing, swimming, fishing, antiquing, covered bridges and foliage drives.

Townshend, West *

Montenieri, Jan & Jim
Rte. 30, P.O. Box 1111, 05359
(802) 874-4853

Amenities: 1,2,6,7,8,10,12,13, 16
Breakfast: F.

Dbl. Oc.: $59.40 - $64.80
Sgl. Oc.: $48.60 - $54.50
Third Person: $10.80 (per cot)
Child: $10.80 (per cot)

The General Fletcher Homestead Bed And Breakfast—The warmth and charm of a historic (circa 1773) farmhouse near the scenic Green Mountains. Three comfortable bedrooms with private baths. Nearby scenery, swimming, hiking, fishing, antiquing, shopping, flea markets and skiing.

Vergennes *

Bargiel, Mary
82 W. Main St., 05491
(802) 877-3337

Amenities: 1,2,6,7,8,9,10,12,13,15,16,17,18
Breakfast: F.
Dbl. Oc.: $59.40 - $118.80
Sgl Oc.: $48.60 - $108.00
Third Person: $10.00
Child: $10.00

Strong House Inn—Elegant lodging in an 1834 Federal home located in the heart of the Champlain Valley. Superb cycling, nearby lake, hiking, golf and the Shelburne Museum. Eight rooms, five private baths, three working fireplaces and full country breakfast. Come feel the spirit of Vermont.

1. No Smoking	5. Tennis Available	9. Credit Cards Accepted	13. Lunch Available	17. Shared Baths
2. No Pets	6. Golf Available	10. Personal Check Accepted	14. Conference Rooms Avail.	18. Afternoon Tea
3 Off Season Rates	7. Swimmming Avail.	11. Reservations Necessary	15. Group Seminars Avail.	* Commisions given
4. Senior Citizen Rates	8. Skiing Available	12. Dinner Available	16. Private Baths	to Travel Agents

VERMONT

Vergennes

Emerson, Patricia
82 Main St., 05491
(802) 877-3293

Amenities: 1,2,3,5,6,7,10,16, 17
Breakfast: F.

Dbl. Oc.: $54.00 - $70.20
Sgl. Oc.: $43.20
Third Person: $10.80
Child: $10.80

Emersons' Guest House - Bed And Breakfast—Enjoy a comfortable stay in a beautifully decorated old (circa 1850) Victorian home. Four double rooms and 1-1/2 shared baths. A full breakfast includes delicious homemade bread, muffins and jams served in a country kitchen.

Waitsfield *

Gorman, Joan & Thomas
RD, Box 62, 05673
(802) 496-2405

Amenities: 1,3,5,6,7,8,9,10, 12,16,17
Breakfast: F.

Dbl. Oc.: $54.00 - $65.00
Sgl. Oc.: $38.00 - $43.00

Millbrook Inn—A classic Cape-style farmhouse decorated with antiques, handmade quilts and hand stenciling. Reputation for fine dining. Homemade soups, breads, desserts and pasta made with fresh, local ingredients. Candlelight atmosphere with fireside dining. B&B rates in sumer only.

Waitsfield *

Newton, Nick
Rte. 100, Box 159, 05673
(802) 496-7555

Amenities: 1,2,3,5,6,7,8,9,10, 11,14,16,18
Breakfast: F.
Dbl. Oc.: $75.00 - $105.00
Sgl Oc.: $65.00 - $95.00
Third Person: $20.00
Child: $20.00

Newtons' 1824 House Inn B&B—On the Mad River. Enjoy relaxed elegance. Six guest rooms all with private baths. Wake up to the smell of just-baked muffins, gourmet breakfast, fresh-squeezed orange juice. On 53 acres, even a swiming hole. Ski, golf, play tennis or just relax in the hammock. AAA approved.

Waitsfield *

Pratt, Betsy
Rte. 17, Box 88, 05673
(802) 496-3310

Amenities: 4,5,6,7,8,9,10,11, 12,15,16,18
Breakfast: F.

Dbl. Oc.: $55.00 - $75.00
Sgl. Oc.: $55.00
Third Person: $15.00
Child: Under 10 yrs. - no charge

Mad River Barn—A friendly and informal lodge with 15 rooms, private baths, outdoor pool, gardens and stone walls. Wake up to the quiet of the mountains. Winter rates available.

1. No Smoking	5. Tennis Available	9. Credit Cards Accepted	13. Lunch Available	17. Shared Baths
2. No Pets	6. Golf Available	10. Personal Check Accepted	14. Conference Rooms Avail.	18. Afternoon Tea
3 Off Season Rates	7. Swimming Avail.	11. Reservations Necessary	15. Group Seminars Avail.	* Commisions given
4. Senior Citizen Rates	8. Skiing Available	12. Dinner Available	16. Private Baths	to Travel Agents

VERMONT

Waitsfield *

Simko, Doreen & Jack
E. Warren Rd., 05673
(802) 496-2276

Amenities: 1,2,3,5,6,7,8,9,10, 11,14,15,16,18
Breakfast: F.

Dbl. Oc.: $97.20 - $156.60
Sgl. Oc.: $85.70 - $145.20
Third Person: $24.00

The Inn At The Round Barn Farm—The inn that lives in your imagination. Romantic and classy, 10 elegant guest rooms with fireplaces, jacuzzies, steam showers, canopied beds, scrumptious breakfasts and indoor pool. Curl up by the fire or enjoy Vermont's outdoor activities. Minutes from skiing, golf and more.

Waitsfield *

Stinson, Millie & Bill
Rte. 100,
RR 1, Box 8, 05673
(802) 496-3450, (800) 638-8466

Amenities: 1,2,4,7,8,9,10,11,12,16
Breakfast: F.
Dbl. Oc.: $100.00 - $130.00(MAP - winter)
$49.00 - $79.00 (summer)
Sgl Oc.: $60.00 - $85.00 (MAP - winter)
$49.00 - $69.00 (summer)
Child: Under 6 yrs. - no charge

Valley Inn—An Austrian-style inn with extraordinary appeal and gracious hospitality. All bedrooms have new, private baths and are lovingly decorated with local antiques. Great local skiing, the best ski schools in the east, scenic rides, rollerblading, guided hiking and biking tours.

Wallingford *

McLaughlin, Billie & Doug
7 So. Main
Box 427, 05773
(802) 446-2860, 446-2856

Amenities: 1,2,3,4,5,8,9,11,16,17,18
Breakfast: F.
Dbl. Oc.: $70.25 - $135.00
Sgl Oc.: $61.56 - $126.36

I.B. Munson House—An 1856 Victorian inn boasting canopy and feather bedding, seven fireplaces, clawfoot tubs. Enjoy wine and cheese, player piano, fireside, patio or gazebo. Elegant dining; on Rte. 7; antiquing and leaf-peeping; 15 minutes from Killington, Okemo and Pico.

---

1. No Smoking	5. Tennis Available	9. Credit Cards Accepted	13. Lunch Available	17. Shared Baths
2. No Pets	6. Golf Available	10. Personal Check Accepted	14. Conference Rooms Avail.	18. Afternoon Tea
3 Off Season Rates	7. Swimming Avail.	11. Reservations Necessary	15. Group Seminars Avail.	* Commisions given
4. Senior Citizen Rates	8. Skiing Available	12. Dinner Available	16. Private Baths	to Travel Agents

Warren *

Partsch, Kathy & Frank
RR, Box 38, 05674
(802) 583-3211

Amenities: 2,3,4,5,6,7,8,9,10,
11,16,18
Breakfast: F.

Dbl. Oc.: $90.00
Sgl. Oc.: $60.00
Third Person: $20.00

Sugartree Country Inn—An intimate mountainside country inn featuring handmade quilts atop canopy and brass four-poster beds. Antiques, oil lamps, stained glass and original art. Cool mountain evenings and warm hospitality.

Waterbury *

Gajdos, Anita & George
RR 1, Box 715, 05677
(800) 366-5592

Amenities: 1,2,3,4,5,6,7,8,9,
10,11,16,18
Breakfast: F.

Dbl. Oc.: $65.00 - $100.00
Sgl. Oc.: $55.00 - $75.00
Third Person: $10.00
Child: Under 10 yrs. $10.00

The Black Locust Inn—An 1832 restored farmhouse with large living room. Books, music, 45-inch screen TV and videos. Game area, wood burning stove, antiques, Oriental rugs and comfort. Near all winter and summer activities. Many wonderful restaurants, shops, museums and theatre!

Waterbury *

Gosselin, Pamela
Blush Hill Rd.
Box 1266, 05676
(802) 244-7529, (800) 736-7522

Amenities: 1,2,3,4,5,6,7,8,9,10,16,17,18
Breakfast: F.
Dbl. Oc.: $55.00 - $110.00
Sgl Oc.: $50.00 - $105.00
Third Person: $15.00
Child: Over 6 yrs. - $15.00

Inn At Blush Hill—Stay in a beautiful antique-filled, circa 1790' B&B. Enjoy breathtaking mountain views, fireplaced guest rooms and canopy beds in the heart of Vermont's most popular attractions. Central to Stowe and Sugarbush. Relax in comfort and enjoy the Vermont countryside with us!

---

1. No Smoking
2. No Pets
3 Off Season Rates
4. Senior Citizen Rates

5. Tennis Available
6. Golf Available
7. Swimmming Avail.
8. Skiing Available

9. Credit Cards Accepted
10. Personal Check Accepted
11. Reservations Necessary
12. Dinner Available

13. Lunch Available
14. Conference Rooms Avail.
15. Group Seminars Avail.
16. Private Baths

17. Shared Baths
18. Afternoon Tea
* Commisions given
to Travel Agents

VERMONT

Waterbury *

Sellers, Christopher
Frohman, Mark
RR2, Box 595, Rte. 100 So., 05676
(802) 244-7726, (800) 800-7760

Amenities: 1,3,4,5,6,7,8,9,10,12, 13,14,
Breakfast: F.   15,16,17,18
Dbl. Oc.: $59.40 - $97.20
Sgl Oc.: $37.80 - $54.00
Third Person: $6.48 - $16.20
Child: $6.48 - $16.20

Grunberg Haus Bed And Breakfast—A hand-built Austrian mountain chalet. Fireplace, jacuzzi, sauna, pub, piano entertainment, hiking trails, tennis court, cross-country skiing. Memorable musical breakfasts, balconies and antiques. In Ben & Jerry's hometown, between Stowe and Sugarbush ski resorts. Mobil*.

Waterbury *

Varty, Kelly
RD 2, Box 62, Rte. 100 No., 05676
(800) 292-5911

Amenities: 1,2,3,4,5,6,7,8,9,10,12,14,15,16
Breakfast: C. Plus
Dbl. Oc.: $81.00
Sgl Oc.: $64.80
Third Person: $21.60
Child: Under 12 yrs. - no charge

Thatcher Brook Inn—A cozy full-service country inn with a variety of things to do and see. Visit Ben & Jerry's Ice Cream Factory or watch apple cider being made at Cold Hollow Cider Mill. Enjoy a whirlpool or fireplace, then savor our award-winning country French cuisine. Romantic.

Weathersfield *

Thorburn, Mary Louise
Rte. 106, POB 165, Perkinsville, 05151
(802) 263-9217, (800) 477-4828

Amenities: 2,3,5,6,7,8,9,10,11,12,14,
Breakfast: F.   15,16,18
Dbl. Oc.: $215.25
Sgl Oc.: $143.91
Third Person: $89.18

The Inn At Weathersfield—English 'high tea,' internationally acclaimed, five-course nouvelle cuisine buffet with piano entertainment and six-course breakfasts are served at this 1795 owner-operated colonial inn. Twelve fireplaces. Extensive wine cellar. Rates include meals and high tea.

1. No Smoking	5. Tennis Available	9. Credit Cards Accepted	13. Lunch Available	17. Shared Baths
2. No Pets	6. Golf Available	10. Personal Check Accepted	14. Conference Rooms Avail.	18. Afternoon Tea
3 Off Season Rates	7. Swimming Avail.	11. Reservations Necessary	15. Group Seminars Avail.	* Commisions given
4. Senior Citizen Rates	8. Skiing Available	12. Dinner Available	16. Private Baths	to Travel Agents

VERMONT

West Dover

Sweeney, Robbie
Rte. 100, Box 859, 05356
(800) 332-RELAX,
(802) 464-5281

Amenities: 1,2,3,5,6,7,8,9,10, 11,12,16,17
Breakfast: F.

Dbl. Oc.: $65.00 - $125.00
Third Person: $30.00

Austin Hill Inn—Escape to "timeless relaxation." This completely renovated inn has walls of barnboard, Victorian wallpapers, fireplaces, family heirlooms, pool, afternoon tea and fine dining. Minutes to Mount Snow skiing and championship golf courses. Specialty - murder mystery weekends.

West Hartford *

Fairweather, Gretchen & Robert
Handy Rd., 05084
(802) 295-6082

Amenities: 2,3,4,6,7,8,9,10,15,16
Breakfast: F.
Dbl. Oc.: $108.00
Sgl Oc.: $76.00

The Half Penny Inn—Near Woodstock, Quechee, VT. and Hanover, N.H. Circa 1775. 40 acres of meadows, woods and a spring-fed pond. Tube, kayak or canoe the White River. Hiking and skiing on property. Near major alpine area. Minutes from fine restaurants, museums, antiques and theatre. Come see us.

Weston

Granger, David
Rte. E, #100, Box 104, 05161
(802) 824-6789

Amenities: 1,2,3,5,6,7,8,9,10, 16,17,18
Breakfast: F.

Dbl. Oc.: $60.00 - $80.00
Sgl. Oc.: $55.00 - $75.00

1830 Inn On The Green—A graciously restored dwelling overlooking the village green. Within walking distance of shopping, playhouse and dining. Nearby is the Weston Priory. A full breakfast, afternoon tea and bedtime sweets are served. Open all year.

Weston

Varner, Roy
Lawrence Hill Rd.
Box 106D, 05161
(802) 824-8172

Amenities: 1,2,3,6,8,9,10,11, 16,17,18
Breakfast: F.

Dbl. Oc.: $97.20
Sgl. Oc.: $86.40
Third Person: $26.75
Child: 6-10 yrs. - $16.20

The Wilder Homestead Inn—This 1827 brick home is just a step across the bridge from the village green, shops, museums and summer theatre. Nearby fine restaurants. Four miles to Weston Priory. Common rooms with fireplaces. Antiques, original 1830 stenciling and canopy beds - all in a country atmosphere.

1. No Smoking	5. Tennis Available	9. Credit Cards Accepted	13. Lunch Available	17. Shared Baths
2. No Pets	6. Golf Available	10. Personal Check Accepted	14. Conference Rooms Avail.	18. Afternoon Tea
3 Off Season Rates	7. Swimmming Avail.	11. Reservations Necessary	15. Group Seminars Avail.	* Commisions given
4. Senior Citizen Rates	8. Skiing Available	12. Dinner Available	16. Private Baths	to Travel Agents

VERMONT

Wilder

Sanderson, Gail
119 Christian St., 05088
(802) 295-2600

Amenities: 1,2,5,6,7,8,9, 10,11,16,17
Breakfast: C. Plus

Dbl. Oc.: $108.00
Sgl. Oc.: $91.80
Third Person: $21.60
Child: Under 2 1/2 - no charge

Stonecrest Farm B&B—Located 3-1/2 miles from Dartmouth College, this gracious 1810 home offers a country setting close to all cultural and recreational facilities. Enjoy our antiques, gardens, terraces and barns. We host canoeists' trips on the Connecticut River going from inn to inn. Near I- 91 and I-89.

Williston

Bryant, Sally & Roger
102 Partridge Hill, P.O. Box 52, 05495
(802) 878-4741

Amenities: 1,2,6,10,17
Breakfast: F.

Dbl. Oc.: $60.00
Sgl. Oc.: $35.00

Partridge Hill Bed And Breakfast—On a quiet, wooded hilltop overlooking a panorama of the Green Mountains, 5.8 miles from Burlington Airport. Private entrance to guests' level and common room. King, queen or twin beds. Fireplace in common room. Fourth double bedroom available for families. Open all year.

Wilmington *

Martin, Marie & Thomas
Smith Rd., 05363
(802) 464-3362,
(800) 34-ESCAPE

Amenities: 1,2,3,5,7,8,9, 10,11,16,18
Breakfast: F.

Dbl. Oc.: $112.10
Sgl. Oc.: $112.10
Third Person: $25.00
Child: Under 1 yr. - no charge

The Inn At Quail Run—A quiet and relaxing 15-room inn overlooking Mt. Snow on 12 private acres. Large rooms with private baths. Cross-country skiing, sauna, TV room, game room, exercise room, clay tennis court and heated pool. Marlboro Music Festival. Ski areas and large lake nearby.

Woodstock *

Deignan, Liza
61 River St., Rte. 4, 05091
(802) 457-3896

Amenities: 1,2,3,5,6,7,8, 9,10,14,16,18
Breakfast: F.

Dbl. Oc.: $85.00
Sgl. Oc.: $80.00
Third Person: $20.00
Child: Under 11 yrs. - $10.00

The Woodstocker Bed And Breakfast—Located in the historic Woodstock Village within walking distance of dining, shops and theatre. Enjoy our nine lovely rooms, spacious suites and relaxing whirlpool. The living room provides a library, games and cable TV. Buffet breakfast will start off your special Vermont getaway.

Woodstock

McGinty, Rosemary
Rte. 4W, HCR 68, Box 443, 05091
(802) 672-3713

Amenities: 1,2,3,5,6,7,8,9, 10,11,16
Breakfast: F.

Dbl. Oc.: $75.60 - $102.60
Sgl. Oc.: $54.00 - $64.80
Third Person: $10.00
Child: Under 5 yrs. - no charge

Deer Brook Inn—Beautifully restored 1820 farmhouse with original pine floors, handmade quilts and antiques. Four spacious guest rooms with private baths. Fireplace and cable TV in living room. Generous country breakfast. Minutes to skiing, hiking, swimming and golf. AAA - 3 stars.

---

1. No Smoking	5. Tennis Available	9. Credit Cards Accepted	13. Lunch Available	17. Shared Baths
2. No Pets	6. Golf Available	10. Personal Check Accepted	14. Conference Rooms Avail.	18. Afternoon Tea
3 Off Season Rates	7. Swimmming Avail.	11. Reservations Necessary	15. Group Seminars Avail.	* Commisions given
4. Senior Citizen Rates	8. Skiing Available	12. Dinner Available	16. Private Baths	to Travel Agents

VIRGINIA

The Mother of Presidents

Capitol: Richmond
Statehood: June 25, 1788: the 10th state
State Motto: "Thus Always To Tyrants"
State Song: "Carry Me Back To Old Virginia"
State Bird: Cardinal
State Flower: Flowering Dogwood
State Tree: Sugar Maple

Virginia is perhaps one of the most beautiful and historic states in the union. The climate is never too hot or too cold, an ideal vacation area. There is so much to see in this state, from the beautiful sandy beaches on the east coast to the rolling horse farms in the interior to the natural beauty of the Shenandoah Mountains and the breathtaking Skyline Drive.

The battlefields scars of two wars are here, along with their surrender points, Yorktown and Appomattox Court House. Historians come here to visit historic Jamestown, Colonial Williamsburg, Thomas Jefferson's home, Monticello, and his University of Virginia, as well as Mount Vernon, our first president's home.

Eight presidents of the United States were born here: George Washington, Thomas Jefferson, James Madison, James Monroe, William Harrison, Zachary Taylor, James Tyler and Woodrow Wilson.

Arlington *

McGrath, Marlys & John
6404 No. Washington Blvd., 22205
(703) 534-4607

Amenities: 1,2,5,7,10,11,16,17
Breakfast: C.
Dbl. Oc.: $73.15
Sgl Oc.: $67.93
Child: Over 12 - $10.00 (cot)

Memory House—An ornate 1899 Victorian lovingly decorated with antiques and collectibles. Convenient base for exploring the nation's capitol. One block from subway. Two blocks off I-66. Air-conditioned rooms. A notable house filled with comfort, hospitality and charm. Ten minutes to D.C.

Blacksburg *

Caines, Gilda & Charles
P.O. Box 10937, 24062
(703) 381-1597

Amenities: 1,2,5,6,9,10,11,16, 18
Breakfast: F.

Dbl. Oc.: $73.15 - $114.95
Sgl. Oc.: $67.93 - $109.72
Third Person: $10.45
Child: Over 12 yrs. - $10.45

Sycamore Tree Bed And Breakfast—Gracious home custom built in a picturesque mountain meadow on 126 acres. Six rooms with private baths and A/C. Wildlife, hiking, antiquing and fine restaurants. Near Roanoke, Salem and the Blue Ridge Parkway. No alcoholic beverages. "Come be a part of the magic of the mountains!"

Blacksburg

Good, Vera G.
1867 Mt. Tabor Rd., 24060
(703) 951-1808

Amenities: 1,2,5,6,10,11,16
Breakfast: F.

Dbl. Oc.: $75.00
Third Person: $15.00

L'Arche Farm Bed And Breakfast—A cozy 1790 southwest Virginia farmhouse on five rural acres. Convenient to Virginia Tech, Radford University and scenic and recreational attractions of the New River Valley. Two miles down on Mt. Tabor Road. Good food and gracious hospitality on a country farm.

1. No Smoking	5. Tennis Available	9. Credit Cards Accepted	13. Lunch Available	17. Shared Baths
2. No Pets	6. Golf Available	10. Personal Check Accepted	14. Conference Rooms Avail.	18. Afternoon Tea
3 Off Season Rates	7. Swimmming Avail.	11. Reservations Necessary	15. Group Seminars Avail.	* Commisions given
4. Senior Citizen Rates	8. Skiing Available	12. Dinner Available	16. Private Baths	to Travel Agents

Blacksburg

Huggins, Jo Pat
401 Clay St., S.W., 24060
(703) 953-2604, (800) 272-4707

Amenities: 1,2,5,6,7,9,10,11,16,17
Breakfast: F.
Dbl. Oc.: $78.38
Third Person: $15.68

Per Diem Bed And Breakfast—One block from Virginia Tech campus. Five-minute walk to coliseum, stadium, downtown shops and restaurants. Each guest house has fully appointed, comfortable living areas with porches. Courtyard with large heated pool, gardens, and patios for relaxing.

Boyce *

Niemann, Cornelia S.
Rte. 2, Box 135, 22620
(703) 837-1476,
Fax: (703) 837-2399

Amenities: 2,4,5,6,7,8,9,10, 11,16
Breakfast: F.

Dbl. Oc.: $78.38 - $99.28
Third Person: $10.45
Child: $10.45

The River House—Convenient to historic, scenic and recreational areas, this rural 1780 getaway is near the Shenandoah River. Relaxing book-filled bed/sitting rooms offer fireplaces, air conditioning and private baths. House parties, small workshops and family reunions invited.

Burke *

Bayly, Luisa
6011 Liberty Bell Ct., 22015
(703) 451-1661

Amenities: 10,11,12,13,14,15, 17,18
Breakfast: F.

Dbl. Oc.: $60.00
Sgl. Oc.: $48.00

Heritage House—Tastefully decorated with antiques. Twenty minutes to Mt. Vernon, Old Town Alexandria and Washington, D.C. Weekend rates available. On rail line.

Cape Charles *

Tribble, Joyce
Longo, Al
108 Bay Ave., 23310
(804) 331-2424

Amenities: 1,3,6,7,16,17,18
Breakfast: C. Plus

Dbl. Oc.: $65.00 - $90.00
Sgl. Oc.: $55.00 - $80.00
Third Person: $20.00
Child: Under 12 yrs. - $15.00

The Sunset Inn Bed And Breakfast—Enjoy a spectacular unobstructed sunset of the Chesapeake Bay from our breezy porch or common area. Walk or bike the boardwalk, the historic district, or visit the quaint shops. Experience the unspoiled beauty of the eastern shore. Sun, swim, relax and unwind.

1. No Smoking	5. Tennis Available	9. Credit Cards Accepted	13. Lunch Available	17. Shared Baths
2. No Pets	6. Golf Available	10. Personal Check Accepted	14. Conference Rooms Avail.	18. Afternoon Tea
3 Off Season Rates	7. Swimmming Avail.	11. Reservations Necessary	15. Group Seminars Avail.	* Commisions given
4. Senior Citizen Rates	8. Skiing Available	12. Dinner Available	16. Private Baths	to Travel Agents

VIRGINIA

Cape Charles *

Wells, James
9 Tazewell Ave., 23310-1345
(804) 331-2206

Amenities: 2,6,7,10,16,17,18
Breakfast: F.

Dbl. Oc.: $63.90 - $79.88
Sgl. Oc.: $63.90 - $79.88
Third Person: $15.00
Child: Under 2 yrs. - no charge

Sea-Gate—Located on Virginia's eastern shore. Sea-Gate invites you to rest, relax and recharge. Enjoy our porches, beach bikes. Sunsets are awing! Our home is your home. A full breakfast and afternoon tea completes a perfect getaway in "the land of gentle living."

Charlottesville *

Scassa, Roly
Rte. 21, Box 123, 22902
(804) 293-2664

Amenities: 2,7,9,10,11,16,
17,18
Breakfast: C.

Dbl. Oc.: $120.00
Sgl. Oc.: $95.00

The Inn At Sunnyfields—Historic plantation house across from Jefferson's Monticello. Five minutes from Charlottesville, seat of the University of Virginia. Historic sites and wineries in the beautiful Piedmont of Virginia. We are known for gracious hospitality in a lovely home.

Chincoteague

Bond, Carlton
600 So. Main St., 23336
(804) 336-3221

Amenities: 2,5,6,7,9,10,11,
16
Breakfast: C.

Dbl. Oc.: $75.00 - $90.00
Third Person: $10.00

Year Of The Horse Inn—All rooms on the water. Pier for crabbing or fishing. Ten minutes to wildlife refuge and ocean beach. Home of famous wild ponies. The inn is tastefully decorated and we pride ourselves on the homey atmosphere.

Chincoteague *

Olian, Victoria
Rte. 710, New Church,
23415 (mail)
(804) 824-0672

Amenities: 1,2,3,5,6,7,9,10,
11,12,16,18
Breakfast: C. Plus

Dbl. Oc.: $75.00 - $125.00
Sgl. Oc.: $75.00 - $125.00
Third Person: $15.00
Child: $15.00

The Garden And The Sea Inn—An historic and romantic inn featuring elegant lodging and French-style gourmet dining in the European tradition. Large rooms, large private baths, antiques and Victorian detail. Nearby beautiful beach and Assateague Wildlife Refuge. Historic side trips. Tours arranged. Mobil-3 Stars.

---

1. No Smoking	5. Tennis Available	9. Credit Cards Accepted	13. Lunch Available	17. Shared Baths
2. No Pets	6. Golf Available	10. Personal Check Accepted	14. Conference Rooms Avail.	18. Afternoon Tea
3 Off Season Rates	7. Swimming Avail.	11. Reservations Necessary	15. Group Seminars Avail.	* Commisions given
4. Senior Citizen Rates	8. Skiing Available	12. Dinner Available	16. Private Baths	to Travel Agents

Chincoteague

Wiedenheft, Barbara & David
4141 Main St., 23336
(804) 336-6686

Amenities: 1,2,3,7,10,15,16,17,18
Breakfast: F.
Dbl. Oc.: $69.00 - $125.00
Sgl Oc.: $59.00 - $95.00
Third Person: $20.00

Miss Molly's Inn—A charming Victorian B&B (1886) with five porches, gazebo, sun deck and picket fences. Beautiful sunsets over Chincoteague Bay. All rooms are air-conditioned and furnished with period antiques. Marguerite Henry wrote "Misty" here.

Christiansburg *

Ray, Margaret & Tom
311 E. Main, 24073
(703) 381-1500

Amenities: 1,2,5,6,8,9,10,
          11,14,15,16,18
Breakfast: F.
Dbl. Oc.: $92.20 - $124.75
Sgl Oc.: $81.37 - $113.95
Third Person: $15.00

The Oaks Bed And Breakfast Inn—A classic 1889 Queen Anne Victorian. Relaxed, tranquil, gourmet breakfasts, fine antqiues, fireplaces. A garden gazebo with hot tub. Cottage with sauna. A *Country Inns Magazine* "Top 12 of the Year." Located in the Blue Ridge Mountains. Near 1-81, I-77 and the Blue Ridge Parkway.

Cluster Springs *

Craddock, Pickett
Hwy. 658
P.O. Box 45, 24535
(804) 575-7137

Amenities: 2,6,7,10,11,12,
          15,17
Breakfast: F.

Dbl. Oc.: $50.00
Sgl. Oc.: $45.00
Third Person: $5.00
Child: $5.00

Oak Grove Plantation Bed And Breakfast—Operated May to September by Mary Pickett Craddock, a descendant of one of the original 1820 builders. Full country breakfast served in Victorian dining room. Visitors can hike and bike on 400-acre grounds. Near historic Danville and Baggs Island Lake. Children welcome.

1. No Smoking	5. Tennis Available	9. Credit Cards Accepted	13. Lunch Available	17. Shared Baths
2. No Pets	6. Golf Available	10. Personal Check Accepted	14. Conference Rooms Avail.	18. Afternoon Tea
3 Off Season Rates	7. Swimmming Avail.	11. Reservations Necessary	15. Group Seminars Avail.	* Commisions given
4. Senior Citizen Rates	8. Skiing Available	12. Dinner Available	16. Private Baths	to Travel Agents

Columbia *

Kaz-Jepsen, Ivona
Laurinaitis, Maya
6452 River Rd., W., (Rt. 6) 23038
(804) 842-2240

Amenities: 7,10,11,16,17
Breakfast: F.

Dbl. Oc.: $70.00
Sgl. Oc.: $60.00
Third Person: $30.00

Upper Byrd Farm B&B—A turn-of-the-century farmhouse nestled in the Virginia countryside on 26 acres. Overlooks the James River in the town of Columbia. Visit Ashlawn and Monticello. See the state's capitol or simply relax by the fire surrounded by antiques and original art.

Covington *

Eckert, John D.
207 Thorny Lane, 24426
(703) 965-0196

Amenities: 4,5,6,7,8,9,10,
          12,13,14,16,18
Breakfast: F.
Dbl. Oc.: $90.53
Sgl Oc.: $78.38
Third Person: $10.00
Child: Under 10 yrs. - no charge

Milton Hall Bed And Breakfast Inn—In Virginia Historic Landmarks National Register. Country manor house built by English nobility on 44 acres adjoining national forest. Spacious rooms feature fireplaces, queen beds and private baths. Fine restaurants nearby.

Culpeper *

Walker, Kathi & Steve
609 So. East St., 22701
(800) 476-2944

Amenities: 1,2,5,6,7,8,9,10,
          12,13,14,16,18
Breakfast: C. Plus
Dbl. Oc.: $65.00 - $95.00
Sgl Oc.: $50.00 - $75.00
Third Person: $20.00
Child: $20.00

Fountain Hall B&B—Built in 1859, this grand B&B is furnished with antiques and warmly welcomes business and leisure travelers. Area activities and attractions include wineries, historic battlefields, antique shops, tennis, swimming, golf, Skyline Drive and more.

1. No Smoking	5. Tennis Available	9. Credit Cards Accepted	13. Lunch Available	17. Shared Baths
2. No Pets	6. Golf Available	10. Personal Check Accepted	14. Conference Rooms Avail.	18. Afternoon Tea
3 Off Season Rates	7. Swimmming Avail.	11. Reservations Necessary	15. Group Seminars Avail.	* Commisions given
4. Senior Citizen Rates	8. Skiing Available	12. Dinner Available	16. Private Baths	to Travel Agents

Flint Hill *

Irwin, Philip R.
Rte. 1, Box 2080, 22627
(703) 675-3693

Amenities: 1,2,5,6,7,8,9,10, 11,13,14,16,17,18
Breakfast: F.

Dbl. Oc.: $73.15 - $104.50
Sgl. Oc.: $73.15 - $104.50
Third Person: $31.35

Caledonia Farm Bed And Breakfast—A working cattle farm adjacent to Shenandoah National Park. Elegant 1812 stone home with fireplaces, air conditioning, mountain scenery, outstanding comfort, hospitality and recreation for overnight, vacation or conference. Washington, VA, four miles away; Washington, DC - 68 miles.

Fredericksburg *

Bannan, Alice & Ed
1200 Princess Anne St., 22401
(703) 371-7622

Amenities: 4,9,10,12,13, 14,15,16,18
Breakfast: C. Plus
Dbl. Oc.: $92.00 - $108.23
Sgl Oc.: $82.00 - $104.00
Third Person: $10.00

Kenmore Inn—An elegant, circa 1800, colonial with 13 guest rooms, all with private baths and some with fireplaces. Full-service dining room, English pub and outdoor patio. On historic walking tour, near shops and river. Banquet facilities, meeting rooms and receptions.

Fredericksburg *

Bible, Mary Jo
1203 Prince Edward St., 22401
(703) 373-7674

Amenities: 1,2,3,4,9,10, 11,12,17,18
Breakfast: C. Plus
Dbl. Oc.: $68.00
Sgl Oc.: $45.00

The Mary Josephine Ball Bed And Breakfast—Charming two-story Victorian town home built in 1879 adjoining Mary Washington's property. Beautifully appointed decor, family antiques, small-town ambience, fine restaurants and shops within easy walking distance.

1. No Smoking	5. Tennis Available	9. Credit Cards Accepted	13. Lunch Available	17. Shared Baths
2. No Pets	6. Golf Available	10. Personal Check Accepted	14. Conference Rooms Avail.	18. Afternoon Tea
3 Off Season Rates	7. Swimmming Avail.	11. Reservations Necessary	15. Group Seminars Avail.	* Commisions given
4. Senior Citizen Rates	8. Skiing Available	12. Dinner Available	16. Private Baths	to Travel Agents

VIRGINIA

Fredericksburg

Roethel, Peggy & John
1300 Caroline St., 22401
(703) 371-1267

Amenities: 1,2,10,16
Breakfast: C. Plus

Dbl. Oc.: $75.95
Sgl. Oc.: $65.10
Third Person: $16.28

The Spooner House Bed And Breakfast—Built in 1793 and located in the historic district, within walking distance of restaurants, museums and Amtrak. Breakfast and morning paper served in guest's spacious two-room suite with private bath and entrance. The B&B is near battlefields - between Richmond and DC.

Fredericksburg *

Schiesser, Michele
4420 Guinea Station Rd., 22408
(703) 898-8444

Amenities: 1,2,9,10,11,16
Breakfast: F.

Dbl. Oc.: $85.20
Sgl. Oc.: $65.00
Third Person: $10.65
Child: No charge - $5.33

La Vista Plantation—An 1838 classic revival country home on 10 acres surrounded by woods, pastures, farm fields and stocked pond. Fireplaces, radio, refrigerators, phone, color TV, bicycles and nearby historic attractions. Fresh eggs and homemade jams. Air-conditioned. Antiques.

Fredericksburg

Thrush, Susan
711 Caroline St., 22401
(703) 899-7606

Amenities: 1,2,4,9,10,15,16
Breakfast: C.

Dbl. Oc.: $95.00 - $160.00
Sgl. Oc.: $95.00 - $160.00
Third Person: $10.00
Child: $10.00

Richard Johnston Inn—A nine-room B&B constructed in 1787 that still reflects all the grace and charm of a past era, while providing all the amenities necessary for the traveler of today. Perfect for weekend getaways, weddings, and conferences.

Front Royal *

Wilson, Ann & Bill
43 Chester St., 22630
(703) 635-3937, (800) 621-0441

Amenities: 2,5,6,7,8,9,10,16, 17
Breakfast: C. Plus

Dbl. Oc.: $60.00 - $110.00

Chester House—A Georgian mansion in the historic district. Elegant and relaxed atmosphere. Elaborate gardens. Shenandoah River/Valley, Skyline Drive, caverns and Blue Ridge Mountains. Near antique and gift shops, wineries, sport and recreational activities and excellent restaurants.

---

1. No Smoking	5. Tennis Available	9. Credit Cards Accepted	13. Lunch Available	17. Shared Baths
2. No Pets	6. Golf Available	10. Personal Check Accepted	14. Conference Rooms Avail.	18. Afternoon Tea
3 Off Season Rates	7. Swimming Avail.	11. Reservations Necessary	15. Group Seminars Avail.	* Commisions given
4. Senior Citizen Rates	8. Skiing Available	12. Dinner Available	16. Private Baths	to Travel Agents

Gordonsville *

Allison, Beverly
16280 Blue Ridge Turnpike, 22942
(703) 832-5555

Amenities: 5,6,7,9,10,11,14,16,18
Breakfast: F.
Dbl. Oc.: $63.90 - $101.18
Sgl Oc.: $53.25 - $79.88
Third Person: $21.30 - $47.93
Child: Under 5 yrs. - no charge

Sleepy Hollow Farm—Located on historic Route 231, between Somerset and Gordonsville. Lovely countryside. Restored farmhouse with cottage and pond. Near Montpelier, horse trails, historic sites and fine dining. Dinner and lunch by arrangement.

Lexington *

Roberts, Ellen & John
603 So. Main St., 24450
(703) 463-3235, (800) 882-1145

Amenities: 2,3,4,5,7,9,10, 11,16
Breakfast: F.

Dbl. Oc.: $75.25
Sgl. Oc.: $64.50
Third Person: $10.00

Llewellyn Lodge At Lexington—Lexington's oldest B&B is a short walk from the historic district. A warm, friendly atmosphere. Offers country charm with a touch of class. Home of the Lee Chapel and Stonewall Jackson. A must for Civil War buffs. Many repeat visits just for our breakfast!

Lexington/Staunton

Tichenor, Pat & Jim
Rte. 1, Box 356, Raphine, 24472
(703) 377-2398

Amenities: 1,2,5,6,7,8,9,10, 11,16,18
Breakfast: C. Plus

Dbl. Oc.: $58.58 - $69.23
Sgl. Oc.: $47.93 - $58.58
Third Person: $15.00

Oak Spring Farm And Vineyard—Located between historic Lexington and Stanton is this restored 1826 plantation house with modern comforts on a 40- acre working farm and vineyard. Decorated with antiques of the period. Amenities, warm hospitality, peace and quiet are our trademarks. Lots to see and do.

1. No Smoking	5. Tennis Available	9. Credit Cards Accepted	13. Lunch Available	17. Shared Baths
2. No Pets	6. Golf Available	10. Personal Check Accepted	14. Conference Rooms Avail.	18. Afternoon Tea
3 Off Season Rates	7. Swimmming Avail.	11. Reservations Necessary	15. Group Seminars Avail.	* Commisions given
4. Senior Citizen Rates	8. Skiing Available	12. Dinner Available	16. Private Baths	to Travel Agents

VIRGINIA

Luray *

Mayes, Gary
13 Wallace Ave., 22835
(703) 743-4701

Amenities: 2,3,4,6,8,9,10,11,16,17
Breakfast: C. Plus
Dbl. Oc.: $80.00 - $125.00
Sgl Oc.: $80.00 - $125.00

Spring Farm—Inviting 1795 retreat with four- bedrooms on 10 acres with beautiful mountain views. Old and new combination provide pleasant, comfortable surroundings. Nearby world-famous Luray Caverns, Shenandoah National Park, Skyline Drive, antique shops and Civil War battlefields. From D.C. take 66W. to 211W.

Lynchburg *

Pfister, Lois Ann & Ed
Rte. 1, Box 362,
Madison Heights, 24572
(804) 384-7220

Amenities: 1,2,5,6,7,8,10,11, 14,16,17

Breakfast: F.

Dbl. Oc.: $52.19 - $73.49
Child: Under 12 yrs. - $10.00

Winridge Bed And Breakfast—A grand colonial southern home on peaceful country meadows. Wonderful mountain views. Large shade trees and beautiful gardens with flowers, birds and butterflies abounding. Close to the Blue Ridge Parkway. Come and share our warm, casual atmosphere at Winridge.

Lynchburg

Rothfeldt, Harriet & Jim
Wiseman Rd.
Rte. 6, Box 126, Shelbyville, 37160
(615) 759-4639

Amenities: 2,9,10,16,17
Breakfast: C.

Dbl. Oc.: $43.20
Sgl. Oc.: $37.80
Third Person: $5.00
Child: Under 5 yrs. - no charge

County Line Bed And Breakfast—A two-story house, circa 1908, situated on a horse farm. Located 4-1/2 miles from Lynchburg and 45 minutes from the space center at Huntsville. Close to Jack Daniel Distillery. Miss Mary Bobo's Boarding House and many arts and crafts shops. Homemade breads. Warm hospitality.

Lynchburg *

Smith, Irene & Dale
413 Madison St., 24504
(804) 528-1503

Amenities: 1,2,6,7,9,10, 16,18
Breakfast: F.

Dbl. Oc.: $77.00 - $104.50
Sgl. Oc.: $66.00

Madison House—Authentic Victorian appeal, spacious guest rooms, private baths, telephones, plush terry robes, numerous amenities, generous breakfast on Wedgewood, afternoon high tea at 4 p.m. in Peacock Parlor. Luxury, privacy, central air and off-street parking.

1. No Smoking	5. Tennis Available	9. Credit Cards Accepted	13. Lunch Available	17. Shared Baths
2. No Pets	6. Golf Available	10. Personal Check Accepted	14. Conference Rooms Avail.	18. Afternoon Tea
3 Off Season Rates	7. Swimmming Avail.	11. Reservations Necessary	15. Group Seminars Avail.	* Commisions given
4. Senior Citizen Rates	8. Skiing Available	12. Dinner Available	16. Private Baths	to Travel Agents

VIRGINIA

Morattico

Graham, Mary Chilton
Rte. 3, Box 410,
Lancaster, 22503
(804) 462-7759

Amenities: 7,10,11,16,17
Breakfast: C.

Dbl. Oc.: $35.00 - $40.00
Sgl. Oc.: $30.00 - $35.00
Third Person: $10.00

"Holly Point"—Your hostess at this country home claims to be related to George Washington and will be happy to direct you to the local historic sites. You will enjoy the 120 acres of pine forest and views of the scenic Rappahannock River. Land and water sports. Open May 1 to November 1.

New Market *

Kasow, Dawn
Schoellig, Jean
9329 Congress St., 22844
(703) 740-8030

Amenities: 1,2,5,6,7,8,9,
10,16
Breakfast: F.

Dbl. Oc.: $64.00 - $75.00
Sgl. Oc.: $54.00 - $60.00
Third Person: $10.00
Child: Over 12 yrs. - $10.00

A Touch Of Country—Come and relax at our restord 1870 home. Six comfortable guest rooms plus two common areas along with a warm, friendly atmosphere are provided for your stay. Located in a residential section of New Market's Main Street.

Onancock *

Tweedie, Karen & David
31 North St., 23417
(804) 787-7311

Amenities: 1,2,5,6,7,9,10,
11,14,15,16,18
Breakfast: F.
Dbl. Oc.: $79.88 - $90.53

The Spinning Wheel Bed And Breakfast—An 1890's folk Victorian home in historic waterfront town. Calm Eastern shore getaway from DC, Virginia, Maryland, Delaware and New Jersey. Walk to restaurants, shops and harbor. Arrive by car or boat. Near beach, bay and ocean. Bicycles, antiques, festivals and wildlife refuge.

---

1. No Smoking	5. Tennis Available	9. Credit Cards Accepted	13. Lunch Available	17. Shared Baths
2. No Pets	6. Golf Available	10. Personal Check Accepted	14. Conference Rooms Avail.	18. Afternoon Tea
3 Off Season Rates	7. Swimmming Avail.	11. Reservations Necessary	15. Group Seminars Avail.	* Commisions given
4. Senior Citizen Rates	8. Skiing Available	12. Dinner Available	16. Private Baths	to Travel Agents

Palmyra *

Palmer, Gregory
Rte. 2, Box 1390, 22963
(800) 253-4306

Amenities: 3,6,7,9,10,11,12,
13,14,15,16,18
Breakfast: F.
Dbl. Oc.: $125.00
Sgl Oc.: $95.00
Third Person: $25.00
Child: Under 10 yrs. - $10.00

Palmer Country Manor—Situated on 180 wooded acres. Private cottages with a large living area, fireplace, color TV and deck. Swimming pool, fishing, ballooning, hiking, historic sightseeing, wine tasting and white-water rafting. Call or write for brochure.

Richmond *

Benson, Lyn
2036 Monument Ave., 23220
(804) 355-4885

Amenities: 1,2,4,9,10,16
Breakfast: F.

Dbl. Oc.: $97.50 - $147.50
Sgl. Oc.: $93.08 - $125.93
Third Person: $20.00
Child: $10.00

The Emmanuel Hutzler House—Offering lovely archiectural detailing in historic location, well-proportioned rooms in warm colors, lovely fabrics. Antiques. Each guest room has a private bath. One has a jacuzzi and fireplace. Mahogony paneled living room with fireplace and leaded-glass windows for guests'

Richmond *

Martin, Robert
2304 E. Broad St, 23223
(804) 780-3746

Amenities: 2,3,4,9,10,11,16,
17
Breakfast: F.

Dbl. Oc.: $82.50
Sgl. Oc.: $72.50
Child: Under 12 yrs. - $20.00

The William Catlin House—An 1845 restored home located in the historic district. Richmond's first and oldest bed and breakfast. Queen beds, central air-conditioning, fireplaces, furnished with antiques. Seen in *Colonial Homes* and *Southern Living* magazines. Breakfast by candlelight. All taxes included.

Richmond

West, Jim
Reese, Billie
1107 Grove Ave., 23220
(804) 358-6174

Amenities: 2,10,11,16
Breakfast: F.

Dbl. Oc.: $65.00 & $75.00

West-Bocock House—Circa 1871 historic house in the heart of the Richmond historic district, specializing in southern hospitality. French linens, fresh flowers, antiques and an eclectic art collection. Nearby museums, retaurants and shopping. Off-street parking. Full southern breakfast.

1. No Smoking	5. Tennis Available	9. Credit Cards Accepted	13. Lunch Available	17. Shared Baths
2. No Pets	6. Golf Available	10. Personal Check Accepted	14. Conference Rooms Avail.	18. Afternoon Tea
3 Off Season Rates	7. Swimmming Avail.	11. Reservations Necessary	15. Group Seminars Avail.	* Commisions given
4. Senior Citizen Rates	8. Skiing Available	12. Dinner Available	16. Private Baths	to Travel Agents

Roanoke/Smith Mountain Lake *

Tucker, Mary Lynn & Lee
Rte. 1, Box 533, 24184
(703) 721-3951

Amenities: 1,2,5,6,7,9,10,11,
 13,15,16,17,18
Breakfast: F.
Dbl. Oc.: $75.00 - $100.00

The Manor At Taylor's Store Bed And Breakfast Inn—Escape to this historic 120-acre estate near Blue Ridge Parkway and Roanoke. Luxury amenities include:hot tub, exercise room, movies, billiards, porches, fireplaces, full heart-healthy breakfast and six private ponds to swim, fish or canoe. Romantic, secluded and relaxing!

Smithfield

Hart, Sylvia & Robert
Earl, Joan & Sam
1607 So. Church St., 23430
(804) 357-3176

Amenities: 1,2,4,9,10,14,16
Breakfast: F.

Dbl. Oc.: $62.84
Sgl. Oc.: $52.19
Third Person: $10.65
Child: Under 3 yrs. - no charge

Isle Of Wight Inn—A luxurious inn located in a delightful and historic riverport town. Suites with fireplaces and jacuzzi. Some 60 old homes dating from 1750. Thirty minutes to Williamsburg and Jamestown. Near Norfolk, Hampton and Virginia Beach. Antique and gift shop.

Stanardsville *

Schwartz, Eleanor & Norman
Rte. 2, Box 303, 22973
(804) 985-3782

Amenities: 1,2,9,10,11,16,17
Breakfast: F.
Dbl. Oc.: $78.38
Sgl Oc.: $67.93
Third Person: $20.90
Child: Under 12 yrs. - $10.45

Edgewood Farm Bed And Breakfast—A circa 1790 restored farmhouse on 130 acres in the Blue Ridge foothills. Off the beaten track, yet within 30 miles of Skyline, Monticello, Montpelier, vineyards, antique and craft shops and fine restaurants. For the gardener, visit our herb and perennial nursery.

1. No Smoking	5. Tennis Available	9. Credit Cards Accepted	13. Lunch Available	17. Shared Baths
2. No Pets	6. Golf Available	10. Personal Check Accepted	14. Conference Rooms Avail.	18. Afternoon Tea
3 Off Season Rates	7. Swimmming Avail.	11. Reservations Necessary	15. Group Seminars Avail.	* Commisions given
4. Senior Citizen Rates	8. Skiing Available	12. Dinner Available	16. Private Baths	to Travel Agents

Stanley *

Beers, Marley
Rte. 2, Box 375, 22851
(703) 778-2285

Amenities: 2,5,6,7,9,10,11,12, 13,14,15,16,18
Breakfast: C. and F.

Dbl. Oc.: $140.00 - $180.00
Sgl. Oc.: $115.00 - $155.00
Third Person: $15.00 - $35.00
Child: Under 4 yrs. - no charge

Jordan Hollow Farm Inn—A restored colonial horse-farm inn. Beautiful mountain views. Twenty-two rooms, one with whirlpool and fireplace. Full-service restaurant and pub. Riding stable with trail rides on premises. Near Skyline Drive, Luray Caverns and much more. Rates include breakfast and dinner.

Staunton *

Harman, Evy & Joe
18 E. Frederick St., 24401
(703) 885-4220, (800) 334-5575

Amenities: 1,2,3,4,5,6,7,8,9,10, 12,13,14,15,16,18
Breakfast: F.
Dbl. Oc.: $53.25 - $101.18
Third Person: $20.00
Child: Under 2 yrs. - $5.00

Frederick House—A small hotel and tea room across from Mary Baldwin College in downtown Staunton, the oldest city in the Shenandoah Valley. Comfortable rooms or suites furnished with antiques. Walk to shops, museums and seven gourmet restaurants. Hiking, golf, biking, tennis and swimming.

Swoope

Fannon, Elizabeth & Daniel
Rte. 1, Box 63, 24479
(703) 337-6929

Amenities: 1,2,10,17
Breakfast: F.

Dbl. Oc.: $47.03
Sgl. Oc.: $36.58

Lambsgate Bed And Breakfast—In the historic Shenandoah Valley, six miles west of Staunton on Route 254. A restored 1816 farmhouse in a pastoral setting facing the Allegheny Mountains. This working sheep farm offers cozy, comfortable lodging near antiquing, hiking and scenic attractions.

Virginia Beach

Yates, Barbara
302 24th St., 23451
(804) 428-4690

Amenities: 1,3,5,6,7,11,16, 17
Breakfast: C. Plus

Dbl. Oc.: $52.56 - $70.08
Sgl. Oc.: $41.61 - $59.13
Third Person: $10.00
Child: Under 10 yrs. - $6.00

Angie's Guest Cottage—A cute, clean and cozy beach house in the heart of the resort area, one block from the beach. International atmosphere with casual and comfortable surroundings. Sun deck and cookout facilities available.

1. No Smoking	5. Tennis Available	9. Credit Cards Accepted	13. Lunch Available	17. Shared Baths
2. No Pets	6. Golf Available	10. Personal Check Accepted	14. Conference Rooms Avail.	18. Afternoon Tea
3 Off Season Rates	7. Swimmming Avail.	11. Reservations Necessary	15. Group Seminars Avail.	* Commisions given
4. Senior Citizen Rates	8. Skiing Available	12. Dinner Available	16. Private Baths	to Travel Agents

VIRGINIA

Williamsburg

Cottle, June
8691 Barhamsville Rd.,
Toano, VA, 23168
(804) 566-0177

Amenities: 10,12,16,18
Breakfast: F.

Dbl. Oc.: $48.00 - $58.00
Sgl. Oc.: $48.00 - $58.00
Third Person: $15.00
Child: Under 6 yrs. - $10.00

Blue Bird Haven B&B—June welcomes you to her ranch-style home located 20 minutes from colonial Williamsburg. Guest rooms are in a private wing and feature handmade quilts and rugs. Breakfast includes homemade granola, country ham and blueberry pancakes. Complimentary evening desserts.

Williamsburg *

Hirz, Sandra & Brad
1022 Jamestown Rd., 23185
(804) 253-1260

Amenities: 1,2,5,6,9,10,
11,16
Breakfast: F.

Dbl. Oc.: $103.00 - $179.00
Third Person: $43.50

Liberty Rose—"Enchanting decor," "delightful hospitality." Old Williamsburg home on wooded hilltop near historic area. Antiques, fireplaces, elaborate queen-size beds and extravagant baths. Great breakfasts! Honeymooners, favorite. Awarded highest reviews by AB&BA, *Fodors* and AAA.

Williamsburg

Hite, Faye
704 Monumental Ave., 23185
(804) 229-4814

Amenities: 2,5,6,10,16,17
Breakfast: C. Plus

Dbl. Oc.: $55.00 - $70.00
Sgl. Oc.: $55.00 - $70.00
Third Person: $15.00
Child: Under 10 yrs. - no charge

Hites's B&B—Attractive Cape Cod. Seven-minute walk to colonial Williamsburg. Large rooms cleverly furnished with antiques. Each room has phone, TV, coffee maker and radio plus charming sitting area. Makes breakfast a private affair. Smoking area.

Williamsburg *

Howard, Deborah
616 Jamestown Rd., 23185
(804) 229-3591,
(800) 296-3591

Amenities: 1,2,3,4,5,6,7,9,10,
11,16,17,18
Breakfast: C. Plus

Dbl. Oc.: $95.48 - $73.78
Sgl. Oc.: $73.78 - $84.63
Third Person: $10.00
Child: $10.00

The Cedars Bed And Breakfast—Stately nine— bedroom Georgian brick, furnished in 18th-century antiques and reproductions. Four— poster canopy beds, suites and a country cottage. Ten— minute walk to historic Williamsburg, across from the College of William & Mary.

1. No Smoking	5. Tennis Available	9. Credit Cards Accepted	13. Lunch Available	17. Shared Baths
2. No Pets	6. Golf Available	10. Personal Check Accepted	14. Conference Rooms Avail.	18. Afternoon Tea
3 Off Season Rates	7. Swimmming Avail.	11. Reservations Necessary	15. Group Seminars Avail.	* Commisions given
4. Senior Citizen Rates	8. Skiing Available	12. Dinner Available	16. Private Baths	to Travel Agents

VIRGINIA

Williamsburg

Lucas, Mary Ann & Ed
930 Jamestown Rd., 23185
(804) 220-0524, (800) 462-4722

Amenities: 1,2,3,5,6,9,10, 11,16
Breakfast: F.

Dbl. Oc.: $86.80 - $135.62
Sgl. Oc.: $86.80 - $135.62

The Legacy Of Williamsburg Tavern Bed And Breakfast - The tavern is of true 18th-century tradition. Once you cross the brick entryway you begin your journey to another place in time. Canopy beds, library, tavern game room, billiards. 6 fireplaces. Walking distance to Williamsburg. We built our legacy by being the best.

Williamsburg

Orendorff, Robert
701 Monumental Ave., 23185
(804) 229-6914, (800) 292-3699

Amenities: 2,4,5,9,10,11,16
Breakfast: C. Plus
Dbl. Oc.: $78.00
Sgl. Oc.: $68.00
Third Person: $20.00
Child: Under 6 yrs. - $15.00

Fox Grape Bed And Breakfast—Warm hospitality awaits you just a seven-minute walk north of Virginia's restored colonial capitol. Furnishings include antiques, counted cross-stitch, stained glass, duck decoys and a cup and plate collection. Bob carves walking sticks and Pat enjoys needlepoint and reading.

Williamsburg *

Sisane, Helen & Ike
922 Jamestown Rd., 23185
(804) 253-0398. (800) 722-1169

Amenities: 1,2,5,6,7,10, 11,16
Breakfast: F.

Dbl. Oc.: $80.00 - $90.00
Sgl. Oc.: $80.00 - $90.00

Williamsburg Sampler Bed & Breakfast—Elegant plantation-style, six- bedroom colonial. Richly furnished with antiques, pewter, samplers. King/queen beds with colonial decor. Warm atmosphere. Private baths. Beautiful grounds with 18th century replica of CW's Coke-Garrett Carriage House. "Skip lunch" breakfast. AAA. 3— Diamond award.

Williamsburg *

Strout, Fred
605 Richmond Rd., 23185
(800) 899-APLE

Amenities: 1,2,3,5,6,7,9,10, 11,16,18
Breakfast: C. Plus

Dbl. Oc.: $70.52 - $108.50
Sgl. Oc.: $54.25 - $92.25
Third Person: $15.00
Child: Under 12 yrs. - $10.00

Applewood Colonial Bed And Breakfast—The owner's unique apple collection is evidenced throughout this colonial home. Four elegant guest rooms with private baths. Enjoy the fireplace in the suite. The romantic atmosphere and antiques make your stay memorable. Sit-down breakfast in the dining room and afternoon tea.

1. No Smoking	5. Tennis Available	9. Credit Cards Accepted	13. Lunch Available	17. Shared Baths
2. No Pets	6. Golf Available	10. Personal Check Accepted	14. Conference Rooms Avail.	18. Afternoon Tea
3 Off Season Rates	7. Swimmming Avail.	11. Reservations Necessary	15. Group Seminars Avail.	* Commisions given
4. Senior Citizen Rates	8. Skiing Available	12. Dinner Available	16. Private Baths	to Travel Agents

Williamsburg *

Supplee, Kelly & Paul
330 Indian Springs Rd., 23185
(804) 220-0726

Amenities: 1,2,10,11,16,18
Breakfast: F.

Dbl. Oc.: $63.00 - $90.00
Third Person: $11.00
Child: Under 5 yrs. - no charge

Indian Springs Bed And Breakfast—A quiet, wooded retreat three blocks from restored area. Gracious hosts are dedicated to making your visit memorable and fun. Enjoy bird watching, library and game room. A hearty breakfast is always a delight.

Wintergreen *

Dinwiddie, Betty & Ed
P.O. Box 280,
Wintergreen Dr., Nellysford, 22958
(804)325-9126(9 a.m.-8 p.m.)
(800)325-9126(reservations

Amenities: 2,5,6,7,8,9,10,11,12,15,16,18
Breakfast: F.
Dbl. Oc.: $83.60 - $99.28
Sgl Oc.: $67.93 - $78.38
Third Person: $36.58
Child: Under 3 yrs. - $10.00

Trillium House—Located within the 10,000-acre resort of Wintergreen. One mile from Blue Ridge Parkway. Selected for "Independent Innkeeper Association", AAA - 3 Diamond, Mobile Guide - 3 Stars. Dinner: Friday and Saturday - 7:30 p.m., by reservation only, $24.00 - $26.00.

Woodstock

Hallgren, Bette
402 No. Main St., 22664
(703) 459-4828

Amenities: 1,2,9,10,16,17
Breakfast: C.

Dbl. Oc.: $69.20
Sgl. Oc.: $37.30
Third Person: $10.00
Child: Under 12 yrs. - $10.00

The Country Fare—A small and cozy country inn where old-fashioned hospitality has not gone out of style. Relax and unwind in one of the three hand-stenciled bedrooms furnished with a comfortable blend of country and collectibles. A continental breakfast of home-baked breads is served.

Woodstock

McDonald, Margaret & Price
551 So. Main St., 22664
(703) 459-3500

Amenities: 1,2,5,6,7,8,9,10,
11,12,13,16,17,18
Breakfast: F.

Dbl. Oc.: $50.00 - $70.00
Sgl. Oc.: $40.00
Third Person: $15.00
Child: Under 15 yrs. - $15.00

Azalea House—A Victorian home (circa 1892) furnished with family antiques. Stenciled ceilings. Balconies. Porches overlooking mountains. Near to Skyline Drive, Civil War battlefields, antique shops, hiking, skiing, horse riding, wineries, orchards and fishing on the beautiful Shenandoah River.

1. No Smoking	5. Tennis Available	9. Credit Cards Accepted	13. Lunch Available	17. Shared Baths
2. No Pets	6. Golf Available	10. Personal Check Accepted	14. Conference Rooms Avail.	18. Afternoon Tea
3 Off Season Rates	7. Swimmming Avail.	11. Reservations Necessary	15. Group Seminars Avail.	* Commisions given
4. Senior Citizen Rates	8. Skiing Available	12. Dinner Available	16. Private Baths	to Travel Agents

WASHINGTON

The Evergreen State

Capitol: Olympia
Statehood: November 11, 1889; the 42nd state
State Motto: "Alki (Bye & Bye)"
State Song: "Washington, My Home"
State Bird: Willow Goldfinch
State Flower: Coast Rhododendron
State Tree: Western Hemlock

The state of Washington receives an abundance of rain. Because of this, it has great forests and lumber is its major industry. It also is known as great land for hunting and fishing.

Olympia, the capitol, and the other cities on Puget Sound are sheltered from most of the heavy rain and are able to maintain a busy harbor to send supplies north to Alaska and receive in return oil to be refined.

There are also farmlands here irrigated by means of the harnessing of the water by dams. The chief dam being the Coulee Dam, is considered to be one of the greatest pieces of engineering ever completed.

The state of Washington is also well known for her delicious Washington state apples.

WASHINGTON

Anacortes *

Hasty, Melinda & Mikea
1312 8th St., 98221
(206) 293-5773

Amenities:1,2,9,10,16,17
Breakfast: F.

Dbl. Oc.: $64.50 - $86.00
Sgl. Oc.: $64.50 - $86.00
Third Person: $15.00

Hasty Pudding House—A delightfully romantic 1913 craftsman home located in quiet historic neighborhood. Antiques, fresh flowers and cozy window seats add to the tasteful decor. Walk to nearby restaurants and shops. Breakfast is full and luscious. Heart smart by request.

Anacortes *

McIntyre, Pat & Dennis
2902 Oakes Ave., 98221
(206) 293-9382

Amenities: 1,2,3,9,10,16,17
Breakfast: F.

Dbl. Oc.: $74.18 - $95.68
Sgl. Oc.: $63.43 - $95.68
Third Person: $20.00
Child: $20.00

Channel House—A classic 1902 island home located within minutes of the ferry dock. We offer comfortable rooms (two with fireplaces), private and shared baths and views. Guests enjoy use of our living room, library and hot tub.

Anacortes *

Robinson, Ralph
608 H. Ave., 98221
(206) 293-3505

Amenities: 1,2,3,5,6,7,9,10,
11,16
Breakfast: F.

Dbl. Oc.: $86.00 & $91.38
Third Person: $15.00

Outlook Bed And Breakfast—Lovingly restored 1916 vintage Robinson home with 180 degrees of unobstructed views of Mt. Baker and San Juan Islands. Watch kyaks to ocean-going ships pass by. Only eight blocks to "downtown." Ferry service to islands is 10 minutes away. Heart smart or sumptuous breakfasts.

Anacortes *

Short, Marilyn & Cecil
5708 Kingsway W., 98221
(206) 293-0677

Amenities: 1,3,6,8,9,10,11,16
Breakfast: F.
Dbl. Oc.: $60.00 - $75.00
Sgl Oc.: $55.00 - $75.00
Third Person: $20.00
Child: Under 2 yrs. - no charge

Albatross Bed & Breakfast—A charming Cape Cod-style home with a large viewing deck across the street from the Skyline Marina, charter boats and restaurant. Near Washington Park and ferries to the San Juan Islands and Victoria, B.C. Airport/ferry pick-up. Four rooms with king and queen beds and private baths. AAA approved

---

1. No Smoking	5. Tennis Available	9. Credit Cards Accepted	13. Lunch Available	17. Shared Baths
2. No Pets	6. Golf Available	10. Personal Check Accepted	14. Conference Rooms Avail.	18. Afternoon Tea
3 Off Season Rates	7. Swimmming Avail.	11. Reservations Necessary	15. Group Seminars Avail.	* Commisions given
4. Senior Citizen Rates	8. Skiing Available	12. Dinner Available	16. Private Baths	to Travel Agents

WASHINGTON

Anderson Island

Burg, Annie & Ken
8808 Villa Beach Rd., 98303
(206) 884-9185, (206) 488-8682

Amenities: 1,2,5,6,7,8,9,10,11, 12,13,16

Breakfast: F.

Dbl. Oc.: $71.00 & $98.00
Sgl. Oc.: $71.00 & $98.00
Third Person: $15.00
Child: $15.00

The Inn At Burg's Landing—Catch the ferry from Steilacoom to stay at this 1987 contemporary log homestead. Two guest rooms, master bedroom with queen size "log" bed with skylight and whirlpool bath. Private beach. Spectacular views of Mt. Ranier, Pugett Sound and Cascade Mountains. Families welcome. Ten miles south of Tacoma off I-5.

Ashford *

Darrah, Chad J.
28912 S.R. 706E, 98304
(206) 569-2788

Amenities: 2,3,6,7,8,9,10,11, 16,18

Breakfast: F.

Dbl. Oc.: $82.13 - $93.09
Sgl. Oc.: $71.18
Third Person: $16.43

Mountain Meadows Inn B. & B.—Built in 1910 on 14 acres. Antiques, model trains, nature trails, trout pond, campfire,and S'mores in the evenings. Six miles from Mt. Rainier National Park. Player piano. Cab rides on Mt. Rainier's scenic railroad. Your home-away-from-home. Hospitality at its finest.

Bellevue *

Garnett, Carol & Cy
830-100 Ave. S.E., 98004
(206) 453-1048

Amenities: 1,2,3,4,10,11,12, 13,14,15,16

Breakfast: F.

Dbl. Oc.: $59.51
Sgl. Oc.: $59.51
Third Person: $16.23
Child: Under 1 yr. - no charge

Bellevue Bed & Breakfast—Mountain and city views. Private suite or single rooms with private baths and entrance. Central location. Full breakfast. Gourmet coffee. In *Seattle's Best Places*. Reasonable rates.

Bellingham *

DeFreytas, Barbara & Frank
1014 N. Garden, 98225
(206) 671-7828, (800) 922-6414

Amenities: 1,2,3,9,10,15,16, 17

Breakfast: F.

Dbl. Oc.: $54.00 - $64.00
Sgl. Oc.: $49.00 - $59.00
Third Person: $10.00

North Garden Inn—A Queen Anne Victorian in the Register of Historic Place. Views of Bellingham Bay. Ten elegant guest rooms. Near university, shopping and dining.

Bellingham

McAllister, Donna
4421 Lakeway Dr., 98226
(206) 733-0055

Amenities: 1,2,5,7,9,10,11,16, 18

Breakfast: F.

Dbl. Oc.: $108.00 - $189.00
Sgl. Oc.: $108.00 - $189.00
Third Person: $27.00
Child: Under 10 yrs. - $11.00

Schnauzer Crossing Bed & Breakfast—A luxury contemporary B&B on Lake Whatcom. Suite with fireplace, TV and jacuzzi tub. Cottage with lake view, deck, fireplace and jacuzzi. King and queen beds, outdoor spa, fresh flowers and down comforters. Gardens: blueberries and raspberries. Northwest quiet, northwest magic.

---

1. No Smoking	5. Tennis Available	9. Credit Cards Accepted	13. Lunch Available	17. Shared Baths
2. No Pets	6. Golf Available	10. Personal Check Accepted	14. Conference Rooms Avail.	18. Afternoon Tea
3 Off Season Rates	7. Swimmming Avail.	11. Reservations Necessary	15. Group Seminars Avail.	* Commisions given
4. Senior Citizen Rates	8. Skiing Available	12. Dinner Available	16. Private Baths	to Travel Agents

Camano Island

Harmon, Esther
1462 Larkspur Lane, 98292
(206) 629-4746

Amenities: 1,2,10,15,16,17
Breakfast: F.

Dbl. Oc.: $60.00 - $65.00
Sgl. Oc.: $45.00
Third Person: $17.00
Child: Under 10 yrs. - $17.00

Willcox House Bed & Breakfast—A country-style inn only one mile from the small town of Stanwood, on an island. Pleasantly serene. Furnished with antiques. Wonderful view of Cascades and Mt. Baker. A great place to relax, yet only one hour from Seattle and 30 minutes to historic Snohomish or LaConner.

Coupeville, Whidbey Island *

Fresh, Dolores
602 N. Main
P.O. Box 761, 98239
(206) 678-5305

Amenities: 1,2,9,10,11,14,15,
16,18
Breakfast: F.

Dbl. Oc.: $86.24 - $107.80
Sgl. Oc.: $77.62 - $97.00
Third Person: $16.17
Child: $16.17

The Victorian Bed And Breakfast—A graceful Italianate Victorian in the heart of a historic reserve. Two rooms in the house feature queen beds and private baths. The charming cottage is a private hideaway with queen bedroom, sitting room and bath - $100.00. Gourmet breakfast.

Eatonville *

Gallagher, Catharine
116 Oak St. E.
P.O. Box 543, 98328
(206) 832-6506

Amenities: 1,4,7,8,9,10,16,17
Breakfast: F.
Dbl. Oc.: $60.00 - $80.00
Sgl Oc.: $54.00 - $76.00
Third Person: $15.00
Child: Under 10 yrs. - $5.00

Old Mill House B&B—Your password to the '20s! Built at a time of economic optimism, this lumber baron's home possesses spacious rooms, a shower in the master suite with seven heads and a Prohibition bar off the library. Put a wrinkle in time. Just say, "Joe sent me!"

1. No Smoking	5. Tennis Available	9. Credit Cards Accepted	13. Lunch Available	17. Shared Baths
2. No Pets	6. Golf Available	10. Personal Check Accepted	14. Conference Rooms Avail.	18. Afternoon Tea
3 Off Season Rates	7. Swimmming Avail.	11. Reservations Necessary	15. Group Seminars Avail.	* Commisions given
4. Senior Citizen Rates	8. Skiing Available	12. Dinner Available	16. Private Baths	to Travel Agents

La Conner *

Goldfarb, Peter
1388 Moore Rd., Mt. Vernon (mail), 98273
(206) 445-6805

Amenities: 1,2,9,10,11,16,17
Breakfast: C.
Dbl. Oc.: $80.63 - $129.00
Sgl Oc.: $69.88
Third Person: $27.00

The White Swan Guest House—A storybook Victorian farmhouse. 6 miles to La Conner. 3 guest rooms sharing two baths. Romantic garden cottage. English gardens, chocolate-chip cookies and country charm. 1 hour north of Seattle. Wonderful shops, galleries and restaurants nearby. Close to San Juan ferries and Vancouver, British Columbia.

Langley *

Metcalf, Senator Jack & Mrs. Norma
3273 E. Saratoga Rd., 98260
(206) 321-5483

Amenities: 1,2,5,9,10,16
Breakfast: F.
Dbl. Oc.: $81.55 - $105.11
Third Person: $15.00

Log Castle—Waterfront log lodge on Whidbey Island. Rustic elegance. Turret rooms, wood stoves. Walk out to secluded beach and watch for Eagles and Sea Lions, then curl up by the big stone fireplace. Featured in *USA Weekend* as one of seven of the most unusual lodgings in the U.S.

Leavenworth

Turner, Karen & Monty
9308 E. Leavenworth Rd., 98826
(509) 548-7171, (800) 288-6491

Amenities: 1,2,6,8,9,10,14,15,16,18
Breakfast: F.
Dbl. Oc.: $85.00 - $145.00
Sgl Oc.: $75.00 - $135.00

Run Of The River Bed & Breakfast—The quintessential northwest log bed and breakfast inn. Panoramic Cascade and Icicle River views, hand-hewn log beds and furniture and private baths. Enjoy sun splashed decks and a moonlit hot tub. Mountain bikes available. Smoke free inn and grounds.

1. No Smoking	5. Tennis Available	9. Credit Cards Accepted	13. Lunch Available	17. Shared Baths
2. No Pets	6. Golf Available	10. Personal Check Accepted	14. Conference Rooms Avail.	18. Afternoon Tea
3 Off Season Rates	7. Swimmming Avail.	11. Reservations Necessary	15. Group Seminars Avail.	* Commisions given
4. Senior Citizen Rates	8. Skiing Available	12. Dinner Available	16. Private Baths	to Travel Agents

Olympia *

Williams-Young, Penny & Bob
1304 7th Ave. W., 98502
(206) 357-5520

Amenities: 1,3,5,6,7,10,11,14, 16
Breakfast: F.

Dbl. Oc.: $59.35
Sgl. Oc.: $53.95
Third Person: $5.39
Child: Under 6 yrs. - no charge

The Cinnamon Rabbit Bed And Breakfast—A comfortable, older home in a quiet neighborhood. Close to downtown, Capital Mall and bus line. Relax in the hot tub, play the piano or borrow a cat for the evening. Check-in after 4:00 p.m. unless prearranged. No dogs, please.

Port Townsend

Kelly, Michael
2037 Haines, 98368
(206) 385-6059

Amenities: 1,2,5,6,7,9,10,14, 15,16,17,18
Breakfast: F.

Dbl. Oc.: $60.00 - $100.00
Sgl. Oc.: $60.00 - $100.00
Third Person: $10.00

Trenholm House Bed & Breakfast—An 1890 Victorian farmhouse inn. Original woodwork. Five guest rooms and cottage furnished in country antiques. Gourmet breakfast. Beautiful lagoon and bay views. Make every stay memorable.

Port Townsend *

Sokol, Edel
744 Clay St., 98368
(206) 385-3205

Amenities: 1,2,3,5,6,7,8,9,10,14,15,16,18
Breakfast: F.
Dbl. Oc.: $75.00 - $175.00
Sgl Oc.: $75.00 - $175.00
Third Person: $25.00

Ann Starrett Mansion B&B—103 year old Victorian mansion furnished with truly authentic antiques. Frescoed ceilings and a mysterious spiral staircase. Walking distance to restaurants, beach and galleries. Decadent breakfast prepared according to our original recipes. Relax in a magical living legacy.

Seattle *

Brown, Jerry
1001 Fairview Ave., N., 98109
(206) 340-1201

Amenities: 1,2,3,7,9,10,11,12, 13,14,15,16,17
Breakfast: F.

Dbl. Oc.: $70.00 - $225.00
Sgl. Oc.: $50.00 - $225.00
Third Person: $20.00
Child: Under 10 yrs. - $20.00

Tugboat Challenger—Fully functional tugboats with granite fireplace, laundry and hot-water heat. Downtown Seattle. TV, VCR, rental boats and views. Restaurants, shopping, Seattle Center and Seattle Convention Center are all within six blocks. Recognized in major publications (*McCalls*).

1. No Smoking	5. Tennis Available	9. Credit Cards Accepted	13. Lunch Available	17. Shared Baths
2. No Pets	6. Golf Available	10. Personal Check Accepted	14. Conference Rooms Avail.	18. Afternoon Tea
3 Off Season Rates	7. Swimmming Avail.	11. Reservations Necessary	15. Group Seminars Avail.	* Commisions given
4. Senior Citizen Rates	8. Skiing Available	12. Dinner Available	16. Private Baths	to Travel Agents

WASHINGTON

Seattle *

Hagemeyer, Bunny & Bill
5005-22nd Ave. NE., 98105
(206) 522-2536

Amenities: 1,2,5,6,7,8,9,10,11,
      14,15,16,17,18
Breakfast: F.
Dbl. Oc.: $72.50 - $95.00
Sgl Oc.: $65.00 - $87.50
Third Person: $15.00
Child: Under 12 yrs. - $10.00

Chambered Nautilus Bed & Breakfast Inn—Seattle's finest! A magnificent Georgian colonial set high on a hill in a convenient university district. Ten minutes from downtown. Carved ceilings, fireplaces, fully stocked bookcases and Persian rugs. English and American antiques. "NATIONALLY - RENOWNED -BREAKFASTS!"

Seattle *

Jones, Dick
4915 Linden Ave. N., 98103
(206) 547-6077

Amenities: 1,2,3,4,5,6,7,9,10,
      11,16,18
Breakfast: F.

Dbl. Oc.: $86.00 - $102.00
Sgl. Oc.: $80.00 - $97.00

Chelsea Station B&B Inn—Nestled amidst the city's activities and amenities in a peaceful, wooded setting. Near Greenlake and Seattle Zoo. Keep the comforts of home. Private baths, hot tub, full breakfast and bottomless cookie jar!

Seattle *

Sarver, Mildred J.
1202-15th Ave. E., 98112
(206) 325-6072

Amenities: 1,2,5,6,7,8,9,10,11,17,18
Breakfast: F.
Dbl. Oc.: $71.00
Sgl Oc.: $60.00
Third Person: $15.00
Child: Under 3 yrs. - no charge

Mildred's Bed & Breakfast—A traditional 1890 Victorian in an elegant style. Old-fashioned hospitality awaits. Across the street is an art musuem, flower conservatory, and historic 44-acre volunteer park. Electric trolley at the front door. Minutes to the city center and all points of interest.

1. No Smoking	5. Tennis Available	9. Credit Cards Accepted	13. Lunch Available	17. Shared Baths
2. No Pets	6. Golf Available	10. Personal Check Accepted	14. Conference Rooms Avail.	18. Afternoon Tea
3 Off Season Rates	7. Swimmming Avail.	11. Reservations Necessary	15. Group Seminars Avail.	* Commisions given
4. Senior Citizen Rates	8. Skiing Available	12. Dinner Available	16. Private Baths	to Travel Agents

Sequim *

Melang, Peggy & Bill
177 Keeler Rd., 98382
(206) 683-5889

Amenities: 1,2,3,6,7,8,9,10,
14,16
Breakfast: F.

Dbl. Oc.: $66.84- $118.58
Third Person: $21.56

Greywolf Inn—A five— acre, rural retreat at the foot of the mighty Olympics. Located just one mile east of Sequim, Greywolf offers easy access to shops and restaurants and is your springboard to adventure on the magnificent Olympic Peninsula. Six guest rooms.

So. Cle Elum *

Sherwood, Cindy & Eric
526 Marie St.
Box 629, 98943
(509) 674-5939

Amenities: 1,2,5,6,7,8,9,10,
12,13,15,16,17
Breakfast: F.

Dbl. Oc.: $45.00 - $105.00
Sgl. Oc.: $45.00 - $105.00
Third Person: $10.00
Child: $10.00

The Moore House Bed & Breakfast Country Inn—Relive the grand era of railroading at this historic eleven room inn. Bring your family and stay in a genuine caboose. Bring your loved one and enjoy the intimacy of the elegant bridal suite with private jacuzzi. Visit historic Roslyn, home of CBS TV series "Northern Exposure".

Spokane *

Bender, Jo Ann
E. 1729 18th St., 99203
(509) 534-1426 (day),
(509) 535-1893 (night)

Amenities: 1,2,9,14,15,17
Breakfast: C. and F.
Dbl. Oc.: $55.00
Sgl Oc.: $48.00
Third Person: $15.00
Child: $15.00

Hillside House B&B—A house on a hillside overlooking the city and mountains. Hospitable hosts cater to traveling reps as well as tourists. Quick or gourmet breakfasts. Adaptable to guests' needs. Nearby parks. Three miles to town. Airport pick-up. A member of the Spokane B&B Association.

Spokane *

Maguire, Phyllis
427 E.Indiana, 99207
(509) 483-4316

Amenities: 1,2,9,10,16,17
Breakfast: F.

Dbl. Oc.: $74.52
Sgl. Oc.: $63.40
Third Person: $10.00
Child: Over 10 yrs. - $10.00

Marianna Stoltz House B & B—Antique quilts, lace curtains and old world charm await you in our historic home. Easy access to freeway, close to downtown convention center arena, shopping and bus. Enjoy Stoltz House strada and peach melba parfets. Come stay with us when visiting Spokane, you will love it.

1. No Smoking	5. Tennis Available	9. Credit Cards Accepted	13. Lunch Available	17. Shared Baths
2. No Pets	6. Golf Available	10. Personal Check Accepted	14. Conference Rooms Avail.	18. Afternoon Tea
3 Off Season Rates	7. Swimmming Avail.	11. Reservations Necessary	15. Group Seminars Avail.	* Commisions given
4. Senior Citizen Rates	8. Skiing Available	12. Dinner Available	16. Private Baths	to Travel Agents

Tacoma *

Kaufmann, Sharon & Bill
3312 N. Union Ave., 98407
(206) 752-8175

Amenities: 1,2,9,10,11,16,17 **Dbl. Oc.:** $98.82
Breakfast: C.

Commencement Bay Bed And Breakfast—An elegant view home in scenic north Tacoma, near downtown shops and trails. Large rooms, secluded hot tub, elegant fireside reading area, game room and office for business travelers. Enjoy our fresh ground coffee watching boats on the bay at sunrise.

Tacoma *

Taut, Mrs. Gertrude
15313 17th Ave. Ct. E., 98445
(206) 535-4422

Amenities: 1,2,4,5,6,7,8,9,10, **Dbl. Oc.:** $20.00 - $60.00
11,12,13,14,15,16, **Sgl. Oc.:** $25.00 - $55.00
17 **Third Person:** $15.00
Breakfast: C. and F. **Child:** Under 18 yrs. - $15.00

Adventure Traudel's Haus—Unwind among antiques, old clocks, feather beds, fireplace, color TV and private bath. Near Pacific Lutheran University and Interstate 5. Central to Seatac Airport, Mt. Rainier and Mt. St. Helens. Experience Old-World German hospitality.

Vashon Island *

Clayton, Jacqueline
16529 - 91st Ave. SW, 98070
(206) 463-2583

Amenities: 1,2,6,10,16 **Dbl. Oc.:** $65.00
Breakfast: C. **Sgl. Oc.:** $65.00

Artist's Studio Loft—A lovely, private and spacious studio. Oak parquet floors, cathedral ceiling, skylights, stained glass and sun deck. Five acres. Features queen-size bed, TV, stereo, Mr. Coffee, refrigerator, microwave and bathroom with shower. Also, a wonderfully relaxing hot tub, deck and gazebo.

Winthrop *

Herman, Joan
Rader Rd., 98862
(509) 996-2173

Amenities: 1,5,6,7,8,9,10,11, **Dbl. Oc.:** $53.75
17 **Third Person:** $10.75
Breakfast: F.

Rader Road Inn—Situated on 11 1/2 wooded acres in the beautiful Methow Valley. Within walking distance to historic downtown, Winthrop shops and restaurants. Enclosed pool and hot tub. Fifty yards from Methow River.

1. No Smoking
2. No Pets
3 Off Season Rates
4. Senior Citizen Rates
5. Tennis Available
6. Golf Available
7. Swimming Avail.
8. Skiing Available
9. Credit Cards Accepted
10. Personal Check Accepted
11. Reservations Necessary
12. Dinner Available
13. Lunch Available
14. Conference Rooms Avail.
15. Group Seminars Avail.
16. Private Baths
17. Shared Baths
18. Afternoon Tea
* Commisions given to Travel Agents

WEST VIRGINIA

The Mountain State

Capitol: Charleston
Statehood: June 20, 1863; the 35th state
State Motto: "Mountaineers Are Always Free"
State Song: "The West Virginia Hills" and
                    "West Virginia, My Home Sweet Home"
State Bird: Cardinal
State Flower: Rhododendron
State Tree: Sugar Maple

The state of West Virginia is an outgrowth of the Civil War. Unable to reconcile themselves to the southern philosophy, these western Virginians separated from Virginia at the height of the War and became allied with the union states and subsequently called this area West Virginia.

West Virginia has some of the same beautiful scenery that Virginia has, along with mineral springs and plenty of hunting and fishing that brings delight t the many fishermen and hunters who come here every year.

The land is very mountainous and rugged and has extensive bituminous coal beds. The major industry here has been and is coal mining.

Its pleasant climate, hunting, fishing and mineral springs has made it a most attractive state for tourists.

WEST VIRGINIA

Charles Town

Heiler, Jean
P.O. Box 1104, 254
(304) 725-0637

Amenities: 2,3,6,9,10, 14,15,16,18
Breakfast: F.

Dbl. Oc.: $85.00 - $130.00
Sgl Oc.: $50.00 (weekdays)
Third Person: $20.00

Gilbert House—A beautiful, historic stone house (circa 1760) near Harpers Ferry and Antietam Battlefield. Close to I-81. Tasteful antiques, spacious rooms and bridal suite. Fireplace and private baths. Nearby stream and gazebo. Located in a quaint village with its own ghost!

Charles Town *

Simpson, Eleanor
Kabletown Rd. & Mill Lane
RR 2, Box 61-S, 25414
(304) 725-3371

Amenities: 2,5,6,9,10,15,16, 18
Breakfast: F.

Dbl. Oc.: $81.75 - $114.45
Sgl. Oc.: $70.85
Third Person: $10.00
Child: Under 5 yrs. - $10.00

Cottonwood Inn—A beautifully restored Georgian farmhouse with six secluded acres on Bullskin Run. Seven guest rooms have private baths, TV, A/C, queen-size beds and sitting areas. Afternoon tea and sumptuous breakfasts are included. Children welcome.

Elkins

Beardslee, Anne & Paul
Route 1, Box 59-1, 26241
(304) 636-1684

Amenities: 2,4,5,6,7,8,10,16
Breakfast: F.

Dbl. Oc.: $54.50 - $65.40
Sgl. Oc.: $49.05 - $59.95
Third Person: $16.35

Tunnel Mountain Bed And Breakfast—A charming three-story fieldstone home nestled on 5 private wooded acres. Each romantic room has a private bath, antiques and sensational views. Near many state and national parks. Hiking, skiing, canoeing, spelunking, fishing, rafting, antiques and festivals galore.

Huttonsville *

Murray, Loretta
P.O. Box 88, 26273
(304) 335-6701, (800) 234-6701

Amenities: 1,2,4,8,9,10,12,13, 16,17
Breakfast: F.

Dbl. Oc.: $50.00 - $75.00
Sgl. Oc.: $45.00 - $70.00
Third Person: $10.00
Child: Under 10 yrs. - $5.00

The Hutton House—Enjoy our historically registered Queen Anne home which is ideally located near outdoor and cultural attractions. Gaze at the Laurel Mountains while relaxing on our wrap-around porch and being served refreshments at your leisure rather than a predetermined time.

---

1. No Smoking	5. Tennis Available	9. Credit Cards Accepted	13. Lunch Available	17. Shared Baths
2. No Pets	6. Golf Available	10. Personal Check Accepted	14. Conference Rooms Avail.	18. Afternoon Tea
3 Off Season Rates	7. Swimmming Avail.	11. Reservations Necessary	15. Group Seminars Avail.	* Commisions given
4. Senior Citizen Rates	8. Skiing Available	12. Dinner Available	16. Private Baths	to Travel Agents

WEST VIRGINIA

White Sulphur Springs

Griffith, Cheryl
208 E. Main St., 24986
(304) 536-9444

Amenities: 1,2,9,10,16,17
Breakfast: F.

Dbl. Oc.: $65.00
Sgl. Oc.: $60.00
Third Person: $10.00
Child: $10.00

The James Wylie House—Located near the five-star resort (The Greenbier) in White Sulphur Springs. It is listed in the the the Register of Historic Places. Less than a mile from I-64. Nearby fine restaurants, shops, theatre and state parks. Nearby ski resorts. Two-bedroom suite and guest cottage are available.

1. No Smoking	5. Tennis Available	9. Credit Cards Accepted	13. Lunch Available	17. Shared Baths
2. No Pets	6. Golf Available	10. Personal Check Accepted	14. Conference Rooms Avail.	18. Afternoon Tea
3 Off Season Rates	7. Swimmming Avail.	11. Reservations Necessary	15. Group Seminars Avail.	* Commisions given
4. Senior Citizen Rates	8. Skiing Available	12. Dinner Available	16. Private Baths	to Travel Agents

WISCONSIN

The Badger State

Capitol: Madison
Statehood: May 29, 1848; the 30th state
State Motto: "Forward"
State Song: "On Wisconsin"
State Bird: Robin
State Flower: Wood Violet
State Tree: Sugar Maple

Wisconsin means gathering of the waters. Water is everywhere in this state and water means fun. There is much boating and swimming and general all-around recreational activities. The cold and snow of winter brings downhill and cross-country skiing, with great ice-skating on the many ponds and lakes.

Dairy products and farming are the major industries here. Wisconsin is famous for its cheese. The early settlers from Switzerland and Germany brought their knowledge of how to make cheese with them and it has been something Wisconsin has been famous for since those early times. The farms here also produce wonderful apples and berries.

The people of Wisconsin are proud of their state and are most hospitable and eager that you come and enjoy all their state has to offer.

WISCONSIN

Algoma

Warren, Jan
No. 7136 Hwy. 42
Lakeshore Dr., 54201
(414) 487-3471

Amenities: 1,4,5,6,7,9,10,11, 15,16
Breakfast: F.

Dbl. Oc.: $57.75 - $89.25
Third Person: $10.00
Child: $10.00

Amberwood Inn—Lake Michigan luxury suites. Private baths and French doors that open to the beach. Sleep to the sound of the waves, awaken to a spectacular sunrise over the water. Walk, bike, golf, swim, fish or relax. Romantic Cape Cod ambience. Some suites with wet bars. Ten minutes to Door Cnty.

Cedarburg

Brown, Elizabeth & Brook
W61, N520 Washington, 53012
(414) 375-0208

Amenities: 1,2,3,5,6,8,9,10, 16
Breakfast: C. Plus

Dbl. Oc.: $68.58
Sgl. Oc.: $58.03
Third Person: $10.00
Child: Under 2 yrs. - no charge

Stagecoach Inn Bed And Breakfast—Historically restored 1853 Greek Revival stone building in the National Register. Thirteen guest rooms, five whirlpool suites, antiques, pub and chocolate shop. Breakfast includes croisssants, muffins, juice, fresh ground coffee and tea.

Cedarburg *

Porterfield, Wendy
W62 N573 Washington Ave.,
53012
(414) 375-3550, (800) 554-4717

Amenities: 4,9,10,14,16,18
Breakfast: C. Plus
Third Person: $10.00

Dbl. Oc.: $62.25 - $146.65
Sgl. Oc.: $62.25 - $146.65
Child: $10.00

Washington House Inn—Located 25 minutes north of Milwaukee, in historic Cedarburg. Twenty-nine rooms, all with private baths, most with whirlpools and some with fireplaces. Features country and Victorian rooms with antiques and down quilts. Meeting room and sauna available.

Eagle *

Herriges, Riene & Dean
W370, 59590, Hwy. 67, 53119
(414) 363-4700

Amenities: 1,2,6,7,8,9,10,16
Breakfast: F.

Dbl. Oc.: $82.95 - $115.75
Third Person: $15.75

Eagle Centre House Bed And Breakfast—A replicated 1850s Greek Revival stagecoach inn full of antiques. Five guest rooms. Whirlpools. In Southern Kettle Moraine Forest near Old World, Wisconsin. Outdoor Living History Museum. Ninety miles from Chicago and 30 miles from Milwaukee. Bike, hike and ski. Antique shops.

1. No Smoking	5. Tennis Available	9. Credit Cards Accepted	13. Lunch Available	17. Shared Baths
2. No Pets	6. Golf Available	10. Personal Check Accepted	14. Conference Rooms Avail.	18. Afternoon Tea
3 Off Season Rates	7. Swimmming Avail.	11. Reservations Necessary	15. Group Seminars Avail.	* Commisions given
4. Senior Citizen Rates	8. Skiing Available	12. Dinner Available	16. Private Baths	to Travel Agents

Eagle River *

Kalous, Darlene
1429 Silver Lake Rd., 54521
(715) 479-2215

Amenities: 2,3,5,6,7,8,10,15, 16
Breakfast: F.

Dbl. Oc.: $88.00
Sgl. Oc.: $88.00

Cranberry Inn—A converted coach house in a north woods setting. Clean and comfortable rooms. Situated on eight acres on Yellow Birch Lake, a chain of 28 lakes. Fishing and boating. Adjacent to authentic Finnish sauna. One mile to town; 3-20 miles to Nicolet and Ottowa National Forests.

East Troy *

Leibner, Ruth
770 Adam's Church Rd., 53120
(414) 495-8485

Amenities: 2,9,10,11,17
Breakfast: F.

Dbl. Oc.: $52.75 - $63.30
Sgl. Oc.: $47.47 - $58.03
Third Person: $10.55
Child: Under 10 yrs. - $5.28

Greystone Farms Bed & Breakfast—On a quiet country road in the heart of Kettle Moraine Recreational Area. This lovely old farm home has Victorian decor and downhome charm - like a visit to grandma's. Famous breakfast. Near Old World Wisconsin shop. Nearby are a quaint town or big city mall. Relax. 27 acres.

Fish Creek

Falck-Pedersen, Christine & Sverre
4135 Bluff Rd.
P.O. Box 490, 54212
(414) 868-2444

Amenities: 1,2,3,5,6,7,8,10,16
Breakfast: C.
Dbl. Oc.: $73.85 - $121.33
Sgl Oc.: $68.58 - $116.05

Thorp House Inn—On a quiet street in the heart of the village - harbor view - walk to park entrance. Gracious air-conditioned guest rooms feature fine antiques and private baths (one with whirlpool). Housekeeping cottages feature fireplaces, country antiques and decks. Open all year.

Hudson *

Miller, Sharon
1109 3rd St., 54016
(715) 386-7111

Amenities: 1,2,3,6,7,8,10,15, 16,18
Breakfast: C.(weekday), F.(weekends)

Dbl. Oc.: $96.57 - $161.67
Sgl. Oc.: $70.53
Third Person: $20.00
Child: 9 - 18 yrs. - $10.00

Jefferson-Day House—This 1857 antique-filled Italianate home on a historic tree- lined street is two blocks from the St. Croix River. All rooms have private baths, queen beds, air-conditioning, whirlpools for two and three rooms have gas fireplaces. Romantic three-room suite available. Three course fireside breakfasts.

1. No Smoking	5. Tennis Available	9. Credit Cards Accepted	13. Lunch Available	17. Shared Baths
2. No Pets	6. Golf Available	10. Personal Check Accepted	14. Conference Rooms Avail.	18. Afternoon Tea
3 Off Season Rates	7. Swimming Avail.	11. Reservations Necessary	15. Group Seminars Avail.	* Commisions given
4. Senior Citizen Rates	8. Skiing Available	12. Dinner Available	16. Private Baths	to Travel Agents

WISCONSIN

Merrill *

Staniak, Dan
700 W. Main St., 54452
(715) 536-7744

Amenities: 1,2,5,6,7,8,9,10, 16

Breakfast: F.

Dbl. Oc.: $50.00 - $95.00
Third Person: $10.00

Candlewick Inn—Warm, inviting and elegant. This 19th-century lumber baron's mansion welcomes you. Restored to its original beauty with period furnishings, it offers the best of B&B tradition. Spacious screened porch, fireplaces and gift shop. Hiking, biking and state park.

Merrill

Ullmer, Kris & Randy
108 S. Cleveland St., 54452
(715) 536-3230

Amenities: 1,2,5,6,7,8,9,10, 17

Breakfast: F.

Dbl. Oc.: $50.00 - $55.00
Sgl. Oc.: $45.00 - $50.00
Third Person: $10.00

The Brick House Bed And Breakfast—Sparkling beveled-glass doors lead to a glowing fireplace, enticing you to relax after an active day. Warm woods and the handsome simplicity of Mission furnishings comfortably surround you in this 1915 prarie-style home. Nearby cross-country and bike trails.

Sparta *

Justin, Donna & Don
Route 1, Box 274, 54656
(608) 269-4522, (800) 488-4521

Amenities: 1,2,8,9,10,11,16
Breakfast: F.

Dbl. Oc.: $65.00 - $195.00
Sgl. Oc.: $55.00 - $185.00
Child: No charge

Just-N-Trails B&B Farm Vacation—We specialize in recreation: bicycling, hiking, cross-country skiing, relaxation, bird watching, star gazing, romance. Double whirlpools, fireplaces, fluffy pillows, Laura Ashley linenes. Tranquility, "Little House On The Prarie", "The Granary" and working dairy farm.

1. No Smoking	5. Tennis Available	9. Credit Cards Accepted	13. Lunch Available	17. Shared Baths
2. No Pets	6. Golf Available	10. Personal Check Accepted	14. Conference Rooms Avail.	18. Afternoon Tea
3 Off Season Rates	7. Swimmming Avail.	11. Reservations Necessary	15. Group Seminars Avail.	* Commisions given
4. Senior Citizen Rates	8. Skiing Available	12. Dinner Available	16. Private Baths	to Travel Agents

WYOMING

The Equality State

Capitol: Cheyenne
Statehood: July 10, 1890; the 44th state
State Motto: "Equal Rights"
State Song: "Wyoming"
State Bird: Meadow Lark
State Flower: Indian Paintbrush
State Tree: Cottonwood

This is a very beautiful and scenic state. Its climate is dry and sunny with cold and snowy winters and warm summers. The majestic Rocky Mountain peaks tower over much of this land. The oldest national park, Yellowstone, was founded here by John Colter in 1807. The first national monument, Devil's Tower, was dedicated by President Teddy Roosevelt. The beautiful Teton Park and Fort Laramie, established in 1840 to protect the white man from Indians as he crossed this state in covered wagons, contributed to the fascination of this state for tourists.

Women won the right to vote here in 1869 and in 1870, Esther Morris became the first Justice of the Peace in the U.S. In 1925, Nellie Taylor Ross became the first woman to become Governor.

WYOMING

Casper *

Frigon, Don & Sherry
843 So. Durbin, 82601
(307) 577-5774

Amenities: 1,2,4,6,7,8,9,11, 12,14,17
Breakfast: F.

Dbl. Oc.: $47.70 - $63.60
Sgl. Oc.: $37.10 - $53.00
Third Person: $10.60

Durbin Street Inn Bed & Breakfast—75 year old home, comfortably decorated in Victorian period. Clean, relaxed friendly atmosphere. Good food. A lot to see and do in the area, or just relax. Central to everything. Good skiing on Casper Mountain. Two golf courses - 18 holes, events center and museums nearby.

Casper *

McInroy, Opal
5120 Alcova Rte.
P.O. Box 40, 82604
(307) 265-6819

Amenities: 1,2,6,7,8,9,10,11, 12,13,17
Breakfast: F.

Dbl. Oc.: $45.00
Sgl. Oc.: $35.00
Third Person: $10.00
Child: $10.00

Bessemer Bend Bed And Breakfast—A large home in a scenic area 10 miles southwest of Casper, on North Platte River. Two miles from fish hatchery. Historic area with wildlife. Tours arranged. Fishing, hiking, bird watching, horseshoes, recreation room and photography.

Cheyenne

Drege, Nancy & John
219 E. 18th St., 82001
(307) 638-2337

Amenities: 1,2,3,4,9,10,14,16
Breakfast: F.
Dbl. Oc.: $80.25 - $101.65
Sgl Oc.: $80.25 - $101.65

Rainsford Inn B&B—National historic restored home near downtown Cheyenne. Five suites, each with private bath, featuring whirlpool tub and separate shower. Handicapped accessible. Reservations recommended. Reminds guests of a visit to Grandma's house.

Clearmont *

Bumbaca, Lily & Rich
4355 US Hwy. 14 - 16 E., 82835
(307) 758-4387

Amenities: 1,9,13
Breakfast: F.
Dbl. Oc.: $65.00
Sgl Oc.: $65.00
Third Person: $15.00

RBL Bison Ranch Bed And Breakfast—A working Bison ranch on 3,500 acres. Bison herd tours. All meals include bison meat unless other meat desired. Dinner by reservation. 1/2 bath in each room with men's and women's shower rooms. Deer and antelope almost always in view. Some rodeo events.

1. No Smoking	5. Tennis Available	9. Credit Cards Accepted	13. Lunch Available	17. Shared Baths
2. No Pets	6. Golf Available	10. Personal Check Accepted	14. Conference Rooms Avail.	18. Afternoon Tea
3 Off Season Rates	7. Swimmming Avail.	11. Reservations Necessary	15. Group Seminars Avail.	* Commisions given
4. Senior Citizen Rates	8. Skiing Available	12. Dinner Available	16. Private Baths	to Travel Agents

WYOMING

Dubois *

Bridges, Irene
Fish Hatchery Rd.
P.O. Box 635, 82513
(307) 455-2769

Amenities: 1,2,6,8,9,10,11,12, 17
Breakfast: F.

Dbl. Oc.: $63.00
Sgl. Oc.: $63.00
Third Person: $10.50
Child: Under 6 yrs. - $5.25

Jakey's Fork Bed And Breakfast—Secluded hillside home of simple elegance. Rooms have mountian views. Relax in the jacuzzi or sauna or by the fireplace. Historic homestead and clear mountain stream are adjacent. Hiking, backpacking, horseback riding, cross- country skiing, hunting, fishing and mountain biking.

Encampment

Platt, Mayvon
Star Route 49, 82325
(307) 327-5539

Amenities: 1,8,10,11,15,17
Breakfast: F.

Dbl. Oc.: $58.30
Sgl. Oc.: $37.10
Child: No charge - half price

Platt's Rustic Mountain Lodge—Peaceful mountain view and wholesome country atmosphere. Western hospitality on a working farm. Horseback riding, fishing, hiking and rock hounding. Guided tours. Enjoy the flora and fauna, historic trails, mining camps, snowmobiling and cross-country skiing. Cabin rental available for groups.

Jackson

Jern, Sherrie
3725 Teton Village Road
P.O. Box 3724, 83001
(307) 733-4710

Amenities: 1,2,5,6,7,8,9,10, 11,16
Breakfast: F.

Dbl. Oc.: $120.00 - $130.00
Third Person: $20.00
Child: Under 11 yrs. - no charge

The Wildflower Inn—A lovely log home on three acres with five sunny guest rooms, all with private baths. A full breakfast is served. You are invited to soak in a large hot tub and enjoy the beautiful views. Close to all mountain activities and yet you still have a real sense of solitude.

Jackson Hole *

Becker, Chris & Denny
Box 550, Wilson, 83014
(307) 733-3233

Amenities: 1,2,3,5,6,7,8,9,10, 11,16
Breakfast: F.

Dbl. Oc.: $101.65 - $123.05
Sgl. Oc.: $96.30 - $117.70
Third Person: $16.05
Child: $16.05

Teton Tree House—Our secluded but convenient mountain lodge which the *J.H. News* said "combines rustic charm and elegance" is a classic B&B inn. Warm, on-premise hosts, are 30 year locals, guides and travelers delight in sharing information.

1. No Smoking	5. Tennis Available	9. Credit Cards Accepted	13. Lunch Available	17. Shared Baths
2. No Pets	6. Golf Available	10. Personal Check Accepted	14. Conference Rooms Avail.	18. Afternoon Tea
3 Off Season Rates	7. Swimmming Avail.	11. Reservations Necessary	15. Group Seminars Avail.	* Commisions given
4. Senior Citizen Rates	8. Skiing Available	12. Dinner Available	16. Private Baths	to Travel Agents

WYOMING

Lander *

White, Edna
53 N. Fork Rd., 82520
(307) 332-3175

Amenities: 1,10,12,17
Breakfast: F.

Dbl. Oc.: $42.00
Sgl. Oc.: $29.50
Child: $7.50

Edna's Bed And Breakfast—Five miles northwest of Lander and three hours from Yellowstone National Park. A very quiet, informal, working— family ranch homestay with upstairs bedrooms. Observe cattle ranch activities. We love to visit with our guest or you can take a quiet country walk.

Laramie

Acuff, Ann
819 University Ave., 82070
(307) 721-4177

Amenities: 1,2,9,10,11,17
Breakfast: C. Plus

Dbl. Oc.: $53.50 - $64.20
Sgl. Oc.: $42.80 - $53.50
Third Person: $10.00

Annie Moore's Guest House—A cheerfully decorated Queen Anne-style home. Six guest rooms with sunny common areas. Across the street from the University of Wyoming. Close to downtown shops and restaurants. Thirty minutes from spectacular and uncrowded wilderness. Skiing, hiking and fishing.

Pinedale

McClain, Leanne
10151 Hwy. 191, 82941
(307) 367-2600

Amenities: 1,3,6,8,9,10,12,13, 14,15,17
Breakfast: F.

Dbl. Oc.: $66.95
Sgl. Oc.: $56.65
Third Person: $20.60
Child: Under 5 yrs. - no charge
5 - 10 yrs. - $10.30

Window On The Winds—The McKay's invite you to their log home. Lodge pole pine, queen beds, large common room decorated in stunning Western and Plains Indian decor. Enjoy the breathtaking view of "the winds" or relax in the hot tub after a day of mountain adventures. Open year-round.

1. No Smoking	5. Tennis Available	9. Credit Cards Accepted	13. Lunch Available	17. Shared Baths
2. No Pets	6. Golf Available	10. Personal Check Accepted	14. Conference Rooms Avail.	18. Afternoon Tea
3 Off Season Rates	7. Swimmming Avail.	11. Reservations Necessary	15. Group Seminars Avail.	* Commisions given
4. Senior Citizen Rates	8. Skiing Available	12. Dinner Available	16. Private Baths	to Travel Agents

BED AND BREAKFAST

HOMES AND INNS

IN THE PROVINCES OF CANADA

ALBERTA

The Westernmost Prairie Province of Canada

Capitol: Edmonton
Entered The Dominion: September 1, 1905; the 8th province
The Floral Emblem: Wild Rose

Alberta is the largest of the prairie provinces. Because of the oil boom in 1947, it is one of the wealthiest provinces as well.

Some of the most attractive scenery to be found is in this area: the majestic snow-capped Canadian Rockies and Banff and Jasper National Parks. Tourists can ride horseback through these areas as well as enjoy boating, golfing and swimming.

ALBERTA

Calgary

Turgeon, Eileen & Denis
4903 Viceroy Dr., N.W.
T3A 0V2
(403) 288-0494

Amenities: 1,2,5,6,7,8,11,12, 17
Breakfast: F.

Dbl. Oc.: $45.00(CN)
Sgl. Oc.: $30.00(CN)

Turgeons Bed And Breakfast—Experience true western hospitality in a comfortable bungalow with bricked patio, air-conditioning and a fireplace. Close to transit, shopping, Univeristy of Calgary and many attractions. Dog and cat on the premises. Enjoy home-cooked muffins and preserves.

Canmore

Doucette, Mrs. Patricia
P.O. Box 1162 , T0L 0M0
(403) 678-4751

Amenities: 1,2,5,6,7,8,13,17
Breakfast: F.

Dbl. Oc.: $55.00 - $60.00(CN)
Sgl. Oc.: $35.00(CN)
Third Person: $15.00(CN)
Child: $5.00 - $10.00(CN)

Cougar Creek Inn—A quiet, rustic cedar chalet with mountain views in each direction. Grounds border Cougar Creek. Walk along creek into mountains where wildlife is often seen. Area offers skiing, hiking, mountain biking, backpacking, tennis and golf. Relax by the fire or picnic in the back yard.

Claresholm*

Laing, Anola & Gordon
Box 340, T0L 0T0
(403) 625-4389

Amenities: 1,2,17,18
Breakfast: F.

Dbl. Oc.: $50.00 - $95.00(CN)
Sgl. Oc.: $35.00(CN)

Anola's Bed And Breakfast—Stay in our lovingly restored cottage decorated in early 1900s or in our farmhouse. Private two-bedroom suite. Hot tub. Browse through grandad's museum. A 3,800-acre grain farm located on Highway 520; 30 minutes from Head Smashed in Buffalo Jump, northwest of Lethbridge.

Disbury *

Ausenhus, Bev & Cal
R.R. 2 , T0M 0W0
(403) 335-4736

Amenities: 1,2,5,6,10,11,12, 17,18
Breakfast: F.

Dbl. Oc.: $55.00(CN)
Sgl. Oc.: $45.00(CN)
Third Person: $20.00(CN)

The Ausen Hus Bed And Breakfast—Located 40 miles north of Calgary, just off Highway 2, o n the way to the Dinosaur Museum or West Edmonton Mall. Enjoy our quiet, rural setting while taking in Calgary attractions. Outdoor hot tub, gazebo and walking trail on property. Antiques, fireplace and comfortable luxury.

1. No Smoking	5. Tennis Available	9. Credit Cards Accepted	13. Lunch Available	17. Shared Baths
2. No Pets	6. Golf Available	10. Personal Check Accepted	14. Conference Rooms Avail.	18. Afternoon Tea
3 Off Season Rates	7. Swimmming Avail.	11. Reservations Necessary	15. Group Seminars Avail.	* Commisions given
4. Senior Citizen Rates	8. Skiing Available	12. Dinner Available	16. Private Baths	to Travel Agents

BRITISH COLUMBIA

Canada's Third Largest Province

Capitol: Victoria
Entered The Dominion: July 20, 1871; the 6th province
Motto: "Unfailing Splendor"
The Floral Emblem: Flowering Dogwood

British Columbia is the western most province of Canada. It is a powerful province with great potential. It possesses great lands that can be used to grow crops, large mineral deposits and enormous tracts of forest.

Victoria is the capitol of this province and has an excellent harbor. Visitors come from all over to purchase imported goods that come into this harbor as well as Vancouver's harbor on this southwestern coast.

The temperature is pleasant. Because of the mild winds from the Pacific Ocean, British Columbia's coast in the winter is fairly warm and cool in the summer. This kind of moderate climate makes for a wide range of recreational advantages.

BRITISH COLUMBIA

Abbotsford *

Friesen, Ina & Walter
Southridge Pl., V3G 1E2
(604) 852-5787

Amenities:1,2,6,10,11
16,17,18
Breakfast: F.

Dbl. Oc.: $55.00 & $69.00 (US)
Sgl. Oc.: $45.00 (US)

The Cliff House — Offers a beautiful view of Mt. Baker. It is 40 miles east of Vancouver, B.C., 3/4 of a mile off the #401 Freeway, Exit 95. Wonderland Amusement Park, golf and restaurants nearby. Meals served on the large patio weather permitting.

Dawson Creek

Kux-Kardos, Heidy & Charles
10209-10 St.
P.O. Box 246, V1G 4G7
(604) 782-7998

Amenities: 3,5,6,7,8,9,12,13,14,15,16,17,18
Breakfast: C., C. plus, or F.
Dbl. Oc.: $51.75(CN)
Sgl Oc.: $40.25(CN)
Third Person: $17.25(CN)

Hotel Alaska—Located in Mile Zero Plaza. Combines the spirit of Northern adventure with Old World charm. World -famous restaurant. Dew Drop Inn pub - live entertainment. The best place to begin and end your Alaska highway adventure.

Dawson Creek

Shandro, Norine & Donn
933-111 Ave., V1G 2X4
(604) 782-4148

Amenities: 1,2,3,5,6,7,8,10,
17
Breakfast: F. or C. Plus

Dbl. Oc.: $55.00(CN)
Sgl. Oc.: $45.00(CN)

Inn Margaree—Homemade breakfast of bread, rolls, scones or muffins - fresh daily. Two spacious bedrooms with king- and queen- size beds, guest bathroom, relaxing living room, adult oriented, private back yard, centrally located, period decor, fine china and silverware. Late tea and dainties.

Fort Nelson

Muss, Ann & Ken
5437 - 47th St.,Box 58, V0C 1R0
(604) 774-6050

Amenities: 1,2,3,5,6,7,11,17
Breakfast: C. or F.

Dbl. Oc.: $50.00 - $55.00(CN)
Sgl. Oc.: $45.00 - $50.00(CN)

Fort Nelson Bed And Breakfast—Located on Mile 300, Alaska Highway. Quiet, comfortable home near downtown with laundry facilities and offering a home-style breakfast.

---

1. No Smoking
2. No Pets
3 Off Season Rates
4. Senior Citizen Rates

5. Tennis Available
6. Golf Available
7. Swimmming Avail.
8. Skiing Available

9. Credit Cards Accepted
10. Personal Check Accepted
11. Reservations Necessary
12. Dinner Available

13. Lunch Available
14. Conference Rooms Avail.
15. Group Seminars Avail.
16. Private Baths

17. Shared Baths
18. Afternoon Tea
* Commisions given
to Travel Agents

BRITISH COLUMBIA

Fort St. John

Hetrick, Cecil & Jaye
SS# 2, Site 7,
Comp. 24, V1J 4M7
(604) 785-3532

Amenities: 1,6,17
Breakfast: F.

Dbl. Oc.: $55.00
Sgl. Oc.: $45.00
Third Person: $10.00
Child: $10.00

Alaska Highway Bed And Breakfast—We invite you to stay and relax in our spacious and comfortable home overlooking the city and the famous Alaska Highway. You will delight in your quiet, country-style rooms. We are located near Charlie Lake, renowned for bird watching, fishing, hiking and golfing.

Mill Bay *

Clarke, Barbara & Clifford
3191 Mutter Rd., V0R 2P0
(604) 743-4083

Amenities: 1,2,3,9,10,11,16
Breakfast: F.

Dbl. Oc.: $75.00 - $95.00(CN)
Sgl. Oc.: $60.00 - $75.00(CN)
Third Person: $15.00(CN)

Pine Lodge Farm Bed And Breakfast—A lovely pine lodge built on a hillside overlooking the ocean and islands, with walking trails, farm animals, wild deer, magnificent arbutus trees: fir, alder, cedar, hemlock and dogwood, all contributing to the paradise-like setting. Central to Victoria and Upper Island.

Nanoose Bay*

Wilkie, Marj & Herb
3381 Dolphin Dr., RR 2, V0R 2R0
(604) 468-9796

Amenities: 1,2,3,5,6,7,8,10,
11,16,17
Breakfast: F.

Dbl. Oc.: $50.00 - $70.00 (CN)
Sgl. Oc.: $40.00(CN)
Third Person: $20.00(CN)

"The Lookout" Bed And Breakfast And Vacation Suite—Mid-way from Victoria and Tofino. Spectacular view of Georgia Strait. Relax on wrap-around deck and enjoy boats, cruise ships, eagles and majestic mountains. Fairwinds golf, marina and resort two minutes away. Warm, friendly hosts. Ample parking. Paradise!

Vancouver *

Johnson, Sandy
2278 W. 34th Ave., V6M 1G6
(604) 266-4175

Amenities: 1,2,3,10,16,17
Breakfast: F.

Dbl. Oc.: $55.00 - $90.00(CN)
Sgl. Oc.: $45.00 - $80.00(CN)
Third Person: $15.00(CN)
Child: Over 8 yrs. - $15.00(CN)

Johnson House Bed And Breakfast—Nestled into a quiet tree-lined avenue but close to good restaurants, city buses and most services. Tourist attractions, downtown and airport are within minutes. Homey antique decor includes carousel horses and brass beds. Healthy homemade breakfasts to please you.

1. No Smoking	5. Tennis Available	9. Credit Cards Accepted	13. Lunch Available	17. Shared Baths
2. No Pets	6. Golf Available	10. Personal Check Accepted	14. Conference Rooms Avail.	18. Afternoon Tea
3 Off Season Rates	7. Swimming Avail.	11. Reservations Necessary	15. Group Seminars Avail.	* Commisions given
4. Senior Citizen Rates	8. Skiing Available	12. Dinner Available	16. Private Baths	to Travel Agents

BRITISH COLUMBIA

Vancouver, No.

Poole, Doreen
421 W. St. James Rd.
V7N 2P6
(604) 987-4594

Amenities: 1,2,3,7,8,10,17
Breakfast: Full

Dbl. Oc.: $50.00(CN)
Sgl. Oc.: $35.00(CN)
Third Person: $10.00(CN)
Child: Under 6 yrs. - no charge

Poole's Bed And Breakfast—Quiet home, relaxed surroundings, lovely residential district. Close to restaurants, bus, downtown Vancouver, Stanley Park, Capilano Suspension Bridge and Grouse Mt. Vancouver Island ferry. Retired hosts are happy to assist you with information and directions.

*Victoria**

Allison, Marilyn & Douglas
116 Eberts St.V8S 3H7
(604) 360-0747
Fax: (604) 383-3550

Amenities: 1,2,3,5,6,7,9,11,
16,17
Breakfast: C. or F.

Dbl. Oc.: $75.00 - $95.00(CN)
Sgl. Oc.: $55.00(CN)
Third Person: $20.00(CN)
Child: Over 5 yrs. - $25.00(CN)

Maridou House—Charming 1909 Edwardian with antique furnishings, canopied beds and down comforters. Shared or private baths with Jacuzzi bathtub. Children welcome in 3 bedroom self contained suite. Our home offers large cheerful rooms, one with twin beds and warm Scottish hospitality.

*Victoria **

Barr, Rene
3844 Hobbs St.V8N 4C4
(604) 477-6558

Amenities: 1,2,5,6,7,9,10,11,
16,17,18
Breakfast: F.

Dbl. Oc.: $55.00 - $70.00(CN)
Sgl. Oc.: $40.00(CN)
Third Person: $20.00(CN)
Child: Under 12 yrs.-
$15.00(CN)

Cadboro Bay Bed And Breakfast—A short walk to the university, beach, parks (with windsurfing),tennis, and restaurants and village pub. Only 15 minutes to downtown Victoria and all local attractions. Delightful accommodations include a separate guest cottage and a generous gourmet breakfast which changes daily.

*Victoria**

Dashwood, Derek
1 Cook St., V8V 3W6
(604) 385-5517

Amenities: 1,3,4,9,10,11,16
Breakfast: F.

Dbl. Oc.: $75.00 - $235.00(CN)
Sgl. Oc.: $65.00 - $225.00(CN)
Third Person: $35.00
Child: Under 18 yrs. -
$25.00(CN)

Dashwood Seaside Manor—Victoria's only seaside B&B inn. Next to Beacon Hill Park. On scenic Marine Drive, minutes to town. A 1912 Tudor mansion with 14 suites, each your own home. Help yourself to breakfast in your own suite. Beam ceilings. Some fireplaces. Enjoy a glass of sherry in the library.

---

1. No Smoking	5. Tennis Available	9. Credit Cards Accepted	13. Lunch Available	17. Shared Baths
2. No Pets	6. Golf Available	10. Personal Check Accepted	14. Conference Rooms Avail.	18. Afternoon Tea
3 Off Season Rates	7. Swimmming Avail.	11. Reservations Necessary	15. Group Seminars Avail.	* Commisions given
4. Senior Citizen Rates	8. Skiing Available	12. Dinner Available	16. Private Baths	to Travel Agents

Victoria

Gray, Sandra
3808 Heritage Lane, V8Z 7A7
(604) 479-0892

Amenities: 1,2,9,11,15,17,18
Breakfast: F.
Dbl. Oc.: $95.00(CN)
Sgl Oc.: $70.00(CN)
Third Person: $35.00(CN)

Heritage House Bed And Breakfast—Designated heritage home on 3/4 of an acre. Quiet private road. Lounging veranda, large rooms, guest parlor with fireplace, fireplace in library/den. Adult oriented. Complimentary house wine. Convenient to ferries, town and all highways.

*Victoria**

Jessen, Marilyn
1121 Faithful St., V8V 2R5
(604) 383-9948

Amenities: 1,2,3,5,9,11,16,17
Breakfast: F.
Dbl. Oc.: $75.00 - $85.00(CN)
Sgl Oc.: $65.00 - $75.00(CN)
Third Person: $20.00(CN)

Ambleside B&B—A relaxing, warm and friendly retreat within walking distance of downtown Victoria and 30 minutes to famous Butchart Gardens. Stroll along scenic ocean beaches or through 187 acres of gardens and parkland, both just one block from our beautifully restored character home.

*Victoria **

McKechnie, William
998 Humboldt St., V8V 2Z6
(604) 384-8422

Amenities: 1,2,3,9,10,16
Breakfast: F.
Dbl. Oc.: $100.00 - $198.00(CN)
Sgl. Oc.: $100.00 - $198.00(CN)
Third Person: $26.00(CN)
Child: Under 10 yrs. - no charge

The Beaconsfield—An award-winning restored English mansion A few blocks from downtown Victoria. Enter into a world of rich textures: velvets, leather, warm woods and goosedown quilts. Antiques throughout. Delicious breakfast and service to pamper you.

1. No Smoking	5. Tennis Available	9. Credit Cards Accepted	13. Lunch Available	17. Shared Baths
2. No Pets	6. Golf Available	10. Personal Check Accepted	14. Conference Rooms Avail.	18. Afternoon Tea
3 Off Season Rates	7. Swimmming Avail.	11. Reservations Necessary	15. Group Seminars Avail.	* Commisions given
4. Senior Citizen Rates	8. Skiing Available	12. Dinner Available	16. Private Baths	to Travel Agents

BRITISH COLUMBIA

*Victoria**

Musar, Marty	**Amenities:** 1,3,9,11,15,16,17	**Dbl. Oc.:** $92.43 - $107.64(CN)
5259 Patricia Bay Hwy.,	**Breakfast:** F.	**Sgl. Oc.:** $64.35(CN)
V8Y 1S8		**Third Person:** $23.40(CN)
(604) 658-8879		**Child:** Over 12 yrs. - $23.40(CN)

Elklake Lodge—Unique and grand home built in 1910. Attractive, comfortable guest rooms with private baths. Beautiful gardens. large deck, outdoor hot tub, full breakfast. Close to ferry and airport. Ten minutes from downtown Victoria.

Victoria

Ranzinger, Sue & Inge	**Amenities:** 1,2,3,5,6,7,9,10,	**Dbl. Oc.:** $65.00 - $90.00(CN)
66 Wellington Ave., V8V 4H5	11,16	**Sgl. Oc.:** $45.00(CN)
(604) 383-5976	**Breakfast:** F.	**Third Person:** $15.00(CN)

Wellington Bed And Breakfast—A designer's delight! Large, beautifully furnished rooms with queen or king beds, walk-in closets and private baths. Close to downtown, 1/2 block from bus and beaches. Enjoy great hospitality, superb breakfasts and a good sleep! Relax in the living room, sun deck or on the sunporch.

Victoria

Waibel, Peggy	**Amenities:** 5,6,7,10,11,16,17	**Dbl. Oc.:** $100.00(CN) & up
279 Coal Point Lane	**Breakfast:** F.	**Sgl. Oc.:** $100.00(CN) & up
R.R. #1, Sydney, B.C., V8L 3R9		**Third Person:** $20.00(CN)
(604) 656-5656		**Child:** Under 10 yrs. - $10.00(CN)

Peggy's Cove Bed And Breakfast—Spoil yourself! Come join me in my beautiful home surrounded by ocean on three sides. Watch eagles and whales. In the evening spend a romantic moment in our hot tub under the stars. Butchart Gardens and ferries are close by. Peggy's Cove is a honeymooners' paradise.

*Whistler **

Morel, Ursula	**Amenities:** 1,2,4,5,6,7,8,9,10,11	**Dbl. Oc.:** $69.03 - $115.83(CN)
7162 Nancy Greene Dr., V0N 1B0	12,13,14,15,16,18	**Sgl. Oc.:** $57.33 - $104.13(CN)
(604) 932-3641		**Third Person:** $23.40(CN)
Fax: (604) 938-1746	**Breakfast:** F.	**Child:** Under 6 yrs. - $11.70(CN)

Edelweiss Pension—Traditional European hospitality. Rooms with a view, balconies, down comforters, private bathroom, sauna, whirlpool and fireside guest lounge. Rates include full breakfast. Easy walk to lifts, village and park. Non-smoking

1. No Smoking	5. Tennis Available	9. Credit Cards Accepted	13. Lunch Available	17. Shared Baths
2. No Pets	6. Golf Available	10. Personal Check Accepted	14. Conference Rooms Avail.	18. Afternoon Tea
3 Off Season Rates	7. Swimmming Avail.	11. Reservations Necessary	15. Group Seminars Avail.	* Commisions given
4. Senior Citizen Rates	8. Skiing Available	12. Dinner Available	16. Private Baths	to Travel Agents

BRITISH COLUMBIA

Whistler *

Zinsli, Luise & Eric
7461 Ambassador Crescent
P.O. Box 352, V0N 1B0
(604) 932-4187
Fax; (604) 938-1531

Amenities: 1,2,4,5,6,7,8,9,10,
11,13,14,15,16,18
Breakfast: F.

Dbl.Oc.: $81.00 - $128.00(CN)
Sgl. Oc.: $69.00 - $116.00(CN)
Third Person: $29.00(CN)
Child: Under 10 yrs.-
$12.00(CN)

Chalet Luise Pension B&B Inn—Traditional Swiss hospitality. Rooms with a view, balconies, down quilts, ensuite bathrooms, whirlpool, sauna, fireside guest lounge and garden/patio. Non-smoking establishment. An easy walk to lifts, village, lost lake park and trails. Home-baked bread.

1. No Smoking	5. Tennis Available	9. Credit Cards Accepted	13. Lunch Available	17. Shared Baths
2. No Pets	6. Golf Available	10. Personal Check Accepted	14. Conference Rooms Avail.	18. Afternoon Tea
3 Off Season Rates	7. Swimmming Avail.	11. Reservations Necessary	15. Group Seminars Avail.	* Commisions given
4. Senior Citizen Rates	8. Skiing Available	12. Dinner Available	16. Private Baths	to Travel Agents

NEW BRUNSWICK

One of Canada's Four Atlantic Provinces

Capitol: Fredericton
Entered The Dominion: July 1, 1867
Provincial Motto: "Hope Restored"
Floral Emblem: Purple Violet

New Brunswick is one of the original provinces of Canada. It has great natural beauty. Forest covers about 90% of the land yet in the St. John River Valley area there is rich farmland where potatoes are grown in great abundance.

More than one half of the people of this province live in the cities and towns. St. John is the largest city and chief industrial and shipping center. Most of the people are French descent, some are descendents from the United Empire Loyalists who left the U.S. after the Revolutionary War. This event of 1783 is still celebrated every year on May 18th in St. John.

New Brunswick has one of the best fishing grounds in North America. Thousands of visitors come here yearly to enjoy fishing, boating and swimming off the banks of the Bay of Fundy and the Gulf of St. Lawrence.

NEW BRUNSWICK

Grand Manan

Bowden, Cecilia
North Head, E0G 2M0
(506) 662-8570,
Off Season: (506) 446-5906

Amenities: 1,5,6,7,9,10,11,12, 13,17,18

Breakfast: F.

Dbl. Oc.: $64.14(CN)
Sgl. Oc.: $47.51(CN)
Child: Under 2 yrs. - no charge

The Compass Rose—Consists of two charming old houses by the sea, close to the ferry wharf. Two ferries operate during the summer months for the 1-1/2 hour crossing from the mainland. Whale watching, hiking, bird watching, photography and an excellent museum.

St. Andrews

Lazare, Kathleen & Michael
59 Carleton St.
P.O. Box 349, E0G 2X0
(506) 529-3834

Amenities: 1,5,6,7,9,10,12,13, 15,17,18

Breakfast: F.

Dbl. Oc.: $90.00(CN)
Sgl. Oc.: $80.00(CN)
Third Person: $20.00(CN)
Child: $20.00(CN)

Pansy Patch—Located in the resort town of St. Andrews. It has a well-deserved reputation for its beautifully furnished rooms, superb water view and the warmth and charm of its atmosphere. The house itself is the most photographed building in New Brunswick.

---

1. No Smoking	5. Tennis Available	9. Credit Cards Accepted
2. No Pets	6. Golf Available	10. Personal Check Accepted
3 Off Season Rates	7. Swimmming Avail.	11. Reservations Necessary
4. Senior Citizen Rates	8. Skiing Available	12. Dinner Available

13. Lunch Available	17. Shared Baths
14. Conference Rooms Avail.	18. Afternoon Tea
15. Group Seminars Avail.	* Commisions given
16. Private Baths	to Travel Agents

NOVA SCOTIA

One Of the Four Atlantic Provinces of Canada

Capitol : Halifax
Entered The Dominion: July 1, 1867;
                    one of the four original provinces.
Provincial Motto: "One Offends and The Other Conquers."
The Floral Emblem: Trailing Arbutus

Halifax is the capitol of Nova Scotia and was founded in 1749 by an English Governor named Cornwallis. He made this city the capitol and to this day it has remained very pro- English and proud of its British connection.

Halifax is an extremely busy and large shipping port, perhaps one of the busiest in the world.

The beaches and resorts of Nova Scotia are beautiful and visitors travel from all over to see and enjoy them. There is great hunting and fishing in this area as well. The climate is conducive to many sports; it never gets too hot nor too cold.

You can read more about Nova Scotia and its early times in Henry Wadsworth Longfellow's poem, Evangeline.

Lunenburg

Heubach, Merrill & Al
Blue Rocks Rd.
RR#l, BOJ 2CO
(902) 634-3426

Amenities: 1,2,3,6,9,16,17
18
Breakfast: F.

Dbl. Oc.: $50.00 - $60.00
Sgl. Oc.: $35.00 - $45.00
Third Person: $12.00
Child: Under 6 yrs. - $5.00

Blue Rocks Road Bed And Breakfast—Join us in our home one mile from Lunenburg on the road to scenic Blue Rocks. Relax in lovely surroundings on Lunenburg Bay. Firm beds, quiet nights, great breakfast with our farm-fresh eggs. Home of the bicyle barn. Everything for the bike tourist. Rentals, too!

1. No Smoking	5. Tennis Available	9. Credit Cards Accepted	13. Lunch Available	17. Shared Baths
2. No Pets	6. Golf Available	10. Personal Check Accepted	14. Conference Rooms Avail.	18. Afternoon Tea
3 Off Season Rates	7. Swimmming Avail.	11. Reservations Necessary	15. Group Seminars Avail.	* Commisions given
4. Senior Citizen Rates	8. Skiing Available	12. Dinner Available	16. Private Baths	to Travel Agents

ONTARIO

Canada's Second Largest Province

Capitol: Toronto
Entered The Dominion: July 1, 1867;
                        — one of the four original provinces.
Motto: "Loyal She Began, Loyal She Remains"
The Floral Emblem: White Trillium

Ontario is most prosperous in agriculture and industry. There are still large farms in this province, even though more than half of its population is urbanized.

Ottawa, the capitol of Canada, is situated in this province and here most of the population is employed by the government. Toronto, the capitol of Ontario, is large and modern and gradually becoming the metropolis and center for all English Canada.

The history of this province is interesting. It was first settled by British loyalists who left the American colonies after the Revolutionary War ended in defeat for the English. As a result, they set the pattern for social behavior, architecture and style of living, which gives it a strong American bond.

There are many lakes which offer a variety of vacation attractions in Ontario. The southern areas along Lake Erie and Ontario are sunny and make for enjoyable vacationing.

The Dionne quintuplets were born here in Callander in 1934 and insulin was discovered here by Frederick Banting and Charles Best in 1921.

ONTARIO

Braiside

McGregor, Noreen & Steve
R.R. #1, K0A 1G0
(613) 432-6248

Amenities: 1,2,12,13,16,18
Breakfast: F.

Dbl. Oc.: $45.00 & $50.00(CN)
Sgl. Oc.: $35.00(CN)
Third Person: $10.00(CN)
Child: Under 6 yrs. -
$10.00(CN)

Glenroy Farm—Our heritage stone home was built over 100 years ago by host's grandfather. Family antiques help to furnish our home and make interesting conversation pieces. Pleasant and practical facilities on our working family farm. Enjoy Ottawa Valley hospitality and scenery.

Branford

McVicar, Sandra
143 Tutela Heights Rd.
R.R. #3, N3T 5L6
(519) 752-2972

Amenities: 3,6,9,16
Breakfast: F.

Dbl. Oc.: $90.00(CN)
Sgl. Oc.: $85.00(CN)

On The Grand Bed & Breakfast—One hour from Toronto, Stratford, & Niagara. Spacious century home on over 1 acre with panormaic views from every room of the Grand River, city lights, & farmland. Historic site. Hike, ski, or fish. Furnished in antiques which are available from our gift store. A warm welcome awaits you.

*Drayton**

McIsaac, Virginia & John
19 King St.
Box 263, NOG 1PO
(519) 638-2190

Amenities: 1,2,8,9,10,11,12,
16,17,18
Breakfast: F.

Dbl. Oc.: $45.00
Sgl. Oc.: $30.00

The McIsaac's—Located in a quiet area of a small town. Home of Drayton Opera House and Old Thyme Jamboree in August. Fiddle and step dancing. Large lawn with lots of trees for shade or to rest under. Member of S.O.C.V.A and F.O.B.B.A.

*Gananoque**

Franks, Carol
279 King St., W., K7G 2G7
(613) 382-3368

Amenities: 1,2,3,4,9,14,15,
16
Breakfast: C.

Dbl. Oc.: $88.00(CN)
Sgl. Oc.: $78.00(CN)
Child: Under 10 yrs. - no charge

The Victoria Rose Inn—A majestic mansion, circa 1872, offering eight guest rooms tastefully furnished in Canadian antiques. All with en suite baths, and Jacuzzis. Five marble fireplaces. Air-conditioned. Silver service at breakfast. Two acres of gardens. Fine dining nearby.

1. No Smoking	5. Tennis Available	9. Credit Cards Accepted	13. Lunch Available	17. Shared Baths
2. No Pets	6. Golf Available	10. Personal Check Accepted	14. Conference Rooms Avail.	18. Afternoon Tea
3 Off Season Rates	7. Swimmming Avail.	11. Reservations Necessary	15. Group Seminars Avail.	* Commisions given
4. Senior Citizen Rates	8. Skiing Available	12. Dinner Available	16. Private Baths	to Travel Agents

ONTARIO

Grafton *

Corcoran, James
RR #1, K0K 2G0
(416)349-2493

Amenities: 1,2,3,5,6,7,9,10,
11,12,13,14,16
Breakfast: F.

Dbl. Oc.: $134.40(CN) and up
Sgl. Oc.: $$95.20(CN) and up
Third Person: $16.80(CN)

St. Anne's Inn—A country castle just one hour from the center of Toronto. This inn is beautifully set in the Northumberland Hills on 560 acres of land overlooking Lake Ontario. All rooms are furnished with antiques and tastefully decorated. Weekend packages include two nights, meals and spa service.

Hunta

Landis, Judy & Larry
P0L 1P0
(705) 272-6302

Amenities: 3,6,7,8,12,16,17
Breakfast: F.

Dbl. Oc.: $50.00(CN)
Sgl. Oc.: $40.00(CN)
Third Person: $10.00(CN)
Child: Under 5 yrs. - $5.00(CN)

Long Lake Farm—In northern Ontario, amid many lakes and rivers. Our log house has three bedrooms for guests. Breakfast is served in the great room or solarium. A log cottage with fireplace, three bedrooms, 1-1/2 baths, overlooking a river is available for $500.00 (CN) per week. Come and relax!

*Kingston-Gananoque**

Hart, Nensi
Hart Country Estate
RR #4, Lansdowne, K0E 1L0(mail)
(613) 659-2873

Amenities: 1,7,11,12,13,17
Breakfast: C. or F.

Dbl. Oc.: $55.00(CN)
Sgl. Oc.: $40.00(CN)
Child: Under 12 yrs.-
$10.00(CN)

Hart Country Estate—In the 1,000 Islands. Large red brick 1890 farmhouse on 75 acres. Menagerie of farm animals. Quiet spot for a getaway. Close to beaches and U.S. border. Children are especially welcome. Enjoy a home-grown dinner on arrival. Write for brochure.

Kitchener

Holl, Maria & Frank
90 Franklin St. No., N2A 1X9
(519)893-4056

Amenities: 1,2,11,17
Breakfast: F.

Dbl. Oc.: $45.00(CN)
Sgl. Oc.: $35.00(CN)

Austrian Home—Enjoy bed and breakfast in our Austrian-style home in Kitchener. The bedrooms have been newly decorated. Kitchener is 80KM east of Metro Toronto and is well known for Oktoberfest, the Farmers' Market Centre in the Square, Mennonites and fine restaurants.

1. No Smoking	5. Tennis Available	9. Credit Cards Accepted	13. Lunch Available	17. Shared Baths
2. No Pets	6. Golf Available	10. Personal Check Accepted	14. Conference Rooms Avail.	18. Afternoon Tea
3 Off Season Rates	7. Swimmming Avail.	11. Reservations Necessary	15. Group Seminars Avail.	* Commisions given
4. Senior Citizen Rates	8. Skiing Available	12. Dinner Available	16. Private Baths	to Travel Agents

ONTARIO

Lakefield *

Wilkins, Joan & Wally
Selwyn, RR 3, K0L 2H0
(705) 652-6290,
Fax: (705) 652-6949

Amenities: 1,2,6,7,8,13,15,16, 17
Breakfast: F.

Dbl. Oc.: $50.00 - $70.00(CN)
Sgl. Oc.: $40.00(CN)
Third Person: $12.00(CN)
Child: $12.00(CN)

Windmere Farm Bed And Breakfast—Our spacious, air-conditioned, century stone farm home is an oasis of country comfort in the heart of the Kawartha Lakes. Local attractions include wildlife art galleries, world's highest boat liftlock, walking trails, fishing and swimming.

Leamington

Tiessen, Agatha
115 Erie St. So., N8H 3B5
(519)326-7169

Amenities: 1,6,7,10,11,16,17,18
Breakfast: F.
Dbl. Oc.: $50.00 - $60.00(CN)
Sgl Oc.: $40.00(CN)
Child: Under 5 yrs. - $5.00(CN)

Home Suite Home Bed And Breakfast—Enjoy warm hospitality in our turn-of-the-century home. Country and Victorian, plush carpeting, hand-sewn quilts, air-conditioned, 40 minutes from Detroit, en route to Niagara Falls. Fine beaches, cycling, canoeing, near Point Pelee National Park. Plan to have a good time.

Niagara Falls

Whiteley, Kathy & Stephen
4835 River Rd., L2E 3G4
(416) 374-8515

Amenities: 2,3,5,6,7,10,11,16,17
Breakfast: F.
Dbl. Oc.: $59.00(US)
Sgl Oc.: $40.00(US)
Third Person: $12.00(US)
Child: Under 12 yrs. - $8.00(US)

Bedham Hall B&B—Welcome to our Victorian, circa 1880, home overlooking the Niagara River. Kathy, formerly from Yorkshire, England, offers a bit of old England in Canada. Perfectly located between the falls, Niagara on the Lake and Shaw Theatre. Bikes available.

---

1. No Smoking	5. Tennis Available	9. Credit Cards Accepted	13. Lunch Available	17. Shared Baths
2. No Pets	6. Golf Available	10. Personal Check Accepted	14. Conference Rooms Avail.	18. Afternoon Tea
3 Off Season Rates	7. Swimmming Avail.	11. Reservations Necessary	15. Group Seminars Avail.	* Commisions given
4. Senior Citizen Rates	8. Skiing Available	12. Dinner Available	16. Private Baths	to Travel Agents

ONTARIO

Niagara-On-The-Lake

Hernder, Pat & Art	**Amenities:** 1,2,5,6,7,16,17	**Dbl. Oc.:** $60.00 - $75.00(CN)
753 Line 3, RR 2, L0S 1J0	**Breakfast:** F.	**Sgl. Oc.:** $55.00 (CN)
(416) 468-3192		**Third Person:** $15.00(CN)
		Child: Under 5 yrs. - no charge

Hernder's Country Home—Located on the wine route in the heart of Niagara's fruitland, our modern and spacious air-conditioned home offers the best of both worlds. A quiet country setting with queen-size beds. Five minutes to Shaw Festival Theatre and shops. Ten minutes to Niagara Falls.

Niagara-On-The-Lake

Hiebert, Marlene & Otto	**Amenities:** 1,2,3,5,6,7,10,11,	**Dbl. Oc.:** $55,00 - $85.00 (CN)
275 John St., W.	16,17	**Sgl. Oc.:** $50.00 - $80.00 (CN)
Box 1371, L0S 1J0	**Breakfast:** F.	**Third Person:** $15.00(CN)
(416) 468-3687		**Child:** under 13 yrs.-
		$10.00(CN)

Hiebert's Guest House—Our quaint, historic town is located 15 miles north of Niagara Falls. The Shaw Festival Theatre, shops, wineries and historic sites are some of the area's attractions. Guest rooms with private or semi-private baths. Non-smoking home. Air-conditioned. Open all year.

Norland

Lowry, Derek	**Amenities:** 2,6,7,8,9,11,12,14,	**Dbl. Oc.:** $75.00(CN)
RR 1, Hwy. 35, K0M 2L0	16,18	**Sgl. Oc.:** $59.00(CN)
(705) 454-1753	**Breakfast:** F.	

Moore Lake Inn—Two hours from Toronto in Haliburton. A turn-of-the-century farmhouse/tavern offering comfort, civility and cuisine. Six double rooms, all with private baths. Our restaurant is considered the best for miles. Close to riding, marinas, winter sports and antiques.

Ottawa *

Bradley, Donna	**Amenities:** 3,4,5,8,9,10,14,15,	**Dbl. Oc.:** $54.00 - $83.00(CN)
172 O'Connor St., K2P 1T5	16,17,18	**Sgl. Oc.:** $49.00 - $78.00(CN)
(613) 236-4221,	**Breakfast:** F.	**Third Person:** $10.00(CN)
, Fax: (613) 236-4232		**Child:** Under 12 yrs. - no charge

O'Connor House Bed And Breakfast—Most centrally located B&B. in Ottawa, a short walk to Parliament buildings, National Gallery, shopping and restaurants. Friendly, pleasant accommodations, air- conditioned rooms. Bicycles, ice skates and tennis. Fantastic breakfast. Minutes to beaches and skiing.

1. No Smoking	5. Tennis Available	9. Credit Cards Accepted	13. Lunch Available	17. Shared Baths
2. No Pets	6. Golf Available	10. Personal Check Accepted	14. Conference Rooms Avail.	18. Afternoon Tea
3 Off Season Rates	7. Swimmming Avail.	11. Reservations Necessary	15. Group Seminars Avail.	* Commisions given
4. Senior Citizen Rates	8. Skiing Available	12. Dinner Available	16. Private Baths	to Travel Agents

ONTARIO

Ottawa

Delroy, Cathy & John
478 Albert St., K1R 5B5
(800) 267-1982, (613) 236-4479

Amenities: 2,3,9,11,14,16,18
Breakfast: F.

Dbl. Oc.: $69.00 - $89.00(CN)
Sgl. Oc.: $59.00 - $79.00(CN)
Third Person: $10.00(CN)

Albert House—Our large Victorian home, built in 1875, is in the heart of downtown Ottawa. All guest rooms are individually decorated and have en-suite facilities. Famous Albert House breakfast. We have two large, but very, friendly dogs.

Ottawa

McElman, Connie
264 Stewart St., K1N 6K4
(613) 233-4433

Amenities: 1,2,17,18
Breakfast: F.

Dbl. Oc.: $65.00(CN)
Sgl. Oc.: $50.00(CN)
Third Person: $15.00(CN)

Ottawa House Bed And Breakfast—A very special place to stay. Downtown location, sumptuous breakfasts, three charming guest rooms, antique furnishings, free parking, walking distance to Parliament, National Gallery and restaurants.

Ottawa

Waters, Carol
35 Marlborough Ave., K1N 8E6
(613) 235-8461

Amenities: 2,3,10,16,17,18
Breakfast: F.

Dbl. Oc.: $45.00 - $60.00(CN)
Sgl. Oc.: 38.00(CN)
Third Person: $15.00(CN)

Australis Guest House—Award-winning, oldest-established B&B in Ottawa. Classic residence with leaded windows and fireplaces. Close to downtown and all amenities in an area of parks, embassies and Rideau River. Hosts have Australian and English backgrounds. Off-street parking. Great breakfasts, baby sitting and rail and bus pick-up.

St. Clements

Frey, Mrs. Amsey
R.R.# 1, N0B 2M0
(516) 699-4668

Amenities: 1,2,3,17
Breakfast: F.

Dbl. Oc.: $45.00(CN)
Sgl. Oc.: $30.00(CN)

The Cottage Bed And Breakfast—A new bungalow on the edge of a small village, beside a wood lot, overlooking a large pond. We are surrounded by a unique rural lifestyle. There are tourist areas of interest, theatres, or you can enjoy a quiet walk in the country.

1. No Smoking	5. Tennis Available	9. Credit Cards Accepted	13. Lunch Available	17. Shared Baths
2. No Pets	6. Golf Available	10. Personal Check Accepted	14. Conference Rooms Avail.	18. Afternoon Tea
3 Off Season Rates	7. Swimming Avail.	11. Reservations Necessary	15. Group Seminars Avail.	* Commisions given
4. Senior Citizen Rates	8. Skiing Available	12. Dinner Available	16. Private Baths	to Travel Agents

ONTARIO

St. Clements

Wideman, Sharon Lee & Jim
Box 212, NOB 2MO
(519) 699-4430

Amenities: 1,5,6,7,8,10,11,16, 17
Breakfast: F.

Dbl. Oc.: $50.00(CN)
Sgl. Oc.: $40.00(CN)
Third Person: $10.00(CN)
Child: Under 5 yrs. - no charge

Riverhouse Bed And Breakfast—Relax on the multi-level deck on the bank of the Conestoga River with a panoramic view of the surrounding farms or take a ride on the paddle boat or canoe. Five minutes to the village of St. Jacobs. Informed hosts will share the rich heritage of the area with you.

Toronto *

Bosher, Kenneth
322 Palmerston Blvd., M6G 2N6
(416) 920-7842, Fax: (416) 960-9529

Amenities: 1,2,9,11,17
Breakfast: C. Plus
Dbl. Oc.: $68.00 - $73.00(CN)
Sgl Oc.: $51.00 - $62.00(CN)
Third Person: $30.00(CN)

Burken Guest House—Stately home located on a quiet residential boulevard adjacent to downtown. Eight tastefully appointed guest rooms with private phones and wash basins. Limited free parking on premises; 24-hour public transit nearby. Eight years of operation, excellent reputation.

Toronto*

Ketchen, Donna
92 Orchard View Blvd., M4R 1C2
(416) 488-6826

Amenities: 1,2,16,17
Breakfast: F.

Dbl. Oc.: $55.00 - $60.00(CN)
Sgl. Oc.: $50.00(CN)

Orchard View—Chosen for "best places to B&B in Ontario." Our spacious 1911 home is uniquely decorated for the 1990s. The double has a private ensuite, the twin, a sitting room and separate entrance to main bath. Centrally located, stroll to shops and restaurants. A $5.00 surcharge for one night.

Toronto

McLoughlin, Katya & Bernard
38 Beaconsfield Ave., M6J 3H9
(416) 535-3338

Amenities: 1,2,11,16,17
Breakfast: F.

Dbl. Oc.: $65.00 - $95.00(CN)
Sgl. Oc.: $55.00(CN)
Third Person: $15.00(CN)
Child: Under 10 yrs. - $5.00(CN)

Beaconsfield B&B—Artist's unconventional 1882 Victorian home full of paintings, plants and pizzazz on quiet downtown avenue. Unique rooms, also private suite. Kitchen facilities, sun decks and many extras. Recipients of Government of Canada Tourism Ambassador Award.

---

1. No Smoking	5. Tennis Available	9. Credit Cards Accepted	13. Lunch Available	17. Shared Baths
2. No Pets	6. Golf Available	10. Personal Check Accepted	14. Conference Rooms Avail.	18. Afternoon Tea
3 Off Season Rates	7. Swimmming Avail.	11. Reservations Necessary	15. Group Seminars Avail.	* Commisions given
4. Senior Citizen Rates	8. Skiing Available	12. Dinner Available	16. Private Baths	to Travel Agents

ONTARIO

Toronto*

Ricciuto, William
235 Beverley St., M5T 1Z4
(416) 977-0077

Amenities: 1,16,17
Breakfast: F.

Dbl. Oc.: $60.00 - $85.00(CN)
Sgl. Oc.: $45.00(CN)
Third Person: $15.00(CN)

Beverly Place—An 1887 Victorian house lovingly restored to its original beauty, complete with exquisite antique furnishings. Grand piano for the music lover. Stroll to all attractions: City Hall, historic Queen's Park, Royal Ontario Museum, art gallery, University of Toronto, Convention Centre and more.

Westport

Saunders, Madeline
Centreville Rd.
R.R. 2, KOG 1XO
(613) 273-3806

Amenities: 1,2,6,7,8,9,11,16,18
Breakfast: F.
Dbl. Oc.: $70.00 - $80.00
Sgl Oc.: $50.00
Third Person: $25.00

Stepping Stone Inn—Beautifully restored and appointed heritage stone home on 150 scenic acres. Quiet environment with three guest rooms. Superb home cooking, fresh country eggs and produce. Swimming, nature walks, golf, many local attractions. Four Kms. south of Westport off #10 Highway.

---

1. No Smoking	5. Tennis Available	9. Credit Cards Accepted	13. Lunch Available	17. Shared Baths
2. No Pets	6. Golf Available	10. Personal Check Accepted	14. Conference Rooms Avail.	18. Afternoon Tea
3 Off Season Rates	7. Swimmming Avail.	11. Reservations Necessary	15. Group Seminars Avail.	* Commisions given
4. Senior Citizen Rates	8. Skiing Available	12. Dinner Available	16. Private Baths	to Travel Agents

PRINCE EDWARD ISLAND

Capitol: Charlottetown
Entered The Dominion: July 1, 1873; the 7th province
Provincial Motto: "The Small Under The Protection
Of The Great"
The Floral Emblem: :Lady's Slipper

P. E. I. as it is often referred to, is the smallest yet the most densely populated province of the Canadian provinces. It is the only one of the provinces that is separated from the main land of North America.

The people of this island depend greatly upon its green meadows and rich red soil for the agriculture which brings them their yearly income.

Tourism helps the economy, too. Over 600,000 vacationers visit Prince Edward Island each year. The climate is mild during the summer and the beaches are beautiful.

The biggest event of the year takes place in August in the capitol of Charlottetown. It is called Old Home Week. People come from all over to enjoy this happy event.

Montague

Currie, Catherine
RR #4, Murray Harbor No.
C0A 1R0
(902) 962-3426

Amenities: 3,6,7,8,9,11,17,18
Breakfast: F.
Dbl. Oc.: $41.80 - $47.30(CN)
Sgl Oc.: $41.80(CN)
Third Person: $8.80 (CN)

Lady Catherine's Bed And Breakfast—Stay in a large Victorian-style home overlooking the Northumberland Strait on the scenic Kings Byway. Rated three stars. Miles of beaches for walking and swimming; two golf courses nearby; antique shop on the grounds; bicycles available for guests.

*Montague**

Partridge, Gertrude
RR 2, Pamure Island
C0A 1R0
(902) 838-4687

Amenities: 1,5,6,7,9,10,11,16, 17
Breakfast: F.

Dbl. Oc.: $50.00(CN)
Sgl. Oc.: $30.00(CN)
Third Person: $10.00(CN)
Child: Under 12 yrs. - no charge

Partridge Bed And Breakfast—Families welcome. Five minutes to white sandy beach, canoe, rowboat and sail s to rent. Bird watching. Baby cribs and highchairs available. Good restaurants nearby. Kitchen for guests' use, private baths, beautiful flowers and comfortable beds.

North Bedeque

Waugh, June & Willard
C1N 4J9
(902) 436-4843

Amenities: 1,2,7,10,11,16,17
Breakfast: C.

Dbl. Oc.: $38.50 (CN)
Sgl. Oc.:$35.00 (CN)
Third Person: $10.00 (CN)

Blue Heron Country B&B — We are located on Rte. IA, 20 minutes from the ferry terminal. 4 spacious, bright and individually decorated guest rooms, one with private bath. Out 1,000 acres family operated grows potatoes. Relax and enjoy complimentary coffee in the evening. 2 miles from summerside.

1. No Smoking	5. Tennis Available	9. Credit Cards Accepted	13. Lunch Available	17. Shared Baths
2. No Pets	6. Golf Available	10. Personal Check Accepted	14. Conference Rooms Avail.	18. Afternoon Tea
3 Off Season Rates	7. Swimming Avail.	11. Reservations Necessary	15. Group Seminars Avail.	* Commisions given
4. Senior Citizen Rates	8. Skiing Available	12. Dinner Available	16. Private Baths	to Travel Agents

QUEBEC

The Largest Province Of Canada

Capitol: Quebec
Entered The Dominion: July 1, 1867
Provincial Motto: "I Remember"
The Floral Emblem: White Garden Lily
Provincial Tree: Sugar Maple

The province of Quebec is quite different from all the other provinces. Most of its people speak French and adhere to French customs. Old Quebec is a site of much history and visitors come here and enjoy the charm of this city and its 300-year-old winding and cobblestone streets.

Montreal is the largest city in this province and it is a beautiful city. It has lovely parks and shops and a large community of business from around the world. It has a metropolitan air about it.

In Montreal, the University of McGill is located. This particular university is English speaking.

Quebec is known for its great religious faith. There are many Catholic and Protestant churches available for the people. Tourists love Quebec and return here by the thousands every day.

QUEBEC

Beauport

Tremblay, Gisele
2515 Ave. Royale, G1C 1S2
(418) 666-4755

Amenities: 2,5,6,7,8,12,13,15, 16,17
Breakfast: F.

Dbl. Oc.: $45.00(CN)
Sgl. Oc.: $35.00(CN)
Third Person: $20.00(CN)
Child: Under 12 yrs.- $10.00(CN)

En Haut De La Chute—Family run B&B home with five rooms; both shared and private baths. Full family-style breakfast is served. Ten minutes from Quebec City and 30 minutes to great skiing areas. Public bus stop right outside the front door.

DeLery

Raymond, Claire
32 Ch Du Lac St. Louis, J6N 1A1
(514) 692-6438

Amenities: 2,6,11,17
Breakfast: F.
Dbl. Oc.: $50.00(CN)
Sgl Oc.: $35.00 - $40.00(CN)
Child: Under 3 yrs. - $10.00(CN)

"La Feuilleraie"—Fifteen miles from Montreal, 12 miles from Dorval Airport. Comfortable, luxurious house on park -like property with trees, green lawns, flowers and panoramic views of St. Louis lake. Relaxing and peaceful. Sailing available.

La Conception

Gosselin, Madeleine & Rolland
2388 Chemin des Pins Blancs,
J0T 1M0
(819) 686-2807

Amenities: 2,3,4,5,6,7,8,12, 13,15,16,17
Breakfast: F.

Dbl. Oc.: $50.00 - $60.00(CN)
Sgl. Oc.: $40.00(CN)
Third Person: $20.00(CN)
Child: $15.00(CN)

Enchanting location by the water. The crystal water and the view are part of the surroundings. Montreal Highway 15 north and Rte. 117 north to La Conception after the bridge and the flashing lights, left on Rue Des Erables, at the sign for Lac-Xavier Chemin Des Pins Blancs turn left.

---

1. No Smoking	5. Tennis Available	9. Credit Cards Accepted	13. Lunch Available	17. Shared Baths
2. No Pets	6. Golf Available	10. Personal Check Accepted	14. Conference Rooms Avail.	18. Afternoon Tea
3 Off Season Rates	7. Swimmming Avail.	11. Reservations Necessary	15. Group Seminars Avail.	* Commisions given
4. Senior Citizen Rates	8. Skiing Available	12. Dinner Available	16. Private Baths	to Travel Agents

QUEBEC

Montreal*

Blondel, Lena Forss
3000 De Breslax, H3Y 2G7
(514) 935-2312

Amenities: 1,11,17
Breakfast: F.
Dbl. Oc.: $60.00 - $70.00(CN)
Sgl Oc.: $55.00 - $65.00(CN)
Third Person: $25.00(CN)
Child: Under 12 yrs.- $10.00(CN)

Montreal Oasis Bed And Breakfast—A spacious home in elegant Driest Farm District, safest neighborhood in downtown Montreal. Near museum, restaurants and shopping. Your Swedish host is world traveled, loves music, food and African art. Friendly Siamese cat. Gourmet breakfast.

Montreal *

Chang, Liling Tokes
3497 Girouard Ave., H4A 3C5
(514) 489-9441

Amenities: 2,3,4,11,17
Breakfast: F.

Dbl. Oc.:$45/00 (CN)
Sgl. Oc. $40.00 (CN)
Third Person: $10.00 (CN)
Child: Under 12 yrs. - $5.00 (CN)

Bed & Breakfast Overseas— There is no better way to be in Montreal than a private home offering you comfort and friendly service at the right price. Five minutes from downtown.

Montreal

Jouhannet, Claude
3422 Stanley St., H3A 1R8
(514) 288-6922
 Fax: (514) 288-5757

Amenities: 3,9,11,16,17
Breakfast: C.

Dbl. Oc.: $69.55(CN)
Sgl. Oc.: $64.20(CN)
Third Person: $10.00(CN)
Child: Under 12 yrs - no charge

Manoir Ambrose—Downtown Victorian-style mansion with 22 rooms - comfortable and quiet at reasonable rates. Right in the heart of the action. Walking distance of Metro Peel shopping area, restaurants and theatres. Cable TV and phone. Your personal host is Lucie.

Montreal

Lauzon, Jean-Paul
4660 de Grand-Pre, H2T 2H7
(514) 843-6458

Amenities: 3,11,17
Breakfast: F.

Dbl. Oc.: $65.00 - $70.00(CN)
Sgl. Oc.: $45.00 - $50.00(CN)

La Maison De Grand Pre—A cozy and quiet 19th-century house with warm hospitality. Near the famous St.-Denis Street, with its restaurants, boutiques and open-door cafes. Two minutes from subway and 15 minutes from the business district. Breakfast has four different menus, fruits and hot bread.

---

1. No Smoking	5. Tennis Available	9. Credit Cards Accepted	13. Lunch Available	17. Shared Baths
2. No Pets	6. Golf Available	10. Personal Check Accepted	14. Conference Rooms Avail.	18. Afternoon Tea
3 Off Season Rates	7. Swimmming Avail.	11. Reservations Necessary	15. Group Seminars Avail.	* Commisions given
4. Senior Citizen Rates	8. Skiing Available	12. Dinner Available	16. Private Baths	to Travel Agents

QUEBEC

Montreal *

Morvan, Annick
151 Sherbrooke Est, H2X 1C7
(516) 285-0895, (516) 285-0140
Fax: (516) 284-1126

Amenities: 2,3,4,9,15,16,17
Breakfast: C.

Dbl. Oc.: $42.00 - $59.00(CN)
Sgl. Oc.: $32.00 - $53.00(CN)
Third Person: $8.00(CN)
Child: Under 12 yrs. - no charge

Armor Inn—A small inn with typical European character. Situated in the heart of Montreal, it offers its guests a warm family atmosphere.. The area contains a great many of Montreal's most fashionable shops and is central to the city's historic district.

Mont Tremblant*

Riddell, Judy & Alex
616 Montee Ryan, J0T 1Z0
(819) 425-7275, 843-1742

Amenities: 1,2,3,5,6,7,8,10, 16,17
Breakfast: F.

Dbl. Oc.: $52.00(CN)
Sgl. Oc.: $26.00(CN)

Chateau Beauvallen—An intimate country inn on private beach and wooded property. The inn possesses a collection of antique Quebecois needlepoint tapestries on display in the pine-paneled lounge and guest rooms. All summer and winter activities available.

New Carlisle West

Sawyer, Helen
337 Rte. 132
Main Hwy.,, G0C 1Z0
(418) 752-2725, 752-6718

Amenities: 2,5,6,7,8,12,13,14,15,17,18
Breakfast: F.
Dbl. Oc.: $35.00(CN)
Sgl Oc.: $25.00(CN)
Third Person: $10.00(CN)
Child: Under 12 yrs. - $5.00(CN)

Bay View Farm B&B—Located on beautiful Gaspe Peninsula. Seaside home with five cozy guest rooms. Home-baked, farm-fresh meals. Crafts, quilts, baking and jams on sale. Quiet, restful. Hiking, bird watching and golf. Spectacular panoramic views. Cottage. Folk music and dance festival in August.

Quebec City*

Butler-Coutts, Joyce
2156 Rue Dickson-Sillery, G1T 1C9
(418) 683-3847

Amenities: 1,5,6,7,8,11,17, 18
Breakfast: F.

Dbl. Oc.: $55.00 - $65.00(CN)
Sgl. Oc.: $55.00(CN)
Third Person: $15.00(CN)
Child: $15.00(CN)

"Fernlea"—A beautiful home with a lovely garden. Quiet residential neighborhood where one can jog, cycle or just stroll. Ten minutes to large shopping malls. One minute to bus for Old Quebec. Easy access to hundreds of fine restaurants. Superb skiing in mid-December. Pick-up tours at door.

1. No Smoking	5. Tennis Available	9. Credit Cards Accepted	13. Lunch Available	17. Shared Baths
2. No Pets	6. Golf Available	10. Personal Check Accepted	14. Conference Rooms Avail.	18. Afternoon Tea
3 Off Season Rates	7. Swimmming Avail.	11. Reservations Necessary	15. Group Seminars Avail.	* Commisions given
4. Senior Citizen Rates	8. Skiing Available	12. Dinner Available	16. Private Baths	to Travel Agents

QUEBEC

Quebec City

Dumais, Dolores
820 Eymard, G1S 4A1
(418) 681-6804

Amenities: 6,8,11,17
Breakfast: F.

Dbl. Oc.: $45.00(CN)
Sgl. Oc.: $35.00(CN)
Third Person: $15.00(CN)

The Battlefield Bed And Breakfast—Between Laval Campus and Walled City. Quebec is a place of history, culture, gastronomy, heritage, nature and distinctiveness. Starting point to Ile-D'Orleans, Ste.-Anne De Beaupre Shrine, Jacques Carteir, Saguenay and St.- Lawrence Valleys and restaurants.

Sacre-Coeur *

Deschenis, Adeline & Jean Pierre
65 Rue Morin Est, G0T 1Y0
(418) 236-4307

Amenities: 5,6,7,17
Breakfast: F.

Dbl. Oc.: $45.00(CN)
Sgl. Oc.: $35.00(CN)
Third Person: $10.00(CN)
Child: $10.00(CN)

"Les Marguerites"—In a scented garden you can smell the homemade bread and fresh jams. Welcome and relax. Located within fjord, Salmon river, lake and Sugar Shack, 15 km from Tadoussac. Whale watching. From Tadoussac, Rte. 138 E. and 172 to Sacre-Coeur. Turn left on Rue Lavoie and right on Morin.

Sillery*

Perigny, Lily
1067 Maguire, G1T 1Y3
(418) 681-3212

Amenities: 1,2,3,8,10,11,16, 17,18
Breakfast: F.

Dbl. Oc.: $50.00 & $60.00(CN)
Sgl. Oc.: $40.00(CN)
Third Person: $10.00(CN)
Child: $10.00(CN)

B&B Bienvenue A Quebec And Sillery—Private and quiet house central to town. Ten minutes to Old Quebec. Single and double beds, private bath. Homemade bread. French hospitality. Love children. Skiing all around. Hosts offer friendly travel ideas. Near bus routes. Hosts will pick up when possible. Welcome home.

St. Bruno De Montarville *

Richard, Dominique
1959 Montarville, J3V 3V8
(514) 653-2149

Amenities: 5,6,7,12,17
Breakfast: F.

Dbl. Oc.: $50.00(CN)
Sgl. Oc.: $30.00(CN)
Third Person: $15.00(CN)

Gite St. Bruno B&B—Offers quick and easy access to Montreal or airports. Quebec City or Ottawa are 2-1/2 hours away via Highway 20. Acre of land, fruit trees, vegetable and flower garden. Barbeque and picnic area. Screenhouse for guests. French, Dutch and English spoken. Open April-November.

1. No Smoking	5. Tennis Available	9. Credit Cards Accepted	13. Lunch Available	17. Shared Baths
2. No Pets	6. Golf Available	10. Personal Check Accepted	14. Conference Rooms Avail.	18. Afternoon Tea
3 Off Season Rates	7. Swimming Avail.	11. Reservations Necessary	15. Group Seminars Avail.	* Commisions given
4. Senior Citizen Rates	8. Skiing Available	12. Dinner Available	16. Private Baths	to Travel Agents

QUEBEC

St. Jean, Ile d'Orleans

Godolphin, Lorraine & John
170 Chemin Marie-Carreau,
G0A 3W0
(418) 829-2613, 829-2871

Amenities: 1,6,7,10,16
Breakfast: F.

Dbl. Oc.: $70.00 - $85.00(CN)
Sgl. Oc.: $60.00(CN)

La Vigie Du Pilote (The Pilot's Lookout)—Come and stay at the river pilot's home. Our tranquil cliff-top setting on four acres of land gives our luxurious home magnificent views of the St. Lawrence River and shipping channel. Only 30 minutes from Quebec City. Fluent English and French spoken.

St. Marc *

Handfield, Conrad
555 Richelieu, J0L 2E0
(514) 584-2226

Amenities: 2,5,6,7,8,9,12,13,
15,16,18
Breakfast: F.

Dbl. Oc.: $61.20(CN)
Sgl. Oc.: $51.19(CN)
Third Person: $11.13(CN)
Child: Under 10 yrs. - no charge

Handfield Inn—Quintessentially French is this inn on the Richelieu River. The rustic decor of this 160-year-old home is complemented with antiques and locally crafted furnishings. Outstanding cuisine, marina and other facilities. Health spa with massotherapy algatherapy, hydrotherapy and beauty care.

Tadoussac

Hovington, Lise & Paulin
285 Des Pionniers, G0T 2A0
(418) 235-4466

Amenities: 3,9,11
Breakfast: C.

Dbl. Oc.: $65.00(CN)
Sgl. Oc.: $60.00(CN)
Third Person: $15.00(CN)
Child: $15.00(CN)

Maison Hovington—In the center of Tadoussac Village facing the St. Lawrence and Saguenay Rivers. Public transportation every day. Fine restaurants and shops. Charming ancestral home. Quiet and relaxed. The country of whales with marvelous scenery and great views.

Val-David

Bourque, Camil & Lise
1267 Ch. de la Sapiniere,
J0T 2N0
(819) 322-6379

Amenities: 1,2,8,10,11,17
Breakfast: C.

Dbl. Oc.: $40.00(US)
Sgl. Oc.: $25.00(US)
Third Person: $10.00(US)
Child: Under 12 yrs.-
$10.00(US)

La Chaumiere Aux Marguerites—One hour north of Montreal. Enjoy a healthy breakfast and relaxing music by the fireplace in this log house. In winter there is a downhill and cross-country skiing area. In summer there is bush walking and mountain climbing. Fine restaurants and genuine art and crafts shops.

1. No Smoking	5. Tennis Available	9. Credit Cards Accepted	13. Lunch Available	17. Shared Baths
2. No Pets	6. Golf Available	10. Personal Check Accepted	14. Conference Rooms Avail.	18. Afternoon Tea
3 Off Season Rates	7. Swimmming Avail.	11. Reservations Necessary	15. Group Seminars Avail.	* Commisions given
4. Senior Citizen Rates	8. Skiing Available	12. Dinner Available	16. Private Baths	to Travel Agents

SASKATCHEWAN

One of the Prairie Provinces of Canada

Capitol: Regina
Entered the Dominion: September 1, 1905
Motto: From Many People Strength
The Floral Emblem: The Prairie Lilly

Saskatchewan is the greatest wheat growing region in North America, producing half of Canada's wheat. The world's largest Grain Handling Cooperative is located in Regina. Saskatchewan has 2/5th of the farmland in all of Canada. More than any of the other Provinces.

The Province got its name from the Sashat River, named by the Cree Indians. It ranks 6th among the Canadian Provinces, and from 1883 to 1905 was the capitol of the Northwest Territories. The Royal Canadian Mounted Police have their training center in Regina.

Ile-a-la-Crosse

Cornett, Ken
Box 238
Ile-a-la-Crosse, S0M 1C0
(306) 833-2590

Amenities: 1,2,4,6,7,8,9,10,
12,13,17,18
Breakfast: F.

Dbl. Oc.: $60.00(CN)
Sgl. Oc.: $44.00(CN)
Third Person: $10.00(CN)
Child: Under 6 yrs. - no charge

Rainbow Ridge Bed And Breakfast—Become one of the family in one of our six luxurious rooms located on a beautiful 14-acre peninsula. To our guests we provide complimentary boats, canoes, Ski-Doo and mini-golf. A very quiet, peaceful and scenic location.

1. No Smoking	5. Tennis Available	9. Credit Cards Accepted	13. Lunch Available	17. Shared Baths
2. No Pets	6. Golf Available	10. Personal Check Accepted	14. Conference Rooms Avail.	18. Afternoon Tea
3 Off Season Rates	7. Swimmming Avail.	11. Reservations Necessary	15. Group Seminars Avail.	* Commisions given
4. Senior Citizen Rates	8. Skiing Available	12. Dinner Available	16. Private Baths	to Travel Agents

NORTHWEST TERRITORIES

Yellowknife *

MacDonald, Jesse
Hearne Hill
X1A 2E6
(403) 920-2061, Fax: (403) 873-8310

Amenities: 1,2,6,7,8,9,11,17
Breakfast: F.

Dbl. Oc.: $70.00(CN)
Sgl. Oc.: $60.00(CN)
Third Person: $15.00(CN)
Child: Over 12 yrs. - no charge

Artic House B&B—A bed and breakfast for the adventurous. Lake view, near floatplanes and Wild Cat cafe. Features good conversation over a sumptuous breakfast. Multiple-night discounts. Airport pick-up with prepaid bookings. Bike, canoe, boating and camping equipment. Tour packages.

YUKON

Dawson City

Magnusson, Inday & Jon
451 Craig St.
Box 954, Dawson City,
Y0B 1G0
(403) 993-5649; Fax (403) 993-5648

Amenities: 1,2,3,4,8,9,10,11,
12,13,16,17,18
Breakfast: C.(summer) &
F.(winter)

Dbl. Oc.: $69.00 - $79.00(CN
Sgl. Oc.: $59.00(CN)
Third Person: $18.00(CN)
Child: Under 6 yrs. -
no charge

Dawson City Bed And Breakfast—Located in a quiet setting at the junction of the Klondike and Yukon Rivers. Northern hospitality with an Oriental theme. Walking distance of downtown attractions. Complimentary airport, bus and waterfront transportaion provided. Open year-round. Free brochure.

---

1. No Smoking	5. Tennis Available	9. Credit Cards Accepted	13. Lunch Available	17. Shared Baths
2. No Pets	6. Golf Available	10. Personal Check Accepted	14. Conference Rooms Avail.	18. Afternoon Tea
3 Off Season Rates	7. Swimmming Avail.	11. Reservations Necessary	15. Group Seminars Avail.	* Commisions given
4. Senior Citizen Rates	8. Skiing Available	12. Dinner Available	16. Private Baths	to Travel Agents

BED AND BREAKFAST

HOMES AND INNS

IN THE CARIBBEAN

BERMUDA

Hamilton *

Smith, Mrs. James
P.O. Box 374,
(809) 295-0503,
Fax: (809) 295-0250

Amenities: 3,5,6,7,11,16
Breakfast: C.
Dbl. Oc.: $136.38
Sgl. Oc.: $114.84
Third Person: $31.32

Oxford Guest House—Closest guest house to Hamilton. Easy walk to bus, ferry and restaurants. All bathrooms en suite with air conditioning, TV and telephone. Sightseeing and sports activities easily arranged. Twelve rooms.

COSTA RICA

Watkins, John A.
Box 1, 3017 San Isidro de Heredia
Box 308, Greenfield, MO 65661(mail)
(417) 637-2066 (U.S.),
(506) 39-8096 (Costa Rica)

Amenities: 9,12,14,15,16
Breakfast: F.

Dbl. Oc.: $45.20
Sgl. Oc.: $39.55
Third Person: $11.30

La Posada De La Montana—Great headquarters for birding trips. Less than three hours to either the Pacific or the Atlantic. Best climate in the country with clean air at 4,500-foot elevation. 5- 1/2 acres. Terrific mountain views. 20 minutes to San Jose. Grow own coffee, fruit and melons. American owned.

SANTO DOMINGO

*Santo Domingo**

Villalona, Mercedes
Dr. Baez #22,
(202) 387-3884, (809) 687-9244

Amenities: 10,15,16,17,18
Breakfast: C.

Dbl. Oc.: $50.00
Sgl. Oc.: $45.00
Third Person: $5.00
Child: Under 3 yrs. - no charge

Mercedes' B&B—Victorian elegance just four houses away from the Presidential Palace. Transportation nearby. Museums, theatres and restaurants within walking distance. Beaches only 45 minutes away. A great Spanish patio to realax on and chat.

---

1. No Smoking	5. Tennis Available	9. Credit Cards Accepted	13. Lunch Available	17. Shared Baths
2. No Pets	6. Golf Available	10. Personal Check Accepted	14. Conference Rooms Avail.	18. Afternoon Tea
3 Off Season Rates	7. Swimmming Avail.	11. Reservations Necessary	15. Group Seminars Avail.	* Commisions given
4. Senior Citizen Rates	8. Skiing Available	12. Dinner Available	16. Private Baths	to Travel Agents

PUERTO RICO

Ceiba *

Treat, Nicki
Carr #977, KM 1.2, 00735
(809) 885-0471

Amenities: 2,9,13,15,16
Breakfast: C. Plus

Dbl. Oc.: $55.00
Sgl. Oc.: $45.00
Third Person: $10.00
Child: Under 1 yr. - no charge

Ceiba Country Inn—A nine-room tropical inn located in the hills above town. A magnificent view of the ocean and the Isle of Culebra. A cozy cocktail lounge and sunny breakfast room. Three miles to Roosevelt Roads Navy Base. Thirty-five miles to the nightlife of San Juan.

UNITED STATES VIRGIN ISLANDS

St. John *

Straubinger, Eric
P.O. Box 350, 00831
(809) 776-6378, (800) 221-1637

Amenities: 2,3,5,9,12,13,16, 17
Breakfast: C.

Dbl. Oc.: $58.00 & up

The Inn At Tamarind Court— Secure, intimate, 20 room inn located just two blocks from the ferry dock. A most convenient retreat while you explore St. John's National Park and unspoiled beaches.

WEST INDIES

Petit Valley, Trinidad *

Theophilus, Rupert
L40 Majuba Cross Rd.,
(809) 632-0113

Amenities: 3,4,5,6,7,11,16
Breakfast: C. Plus

Dbl. Oc.: $69.00
Sgl. Oc.: $50.00
Third Person: Under 10 yrs. - $10.00

Caribbean Condo Villas—Cool suburbs, 10 minutes to town, restaurants and other cultural events. 30 minutes to beaches. Sport malls nearby. Three modern, two bedroom vacation suites that sleep four. Tourism authority approved. Helpful host on site. Public transportation at door. Weekly rates $375.00 - $450.00.

---

1. No Smoking	5. Tennis Available	9. Credit Cards Accepted	13. Lunch Available	17. Shared Baths
2. No Pets	6. Golf Available	10. Personal Check Accepted	14. Conference Rooms Avail.	18. Afternoon Tea
3 Off Season Rates	7. Swimmming Avail.	11. Reservations Necessary	15. Group Seminars Avail.	* Commisions given
4. Senior Citizen Rates	8. Skiing Available	12. Dinner Available	16. Private Baths	to Travel Agents

RESERVATION SERVICES

ALABAMA

Leeds

Redhorse, Kay
Rte. 2, Box 275, 35094
(205) 699-9841

Amenities: 4,6

Dbl. Oc.: $50.00 - $110.00
Sgl. Oc.: $45.00 - $100.00

Bed And Breakfast Birmingham—Southern hospitality assured from north Alabama to the Gulf Coast. Homes in a variety of settings and state-wide locations. Descriptive directory available for $2.00.

Areas covered: Birmingham, Anniston, Huntsville, Decatur, Arab, Mobile area, Muscle Shoals, Alabama and some of Florida.

ALASKA

Anchorage

Mercy, Dennis
P.O. Box 200047, 99520-0047
(907) 258-1717

Amenities: 1,3,4,5,6

Dbl. Oc.: $50.00 - $125.00
Sgl. Oc.: $40.00 - $110.00

Alaska Private Lodging—Offers travelers a selection of accommodations in pleasant private homes. Downtown to wilderness, a great way to discover Alaska and enjoy genuine Alaskan hospitality.

Areas covered: South central Alaska.

Anchorage

Parsons, Jean M.
3605 Arctic Blvd., Ste. 173, 99503
907) 278-8800

Amenities: 1,3,4,5,6,7,8

Dbl. Oc.: $55.00 - $115.00
Sgl. Oc.: $45.00 - $85.00

Accommodations Alaska Style - Stay With A Friend—Alaska bed and breakfasts are extra rooms in private homes. Quality and price sometimes governed by town size as well as location. Homes in larger cities usually offer more amenities: private bath, view, full breakfast. All B&Bs are inspected and rated by guests. One call.

Areas covered: Anchorage, Fairbanks, Palmer, Wasila, Denali Park, Willow, Glennallen, Valdez, Soldotna, Kenai, Homer, Haines, Juneau and Sitka.

Juneau

Hart, Karla & Betty Lou
P.O. Box 21890, 99801
(907) 586-2959

Amenities: 6

Dbl. Oc.: $60.00 - $100.00
Sgl. Oc.: $50.00 - $70.00

Alaska Bed And Breakfast Association—Members are eager to welcome you into their homes, inns and cabins. To enhance your B&B stays, we can also book quality tours. We suggest you plan to spend at least two nights in each home so you have time to truly see Alaska!

Areas covered: Anchorage, Fairbanks, Gustavus (Glacier Bay), Haines Ketchikan, Pelican, Petersburg, Sitka and Skagway.

1. American Express	3. VISA	5. MasterCard	7. Discover
2. Senior Citizen Rates Availble	4. Personal Check accepted	6. Brochure Available	8. Diners Club

ARIZONA

Scottsdale

Thomas, Thomas
P.O. Box 8628, 85252
(602) 995-2831, (800) 266-7829

Amenities: 1,3,4,5,6,7

Dbl. Oc.: $45.00 - $140.00
Sgl. Oc.: $40.00 - $120.00

Bed And Breakfast In Arizona—Experience the heart of the Southwest with our hospitable B&B hosts. All inspected, tops in friendliness, cleanliness. Call us for the best quality B&Bs in Arizona and New Mexico.

Areas covered: Arizona and New Mexico.

Tempe

Young, Ruth
P.O. Box 950, 85280-0950
(800) 456-0682, Fax: (602) 990-3390

Amenities:

Dbl. Oc.: $40.00 - $150.00
Sgl. Oc.: $35.00 - $150.00

Mi Casa Su Casa—Gracious, friendly hosts in inspected and approved homestays, guest cottages, inns and ranches. All are Gold Medallion facilities (highest standards in B&B). Reservation service established in 1981. Directory, available for $9.50, has complete descriptions and rates.

Areas covered: Arizona state wide. (Flagstaff, Phoenix, Scottsdale, Sedna, Tucson etc.), New Mexico and Utah.

Tucson

Janssen, William A.
5644 E. 6th St., 85711
(800) 333-9776, Fax: (602) 790-2399

Amenities: 6

Dbl. Oc.: $40.00 - $105.00
Sgl. Oc.: $35.00 - $85.00

Old Pueblo Homestay B&B R.S.O.— Serving S.E. Arizona, Kino Bay and Mexico.

Areas covered: Bisbee, Green Valley, southeastern Arizona, Tombstone, Tucson and the Kino Bay area of Mexico.

CALIFORNIA

Altadena *

Judkins, Ruth & Cox, Betty
P.O. Box 694, 91003
(213) 684-4428, (818) 797-2055, Fax:(818)798-3640

Amenities: 3,4,5,6

Dbl. Oc.: $40.00 - $80.00
Sgl. Oc.: $30.00 - $75.00

Eye Openers Bed And Breakfast Reservations—Strives to match traveler's requests with a wide range of bed and breakfast homes and inns throughout California. Office hours: Monday - Friday 10:00 a.m. to 6:00 p.m.

Areas covered: California.

---

1. American Express	3. VISA	5. MasterCard	7. Discover
2. Senior Citizen Rates Availble	4. Personal Check accepted	6. Brochure Available	8. Diners Club

RESERVATION SERVICES

Fullerton

Garrison, Theresa
1943 Sunny Crest Dr., # 304, 92635
(714) 738-8361, Fax: (714) 525-0702

Amenities: 1,4,5,6

Dbl. Oc.: $45.00 - $160.00
Sgl. Oc.: $35.00 - $150.00

Bed And Breakfast Of Southern California—Private homes with guest rooms, bed and breakfast inns, furnished houses and studios. From San Diego to San Francisco's coastline, Yosemite, mountain areas, Los Angeles, wine country, Los Cabos, Mexico, anywhere in California. "Getaway!"

Areas covered: All of California: Anaheim, Laguna Beach, Orange County, San Berardino, San Diego, San Francisco and Santa Barbara.

San Francisco

Klein, Sharene
P.O. Box 282910, 94128-2910
(415) 696-1690

Amenities: 1,3,4,5,6

Dbl. Oc.: $125.00
Sgl. Oc.: $58.00

Bed And Breakfast International—One of the oldest reservation services in the U.S. It represents over 350 private homes, inns and guest houses throughout California and Nevada. Victorians, carriage houses, even houseboats. San Francisco, the wine country, Monterey, Yosemite to Los Angeles.

Areas covered: All of California and Nevada.

San Francisco

Kreibich, Susan
P.O. Box 420009, 94142
(415) 479-1913

Amenities: 1,3,4,6

Dbl. Oc.: $55.00 - $200.00
Sgl. Oc.: $45.00 - $150.00

Bed And Breakfast San Francisco—The real hospitality of San Franciscans. Accommodations include Victorian mansions, yachts, houseboats and friendly hosted homestays. Also wonderful B&Bs on the California coast as well as Yosemite and the wine country. All accommodations include full breakfasts.

Areas covered: Carmel, Monterey, San Francisco, wine country, Yosemite and Pacific coast.

San Luis Obispo

Segor, Joyce
1776 Royal Way, 93405
(805) 544-4406

Amenities: 4,6

Dbl. Oc.: $60.00 - $150.00
Sgl. Oc.: $50.00 - $150.00

Meghan's Friends B&B Reservation Service—California central coast. One-time membership fee. Non-smoking private homes and cabins. Ocean beaches, wineries and golfing. See Hearst Castle. Visit Solvang.

Areas covered: Arroyo Grande, Cambria, Morro Bay, Los Osos, Pismo, Sunset Palisades, Paso Roble, Solvang, counties of San Luis Obispo and Santa Barbara and central coast of California.

---

1. American Express	3. VISA	5. MasterCard	7. Discover
2. Senior Citizen Rates Availble	4. Personal Check accepted	6. Brochure Available	8. Diners Club

RESERVATION SERVICES

Whittier

Davis, Coleen
(310) 699-8427

Amenities: 4,6

Dbl. Oc.: $40.00 - $85.00
Sgl. Oc.: $35.00 - $65.00

CoHost, America's Bed And Breakfast—CoHosts enjoy guests, full breakfast, clean bath and a good bed. Extras include: baby-sitting, guided tours, dinner, lunch, picnic baskets, breakfast in bed, aid with travel planning, wine and cheese with conversation on the deck or patio at homes up and down the coast and inland.

Areas covered: All of California: San Diego, Los Angeles, north and south coasts, San Francisco; inland: Yosemite, Lake Tahoe. Selected towns and establishments throughout the U.S.

COLORADO

Denver

Carroll, Cheryl
906 So. Pearl St., 80209
(800) 733-8415, Fax:(303) 733-3615

Amenities: 1,3,5

Dbl. Oc.: $32.00 & up
Sgl. Oc.: $27.00 & up

Bed And Breakfast - Rocky Mountains—A free reservation service for the Rocky Mountain region. Over 200 inns and homestays.

Areas covered: Colorado, Utah and New Mexico.

CONNECTICUT

Guilford *

Taddei, Ernie
329 Lake Dr., 06437
(800) 582-0853

Amenities: 3,4,5,6

Dbl. Oc.: $45.00 - $100.00 & up
Sgl. Oc.: $35.00 - $85.00

Bed And Breakfast/Inns Of New England—Gracious owner hospitality at over 100 locations. Scenic seaport villages, lake front and mountainside retreats. Be close to all major attractions, colleges and businesses. Enjoy 18th-century colonial inns, Victorians, or Georgian mansions. All offer hearty country breakfasts and snacks.

Areas covered: All six New England states: Connecticut, Maine, Massachusetts, New Hampshire, Rhode Island and Vermont.

1. American Express	3. VISA	5. MasterCard	7. Discover
2. Senior Citizen Rates Availble	4. Personal Check accepted	6. Brochure Available	8. Diners Club

RESERVATION SERVICES

New Haven

Argenio, Jack
P.O. Box 216, 06513
(203) 469-3260

Amenities: 4,6

Dbl. Oc.: $50.00 - $75.00
Sgl. Oc.: $45.00 - $60.00

Bed And Breakfast, Ltd.—Offers 125 listings of B&Bs throughout Connecticut, from elegantly simple to simply elegant! Our emphasis is on variety, personal attention and affordability. A quick call assures you of current availability, description and accurate prices. Now in our 10th year!

Areas Covered: Connecticut and some listings in Massachusetts and Rhode Island.

West Hartford

Souza, Michelle
P.O. Box 1117, 06127-1117
(203) 236-6698

Amenities: 1,3,4,5,6

Dbl. Oc.: $45.00 - $150.00
Sgl. Oc.: $45.00 - $90.00

Nutmeg Bed And Breakfast Agency—Connecticut's most comprehensive reservation service offers the best affordable accommodations. Specializing in unique getaways, business travel and reloction. Call from 9:30 a.m. - 5:00 p.m.

Areas covered: Connecticut and a few bordering towns.

DELAWARE

Wilmington

Alford, Millie
Box 177, 3650 Silverside Rd., 19810
(302) 479-9500

Amenities: 2,3,4,5

Dbl. Oc.: $60.00 - $160.00
Sgl. Oc.: $40.00 - $90.00

Bed And Breakfast Of Delaware—Accommodations in private homes and historic small inns. Throughout Delaware, Maryland and Virginia's Chesapeake Bay. Pennsylvania's beautiful Brandywine Valley; Wyeth, Hagley, Winterthur Museums and Longwood.

Areas Covered: State of Delaware: Bridgeville, Dagsboro, Dover, Laurel, Lewes, Milford, Milton, New Castle, Newark, Odessa, Selbyville and Wilmington. State of Maryland: Cambridge, Chesapeake City, Elkton, Oxford and St. Michaels. State of Virginia: Chesapeak Bay area on the eastern shore.

1. American Express	3. VISA	5. MasterCard	7. Discover
2. Senior Citizen Rates Availble	4. Personal Check accepted	6. Brochure Available	8. Diners Club

DISTRICT OF COLUMBIA

Washington

Gillespie, Helen
P.O. Box 12011, 20005
(202) 328-3510

Amenities: 1,3,4,5,6,8

Dbl. Oc.: $50.00 - $225.00
Sgl. Oc.: $40.00 - $100.00

Bed And Breakfast A Featuring accommodations in private homes, apartments, guest houses and inns. Many are historic properties decorated with antiques, some have pools. All are close to public transportation. Friendly and informed owners will assure that your stay is memorable.

Areas covered: Washington, D.C. and nearby Maryland and Virginia.

Washington

Groobey, Millie
P.O. Box 9490, 20016
(202) 363-7767

Amenities: 1,3,4,5,6,8

Dbl. Oc.: $62.55 - $140.25
Sgl. Oc.: $45.90 - $123.60

Bed And Breakfast League/Sweet Dreams And Toast—Represents privately owned homes and apartments in the best, safe sections of the city. Most homes are in the historic districts. All offer easy access to public transportation, many offer parking. All B&Bs are carefully screened and selected.

Areas covered: Washington, D.C., Virginia and Maryland suburbs.

FLORIDA

Anna Maria

Kern, Becky
P.O. Box 628, 34217
(813) 778-6858, (813) 778-4369

Amenities: 1,3,4,5

Dbl. Oc.: $60.50 - $93.50
Sgl. Oc.: $55.50 - $88.00

Rebecca's Bed And Breakfast Accommodations—Specializing in beachside communities for the vacationer or business traveler. Accommodations include hosted and non-hosted homestays and bed and breakfast inns.

Areas covered: Florida's west coast.

Tallahassee

Mahlert, Dianne
106 Hoffman Dr., 32312
(904) 386-8196

Amenities: 3,4,6

Dbl. Oc.: $50.00 - $120.00
Sgl. Oc.: $37.50 - $120.00

Bed And Breakfast Scenic Florida—Outstanding B&B locations from cities to towns, all across north Florida and some beyond. Styles range from Victorian to steamboat Gothic to a vintage yacht. Near business centers, unique recreational spots and beaches. All inspected and approved.

Areas covered: North Florida including Jacksonville, Tallahassee, Ocala, Gainesville and Panama city.

1. American Express	3. VISA	5. MasterCard	7. Discover
2. Senior Citizen Rates Availble	4. Personal Check accepted	6. Brochure Available	8. Diners Club

RESERVATION SERVICES

GEORGIA

Savannah

Fort, Alan **Amenities:** 3,4,5,6 **Dbl. Oc.:** $65.00 - $250.00
(912)232-7787, (800)729-7787, Fax:(912) 236-2880 **Sgl. Oc.:** $60.00 - $100.00

R.S.V.P. Savannah B&B Reservation Service—For wonderful B&B inns and guest houses in Savannah's landmark historic district and down the Georgia coastline. Also Atlanta, Macon and Swainsboro. Charming offerings in Beaufort and Charleston, SC. Call Mon - Fri., 9:30 a.m. - 5:30 p.m. Some accept pets. FAX: (912) 236-2880.

Areas covered: Atlanta, Brunswick, Darien, Macon, Savannah, St. Mary's, St. Simons Island, Swainsboro, Tybee Island, GA; Beaufort and historic Charleston, SC

Thomasville

Watt, Mercer **Amenities:** 4,6 **Dbl. Oc.:** $40.00 - $75.00
Lanigan, Kathy **Sgl. Oc.:** $40.00 - $65.00
1104 Old Monticello Rd., 31792
(912) 226-7218, (912) 226-6882

Quail Country Bed And Accommodations in private homes and guest cottages in Thomasville. Activities of interest include plantation tours, Pebble Plantation, the Lapham-Patterson House, historic restorations, the April Rose Festival and nearby hunting preserves.

Areas covered: Thomasville

HAWAII

Hilo

Diamond, Fred **Amenities:** 4,6 **Dbl. Oc.:** $60.00 & up
P.O. Box 11418, 96721 **Sgl. Oc.:** $50.00 & up
(800)662-8483 (Mainland US),(808)935-4178 (Hawaii)

Go Native..Hawaii—A celebratiion of aloha! Go Native..Hawaii offers a rainbow of choices from mac nut farm on Kauai to a romantic cliff-top gazebo on Maui. From modest to luxury, our island B&Bs are special. A native view of Paradise. Call or write for details.

Areas covered: Each major island in the state of Hawaii.

Honolulu

Bridges, Gene **Amenities:** 3,5,6 **Dbl. Oc.:** $40.00 and up
3242 Kaohiniani Dr., 96817 **Sgl. Oc.:** $35.00 and up
(800) 288-4666, (808) 595-7533, Fax:(808)595-2030

Bed And Breakfast Honolulu—Hawaii's largest B&B agency! Over 350 homestays and studios. Free brochure. Toll-free reservations. Low rates on rental cars and inter-island air coupons. Homestays are like having friends in the islands! AND ONE CALL DOES IT ALL!

Areas covered: All islands in the state of Hawaii.

1. American Express	3. VISA	5. MasterCard	7. Discover
2. Senior Citizen Rates Availble	4. Personal Check accepted	6. Brochure Available	8. Diners Club

RESERVATION SERVICES

Kailua

Carlin, Ann
823 Kainui Dr., 96734
(800) 542-0344

Amenities: 1,3,4,5,6

Dbl. Oc.: $49.05 - $293.40
Sgl. Oc.: $49.05

All Islands Bed And Breakfast—Over 400 unique private homes, studios and cottages. Modest to luxurious. Inspected. Excellent rates for rental cars and inter-island air fares. Call our toll-free number for information and reservations.

Areas covered: All of the Hawaiian islands.

Kailua

Epp, Doris
19 Kai Nani Pl., 96734
(808)262-6026/4848,(800)999-6026,Fax:(808)261-6573

Amenities: 3,4,5,6

Dbl. Oc.: $45.00 - $105.00
Sgl. Oc.: $45.00 - $105.00

Bed And Breakfast Pacific - Hawaii—Beach-front retreats, white-sand beach, ideal swimming or just walking the two-mile stretch of beach. Executive-type homes. Non-tourist environment, yet only 15-minute drive to downtown Honolulu or 30-minute drive to Wakiki.

Areas covered: All the islands of Hawaii.

Kapaa, Kauai

Warner, Evie
P.O. Box 449, 96746
(800) 733-1632, (808) 822-7771

Amenities: 3,4,5,6

Dbl. Oc.: $43.60 - $136.25
Sgl. Oc.: $43.60 - $109.00

Bed And Breakfast Hawaii—A reservation service covering all the Hawaiian islands. We can arrange car rentals as well. B&Bs, suites, cottages in tropical settings. Ask about our guidebook and directory with color pictures and descriptions. Aloha!

Areas covered: All the islands of Hawaii.

ILLINOIS

Chicago

Shaw, Mary
P.O. Box 14088, 60614-0088
(312) 951-0085

Amenities: 1,3,4,5,6

Dbl. Oc.: $65.00 - $85.00
Sgl. Oc.: $55.00 - $75.00

Bed And Breakfast/Chicago, Inc.—We provide pleasant, reasonably priced lodging in guest rooms in private homes, furnished self-contained apartments and small inns. There are over 70 accommodations for you to choose from. Brochure and list upon request. Come stay with us!

Areas covered: Chicago, north shore suburbs and along the shore of Lake Michigan.

1. American Express	3. VISA	5. MasterCard	7. Discover
2. Senior Citizen Rates Availble	4. Personal Check accepted	6. Brochure Available	8. Diners Club

RESERVATION SERVICES

Hoffman Estates

McDonald-Swan, Martha
P.O. Box 95503, 60195-0503
(800) 342-2632

Amenities: 3,5,6,7

Dbl. Oc.: $58.00 - $175.00
Sgl. Oc.: $48.00 & up

B&B Midwest Reservations—Reservations for northern Illinois, from Chicago suburbs to Galena and various locations in southern Illinois, Indiana and Ohio. Private and shared baths, some with Jacuzzis or fireplaces. Call for free borchure and listing. Some homes require two-night minimum. All homes are inspected.

Areas covered: Predominantly northern Illinois (exclusive of Chicago proper), southern Illinois, Indiana and Ohio.

LOUISIANA

New Orleans

Brown, Sarah
3660 Gentilly Blvd., 70005
(504) 947-3401

Amenities: 1,3,5,6,7

Dbl. Oc.: $55,00 (minimum)
Sgl. Oc.: $40.00 (minimum)

New Orleans Bed And Breakfast And Accommodations—Sarah Margaret offers a range from the youth-hostel type to modest accommodations to deluxe in lovely and historic locations. If past intrigues, treat yourself to a visit to our city. Rates increase during Mardi Gras, Jazz Festival, Sugar Bowl; decrease for longer stays.

Areas covered: New Orleans and vicinity.

MARYLAND

Baltimore

Grater, Betsy
1428 Park Ave., 21217-4230
(410) 225-0001

Amenities: 1,3,4,5,6

Dbl. Oc.: $60.00 & up
Sgl. Oc.: $50.00 & up

Amanda's Bed And Breakfast Reservation Service—Private homes, small inns and yachts. Selected properties, urban and rural. In Baltimore, walk or ride the new lightrail to Oriole Park at Camden Yards or venture further afield throughout Maryland.

Areas covered: Exceptional sites in Maryland, Virginia, Pennsylvania, West Virginia, Delaware, New Jersey and D.C.

1. American Express	3. VISA	5. MasterCard	7. Discover
2. Senior Citizen Rates Availble	4. Personal Check accepted	6. Brochure Available	8. Diners Club

MASSACHUSETTS

Bedford

Phillips, Phyllis
48 Springs Rd., 01730
(617) 275-9025

Amenities: 4,6

Dbl. Oc.: $50.00 - $90.00
Sgl. Oc.: $40.00 - $70.00

Bed And Breakfast Folks—A B&B reservation service offering a warm, homey alternative to hotels and motels. Located in 14 towns north and west of Boston.

Areas covered: North and west of Boston, Massachusetts.

Billerica

Carr, Jr., Leo Charles
446 Boston Rd., Ste. 305, 01821-2701
(800) 832-9939

Amenities: 1,3,5

Dbl. Oc.: $30.00 - $120.00
Sgl. Oc.: $20.00 - $110.00

Panda Bed And Breakfast—A bed and breakfast reservation service featuring accommodations of distinction across North America and other countries. Let the travel agent book your transportation, let us book your accommodations.

Areas covered: International.

Boston

Mintz, Ferne
47 Commercial Wharf, 02110
(800) 248-9262

Amenities: 3,4,5,6

Dbl. Oc.: $55.00 - $100.00
Sgl. Oc.: $45.00 - $90.00

A Bed And Breakfast Agency Of Boston—Downtown Boston's largest selection of historic, private homes, including Federal and Victorian townhouses and fully furnished apartments. Exclusive locations include the waterfront/Faneuil Hall, Back Bay, Beacon Hill and Copley Square.

Areas covered: Downtown Boston, Brookline, Cambridge, Cape Cod, Martha's Vineyard, Newton, Nantucket and the north shore.

Boston *

Mitchell, Marilyn
P.O. Box 57166, Babson Park, 02157-0166
(617) 449-5302, (800) 347-5088, Fax:(617) 449-5958

Amenities: 1,3,4,5,6,8

Dbl. Oc.: $60.00 - $125.00
Sgl. Oc.: $50.00 - $90.00

Bed And Breakfast Associates Bay Colony, Ltd.—Friendly, experienced reservationists will help you select just the right B&B or inn for your visit from 150 fully inspected accommodations in desirable locations near public transportation. Call us weekdays from 10:00 a.m. - 5:00 p.m. for the very best B&Bs throughout eastern

Areas Covered: Boston, Brookline, Cambridge, surrounding suburbs, north and south shores and Cape Cod.

---

1. American Express	3. VISA	5. MasterCard	7. Discover
2. Senior Citizen Rates Availble	4. Personal Check accepted	6. Brochure Available	8. Diners Club

RESERVATION SERVICES

Boston

Whittington, Marcia   **Amenities:** 1,3,4,5,6   **Dbl. Oc.:** $54.00 - $120.00
P.O. Box 117, Waban Branch, 02168   **Sgl. Oc.:** $45.00 - $85.00
(617) 244-1308

Host Homes Of Boston—Since 1982, Marcia has culled the best B&B homes close to historic, cultural and business sites. Cordial hosts at exclusive addresses include Beacon Hill, Back Bay, Faneuil Hall and nearby suburbs on the "T." Two-night minimum. Call Monday-Friday, 9:00-4:30. Free directory.

Areas covered: Boston, Brookline, Cambridge, Cape Cod, Cohasset, Marblehead, Milton, Needham, Newton, Swampscott, Wellesley, Westwood and Weymouth.

Brookline

Simonelli, Lauren   **Amenities:** 1,3,4,5,6   **Dbl. Oc.:** $47.00 - $125.00
P.O. Box 1142, 02146   **Sgl. Oc.:** $45.00 - $90.00
(617) 277-5430

Greater Boston Hospitality—Outstanding Georgians, Federals, colonials, and Victorian homes and inns throughout the greater Boston area. Many include parking, most are near public transportation. Excellent values. Visit Boston as a native. Let us make your stay here unusual and memorable.

Areas covered: Boston, Brookline, Cambridge, Charlestown, Danvers, Gloucester, Marblehead, Needham, Newton and Wellesley.

Cambridge

Carruthers, Pamela   **Amenities:** 1,3,5   **Dbl. Oc.:** $60.00 - $105.00
P.O. Box 665, 02140   **Sgl. Oc.:** $50.00 - $95.00
(617) 576-1492, (800) 888-0178

Bed And Breakfast Cambridge And Greater Boston B&B—Attractive, comfortable lodging in private B&B homes. Many have private baths. Excellent public transportation allows you to see everything without a car. Homes inspected regularly. Call us Mon. - Fri.: 10-6, Sat.: 10-3. Brochure available. Come home to us!

Areas covered: In-town Boston, Cambridge, Lexington and Lincoln.

Orleans

Griffin, Richard E.   **Amenities:** 1,2,3,4,5,6   **Dbl. Oc.:** $48.00 - $250.00
Box 1881, 02653   **Sgl. Oc.:** $35.00 - $150.00
(800) 666-HOST

House Guests Cape Cod And The Islands—Features B&B lodgings in expertly restored sea- and whaling- captains' homes dating from 1712. Many are in lovely, wooded settings; others are oceanfront or water view. A selection of cottages and apartments is also available. Send for free 68-page illustrated directory.

Areas covered: Cape Cod, Martha's Vineyard and Nantucket.

1. American Express	3. VISA	5. MasterCard	7. Discover
2. Senior Citizen Rates Availble	4. Personal Check accepted	6. Brochure Available	8. Diners Club

RESERVATION SERVICES

Plymouth

Gillis, Diane
P.O. Box 1333, 02360
(617) 837-9867

Amenities: 1,3,4,5,6

Dbl. Oc.: $60.00 - $125.00
Sgl. Oc.: $45.00 - $65.00

Be Our Guest Bed And Breakfast, Ltd.—Homes range from historic to traditional New England. Hosted by people dedicated to making your stay a memorable one. Visit Plymouth Rock, the Mayflower, Boston and Cape Cod. Enjoy the ocean, fine restaurants and antiquing. Easy commute to all points of interest. Brochure: $1.00.

Areas covered: Cape Cod, Cohasset, Falmouth, Hanover, Kingston, Marshfield, Plymouth, Scituate and south of Boston.

Revere

Schmidt, Leah A.
640 Revere Beach Blvd., 02151
(617) 289-1053, (800) 892-3231

Amenities: 3,4,5,6

Dbl. Oc.: $50.00 - $115.00
Sgl. Oc.: $40.00 - $70.00

Golden Slumber Accommodations—Features an array of exquisite homes, small, gracious inns and courteous hosts representing the finest in affordable, personalized lodging in the favored New England tradition. Children welcome. Limousine service. Hours Monday - Saturday 8 a.m. - 9 p.m.

Areas covered: Massachusetts seacoast including Cape Cod, Greater Boston and south and north shores.

West Hyannis

Diehl, Clark
P.O. Box 341, 02672-0341
(508) 775-2772, Fax: (508) 775-2884

Amenities: 1,3,4,5,6,7

Dbl. Oc.: $48.00 - $185.00
Sgl. Oc.: $40.00 - $60.00

Bed And Breakfast Cape Cod—Select from 90 historic inns or host homes. All inspected and approved. Ocean views, fireplaces, jacuzzis and great breakfasts await your visit. We can help you find the right accommodation to make your vacation memorable. Write, call or fax for information or brochure.

Areas covered: Cape Ann, Cape Cod, Cohasset, Gloucester, Marshfield, Martha's Vineyard, Nantucket, north of Boston, Scituate and the south shore of Boston

1. American Express	3. VISA	5. MasterCard	7. Discover
2. Senior Citizen Rates Availble	4. Personal Check accepted	6. Brochure Available	8. Diners Club

RESERVATION SERVICES

MISSOURI

Branson

Cameron, Kay
P.O. Box 295, 65616
(800) 695-1546, (417) 334-4720

Amenities: 4,6

Dbl. Oc.: $35.00 - $145.00
Sgl. Oc.: $30.00 - $145.00

Ozark Mountain Country Bed And Breakfast Service—There are 80 special places waiting for you in the Ozarks! Quaint inns! Gracious homes! Hospitable farms! Cozy cottages! Suites with relaxing hot tubs! Panoramic views of lakes and mountains! All are carefully selected to provide the quality you expect!

Areas covered: S.W. Missouri and N.W. Arkansas.

MISSISSIPPI

Meridan

Hall, Barbara Lincoln
2303 23rd Ave.
P.O. Box 3497, 39303
(601) 482-5483, (800) 633-MISS, Fax: (601)693-7447

Amenities: 1,3,4,5,6

Dbl. Oc.: $55.00 - $160.00
Sgl. Oc.: $45.00 - $150.00

Lincoln Ltd., Mississippi Bed And Breakfast—Gracious Southern hospitality in Mississippi's loveliest historic inns and private homes. Your personal preferences are carefully considered when placing you with one of our charming hosts. Natchez to Memphis one call 9 a.m. - 5 p.m.

Areas covered: Mississippi: Memphis to Natchez(including Mississippi River Plantation country and Mississippi Gulf coast), S.W. Alabama and eastern Louisiana.

MONTANA

Billings

Deigert, Paula
806 Poly Dr.
P.O. Box 20972, 59104-0972
(406) 259-7993

Amenities: 3,4,5,6

Dbl. Oc.: $40.00 - $175.00
Sgl. Oc.: $35.00 - $110.00

Bed And Breakfast Western Adventure—We can make reservations for you at inspected B&B homes, ranches and cabins in Idaho, Montana, Wyoming and the Black Hills of South Dakota. Free brochure. Directory - $5.00.

Areas covered: Black Hills, So. Dakota, Eastern Idaho, Montana and Wyoming.

1. American Express	3. VISA	5. MasterCard	7. Discover
2. Senior Citizen Rates Availble	4. Personal Check accepted	6. Brochure Available	8. Diners Club

RESERVATION SERVICES

Missoula

Nelson, Ann
P.O. Box 20273, 59801
(406) 258-6191, (206) 282-5994, Fax:(206)282-5994

Amenities: 2

Dbl. Oc.: $85.00 - $525.00
Sgl.Oc.: $45.00 - $275.0

High Country Reservation Services, Inc.—Located in the Blackfoot River Valley. We specialize in Bed and breakfsat homes, ranches and mountians inns. Whatever your dream of a high country vacation; hiking 'The Bob', fly-fishing the wild rivers, hunting or ski-trekiing. 'Packing in', or 'punching cows', call us for assistance.

Areas covered: Glacier and Yellowston Parks, Flathead lake. All wilderness area, including The Bob Marshall Wilderness.

NEW HAMPSHIRE

Guilford, CT

Taddei, Ernest
329 Lake Dr., 06437
(800) 582-0853

Amenities: 3,4,5,6

Dbl. Oc.: $45.00 - $100.00 & up
Sgl. Oc.: $35.00 - $85.00

New Hampshire Bed And Breakfast—Over 100 hosts close to four- season recreation, scenic mountain, lakes and seacoast views. Experience 18th-century colonial inns, lake-front homes, New England village settings, close to colleges, businesses, antiques and atttractions. All with gracious owner hospitality.

Areas covered: All of Connecticut, Maine, Massachusetts, New Hampshire, Rhode Island and Vermont,

Strafford

Raiche, Caren
121 Barberry Lane, 03884
(603) 664-5492

Amenities: 1,3,4,5,6,7

Dbl. Oc.: $45.00 - $300.00
Sgl. Oc.: $30.00 - $150.00

Bed And Breakfast Of New England—Reservations can be made for over 100 B&B accommodations located throughout Maine, New Hampshire, Vermont and Massachusetts. Brochure and detailed accommodation list available. Office hours are Monday to Friday - 8 a.m. to 5 p.m.; Saturday - 8 a.m. to 1 p.m.

Areas covered: Maine, Massachusetts, New Hampshire and Vermont.

NEW JERSEY

Princeton

Hurley, John
P.O. Box 571, 08542
(609) 924-3189

Amenities: 6

Dbl. Oc.: $50.00 - $65.00 & up
Sgl. Oc.: $40.00 - $55.00 & up

Bed And Breakfast Of Princeton—Provides a pleasant alternative to local hotel lodging. Private homes that are either a few miles drive or within walking distance of the town center and universities.
Areas covered: Princeton, N.J.

1. American Express	3. VISA	5. MasterCard	7. Discover
2. Senior Citizen Rates Availble	4. Personal Check accepted	6. Brochure Available	8. Diners Club

RESERVATION SERVICES

Toms River

Coccia, Debbie
1905 Breckenridge Pl., 08755
(800) 374-STAY

Amenities: 2,4,6
Breakfast: $65.00 - $170.00

Dbl. Oc.: $55.00 - $110.00

Plain And Fancy Bed And Breakfast Reservation—Service - Debbie's hospitality files offer you a genuine B&B experience including cottages, country inns and farmhouses located in the New Jersey, Pennsylvania area. Local activities include antique shops, cycling, ballooning, beaches and Victorian house tours.

Areas covered: New Jersey; Bay Head, Belmar, Cape May, Lambertville and Stan Hope. Pennsylvania; Ephrata, Holicong, Lancaster, New Hope and Upper Black Eddy.

NEW YORK

Buffalo

Brannan, Georgia A.
466 Amherst St., 14207-2844
(716) 874-8797

Amenities: 3,4,5,6

Dbl. Oc.: $55.00 - $150.00
Sgl. Oc.: $45.00 - $55.00

Rainbow Hospitality, Inc., B&B Reservation Service—Niagara Falls, Buffalo, Rochester, Toronto and Lake Ontario to northern Pennsylvania - one phone call opens the door to over 70 fine, quality bed and breakfast accommodations! We provide the options, you make the choice.

Areas covered: Buffalo, Lake Ontario to northern Pennsylvania, Niagara Falls, Rochester, Syracuse, NY, and Toronto, Ontario.

Delmar *

Copeland, Arthur
4 Greenwood Lane, 12054
(518) 439-7001

Amenities: 1,2,3,4,5,6

Dbl. Oc.: $37.45 - $218.50
Sgl. Oc.: $27.45 - $170.50

The American Country Collection Of Bed And—Breakfast And Country Inns. Relax and enjoy at any of the 118 fully inspected B&Bs/country inn locations. Many of our B&B's are in or near cities, historic locations. They offer a variety of special amenities such as fresh flowers, in-room fireplace, pools and air conditioning.

Areas covered: Eastern New York, western Massachusetts, all of Vermont and St. Thomas, U.S.V.I.

New York City

Goldberg, Leslie
134 W. 32nd, Ste. 602, 10001
(212) 645-8134

Amenities: 4,6

Dbl. Oc.: $75.78 - $311.44
Sgl. Oc.: $54.13 - $64.95

Bed And Breakfast Network Of New York—We represent B&Bs in the most exciting parts of town such as Greenwich Village, midtown and the upper east and west sides. Everything from lofts to brownstones to high-rise condos. Weekly and monthly rates available for both hosted and unhosted accommodations.

Areas covered: New York City.

1. American Express	3. VISA	5. MasterCard	7. Discover
2. Senior Citizen Rates Availble	4. Personal Check accepted	6. Brochure Available	8. Diners Club

RESERVATION SERVICES

Syracuse

Samuels, Elaine   **Amenities:** 4,6   **Dbl. Oc.:** $48.15 & up
4989 Kingston Rd., Elbridge (mail), 13060   **Sgl. Oc.:** $37.45 & up
(315) 689-2082

Elaine's Bed And Breakfast Reservation Service—Modest to elegant home-style rooms in the city ad country. Near lakes, colleges, restaurants, skiing, boutiques, galleries, antiques, theatre, state fair, tennis, golf, concerts, malls, sport events, sightseeing, cruises, arts and crafts and peace. Fresh air. All inspected.

Areas covered: Central New York, Syracuse and suburbs, Finger Lakes, Cazenovia, Rome, Vernon, Savanac Lake, Geneva; the Berkshires in western Massachusetts.

OHIO

Cleveland

Phillips, Ms. E.   **Amenities:** 4,6   **Dbl. Oc.:** $85.00
P.O. Box 18590, 44118   **Sgl. Oc.:** $35.00
(216) 249-0400

Private Lodgings, Inc.—Many unique and historic homes located close to Cleveland's cultural, business, medical centers as well as country and recreational areas. Daily, weekly and monthly stays. Houses and apartments also available. Open: 9 a.m. - 12 p.m and 3 p.m. - 5 p.m. Closed Wednesday.

Areas covered: Greater Cleveland area.

PENNSYLVANIA

Devon (Philadelphia)

Gregg, Peggy   **Amenities:** 1,3,4,5,6   **Dbl. Oc.:** $40.00 - $195.00
Scribner, Lucy   **Sgl. Oc.:** $30.00 - $125.00
P.O. Box 21, 19333
(215) 687-3565, (800) 448-3619

Bed And Breakfast Connections—Gracious hosts welcome you to pre-Revolutionary colonials, quaint 1800s townhouses and farmhouses, contemporary homes and turn-of-the-century mansions. Also quaint country inns. All personally inspected and Gold Medallion certified. Reservations: Monday - Saturday, 9 a.m. - 9 p.m.

Areas covered: Philadelphia, suburbs, Valley Forge, Brandywine Valley, Pennsylvania Dutch country, York and Reading.

1. American Express	3. VISA	5. MasterCard	7. Discover
2. Senior Citizen Rates Availble	4. Personal Check accepted	6. Brochure Available	8. Diners Club

RESERVATION SERVICES

Gettysburg

Rice, Nancy
240 Baltimore St., 17325
(800) 247-2216

Amenities: 3,4,6

Dbl. Oc.: $53.00 - $132.50

Inns Of The Gettysburg Area—Privately owned inns located in Gettysburg and surrounding area. All are historic buildings expressing each inn's unique place in history. The hosts will be happy to offer invaluable assistance on what to see. Maps for biking inn-to-inn are available.

Areas covered: Pennsylvania; Gettysburg, Hanover and East Berlin. Maryland: Taneytown and Emmitsburg.

Philadelphia

Ralston, Joan R.
1616 Walnut St., Ste. 1120, 19103
(800) 733-4747, (215) 358-4747

Amenities: 1,3,4,5,6

Dbl. Oc.: $35.00 - $125.00
Sgl. Oc.: $25.00 - $85.00

Bed And Breakfast Philadelphia—Pennsylvania's original bed and breakfast service. Center of city townhouses, suburban manors, country inns and farms. Short- and long-term stays. Monday - Friday 9 a.m. - 7 p.m.; Saturday 10 a.m. - 4 p.m.

Areas covered: Historic areas, Valley Forge, New Hope, Brandywine Valley and Amish country.

Valley Forge

Williams, Carolyn
P.O. Box 562, 19481-0562
(215) 783-7838, (800) 344-0123, Fax:(215) 783-7783

Amenities: 1,3,4,5,6,8

Dbl. Oc.: $42.40 - $132.50
Sgl. Oc.: $21.20 - $79.50

All About Town B&B—There is a B&B for you! Business, vacation, getaways, relocating. Request B&B near your destination, family plan, jacuzzi, pool, dinner/theatre reservations, descriptive directory $3.00. Estate cottages, inns, town, historic & ski locations. Featured in Philadelphia Magazine.

Areas covered: Brandywine, Bucks county and Lancaster county, Philadelphia and Valley Forge.

West Chester

Archbold, Janice K.
Box 2137, 19380
(215) 692-4575, Fax: (215) 692-4451

Amenities: 1,3,4,5,6

Dbl. Oc.: $70.00 - $200.00 & up
Sgl. Oc.: $65.00 - $200.00 & up

Guesthouses, Inc.—Specializing in historic private and public landmarks and National Register sites. "Brandywine Breakaway" package - three days, two nights, admissions, dinner - $320.00 per couple. Includes taxes and gratuities. Call Monday-Friday, 12 p.m. - 4 p.m. to make reservations.

Areas covered: Delaware, District of Columbia, Chesapeake Bay, Maryland, New Jersey and Pennsylvania.

---

1. American Express
2. Senior Citizen Rates Availble
3. VISA
4. Personal Check accepted
5. MasterCard
6. Brochure Available
7. Discover
8. Diners Club

RHODE ISLAND

Newport

Meiser, Joy
38 Bellevue Ave., 02840
(401) 849-1298(reservations), (800) 628-INNS(info)

Amenities: 1,3,4,5

Dbl. Oc.: $45.00 - $115.00
Sgl. Oc.: $50.00 - $115.00

Bed And Breakfast Of Rhode Island—We have selected B&Bs that will add to your comfort during your visit to Rhode Island. Personally inspected. All our B&Bs meet our high standards of cleanliness, comfort and represent a wide range of styles and prices.

Areas covered: Rhode Island and southern Massachusetts.

SOUTH CAROLINA

Charleston

Fairey, Charlotte
43 Legare St., 29401
(803) 722-6606

Amenities: 1,3,4,5,6

Dbl. Oc.: $55.00 - $135.00
Sgl. Oc.: $55.00 - $135.00

Historic Charleston And South Carolina Bed And—Breakfast - A reservation service for the state of South Carolina with the largest number of homes in Charleston's historic district. Many historic homes, two plantations and several inns are included in our listings. Near beaches, lakes, museums and many cultural activities.

Areas covered: Charleston, Columbia, Hilton Head and Summerville.

TENNESSEE

Hampshire

Jones, Kay
P.O. Box 193, 38461
(615) 285-2777, (800) 377-2770

Amenities: 3,4,5,6

Dbl. Oc.: $50.00 - $125.00
Sgl. Oc.: $45.00 - $108.00

Natchez Trace Bed And Breakfast Reservation Serv.—A favorite of history buffs, the Natchez Trace is a scenic national parkway from Nashville, TN, to antebellum Natchez, Mississippi. Kay's information about the Trace and her interesting homes along the way make your trip an unhurried excursion into yesteryear.

Areas covered: Mississippi: Columbus, Corinth, French Camp, Kosciusko and Vicksburg.

Memphis

Denton, Helen V.
P.O. Box 41621, 38174-1621
(901) 726-5920

Amenities: 3,4,5,6

Dbl. Oc.: $50.96 - $159.00
Sgl. Oc.: $50.96 - $159.00

Bed And Breakfast In Memphis—Lxury accommodations in private homes, fully furnished apartments and condos in carefully selected locations throughout the city. Weekly and monthly rates available.

Areas covered: Statewide.

1. American Express	3. VISA	5. MasterCard	7. Discover
2. Senior Citizen Rates Availble	4. Personal Check accepted	6. Brochure Available	8. Diners Club

RESERVATION SERVICES

Nashville

Odom, Fredda
P.O. Box 110227, 37222
(615) 331-5244

Amenities: 1,3,4,5,6,7

Dbl. Oc.: $55.00 - $125.00
Sgl. Oc.: $45.00 - $100.00

Bed And Breakfast - Tennessee—Use our service to save toll calls for domestic and international reservations in over 700 inns and homestays all over the world. A small processing fee will be accessed and a credit-card number is required.

Areas covered: State of Tennessee.

TEXAS

San Antonio

Campbell, Lavern
166 Rockhill, 78209
(512) 824-8036, Fax: (800) 356-1605

Amenities: 1,2,3,4,5,6,7

Dbl. Oc.: $62.15 - $124.30
Sgl. Oc.: $48.03 - $121.90

Bed And Breakfast Hosts Of San Antonio—Friendly hosts welcome you to our historic, romantic city. Don't miss the Alamo, Paseo Del Rio (bustling river walk), Sea World, Fiesta Texas, the Missions, Brackenridge Park Zoo, Botanical center, art museums, El Mercado (Mexican and farmer's market). Wonderful shopping and dining.

Areas covered: San Antonio and outlying areas of south Texas.

VIRGINIA

Alexandria

Mansmann, Mr. E.Ô.
819 Prince St., 22314
(703) 683-2159

Amenities: 4

Dbl. Oc.: $78.38 - $88.83

Princely Bed and Breakfast, Ltd.—Delux program, historic homes (1750) - 1870) many with museum quality antiques. Closest area to Washington D.C. New metro subway is fast, frequent, immaculate - 15 minutes to D.C. Call Mondays, Thursdays or Fridays.

Areas covered: Alexandria.

Berryville

Duncan, Rita
Rte. 2, Box 3895, 22611
(703) 955-1246, (800) 296-1246

Amenities:

Dbl. Oc.: $50.00 - $180.00
Sgl. Oc.: $45.00 - $90.00

Blue Ridge Bed & Breakfast—Historic farms, gracious homes and quaint inns with romantic rooms. Fishing, canoeing, skiing, hiking, hunting, antique shopping, swimming, horseracing, mountains, fall foliage, Shenandoah Valley, Appalachian Trail and Harpers' Ferry.

Areas covered: Maryland, Pennsylvania,Virginia and West Virginia.

1. American Express	3. VISA	5. MasterCard	7. Discover
2. Senior Citizen Rates Availble	4. Personal Check accepted	6. Brochure Available	8. Diners Club

RESERVATION SERVICES

Charlottesville

Capertown, Mary Hill
P.O. Box 5737, 22903
(804) 979-7264(12-5p.m.)

Amenities: 1,3,4,5,6

Dbl. Oc.: $52.98 - $141.50
Sgl. Oc.: $56.42 - $162.75

Guesthouses B&B Inc.—Accommodations in distinctive, private homes, suites and guest cottages. Country and town locations near Jefferson's Monticello, the University of Virginia and the Blue Ridge Mountains. Call or send for descriptive brochure - $1.00. Call 12 p.m - 5 p.m. weekdays.

Areas covered: Charlottesville and Albemarle County, Virginia.

Norfolk

Furr, Betty
Ridgely, Nash
P.O. Box 6226, 23508
(804) 627-1983

Amenities: 4,6

Dbl. Oc.: $55.00 - $150.00
Sgl. Oc.: $50.00 - $100.00

Bed And Breakfast Of Tidewater Virginia—Select homes, inns and yachts. Historic and resort areas on the Atlantic Ocean, Chesapeake Bay, Rappahannock and Elizabeth River. Day cruises, antiques, museums, medical center. Swim, fish, sail. Seafood. Town or country.

Areas covered: Eastern Virginia (coastal), Norfolk, Virginia Beach, the eastern shore, northern neck and Matthews county.

Richmond

Benson, Lyn
2036 Monument Ave., 23220
(804) 353-6900

Amenities: 4,6

Dbl. Oc.: $69.23 - $147.50
Sgl. Oc.: $69.23 - $147.50

Bensonhouse Reservation Service Of Virginia—Representing 40 carefully selected small inns and private homes in Fredericksburg, Richmond, Williamsburg, Norfolk and the eastern shore. Most are of architectural interest and in historic areas. Most have private baths and some have fireplaces and jacuzzis.

Areas covered: Fredericksburg, Norfolk, Petersburg, Richmond, Williamsburg and the eastern shore of Virginia.

Williamsburg

Zubkoff, Sheila R.
P.O. Box 838, 23187
(804) 253-1571

Amenities: 4,6

Dbl. Oc.: $52.40 - $101.18
Sgl. Oc.: $42.08 - $90.53

The Travel Tree Reservation Service—Williamsburg's B&B reservation service offers the finest accommodations: quaint dormered rooms, elegant suites, a cozy cottage and more! Choose gracious private homes or small inns, some within walking distance of historic area, others within 1-4 miles. Mon. - Fri., 6 p.m. - 9 p.m.

Areas covered: U.S., Canada and overseas.

---

1. American Express	3. VISA	5. MasterCard	7. Discover
2. Senior Citizen Rates Availble	4. Personal Check accepted	6. Brochure Available	8. Diners Club

CANADA

Vancouver, British Columbia

Burich, Helen
2803 W. 4th Ave.
Box 74542, V6K 1K2
(604) 731-5942

Dbl. Oc.: $65.00 - $150.00(CN)
Sgl. Oc.: $45.00 - $65.00(CN)

Town And Country Bed And Breakfast In British—Columbia Reservation Service offering modest to luxurious accommodations with rates accordingly. Some cottages available. Guide listing 200 homes in British Columbia available for $13.00 (U.S.) from above address. We have been established since 1980.

Areas covered: Vancouver, Victoria and Vancouver Island.

Vancouver, British Columbia

Tyndall, Vicki
1226 Silverwood Crescent
North Vancouver, V7P 1J3
(604) 986-5069, Fax: (604) 986-8810

Amenities: 3,5,6

Dbl. Oc.: $60.00 - $120.00(CN)
Sgl. Oc.: $45.00 - $90.00(CN)

Old English Bed And Breakfast Registry—A professional reservation service. We represent personally inspected homes in Vancouver and Victoria. These homes will provide you a friendly, ho ospitable, relaxing stay. One telephone call is all it takes.

Areas covered: Greater Vancouver and Victoria.

Victoria, British Columbia

Catterill, Kate
P.O. Box 5511 Stn. 'B'
Victoria, V8R 6S4
(604) 595-2337

Amenities: 3,5

Dbl. Oc.: $65.00 - $190.00(CN)
Sgl. Oc.: $45.00 - $90.00(CN)

All Seasons Bed And Breakfast Agency, Inc.—There is an accommodation style for everyone. Personally inspected B&Bs in heritage, garden and waterfront homes. Brochure available. We are a personalized service geared to the discriminating traveler.

Areas covered: Victoria, Vancouver Island and Gulf Islands.

Victoria, British Columbia

Wensley, Doreen
660 Jones Terrace, V8Z 2L7
(604) 479-1986, 479-9999

Amenities: 1,3,5

Dbl. Oc.: $55.00 - $190.00(CN)
Sgl. Oc.: $40.00 - $75.00(CN)

Garden City B&B Reservation Service—No booking fee. Catering to vacationers, honeymooners and itineraries, etc. Majestic heritage to demure cozy cottage in excellent locations. Doreen's caring attention to detail ensures the best possible accommodations. Phone 7:30 a.m. - 10 p.m., Mon.-Sat. Sunday 2 p.m. - 8 p.m.

Areas covered: Victoria, Vancouver Island and Gulf Island

1. American Express	3. VISA	5. MasterCard	7. Discover
2. Senior Citizen Rates Availble	4. Personal Check accepted	6. Brochure Available	8. Diners Club

RESERVATION SERVICES

Leamington, Ontario

Tiessen, Agatha   **Amenities:**4   **Dbl. Oc.:** $50.00 - $60.00(CN)
115 Erie St., N8H 3B5   **Sgl. Oc.:** $40.00 - $47.00(CN)
(519) 326-7169

Point Pelee Bed & Breakfast Reservation Service — Welcome to the southern most tip of the Canadian mainland, Point Pelee National Park, world famous for bird watching. 40 minutes from Detroit beaches. Cycling, canoeing, golfing, dinner theatres, and winery tours. Early bird breakfast for bird watchers. Great restaurants in the area.

Areas covered: Leamington.

Ottawa, Ontario

Rivoire, Robert   **Amenities:** 6   **Dbl. Oc.:** $50.00 (CN)
488 Cooper St., K1R 5H9   **Sgl. Oc.:** $40.00 (CN)
(613) 563-0161

Ottawa Bed & Breakfast: Welcome to friendly and affordable accommodations in Canada's capital. Your hosts are residents of Ottawa who are anxious to meet you and show you their homes and provide you with much advice about out city.

Areas covered: Ottawa.

Toronto, Ontario

Gray, Niloufer   **Amenities:** 3,4,6   **Dbl. Oc.:** $55.00 - $75.00(CN)
P.O. Box 190, Stn. B., M5T 2W1   **Sgl. Oc.:** $45.00 - $65.00(CN)
(416) 690-1724

Downtown Tour Association Of B&B Guesthouses—In our 11th year with the largest selection of downtown properties. All non-smoking. Parking. Apartments, suites, private homes and en suites, some air-conditioned. Six languages spoken. All hosts are active in the arts-and-hospitality industry. Tell us your needs.

Areas covered: Toronto.

Toronto, Ontario

Ketchen, Donna   **Amenities:** 6   **Dbl. Oc.:** $40.00 - $65.00(CN)
P.O. Box 46093   **Sgl. Oc.:** $30.00 - $55.00(CN)
College Park P.O., M5B 2L8
(416) 363-6362

Bed And Breakfast Homes Of Toronto—An established B&B association with a refreshing difference. A cooperative of 20 friendly, independent homes allows you to speak directly with the host of your choice before booking. Standards are high, yet room rates are low. No hidden commissions.

Areas covered: Metropolitan Toronto.

1. American Express	3. VISA	5. MasterCard	7. Discover
2. Senior Citizen Rates Availble	4. Personal Check accepted	6. Brochure Available	8. Diners Club

RESERVATION SERVICES

Toronto, Ontario

Page, Larry
P.O. Box 269,
253 College St., M6G 3A7
(416) 588-8800

Amenities: 3,5,6,8

Dbl. Oc.: $50.00 - $85.00(CN)
Sgl. Oc.: $40.00 - $75.00(CN)

Toronto Bed & Breakfast—Toronto's oldest professional bed and breakfast reservation service. A quality registry, now in its 14th year. 25 selected hosts help you discover Toronto with a variety of homes throughout the metropolitan area. A free brochure is available upon request.

Areas covered: Toronto.

Montreal, Quebec

Finkelstein, Bob
3458 Laval Ave. (at Sherbrooke St.)
Montreal, H2X 3C8
(514) 289-9749, Fax: (514) 287-7386

Amenities: 3,5,6

Dbl. Oc.: $35.00 - $55.00(CN)
Sgl. Oc.: $25.00 - $40.00(CN)

A Bed And Breakfast - A Downtown Network—A network of fine private homes offering comfortable accommodations, including a complete breakfast, at prices you can well afford. Downtown Old Montreal, Latin Quarter our specialty. One of Canada's oldest bed and breakfast networks.

Areas covered: Montreal (particuly downtown), Old Montreal and the Latin Quarter.

Quebec, Quebec

Blanchet, Raymond
3765 Rd. Monaco,G1P 3J3
(418) 527-1465

Amenities: 4,6

Dbl. Oc.: $45.00 - $95.00(CN)
Sgl. Oc.: $35.00 - $45.00(CN)

Bed And Breakfast Bonjour Quebec—For reservations: write or phone to the above. Denise and Raymond Blanchet will forward, by mail, information as well as a city map with directions. The first R.S.O. of Quebec represents 11 homes selected to make your visit a genuine French experience.

Areas covered: Quebec City.

UNITED STATES VIRGIN ISLANDS

St. John

Zalis, Annellen
P.O. Box 191, 00830
(809) 779-4094, (809) 776-7836

Amenities: 6

Dbl. Oc.: $75.00 - $115.00
Sgl. Oc.: $60.00 - $105.00

V.I. B&B Homestays—Stay in a hillside home with breathtaking ocean views or in a luxurious waterfront setting. V.I.B&B will reserve your host home. Let us arrange it for you: jeep rentals, island tours, day sails, diving trips and space on the most beautiful beaches in the world!

1. American Express	3. VISA	5. MasterCard	7. Discover
2. Senior Citizen Rates Availble	4. Personal Check accepted	6. Brochure Available	8. Diners Club

RESTAURANTS

RESTAURANTS

ALASKA

Anchorage

Sacks Cafe
625 W. 5th Ave., 99501
(907) 274-4022

Amenities: 1,3,4,9,13
Lunch: $4.50 - $9.00

Appetizer: $6.75 - $9.00
Entree: $11.00 - $18.50
Dessert: $4.75

Located in downtown Anchorage, featuring fresh seafood, daily specials, fresh pasta, unique sandwiches, salads and desserts. Light, airy and relaxed atmosphere.

Hours: 11 a.m. - 5 p.m. (Mon. - Sun.), 11 a.m. - 11 p.m . (Fri. & Sat.),
   Sunday Brunch: 11 a.m. - 2:30 p.m.

ARIZONA

Pinetop/Lakeside

The Dining Room At The Meadows Inn
453 N. Woodland Rd., 85929
(602) 367-8200

Amenities: 1,3,4,7,9,10,12
Breakfast: $7.00 - $10.00
Lunch: $10.00 - $20.00
Appetizer: $4.00 - $6.00
Entree: $15.00 - $20.00
Dessert: $4.00 - $6.00

Enjoy our country breakfast and gourmet lunches in "The Dining Room" or on the veranda. Homemade soups and desserts. Wonderful salads, sandwiches and specialties from The Meadows' own chef. Relax in our cozy wine bar and experience one of our exceptional wines.

Hours: Breakfast 7 a.m. - 10 a.m., Lunch: 11:30 a.m. - 3 p.m., Open for dinner.

CALIFORNIA

Eureka

Hotel Carter Restaurant
301 L. St., 95501
(707) 444-8062

Amenities: 1,2,3,4,5,7,9,13
Brunch: $11.50 - $7.50
(No charge to hotel guests.)

Entree: $25.00 (includes
   appetizer and dessert.)

Specializing in regional seasonal cuisine, we use only local produce, cheeses and seafood, in addition to herbs and vegetables from our own gardens. Superb wines and service.

Hours: 6 p.m. - 10:10 p.m. (Thus. - Mon.). Sunday Brunch: 8 a.m. - 12 p.m.

1. American Express	4. VISA	7. Public Parking	10. Full Bar 13. Handicap Accessibility
2. Discover	5. Diners Club	8. Valet Parking	11. Senior Citizen Rates
3 MasterCard	6. Reservations Required	9. Beer & Wine Served	12. Function Rooms Available

RESTAURANTS

Nevada City

Country Rosa Cafe
300 Commercial St., 95959
(916) 265-6252

Amenities: 1,3,4,5,9

Lunch.: $5.95 - $9.95

Appetizer: $5.95 - $6.95
Entree: $13.95 - $19.95
Dessert: $2.50 - $3.50

Country French, fresh seafood and blackboard menu. Patio dining. A quaint and charming 1800s brick building. All plates are beautifully presented with the uniqueness of this chef-owned country French cuisine. Homemade desserts, expresso and wine bar for your pleasure.

Hours: Lunch: 11 a.m. - 2:30 p.m.(Mon. - Sat.), Dinner: 5 p.m. - 9 p.m.(daily).

St. Helena

Showley's At Miramonte
1327 Railroad Ave., 94574
(707) 963-1200
Fax: (707) 963-8864

Amenities: 1,2,3,4,7,9,12,13

Lunch: $5.00 - $10.00

Appetizer: $5.00 - $8.00
Entree: $12.00 - $19.50
Dessert: $5.00 - $6.00

California cuisine in a gracious, relaxed environment. Historic building and private garden dining in-season. Award-winning menu and wine list with fine service at affordable prices. Reservations advised.

Hours: Lunch: 11:30 a.m. - 3 p.m. (Tues. - Sun.), Dinner: 6 p.m. - 9 p.m. (Tues - Sun.) Closed Mondays.

Sonoma

Depot 1870 Restaurant
241 First St., W., 95476
(707) 938-2980

Amenities: 1,2,3,4,7,9,12,13

Lunch.: $6.75 - $11.50

Appetizer: $4.75 - $6.25
Entree: $11.50 - $17.50
Dessert: $3.75 - $4.50

National, award-winning north Italian cuisine. Homemade pastas, steaks, veal and fresh seafood. Charming historic stone building with garden terrace and poolside dining. Extensive Sonoma Valley wine list. Near historic plaza and wineries. Free private parking.

Hours: Lunch: 11:30 a.m. - 2 p.m. (Wed- Fri.), Dinner: 5 p.m. - 9 p.m. (Wed. - Sun.).

COLORADO

Denver

Buckhorn Exchange
1000 Osage St., 80204
(303) 534-9505

Amenities: 1,2,3,4,5,7,9,10, 12,13

Lunch.: $4.95 - $10.50

Appetizer: $4.25 - $6.50
Entree: $16.00 - $29.00
Dessert: $2.50 - $3.50

Established in 1893. This is Colorado's oldest and most historic eating-and-drinking emporium. Marvelously hearty fare including prime dry-aged beef steaks, buffalo, ribs and game specialties. Lunch features five enormous burgers and a pot-roast sandwich.

Hours: Lunch: 11 a.m. - 3 p.m. (Mon. - Fri.), Dinner: 5 p.m. - 10:30 p.m. (daily).

1. American Express	4. VISA	7. Public Parking	10. Full Bar	13. Handicap Accessibility
2. Discover	5. Diners Club	8. Valet Parking	11. Senior Citizen Rates
3 MasterCard	6. Reservations Required	9. Beer & Wine Served	12. Function Rooms Available

RESTAURANTS

Telluride

Powder House Restaurant And Bar
226 W. Colorado Ave., 81435   **Amenities:**1,3,4,9,10,12
(303) 728-3622

Appetizer: $5.95 - $9.95
Entree: $13.95 - $28.95
Dessert: $6.00 - $6.50

Every evening we offer our customers duck with its own special sauces, special wild game selections, domestic offerings that include beef, chicken, lamb, catch of the day and pastas. Come join us for a taste of the Rockies.

Hours: 6 p.m. - 10 p.m (daily).

CONNECTICUT

Norwalk, East

Skippers Restaurant
Beach Rd., 06855
(203) 838-2211

Amenities: 1,3,4,5,7,8,9,11, 12
Breakfast: $14.95 (brunch)

Lunch: $4.50 - $8.95
Appetizer: $3.50 - $7.25
Entree: $11.00 - $23.75
Dessert: $2.00 - $3.50

Located on the harbor, enjoy your meal while watching the beautiful boats just outside your table window. Skippers is well known for its food, atmosphere and service. Lobster, prime rib, steaks, chops and homemade desserts. Banquet rooms available. Dancing on Fridays and Saturdays.

Hours: Lunch 11:30 a.m. - 3:30 p.m., Dinner:4 p.m. - 10:30 p.m. (weekdays), 4 p.m. - 10:30 p.m. (Fri. & Sat.). Sunday Brunch: 11:30 a.m. - 2:30 p.m.

FLORIDA

Cedar Key

Historic Island Hotel Restaurant
Second and 'B' St.
P.O. Box 460, 32625
(904) 543-5111

Amenities:3,4,7,10,12,13
Entree: $7.95 - $9.95
Dessert: $4.00

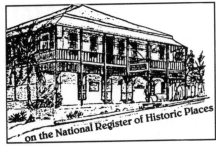

on the National Register of Historic Places

Gourmet seafood in one of Forida's oldest hotels. Local seafood in traditional recipes, including island stonecrab claws, softshell and blue crab, plus the original heart of palm salad. Dine on our romantic porch and relax in the famous Neptune Lounge.

Hours: Dinner: 6 p.m. - 9p.m., (Thurs. - Sun.).

1. American Express	4. VISA	7. Public Parking	10. Full Bar	13. Handicap Accessibility
2. Discover	5. Diners Club	8. Valet Parking	11. Senior Citizen Rates	
3 MasterCard	6. Reservations Required	9. Beer & Wine Served	12. Function Rooms Available	

RESTAURANTS

ILLINOIS

Urbana

The Canterbury Restaurant and Pub
One Lincoln Sq., 61801
(217) 367-3663

Amenities: 1,3,4,7,9,10,13
Lunch: $3.00 - $6.00

Appetizers: $5.00 - $7.00
Entree: $10.00 - $18.00
Desserts: $2.00 - $4.00

Enjoy dining in a relaxed and intimate atmosphere. We feature aged prime beef and fresh seafood. Homemade soups and desserts are a speciality. Make your reservations to spend a special evening with us. "Dedicated to excellence."

Hours: 11 a.m. - 9 p.m. (Mon. - Thurs.), 11 a.m. - 10 p.m. (Fri. & Sat.).

INDIANA

Bluffton

The Ritten- House Restaurant
218 So. Main St., 46714
(219) 824-8112

Amenities: 1,2,3,4,7,9,10,11, 12,13
Lunch: $3.95 - $7.95

Appetizer: $4.95 - $5.95
Entree: $5.45 - $19.95
Dessert: $1.95 - $3.95

Beef Tenderloin, chicken, seafood specials, homemade quiche and breads are just a few of the favorites. Served in elegant Victorian surroundings. Explore this historic home filled with antiques. Browse through the quaint gift shop after dinner.

Hours: 11 a.m. - 9 p.m. (Tues. - Fri.), 4 p.m. - 9 p.m. (Sat.), 11 a.m. - 2:30 p.m. (Sun. brunch).

MAINE

Kennebunkport

Olde Grist Mill
1 Mill Lane, 04046
(207) 967-4781, (800) 27-GRIST

Amenities: 1,2,3,4,5,6,7,9,10, 12,13

Appetizer: $3.75 - $9.25
Entree: $12.75 - $19.75
Dessert: $2.75 - $4.50

One of the nation's few remaining tidewater mills (1749). Specialties are fresh seafood and Maine lobster, along with choice beef selections, poultry, roast duckling, lamb and veal. Home-baked rolls, johnnycake and famous N.E. Indian Pudding. Dining room/lounge overlook the Kennebunk River.

Hours: April - October open daily. Dinner: 5:30 p.m. until closing. (July and August). Closed Mondays during the spring and fall.

1. American Express	4. VISA	7. Public Parking	10. Full Bar	13. Handicap Accessibility
2. Discover	5. Diners Club	8. Valet Parking	11. Senior Citizen Rates	
3 MasterCard	6. Reservations Required	9. Beer & Wine Served	12. Function Rooms Available	

RESTAURANTS

Kennebunkport

The White Barn Inn
Beach St., 04046
(207) 967-2321

Amenities:1,3,4,6,7,10,12,13

Appetizer: $6.95 - $8.95
Entree: $18.75 - $29.95
Dessert: $4.95 - $7.95

Architectually-perserved barns modified only by soaring three-story windows exposing gardens chock-full of seasonal foliage sets the stage for award winning, regional cuisine prepared with a passion for freshness. Four Star, Four Diamond. Member: Relais and Chateaux.

Hours: Open year round.

Kittery

Warren's Lobster House
11 Water St. (U.S. Rte. 1), 03904
(207) 439-1630

Amenities: 1,3,4,7,8,10,12,13
Breakfast: $9.95 (brunch)

Lunch.: $4.50 - $8.95
Appetizer: $2.25 - $5.50
Entree: $9.95 - $16.95
Dessert: $1.49 - $2.95

An outstanding array of lobster, seafood, steak and other specialties complemented by an award-winning salad bar offering over 50 items. An outdoor deck and a picturesque setting on the water. Family restaurant where quality food has been served for 52 years.

Hours: Lunch: 11:30 a.m. - 4p.m. (Mon. - Sat.), Dinner: 4 p.m.- Closing (Mon. - Sat.)
11:30 a.m. - Closing (Sun.), Sunday Brunch: 10 a.m. - 2 p.m.

MASSACHUSETTS

Boston

Another Season
97 Mt. Vernon St., 02108
(617) 367-0880

Amenities: 1,3,4,6,7,9,12,13

Lunch: $5.00 - $10.00
Appetizer.: $4.00 -$8.00
Entree: $13.00 - $24.00
Dessert: $5.00 - $7.00

Attractive dining rooms decorated with turn-of-the-century French murals. Modern menu changes monthly. Featuring fresh and flavorful seasonal ingredients. Prix fixe menu, $22.00 per person, also available Monday - Thursday. Located on historic Beacon Hill.

Hours: Lunch: 12 p.m. - 2 p.m. (Tues. - Fri.), Dinner: 5:45 p.m. - 10 p.m. (Mon. - Sat.).

1. American Express	4. VISA	7. Public Parking	10. Full Bar	13. Handicap Accessibility
2. Discover	5. Diners Club	8. Valet Parking	11. Senior Citizen Rates	
3 MasterCard	6. Reservations Required	9. Beer & Wine Served	12. Function Rooms Available	

RESTAURANTS

Sandwich

Dan'l Webster Inn
149 Main St., 02563
(508) 888-3622

Amenities: 1,2,3,4,5,7,8,9,10,12,13
Lunch.: $5.95 - $9.95
Appetizer: $3.25 - $7.95
Entree: $14.95 - $24.95
Dessert: $2.50 - $4.95

Historic 47-room, four-star inn offers fine dining, warm hospitality, attentive service and outstanding ambience. Fresh native seafood and choice meats are featured specials. Early evening menus also offered.

Hours: Weekdays: 8 a.m. - 10 p.m. (11:30 a.m. - 9 p.m. off-season); Weekends: 8 a.m. - 9 p.m.

MINNESOTA

Lutsen

Village Inn Restaurant
County Rd. 36, Box 87, 55612
(218) 663-7316

Amenities: 1,2,3,4,5,7,10,12

Breakfast: $3.25 - $6.95
Entree: $3.25 - $6.95
Dinner: $6.25 - $13.95

A change of pace, mountainside restaurant in a casual setting surrounded by the warmth of wood and a massive stone fireplace. Enjoy your favorite cocktails with steaks and fish specials or try the North Shore's best homemade pizza. You'll be at home with us.

Hours: Breakfast: 8 a.m. - 12 p.m., Lunch and dinner: 11 a.m. - 12 midnight.

NEW HAMPSHIRE

Bethlehem

Rosa Flamingos
Main St.
P.O. Box 190, 03574
(603) 869-3111

Amenities: 3,4,7,10

Lunch.: $4.50 - $8.95

Appetizer: $3.75 - $5.95
Entree: $5.95 - $16.95
Dessert: $2.25 - $2.75

Creative cuisine with an Italian flair. Luncheon specials include our famous vegetable crust. Dinner entrees include chicken braciolatine or fresh baked seafood sampler. Specialty pizzas such as shrimp and garlic, eggplant and pesto are served all day.

Hours: Sumer Lunch: 11:30 a.m. - 3 p.m. (Mon. - Sun.), Dinner: 5 p.m. - 10 p.m. (Mon. - Sun.).
Winter Lunch: 11:30 a.m. - 3 p.m. (Fri., Sat., & Sun.,), Dinner 5 p.m. - 9 p.m. (Mon. - Sun.).

1. American Express	4. VISA	7. Public Parking	10. Full Bar	13. Handicap Accessibility
2. Discover	5. Diners Club	8. Valet Parking	11. Senior Citizen Rates	
3 MasterCard	6. Reservations Required	9. Beer & Wine Served	12. Function Rooms Available	

RESTAURANTS

Bethlehem

Riverview Restaurant At The Wayside Inn
RR 1, Rte. 302, 03574   **Amenities:**1,2,3,4,5,7,10,13
(603) 869-3364

Appetizer: $1.75 - $5.25
Entree: $8.95 - $15.75
Dessert: $1.50 - $3.00

Swiss hospitality in the White Mountains. Enjoy outstanding veal dishes such as Wienerschnitzel, seafood and fish. Prime rib on Saturdays (summer only). Cheese fondue in winter. Wonderful view from the restaurant of the garden and the Ammonoosuc River.

Hours: May 15 - Oct. 20: 6 p.m. - 9 p.m. (Tue. - Sun.),
      Dec. 26 - March 30: 6 p.m. - 9 p.m. (Fri. & Sat.).

Portsmouth

Oar House
55 Ceres St., 03801
(603) 436-4025

Amenities: 1,3,4,6,8,9,10, 12,13
Sandwiches: $4.95 - $5.95

Lunch.: $5.95 - $12.50
Appetizer: $1.95 - $8.25
Entree: $13.95 - $23.95
Dessert: $3.00 - $3.50

A favorite among locals and a find for visitors. The pleasant surroundings of this beautifully restored, yet rustic, restaurant makes for a truly relaxed dining experience in an atmosphere reminiscent of days gone by. Outdoor dining May - October on the waterfront.

Hours: Lunch: 11:30 a.m. - 2:30 p.m. (Mon. - Sat.), 11:30 a.m. - 4 p.m. (Sun.),
      Dinner: 5:30 p.m. - 9 p.m. (Mon. - Thurs.), 5:30 p.m. - 10 p.m. (Fri. & Sat.),
      Until 8p.m. (Sun.).

NEW JERSEY

W. Cape May

"Peaches At Sunset"
One Sunset Blvd., 08204
(609) 898-0100

Amenities: 3,4,6,7,8,12,13
Brunch: $5.00 - $10.00

Appetizers: $3.00 - $7.00
Entree: $15.00 - $20.00
Desserts: $4.00 - $5.00

Contemporary cuisine in a newly renovated Victorian. Superb international menu, fine sauces and exceptional desserts. Featuring fresh flowers, exotic tropical decor, outdoor deck and pavilion. Ideal for private parties, small weddings, etc. Free on-site parking. B.Y.O.B.

Hours: Sunday brunch: 10 a.m. - 2 p.m., Dinner: 5:30 p.m. - 10 p.m.

1. American Express	4. VISA	7. Public Parking	10. Full Bar 13. Handicap Accessibility
2. Discover	5. Diners Club	8. Valet Parking	11. Senior Citizen Rates
3 MasterCard	6. Reservations Required	9. Beer & Wine Served	12. Function Rooms Available

RESTAURANTS

NEW MEXICO

Santa Fe

Coyote Cafe
132 W. Water St., 87501
(505) 983-1615

Amenities: 1,2,3,4,5,6,10,13

Entree: $7.50 - $12.00
Dinner: $35.00 (Pre Fix for
three courses.)

Mark Miller's nationally acclaimed restaurant serves modern Southwestern cuisine. The imaginative menu is based on history and tradition, like Santa Fe itself, while the exciting and whimsical decor delights the diner.

Hours: Lunch, 11:30 a.m. - 2 p.m. (Sat. & Sun.), Dinner nightly 6 p.m. - 9:30 p.m..
Rooftop Cantina open May 1 - Oct. 31, 11:30 a.m. - 9:30 p.m. (daily).

Taos

Lambert's Of Taos Restaurant
309 Paseo Del Pueblo Sur
P.O. Box 6302, 87571
(505) 758-1009

Amenities: 1,3,4,5,7,9,12,13

Lunch.: $3.00 - $7.50

Appetizer $3.00 - $9.00
Entree: $8.00 - $18.00
Dessert: $3.75

Contemporary American food. Lamb, seafood, steaks and chops. Innovative preparations. Delicious house-made bread and desserts. Located 2-1/2 blocks south of Taos Plaza. Convenient parking. Zeke and Tina Lambert, chef/owners.

Hours: Sunday brunch: 11 a.m. - 2:30 p.m., Lunch: 11:30 a.m. - 2:30 p.m. (Mon. - Fri.),
Dinner: 6 p.m. - 9 p.m. (daily).

NEW YORK

Mohawk

Mohawk Station Restaurant
& Cocktail Lounge
93 E. Main St., 13407
(315) 866-7460

Amenities:1,3,4,5,7,9,10,12
Lunch.: $3.95 - $7.95
Appetizer: $1.25 - $6.95
Entree: $5.50 - $25.50
Dessert: $1.50 - $3.25

Colorful, quaint railroad decor. located at the junction of Routes 5 So., 28 and Exit 30 of I-90. Lunch and dinner served. Banquet and lounge: Serving steaks, seafood and sandwiches; 40-item salad bar.

Hours: 11 a.m. - 9 p.m. (Mon. - Thurs.); 11 a.m. - 10 p.m. (Fri. & Sat.); 11:30 a.m. - 8 p.m. (Sun.).

---

1. American Express	4. VISA	7. Public Parking	10. Full Bar	13. Handicap Accessibility
2. Discover	5. Diners Club	8. Valet Parking	11. Senior Citizen Rates	
3 MasterCard	6. Reservations Required	9. Beer & Wine Served	12. Function Rooms Available	

Saratoga Springs

Olde Bryan Inn
13 Maple Ave., 12866
(518) 587-2990

Amenities: 1,2,3,4,5,7,9,10
Lunch: $4.25 - $6.95
Appetizer: $2.95 - $5.95
Entree: $7.95 - $16.95
Dessert: $2.75 - $3.25

The Olde Bryan Inn

Historic building is a Saratoga landmark. Extensive menu at reasonable prices. From soup, salads, burgers and sandwiches to prime rib, steaks, fresh seafood, poultry and pasta dishes. Daily specials and homemade desserts. Excellent American wine list and wines by the glass.

Hours: 11:30 a.m. - 11 p.m. (Sun. - Thurs.); 11:30 a.m. - 12 midnight (Fri. & Sat.);
Tavern open until 1 a.m.

NORTH CAROLINA

Asheville

Steven's Restaurant
157 Charlotte St., 28801
(704)253-5348

Amenities: 1,2,3,4,7,9,10, 11,12

Appetizer: $4.95 - $8.95
Entree: $9.95 - $18.95
Dessert: $2.25 - $4.50

Steven's Restaurant offers a continental menu amidst a charming Victorian atmosphere in the 2nd floor dining room. The 1st floor English pub serves sandwiches, draft beer and mixed drinks.

Hours: Lunch: 11:30 a.m. - 2 p.m. (Mon. - Fri.), Dinner: from 5 p.m. (daily).

Sylva

Lulu's Cafe
18 W. Main
(704) 586-8989

Amenities: 3,4,7,9
Lunch: $2.25 - $7.95

Appetizer: $1.50 - $4.95
Entree: $8.50 - $11.95
Dessert: $2.25 - $2.95

Delicious homemade soups. Freshest salads. Sandwiches with homemade bread. Full course dinners. Specializing in pasta, chicken, seafood, vegetarian and ethnic dishes. Wonderful homemade desserts. Great daily features.

Hours: Summer: 11 a.m. - 9 p.m. (Mon. - Sat.); Winter: 11 a.m. - 8:30 p.m. (Mon. - Thurs.),
11 a.m. - 9 p.m. (Fri. & Sat.).

1. American Express	4. VISA	7. Public Parking	10. Full Bar	13. Handicap Accessibility
2. Discover	5. Diners Club	8. Valet Parking	11. Senior Citizen Rates
3 MasterCard	6. Reservations Required	9. Beer & Wine Served	12. Function Rooms Available

RESTAURANTS

OHIO

Athens

7 Sauces Restaurant
6 N. Court, 45701
(614) 592-5555

Amenities: 1,3,4,9,10,12
Lunch: $3.50 - $5.95

Appetizer: $3.25 - $7.95
Entree: $8.95 - $14.95
Dessert: $2.50

"Food worth traveling for"- *Ohio Magazine.* Weekly changing menu featuring fresh seafood, steaks, innovative classic, international, American and vegetarian cuisine. Food at its freshest and finest. Entertainment, fine wine and spirits. Open Sunday.

Hours: Lunch: 11 a.m. - 2 p.m. (Mon. - Frid.), Dinner: 5 p.m. - 9 p.m. (Sun. - Thurs.),
5 p.m. - 10 p.m. (Fri. & Sat.).

Millersburg

Hotel Millersburg
35 W. Jackson St., 44654
(216) 674-1457

Amenities: 1,3,4,7,9,10,12,13
Lunch: $3.95 - $16.95
Entree: $5.95 - $16.95

Built in 1847, historic Hotel Millersburg provides you with the quality and charm of a country inn. Dine in our formal dining room, lounge, or our brick country yard. The only complex of its kind in Holmes County. Call for our entertainment schedule.

Hours: Lunch: 11 a.m. - 2 p.m., Dinner: 5 p.m. - 10 p.m., Lounge open 11 a.m. - 1 a.m.

OREGON

Florence

The Blue Hen Cafe
1675 Hwy. 101, 97439
(503) 997-3907

Amenities: 2,3,4,7,9,13
Breakfast: $2.25 - $7.95

Lunch: $3.95 - $6.95
Entree: $5.95 - $8.95
Dessert: $1.75 - $2.95

Award-winning chicken, breakfasts' clam chowder and gourmet hamburgers. Real home cooking, homemade bread, biscuits and desserts.

Hours: 7 a.m. - 8 p.m. (Mon. - Sat.), 7 a.m. - 7 p.m. (Sun.).

Florence

Canyon Way Restaurant
1216 S.W. Canyon Way
(503) 265-8319

Amenities: 1,2,3,4,7,9,10,13
Lunch: $4.50 - $9.95

Appetizer: $5.50 - $7.95
Entree: $10.95 - $19.95
Dessert: $2.95 - $4.25

Twenty years of excellent cuisine. Voted "Best Seafood in Oregon" by *Pacific Northwest Magazine* readers' poll. Featuring fresh daily seafood, steaks, vegetarian dishes, fine homemade pasta dishes, soups, pastries and desserts. Full take-out delicatessen open daily.

Hours: Lunch: 11 a.m. - 3 p.m. (Mon. - Thurs.), Dinner: 5 p.m. - 9 p.m. (Tue. - Sat.).

1. American Express	4. VISA	7. Public Parking	10. Full Bar	13. Handicap Accessibility
2. Discover	5. Diners Club	8. Valet Parking	11. Senior Citizen Rates	
3 MasterCard	6. Reservations Required	9. Beer & Wine Served	12. Function Rooms Available	

RESTAURANTS

PENNSYLVANIA

Ephrata

The Restaurant At Doneckers
333 N. State St., 17522
(717) 738-2421

Amenities: 1,2,3,4,5,7,9,10, 12,13
Lunch: $6.75 - $12.75

Appetizer: $3.95 - $9.25
Entree: $16.95 - $22.95
Dessert: $2.25 - $4.25

Classic French cuisine with an innovative American flair. Attentive service and gracious surroundings. Heart-healthy dining options on all menus. Banquet facilities for groups from 12 to 200. Near Doneckers fashion stores and art galleries. An elegant country inn. Supper menu available.

Hours: 11 a.m. - 10 p.m. (daily), Sunday brunch: 11:30 a.m. - 3 p.m. Closed Wednesdays.

TENNESSEE

Memphis

The Original Grisanti's Restaurant
1489 Airway Blvd., 38114
(901) 458-2648

Amenities: 1,2,3,4,5,7,8,9,10,12,13
Lunch: $3.75 - $7.50
Entree: $10.00 - $22.00

Northern Italian menu. Bar, wine cellar. Specialties include: Canneloni ala Gusi, baked manicotti, fresh fish, prime rib. Specially prepared gourmet menu on request. Chef owned.

Hours: Lunch: (Mon. - Fri.), Dinner: (Mon. - Sat.).

UTAH

Moab

Center Cafe
92 E. Center St., 84532
(801) 259-4295

Amenities: 1,3,4,7,9,13

Entree: $9.95 - $18.95
Dessert: $3.95
Appetizer: $3.95 - $5.95

"Contemporary American cuisine." Fresh fish, grilled meats, pasta, fine desserts, espresso. Fine dining with casual elegance. Chef Tim Buckingham praised as one of the 10 "new American star chefs" by Food and Wine Companion - October 1990.

Hours: Dinner: 6 - 10 p.m. (Mon. - Sat.).

---

1. American Express	4. VISA	7. Public Parking	10. Full Bar 13. Handicap Accessibility
2. Discover	5. Diners Club	8. Valet Parking	11. Senior Citizen Rates
3 MasterCard	6. Reservations Required	9. Beer & Wine Served	12. Function Rooms Available

RESTAURANTS

VERMONT

Arlington

Arlington Inn
Historic Rt. 7A, 05250
(802) 375-6532

Amenities: 1,2,3,4,5,6,7,9
10,12
Brunch: $7.95 - $11.95

Entree: $16.00 - $24.00
Dessert: $3.75 - $4.50

Relax and savor award-winning American cuisine and a selection from our outstanding wine list. Enjoy old fashioned country hospitality by romantic candlelight in our antique filled 1848 Greek Revival mansion.

Hours: Dinner from 5:30 p.m., Sunday Brunch: 12 p.m. - 2 :30p.m.

Isle La Motte

Ruthcliffe Lodge & Restaurant
Box 32, Old Quarry Rd., 05463
(802) 928-3200

Amenities: 3,4,7,9,10

Brunch: $7.95 - $11.95

Breakfast: $1.00 - $7.00
Lunch: $4.95 - $8.95
Dinner: $10.95 - $22.95

Chef owned and operated overlooking beautiful Lake Champlain. Dine on our outdoor patio or in our rustic pine dining room. Featuring Italo-American cuisine. Fresh seafood, handcut steaks, poultry and veal. Other Italian specialties priced from $7.95 - $18.95.

Hours: Breakfast: 8:30 a.m. - 11 a.m. (daily), Lunch: 12 p.m. - 2 p.m. (Tues. - Sun., closed Mondays for lunch), Dinner: 5 p.m. - 9 p.m. (daily).

VIRGINIA

Charlottesville

Le Snail Restaurant
320 W. Main St., 22903
(804) 295-4456

Amenities: 1,2,3,4,5,8,9,12

Tradition of excellence since 1979. Outstanding classic French cuisine. Home of Viennese chef. Elegant surroundings in historic home convenient to downtown mall area and University of Virginia. Award-winning wine list. Reservations recommended. Dress code.

Hours: Dinner: 6 - 10 p.m. (Mon. - Sat.), Prix-fixe menu (Mon. - Thurs.),
A La Carte menu (Mon - Sat.).

1. American Express	4. VISA	7. Public Parking	10. Full Bar 13. Handicap Accessibility
2. Discover	5. Diners Club	8. Valet Parking	11. Senior Citizen Rates
3 MasterCard	6. Reservations Required	9. Beer & Wine Served	12. Function Rooms Available

RESTAURANTS

Chincoteague

aj's... on the creek
6585 Maddox Blvd., 23336
(804) 336-1539

Amenities: 1,2,3,4,5,7,9,10,
11,13
Lunch.: $2.75 - $7.95

Appetizer: $2.95 - $7.95
Entree: $8.95 - $17.95
Dessert: $3.00

Exceptional dining in casual elegance. Enjoy the bounty of our waters - the finest the land has to offer. Seafood, pasta, hand-cut steaks and veal. We'll surround you with the richness of life and the value that makes it worthwhile. Vegetarian menu available. Open year-round.

Hours: 11:30 a.m. - 10 p.m. (seven days a week). No lunch served on Sundays.
Lounge open 11a.m. - 12 midnight.

Fredericksburg

Le La Fayette Restaurant,
623 Caroline St., 22401
(703) 373-6895

Amenities: 1,2,3,4,5,6,9,10
Lunch: $10.00

Appetizer: $3.50 - $4.00
Entree: $12.00 - $21.00
Dessert: $3.75 - $4.50

Elegant dining in a charming 18th-century atmosphere. French, Virginia, American regional cuisine. Sunday brunch. Banquet ad party facilities. Located in the Chimneys historic landmark, circa 1709.

Hours: Lunch: 11:30 a.m. - 3:30 p.m.(Mon. - Sun.), Dinner: 5:30 p.m. - 10 p.m. (Mon. - Sat.),
5:30 p.m. - 9p.m. (Sun.).

WASHINGTON

Seattle

Ray's Boathouse Restaurant & Cafe
6049 Seaview Ave., N.W., 98107
(206) 789-3770

Amenities: 1,3,4,5,6,7,8,9,10,12,13
Lunch: $4.95 - $10.50
Appetizer: $2.95 - $8.95
Entree: $5.95 - $19.95
Dessert: $1.95 - $5.95

Providing the freshest available northwest seafood, meat and produce, has earned Ray's the reputation of being the "if-you-only-have-one-meal-in-Seattle-have-it-here"restaurant. In addition to our dining room, the Cafe upstairs is a casual spot for catchin' Ray's.

Hours: Lunch: 11:30 a.m. - 2 p.m.(Mon. - Sun.). Dinner: 5 p.m. - 10 p.m. (Mon. - Sun.).

---

1. American Express	4. VISA	7. Public Parking	10. Full Bar	13. Handicap Accessibility
2. Discover	5. Diners Club	8. Valet Parking	11. Senior Citizen Rates	
3 MasterCard	6. Reservations Required	9. Beer & Wine Served	12. Function Rooms Available	

RESTAURANTS

WISCONSIN

Genesee Depot

The Union House
S42 W31320 Hwy 83, 53127
(414) 968-4281

Amenities: 1,3,4,5,6,7,8,9, 10,12,13

Appetizer: $4.00 - $8.00
Entree: $12.00 - $25.00
Dessert: $3.00 - $5.00

Country gourmet style of cuisine. Fresh ingredients insure quality. Charming turn-of-the-century Greek revival style building. Excellent wine list. Premium rail drinks. Reservations always recommended. Experience the warmth and hospitality of The Union House.

Hours: 5 p.m. - 9 p.m. (Tues., Wed., & Thurs.), 5 p.m. - 10 p.m. (Fri. & Sat.).

BRITISH COLUMBIA, CANADA

Victoria

Tio's Casual Dining
4496 w. saanich rd., v8z 3e9
(604) 479-2123

Amenities: 1,3,4,5,6,7,10

Appetizer: $4.95 - $7.95
Entree: $8.95 - $19.95
Dessert: $3.95 - $5.95

one of victoria's most thriving and oldest dining sites, a swiss chalet in the royal oak area... steaks, chicken, seafood, veal, lamb and pasta dishes. prepared without preservatives such as m.s.g. in the continental and indonesian tradition of home cooking.

Hours: 4:30 p.m. - 11:30 p.m. (Mon. - Sun.). Closed Sundays.

1. American Express
2. Discover
3 MasterCard
4. VISA
5. Diners Club
6. Reservations Required
7. Public Parking
8. Valet Parking
9. Beer & Wine Served
10. Full Bar
11. Senior Citizen Rates
12. Function Rooms Available
13. Handicap Accessibility

THE NATIONAL BED & BREAKFAST GUIDE • (Comments)

Help us serve you better!
Aidez-nous à vous mieux servir!
¡Ayúdennos servirles mejor!

Name of B. & B. _____

Address_____

I found this B. & B. to be   Excellent _____   Good _____   Poor _____

J'ai trouvé cette pension   Excellente _____   Bonne _____   Mauvaise _____

Encontré esta pensión   Excelente _____   Bueno _____   Malo _____

Signature _____

Address_____

Comments _____

Remarques _____

Comentos_____

THE NATIONAL BED & BREAKFAST GUIDE • (Comments)

Help us serve you better!
Aidez-nous à vous mieux servir!
¡Ayúdennos servirles mejor!

Name of B. & B. _____

Address_____

I found this B. & B. to be   Excellent _____   Good _____   Poor _____

J'ai trouvé cette pension   Excellente _____   Bonne _____   Mauvaise _____

Encontré esta pensión   Excelente _____   Bueno _____   Malo _____

Signature _____

Address_____

Comments _____

Remarques _____

Comentos_____

NATIONAL B. & B. ASSOCIATION
P.O. Box 332
Norwalk, CT 06852

NATIONAL B. & B. ASSOCIATION
P.O. Box 332
Norwalk, CT 06852

MEMBERSHIP CARD

Please send me at the address below, an application for membership
in The National Bed & Breakfast Assoc. which will entitle me to a listing
in your Bed & Breakfast Guide for the U.S. & Canada.

_____

_____

_____

_____
                                              Zip Code

Thank you,
Phyllis Featherston, President
Barbara F. Ostler, Vice President

MEMBERSHIP CARD

Please send me at the address below, an application for membership
in The National Bed & Breakfast Assoc. which will entitle me to a listing
in your Bed & Breakfast Guide for the U.S. & Canada.

_____

_____

_____

_____
                                              Zip Code

Thank you,
Phyllis Featherston, President
Barbara F. Ostler, Vice President

NATIONAL B. & B. ASSOCIATION
P.O. Box 332
Norwalk, CT 06852

NATIONAL B. & B. ASSOCIATION
P.O. Box 332
Norwalk, CT 06852

TRAVELERS NOTES

TRAVELERS NOTES

TRAVELERS NOTES

TRAVELERS NOTES